U.S. Department of Homeland Security

United States Coast Guard

MW00890166

LIGHT LIST

Volume I

ATLANTIC COAST

St. Croix River, Maine to Shrewsbury River, New Jersey

This Light List contains a list of lights, sound signals, buoys, daybeacons, and other aids to navigation.

IMPORTANT
THIS LIGHT LIST SHOULD BE CORRECTED
EACH WEEK FROM THE LOCAL NOTICES TO MARINERS
OR NOTICES TO MARINERS AS APPROPRIATE.

2024

COMDTPUB P16502.1

LIMITS OF LIGHT LISTS PUBLISHED BY

U.S. COAST GUARD

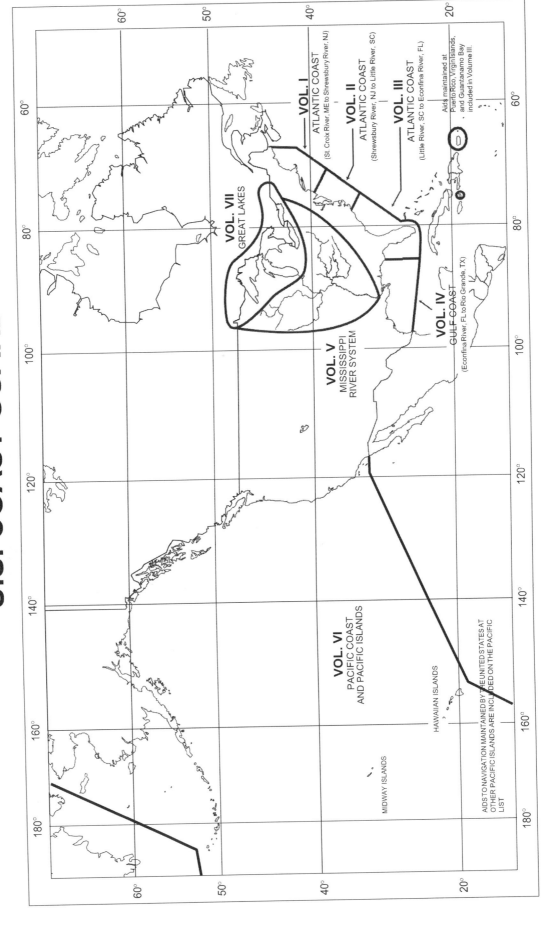

VOL. I
ATLANTIC COAST
(St. Croix River, ME to Shrewsbury River, NJ)

VOL. II
ATLANTIC COAST
(Shrewsbury River, NJ to Little River, SC)

VOL. III
ATLANTIC COAST
(Little River, SC to Econfina River, FL)

Aids maintained at
Puerto Rico, Virgin Islands,
and Guantanamo Bay
included in Volume III.

VOL. VII
GREAT LAKES

VOL. V
MISSISSIPPI
RIVER SYSTEM

VOL. IV
GULF COAST
(Econfina River, FL to Rio Grande, TX)

VOL. VI
PACIFIC COAST
AND PACIFIC ISLANDS

HAWAIIAN ISLANDS

MIDWAY ISLANDS

AIDS TO NAVIGATION MAINTAINED BY THE UNITED STATES AT
OTHER PACIFIC ISLANDS ARE INCLUDED ON THE PACIFIC
LIST

U.S. AIDS TO NAVIGATION SYSTEM
on navigable waters except Western Rivers

LATERAL SYSTEM AS SEEN ENTERING FROM SEAWARD

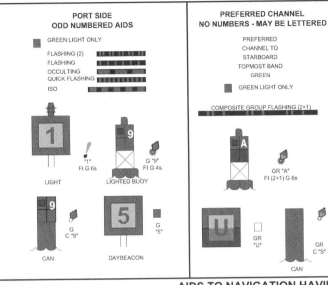

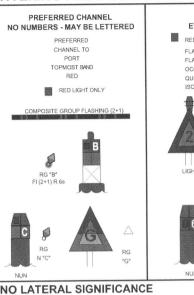

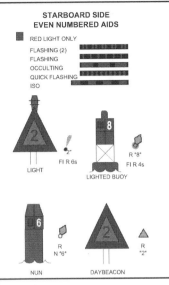

AIDS TO NAVIGATION HAVING NO LATERAL SIGNIFICANCE

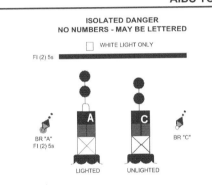

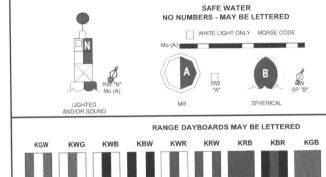

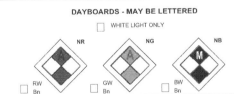

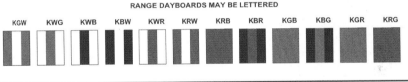

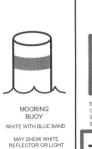

Aids to Navigation marking the Intracoastal Waterway (ICW) display unique yellow symbols to distinguish them from aids marking other waters. Yellow triangles △ indicate aids should be passed by keeping them on the starboard (right) hand of the vessel. Yellow squares ■ indicate aids should be passed by keeping them on the port (left) hand of the vessel. A yellow horizontal band ▬ provides no lateral information, but simply identifies aids as marking the ICW.

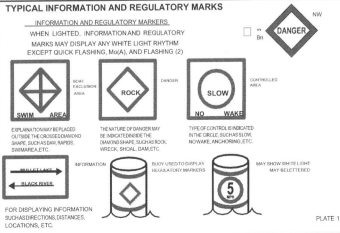

PLATE 1

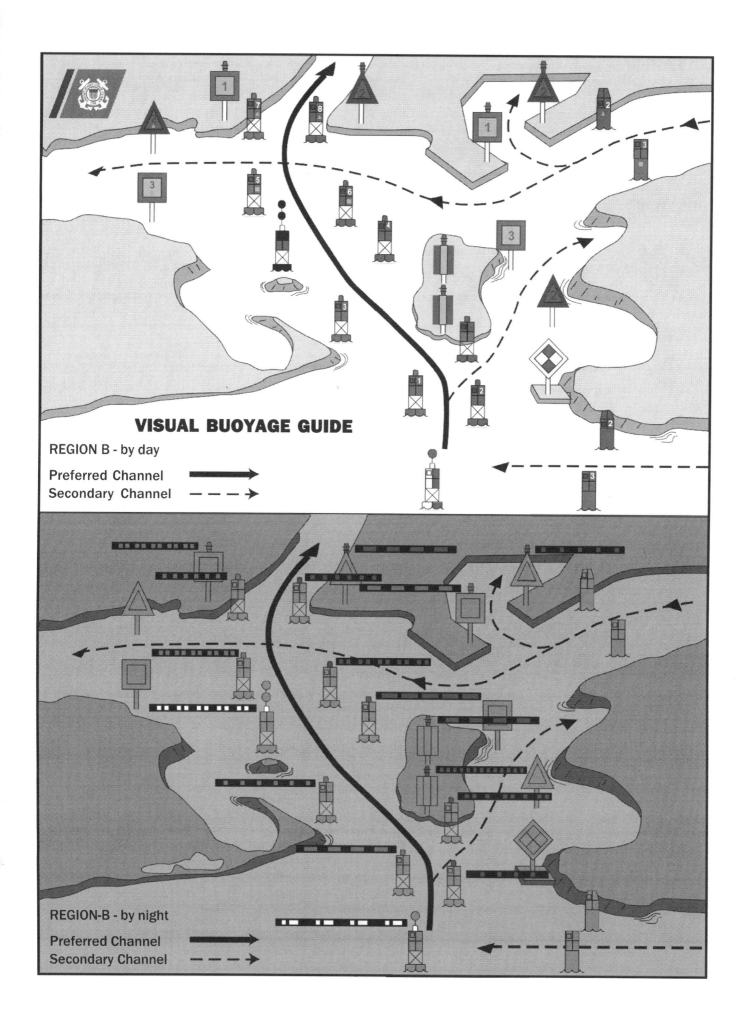

VISUAL BUOYAGE GUIDE

REGION B - by day

Preferred Channel ➝

Secondary Channel ⇢

REGION-B - by night

Preferred Channel ➝

Secondary Channel ⇢

FICTITIOUS NAUTICAL CHART

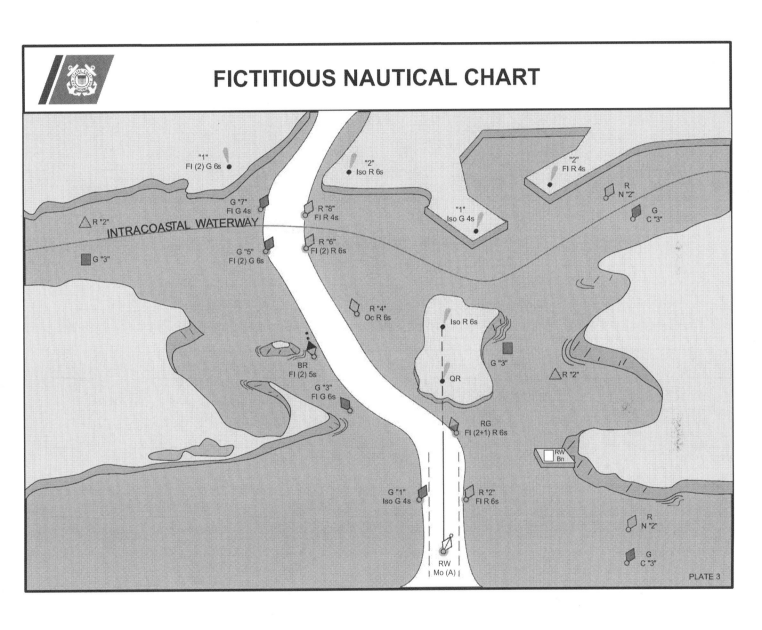

INTRACOASTAL WATERWAY

"1"
Fl (2) G 6s

"2"
Iso R 6s

"2"
Fl R 4s

R
N "2"

G "7"
Fl G 4s

R "8"
Fl R 4s

"1"
Iso G 4s

G
C "3"

R "2"

G "3"

G "5"
Fl (2) G 6s

R "6"
Fl (2) R 6s

R "4"
Oc R 6s

Iso R 6s

G "3"

R "2"

BR
Fl (2) 5s

QR

G "3"
Fl G 6s

RG
Fl (2+1) R 6s

RW
Bn

G "1"
Iso G 4s

R "2"
Fl R 6s

R
N "2"

G
C "3"

RW
Mo (A)

PLATE 3

AIDS TO NAVIGATIONSYSTEM
on the Western River System

AS SEEN ENTERING FROM SEAWARD

PORT SIDE
OR RIGHT DESCENDING BANK

■ GREEN OR □ WHITE LIGHTS

FLASHING
ISO

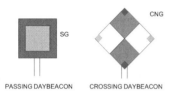

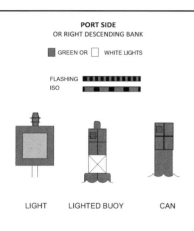

LIGHT   LIGHTED BUOY   CAN

SG

CNG

PASSING DAYBEACON   CROSSING DAYBEACON

176.9
MILE BOARD

PREFERRED CHANNEL
MARK JUNCTIONS AND OBSTRUCTIONS
COMPOSITE GROUP FLASHING (2+1)

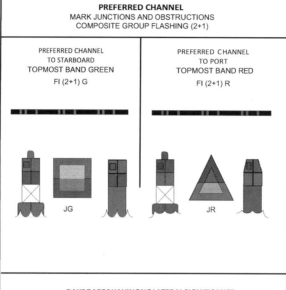

PREFERRED CHANNEL
TO STARBOARD
TOPMOST BAND GREEN
FI (2+1) G

PREFERRED CHANNEL
TO PORT
TOPMOST BAND RED
FI (2+1) R

JG

JR

DAYBOARDS HAVING NO LATERAL SIGNIFICANCE

MAY BE LETTERED   □ WHITE LIGHT ONLY

NB
A

STARBOARD SIDE
OR LEFT DESCENDING BANK

■ RED OR □ WHITE LIGHTS

FLASHING (2)
ISO

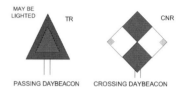

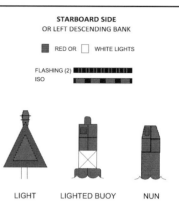

LIGHT   LIGHTED BUOY   NUN

MAY BE
LIGHTED   TR

CNR

PASSING DAYBEACON   CROSSING DAYBEACON

123.5
MILE BOARD

SPECIAL MARKS--MAY BE LETTERED

A
C

NY
A

B

UNLIGHTED   LIGHTED

SHAPE: OPTIONAL--BUT SELECTED TO BE APPROPRIATE
FOR THE POSITION OF THE MARK IN RELATION TO THE
NAVIGABLE WATERWAY AND THE DIRECTION
OF BUOYAGE.

 YELLOW LIGHT ONLY
FIXED
FLASHING

MOORING
BUOY
WHITE WITH BLUE BAND

MAY SHOW WHITE
REFLECTOR OR LIGHT

TYPICAL INFORMATION AND REGULATORY MARKS

NW □ WHITE LIGHT ONLY

INFORMATION AND REGULATORY MARKERS

WHEN LIGHTED, INFORMATION AND REGULATORY MARKS
MAY DISPLAY ANY LIGHT RHYTHM EXCEPT QUICK FLASHING, Mo(a)
AND FLASHING (2)

DANGER

BOAT
EXCLUSION
AREA

SWIM   AREA

EXPLAINATION MAY BE PLACED
OUTSIDE THE CROSSED DIAMOND
SHAPE, SUCH AS DAM, RAPIDS,
SWIM AREA, ETC.

ROCK

DANGER

THE NATURE OF DANGER MAY
BE INDICATED INSIDE THE
DIAMOND SHAPE, SUCH AS ROCK,
WRECK, SHOAL, DAM, ETC.

SLOW

NO   WAKE

CONTROLLED
AREA

TYPE OF CONTROL IS INDICATED
IN THE CIRCLE, SUCH AS SLOW,
NO WAKE, ANCHORING, ETC.

MULLET LAKE
BLACK RIVER

INFORMATION

FOR DISPLAYING INFORMATION
SUCH AS DIRECTIONS, DISTANCES,
LOCATIONS, ETC.

BUOY USED TO DISPLAY
REGULATORY MARKERS

5
MPH

MAY SHOW WHITE LIGHT
MAY BE LETTERED

STATE WATERS

3   2

INLAND (STATE) WATERS OBSTRUCTION MARK

MAY SHOW WHITE
REFLECTOR OR QUICK FLASHING WHITE LIGHT

BLACK-STRIPED
WHITE BUOY

Used to indicate an obstruction to navigation,
extends from the nearest shore to the buoy. This
means "do not pass between the buoy and the
nearest shore." This aid is replacing the red and
white striped buoy within the USWMS, but cannot
be used until all red and white striped buoys on a
waterway have been replaced.

PLATE 4

LUMINOUS RANGE DIAGRAM

The nominal range given in this Light List is the maximum distance a given light can be seen when the meteorological visibility is 10 nautical miles. If the existing visibility is less than 10 NM, the range at which the light can be seen will be reduced below its nominal range. And, if the visibility is greater than 10 NM, the light can be seen at greater distances. The distance at which a light may be expected to be seen in the prevailing visibility is called its luminous range.

This diagram enables the mariner to determine the approximate luminous range of a light when the nominal range and the prevailing meteorological visibility are known. The diagram is entered from the bottom border using the nominal range listed in column 6 of this book. The intersection of the nominal range with the appropriate visibility curve (or, more often, a point between two curves) yields, by moving horizontally to the left border, the luminous range.

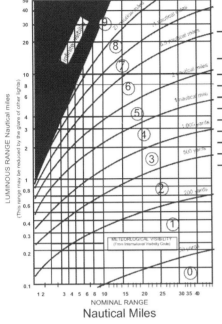

Nautical Miles

METEOROLOGICAL VISIBILITY
(From International Visibility Code)

Code	Metric	Nautical (approximate)
0	less than 50 meters	less than 50 yards
1	50-200 meters	50-200 yards
2	200-500 meters	200-500 yards
3	500-1,000 meters	500-1,000 yards
4	1-2 kilometers	1,000-2,000 yards
5	2-4 kilometers	1-2 nautical miles
6	4-10 kilometers	2-5.5 nautical miles
7	10-20 kilometers	5.5-11 nautical miles
8	20-50 kilometers	11-27 nautical miles
9	greater than 50 km	greater than 27 nm

CAUTION
When using this diagram it must be remembered that:

1. The ranges obtained are approximate.
2. The transparency of the atmosphere may vary between observer and light.
3. Glare from background lighting will reduce the range that lights are sighted.
4. The rolling motion of a vessel and/or of a lighted aid may reduce the distance that lights can be detected or identified.

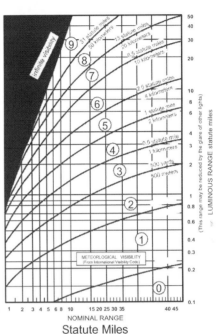

Statute Miles

GEOGRAPHIC RANGE TABLE

The following table gives the approximate geographic range of visibility for an object which may be seen by an observer at sea level. It is necessary to add to the distance for the height of any object the distance corresponding to the height of the observer's eye above sea level.

Height Feet/Meters	Distance Nautical Miles (NM)	Height Feet/Meters	Distance Nautical Miles (NM)	Height Feet/Meters	Distance Nautical Miles (NM)
5/1.5	2.6	70/21.3	9.8	250/76.2	18.5
10/3.1	3.7	75/22.9	10.1	300/91.4	20.3
15/4.6	4.5	80/24.4	10.5	350/106.7	21.9
20/6.1	5.2	85/25.9	10.8	400/121.9	23.4
25/7.6	5.9	90/27.4	11.1	450/137.2	24.8
30/9.1	6.4	95/29.0	11.4	500/152.4	26.2
35/10.7	6.9	100/30.5	11.7	550/167.6	27.4
40/12.2	7.4	110/33.5	12.3	600/182.9	28.7
45/13.7	7.8	120/36.6	12.8	650/198.1	29.8
50/15.2	8.3	130/39.6	13.3	700/213.4	31.0
55/16.8	8.7	140/42.7	13.8	800/243.8	33.1
60/18.3	9.1	150/45.7	14.3	900/274.3	35.1
65/19.8	9.4	200/61.0	16.5	1000/304.8	37.0

Example: Determine the geographic visibility of an object, with a height above water of 65 feet, for an observer with a height of eye of 35 feet.

Enter above table;

Height of object 65 feet= 9.4 NM
Height of observer 35 feet= 6.9 NM
Computed geographic visibility= 16.3NM

This Page Intentionally Left Blank

TABLE OF CONTENTS

This Page Intentionally Left Blank

Federal AIS ATON Broadcast Sites

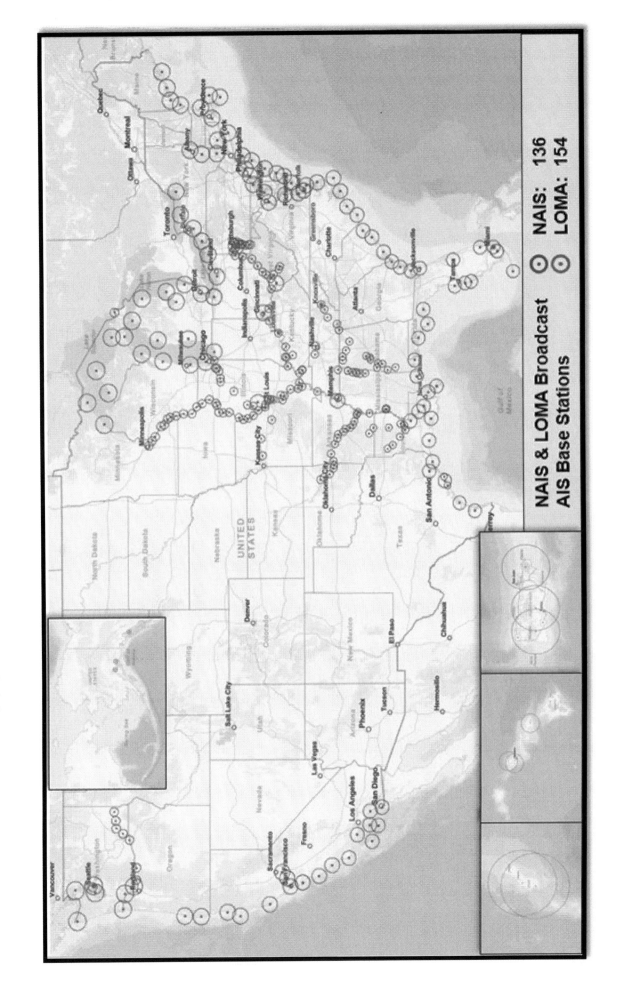

NAIS & LOMA Broadcast	NAIS: 136
AIS Base Stations	LOMA: 154

The following is a description of the geographic coverage of each volume:

Volume	Coast Guard District(s)	Geographic Description
I	**First Coast Guard District** 408 Atlantic Avenue Boston, MA 02110-3350 Tel: 617-223-8356 http://www.uscg.mil/d1	Maine, New Hampshire, Massachusetts, Vermont (Lake Champlain), Rhode Island, Connecticut and New York to Shrewsbury River, New Jersey.
II	**Fifth Coast Guard District** Federal Building 431 Crawford Street Portsmouth, VA 23704-5004 Tel: (757)398-6486 (757) 398-6552 http://www.uscg.mil/d5	Shrewsbury River, New Jersey to Little River South Carolina.
III	**Seventh Coast Guard District** Brickell Plaza Federal Building 909 SE 1st Avenue; Rm:406 Miami, FL 33131-3050 Tel: (305) 415-6752 or (305) 415-6800 http://www.uscg.mil/d7	South Carolina, Georgia, Florida to Econfina River (083°50' W), and Puerto Rico and the U.S. Virgin Islands.
IV	**Eight Coast Guard District** Hale Boggs Federal Building 500 Poydras Street New Orleans, LA 70130-3310 Tel: (504) 671-2327 (504) 671-2137 http://www.uscg.mil/d8	Econfina River (083°50' W), Florida to Rio Grande, Texas.
V		Mississippi River system and its navigable tributaries, Tenn-Tom Waterway, Alabama, Atchafalaya, and the Apalachicola-Chattahoochee-Flint River Systems.
VI	**Eleventh Coast Guard District** **(California, Nevada, Utah, Arizona)** Coast Guard Island Building 50-2 Alameda, CA 94501-5100 Tel: (510) 437-2975 http://www.uscg.mil/d11 **Thirteenth Coast Guard District** **(Oregon, Washington, Idaho, Montana)** Federal Building 915 Second Ave, Suite 3510 Seattle, WA 98174-1067 Tel: (206)220-7280 (206) 220-7001 http://www.uscg.mil/d13 **Fourteenth Coast Guard District** **(Hawaiian, American Samoa, Marshall, Marianas, and Caroline Islands)** Prince Kalanianaole Federal Bldg. 300 Ala Moana Blvd 9th Floor, Room 9-220 Honolulu, HI 96850-4982 Tel: (808) 535-3409 (808) 535-3414 http://www.uscg.mil/d14 **Seventeenth Coast Guard District** **(Alaska)** PO Box 25517 Juneau, AK 99802-5517 Tel: (907) 463-2269 http://www.uscg.mil/d17	Pacific Coast, Pacific Islands, and the Coast of Alaska.
VII	**Ninth Coast Guard District** 1240 East 9th Street Cleveland, OH 44199-2060 Tel: (216)902-6060 or (216) 902-6117 http://www.uscg.mil/d9	Great Lakes and the St. Lawrence River above the St. Regis River.

U. S. COAST GUARD
FIRST DISTRICT ATON UNIT LISTING

AIDS TO NAVIGATION TEAMS

ANT Boston
427 Commercial St.
Boston, MA 02109-1027
Tel: (617) 223-3293

ANT Bristol
1 Thames St
P.O. Box 1050
Bristol, RI 02809-1050
Tel: (401) 253-9585

ANT Long Island Sound
120 Woodward Ave
New Haven, CT 06512- 3698
Tel: (203) 468-4513

ANT Moriches
100 Foster Avenue
Hampton Bays, NY 11946-3233
Tel: (631) 728-6981

ANT New York
85 Port Terminal Blvd.
Slip 6
Bayonne, NJ 07002-5041
Tel: (201) 443-6298

ANT Saugerties
154 Lighthouse Dr.
Saugerties, NY 12477-9101
Tel: (845) 246-7612

ANT South Portland
259 High St
South Portland, ME 04106-0007
Tel: (207) 767-0392

ANT Southwest Harbor
184 Clark Point Road
Southwest Harbor, ME 04679- 5000
Tel: (207) 244-4281

ANT Woods Hole
1 Little Harbor Road
Woods Hole, MA 02543-1099
Tel: (508) 457-3329

ANT Burlington
1 Depot Street
Burlington, VT 05401-5226
Tel: (802) 951-6792

BUOY TENDERS

USCGC ABBIE BURGESS (WLM-553)
54 Tillson Avenue
Rockland, ME 04841-3417 Tel: (207) 594-2663

USCGC IDA LEWIS (WLM-551)
47 Chandler St, Pier 2
Newport, RI 02841-1716
Tel: (401) 367-1647

USCGC SYCAMORE (WLB 209)
47 Chandler St, Pier 2,
Newport, RI 02841-1716
Tel: (401) 367-1645

USCGC KATHERINE WALKER (WLM-552)
85 Port Terminal Blvd. Slip #1
Bayonne, NJ 07002-5041
Tel: (201) 443-5311

USCGC MARCUS HANNA (WLM-554)
259 High Street
South Portland, ME 04106-0007
Tel: (207) 767-0380

USCGC OAK (WLB 211)
47 Chandler St, Pier 2
Newport, RI 02841-1716
Tel: (401) 367-1646

Light List Volume I

This Light List is corrected through Coast Guard District Local Notice to Mariners No. 53/23, and

National Geospatial-Intelligence Agency (NGA) Notice to Mariners No. 53/23.

The 2024 edition supersedes the 2023 edition.

RECORD OF CORRECTIONS YEAR 2024

1/24	2/24	3/24	4/24	5/24	6/24	7/24	8/24
9/24	10/24	11/24	12/24	13/24	14/24	15/24	16/24
17/24	18/24	19/24	20/24	21/24	22/24	23/24	24/24
25/24	26/24	27/24	28/24	29/24	30/24	31/24	32/24
33/24	34/24	35/24	36/24	37/24	38/24	39/24	40/24
41/24	42/24	43/24	44/24	45/24	46/24	47/24	48/24
49/24	50/24	51/24	52/24	53/24			

PREFACE

Lights and other marine aids to navigation maintained by or under authority of the U.S. Coast Guard and located on waters used by general navigation are described in the 7 volumes of the U.S. Light List. The Light List describes many aids to navigation owned or maintained by private entities; however, not all such aids are described.

The following is a description of the geographic coverage of each volume:

Volume	Coast Guard District(s)	Geographic Description
I	**First Coast Guard District** 408 Atlantic Avenue Boston, MA 02110-3350 Tel: 617-223-8356 http://www.uscg.mil/d1	Maine, New Hampshire, Massachusetts, Vermont (Lake Champlain), Rhode Island, Connecticut and New York to Shrewsbury River, New Jersey.
II	**Fifth Coast Guard District** Federal Building 431 Crawford Street Portsmouth, VA 23704-5004 Tel: (757)398-6486 (757) 398-6552 http://www.uscg.mil/d5	Shrewsbury River, New Jersey to Little River South Carolina.
III	**Seventh Coast Guard District** Brickell Plaza Federal Building 909 SE 1st Avenue; Rm:406 Miami, FL 33131-3050 Tel: (305) 415-6752 or (305) 415-6800 http://www.uscg.mil/d7	South Carolina, Georgia, Florida to Econfina River (083°50' W), and Puerto Rico and the U.S. Virgin Islands.
IV	**Eight Coast Guard District** Hale Boggs Federal Building 500 Poydras Street New Orleans, LA 70130-3310 Tel: (504) 671-2327 (504) 671-2137 http://www.uscg.mil/d8	Econfina River (083°50' W), Florida to Rio Grande, Texas.
V		Mississippi River system and its navigable tributaries, Tenn-Tom Waterway, Alabama, Atchafalaya, and the Apalachicola-Chattahoochee-Flint River Systems.
VI	**Eleventh Coast Guard District** **(California, Nevada, Utah, Arizona)** Coast Guard Island Building 50-2 Alameda, CA 94501-5100 Tel: (510) 437-2975 http://www.uscg.mil/d11 **Thirteenth Coast Guard District** **(Oregon, Washington, Idaho, Montana)** Federal Building 915 Second Avenue 35th Floor, Rm3510 Seattle, WA 98174-1067 Tel: (206)220-7270 (206) 220-7004 http://www.uscg.mil/d13 **Seventeenth Coast Guard District** **(Alaska)** PO Box 25517 Juneau, AK 99802-5517 Tel: (907)463-2029 or (907) 463-2269 http://www.uscg.mil/d17	Pacific Coast, Pacific Islands, and the Coast of Alaska.
VII	**Ninth Coast Guard District** 1240 East 9th Street Cleveland, OH 44199-2060 Tel: (216)902-6060 or (216) 902-6117 http://www.uscg.mil/d9	Great Lakes and the St. Lawrence River above the St. Regis River.

CAUTION: Mariners attempting to pass a buoy close aboard risk collision with a yawing buoy or with the obstruction that the buoy marks. Mariners must not rely on buoys alone for determining their positions due to factors limiting buoy reliability.

PRIVATE AIDS TO NAVIGATION

Class I aids to navigation: These are aids located on marine structures or other works that the owners are legally obligated to establish, maintain, and operate as prescribed by the Coast Guard. These are included in the Light List.

Class II aids to navigation: These are aids, exclusive of Class I, that are located in waters used by general navigation. These are included in the Light List.

Class III aids to navigation: These are aids, exclusive of Class I and Class II that are located in waters not ordinarily used by general navigation. These are not included in the Light List.

LIGHT LIST AVAILABILITY

This Light List is annually published in electronic format and is intended to furnish more information concerning aids to navigation than can be conveniently shown on charts (U.S. Coast Guard Light List volumes can be found US Coast Guard Navigation Center website (USCG Light Lists). This Light List is not intended to be used in place of charts or the United States Coast Pilot®. Charts should be consulted for the location of all aids to navigation. It may be dangerous to use aids to navigation without reference to charts.

Note: NOAA has announced the phased shutdown of its traditional paper and raster chart production system. Cancellation of traditional NOAA paper nautical charts, RNCs, and other associated raster chart products will begin in 2021 and will be completed by January 2025. Use NOAA ENCs for the most up-to-date information.

This list is corrected to the date of the notices to mariners shown on the title page. Changes to aids to navigation during the year are advertised in U.S. Coast Guard Local Notices to Mariners and National Geospatial-Intelligence Agency (NGA) Notices to Mariners. Important changes to aids to navigation may also be broadcast through Coast Guard or Naval radio stations and NAVTEX. Mariners should keep their Light Lists corrected from these notices and should consult all notices issued after the date of publication of this Light List. Additionally, the U.S. Coast Guard maintains weekly updated Light Lists corrected through the current LNM week and are available in **XML** and **PDF** on the Weekly Light List Page of the U.S. Coast Guard Navigation Center (NAVCEN) website.

IMPORTANT: A summary of corrections for this publication, which includes corrections from the dates shown on the title page to the date of availability, is advertised in the Local Notice to Mariners and the Notice to Mariners. These corrections must be applied to bring the Light List up to date. Additionally, this publication should be corrected weekly from the Local Notices to Mariners or the Notices to Mariners, as appropriate.

Mariners and others are requested to bring any apparent errors or omissions in these lists to the attention of the cognizant U.S. Coast Guard District or NAVCEN at **TIS-PF-NISWS@USCG.MIL**

INTRODUCTION

How the Light List is Arranged

Aids to navigation on the Coastal United States are listed in geographic order clockwise from north to south along the Atlantic coast, east to west along the Gulf of Mexico, and south to north along the Pacific coast. On the Great Lakes, aids to navigation are listed from east to west and from south to north, except on Lake Michigan, which is listed from north to south. Seacoast aids to navigation are listed first, followed by entrance and harbor aids to navigation, which are listed in the order proceeding towards the head of navigation from seaward.

Names of aids to navigation are printed as follows to help distinguish immediately the type of aid to navigation.

Seacoast/Lake Coast Lights
Secondary Lights, RACONS
Sound Signals
RIVER, HARBOR, OTHER LIGHTS, V-AIS
Lighted Buoys
Daybeacons, Unlighted Buoys

Light List numbers are assigned to all Federal and Private aids to navigation for reference in the Light List. Aids to navigation are generally numbered by fives in accordance with their order of appearance in each volume of the Light List. Other numbers and decimal fractions are assigned where newly established aids to navigation are listed between previously numbered aids to navigation. The Light Lists are renumbered periodically to assign whole numbers to all aids to navigation.

International numbers are assigned to certain aids to navigation in cooperation with the International Hydrographic Organization. They consist of an alphabetic character followed by three or four numeric characters. A cross reference listing appears after the index.

Description of Columns

Column (1):   Light List Number.

Column (2):   Name and location of the aid to navigation.

Bearings are in degrees true, read clockwise from 000° through 359°.

Bearings on range lines are given in degrees and tenths where applicable.

(C) indicates Canadian aid to navigation.

Note: A dash (-) is used to indicate the bold heading is part of the name of the aid to navigation. When reporting discrepancies or making references to such an aid to navigation in correspondence, the full name of the aid including the geographic heading, should be given.

Column (3):   Geographic position (WGS-84) of the aid to navigation in latitude and longitude.

Column (4):   Light characteristic for lighted aids to navigation.

Column (5):   Height above water from the focal plane of the fixed light to mean high water, listed in feet. -For Volume 5 (Western Rivers), height above water is not indicated for aids to navigation. Clearances for bridges, etc. are contained in the remarks column and indicate water level for each instance.

For Volume 7 (Great Lakes), height above water from the focal plane of the fixed light to low water datum, listed in feet and meters.

Column (6):   Nominal range of lighted aids to navigation, in nautical miles, listed by color for sector and passing lights. Nominal Range is not listed for ranges, directional lights, or private aids to navigation.

For Volume 7 (Great Lakes), nominal range is expressed in statute miles.

Column (7):   The structural characteristic of the aid to navigation, including: dayboard (if any), description of fixed structure, color and type of buoy, height of structure above ground for major lights.

Column (8):   Aid remarks, sound signal characteristics, including: VHF-FM channel if remotely activated, RACON characteristic, light sector arc of visibility, radar reflector, emergency lights, seasonal remarks, and private aid to navigation identification. AIS specific information may include its unique Maritime Mobile Service Identity (MMSI), the MMSI(s) of its source AIS transmission, and the application identifier of any Application Specific Messages (ASM) it may also be transmitting.

U.S. Coast Guard Light List Distribution

U.S. Regulations require that most commercial vessels maintain on board a currently corrected copy or pertinent extract of the U.S. Coast Guard Light Lists, which are available for free and are updated weekly on the Coast Guard Navigation Center's website at USCG NAVCEN. For our policy on the use of electronic publications and charts, see Navigation and Vessel Inspection Circular (NVIC) 01-16 CH-2 which can be found here: https://www.dco.uscg.mil/Our-Organization/NVIC/Year/2010/ .

Nautical Charts & Publications

Nautical charts covering the coastal waters of the United States and its territories are produced by the National Oceanic and Atmospheric Administration (NOAA). These chart products include the NOAA electronic navigational chart (NOAA ENC®), NOAA raster navigational chart (NOAA RNC®), and traditional paper nautical charts. Information about ENCs may be found here: https://nauticalcharts.noaa.gov/charts/noaa-enc.html. Information about paper nautical charts and associated raster chart products may be found here: https://nauticalcharts.noaa.gov/charts/noaa-raster-charts.html.

ENCs, RNCs, and traditional chart images may be downloaded from the NOAA Chart Locator at: https://www.charts.noaa.gov/InteractiveCatalog/nrnc.shtml. Paper copies of traditional nautical charts may be purchased from any of the NOAA certified chart agents listed at: https://www.nauticalcharts.noaa.gov/publications/print-agents.html#paper-charts.

Note: NOAA has announced the phased shutdown of its traditional paper and raster chart production system. Cancellation of traditional NOAA paper nautical charts, RNCs, and other associated raster chart products will begin in 2021 and will be completed by January 2025. Use NOAA ENCs for the most up-to-date information.

Inland Electronic Navigational Charts (IENC) and chart books are published by the U.S. Army Corps of Engineers (USACE) and are available online at https://www.agc.army.mil/echarts

Tide Tables and Tidal Current Tables are no longer printed or distributed by NOAA. NOAA Tide and Current predictions are available online at NOAA Tides & Currents. Commercially printed versions that use NOAA data are also available.

Notices to Mariners

Several maritime information products produced by the U. S. Government use some version of the name "Notice to" or "Notice to Mariners". This section will describe each and explain how they can be obtained or accessed.

U.S. Notice to Mariners, published weekly by the National Geospatial Intelligence Agency (NGA), is prepared jointly by the NGA, the U. S. Coast Guard, and the National Ocean Service. Its purpose is to provide corrections to U. S. nautical charts used by ocean-going vessels, and corrections for a variety of publications, including the U. S. Coast Pilot, NGA List of Lights, and the USCG Light List, among others. The Notice to Mariners also catalogues recent maritime safety information that has been distributed for the benefit of oceangoing vessels. These include NAVAREA Warnings, HYDROLANTS, HYDROPACS, and HYDROARCS. Visit NGA at https://msi.nga.mil/NTM to obtain the latest and previous U. S. Notice to Mariners. For more information about such information is distributed worldwide through the Global Maritime Distress and Safety System (GMDSS), refer to NGA Publication 117: https://msi.nga.mil/Publications/RNA

Local Notice to Mariners are published weekly by each of the nine U. S. Coast Guard Districts, and provide the following information for waters within the District: the status of federal and private aids to navigation (such as discrepancies or temporary or proposed changes); special notices about maritime events, operations, and hazards; information about bridges; and, chart corrections for all National Ocean Service Charts in the District. Current and previous Local Notice to Mariners for each CG District can be found at the Coast Guard Navigation Center Website: https://www.navcen.uscg.gov/?pageName=lnmMain

U.S. Army Corps of Engineers (USACE) Notice to Navigation Interests (NTNI Notices) website contains navigation notices and policies issued by USACE Districts with a waterway navigation mission. These documents are disseminated to inform mariners of information describing events that affect waterway navigation such as maintenance projects, hazards to navigation, and other pertinent information. The notices are removed from the page seven days past the end date on the latest amendment. The site also has Policy Notices that remain in place until superseded. This site does not contain all notices such as those published by other agencies.

Broadcast Notices to Mariners (BNM) are transmitted using voice over VHF radio (channel 22) by each Coast Guard District to communicate local information about hazards, emergent situations, and the status of federal aids to navigation. Broadcasts occur at scheduled times, or as needed, and are normally announced first on VHF channel 16, before transmission on channel 22. BNMs provide in near real-time much of the same information that will later be published in the Local Notice to Mariners. The Coast Guard is enhancing the delivery and accessibility of Broadcast Notices to Mariners (BNMs) by initiating email distribution service. In addition to traditional methods, mariners can now receive BNMs directly to their email, ensuring timely and convenient updates. Furthermore, BNMs are being archived on the website www.navcen.gov, making them readily available for access via wireless mobile devices. This nationwide service will improve the reach and efficiency of maritime safety information and communications. To subscribe to the email service, mariners can visit the following link: https://www.navcen.uscg.gov/subscribe-email-rss-feeds.

Urgent broadcasts applicable to situations or locations beyond the range of VHF land stations and out to approximately 100 miles have also been broadcast via the medium frequency NAVTEX system.

Discrepancies to Aids to Navigation

The U.S. Aids to Navigation System is a publicly monitored system that relies on mariners to inform U.S. Coast Guard units of observed discrepancies or outages. Therefore, for the safety of all mariners, anyone who observes an aid to navigation that is either off station or exhibiting characteristics other than those listed in the Light Lists should promptly notify the nearest Coast Guard unit. Radio messages should be prefixed "COAST GUARD" and transmitted on VHF-FM channel 16. In addition to notifying the nearest Coast Guard unit by radio, a discrepant aid to navigation can be reported online at http://www.navcen.uscg.gov/?pageName=atonOutageReport, or by calling (703) 313-5900, or emailing the Navigation Information Service (NIS) watch at TIS-SMB-NISWS@USCG.MIL .

GENERAL

U.S. AIDS TO NAVIGATION SYSTEM

The navigable waters of the United States are marked to assist navigation using the U.S. Aids to Navigation System, a system consistent with the International Association of Marine Aids to Navigation and Lighthouse Authorities (IALA) Maritime Buoyage System. The IALA Maritime Buoyage System is followed by most of the world's maritime nations and improves maritime safety by encouraging conformity in buoyage systems worldwide. IALA buoyage is divided into two regions made up of Region A and Region B. All navigable waters of the United States follow IALA Region B, except U.S. possessions west of the International Date Line and south of 10° north latitude, which follow Region A. Lateral aids to navigation in Region A vary from those located within Region B. Non-lateral aids to navigation in Region A are the same as those used in Region B. Appropriate nautical charts and publications should be consulted to determine whether the Region A or Region B marking schemes are in effect for a given area.

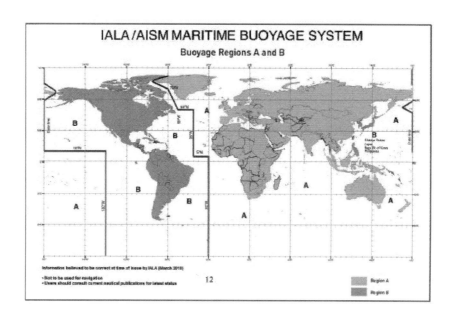

Aids to navigation are developed, established, operated, and maintained by the U.S. Coast Guard to accomplish the following:

1. Assist navigators in determining their position,
2. Assist the navigator in determining a safe course,
3. Warn the navigator of dangers and obstructions,
4. Promote the safe and economic movement of commercial vessel traffic, and
5. Promote the safe and efficient movement of military vessel traffic, and cargo of strategic military importance.

The U.S. Aids to Navigation System is designed for use with nautical charts. Nautical charts portray the physical features of the marine environment, which include soundings, landmarks, hazards to navigation, and aids to navigation. To best understand the purpose of a specific aid to navigation, mariners should consult the associated nautical chart, which illustrates the relationship of the aid to navigation to channel limits, obstructions, hazards to navigation, and to the aids to navigation system as a whole. Seasonal aids to navigation are placed into service, withdrawn, or changed at specified times of the year. The dates shown in the Light Lists are approximate and may vary due to adverse weather or other conditions. These aids will be changed on Electronic Navigational Charts (ENC) based on Light List dates and electronic navigation system settings.

Mariners should maintain and consult suitable publications and navigation equipment depending on the vessel's requirements. This shipboard navigation equipment is separate from the aids to navigation system but is often essential to its use.

The Coast Guard establishes, maintains, and operates a system of aids to navigation consisting of visual, audible, and electronic signals designed to assist the prudent mariner in the process of navigation. The U.S. Aids to Navigation System is primarily a lateral system, which employs a simple arrangement of colors, shapes, numbers, and light characteristics to mark the limits of navigable routes. This lateral system is supplemented with electronic signals such as AIS-ATON and non-lateral aids to navigation where appropriate.

The U.S. Aids to Navigation System contains the following subsystems:

1. **Intracoastal Waterway**: The aids to navigation marking the Intracoastal Waterway are arranged geographically from north to south on the Atlantic Coast and generally east to west on the coast of the Gulf of Mexico. Red lights (if so equipped), even numbers, and red buoys or triangle shaped daymarks are located on the southbound/westbound starboard waterway boundary. Green lights (if so equipped), odd numbers, and green buoys or square shaped daymarks are on the southbound/westbound port waterway boundary.

2. **Western Rivers**: The Western Rivers System is employed on the Mississippi River System, in addition to the Tennessee-Tombigbee Waterway and the Alabama, Atchafalaya, and Apalachicola-Chattahoochee-Flint River Systems. The Western Rivers System consists of the following characteristics:

   a. Buoys are not numbered.
   b. Numbers on beacons do not have lateral significance, but rather indicate mileage from a fixed point (normally the river mouth).
   c. Diamond shaped non-lateral dayboards, red and white or green and white as appropriate, are used to indicate where the river channel crosses from one bank to the other.
   d. Lights on green aids to navigation show a single-flash characteristic, which may be green or white.
   e. Lights on red aids to navigation show a group-flash characteristic, which may be red or white.
   f. Isolated danger marks are not used.

3. **Bridge Markings:** Bridges across navigable waters are marked with red, green and/or white lights for nighttime navigation. Red lights mark piers and other parts of the bridge. Red lights are also placed on drawbridges to show when they are in the closed position. Green lights are placed on drawbridges to show when they are in the open position. The location of these lights will vary according to the bridge structure. Green lights are also used to mark the centerline of navigable channels through fixed bridges. If there are two or more channels through the bridge, the preferred channel is also marked by three white lights in a vertical line above the green light.

   Red and green retro-reflective panels may be used to mark bridge piers and may also be used on bridges not required to display lights. Lateral red and green lights and dayboards may mark main channels through bridges. Adjacent piers are marked with fixed yellow lights when the main channel is marked with lateral aids to navigation. Centerlines of channels through fixed bridges may be marked with a safe water mark and an occulting white light when lateral marks are used to mark main channels.

   The centerline of the navigable channel through the draw span of floating bridges may be marked with a special mark. The mark will be a yellow diamond with yellow retro-reflective panels and may exhibit a yellow light that displays a Morse code "B" (a long flash followed by three short flashes). AIS-ATON and RACONs may be placed on the bridge structure to mark the centerline of the navigable channel through the bridge.

   Vertical clearance gauges may be installed to enhance navigation safety. The gauges are located on the right channel pier or pier protective structure facing approaching vessels. Clearance gauges indicate the vertical distance between "low steel" of the bridge channel span (in the closed to navigation position for drawbridges) and the level of the water, measured to the bottom of the foot marks, read from top to bottom.

Drawbridges equipped with radiotelephones display a blue and white sign which indicates what VHF radiotelephone channels should be used to request bridge openings.

4. **Private** aids to navigation include aids to navigation that are either operated by private persons and organizations, or that are operated by states. Private aids to navigation are classified into three categories:

   a. **Class I**: Aids to navigation on marine structures or other works that the owners are legally obligated to establish, maintain, and operate as prescribed by the U.S. Coast Guard.
   b. **Class II:** Aids to navigation that, exclusive of Class I aids, are in waters used by general navigation.
   c. **Class III:** Aids to navigation that, exclusive of Class I and Class II aids, are in waters not ordinarily used by general navigation.

Authorization for the establishment of a Class II or Class III private aid to navigation by the U.S. Coast Guard imposes no legal obligation that the aid be established and operated. It only specifies the location and operational characteristics of the aid for which the authorization was requested. Once the aid is established, however, the owner is legally obligated to maintain it in good working order and properly painted.

5. **Lights and sound signals on oil wells or other offshore structures** in navigable waters are private aids to navigation and are generally not listed in the Light List unless they are equipped with a RACON or AIS-ATON. Where space allows, the structures are shown on the appropriate nautical charts. Information concerning the location and characteristics of those structures which display lights and sound signals not located in obstruction areas are published in Local and/or weekly Notices to Mariners. In general, during the nighttime, a series of white lights are displayed extending from the platform to the top of the derrick when drilling operations are in progress. At other times, structures are usually marked with one or more quick flashing white, red, or yellow lights, visible for at least one nautical mile during clear weather. Obstructions, which are a part of the appurtenances to the main structure, such as mooring piles, anchors, and mooring buoys, etc., are not normally lighted. In addition, some structures are equipped with a sound signal that produces a single two-second blast every 20 seconds.

6. **Lighting and Marking of Windfarm Structures.** The United States follows the International Association of Marine Aids to Navigation and Lighthouse Authorities IALA) Guideline G1162 on The Lighting and Marking of Offshore Man-Made Structures, except as follows: Uniform Alphanumeric Marking of Installations, Facilities and Structures (IFSs): Each IFS in an OREI lease area should be marked with its unique alphanumeric character, a National Oceanic and Atmospheric Administration charted designator, enabling quick recognition and reference for search and rescue, law enforcement, and other purposes. Markings on each IFS should be at least 8 feet (ft.) (2.5 meters (m)) and as close to 10 ft. (3 m) in height as possible, posted between 30 to 50 ft. above Mean Higher High water, such that they are visible all-round (360-degree arc) from the water's surface. Use of retro-reflective paint or materials for lettering and numbering is highly recommended. Each IFS' unique marking should be duplicated on top of its nacelle to aid identification from the air. Lighting and Sound Signals of Significant Peripheral Structure (SPS), normally a corner structure and other significant points on the boundary of the wind farm.

The following guidance provides additional information to augment compliance with lighting and marking of OREIs on the Outer Continental Shelf (OCS). Lighting and Marking: The nominal distance between SPSs and any adjacent SPS or Intermediate Peripheral Structure should not exceed 3 nautical miles (NM). In addition to its marking, each SPS should be fitted with the following:

- Quick flashing yellow light (QY, 0.3s on/0.7s off) that is visible at least 5NM and synchronized with all other SPS lights; and
- Sound signal that produces a 4s blast every 30s with rated range of 2NM when the visibility in any direction is less than 5NM or when activated by keying marine VHF-FM Channel 1083 (157.175 MHz, previously 83A) five times within ten seconds—Mariner Radio Activated Sound Signal (MRASS).

Lighting of Intermediate Peripheral Structures: Outer boundary non-SPS IFS are called Intermediate Peripheral Structures (IPS). IPS should be fitted with a 2.5 second flashing yellow light (FL Y 2.5s, 1.0s on/1.5s off) that is visible at least 3NM away and synchronized with all other IPS lights.

Lighting of IFS: Interior IFS should be fitted with a 6 second flashing yellow light (FL Y 6s, 1.0s on/5.0s off) or a 10 second flashing yellow light (FL Y 10s, 1.0s on/9.0s off) that is visible at least 2NM and should be synchronized with all other Interior IFS lights.

Lighting of SPS: SPS should be Quick Flashing Yellow 5 NM IPS Flashing 2.5 Seconds Yellow 3 NM Interior Towers Flashing 6, 10 or 15 Sec. Yellow 2NM. Each SPS, and IPS adjacent to a fairway or used to identify a designated vessel transit route through the farm or closely adjacent farms, shall be identified by a properly encoded AIS Message 21. These broadcasts shall be made autonomously and continuously (99 percent availability), at least every 6 minutes, alternating on AIS channel 1 and 2, at sufficient power to provide a relatively uniform coverage recommended to extend at least 8NM beyond the periphery of the wind farm to allow sufficient time for ship operators to detect and make any necessary course or speed alterations. IPS, or other IFS within the farm, may be additionally marked with physical or synthetic AIS Message 21 if circumstances warrant; but not such to overload the VHF data link in or near congested waters. Additionally, AIS Message 21 broadcasts should indicate current "ATON status" (i.e., good health, light discrepancies, etc.). ATON status "alarms" may be accompanied by an AIS Safety Related Broadcast (AIS Message 14). Use of AIS requires submission of a USCG AIS Private ATON Application (see Form CG-4143) and subsequent Federal Communications Commission licensing.

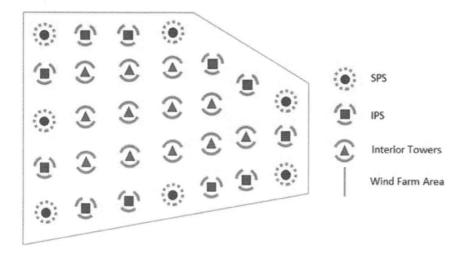

Example of SPS and IPS identified in a windfarm layout (not to scale).

BUOYS, BEACONS, AND AIS-ATON

The primary components of the U.S. Aids to Navigation System are buoys, beacons, and AIS-ATON.

Buoys are floating aids to navigation used extensively throughout U.S. waters. They are moored to sinkers by varying lengths of chain and may shift due to sea conditions and other causes. Buoys may also be carried away, capsized, or sunk. Prudent mariners will not rely solely on any single aid to navigation, particularly floating aids.

Buoy positions represented on nautical charts are approximate position only, due to the practical limitations of positioning and maintaining buoys and their sinkers in precise geographical locations.

Positions of Federal buoys are verified during periodic maintenance visits. Between visits, environmental conditions such as atmospheric and sea conditions or seabed slope and composition may shift buoys off their charted positions. Buoys may also be dragged off station, sunk, or capsized by a collision with a vessel.

Beacons are aids to navigation which are permanently fixed to the earth's surface. They range from large lighthouses to small single-pile structures and may be located on land or in the water. Lighted beacons are called lights; unlighted beacons are called daybeacons. Lighthouses are placed on shore or on marine sites and most often do not indicate lateral significance. Lighthouses with no lateral significance exhibit a white light.

Beacons exhibit a daymark. For small structures, these are colored geometric shapes that make an aid to navigation readily visible and easily identifiable against background conditions. Generally, the daymark conveys to the mariner during daylight hours the same significance as the aid's light or reflector does at night. The daymark of towers, however, consists of the structure itself. As a result, these daymarks do not imply lateral significance.

Ranges (Leading Lights) are non-lateral aids to navigation composed of two beacons, which when sighted in line with one another, define a particular bearing or course. The appropriate nautical chart must be consulted when using ranges to determine whether the range marks the centerline of the navigable channel and what section of the range may be safely traversed. Ranges typically display rectangular dayboards of various colors and are generally, but not always lighted. Ranges may display lights during daylight and at night. When lighted, ranges may display lights of any color.

Caution: Vessels should not pass beacons close aboard due to the danger of collision with riprap or structure foundations, or with the obstruction or danger being marked.

Automatic Identification System (AIS) is a maritime navigation safety communications protocol defined by the International Telecommunication Union and adopted by the International Maritime Organization for the autonomous and continuous exchange of pertinent navigation information between seagoing ships and other mandated vessels, such as identity, call-sign, position, dimensions, type, and navigation status. In addition to ship-to-ship broadcasts, AIS may communicate between ship and shore stations and be used for other navigation safety purpose, such as augmenting the presence (on radar) and/or providing the status of an existing ATON.

Automatic Identification System-ATON (AIS-ATON) ATON may be enhanced using AIS communications protocol. AIS-ATON can be used to autonomously and at fixed intervals broadcast the name, position, dimensions, type, characteristics, and status from or concerning an aid to navigation. AIS-ATON information can only be "seen" on AIS capable navigation display systems, such as those that meet IEC 62288 Navigation Presentation standards or are supported by other proprietary means used by non-IEC compliant manufacturers. The figures below show how some are represented on AIS compliant navigation displays. AIS-ATON reports may have lateral significance and thus are charted to mimic a physical buoy or beacon. They may also be used to provide other marine safety information, such as when a charted restricted area is open or closed, or to highlight a temporary condition that may not be charted, e.g., rocket launch areas. AIS, as provided by the U.S. Army Corp of Engineers, can also provide reports on environmental conditions, wind speed and direction, current data, lock status, etc.

AIS-ATON reports are characterized in one of three ways: **physical** (meaning the AIS transmitter is physically located on the aid to navigation it is associated with, such as a ATON), **synthetic** (meaning the AIS message or symbol associated with a particular ATON or beacon is being broadcast from a different physical location, such as from an AIS antenna on shore), or **virtual** (meaning no physical ATON or beacon exists, but that an AIS message or symbol is being broadcast in order to be portrayed in a particular location). In the Light List, physical and virtual aids will be listed as such in column (8), the remarks section. If an AIS-ATON listed in the Light List does not have the words "physical" or "virtual" in the remarks section, it should be presumed by the mariner to be a synthetic AIS-ATON. Column (8) will also identify the source Maritime Mobile Service Identity (MMSI) of the broadcast station(s). For example:

	(8) Remarks
	[Physical/Virtual] AIS AIS: 993666 $X_1X_2X_3X_4$ SOURCE AIS: 00366$X_1X_2X_3X_4$, ASM: 8/67:33v3 [If more than 1 source station] 00366 $X_1X_2X_3X_4$

Caution: When encountering an AIS-ATON, especially one associated with an ATON, mariners should consult the Light List carefully to understand whether the AIS transmitter is located on the aid or not. This is critical information necessary for interpreting the situation. For example, if the AIS transmitter is located on the ATON it is associated with (physical AIS-ATON), the location of the AIS signal will always correspond to the ATON's actual position. If off-station, its broadcasted report will state so (i.e., off-position indicator, 0 = on position, 1 = off position); and additionally, will broadcast an AIS safety-related text message stating: ATON OFF-POSITION. These ATON are usually charted and denoted by a magenta circle and "AIS" label.

Synthetic AIS-ATON do not have this capability; when employed with a ATON, synthetic AIS-ATON always appear on the ATON's assigned (charted) position, even if the ATON is off-station, damaged, missing, etc.

Caution: Mariners may find it difficult to distinguish between a synthetic and physical AIS-ATON by examining only the chart. Physical AIS-ATON is encircled in magenta, while synthetic AIS-ATON is not. Charts may not necessarily reflect the existence of a Synthetic AIS-ATON, nor its source station. If unsure, the Light List should be consulted. Virtual AIS-ATON are always listed as "VAIS" on the chart.

For virtual and synthetic AIS-ATON, the Light List may list the Maritime Mobile Service Identity (MMSI) of its (source) broadcast station. Where provided, this information is intended to aid mariners in determining whether they are near enough for their equipment to detect such AIS-ATON. For voyage planning purposes, mariners should note that an ATON's broadcasted position may be up to 25 nautical miles away from the source station.

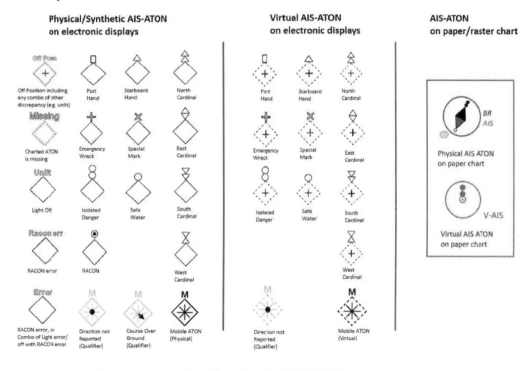

As per current IEC 62288:2021 & IHO S-52

The technology associated with AIS-ATON allows for other types of information to be broadcast to the mariner. Examples could include information about the health or status of AIS-ATON, environmental or other safety information, navigation warnings, or information about the status of bridges. Mariners should look for updates to the Light List to understand how the Coast Guard is implementing this technology. Although all existing AIS mobile devices can receive AIS ATON Reports and Application Specific Messages (ASM), they may not readily appear on an AIS Minimal Keyboard Display or other shipboard navigational display systems (Radar), which would require software updates to make these systems compliant with international navigation presentation standards (i.e., IEC 62288 (series), IHO S-52 (series)). The data content of AIS Application Specific Messages can found at https://www.iala-aism.org/asm.

They are identified by their: AIS message number (i.e. 6, 8, 25 or 26), Designated Area Code (DAC), Function Identifier (FI), and Version Number.

Application Specific Message ASM:X/YYY.ZZ.V, where:
X identifies the AIS message number (i.e. 6, 8, 25 or 26),
YYY its Designated Area Code (DAC),
ZZ its Function Identifier (FI), and V its Version Number,

e.g. ASM:8/367.22.2 denotes U.S. Geographic Notice, Application Specific Message 8, DAC = 367, FL = 22, Version =2.

Symbology used for Application Specific Messages per International Navigation Displays Standard (IEC 62288)

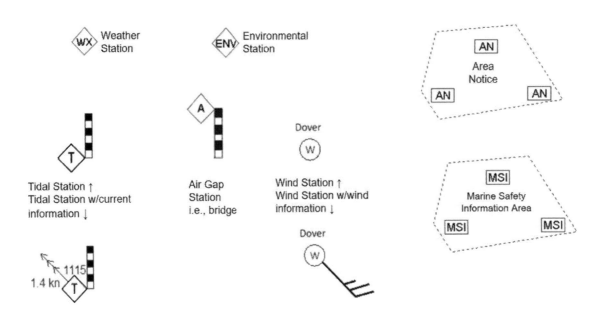

Nationwide Automatic Identification System (NAIS) consists of approximately 200 VHF receiver sites located throughout the coastal continental United States, inland rivers, Alaska, Hawaii, Puerto Rico, and Guam. NAIS couples AIS technology with a comprehensive network infrastructure to achieve ship to-shore and shore-to-ship data transmission throughout the navigable waters of the United States. The system enables AIS-equipped vessels to receive important marine information such as safety and security messages, weather alerts, and electronic aids to navigation. A list of NAIS Base Stations and their corresponding MMSI numbers can be found in the table at the end of this section.

NAIS is designed to collect safety and security data from AIS-equipped vessels in navigable waters of the United States and share that data with Coast Guard operators and other government and port partners. The primary goal of NAIS is to increase situational awareness through data dissemination via a network infrastructure, particularly focusing on improving maritime security, marine and navigational safety, search and rescue, and environmental protection services. Collected AIS data improves the safety of vessels and ports through collision avoidance and the safety of the nation through detection, identification, and classification of vessels. NAIS broadcasts navigation enhancing safety related messages such as Synthetic AIS ATON Reports and Application Specific Messages.

For more information about AIS see:
- AIS messages at: NAVCEN AIS Messages
- IMO Safety of Navigation Circular 289 and 290 regarding Application Specific Messages (ASM) at: NAVCEN AIS References
- IALA AIS ASM Catalog at: www.e-navigation.nl/asm, and
- USCG Special Notice 14-02 regarding AIS Aids to Navigation at: NAVCEN AIS FAQ #21

The U.S. Army Corps of Engineers (USACE) operates AIS-ATONs extensively throughout the Western Rivers, Columbia River and at the Sault Ste Marie lock and dam. USACE AIS Stations broadcast a variety of information including ATON, Environmental, and Geographic Notices in support of navigation safety and efficient movement of vessels though U.S. inland waterways through their Lock Operations and Management Application (LOMA).

The Marine Exchange of Alaska (MXAK) is a nonprofit maritime organization based in Juneau, Alaska. The organization was established to broker information, that aids safe, secure, efficient, and environmentally sound maritime operations in Alaska. MXAK operates a network of Automatic Identification System (AIS) Stations to broadcast a variety of information including ATON, Environmental, and Geographic Notices in support of navigation safety and efficient movement of vessels throughout Alaska.

The U.S. Coast Guard and some other approved entities (i.e., U.S. Army Corps of Engineers, National Oceanic and Atmospheric Administration, Marine Exchange of Alaska, etc.) have been transmitting AIS ATON Reports and marine safety information via AIS since 2014 (see our Special Notice 01-2014). The exact content, location, and times of these transmissions are announced in the Coast Guard Local Notices to Mariners (LNM) and denoted in Coast Guard Light List.

Note, AIS ATON stations operated in the U.S., other than by the U.S. Coast Guard, require Federal Communications Commission (FCC) or National Telecommunication Information Agency (NTIA) radio determination service licensing/authorization; which they will not grant without prior approval from the U.S. Coast Guard. Requests for such approvals may be sent to cgnav@uscg.mil via a USCG Private Aid to Navigation (PATON) application (either CG Form 2554 or 4143) and this Addendum. For further information on AIS ATON see our AIS Frequently Asked Question 21 and the International Association of Marine Aid to Navigation and Lighthouse Authorities' (IALA) publications on the subject.

For further information on AIS ATON, please refer to the various IALA Guidelines and Recommendations and their uses. The U.S. Coast Guard and some other approved entities (i.e., U.S. Army Corps of Engineers, National Oceanic and Atmospheric Administration, Marine Exchange of Alaska, etc.) have been transmitting AIS ATON Reports and marine safety information via AIS since 2014 (see our Special Notice 01-2014). The exact content, location, and times of these transmissions are announced in the Coast Guard Local Notices to Mariners (LNM) and denoted in Coast Guard Light List.

TYPES OF SIGNALS

Lighted aids to navigation are, for the most part, equipped with daylight controls which automatically cause the light to operate during darkness and to be extinguished during daylight. These devices are not of equal sensitivity; therefore, all lights do not come on or go off at the same time. Mariners should ensure correct identification of aids to navigation during twilight periods when some lighted aids to navigation are lit while others are not. The lighting apparatus is serviced at periodic intervals to assure reliable operation, but there is always possibility of a light being extinguished or operating improperly.

Only aids to navigation with green or red lights have lateral significance and exhibit either flashing, quick flashing, group flashing, occulting, or isophase light rhythms. When proceeding in the conventional direction of buoyage, the mariner in IALA Region B, may see the following lighted aids to navigation:

Green lights on aids to navigation mark port sides of channels and locations of wrecks or obstructions that must be passed by keeping these lighted aids to navigation on the port hand of a vessel. Green lights are also used on preferred channel marks where the preferred channel is to starboard (i.e., aid to navigation left to port when proceeding in the conventional direction of buoyage). Red lights on aids to navigation mark starboard sides of channels and locations of wrecks or obstructions that must be passed by keeping these lighted aids to navigation on the starboard hand of a vessel. Red lights are also used on preferred channel marks where the preferred channel is to port (i.e., aid to navigation left to starboard when proceeding in the conventional direction of buoyage).

White and yellow lights have no lateral significance. The shapes, colors, letters, and light rhythms may determine the purpose of aids to navigation exhibiting white or yellow lights.

Different colored light emitting diode (LED) lights used in conjunction or sectors of colored glass are placed in the lanterns of some lights to produce a system of light sectors of different colors. In general, red sectors are used to mark shoals or to warn the mariner of other obstructions to navigation or of nearby land. Such lights provide approximate bearing information since observers may note the change of color as they cross the boundary between sectors. These boundaries are indicated in the Light List (Col. 8) and by dotted lines on charts. These bearings, as all bearings referring to lights, are given in true degrees from 000° to 359°, as observed from a vessel toward the light.

When navigating, mariners should not rely on a line of bearing defined by the boundary between light sectors. These sectors are not designed to define an accurate observed line of bearing. Using a compass bearing to the light is recommend as more accurate. Be guided instead by the correct compass bearing to the light and do not rely on being able to accurately observe the point at which the color changes. This is difficult to determine because the edges of a colored sector cannot be cut off sharply. On either side of the line of demarcation between white, red, or green sectors, there is always a small arc of uncertain color. Moreover, when haze or smoke is present in the intervening atmosphere, a white sector might have a reddish hue.

The arc drawn on charts around a light is not intended to give information as to the distance at which it can be seen. The arc indicates the bearings between which the variation of visibility or obstruction of the light occurs.

Most aids to navigation are fitted with retro reflective material to increase their visibility in darkness. Colored reflective material is used on aids to navigation that, if lighted, will display lights of the same color.

Preferred channel marks exhibit a composite group-flashing light rhythm of two flashes followed by a single flash.

Safe water marks exhibit a white Morse code "A" rhythm (a short flash followed by a long flash).

Isolated danger marks exhibit a white flashing (2) rhythm (two flashes repeated regularly).
Special marks exhibit yellow lights and exhibit a flashing or fixed rhythm.

Information and regulatory marks exhibit a white light with any light rhythm except quick flashing, flashing (2) and Morse code "A."

For situations where lights require a distinct cautionary significance, as at sharp turns, sudden channel constrictions, wrecks, or obstructions, a quick flashing light rhythm will be used.

Conditions which may affect a Light

The condition of the atmosphere has a considerable effect upon the distance at which lights can be seen. Sometimes lights are obscured by fog, haze, dust, smoke, or precipitation which may be present at the light, or between the light and the observer, and which is possibly unknown by the observer. Atmospheric refraction may cause a light to be seen farther than under ordinary circumstances.

A light of low intensity will be easily obscured by unfavorable conditions in the atmosphere and little dependence can be placed on it being seen. For this reason, the intensity of a light should always be considered when expecting to sight it in reduced visibility. Haze and distance may reduce the apparent duration of the flash of a light. In some atmospheric conditions, white lights may have a reddish hue. Lights placed at high elevations are more frequently obscured by clouds, mist, and fog than those lights located at or near sea level.

In regions where ice conditions prevail in the winter, the lantern panes of lights may become covered with ice or snow, which will greatly reduce the visibility of the lights and may also cause colored lights to appear white.

The increasing use of brilliant shore lights for advertising, illuminating bridges, and other purposes, may cause marine navigational lights, particularly those in densely inhabited areas, to be outshone and difficult to distinguish from the background lighting. Mariners are requested to report such cases in order that steps may be taken to improve the conditions.

The "loom" (glow) of a powerful light is often seen beyond the limit of visibility of the actual rays of the light. The loom may sometimes appear sufficiently sharp enough to obtain a bearing. At short distances, some flashing lights may show a faint continuous light between flashes.

The distance of an observer from a light cannot be estimated by its apparent intensity. Mariners should always check the characteristics of lights to avoid mistaking powerful lights, visible in the distance, for nearby lights (such as those on lighted buoys) showing similar characteristics of low intensity. If lights are not sighted within a reasonable time after prediction, a dangerous situation may exist, requiring prompt resolution or action to ensure the safety of the vessel.

The characteristic of a lights can appear to change based on the observer's distance from it. Consider the case of a light with a rather complex characteristic: Fixed white with an alternating red and white. From a distance the light might appear to only be a flashing white. At a shorter distance it may look like an alternating red and white. Only up close might an observer be able to see the true characteristic. Fixed white with an alternating red and white.

If a vessel has considerable vertical motion due to pitching in heavy seas, a light sighted on the horizon may alternatively appear and disappear. This may lead the unwary to assign a false characteristic and hence, to error in its identification. The true characteristic will be evident after the distance has been sufficiently decreased or by increasing the height of eye of the observer.

Similarly, the effect of wave motion on lighted buoys may produce the appearance of incorrect light phase characteristics when certain flashes occur but are not viewed by the mariner. In addition, buoy motion can reduce the distance at which buoy lights are detected.

Shapes are used to provide easy identification on certain unlighted buoys and dayboards on beacons. These shapes are laterally significant only when associated with laterally significant colors. In IALA Region B, cylindrical buoys (referred to as "can buoys") and square dayboards mark the port side of a channel when proceeding in the conventional direction of buoyage. These aids to navigation are associated with solid green or green and red-banded marks where the topmost band is green. Conical buoys (referred to as "nun buoys") and triangular dayboards mark the starboard side of the channel when proceeding from seaward. These aids to navigation are associated with solid red or red and green-banded marks where the topmost band is red.

Unless fitted with topmarks; lighted, sound, pillar, and spar buoys have no shape significance. Their numbers, colors, and light characteristics convey their meanings.

Dayboards throughout the U.S. Aids to Navigation System are described using standard designations that describe the appearance of each dayboard. A brief explanation of the designations and of the purpose of each type of dayboard in the system is given below, followed by a verbal description of the appearance of each dayboard type.

Designations:

1. First Letter – Shape or Purpose

    C: Crossing (Western Rivers only) diamond-shaped, used to indicate the points at which the channel crosses the river.

    J: Junction (square or triangle) used to mark (preferred channel) junctions or bifurcations in the channel, or wrecks or obstructions which may be passed on either side; color of top band has lateral significance for the preferred channel.

K: Range (rectangular) when both the front and rear range dayboards are aligned on the same bearing, the observer is on the azimuth of the range, usually used to mark the center of the channel.

M: Safe Water (octagonal) used to mark the fairway or middle of the channel.

N: No lateral significance (diamond or rectangular) used for special purpose, warning, distance, or location markers.

S: Square used to mark the port side of channels when proceeding from seaward.

T: Triangle used to mark the starboard side of channels when proceeding from seaward.

2. Second Letter – Key Color

   B – Black   G – Green   R – Red   W – White   Y – Yellow

3. Third Letter – Color of Center Stripe (Range Dayboards Only)

4. Additional Information after a (-)

   -I: Intracoastal Waterway; a yellow reflective horizontal band on a dayboard; indicates the aid to navigation marks the Intracoastal Waterway.

   -SY: Intracoastal Waterway; a yellow reflective square on a dayboard; indicates the aid to navigation is a port hand mark for vessels traversing the Intracoastal Waterway. May appear on a triangular daymark where the Intracoastal Waterway coincides with a waterway having opposite conventional direction of buoyage.

   -TY: Intracoastal Waterway; a yellow reflective triangle on a dayboard; indicates the aid to navigation is a starboard hand mark for vessels traversing the Intracoastal Waterway. May appear on a square daymark where the Intracoastal Waterway coincides with a waterway having opposite conventional direction of buoyage.

Descriptions:

CNG: Diamond-shaped dayboard divided into four diamond-shaped colored sectors with the sectors at the side corners white and the sectors at the top and bottom corners green, with green reflective diamonds at the top and bottom corners and white reflective diamonds in the side corners (Western Rivers only).

CNR: Diamond-shaped dayboard divided into four diamond-shaped colored sectors with the sectors at the side corners white and the sectors at the top and bottom corners red, with red reflective diamonds at the top and bottom corners and white reflective diamonds in the side corners (Western Rivers only).

JG: Dayboard bearing horizontal bands of green and red, green band topmost, with corresponding reflective borders.

JG-I: Square dayboard bearing horizontal bands of green and red, green band topmost, with corresponding reflective borders and a yellow reflective horizontal band.

JG-SY: Square dayboard bearing horizontal bands of green and red, green band topmost, with corresponding reflective borders and a yellow reflective square.

JG-TY: Square dayboard bearing horizontal bands of green and red, green band topmost, with corresponding reflective borders and a yellow reflective triangle.

JR: Dayboard bearing horizontal bands of red and green, red band topmost, with corresponding reflective borders.

JR-I: Triangular dayboard bearing horizontal bands of red and green, red band topmost, with corresponding reflective borders and a yellow reflective horizontal band.

JR-SY: Triangular dayboard bearing horizontal bands of red and green, red band topmost, with corresponding reflective borders and a yellow reflective square.

JR-TY: Triangular dayboard bearing horizontal bands of red and green, red band topmost, with corresponding reflective borders and a yellow reflective triangle.

KBG: Rectangular black dayboard bearing a central green stripe.

KBG-I: Rectangular black dayboard bearing a central green stripe and a yellow reflective horizontal band.

KBR: Rectangular black dayboard bearing a central red stripe.

KBR-I: Rectangular black dayboard bearing a central red stripe and a yellow reflective horizontal band.

KBW: Rectangular black dayboard bearing a central white stripe.

KBW-I: Rectangular black dayboard bearing a central white stripe and a yellow reflective horizontal band.

KGB: Rectangular green dayboard bearing a central black stripe.

KGB-I: Rectangular green dayboard bearing a central black stripe and a yellow reflective horizontal band.

KGR: Rectangular green dayboard bearing a central red stripe.

KGR-I: Rectangular green dayboard bearing a central red stripe and a yellow reflective horizontal band.

KGW: Rectangular green dayboard bearing a central white stripe.

KGW-I: Rectangular green dayboard bearing a central white stripe and a yellow reflective horizontal band.

KRB: Rectangular red dayboard bearing a central black stripe.

KRB-I: Rectangular red dayboard bearing a central black stripe and a yellow reflective horizontal band.

KRG: Rectangular red dayboard bearing a central green stripe.

KRG-I: Rectangular red dayboard bearing a central green stripe and a yellow reflective horizontal band.

KRW: Rectangular red dayboard bearing a central white stripe.

KRW-I: Rectangular red dayboard bearing a central white stripe and a yellow reflective horizontal band.

KWB: Rectangular white dayboard bearing a central black stripe.

KWB-I: Rectangular white dayboard bearing a central black stripe and a yellow reflective horizontal band.

KWG: Rectangular white dayboard bearing a central green stripe.

KWG-I: Rectangular white dayboard bearing a central green stripe and a yellow reflective horizontal band.

KWR: Rectangular white dayboard bearing a central red stripe.

KWR-I: Rectangular white dayboard bearing a central red stripe and a yellow reflective horizontal band.

MR: Octagonal dayboard bearing stripes of white and red, with a white reflective border.

MR-I: Octagonal dayboard bearing stripes of white and red, with a white reflective border and a yellow reflective horizontal band.

NB: Diamond-shaped dayboard divided into four diamond-shaped colored sectors with the sectors at the side corners white and the sectors at the top and bottom corners black, with a white reflective border.

ND: Rectangular white mileage marker with black numerals indicating the mile number (Western Rivers only).

NG: Diamond-shaped dayboard divided into four diamond-shaped colored sectors with the sectors at the side corners white and the sectors at the top and bottom corners green, with a white reflective border.

NL: Rectangular white location marker with an orange reflective border and black letters indicating the location.

NR: Diamond-shaped dayboard divided into four diamond-shaped colored sectors with the sectors at the side corners white and the sectors at the top and bottom corners red, with a white reflective border.

NW: Diamond-shaped white dayboard with an orange reflective border and black letters describing the information or regulatory nature of the mark.

NY: Diamond-shaped yellow dayboard with yellow reflective border.

SG: Square green dayboard with a green reflective border.

SG-I: Square green dayboard with a green reflective border and a yellow reflective horizontal band.

SG-SY: Square green dayboard with a green reflective border and a yellow reflective square.

SG-TY: Square green dayboard with a green reflective border and a yellow reflective triangle.

SR: Square red dayboard with a red reflective border. (IALA Region "A")

TG: Triangular green dayboard with a green reflective border. (IALA Region "A")

TR: Triangular red dayboard with a red reflective border.

TR-I: Triangular red dayboard with a red reflective border and a yellow reflective horizontal band.

TR-SY: Triangular red dayboard with a red reflective border and a yellow reflective square.

TR-TY: Triangular red dayboard with a red reflective border and a yellow reflective triangle. These abbreviated descriptions are used in column (7) and may also be found on the illustrations of the U.S. Aids to Navigation System.

Numbers are used to provide easy identification of aids to navigation. In IALA Region B, all solid red and solid green aids are numbered, except for buoys located on the Western Rivers. Red aids to navigation have even numbers and green aids to navigation have odd numbers. The numbers for each increase from seaward when proceeding in the conventional direction of buoyage. Numbers are kept in approximate sequence on both sides of the channel by omitting numbers where necessary.

Letters may be used to augment numbers when lateral aids to navigation are added to channels with previously completed numerical sequences. Letters will increase in alphabetical order, proceeding in the conventional direction of buoyage, and are added to numbers as suffixes. Letters are not used for buoys on the Western Rivers. No other aids to navigation are numbered. Preferred channel, safe water, isolated danger, special marks, and information and regulatory aids to navigation may be lettered, but not numbered.

Sound signal is a generic term used to describe aids to navigation that produce an audible signal designed to assist the mariner in periods of reduced visibility. These aids to navigation can be activated by several means e.g., manually, remotely, or automatically (as in the case of a fog detector). The Coast Guard is replacing many fog detectors with mariner radio activated sound signals (MRASS). To activate, mariners key their VHF-FM radio a designated number of times on a designated VHF-FM channel. The sound signal is activated for a period of 15, 30, 45, or 60 minutes after which the activated assistance automatically turns off. In cases where a fog detector is in use, there may be a delay in the automatic activation of the signal. Additionally, fog detectors may not be capable of detecting patchy fog conditions.

Sound signals are distinguished by their tone and phase characteristics. Devices producing sound, e.g., diaphones, diaphragm horns, sirens, whistles, bells, and gongs emit a distinct sound.

Phase characteristics are defined by the signal's sound pattern, i.e., the number of blasts and silent periods per minute and their durations. Signals sounded from fixed structures generally produce a specific number of blasts and silent periods each minute when operating. Sound signals installed on buoys are generally activated by the motion of the sea and therefore do not emit a regular signal characteristic. It is common, in fact, for a buoy to produce no sound signal when seas are calm.

The characteristic of a sound signal is listed in column (8) of the Light List. If the sound signal is remotely activated, column (8) will contain the VHF-FM channel and number of times the VHF-FM radio should be keyed. All waterway users equipped with a VHF-FM radio may activate the sound signal, but they are not required to do so. Unless the light list indicates that the sound signal "operates continuously," or the signal is a bell, gong, or whistle on a buoy, mariners can assume that the sound signal only operates during times of fog, reduced visibility, or adverse weather.

Caution: Mariners should not rely on sound signals to determine their position. Distance cannot be accurately determined by sound intensity. Occasionally, sound signals may not be heard in areas close to their location. Signals may not sound in cases where fog exists close to, but not at, the location of the sound signal.

Radar Beacons (RACONS) are radar transponders that when triggered by an X-band radar produce a coded response from its location, which is portrayed radially as a series of dots and dashes on the triggering radar. Although RACONS may be used on both laterally significant and non-laterally significant aids to navigation, their signal should just be used for identification purposes only.

RACONS have a typical output of 600 milliwatts and are considered a short-range aid to navigation. Reception varies from a nominal range of 6 to 8 nautical miles (when mounted on a buoy) to as much as 17 nautical miles for a RACON mounted on a fixed structure. It must be understood that these nominal ranges are dependent upon many factors.

The beginning of the RACON presentation occurs about 50 yards beyond the RACON's actual position and will persist for a number of revolutions of the radar antenna (depending on its rotation rate).

Radar operators may notice some broadening or spoking of the RACON presentation when their vessel approaches closely to the source of the RACON. This effect can be minimized by adjusting the IF gain or sweep gain control of the radar. If desired, the RACON presentation can be virtually eliminated by operation of the FTC (fast time constant) controls of the radar.

Radar Reflectors are special fixtures, incorporated into both lighted and unlighted aids to navigation, to enhance the reflection of radar energy. These fixtures make equipped ATON more detectable. However, they do not positively identify a radar target as an ATON.

GPS and Navigation – Related Services Operated by the US Coast Guard

Global Positioning System (GPS) is a satellite-based navigation system, operated and controlled by the Department of Defense (DOD) under U.S. Air Force management, which provides precise, worldwide, three-dimensional navigation capabilities. The system was originally designed for military application; however, it is now available to all and used almost ubiquitously. The United States is committed to maintaining the availability of at least 24 operational GPS satellites, in six precise orbital planes, each of which complete a circular 10,900 nautical mile orbit of the earth once every 12 hours. At least three satellites are required for a two-dimensional solution. However, GPS does not provide integrity information and mariners should exercise extreme caution when using GPS in restricted waterways. Ideally, a minimum of four satellites will be visible from any position on the earth and will provide positions with a global horizontal accuracy within 3 meters, 95% percent of the time. Whenever possible, advance notice of when GPS satellites should not be used will be provided by the DOD and made available by the US Coast Guard through GPS status messages.

Navigation Information Service (NIS): The U.S. Coast Guard Navigation Center (NAVCEN) is the official government source of information for civil users of the Global Positioning System (GPS). The Navigation Information Service (NIS) is available 24 hours a day, seven days a week, for all Radio Navigation and maritime related needs via phone, fax or e-mail. The NIS provides users the ability to access real time or archived GPS, and LNM information at WWW.NAVCEN.USCG.gov, as well as subscribe to an automated list service which enables users to receive GPS status messages and Notice to NAVSTAR User (NANU) messages via direct Internet e-mail. The NAVCEN also disseminates GPS safety advisory broadcast messages through USCG broadcast stations utilizing VHF-FM voice, HF-SSB voice, and NAVTEX broadcasts. The broadcasts provide the GPS user in the marine environment with the status of the navigation systems, as well as any planned/unplanned system outages that could affect GPS navigational accuracy.

To comment on any of these services or ask questions about the service offered, contact the NAVCEN at:

Commanding Officer U.S. Coast Guard NAVCEN (NIS) MS 7310
7323 Telegraph Road Alexandria, VA 20598-7310
Phone: (703) 313-5900
FAX: (703) 313-5920
http://www.navcen.uscg.gov

USCG Navigation Center Website: The USCG Navigation Center (NAVCEN) operates a website that provides the maritime public with marine safety information (MSI) dissemination and reporting services. The NAVCEN website is www.navcen.uscg.gov. NAVCEN MSI dissemination services include GPS status messages, Notice Advisory to NAVSTAR Users (NANU) messages, Local Notice to Mariners, Broadcast Local Notice to Mariners, and the USCG Light List. Methods of MSI dissemination include VHF, NAVTEX, MF/HF SSB broadcasts, RSS feeds, and email subscription services. NAVCEN reporting services include web-based form discrepancy reporting for aids to navigation (ATON), global positioning system (GPS), automatic identification system (AIS), and Long Range Identification System (LRIT).

ABBREVIATIONS

Various abbreviations are utilized in Broadcast Notices to Mariners, Local Notices to Mariners, on charts, and in the Light Lists. Refer to the following list.

Light Characteristics		Sound Signal Characteristics	
Alternating Characteristic	AL CHAR	Blast Every	BL EV
Composite Group-Flashing	FL (2+1)	Seconds	S
Composite Group-Occulting	OC (2+1)	Silent	SI
Continuous Quick-Flashing	Q	**Colors***	
		Black	B
Eclipse	EC FFL	Blue	BU
Fixed and Flashing		Green	G
Fixed	F	Orange	OR
Group-Flashing	FL (3)	Red	R
Group-Occulting	OC (2)	White	W
Interrupted Quick-Flashing	IQ	Yellow	Y
Isophase	ISO	*NOTE: Color refers to characteristics of aids to navigation only.	
Morse Code	MO (A)		
Occulting	OC	**Aids to Navigation**	
Single-Flashing	FL	Aeronautical Radiobeacon	AERO RBN
Organizations		Automatic Identification System	AIS
Commander, Coast Guard District	CCGD (#)	Daybeacon	DBN
		Destroyed	DESTR
Coast Guard	CG	Discontinued	DISCONTD
U.S. Army Corps of Engineers	USACE	Established	ESTAB
		Exposed Location Buoy	ELB
National Geospatial-Intelligence Agency	NGA	Extinguished	EXT
		Fog Signal Station	FOG SIG

National Ocean Service	NOS	Light List Number	LLNR
National Weather Service	NWS	Light	LT
		Lighted Bell Buoy	LBB
Vessels		Lighted Buoy	LB
Aircraft	A/C	Lighted Gong Buoy	LGB
Fishing Vessel	F/V	Lighted Horn Buoy	LHB
Liquefied Natural Gas Carrier	LNG	Lighted Whistle Buoy	LWB
Motor Vessel (includes Steam Ship, Container Ship, Cargo Vessel, Tanker etc)	M/V	Mariner Radio Activated Sound Signal	MRASS
		Ocean Data Acquisition System	ODAS
Pleasure Craft	P/C	Privately Maintained	PRIV MAINTD
Research Vessel	R/V	Radar Reflector	RA REF
Sailing Vessel	S/V	Radar Responder Beacon	RACON
		Remote Radio Activated Sound Signal	RRASS
Various		Single Point Mooring Buoy	SPM
Anchorage	ANCH	Sound Signal	SS
Anchorage Prohibited	ANCH PROHIB	Temporarily Replaced by Lighted Buoy	TRLB
Approximate	APPROX	Temporarily Replaced by Unlighted Buoy	TRUB
Atlantic	ATL	Topmark	TMK
Authorized	AUTH	Virtual AIS Aid to Navigation	V-AIS
Average	AVG	Whistle	WHIS
Bearing	BRG		
Breakwater	BKW		
Broadcast Notice to Mariners	BNM		
Canadian Aid	(C)		
Captain of the Port	COTP		
Channel	CHAN		
Code of Federal Regulations	CFR		
Continue	CONT		
Degrees (temp, geo, pos)	DEG		
Diameter	DIA		
Edition	ED		
Effect/Effective	EFF		
Entrance	ENTR		

Days of the Week

Monday	MON
Tuesday	TUE
Wednesday	WED
Thursday	THU
Friday	FRI
Saturday	SAT
Sunday	SUN

Compass Directions

North	N
South	S
East	E
West	W
Northeast	NE
Northwest	NW
Southeast	SE
Southwest	SW

Explosive Anchorage	EXPLOS ANCH		
Fathom(s)	FM(S)		
Foot/Feet	FT		
Harbor	HBR		
Height	HT		
Hertz	HZ		
Horizontal Clearance	HOR CL		
Hour	HR		
International Regulations for Preventing Collisions at Sea	COLREGS		
Kilohertz	KHZ		
Kilometer	KM		
Knot(s)	KT(S)		
Minute (time, geo, pos)	MIN		
Megahertz	MHZ		
Maritime Mobile Service Identity	MMSI		
Moderate	MOD		
Mountain, Mount	MT		
Nautical Mile(s)	NM		
Notice to Mariners	NTM		
Obstruction	OBSTR		
Occasion/ Occasionally	OCCASION		
Operating Area	OPAREA		
Pacific	PAC		
Point(s)	PT(S)		
Position	POS		
Position Approximate	PA		
Pressure	PRES		
Private, Privately	PRIV		
Prohibited	PROHIB		
Publication	PUB		
Range	RNG		
Reported	REP		
Restricted	RESTR		

Months

January	JAN
February	FEB
March	MAR
April	APR
May	MAY
June	JUN
July	JUL
August	AUG
September	SEP
October	OCT
November	NOV
December	DEC

Countries and States

Alabama	AL
Alaska	AK
American Samoa	AS
Arizona	AZ
Arkansas	AR
California	CA
Canada	CN
Colorado	CO
Connecticut	CT
Delaware	DE
District of Columbia	DC
Florida	FL
Georgia	GA
Guam	GU
Hawaii	HI
Idaho	ID
Illinois	IL
Indiana	IN
Iowa	IA
Kansas	KS
Kentucky	KY
Louisiana	LA
Maine	ME
Maryland	MD
Marshall Islands	MH
Massachusetts	MA

River	RIV	Missouri	MO
Rock	RK	Mississippi	MS
Saint	ST	Mexico	MX
Second (time, geo, pos)	SEC	Michigan	MI
		Minnesota	MN
Signal Station	SIG STA	Montana	MT
Station	STA	Nebraska	NE
Statute Mile(s)	SM	Nevada	NV
Storm Signal Station	S SIG STA	New Hampshire	NH
		New Jersey	NJ
Temporary	TEMP	New Mexico	NM
Thunderstorm	TSTORM	New York	NY
Through	THRU	North Carolina	NC
True	T	North Dakota	ND
Uncovers, Dries	UNCOV	Northern Marianas	MP
Universal Coordinate Time	UTC	Ohio	OH
		Oklahoma	OK
Urgent Marine Information Broadcast	UMIB	Oregon	OR
		Pennsylvania	PA
Velocity	VEL	Puerto Rico	PR
Vertical Clearance	VERT CL	Rhode Island	RI
Vessel Traffic Service	VTS	South Carolina	SC
		South Dakota	SD
Visibility	VIS	Tennessee	TN
Yard(s)	YD	Texas	TX
Warning	WARN	United States	US
Weather	WX	Utah	UT
Wreck	WK	Vermont	VT
		Virgin Islands	VI
		Washington	WA
		West Virginia	WV
		Wisconsin	WI
		Wyoming	WY

GLOSSARY OF AIDS TO NAVIGATION TERMS

Adrift: Afloat and unattached in any way to the shore or seabed.

Aid to Navigation: Any device external to a vessel or aircraft specifically intended to assist navigators in determining their position or safe course, or to warn them of dangers or obstructions to navigation.

Automatic Identification System Aid to Navigation (AIS-ATON): An aid to navigation signal that is broadcast through AIS. They can be physical, synthetic, or virtual.

Alternating Lights: A rhythmic light showing light of alternating colors.

Arc of Visibility: The portion of the horizon over which a lighted aid to navigation is visible from seaward.

Articulated Beacon: A beacon-like buoyant structure, tethered directly to the seabed and having no watch circle. Called articulated light or articulated daybeacon, as appropriate.

Assigned Position: The latitude and longitude position for an aid to navigation.

Beacon: A lighted or unlighted fixed aid to navigation attached directly to the earth's surface. (Lights and Daybeacons both constitute beacons.

Bearing: The horizontal direction of a line of sight between two objects on the surface of the earth.

Bell: A sound signal producing bell tones by means of a hammer actuated by electricity on fixed aids and by sea motion on buoys.

Bifurcation: The point where a channel divides when proceeding from seaward. The place where two tributaries meet.

Broadcast Notice to Mariners: A radio broadcast designed to provide important marine information.

Buoy: A floating object of defined shape and color, which is anchored at a given position and serves as an aid to navigation.

Characteristic: The audible, visual, or electronic signal displayed by an aid to navigation to assist in the identification of an aid to navigation. Characteristic refers to lights, sound signals, RACONS, and Daybeacons.

Commissioned: The action of placing a previously discontinued aid to navigation back in service.

Composite Group Flashing Light: A group flashing light in which the flashes are combined in successive groups of different numbers of flashes.

Composite Group-Occulting Light: A light like a group occulting light except that the successive groups in a period have different numbers of eclipses.

Conventional Direction of Buoyage: The general direction taken by the mariner when approaching a harbor, river, estuary, or other waterway from seaward, or proceeding upstream or in a direction of the main stream of flood tide, or in the direction indicated in appropriate nautical documents (normally, following a clockwise direction around land masses).

Daybeacon: An unlighted fixed structure which is equipped with a dayboard for daytime identification.

Dayboard: The daytime identifier of an aid to navigation presenting one of several standard shapes (square, triangle, rectangle) and colors (red, green, white, orange, yellow, or black).

Daymark: The daytime identifier of an aid to navigation. (See column 7 of the Light List)

Diaphone: A sound signal which produces sound by means of a slotted piston moved back and forth by compressed air. A "two- tone" diaphone produces two sequential tones with a second tone of lower pitch.

Directional Light: A light illuminating a sector or very narrow angle and intended to mark a direction to be followed.

Discontinued: To remove from operation (permanently of temporarily) a previously authorized aid to navigation.

Discrepancy: Failure of an aid to navigation to maintain its position or function as prescribed in the Light List.

Discrepancy Buoy: An easily transportable buoy used to temporarily replace an aid to navigation not watching properly.

Dolphin: A minor aid to navigation structure consisting of a number of piles driven into the seabed or riverbed in a circular pattern and drawn together with rope.

Eclipse: An interval of darkness between appearances of a light.

Emergency Light: A light of reduced intensity displayed by certain aids to navigation when the main light is extinguished.

Establish: To place an authorized aid to navigation in operation for the first time.

Extinguished: A lighted aid to navigation which fails to show a light characteristic.

Fixed Light: A light showing continuously and steady, as opposed to a rhythmic light. (Do not confuse with

"fixed" as used to differentiate from "floating".)

Flash: A relatively brief appearance of a light, in comparison with the longest interval of darkness in the same characteristic.

Flash tube: An electronically controlled high-intensity discharge lamp with a very brief flash duration.

Flashing Light: A light in which the total duration of the light in each period is clearly shorter than the total duration of the darkness and in which the flashed of light are all of equal duration. (Commonly used for a single-flashing light which exhibits only single flashes which are repeated at regular intervals.)

Floating Aid to Navigation: A buoy, secured in its assigned position by a mooring.

Fog Detector: An electronic device used to automatically determine conditions of visibility which warrant the activation of a sound signal or additional light signals.

Fog Signal: See sound signal.

Geographic Range: The greatest distance the curvature of the earth permits an object of a given height to be seen from a particular height of eye without regard to luminous intensity or visibility conditions.

Global Positioning System (GPS): A satellite-based radio-navigation system providing continuous worldwide coverage. It provides navigation, position, and timing information to air, marine, and land users.

Gong: A wave actuated sound signal on buoys which uses a group of saucer- shaped bells to produce different tones.

Group Flashing Light: A flashing light in which a group of flashes, specified in number, is regularly repeated.

Group Occulting Light: An occulting light in which a group of eclipses, specified in number, regularly repeated.

Horn: A sound signal which uses electricity or compressed air to vibrate a disc diaphragm.

Inoperative: Sound signal or electronic aid to navigation out of service due to a malfunction.

Intermediate Peripheral Structure: are structures on the edge of a wind farm.

Interrupted Quick Flash: A quick flashing light in which the rapid alternations are interrupted at regular intervals by eclipses of long duration.

Isolated Danger Mark: A mark erected on, or moored above or very near, an isolated danger which has navigable water all around it.

Isophase Light: A rhythmic light in which all durations of light and darkness are equal.

Junction: The point where a channel divides when proceeding seaward. The place where a distributary departs from the mainstream.

Lateral System: A system of aids to navigation in which characteristics of buoys and beacons indicate the sides of a channel or route relative to a Conventional Direction of Buoyage (usually upstream).

Light: The signal emitted by a lighted aid to navigation. The illuminating apparatus used to emit the light signal. A lighted aid to navigation on a fixed structure.

Light Sector: The arc over which a light is visible, described in degrees true, as observed from seaward towards the light. May be used to define distinctive color difference of two adjoining sectors, or an obscured sector.

Lighted Ice Buoy (LIB): A lighted buoy without a sound signal and designed to withstand the forces of shifting and flowing ice. Used to replace a conventional buoy when that aid to navigation is endangered by ice.

Lighthouse: A lighted beacon of major importance.

Local Notice to Mariners: A written document issued by each U.S. Coast Guard district to disseminate important information affecting aids to navigation, dredging, marine construction, special marine activities, and bridge construction on waterways within that district.

Luminous Range: The greatest distance a light can be expected to be seen given its nominal range and the prevailing meteorological visibility.

Mariner Radio Activated Sound Signal (MRASS): A system that allows the mariner to activate an ATON sound signal or light signal if the aid is so equipped. Once activated, the signal will continue to sound or remain lit for a period of time noted in the Light List before shutting down and going into standby mode again. The signal is activated by keying the microphone 5 consecutive times on VHF/FM channel 81A/157.075Mhz.

Mark: A visual aid to navigation. Often called navigational mark, including floating marks (buoys) and fixed marks (beacons).

MATON: A Mobile Aid to Navigation in which a mark is attached to floating objects which may be a collision hazard. A MATON has a defined light characteristic of three flickering flashes, followed by two regular flashes.

Meteorological Visibility: The greatest distance at which a black object of suitable dimension could be seen and recognized against the horizon sky by day, or in case of night observations, could be seen and recognized if the general illumination were raised to the daylight level.

Mileage Number: A number assigned to aids to navigation which gives the distance in sailing miles along the river from a reference point to the aid to navigation. The number is used principally in the Mississippi River

Nominal Range: The maximum distance a light can be seen in clear weather (meteorological visibility of 10 nautical miles). Listed for all lighted aids to navigation except range lights, directional lights, and private aids to navigation.

Occulting Light: A light in which the total duration of light in each period is clearly longer than the total duration of the darkness and in which the intervals of darkness (occultations) are all of equal duration. Commonly used for single occulting light which exhibits only single occultation which are repeated at regular intervals.

Ocean Data Acquisition System (ODAS): Certain large buoys in deep water for the collection of oceanographic and meteorological information. All ODAS buoys are yellow in color and display a yellow light.

Offshore Tower: Monitored light stations built on exposed marine sites to replace lightships.

Off Station: A floating aid to navigation that is not on its assigned position.

Passing Light: A low intensity light which may be mounted on the structure of another light to enable the mariner to keep the latter light in sight when passing out of its beam during transit.

Period: The interval of time between the commencements of two identical successive cycles of the characteristic of the light or sound signal.

Physical AIS-ATON: AIS-ATON message broadcast from a transponder affixed to the corresponding buoy and beacon.

Pile: A long, heavy steel, concrete or timber driven into the seabed or riverbed to serve as a support for an ATON.

Port Hand Mark: A buoy or beacon which is left to the port hand when proceeding in the "Conventional Direction of Buoyage".

Preferred Channel Mark: A lateral mark indicating a channel junction or bifurcation, or a wreck or other obstruction which after consulting a chart, may be passed on either side.

Primary Aid to Navigation: An aid to navigation established for the purpose of making landfalls and coastwise passages from headland to headland.

Quick Light: A light exhibiting very rapid regular alternations of light and darkness, normally 60 flashes per minute.

RACON: A radar beacon which produces a coded response or radar paint, when triggered by a radar signal.

Radar: An electronic system designed to transmit radio signals and receive reflected images of those signals from a "target" in order to determine the bearing and distance to the "target".

Radar Reflector: A special fixture fitted to or incorporated into the design of certain aids to navigation to enhance their ability to reflect radar energy. In general, these fixtures will materially improve the aid to navigation for use by vessels with radar.

Range: A line formed by the extension of a line connecting two charted points.

Range lights: Two lights associated to form a range which often, but not necessarily, indicates the channel centerline. The front range light is the lower of the two, and nearer to the mariner using the range. The rear light is higher and further from the mariner.

Rebuilt: A fixed aid to navigation, previously destroyed, which has been restored as an aid to navigation.

Regulatory Marks: A white and orange aid to navigation with no lateral significance. Used to indicate a special meaning to the mariner, such as danger, restricted operations, or exclusion area.

Relighted: An extinguished aid to navigation returned to its advertised light characteristics.

Replaced: An aid to navigation previously off station, adrift, or missing, restored by another aid to navigation of the same type and characteristics.

Replaced (temporarily): An aid to navigation previously off station, adrift, or missing restored by another aid to navigation of a different type and/or characteristic.

Reset: A floating aid to navigation previously off station, adrift or missing, returned to its assigned position (station).

Rhythmic Light: A light showing intermittently with a regular periodicity.

Sector: See light sector.

Setting a Buoy: The act of placing a buoy on assigned position in the water.

Significant Peripheral Structure (SPS): normally a corner structure and other significant points on the boundary of a wind farm.

Siren: A sound signal which uses electricity or compressed air to actuate either a disc or a cup shaped rotor.

Skeleton Tower: A tower, usually of steel, constructed of heavy corner members and various horizontal and diagonal bracing members.

Sound Signal: A device which transmits sound, intended to provide information to mariners during periods of restricted visibility and foul weather.

Starboard Hand Mark: A buoy or beacon which is right to the starboard hand when proceeding in the Conventional Direction of Buoyage.

Synthetic AIS-ATON: AIS ATON message broadcast (typically from shore) to an assigned position with a corresponding buoy or beacon.

Top mark: One or more relatively small objects of characteristic shape and color placed on aid to identify its purpose.

Traffic Separation Scheme: Shipping corridors marked by buoys which separate incoming from outgoing vessels. Improperly called SEA LANES.

Virtual AIS-ATON: AIS ATON message broadcast (typically from shore) to an assigned position with no corresponding buoy or beacon.

Watching Properly: An aid to navigation on its assigned position exhibiting the advertised characteristics in all respects.

Whistle: A wave actuated sound signal on buoys which produces sound by emitting compressed air through a circumferential slot into a cylindrical bell chamber.

Wind Farm: A grouping of structures in a designated area used for wind power generation.

Winter Marker: An unlighted buoy without a sound signal, used to replace a conventional buoy when an aid to navigation is endangered by ice.

Winter Light: A light which is maintained during those winter months when the regular light is extinguished. It is of lower candlepower than the regular light, but usually the same characteristic.

Withdrawn: The discontinuance of an aid to navigation or equipment on an aid to navigation during severe ice conditions or for the winter season.

CHARACTERISTICS OF LIGHTS

Illustration	**Type Description**	**Abbreviation**

1. FIXED. — **F**
A light showing continuously and steadily.

2. OCCULTING.
A light in which the total duration of light in a period is longer than the total duration of darkness and the intervals of darkness (eclipses) are usually of equal duration

2.1 Single-occulting. — **Oc**
An occulting light in which an eclipse is regularly repeated.

2.2 Group-occulting. — **Oc (2)**
An occulting light in which a group of eclipses, specified in numbers, is regularly repeated.

2.3 Composite group-occulting. — **Oc (2+1)**
A light, similar to a group-occulting light, except that successive groups in a period have different numbers of eclipses.

3. ISOPHASE. — **Iso**
A light in which all durations of light and darkness are equal.

4. FLASHING.
A light in which the total duration of light in a period is shorter than the total duration of darkness and the appearances of light (flashes) are usually of equal duration.

4.1 Single-flashing. — **Fl**
A flashing light in which a flash is regularly repeated (frequency not exceeding 30 flashes per minute).

4.2 Group-flashing. — **Fl (2)**
A flashing light in which a group of flashes, specified in number, is regularly repeated.

4.3 Composite group-flashing. — **Fl (2+1)**
A light similar to a group flashing light except that successive groups in the period have different numbers of flashes.

5. QUICK.
A light in which flashes are produced at a rate of 60 flashes per minute.

5.1 Continuous quick. — **Q**
A quick light in which a flash is regularly repeated.

5.2 Interrupted quick. — **I Q**
A quick light in which the sequence of flashes is interrupted by regularly repeated eclipses of constant and long duration.

6. MORSE CODE. — **Mo (A)**
A light in which appearances of light of two clearly different durations (dots and dashes) are grouped to represent a character or characters in the Morse code.

7. FIXED AND FLASHING. — **F Fl**
A light in which a fixed light is combined with a flashing light of higher luminous intensity.

8. ALTERNATING. — **Al RW**
A light showing different colors alternately

LIST OF NAIS AND LOMA BROADCAST BASE STATIONS AND THEIR LOCATIONS
(Table sorted by MMSI)

AIS BASE STATION TYPE	MMSI	LOCATION	LATITUDE	LONGITUDE
LOMA	TBD	Red Bud	38-11-20.544N	89-53-25.260W
LOMA	100553	Lexington	39-9-29.844N	93-54-44.244W
LOMA	101135	Knoxville - TVA	35-57-58.032N	83-55-14.088W
LOMA	830361	Port of Decatur	34-37-12.342N	86-59-15.709W
LOMA	3660554	Mississippi L&D 22	39-38-9.624N	91-14-58.618W
LOMA	3660556	MVD Test Site	32-20-55.194N	90-52-53.220W
NAIS	3660608	Bethany	41-24-17.399N	072-59-58.301W
NAIS	3660609	Shinnecock	40-50-52.800N	072-30-10.501W
NAIS	3660610	Cohasset	42-14-35.999N	070-50-11.000W
NAIS	3660611	Greenbury Point	38-58-44.501N	076-27-15.199W
NAIS	3660612	Alexandria	38-45-14.090N	077-07-35.692W
NAIS	3660613	Ongunquit	43-14-51.690N	070-38-21.640W
NAIS	3660614	Swans Island	44-09-41.918N	068-25-21.788W
NAIS	3660615	Westbrook	43-44-38.000N	070-20-03.001W
NAIS	3660616	Putnam Valley	41-25-54.901N	073-52-49.598W
NAIS	3660617	Troy	42-47-08.999N	073-37-41.002W
NAIS	3660618	Miacomet	41-15-05.050N	070-07-43.900W
NAIS	3660619	Orleans	41-47-29.699N	069-59-35.999W
NAIS	3660620	Warwick	41-39-53.302N	071-31-18.300W
NAIS	3660622	Buxton	35-14-43.879N	075-32-02.609W
NAIS	3660623	Mamie	36-08-08.830N	075-49-27.131W
NAIS	3660624	Stacy	34-52-24.920N	076-24-53.890W
NAIS	3660625	Sneads Ferry	34-31-05.081N	077-26-53.059W
NAIS	3660626	Southport	33-56-56.000N	078-00-42.001W
NAIS	3660627	Carnigan	31-27-52.898N	081-29-05.690W
NAIS	3660628	Garden City	33-36-03.218N	079-03-04.342W
NAIS	3660629	McClellanville	33-05-21.502N	079-29-25.001W
NAIS	3660630	Port Royal	32-25-11.410N	080-28-30.360W
NAIS	3660631	Jacksonville	30-16-35.000N	081-33-51.998W
NAIS	3660632	Saint Cloud	28-16-45.300N	081-01-23.999W
NAIS	3660633	Princeton	25-32-23.798N	080-28-06.499W
NAIS	3660634	Truman Annex	24-33-01.102N	081-48-20.902W
NAIS	3660635	Lake Worth	26-35-21.199N	080-12-43.279W
NAIS	3660636	Monte Del Estado	18-09-07.999N	066-59-26.999W
NAIS	3660637	Cerro Maravilla	18-09-10.810N	066-33-14.830W
LOMA	3660638	Dardanelle L&D (#10)	35-15-0.360N	93-10-4.908W
LOMA	3660641	Ozark L&D (#11)	35-28-18.582N	93-48-44.338W
LOMA	3660643	Murray L&D (7)	34-47-26.292N	92-21-30.240W
LOMA	3660650	Marmet L&D	38-15-17.646N	81-33-57.222W

AIS BASE STATION TYPE	MMSI	LOCATION	LATITUDE	LONGITUDE
LOMA	3660657	Fort Loudoun L&D	35-47-22.560N	84-14-30.120W
LOMA	3660658	Wheeler Gen Joe L&D	34-48-50.724N	87-22-59.412W
LOMA	3660661	Thatcher L&D	33-18-23.568N	92-29-0.060W
LOMA	3660667	Thomas J. Obrien L&D	41-39-5.724N	87-34-3.000W
LOMA	3660669	Red River L&D 3	31-31-18.036N	92-43-39.000W
LOMA	3660670	Dashields L&D	40-32-55.752N	80-12-23.868W
LOMA	3660673	Mississippi L&D 10	42-47-9.708N	91-5-45.359W
LOMA	3660674	Mississippi L&D 2	44-45-35.868N	92-52-9.358W
LOMA	3660675	Mississippi L&D 4	44-19-33.600N	91-55-8.278W
LOMA	3660676	Mississippi L&D 5	44-9-36.792N	91-48-46.019W
LOMA	3660677	Mississippi L&D 6	44-0-1.326N	91-26-15.180W
LOMA	3660678	Mississippi L&D 7	43-51-57.726N	91-18-36.299W
LOMA	3660679	Mississippi L&D 8	43-34-15.120N	91-13-46.319W
LOMA	3660682	Dresden L&D	41-23-51.720N	88-16-56.172W
LOMA	3660683	Emsworth L&D	40-30-18.000N	80-5-18.708W
LOMA	3660684	Melvin Price L&D	38-52-16.061N	90-9-5.940W
LOMA	3660687	La Grange L&D	39-56-28.284N	90-32-5.208W
LOMA	3660688	Mississippi L&D 11	42-32-26.808N	90-38-33.180W
LOMA	3660689	Mississippi L&D 12	42-15-38.874N	90-25-22.559W
LOMA	3660690	Mississippi L&D 13	41-53-51.912N	90-9-15.959W
LOMA	3660691	Mississippi L&D 14	41-34-25.398N	90-24-11.819W
LOMA	3660692	Mississippi L&D 15	41-31-3.228N	90-33-48.838W
LOMA	3660693	Mississippi L&D 16	41-25-29.940N	91-0-35.100W
LOMA	3660694	Mississippi L&D 17	41-11-32.688N	91-3-26.158W
LOMA	3660695	Mississippi L&D 18	40-52-54.504N	91-1-25.198W
LOMA	3660696	Mississippi L&D 19	40-23-48.192N	91-22-29.460W
LOMA	3660697	Mississippi L&D 20	40-8-38.376N	91-30-56.459W
LOMA	3660698	Mississippi L&D 21	39-54-11.772N	91-25-43.079W
LOMA	3660699	Mississippi L&D 24	39-22-25.530N	90-54-22.619W
LOMA	3660700	Mississippi L&D 25	39-0-11.388N	90-41-22.258W
LOMA	3660701	Lockport L&D	41-34-6.402N	88-4-37.618W
LOMA	3660702	Marseilles L&D	41-19-42.031N	88-45-11.880W
LOMA	3660703	Peoria L&D	40-37-55.626N	89-37-27.480W
LOMA	3660704	Columbia L&D	32-10-0.588N	92-6-36.720W
LOMA	3660706	Old Hickory L&D	36-17-43.998N	86-39-23.998W
LOMA	3660709	Wilson L&D	34-48-17.106N	87-37-40.620W
LOMA	3660710	Felsenthal L&D	33-3-34.560N	92-7-22.332W
LOMA	3660711	Waggonner Jr., Joe D. L&D	32-14-59.496N	93-29-46.680W
LOMA	3660712	John H. Overton L&D	31-11-16.152N	92-17-32.820W
LOMA	3660713	Jonesville L&D	31-28-58.512N	91-51-37.188W

AIS BASE STATION TYPE	MMSI	LOCATION	LATITUDE	LONGITUDE
LOMA	3660714	Lindy Claiborne Boggs L&D	31-15-14.591N	91-57-32.544W
LOMA	3660715	Russell B. Long L&D (L&D 4)	31-56-23.111N	93-16-13.966W
LOMA	3660717	Allegheny L&D 4	40-36-49.464N	79-43-10.272W
LOMA	3660726	Terry, David D. L&D (6)	34-39-58.272N	92-9-20.999W
LOMA	3660727	Emmett Sanders L&D	34-14-50.064N	91-54-20.412W
LOMA	3660728	James W. Trimble L&D (13)	35-20-54.744N	94-17-52.908W
LOMA	3660729	Joe Hardin L&D (3)	34-9-50.004N	91-40-40.728W
LOMA	3660730	Norrell L&D (1)	34-1-11.988N	91-11-43.019W
LOMA	3660731	R. S. Kerr Lake L&D (15)	35-20-52.998N	94-46-43.979W
LOMA	3660732	Toad Suck Ferry L&D (#8)	35-4-34.998N	92-32-21.959W
LOMA	3660733	W. D. Mayo L&D (14)	35-18-52.998N	94-33-34.978W
LOMA	3660734	Webbers Falls Lake L&D (16)	35-33-16.002N	95-10-4.980W
LOMA	3660738	Starved Rock L&D	41-19-28.782N	88-59-7.980W
LOMA	3660744	Ensley Engineering Yard	35-4-12.011N	90-7-21.396W
LOMA	3660839	Green River L&D 2	37-31-54.084N	87-15-55.188W
LOMA	3660842	Kaskaskia River Nav. L&D	37-59-3.012N	89-56-47.256W
LOMA	3660846	Mississippi L&D 3	44-36-35.838N	92-36-39.298W
LOMA	3660848	Gray's Landing L&D	39-49-28.956N	79-55-13.656W
LOMA	3660850	Monongahela R L&D 3	40-15-50.268N	79-53-56.699W
LOMA	3660851	Monongahela R L&D 4 (Charleroi)	40-8-49.986N	79-53-56.159W
LOMA	3660854	Point Marion L&D	39-43-41.243N	79-54-44.748W
LOMA	3660855	Hannibal L&D	39-39-54.900N	80-51-57.060W
LOMA	3660856	John T. Myers L&D	37-47-41.640N	87-59-33.108W
LOMA	3660858	Olmsted L&D	37-11-0.918N	89-3-49.799W
LOMA	3660859	Markland L&D	38-46-27.642N	84-57-58.032W
LOMA	3660860	McAlpine L&D	38-16-44.562N	85-47-28.464W
LOMA	3660861	Montgomery L&D (OH)	40-38-52.710N	80-23-6.958W
LOMA	3660862	New Cumberland L&D	40-31-32.928N	80-37-41.340W
LOMA	3660863	Newburgh L&D	37-55-56.034N	87-22-26.098W
LOMA	3660865	Smithland L&D	37-9-59.216N	88-25-41.506W
LOMA	3660870	USACE AREC	38-35-25.800N	90-12-21.960W
LOMA	3660872	St. Mary's (Soo Locks)	46-30-9.529N	84-20-56.314W
LOMA	3660875	Fulton L&D	34-15-27.396N	88-25-26.544W
LOMA	3660876	Glover Wilkins L&D	34-3-53.536N	88-25-33.118W
LOMA	3660877	Howell Heflin L&D	32-50-13.344N	88-8-10.392W
LOMA	3660878	Stennis John C. L&D	33-31-3.828N	88-29-22.488W
LOMA	3660879	G.V. "Sonny" Montgomery L&D (TT)	34-31-18.840N	88-19-24.240W
LOMA	3660881	Bevill, Tom L&D	32-12-37.008N	88-17-13.992W
LOMA	3660882	Whitten, Jamie L&D	34-31-18.768N	88-19-24.420W
LOMA	3660886	Newt Graham L&D (18)	36-3-33.000N	95-32-10.979W

AIS BASE STATION TYPE	MMSI	LOCATION	LATITUDE	LONGITUDE
LOMA	3660890	Montgomery Point L&D	33-56-42.048N	91-5-15.058W
LOMA	3660891	Wilbur D. Mills L&D (2)	34-1-35.166N	91-14-48.538W
LOMA	3661113	Glasgow	39-14-27.852N	92-47-18.384W
NAIS	3669100	Burlington	39-58-13.300N	074-53-55.601W
NAIS	3669101	Cape May	38-56-40.981N	074-53-02.069W
NAIS	3669102	Manasquan	40-06-55.879N	074-02-00.910W
NAIS	3669135	Cape Mendocino	40-26-31.499N	124-23-46.788W
NAIS	3669136	Point Arena	38-53-52.800N	123-37-52.788W
NAIS	3669137	Walker Ridge	41-05-57.682N	124-07-36.624W
NAIS	3669138	Cambria	35-31-06.701N	121-03-35.784W
NAIS	3669139	Catalina Island	33-22-46.402N	118-24-58.896W
NAIS	3669140	Honda Ridge	34-35-17.498N	120-36-20.016W
NAIS	3669141	Laguna Peak	34-06-26.302N	119-03-54.000W
NAIS	3669142	Point Loma	32-40-13.400N	117-14-24.900W
NAIS	3669143	Eagle Rock	37-08-08.491N	122-11-46.932W
NAIS	3669144	Post Ranch	36-13-44.339N	121-46-05.041W
NAIS	3669145	Presidio	37-47-39.458N	122-27-53.064W
NAIS	3669146	Walnut Grove	38-14-22.900N	121-30-05.970W
NAIS	3669147	Elkhorn Mountain	45-44-21.901N	122-22-20.892W
NAIS	3669148	Kelso Notch	46-09-49.460N	122-51-09.576W
NAIS	3669149	Megler Mountain	46-15-43.999N	123-53-18.312W
NAIS	3669150	Rogue River	42-26-24.170N	124-25-02.200W
NAIS	3669151	Bahokus Peak	48-22-14.401N	124-40-22.692W
NAIS	3669152	Gold Mountain	47-32-55.930N	122-47-07.440W
NAIS	3669153	Mount Erie	48-27-14.290N	122-37-34.300W
NAIS	3669154	Seattle	47-36-56.999N	122-18-32.004W
NAIS	3669155	Mount Alutom	13-25-58.501N	144-42-45.299E
NAIS	3669156	Kawela	21-39-53.750N	158-00-00.910W
NAIS	3669157	Mauna Kapu	21-24-12.630N	158-05-52.640W
NAIS	3669158	Anchorage	61-16-09.420N	149-38-19.000W
NAIS	3669163	Proctor	35-06-02.185N	090-17-29.231W
NAIS	3669164	Ft Thomas	39-03-47.966N	084-26-29.868W
NAIS	3669165	Huntington	38-23-30.343N	082-29-29.760W
NAIS	3669166	Pittsburgh PA	40-28-19.056N	079-59-39.635W
NAIS	3669167	Imperial	39-23-18.377N	090-22-20.100W
NAIS	3669168	Bristol	43-54-59.003N	069-29-05.400W
NAIS	3669169	Catskill	42-12-34.160N	073-53-57.220W
NAIS	3669170	Montgomery	31-56-31.900N	081-07-17.490W
NAIS	3669171	Brunswick	30-49-39.800N	081-44-26.400W
NAIS	3669172	Palmetto	27-32-43.100N	082-34-27.330W

AIS BASE STATION TYPE	MMSI	LOCATION	LATITUDE	LONGITUDE
NAIS	3669173	Caney Creek	28-50-40.210N	095-39-29.130W
NAIS	3669175	Baton Rouge	30-22-50.040N	091-03-16.500W
NAIS	3669176	Grammercy	30-04-25.200N	090-42-13.900W
NAIS	3669181	Bay City	43-32-33.100N	083-39-37.000W
NAIS	3669182	Maumee Bay	41-38-13.400N	083-22-01.600W
NAIS	3669183	Gulliver	46-03-26.000N	085-58-42.000W
NAIS	3669184	San Nicolas Island	33-14-22.000N	119-30-18.100W
NAIS	3669185	San Clemente Island	32-53-29.500N	118-27-33.900W
NAIS	3669186	San Onofre Peak	33-21-43.800N	117-29-45.800W
NAIS	3669187	Bush Bluff	37-08-08.260N	122-11-47.800W
NAIS	3669188	Pittsburg	37-58-09.000N	121-54-15.000W
NAIS	3669189	Seven Devils	43-16-27.000N	124-22-12.000W
NAIS	3669190	Merizo	13-16-51.400N	144-40-26.400E
NAIS	3669191	Biscayne Bay	25-32-24.972N	080-28-06.492W
NAIS	3669192	Miami	25-45-33.000N	080-11-30.800W
NAIS	3669193	Wilmette	42-04-37.850N	087-41-03.070W
NAIS	3669743	Swedesboro	39-43-32.498N	075-20-39.599W
NAIS	3669744	Tuckerton	39-37-54.910N	074-21-12.850W
NAIS	3669745	Merrick	37-33-27.202N	075-49-43.000W
NAIS	3669746	Nokomis	27-09-04.000N	082-27-50.000W
NAIS	3669747	Tarpon Springs	28-10-57.670N	082-46-04.330W
NAIS	3669748	Chincoteague	37-55-52.871N	075-22-56.759W
NAIS	3669749	Farnham	37-53-15.000N	076-37-59.999W
NAIS	3669750	Berlin	38-19-39.740N	075-11-48.080W
NAIS	3669751	Newport News	37-09-49.000N	076-32-08.050W
NAIS	3669752	Pungo	36-43-48.698N	076-00-32.400W
NAIS	3669753	El Yunque	18-18-38.002N	065-47-34.001W
NAIS	3669754	Sunset Bay	43-30-30.170N	076-22-16.050W
NAIS	3669755	Avon Lake	41-28-54.599N	082-01-25.201W
NAIS	3669756	Port St Joe	29-49-09.360N	085-15-33.870W
NAIS	3669757	Robertsdale	30-36-45.430N	087-38-41.660W
NAIS	3669758	Santa Rosa	30-22-28.200N	086-11-20.198W
NAIS	3669759	Shell Point	30-04-35.198N	084-18-05.198W
NAIS	3669760	Van Cleave	30-29-10.050N	088-42-53.260W
NAIS	3669761	North East	39-33-41.400N	075-55-46.801W
NAIS	3669762	Reggio	29-48-32.320N	089-45-45.950W
NAIS	3669764	C3CEN LAB TOP	36-52-53.7594N	076-21-33.480W
NAIS	3669765	C3CEN LAB TRANS	36-52-53.7594N	076-21-33.480W
NAIS	3669766	Bachelor	30-52-20.701N	091-40-23.700W
NAIS	3669767	Bayou Salle	29-38-18.600N	091-31-02.399W

AIS BASE STATION TYPE	MMSI	LOCATION	LATITUDE	LONGITUDE
NAIS	3669768	Conneaut	41-55-00.520N	080-32-57.008W
NAIS	3669769	Ripley	42-14-11.900N	079-39-33.901W
NAIS	3669770	Eden	42-39-03.701N	078-49-28.402W
NAIS	3669771	Venice	29-17-59.399N	089-22-28.499W
NAIS	3669772	Hamlin	43-18-09.601N	077-54-53.798W
NAIS	3669773	Lake Port	43-07-27.998N	082-31-37.999W
NAIS	3669774	Baytown	29-46-06.899N	095-01-04.598W
NAIS	3669775	High Island	29-33-56.902N	094-23-19.201W
NAIS	3669776	Port Austin	44-01-44.480N	083-00-04.250W
NAIS	3669777	Grand Chenier	29-46-22.699N	092-59-10.100W
NAIS	3669778	Wayne	42-17-04.700N	083-08-24.000W
NAIS	3669779	Ellison Bay	45-14-04.499N	087-05-27.600W
NAIS	3669780	Point Beach	44-12-22.309N	087-36-24.750W
NAIS	3669781	Aransas Pass	27-56-40.171N	097-07-54.451W
NAIS	3669782	Kenedy	26-59-24.270N	097-39-46.020W
NAIS	3669783	Oak Creek	42-51-21.499N	087-50-44.401W
NAIS	3669784	Michigan City	41-38-33.100N	086-59-52.700W
NAIS	3669785	Agnew	42-56-25.300N	086-08-19.100W
NAIS	3669786	Arcadia	44-27-02.300N	086-12-15.800W
NAIS	3669787	Alpena	45-12-42.001N	083-25-59.999W
NAIS	3669788	Bliss	45-41-13.999N	084-53-57.998W
NAIS	3669789	Porcupine Mountain	46-48-45.202N	089-40-08.000W
NAIS	3669792	Larsmont	47-00-17.540N	091-45-54.970W
NAIS	3669795	Maple Hill	47-47-42.000N	090-19-43.000W
NAIS	3669796	Grand Marais	46-38-29.000N	085-59-35.999W
NAIS	3669798	Marquette	41-38-13.190N	083-22-01.460W
NAIS	3669799	Eagle Harbor	47-22-11.399N	088-11-02.501W
LOMA	93661108	Prices Landing	37-1-33.384N	89-21-23.184W
LOMA	993660555	Cannelton L&D	37-53-58.884N	86-42-22.968W
LOMA	993660557	Bonneville L&D	45-38-13.092N	121-56-58.812W
LOMA	993660642	Ormond, Arthur L&D (9)	35-7-27.264N	92-47-8.268W
LOMA	993660644	Barkley L&D	37-1-9.120N	88-13-29.928W
LOMA	993660645	Ballard L&D (Chittenden)	47-39-55.872N	122-23-49.128W
LOMA	993660646	Belleville L&D	39-7-1.056N	81-44-34.188W
LOMA	993660647	Meldahl, Captain Anthony L&D	38-47-50.424N	84-10-21.108W
LOMA	993660648	Greenup L&D	38-38-52.620N	82-51-40.212W
LOMA	993660649	London L&D	38-11-37.296N	81-22-6.359W
LOMA	993660651	Robert C Byrd L&D	38-40-58.002N	82-11-4.978W
LOMA	993660652	Willow Island L&D	39-21-36.870N	81-19-17.638W
LOMA	993660653	Winfield L&D	38-31-39.966N	81-54-55.199W

AIS BASE STATION TYPE	MMSI	LOCATION	LATITUDE	LONGITUDE
LOMA	993660654	Chain of Rocks L&D (Lock 27)	38-42-10.584N	90-10-49.692W
LOMA	993660655	Cheatham L&D	36-19-14.988N	87-13-18.948W
LOMA	993660656	Chickamauga L&D	35-6-21.708N	85-13-41.232W
LOMA	993660659	Guntersville L&D	34-25-35.256N	86-23-29.472W
LOMA	993660660	Kentucky L&D	37-0-54.972N	88-15-55.548W
LOMA	993660662	Ice Harbor L&D	46-15-3.744N	118-52-50.880W
LOMA	993660663	Little Goose L&D	46-34-55.732N	118-1-39.648W
LOMA	993660664	Lower Granite L&D	46-39-36.564N	117-25-42.060W
LOMA	993660665	Lower Monumental L&D	46-33-51.012N	118-32-24.180W
LOMA	993660666	McNary L&D	45-56-26.304N	119-17-58.416W
LOMA	993660668	Braddock, Monongahela R L&D 2	40-23-32.568N	79-51-34.452W
LOMA	993660672	Mississippi L&D 1	44-54-50.658N	93-12-8.280W
LOMA	993660680	Mississippi L&D 9	43-12-42.708N	91-5-54.298W
LOMA	993660685	Racine L&D	38-55-6.162N	81-54-40.558W
LOMA	993660686	Brandon Road L&D	41-30-12.600N	88-6-12.168W
LOMA	993660705	Nickajack L&D	35-0-19.668N	85-37-9.178W
LOMA	993660707	Pickwick Landing L&D	35-3-53.286N	88-15-1.559W
LOMA	993660708	Watts Bar L&D	35-37-19.998N	84-46-45.959W
LOMA	993660716	Allegheny L&D 2	40-29-16.080N	79-54-58.752W
LOMA	993660723	Allegheny L&D 3	40-32-9.996N	79-48-57.960W
LOMA	993660725	Maynard, Col. Charles D. L&D (5)	34-24-46.908N	92-6-4.212W
LOMA	993660737	Black Rock L&D	42-56-2.112N	78-54-18.360W
LOMA	993660738	Bankhead L&D (John Hollis)	33-27-11.052N	87-21-27.072W
LOMA	993660739	Holt L&D	33-15-11.124N	87-26-57.228W
LOMA	993660740	Oliver L&D (William Bacon)	33-12-36.876N	87-35-36.240W
LOMA	993660741	Selden L&D	32-46-29.359N	87-49-50.520W
LOMA	993660753	The Dalles L&D	45-36-56.556N	121-8-15.360W
LOMA	993660835	Brazos East & West L&D	28-53-46.986N	95-23-17.642W
LOMA	993660836	Colorado River East & West L&D	28-41-2.004N	95-58-24.960W
LOMA	993660838	Green River L&D 1	37-51-33.084N	87-24-31.068W
LOMA	993660845	Trailer #1	32-17-56.400N	90-51-55.080W
LOMA	993660855	Gasconade	38-39-51.696N	91-32-21.696W
LOMA	993660864	Pike Island L&D	40-8-52.866N	80-42-4.799W
LOMA	993660873	Aberdeen L&D	33-49-48.450N	88-31-12.990W
LOMA	993660874	Amory L&D	34-0-39.996N	88-29-18.960W
LOMA	993660883	Coffeeville L&D	31-45-23.076N	88-7-42.672W
LOMA	993660884	Demopolis L&D	32-31-9.660N	87-52-46.992W
LOMA	993660885	Chouteau L&D (17)	35-51-25.992N	95-22-14.988W
LOMA	993661101	Maxwell L&D	40-0-4.176N	79-57-39.924W
LOMA	993661103	Vicksburg Bridge	32-18-52.312N	90-54-27.360W

AIS BASE STATION TYPE	MMSI	LOCATION	LATITUDE	LONGITUDE
LOMA	993661104	Greenville Bridge	33-17-8.117N	91-9-21.157W
LOMA	993661106	Brickeys	38-4-30.000N	90-13-23.988W
LOMA	993661107	Florence	39-37-57.904N	90-36-27.677W
LOMA	993661108	Pere Marquette	38-59-50.788N	90-31-3.104W
LOMA	993661110	Grand Tower	37-39-28.872N	89-30-45.108W
LOMA	993661111	Grays Point	37-14-58.812N	89-27-50.303W
LOMA	993661112	Caruthersville	36-11-35.016N	89-40-39.972W
LOMA	993661113	ERDC CHL TEST	32-17-59.755N	90-51-57.694W

(1) No.	(2) Name and Location	(3) Position	(4) Characteristic	(5) Height	(6) Range	(7) Structure	(8) Remarks
			SEACOAST (Maine) - First District				
	BAY OF FUNDY TO CAPE COD						
3	North Rock Light (AIS)	44-32-15.837N 067-05-13.808W					AIS Physical MMSI 993676005.
3.1	North Shoal Iso Danger By (VAIS "NS")	44-31-41.380N 067-06-39.200W					MMSI 993676005.
3.2	South East Shoal Isolated Danger By (VAIS "SE")	44-29-32.240N 067-04-37.160W					MMSI 993676005.
4	*NOAA Data Lighted Buoy 44027*	44-16-59.000N 067-17-59.000W	Fl (4)Y 20s		4	Yellow.	Marked NOAA 44027 Aid maintained by National Oceanic and Atmospheric Administration.
5 2290	**Mount Desert Light**	43-58-07.046N 068-07-42.021W	Fl W 15s	75	14	Granite conical tower. 65	HORN: 2 blasts ev 30s (2s bl-2s si-2s bl-24s si). MRASS-Fog signal is radio activated, during times of reduced visibility, turn marine VHF-FM radio to channel 83A/157.175Mhz. Key microphone 5 times consecutively, to activate fog signal for 60 minutes.
6	*University of Maine Jordan Basin Lighted Buoy M*	43-29-26.400N 067-52-47.400W	Fl Y 4s			Yellow.	Private aid.
10 3195	**Matinicus Rock Light**	43-47-00.538N 068-51-18.129W	Fl W 10s	90	20	Cylindrical gray granite tower. 41	Emergency light of reduced intensity when main light is extinguished. HORN: 1 blast ev 15s (2s bl). MRASS-Fog signal is radio activated, during times of reduced visibility, turn marine VHF-FM radio to channel 83A/157.175Mhz. Key microphone 5 times consecutively, to activate fog signal for 60 minutes.
20 4925	**Monhegan Island Light**	43-45-53.318N 069-18-56.991W	Fl W 15s	178	20	White tower. 47	Within 3 miles of island the light is obscured between west and southwest. Emergency light of reduced intensity when main light is extinguished.
35 5590	**Seguin Light**	43-42-26.936N 069-45-28.911W	F W	180	14	Brick conical tower. 53	HORN: 2 blasts ev 20s (2s bl-2s si-2s bl-14s si). MRASS-Fog signal is radio activated, during times of reduced visibility, turn marine VHF-FM radio to channel 83A/157.175Mhz. Key microphone 5 times consecutively, to activate fog signal for 60 minutes.
40 6675	**Halfway Rock Light**	43-39-20.835N 070-02-12.437W	Fl R 5s	76	14	White tower attached to dwelling. 77	HORN: 2 blasts ev 30s (2s bl-2s si-2s bl-24s si). MRASS-Fog signal is radio activated, during times of reduced visibility, turn marine VHF-FM radio to channel 83A/157.175Mhz. Key microphone 5 times consecutively, to activate fog signal for 60 minutes.
45 7480	*Portland Lighted Whistle Buoy P*	43-31-36.347N 070-05-28.174W	Mo (A) W		6	Red and white stripes with red spherical topmark.	RACON: M (- -) AIS: MMSI 993672144 (21)

(1) No.	(2) Name and Location	(3) Position	(4) Characteristic	(5) Height	(6) Range	(7) Structure	(8) Remarks
			SEACOAST (Maine) - First District				
	BAY OF FUNDY TO CAPE COD						
60 7520	**Cape Elizabeth Light**	43-33-57.899N 070-12-00.220W	Fl (4)W 15s 0.3s fl 2.2s ec. 0.3s fl 2.2s ec. 0.3s fl 2.2s ec. 0.3s fl 7.2s ec.	129	15	White conical tower. 67	Lighted throughout 24 hours. Emergency light of reduced intensity when main light is extinguished. HORN: 2 blasts ev 60s (3s bl-3s si-3s bl-51s si). Horn located 266 yards, 146° from light tower. MRASS-Fog signal is radio activated, during times of reduced visibility, turn marine VHF-FM radio to channel 83A/157.175Mhz. Key microphone 5 times consecutively, to activate fog signal for 60 minutes.
65	Taylor Reef Buoy 3 Off southeast side of reef.	43-33-22.362N 070-11-16.578W				Green can.	
70	Alden Rock Buoy 4 Southwest of rock.	43-33-04.363N 070-09-34.887W				Red nun.	
75 7500	*East Hue and Cry Rock Lighted Buoy 1 (NOAA 44007)* East-southeast of ledge.	43-31-30.397N 070-08-25.576W	Fl G 4s		4	Green.	3 meter discus buoy marked with 44007 on fin. Aid maintained by National Oceanic and Atmospheric Administration.
80	*Old Anthony Lighted Whistle Buoy 2* Southwest of Old Anthony Rock.	43-32-16.343N 070-10-47.177W	Fl R 4s		4	Red.	
85	Watts Ledge Bell Buoy 1	43-32-19.742N 070-12-35.538W				Green.	
95	**Wood Island Light**	43-27-24.735N 070-19-44.611W	Al WG 10s	71	G 13 W 13	White conical tower connected to dwelling. 71	HORN: 2 blasts ev 30s (2s bl-2s si-2s bl-24s si). MRASS-Fog signal is radio activated, during times of reduced visibility, turn marine VHF-FM radio to channel 83A/157.175Mhz. Key microphone 5 times consecutively, to activate fog signal for 45 minutes.
100	Hussey Rock Buoy 1HR	43-25-28.046N 070-20-20.985W				Green can.	
105 8100	**Goat Island Light**	43-21-28.335N 070-25-30.312W	Fl W 6s	38	12	25	HORN: 1 blast ev 15s (2s bl). MRASS-Fog signal is radio activated, during times of reduced visibility, turn marine VHF-FM radio to channel 83A/157.175Mhz. Key microphone 5 times consecutively, to activate fog signal for 60 minutes.
113	*University of Maine Research Lighted Buoy B*	43-10-46.800N 070-25-36.600W	Fl Y 4s			Yellow.	Private aid.
113.1	*University of Maine Research Lighted Buoy E*	43-42-54.400N 069-21-17.100W	Fl Y 4s			Yellow.	Private aid.
113.2	*University of Maine Research Lighted Buoy I*	44-06-10.200N 068-06-43.800W	Fl Y 4s			Yellow.	Private aid.
115	Bibb Rock Buoy BR	43-16-33.157N 070-32-59.232W				Red nun with green bands.	
120	*Perkins Cove Lighted Bell Buoy PC*	43-14-26.728N 070-34-09.272W	Mo (A) W		4	Red and white stripes with red spherical topmark.	

(1) No.	(2) Name and Location	(3) Position	(4) Characteristic	(5) Height	(6) Range	(7) Structure	(8) Remarks
			SEACOAST (Maine) - First District				
	BAY OF FUNDY TO CAPE COD						
125	**Cape Neddick Light**	43-09-54.768N 070-35-27.955W	Iso R 6s	88	13	White conical tower connected to dwelling. 41	Lighted throughout 24 hours Emergency light of reduced intensity when main light is extinguished. HORN: 1 blast ev 10s (1s bl). Fog signal is radio activated, during times of reduced visibility, turn marine VHF-FM radio to channel 83A/157.175Mhz. Key microphone 5 times consecutively, to activate fog signal for 45 minutes.
130	*Boon Island Ledge Lighted Whistle Buoy 22A*	43-07-27.651N 070-24-32.862W	Fl R 4s		4	Red.	
155	**Boon Island Light**	43-07-17.253N 070-28-35.130W	Fl W 5s	137	14	Gray conical tower, connected to dwelling. 133	Emergency light of reduced intensity when main light is extinguished. HORN: 1 blast ev 10s (2s bl). Operates continuously.
160 8258	*York Harbor Lighted Bell Buoy YH*	43-07-45.395N 070-37-01.328W	Mo (A) W		5	Red and white stripes with red spherical topmark.	
165	Stones Rock Buoy 2SR	43-06-24.936N 070-37-57.599W				Red nun.	
170	York Ledge Buoy YL East of ledge.	43-05-35.249N 070-35-15.061W				Red nun with green bands.	
180	Murray Rock Buoy 2MR Southwest of Murray Rock.	43-04-08.359N 070-36-38.194W				Red nun.	
185	West Sister Buoy 2	43-03-35.928N 070-40-09.627W				Red nun.	
195	*Kitts Rocks Lighted Whistle Buoy 2KR* South of Kitts Rocks.	43-02-57.708N 070-41-27.768W	Fl R 2.5s		4	Red.	
200	**Whaleback Light**	43-03-31.569N 070-41-46.713W	Fl (2)W 10s	59	11	Gray conical tower. 49	HORN: 2 blasts ev 30s (2s bl-2s si-2s bl-24s si). Fog signal is radio activated, during times of reduced visibility, turn marine VHF-FM radio to channel 83A/157.175Mhz. Key microphone 5 times consecutively, to activate fog signal for 45 minutes.
			SEACOAST (New Hampshire) - First District				
	PORTSMOUTH TO CAPE ANN						
205	*Gunboat Shoal Lighted Bell Buoy 1* Off northeast point of shoal.	43-01-25.849N 070-41-55.146W	Fl G 4s		4	Green.	
210	Foss Ledges Buoy 1A Marks east end of ledges.	43-00-43.859N 070-43-12.877W				Green can.	
215 8870	*Rye Harbor Entrance Lighted Whistle Buoy RH*	42-59-37.550N 070-43-45.177W	Mo (A) W		6	Red and white stripes with red spherical topmark.	
			SEACOAST (Maine) - First District				
	PORTSMOUTH TO CAPE ANN						
220	Appledore Ledge Buoy 2	42-59-35.424N 070-37-13.150W				Red nun.	
225	Isles of Shoals Bell Buoy IS North of Halfway Rocks.	42-58-52.214N 070-37-15.609W				Red and white stripes with red spherical topmark.	
226	*UNH Isle of Shoals CO2 Research Lighted Buoy*	43-01-14.880N 070-32-33.000W	Fl Y 4s			Yellow.	Private aid.
			SEACOAST (New Hampshire) - First District				
	PORTSMOUTH TO CAPE ANN						
230	Halfway Rock Buoy 4 West of ledge.	42-58-41.388N 070-37-18.373W				Red nun.	

(1) No.	(2) Name and Location	(3) Position	(4) Characteristic	(5) Height	(6) Range	(7) Structure	(8) Remarks
			SEACOAST (New Hampshire) - First District				
	PORTSMOUTH TO CAPE ANN						
235	**Isles of Shoals Light**	42-58-02.074N 070-37-23.778W	Fl W 15s	82	14	White conical tower. 58	Emergency light of reduced intensity when main light is extinguished. HORN: 1 blast ev 30s (3s bl). MRASS -Fog signal is radio activated, during times of reduced visibility, turn marine VHF-FM radio to channel 83A/157.175Mhz. Key microphone 5 times consecutively, to activate fog signal for 45 minutes.
237	Cedar Island Ledge Isolated Danger Buoy DC	42-58-24.995N 070-35-57.828W				Black and red bands with two black spherical topmarks; can.	
237.5	*UNH Jeffrey's Ledge Lighted Research Buoy*	42-53-25.080N 070-03-33.480W	Fl Y 2.5s			Yellow.	Property of the University of New Hampshire. Private aid.
238	*University of New Hampshire Lighted Research Wave Buoy*	42-47-54.600N 070-10-18.500W	Fl (5)Y 20s			Yellow.	Private aid.
240	Anderson Ledge Buoy 2	42-57-36.143N 070-36-08.931W				Red nun.	
245	Little Boars Head Buoy 1C	42-57-06.771N 070-45-18.267W				Green can.	
			SEACOAST (Massachusetts) - First District				
	PORTSMOUTH TO CAPE ANN						
250	*Seabrook Station Buoy T7*	42-55-15.000N 070-46-46.000W				White with orange bands, can.	Private aid.
255	Breaking Rocks Buoy 2 Off northeast end of ledge.	42-51-52.080N 070-47-46.654W				Red nun.	
260	**Newburyport Harbor Light**	42-48-54.865N 070-49-08.196W	Oc (2)G 15s 7s fl 2s ec. 4s fl 2s ec.	50	10	White conical tower. 45	Obscured by shore structure from 165° to 192° and 313° to 344°.
265 8990	*Merrimack River Entrance Lighted Whistle Buoy MR*	42-48-34.367N 070-47-03.193W	Mo (A) W		4	Red and white stripes with red spherical topmark.	
275	Flat Ground Bell Buoy 1	42-41-04.477N 070-34-48.166W				Green.	
280	Flat Ground Southern Rock Buoy 2 At south end of flat ground.	42-40-36.557N 070-34-59.226W				Red nun.	
285	*Dry Salvages Lighted Bell Buoy 1*	42-40-40.353N 070-33-31.849W	Fl G 2.5s		3	Green.	
290	STRAIGHTSMOUTH LIGHT	42-39-44.177N 070-35-17.065W	Fl G 6s	46	6	White cylindrical tower.	HORN: 1 blast ev 15s (2s bl). MRASS-Fog signal is radio activated, during times of reduced visibility, turn marine VHF-FM radio to channel 83A/157.175Mhz. Key microphone 5 times consecutively, to activate fog signal for 45 minutes.
295	**Cape Ann Light**	42-38-12.479N 070-34-29.763W	Fl R 5s	166	17	166	Emergency light of reduced intensity when main light is extinguished. HORN: 2 blasts ev 60s (3s bl-3s si-3s bl-51s si). MRASS-Fog signal is radio activated, during times of reduced visibility, turn marine VHF-FM radio to channel 83A/157.175Mhz. Key microphone 5 times consecutively, to activate fog signal for 60 minutes.
300	Oak Rock Buoy 2	42-38-25.559N 070-35-03.064W				Red nun.	
305	THACHER ISLAND NORTH LIGHT	42-38-21.828N 070-34-30.000W	F Y	162		Gray granite conical tower.	Private aid.

(1) No.	(2) Name and Location	(3) Position	(4) Characteristic	(5) Height	(6) Range	(7) Structure	(8) Remarks
			SEACOAST (Massachusetts) - First District				
	PORTSMOUTH TO CAPE ANN						
310	Thacher Island Buoy 1	42-38-21.169N 070-34-47.624W				Green can.	
315	Londoner Rock Daybeacon	42-38-06.479N 070-33-57.962W				Iron spindle.	
325	Salt Island Ledge Buoy 4	42-37-00.212N 070-36-54.228W				Red nun.	
	GEORGES BANK AND NANTUCKET SHOALS						
330	**Eastern Point Light**	42-34-48.635N 070-39-52.011W	Fl W 5s	57	20	White conical tower, covered way to dwelling. 57 57	Lighted throughout 24 hours. Emergency light of reduced intensity when main light is extinguished.
340	Eastern Point Lighted Whistle Buoy 2	42-34-14.470N 070-39-50.108W	Fl R 4s		3		
350 9975	**Bakers Island Light**	42-32-11.235N 070-47-09.312W	Al WR 20s	111	W 16 R 14	White conical tower. 111	Emergency light, Fl W 10s when main light extinguished. Light and Horn is reduced intensity when main light or horn is extinguished. HORN: 1 blast ev 30s (3s bl). MRASS-Fog signal is radio activated, during times of reduced visibility, turn marine VHF-FM radio to channel 83A/157.175Mhz. Key microphone 5 times consecutively, to activate fog signal for 60 minutes.
355 10383	Newcomb Ledge Lighted Whistle Buoy 1	42-30-27.872N 070-44-23.262W	Fl G 4s		4	Green.	
365	Great Pig Rocks Lighted Buoy 4	42-27-37.602N 070-50-12.568W	Fl R 4s		4	Red.	
367	University of Maine ODAS Lighted Buoy A	42-31-24.600N 070-33-58.800W	Fl Y 4s			Yellow.	Private aid.
368	Neptune LNG Deepwater Port Lighted Buoy North A1	42-29-13.610N 070-36-33.350W	Q Y			Yellow.	Private aid.
368.2	Neptune LNG Deepwater Port Lighted Buoy South B1	42-27-23.350N 070-36-05.540W	Q Y			Yellow.	Private aid.
369.5	Neptune LNG Deepwater Port Lighted Hazard Buoy	42-29-07.572N 070-46-34.638W	Fl W 4s			White and orange.	Private aid.
371	Northeast Gateway Deepwater Port Lighted Buoy A1	42-23-38.379N 070-35-30.955W	Fl Y 2s				Private aid.
373	Northeast Gateway Deepwater Port Lighted Buoy B1	42-23-56.351N 070-37-00.388W	Fl Y 2s				Private aid.
374.1	Northeast Gateway Support Vessel Mooring Buoy	42-24-01.800N 070-38-42.600W					Private aid.
380 10678	The Graves Lighted Whistle Buoy 5	42-22-32.857N 070-51-28.458W	Fl G 4s		4	Green.	
385 10677	Boston Approach Lighted Buoy BG	42-23-26.857N 070-51-29.069W	Mo (A) W		4	Red and white stripes with red spherical topmark.	AIS: MMSI 993672145 (21)
390 10679	**The Graves Light**	42-21-53.634N 070-52-08.712W	Fl (2)W 12s 0.1s fl 1.8s ec. 0.1s fl 10s ec.	98	15	On light gray conical granite tower. 98	Emergency light of reduced intensity when main light is extinguished. HORN: 2 blasts ev 20s (2s bl-2s si-2s bl-14s si). MRASS-Fog signal is radio activated, during times of reduced visibility, turn marine VHF-FM radio to channel 83A/157.175Mhz. Key microphone 5 times consecutively, to activate fog signal for 60 minutes.
395 11334	Three and One-Half Fathom Ledge Lighted Bell Buoy 2	42-21-05.009N 070-50-29.796W	Fl R 4s		4	Red.	
400 11335	Martin Ledge Buoy 4	42-20-45.739N 070-51-12.086W				Red nun.	
405 11336	Boston Ledge Buoy 6	42-20-04.679N 070-51-49.706W				Red nun.	

(1) No.	(2) Name and Location	(3) Position	(4) Characteristic	(5) Height	(6) Range	(7) Structure	(8) Remarks
			SEACOAST (Massachusetts) - First District				
	GEORGES BANK AND NANTUCKET SHOALS						
410 10676	*Boston Lighted Whistle Buoy B*	42-22-42.189N 070-46-58.171W	Mo (A) W		6	Red and white stripes with red spherical topmark.	RACON: B (- . . .) AIS: MMSI 993672065
	WHOI Traffic Separation Scheme Research Lighted Buoy						
415	*- AB-1*	42-20-49.988N 070-40-40.879W	Fl Y 4s			Yellow.	Private aid.
	GEORGES BANK AND NANTUCKET SHOALS						
420	*Boston Approach Lighted Buoy BF NOAA 44013*	42-20-44.048N 070-39-03.927W	Fl (4)Y 20s 0.5s fl 2s ec. 0.5s fl 2s ec. 0.5s fl 2s ec. 0.5s fl 12s ec.		7	Yellow.	Aid maintained by National Oceanic and Atmospheric Administration.
425 11340	**Boston Light**	42-19-40.889N 070-53-24.278W	Fl W 10s	102	27	On white conical tower. 89	Emergency light of reduced intensity when main light is extinguished. Two emergency lights may be visable from 336° to 001° and from 156° to 181°. HORN: 1 blast ev 30s (3s bl). MRASS-Fog signal is radio activated, during times of reduced visibility, turn marine VHF-FM radio to channel 83A/157.175Mhz. Key microphone 5 times consecutively, to activate fog signal for 60 minutes.
430 11333	*Thieves Ledge Lighted Whistle Buoy 1*	42-19-34.101N 070-49-49.343W	Q G		3	Green.	
435 11337	*Harding Ledge Lighted Bell Buoy 1HL*	42-18-34.222N 070-50-37.883W	Fl G 4s		4	Green.	
440	**Minots Ledge Light**	42-16-11.034N 070-45-32.711W	Fl (1+4+3)W 45s 1.5s fl 5s ec. 1.5s fl 1.5s ec. 1.5s fl 1.5s ec. 1.5s fl 1.5s ec. 1.5s fl 5s ec. 1.5s fl 1.5s ec. 1.5s fl 1.5s ec. 1.5s fl 15.5s ec.	85	10	On gray conical tower. 87	HORN: 1 blast ev 10s (1s bl). MRASS-Fog signal is radio activated, during times of reduced visibility, turn marine VHF-FM radio to channel 83A/157.175Mhz. Key microphone 5 times consecutively, to activate fog signal for 60 minutes.
445	*Davis Ledge Lighted Gong Buoy 1DL*	42-16-20.927N 070-44-51.293W	Fl G 2.5s		3	Green.	
450	*Twenty-one Foot Lighted Buoy 21*	42-16-34.796N 070-42-22.069W	Fl G 4s		4	Green.	
453	*Anduril Industries Research Lighted Bell Buoy A*	42-16-37.560N 070-32-54.480W	Fl Y 4s			Yellow.	Property of Anduril Industries. Private aid.
	Scituate Harbor Approach						
455 12256	Tar Pouch Buoy 2	42-13-10.269N 070-42-13.386W				Red nun.	
460 12258	*Scituate Approach Lighted Gong Buoy SA*	42-12-07.579N 070-41-49.355W	Mo (A) W		4	Red and white stripes with red spherical topmark.	AIS: MMSI 993672146 (21)
465 12270	SCITUATE NORTH JETTY LIGHT 2A	42-12-11.356N 070-42-47.495W	Fl R 4s	23	4	TR on white skeleton tower.	Higher intensity beam eastward.
	WHOI Traffic Separation Scheme Research Lighted Buoy						
466	*- AB-2*	42-20-25.404N 070-33-59.940W	Fl Y 4s			Yellow.	Private aid.
467	*- AB-3*	42-20-00.499N 070-27-16.855W	Fl Y 4s			Yellow.	Private aid.
468	*- AB-4*	42-19-33.636N 070-20-32.341W	Fl Y 4s			Yellow.	Private aid.
471	*- AB-5*	42-19-09.005N 070-13-47.460W	Fl Y 4s			Yellow.	Private aid.
472	*- AB-6*	42-18-40.205N 070-07-05.686W	Fl Y 4s			Yellow.	Private aid.
473	*- AB-7*	42-18-09.630N 070-01-54.325W	Fl Y 4s			Yellow.	Private aid.

(1) No.	(2) Name and Location	(3) Position	(4) Characteristic	(5) Height	(6) Range	(7) Structure	(8) Remarks
	**SEACOAST (Massachusetts) - First District**						
	GEORGES BANK AND NANTUCKET SHOALS							
485	**Race Point Light**	42-03-44.434N 070-14-34.911W	Fl W 10s	41	14	On white tower.	"Obscured from 220° to 292°.
					45		
	WHOI Traffic Separation Scheme Research Lighted Buoy						
496	*- AB-8*	42-13-49.577N 069-58-01.988W	Fl Y 4s			Yellow.	Private aid.
497	*- AB-9*	42-09-22.453N 069-54-58.269W	Fl Y 4s			Yellow.	Private aid.
498	*- AB-10*	42-04-55.419N 069-51-46.206W	Fl Y 4s			Yellow.	Private aid.
	GEORGES BANK AND NANTUCKET SHOALS							
500	**Highland Light**	42-02-22.316N 070-03-39.387W	Fl W 5s	170	14	White conical tower. 66	Lighted throughout 24 hours.
510.1	NAUSET BEACH LIGHT	41-51-36.000N 069-57-12.000W	Al WR 10s 0.1s fl 4.9s ec. 0.1s fl 4.9s ec.	120	R W	Conical tower, upper part red, lower part white.	Lighted throughout 24 hours. Private aid.
	**MASSACHUSETTS - First District**						
	NANTUCKET SOUND AND APPROACHES **Chatham Harbor Approach**							
520	*Chatham Beach Lighted Whistle Buoy C*	41-39-12.040N 069-55-30.051W	Mo (A) W		4	Red and white stripes (No topmark).	AIS MMSI; 993672587 (21)
	**SEACOAST (Massachusetts) - First District**						
	GEORGES BANK AND NANTUCKET SHOALS							
525	**Chatham Light**	41-40-16.738N 069-57-00.564W	Fl (2)W 10s 0.1s fl 2s ec. 0.1s fl 7.8s ec.	80	24	White conical tower. 43	Lighted throughout 24 hours. Storm warning signals displayed by day.
545 13650	**Nantucket (Great Point) Light**	41-23-24.634N 070-02-53.810W	Fl W 5s (R sector)	71	W 14 R 12	On white tower. 70	Red from 084° to 106°. Covers Cross Rip and Tuckernuck Shoals.
555	**Sankaty Head Light**	41-17-03.764N 069-57-57.910W	Fl W 7.5s	158	20	White tower with red band in the middle. 70	Lighted throughout 24 hours.
560	*NOAA Data Lighted Buoy 44018*	42-12-11.240N 070-09-14.295W	Fl (4)Y 20s 0.5s fl 2s ec. 0.5s fl 2s ec. 0.5s fl 2s ec. 0.5s fl 12s ec.	7		Yellow.	Marked NOAA 44018. Aid maintained by National Oceanic and Atmospheric Administration.
589	WHOI RESEARCH LIGHT TOWER	41-19-30.000N 070-34-00.000W	Fl Y 4s			Steel tripod with mast.	HORN: 1 blast ev 20s (2s bl). MRASS-Fog signal is radio activated, during times of reduced visibility, turn marine VHF-FM radio to channel 83A/157.175Mhz. Key microphone 5 times consecutively, to activate fog signal for 50 minutes. Private Aid. Private aid.
589.6	*Vineyard Wind Lighted Research Buoy A*	41-06-50.681N 070-28-00.385W	Fl Y 20s			Yellow.	Property of Vineyard Wind. Private aid.
589.7	*Vineyard Wind Lighted Research Buoy B*	41-01-36.480N 070-31-32.700W	Fl Y 20s			Yellow.	Property of Vineyard Wind. Private aid.
589.8	*Vineyard Wind Lighted Research Buoy C*	41-01-39.410N 070-24-59.910W	Fl Y 20s			Yellow.	Property of Vineyard Wind. Private aid.
589.85	*WHOI Lighted Research Buoy WTRIM*	41-03-39.000N 070-29-39.000W	Fl Y 5s			Yellow.	Private aid.
589.9	*Vineyard Wind Acoustic Lighted Research Buoy*	41-09-33.480N 070-38-18.960W	Fl Y 20s			Yellow.	Private aid.
	APPROACHES TO NEW YORK - NANTUCKET SHOALS TO FIVE FATHOM BANK							
590	*Squibnocket Lighted Bell Buoy 1*	41-15-41.774N 070-46-16.433W	Fl G 4s		3	Green.	
595	Squibnocket Shoal Buoy 2 On west side of shoal.	41-17-45.022N 070-48-07.805W				Red nun.	

(1) No.	(2) Name and Location	(3) Position	(4) Characteristic	(5) Height	(6) Range	(7) Structure	(8) Remarks

SEACOAST (Massachusetts) - First District

APPROACHES TO NEW YORK - NANTUCKET SHOALS TO FIVE FATHOM BANK

(1) No.	(2) Name and Location	(3) Position	(4) Characteristic	(5) Height	(6) Range	(7) Structure	(8) Remarks
600	VINEYARD WIND 1 WTG AT40 Vineyard Wind 1 WEA.	41-01-14.971N 070-25-02.155W	Fl Y 6s	70		Mono pile temp NAV structure.	Private aid. Private aid.
600.01	VINEYARD WIND 1 WTG AU39 Vineyard Wind 1 WEA.	41-00-13.977N 070-26-20.148W	Fl Y 6s	70		Mono pile temp NAV structure.	Private Aid. Private aid.
600.02	VINEYARD WIND 1 WTG AP38 Vineyard Wind 1 WEA.	41-05-13.191N 070-27-46.026W	Fl Y 6s	70		Mono pile temp NAV structure.	Private Aid. Private aid.
600.03	VINEYARD WIND 1 WTG AV39 Vineyard Wind 1 WEA.	40-59-13.951N 070-26-18.843W	Fl Y 2.5s	70		Mono Pole Structure.	Private Aid. Private aid.
600.04	VINEYARD WIND 1 WTG AR39	41-03-14.095N 070-26-24.080W	Fl Y 6s	70			Private aid.
600.05	VINEYARD WIND WTG AW38	40-58-12.887N 070-27-36.742W	Q Y	70			Private aid.
600.06	VINEYARD WIND 1 ESP AM37 VWI WEA.	41-07-12.216N 070-29-06.360W	Fl Y 2.5s	70		ESP structure.	Private aid. Private aid.
600.07	VINEYARD WIND 1 WTG AQ38 VW1 WEA.	41-04-13.012N 070-27-44.683W	Q Y	70		Mono pile.	Private aid. Private aid.
600.08	VINEYARD WIND 1 WTG AV38 Vineyard Wind 1 WEA.	40-59-13.898N 070-27-38.038W	Q Y	70		Mono Pile temp NAV.	Private Aid. Private aid.
600.09	VINEYARD WIND 1 WTG AU38 Vineyard Wind 1 WEA.	41-00-12.941N 070-27-39.362W	Q Y	70		Mono pile temp NAV.	Private Aid. Private aid.
600.1	VINEYARD WIND 1 WTG AT39 VW1 WEA.	41-01-14.012N 070-26-21.443W	Q Y	70		Mono pile.	Private aid. Private aid.
600.11	VINEYARD WIND 1 WTG AS39 VW1 WEA.	41-02-14.020N 070-26-22.721W	Q Y	70		Mono pile.	Private aid. Private aid.
600.12	VINEYARD WIND 1 WTG AN37 Vineyard Wind 1 WEA.	41-06-12.164N 070-29-06.712W	Q Y	70		Mono pile temp NAV.	Private Aid. Private aid.
600.13	VINEYARD WIND 1 WTG AS41 VW1 WEA.	41-02-15.972N 070-23-44.131W	Q Y	70		Mono Pile.	Private Aid. Private aid.
600.14	VINEYARD WIND 1 WTG AQ36 VW1 WEA.	41-04-11.075N 070-30-23.364W	Q Y	70		Mono Pile.	Private aid.
600.15	VINEYARD WIND 1 WTG AT41 VW1 WEA.	41-01-15.931N 070-23-42.864W	Q Y	70		Mono pile.	Private Aid. Private aid.
600.16	VINEYARD WIND 1 WTG AQ39 VW1 WEA.	41-04-14.102N 070-26-25.342W	Q Y	70		Mono Pile.	Private Aid. Private aid.
600.17	VINEYARD WIND 1 WTG AS40 VW1 WEA.	41-02-15.035N 070-25-03.449W	Q Y	70		Mono Pile.	Private Aid. Private aid.
600.18	VINEYARD WIND 1 WTG AR38 VW1 WEA.	41-03-13.106N 070-27-43.370W	Q Y	70		Mono Pile.	Private Aid. Private aid.
600.19	VINEYARD WIND 1 WTG AS42 VW1 WEA.	41-02-16.961N 070-22-24.873W	Q Y	70		Mono pole.	Private aid.
600.2	VINEYARD WIND 1 WTG AP39 VW1 WEA.	41-05-14.180N 070-26-26.675W	Q Y	70		Mono pile.	Private aid.
600.21	VINEYARD WIND 1 WTG AN38 VW1 WEA.	41-06-13.207N 070-27-47.356W	Q Y	70		Mono pile.	Private aid.
600.22	VINEYARD WIND 1 WTG AR40 VW1 WEA.	41-03-15.044N 070-25-04.717W	Q Y	70		Mono pile.	Private aid.

(1) No.	(2) Name and Location	(3) Position	(4) Characteristic	(5) Height	(6) Range	(7) Structure	(8) Remarks
		SEACOAST (Massachusetts) - First District					
	APPROACHES TO NEW YORK - NANTUCKET SHOALS TO FIVE FATHOM BANK						
600.23	VINEYARD WIND 1 WTG AR41 VW1 WEA.	41-03-16.036N 070-23-45.417W	Q Y	70		Mono pile.	Private aid.
600.24	VINEYARD WIND 1 WTG AU40 VW1 WEA.	41-00-14.958N 070-25-00.873W	Q Y	70		Mono Pile.	Private aid.
600.25	VINEYARD WIND 1 WTG AQ42 VW1 WEA.	41-04-17.039N 070-22-27.350W	Q Y	70		Mono pile.	Private aid. Private aid.
600.26	VINEYARD WIND 1 WTG AM38 VW! WEA.	41-07-13.249N 070-27-48.702W	Fl Y 6s	70		Mono pile.	Private aid. Private aid.
600.27	VINEYARD WIND 1 WTG AQ41 VW1 WEA.	41-04-16.080N 070-23-46.697W	Q Y	70		Mono pile.	Private aid. Private aid.
600.28	VINEYARD WIND 1 WTG AQ40 VW1 WEA.	41-04-15.117N 070-25-06.030W	Q Y	70		Mono pile.	Private aid. Private aid.
600.29	VINEYARD WIND 1 WTG AR42 VW1 WEA.	41-03-16.999N 070-22-26.102W	Fl Y 2.5s	70		Mono pile.	Private aid. Private aid.
600.3	VINEYARD WIND 1 WTG AP40 VW1 WEA.	41-05-15.148N 070-25-07.313W	Q Y	70		Mono pile.	Private aid.
600.31	VINEYARD WIND 1 WTG AN39 VW1 WEA.	41-06-14.202N 070-26-27.996W	Q Y	70		Mono pile.	Private aid.
600.32	VINEYARD WIND 1 WTG AP41 VW1 WEA.	41-05-16.121N 070-23-47.959W	Q Y	70		Mono pile.	Private aid.
600.33	VINEYARD WIND 1 WTG AM39 VW1 WEA.	41-07-14.269N 070-26-29.298W	Q Y	70		Mono pile.	Private aid.
600.34	VINEYARD WIND 1 WTG AL38 VW1 WEA.	41-08-13.305N 070-27-50.031W	Q Y	70		Mono pile.	Private aid.
600.35	VINEYARD WIND 1 WTG AS37	41-02-12.041N 070-29-01.325W	Q Y	70			Private aid.
600.36	VINEYARD WIND 1 WTG AT37 VW1 WEA.	41-01-12.000N 070-28-59.989W	Q Y	70		Mono pile.	Private aid.
600.37	VINEYARD WIND 1 WTG AQ34	41-04-08.973N 070-33-02.029W	Q Y	70			Private aid.
600.39	VINEYARD WIND 1 WTG AN36	41-06-11.176N 070-30-26.111W	Q Y	70			Private aid.
600.4	VINEYARD WIND 1 WTG AS32	41-02-06.708N 070-35-37.754W	Q Y	70			Private aid.
600.43	VINEYARD WIND 1 WTG AP35	41-05-10.085N 070-31-44.097W	Q Y	70			Private aid.
600.44	VINEYARD WIND 1 WTG AR34	41-03-08.934N 070-33-00.624W	Q Y	70			Private aid.
600.45	VINEYARD WIND 1 WTG AR37	41-03-12.077N 070-29-02.681W	Q Y	70			Private aid.
600.46	VINEYARD WIND 1 WTG AT33	41-01-07.813N 070-34-17.057W	Q Y	70			Private aid.
601	SOUTH FORK OSS AP06 South Fork WEA.	41-04-33.450N 071-10-04.620W	Q Y	77		Mono Pile Temp NAV.	Private Aid. Private aid.
601.01	SOUTH FORK WTG AM07 South Fork WEA.	41-06-34.628N 071-08-49.913W	Q Y	70		Mono pile TEMP NAV.	Private Aid. Private aid.
601.02	SOUTH FORK WTG AP05 South Fork WEA.	41-04-31.620N 071-11-23.968W	Q Y	70		Mono Pile TEMP NAV.	Private AID. Private aid.
601.03	SOUTH FORK WTG AN06 South Fork WEA.	41-05-31.042N 071-10-04.372W	Q Y	70		Mono Pile TEMP NAV.	Private AID. Private aid.
601.04	SOUTH FORK WTG AN08 South Fork WEA.	41-05-36.168N 071-07-24.229W	Q Y	70		Mono Pile TEMP NAV.	Private AID. Private aid.

(1) No.	(2) Name and Location	(3) Position	(4) Characteristic	(5) Height	(6) Range	(7) Structure	(8) Remarks
			SEACOAST (Massachusetts) - First District				
	APPROACHES TO NEW YORK - NANTUCKET SHOALS TO FIVE FATHOM BANK						
601.05	SOUTH FORK WTG AN09 South Fork WEA.	41-05-37.551N 071-06-08.661W	Q Y	70		Mono pile.	Private AID. Private aid.
601.06	SOUTH FORK WTG AP08 South Fork WEA.	41-04-36.245N 071-07-26.103W	Q Y	70		Mono pole.	Private AID. Private aid.
601.07	SOUTH FORK WTG AM06 South Fork WEA.	41-06-33.151N 071-10-09.129W	Q Y	70		Mono pole.	Private AID Private aid.
601.08	SOUTH FORK WTG AP09 South Fork WEA.	41-04-39.001N 071-06-06.796W	Q Y	70		Mono pole.	Private Aid. Private aid.
601.09	SOUTH FORK WTG AP07 South Fork WEA.	41-04-34.616N 071-08-45.373W	Q Y	70		Mono pole.	Private aid. Private aid.
601.1	SOUTH FORK WTG AM05 South Fork WEA.	41-06-31.782N 071-11-23.401W	Q Y	70		Mono pole.	Private aid. Private aid.
601.11	SOUTH FORK WTG AM08 South Fork WEA.	41-06-33.610N 071-07-30.140W	Q Y	70		Mono pole.	Private aid. Private aid.
601.12	SOUTH FORK WTG AN05 South Fork WEA.	41-05-31.652N 071-11-25.986W	Q Y	70		Mono pole.	Private aid. Private aid.
618	Old Man Ledge Buoy 3 On north end of Rocky Shoal.	41-17-04.413N 070-48-35.775W				Green can.	
619	Lone Rock Buoy 5	41-17-18.351N 070-49-17.877W				Green can.	
620 15610	**Gay Head Light**	41-20-54.454N 070-50-03.687W	Al WR 15s 0.2s W fl 7.3s ec. 0.2s R fl 7.3s ec.	175	W 24 R 20	Red brick tower. 51	Obscured from 342° to 359° by Nomans Land; light occasionally visible through notches in hilltop.Emergency light (Fl W 6s) of reduced intensity when main light is extinguished.Lighted throughout 24 hours.
630 15985	**Buzzards Bay Entrance Light**	41-23-49.152N 071-02-04.877W	Fl W 2.5s	67	14	Tower on red square on 3 red piles with large tube in center, worded BUZZARDS on sides. 68	RACON: B (- . . .) HORN: 2 blasts ev 30s (2s bl-2s si-2s bl-24s si). Fog signal is radio activated, during times of reduced visibility, turn marine VHF-FM radio to channel 83A/157.175Mhz. Key microphone 5 times consecutively, to activate fog signal for 45 minutes.
635	*USACE Data Lighted Buoy Station 154/NDBC 44097*	40-58-01.740N 071-07-25.007W	Fl (5)Y 20s		1	Yellow Spere Marked Wave Buoy.	Marked Wave Buoy. Aid maintained by Scripps Institute for USACE. Aid maintained by U.S. Army Corps of Engineers.
636	*WHOI TEMP Lighted Research Buoy T4*	41-08-45.000N 070-56-42.000W	Fl Y 4s				Private aid.
			SEACOAST (Rhode Island) - First District				
	APPROACHES TO NEW YORK - NANTUCKET SHOALS TO FIVE FATHOM BANK						
640	**Block Island Southeast Light**	41-09-12.276N 071-33-07.434W	Fl G 5s	261	17	Red-brick octagonal, pyramidal tower attached to dwelling. 67	Lighted throughout 24 hours. Emergency light of reduced intensity when main light is extinguished. Emergency light is offset from main light. HORN: 1 blast ev 30s (3s bl). MRASS-Fog signal is radio activated, during times of reduced visibility, turn marine VHF-FM radio to channel 83A/157.175Mhz. Key microphone 5 times consecutively, to activate fog signal for 45 minutes.
			SEACOAST (Massachusetts) - First District				
	APPROACHES TO NEW YORK - NANTUCKET SHOALS TO FIVE FATHOM BANK						
645	*Vineyard Northeast Metocean Lighted Research Buoy*	40-40-21.119N 070-13-07.767W	Fl Y 20s			Yellow.	Property of Ocean Tech Services. Private aid.

(1) No.	(2) Name and Location	(3) Position	(4) Characteristic	(5) Height	(6) Range	(7) Structure	(8) Remarks
		SEACOAST (Rhode Island) - First District					
	APPROACHES TO NEW YORK - NANTUCKET SHOALS TO FIVE FATHOM BANK						
650	*Southwest Ledge Lighted Whistle Buoy 2* Marks southwest edge of shoals.	41-06-28.877N 071-40-10.922W	Fl R 2.5s		4	Red.	
		SEACOAST (Massachusetts) - First District					
	APPROACHES TO NEW YORK - NANTUCKET SHOALS TO FIVE FATHOM BANK						
652	BLOCK ISLAND WIND FARM WTG-1	41-07-32.740N 071-30-27.040W	Q Y				Maintained by Orsted. Private aid.
653	BLOCK ISLAND WIND FARM WTG-2	41-07-11.570N 071-30-50.220W	Fl Y 3s				Maintained by Orsted. Private aid.
654	BLOCK ISLAND WIND FARM WTG-3	41-06-52.960N 071-31-16.180W	Fl Y 3s				Maintained by Orsted. Private aid.
654.5	**Block Island Wind Farm WTG-3 Fog Horn**	41-06-52.960N 071-31-16.180W					Maintained by Orsted. MRASS: Fog signal is radio activated, during times of reduced visibility, turn marine VHF-FM radio to channel 83A/157.175Mhz. Key microphone 5 times consecutively, to activate fog signal for 60 minutes. HORN: 1 blast ev 20s (2s bl). Private aid.
656	BLOCK ISLAND WIND FARM WTG-4	41-06-36.540N 071-31-44.620W	Fl Y 3s				Maintained by Orsted. Private aid.
657	BLOCK ISLAND WIND FARM WTG-5	41-06-22.790N 071-32-15.500W	Q Y				Maintained by Orsted. Private aid.
657.5	*AXYS Technologies Research Lighted Buoy SFW*	41-05-16.000N 071-13-22.000W	Fl Y 4s			Yellow.	Private aid.
657.7	*South Fork Wind Wave Lighted Buoy B*	41-04-34.140N 071-11-13.138W	Fl Y 4s			Yellow.	Private aid.
659	*Ocean Tech Lighted Research Buoy TGS-MA*	40-43-57.936N 070-44-28.968W	Fl Y 2s			Yellow.	AIS:993663051 Private aid.
659.5	*WHOI Lighted Research Buoy Orsted*	41-03-40.680N 070-49-56.280W	Fl Y 4s			Yellow.	Property of WHOI. Private aid.
		SEACOAST (New York) - First District					
	APPROACHES TO NEW YORK - NANTUCKET SHOALS TO FIVE FATHOM BANK						
660	**Montauk Point Light**	41-04-15.513N 071-51-25.540W	Fl W 5s	168	14	White conical tower with red stripe. 168	Emergency light Fl W 5s when main light is extinguished. HORN: 1 blast ev 15s (2s bl). MRASS-Fog signal is radio activated, during times of reduced visibility, turn marine VHF-FM radio to channel 83A/157.175Mhz. Key microphone 5 times consecutively, to activate fog signal for 45 minutes.
		SEACOAST (Massachusetts) - First District					
	APPROACHES TO NEW YORK - NANTUCKET SHOALS TO FIVE FATHOM BANK						
661	*SBU Lighted Research Buoy Montauk A*	41-02-09.719N 071-54-46.778W	Fl Y 2s			Yellow.	Property of SBU. Private aid.
662	*SBU Lighted Research Buoy Montauk B*	41-04-01.189N 071-51-17.165W	Fl Y 2s			Yellow.	Property of SBU. Private aid.
		SEACOAST (New York) - First District					
	APPROACHES TO NEW YORK - NANTUCKET SHOALS TO FIVE FATHOM BANK						
665	*NOAA Data Lighted Buoy NOAA 44017*	40-41-34.258N 072-02-56.319W	Fl (4)Y 20s		4	Yellow.	Aid maintained by National Oceanic and Atmospheric Administration.
670 29035	*Shinnecock Inlet Approach Lighted Whistle Buoy SH*	40-49-00.194N 072-28-34.532W	Mo (A) W		4	Red and white stripes with red spherical topmark.	AIS: MMSI 993672254 (21)
675 29025	**Shinnecock Light**	40-50-31.434N 072-28-41.690W	Fl (2)W 15s	75	11	Skeleton tower. 75	
685	*Moriches Inlet Approach Lighted Whistle Buoy M*	40-44-07.891N 072-45-11.873W	Mo (A) W		6	Red and white stripes.	AIS: MMSI 993672256 (21)

(1) No.	(2) Name and Location	(3) Position	(4) Characteristic	(5) Height	(6) Range	(7) Structure	(8) Remarks
			SEACOAST (New York) - First District				
	APPROACHES TO NEW YORK - NANTUCKET SHOALS TO FIVE FATHOM BANK						
695	**Fire Island Light**	40-37-56.790N 073-13-06.890W	Fl W 7.5s	167	167		Lighted throughout 24 hours. Emergency light of reduced intensity when main light is extinguished. Private aid.
			SEACOAST (Massachusetts) - First District				
	APPROACHES TO NEW YORK - NANTUCKET SHOALS TO FIVE FATHOM BANK						
725	*NOAA Data Lighted Buoy 44065*	40-22-10.000N 073-42-10.000W	Fl (4)Y 20s		4		Aid maintained by National Oceanic and Atmospheric Administration.
740	Fishing Grounds Obstruction (VAIS) East	40-25-41.526N 073-50-53.165W					Virtual AIS, short name FG East, MMSI 993672988
742	Fishing Grounds Obstruction (VAIS) West	40-25-25.522N 073-52-19.935W					Virtual AIS, short name FG West, MMSI 993672989
			SEACOAST (Atlantic Ocean)				
	CAPE SABLE TO CAPE HATTERAS						
820	*NOAA Data Lighted Buoy 44005 (ODAS)*	43-12-02.000N 069-07-37.000W	Fl (4)Y 20s			Yellow boat-shaped buoy.	Marked "NOAA" and "44005". Aid maintained by National Oceanic and Atmospheric Administration.
825	*NOAA Data Lighted Buoy 44011 (ODAS)*	41-05-35.000N 066-33-43.000W	Fl (4)Y 20s			Yellow.	Aid maintained by National Oceanic and Atmospheric Administration.
827	*NOAA Data Lighted Buoy 44008 (ODAS)*	40-29-44.000N 069-15-01.000W	Fl (4)Y 20s				Aid maintained by NOAA. Aid maintained by National Oceanic and Atmospheric Administration.
830	*NOAA Data Lighted Buoy 44025*	40-15-03.072N 073-09-51.592W	Fl (4)Y 20s			Yellow.	Aid maintained by National Oceanic and Atmospheric Administration.
			MAINE - First District				
	NEW BRUNSWICK - GRAND MANAN CHANNEL NORTHERN PART						
840	West Quoddy Head Bell Buoy WQ	44-49-24.984N 066-56-41.382W				Red and white stripes with red spherical topmark.	
845	Wormell Ledges Buoy 1A	44-49-26.681N 066-57-53.597W				Green can.	
850	Quoddy Roads Buoy 2	44-49-38.745N 066-57-48.007W				Red nun.	
	Lubec Channel						
855	- Buoy 1	44-50-15.627N 066-58-25.563W				Green can.	
860	- LIGHT	44-50-31.424N 066-58-35.830W	Fl W 6s	53	6	White conical tower on black cylindrical pier.	HORN: 1 blast ev 15s (2s bl). MRASS-Fog signal is radio activated, during times of reduced visibility, turn marine VHF-FM radio to channel 83A/157.175Mhz. Key microphone 5 times consecutively, to activate fog signal for 45 minutes.
865	- Buoy 3	44-50-34.705N 066-58-36.160W				Green can.	
870	- Buoy 4	44-50-33.825N 066-58-31.830W				Red nun.	
875	- Buoy 5	44-51-04.794N 066-58-28.759W				Green can.	
880	- Buoy 6	44-51-02.584N 066-58-22.899W				Red nun.	
883	- Buoy 6A	44-51-16.537N 066-58-33.808W				Red nun.	
885	- Buoy 8	44-51-56.593N 066-58-55.250W				Red nun.	

(1) No.	(2) Name and Location	(3) Position	(4) Characteristic	(5) Height	(6) Range	(7) Structure	(8) Remarks
			MAINE - First District				
	NEW BRUNSWICK - GRAND MANAN CHANNEL NORTHERN PART						
910	Popes Folly Ledge Buoy 9	44-52-11.119N 066-58-58.345W				Green can.	
914	Treat Island Shoal Lighted Buoy 3	44-53-09.538N 066-59-27.391W	Fl G 2.5s		3	Green can.	
915	Buckman Ledge Buoy 2	44-53-41.437N 066-59-05.408W				Red nun.	
925	CLARK LEDGE LIGHT 3	44-54-55.437N 066-59-04.708W	Fl G 4s	25	3	SG on spindle.	
930	DOG ISLAND LIGHT DI	44-55-06.572N 066-59-21.120W	Fl W 6s	35	9	NG on skeleton tower.	HORN: 1 blast ev 30s (3s bl). MRASS -Fog signal is radio activated, during times of reduced visibility, turn marine VHF-FM radio to channel 83A/157.175Mhz. Key microphone 5 times consecutively, to activate fog signal for 60 minutes.
940	Frost Ledge Lighted Bell Buoy 7	44-58-02.650N 067-02-11.435W	Fl G 4s		4	Green.	
	NEW BRUNSWICK - PASSAMAQUODDY BAY AND ST. CROIX RIVER						
	St. Croix River _Floating aids maintained from 1 Apr. to 1 Nov._						
945	- Lighted Buoy 11	45-06-47.312N 067-07-03.953W	Fl G 2.5s		4	Green.	
950	- LIGHT	45-07-41.710N 067-08-01.756W	Fl W 2.5s	101	7	White skeleton tower surmounted by platform.	
955	- Lighted Buoy 13	45-07-48.310N 067-07-45.956W	Fl G 4s		4	Green.	
960	- Buoy 17	45-09-48.994N 067-10-05.522W				Green can.	Maintained from April 15 to October 15.
970	- Lighted Buoy 19	45-10-15.405N 067-12-12.605W	Q G		3	Green.	Maintained from April 15 to October 15.
975	- Buoy 21	45-10-09.627N 067-12-25.872W				Green can.	Maintained from April 15 to October 15.
985	WHITLOCKS MILL LIGHT 25	45-09-45.407N 067-13-38.574W	Iso G 6s	32	5		
990	- Buoy 27	45-09-59.007N 067-13-53.096W				Green can.	Maintained from April 15 to October 15.
995	- Lighted Buoy 29	45-10-26.956N 067-14-38.250W	Fl G 2.5s		4	Green.	Maintained from April 15 to October 15.
	NEW BRUNSWICK - GRAND MANAN CHANNEL NORTHERN PART						
	Cobscook Bay						
1000	Shackford Ledge Buoy 4	44-53-34.499N 067-00-27.229W				Red nun.	
1005	- Buoy 5	44-53-59.437N 067-01-51.008W				Green can.	
1006	DEEP COVE AQUACULTURE LIGHTS (4)	44-54-18.000N 067-01-18.000W	F Y	8		On floating fish pens.	Four or more lights marking aquaculture structures of varying sizes and shapes in a charted fish pen area. Private aid.
1010	- Buoy 7	44-54-28.342N 067-02-56.509W				Green can.	
1013	ORPC Cobscook Bay Lighted Buoy A	44-54-41.000N 067-02-56.000W	Fl W 2.5s			White with orange bands.	Property of ORPC. Private aid.
1013.1	ORPC Cobscook Bay Lighted Buoy B	44-54-37.000N 067-02-33.000W	Fl W 2.5s			White with orange bands.	Property of ORPC. Private aid.
1013.2	ORPC Cobscook Bay Lighted Buoy C	44-54-26.000N 067-02-38.000W	Fl W 2.5s			White with orange bands.	Property of ORPC. Private aid.
1013.3	ORPC Cobscook Bay Lighted Buoy D	44-54-32.000N 067-03-03.000W	Fl W 2.5s			White with orange bands.	Property of ORPC. Private aid.

(1) No.	(2) Name and Location	(3) Position	(4) Characteristic	(5) Height	(6) Range	(7) Structure	(8) Remarks
			MAINE - First District				

NEW BRUNSWICK - GRAND MANAN CHANNEL NORTHERN PART

Cobscook Bay

(1) No.	(2) Name and Location	(3) Position	(4) Characteristic	(5) Height	(6) Range	(7) Structure	(8) Remarks
1015	- Buoy 8	44-54-40.621N 067-03-31.940W				Red nun.	
1020	- Buoy 9	44-54-24.510N 067-06-12.396W				Green can.	

Pennamaquan River

(1) No.	(2) Name and Location	(3) Position	(4) Characteristic	(5) Height	(6) Range	(7) Structure	(8) Remarks
1025	- Buoy 11	44-55-06.320N 067-06-51.947W				Green can.	Maintained from April 15 to October 15.
1030	- Buoy 13	44-55-20.526N 067-07-45.449W				Green can.	Maintained from April 15 to October 15.
1035	- Buoy 15	44-55-26.425N 067-08-09.092W				Green can.	Maintained from April 15 to October 15.

NEW BRUNSWICK - GRAND MANAN CHANNEL NORTHERN PART

(1) No.	(2) Name and Location	(3) Position	(4) Characteristic	(5) Height	(6) Range	(7) Structure	(8) Remarks
1040	**West Quoddy Head Light**	44-48-54.424N 066-57-02.424W	Fl (2)W 15s 2s on 2s ec 2s on 9s ec.	83	14	White tower with red stripes. 49	HORN: 2 blasts ev 30s (2s bl-2s si-2s bl-24s si). MRASS -Fog signal is radio activated, during times of reduced visibility, turn marine VHF-FM radio to channel 83A/157.175Mhz. Key microphone 5 times consecutively, to activate fog signal for 60 minutes.
1045	*Sail Rock Lighted Whistle Buoy 1*	44-48-37.887N 066-56-25.673W	Fl G 4s		5	Green.	
1050	Morton Ledge Buoy 2	44-47-22.587N 066-59-17.196W				Red nun.	
1055	Baileys Mistake Whistle Buoy 2BM	44-45-30.046N 067-02-52.115W				Red.	
1060	Baileys Mistake Entrance Buoy 1	44-45-29.879N 067-03-21.650W				Green can.	

NEW BRUNSWICK - GRAND MANAN CHANNEL SOUTHERN PART

Little River

(1) No.	(2) Name and Location	(3) Position	(4) Characteristic	(5) Height	(6) Range	(7) Structure	(8) Remarks
1075	- Light	44-39-03.223N 067-11-31.552W	Fl W 6s	56	14	35	HORN: 1 blast ev 10s (1s bl). MRASS-Fog signal is radio activated, during times of reduced visibility, turn marine VHF-FM radio to channel 83A/157.175Mhz. Key microphone 5 times consecutively, to activate fog signal for 60 minutes.
1080	- Entrance Bell Buoy LR	44-39-11.273N 067-10-53.411W				Red and white stripes with red spherical topmark.	
1085	- Ledge Buoy 2 Southwest of ledge.	44-39-12.323N 067-11-51.953W				Red nun.	

Cross Island Narrows

(1) No.	(2) Name and Location	(3) Position	(4) Characteristic	(5) Height	(6) Range	(7) Structure	(8) Remarks
1095	- Buoy 1	44-37-10.245N 067-15-22.856W				Green can.	
1100	*Thornton Point Ledge Lighted Bell Buoy 3*	44-37-16.912N 067-16-16.108W	Fl G 4s		5	Green.	
1105	Thornton Point Ledge Daybeacon 4	44-37-20.254N 067-16-33.109W				TR on spindle.	
1110	Mink Island Ledge Buoy 5	44-37-20.552N 067-17-07.289W				Green can.	
1115	Dogfish Rocks Buoy 7	44-37-47.861N 067-18-06.011W				Green can.	

(1) No.	(2) Name and Location	(3) Position	(4) Characteristic	(5) Height	(6) Range	(7) Structure	(8) Remarks
			MAINE - First District				
	MACHIAS BAY TO TIBBETT NARROWS						
	Libby Island						
1120	- Light	44-34-06.022N 067-22-02.563W	Fl (2) W 20s	91	18	White tower. 42	Emergency light of reduced intensity when main light is extinguished. HORN: 1 blast ev 15s (2s bl). MRASS-Fog signal is radio activated, during times of reduced visibility, turn marine VHF-FM radio to channel 83A/157.175Mhz. Key microphone 5 times consecutively, to activate fog signal for 60 minutes.
1120.1	- Light Station Mooring Buoy	44-34-22.375N 067-22-02.018W				White with blue band.	
	Machias Bay						
1125	Seal Cove Ledge Buoy 2	44-35-40.972N 067-19-22.541W				Red nun.	
	Cross Island						
1126.1	- *Aquaculture Lighted Buoy CI-Northwest*	44-37-07.260N 067-19-03.840W	Fl Y 2.5s			Yellow.	Private aid.
1126.2	- *Aquaculture Lighted Buoy CI-Southeast*	44-36-47.880N 067-19-02.940W	Fl Y 2.5s			Yellow.	Private aid.
1126.3	- *Aquaculture Lighted Buoy CI-Southwest*	44-36-54.600N 067-19-19.720W	Fl Y 2.5s			Yellow.	Private aid.
1126.4	- *Aquaculture Lighted Buoy CI-Northeast*	44-36-58.320N 067-18-48.720W	Fl Y 2.5s			Yellow.	Private aid.
1127.1	- *Aquaculture Lighted Buoy CIN A*	44-37-05.790N 067-18-58.782W	Fl Y 2.5s			Yellow.	Private aid.
1127.2	- *Aquaculture Lighted Buoy CIN B*	44-37-13.824N 067-19-14.364W	Fl Y 2.5s			Yellow.	Private aid.
1127.3	- *Aquaculture Lighted Buoy CIN C*	44-37-24.852N 067-19-03.504W	Fl Y 2.5s			Yellow.	Private aid.
1127.4	- *Aquaculture Lighted Buoy CIN D*	44-37-18.246N 067-18-49.476W	Fl Y 2.5s			Yellow.	Private aid.
	Starboard Island						
1130	- Ledge Buoy 1	44-35-07.742N 067-22-50.686W				Green can.	
1131.1	- *Aquaculture Lighted Buoy SI-SW*	44-36-06.000N 067-23-01.000W	Fl Y 2.5s			Yellow.	Private aid.
1131.3	- *Aquaculture Lighted Buoy SI-NW*	44-36-23.000N 067-23-12.000W	Fl Y 2.5s			Yellow.	Private aid.
1131.4	- *Aquaculture Lighted Buoy SI-NE*	44-36-27.250N 067-23-00.530W	Fl Y 2.5s			Yellow.	Private aid.
1131.5	- *Aquaculture Lighted Buoy SI-SE*	44-36-10.940N 067-22-49.000W	Fl Y 2.5s			Yellow.	Private aid.
	Machias Bay						
1140	Seashore Ledge Buoy 5	44-37-07.451N 067-21-39.786W				Green can.	
1145	AVERY ROCK LIGHT AR	44-39-15.347N 067-20-38.806W	Fl W 6s	16	6	NR on tower.	
	Machias River						
1150	- Buoy 1	44-40-36.278N 067-21-13.358W				Green can.	
1155	- Buoy 3	44-40-47.967N 067-21-51.085W				Green can.	
1160	- Buoy 4	44-40-55.298N 067-23-08.010W				Red nun.	
1165	- Buoy 6	44-41-07.488N 067-23-27.041W				Red nun.	
	Englishman Bay						
1170	Foster Channel Buoy 2	44-34-51.251N 067-23-31.036W				Red nun.	
1175	Foster Channel Buoy 1	44-34-48.501N 067-23-44.216W				Green can.	

(1) No.	(2) Name and Location	(3) Position	(4) Characteristic	(5) Height	(6) Range	(7) Structure	(8) Remarks

MACHIAS BAY TO TIBBETT NARROWS

Englishman Bay

(1) No.	(2) Name and Location	(3) Position	(4) Characteristic	(5) Height	(6) Range	(7) Structure	(8) Remarks
1180	Brothers Passage Bell Buoy 1	44-33-38.322N 067-25-50.968W				Green.	
1185	Brothers Passage Buoy 2 Marks ledge east of Green Island.	44-33-45.702N 067-26-08.019W				Red nun.	
1190	Codhead Ledge Buoy 2	44-35-06.561N 067-26-16.870W				Red nun.	
1195	Halifax Island Reef Buoy 3	44-35-22.320N 067-28-28.973W				Green can.	
1200	Boundry Ledges Buoy 5	44-36-02.037N 067-29-58.008W				Green can.	

Chandler Bay

(1) No.	(2) Name and Location	(3) Position	(4) Characteristic	(5) Height	(6) Range	(7) Structure	(8) Remarks
1205	Jumper Ledge Buoy	44-32-33.092N 067-27-49.261W				Red nun with green bands.	
1210	Middle Back Rock Daybeacon	44-32-21.961N 067-29-11.570W				NR on spindle.	
1215	*Little Breaking Ledge Lighted Gong Buoy 1*	44-30-41.019N 067-30-11.751W	Fl G 4s		4	Green.	
1220	West Black Rock Buoy 2	44-31-38.632N 067-30-24.164W				Red nun.	
1225	*Mark Island Lighted Bell Buoy 1*	44-32-11.471N 067-31-43.557W	Fl G 2.5s		3	Green.	
1230	Kelp Ledge Buoy 3	44-32-25.280N 067-33-05.729W				Green can.	
1235	Ballast Island Ledge Buoy 5	44-33-40.269N 067-32-57.060W				Green can.	
1240	Roque Island Reef Buoy 2	44-35-04.672N 067-33-01.721W				Red nun.	
1244	Shorey Cove Coast Guard Mooring Buoy CG	44-35-31.401N 067-31-37.104W				White with blue band.	
1245	Great Bar Buoy 7	44-35-42.193N 067-32-45.327W				Green can.	

Seguin Passage

(1) No.	(2) Name and Location	(3) Position	(4) Characteristic	(5) Height	(6) Range	(7) Structure	(8) Remarks
1250	Seguin Ledge Buoy 1	44-31-23.898N 067-31-59.356W				Green can.	
1260	Long Ledge Buoy 3	44-31-27.171N 067-33-03.218W				Green can.	
1265	Nats Rock Buoy 5	44-31-20.361N 067-33-45.020W				Green can.	
1270	Southwest Ledge Buoy 6	44-31-26.921N 067-33-54.010W				Red nun.	

Moosabec Reach

(1) No.	(2) Name and Location	(3) Position	(4) Characteristic	(5) Height	(6) Range	(7) Structure	(8) Remarks
1275	Bay Ledge Buoy 2	44-32-08.958N 067-32-44.126W				Red nun.	
1280	Gilchrist Rock Daybeacon 3 On rock.	44-31-53.374N 067-32-50.445W				SG on iron spindle.	
1285	Leighton Ledges Buoy 4	44-31-57.791N 067-33-02.609W				Red nun.	
1290	Virgin Island Ledge Buoy 6	44-31-52.271N 067-33-26.630W				Red nun.	
1295	Two Hour Rock Buoy 7	44-31-44.281N 067-33-34.430W				Green can.	
1300	- Buoy 8	44-31-48.041N 067-33-45.560W				Red nun.	
1305	EMMS ROCK LIGHT 9	44-31-44.400N 067-33-56.960W	Fl G 4s	28	6	SG on gray tower.	Breakwater submerged at highwater.
1310	- Buoy 10	44-31-47.170N 067-34-00.501W				Red nun.	
1315	Little Ledge Buoy 11	44-31-43.740N 067-34-06.751W				Green can.	
1320	Moosabec Bar Buoy 12	44-31-46.057N 067-34-17.536W				Red nun.	

16

(1) No.	(2) Name and Location	(3) Position	(4) Characteristic	(5) Height	(6) Range	(7) Structure	(8) Remarks
			MAINE - First District				

MACHIAS BAY TO TIBBETT NARROWS

Moosabec Reach

(1) No.	(2) Name and Location	(3) Position	(4) Characteristic	(5) Height	(6) Range	(7) Structure	(8) Remarks
1325	Snows Rock Daybeacon 13 On ledge.	44-31-38.276N 067-34-22.382W				SG on iron spindle.	
1330	Sand Ledge Buoy 15	44-31-39.512N 067-34-41.290W				Green can.	
1335	*Horse Ledge Lighted Buoy 17*	44-31-40.431N 067-35-12.593W	Fl G 4s		3	Green.	
1340	SAWYERS COVE LIGHT 18	44-31-47.235N 067-35-38.466W	Fl R 4s	28	3	TR on tower on end of breakwater.	
1345	Cummings Ledge Buoy 18A	44-31-33.410N 067-36-41.075W				Red nun.	
1350	- Buoy 20	44-31-17.089N 067-38-38.889W				Red nun.	
1355	- Buoy 21	44-31-06.677N 067-39-19.181W				Green can.	
1360	*Fessenden Ledge Lighted Bell Buoy 22*	44-31-02.780N 067-39-59.311W	Fl R 4s		4	Red.	
1365	Shabbit Island Ledge Buoy 23	44-30-48.039N 067-40-30.751W				Green can.	
1370	Shabbit Island Buoy 25	44-30-25.481N 067-41-11.290W				Green can.	
1375	*Ram Island Ledge Lighted Gong Buoy 27* North from ledge.	44-29-42.320N 067-42-14.894W	Fl G 4s		5	Green.	
1380	Tibbet Ledge Buoy 28	44-29-45.280N 067-42-17.773W				Red nun.	
1385	Tibbet Narrows Bell Buoy 30	44-29-28.810N 067-42-46.164W				Red.	
Eastern Bay							
1390	**Moose Peak Light**	44-28-28.524N 067-31-55.174W	Fl W 30s	72	20	On white tower. 57	HORN: 2 blasts ev 30s (2s bl-2s si-2s bl-24s si). Located 129 yards, 263° from light tower. Fog signal is radio activated, during times of reduced visibility, turn marine VHF-FM radio to channel 83A/157.175Mhz. Key microphone 5 times consecutively, to activate fog signal for 45 minutes.
1395	Mistake Harbor Buoy 1	44-29-13.693N 067-33-08.746W				Green can.	
1400	Calf Island Reef Buoy 3	44-29-24.402N 067-33-13.995W				Green can.	
1401	*Cooke Aquaculture Lighted Buoy NE*	44-29-45.210N 067-33-10.600W	Fl Y 12s			Yellow.	Private aid.
1401.1	*Cooke Aquaculture Lighted Buoy SE*	44-29-32.580N 067-33-02.740W	Fl Y 12s			Yellow.	Private aid.
1401.2	*Cooke Aquaculture Lighted Buoy SW*	44-29-29.770N 067-33-11.570W	Fl Y 12s			Yellow.	Private aid.
1401.3	*Cooke Aquaculture Lighted Buoy NW*	44-29-41.040N 067-33-23.760W	Fl Y 12s			Yellow.	Private aid.
1405	Channel Rock Daybeacon 4 On ledge.	44-30-05.539N 067-33-50.019W				TR on iron spindle.	
1409	SPECTACLE ISLAND AQUACULTURE LIGHTS (3)	44-30-15.300N 067-34-28.000W	Q Y			On floating fish pens.	Three or more lights marking aquaculture structures of varying sizes and shapes in a charted fish pen area. Private aid.
1410	Spectacle Island Buoy 5	44-30-20.361N 067-33-56.410W				Green can.	
1415	Head Harbor Island Buoy 6	44-30-51.835N 067-33-48.417W				Red nun.	
1420	Sheep Island Buoy 7	44-31-04.421N 067-33-43.346W				Green can.	
Pig Island Gut							
1425	- Buoy 2	44-30-49.401N 067-34-35.191W				Red nun.	

(1) No.	(2) Name and Location	(3) Position	(4) Characteristic	(5) Height	(6) Range	(7) Structure	(8) Remarks
			MAINE - First District				

MACHIAS BAY TO TIBBETT NARROWS

Pig Island Gut

1430	- Buoy 3	44-30-57.811N 067-34-40.415W				Green can.	
1435	- Buoy 5	44-31-01.121N 067-34-51.421W				Green can.	
1440	- Buoy 6	44-31-02.271N 067-34-51.942W				Red nun.	
1445	- Buoy 8	44-31-01.651N 067-35-04.395W				Red nun.	
1450	- Buoy 10	44-31-01.542N 067-35-13.642W				Red nun.	
1455	- Buoy 12	44-31-02.021N 067-35-22.122W				Red nun.	
1460	- Buoy 14	44-31-10.060N 067-35-39.233W				Red nun.	

Western Bay

1465	*Seahorse Lighted Bell Buoy 2SR*	44-25-44.985N 067-38-29.984W	Fl R 4s		4	Red.	
1470	Duck Ledges Buoy 1	44-30-00.320N 067-40-09.990W				Green can.	
1475	Pomp Island Ledge Daybeacon 2	44-30-24.331N 067-39-15.699W				TR on spindle.	
1480	Hardwood Island Daybeacon 3	44-30-49.021N 067-39-08.643W				SG on spindle.	
1485	Salt Rock Daybeacon 4	44-31-01.291N 067-38-54.537W				TR on spindle.	

TIBBETT NARROWS TO SCHOODIC ISLAND

Eastern Harbor

1490	- Buoy 1	44-29-42.250N 067-43-58.777W				Green can.	
1495	- Buoy 2	44-29-41.890N 067-43-49.146W				Red nun.	
1500	- Buoy 5	44-30-11.877N 067-43-47.781W				Green can.	
1505	- Buoy 4	44-30-03.469N 067-43-45.739W				Red nun.	

Pleasant Bay

1510	*Nash Island Lighted Whistle Buoy NI*	44-27-51.781N 067-45-28.668W	Mo (A) W		3	Red and white stripes with red spherical topmark.	
1515	Coles Ledge Buoy 1	44-28-45.120N 067-46-24.340W				Green can.	
1520	Norton Island Buoy 2	44-29-24.321N 067-45-18.642W				Red nun.	
1525	Barton Ledge Buoy 2	44-31-28.837N 067-46-05.649W				Red nun.	
1530	Bunker Ledge Buoy 3	44-31-51.217N 067-46-20.121W				Green can.	
1535	Harthorne Ledge Buoy 5	44-33-48.316N 067-45-26.311W				Red nun.	
1536	- CG Mooring Buoy	44-31-54.817N 067-45-21.489W				White with blue band.	

Pleasant River

1540	- Buoy 6	44-34-15.816N 067-45-28.901W				Red nun.	Maintained from May 1 to Nov. 15.
1545	- Buoy 7	44-34-36.767N 067-45-11.933W				Green can.	Maintained from May 1 to Nov. 15.
1550	- Buoy 8	44-34-41.898N 067-45-06.451W				Red nun.	Maintained from May 1 to Nov. 15.
1555	- Buoy 10	44-34-45.904N 067-45-04.027W				Red nun.	Maintained from May 1 to Nov. 15.

(1) No.	(2) Name and Location	(3) Position	(4) Characteristic	(5) Height	(6) Range	(7) Structure	(8) Remarks
			MAINE - First District				
	TIBBETT NARROWS TO SCHOODIC ISLAND						
	Pleasant Bay						
	Pleasant River						
1560	- Buoy 12	44-34-54.880N 067-45-02.686W				Red nun.	Maintained from May 1 to Nov. 15.
1565	- Buoy 14	44-34-59.280N 067-44-58.893W				Red nun.	Maintained from May 1 to Nov. 15.
1570	Bungy Rock Daybeacon 15 On rock.	44-35-18.842N 067-44-52.052W				SG on spindle.	
1575	- Buoy 16	44-35-59.124N 067-44-53.901W				Red nun.	Maintained from May 1 to Nov. 15.
1580	- Buoy 17	44-36-24.613N 067-44-41.355W				Green can.	Maintained from May 1 to Nov. 15.
	Dyer Island Narrows						
1585	Strout Island Ledges Buoy 2	44-30-36.718N 067-47-25.622W				Red nun.	
1590	Strout Island Ledges Buoy 4	44-30-35.268N 067-47-56.827W				Red nun.	
1595	Strout Island Buoy	44-30-59.381N 067-48-32.860W				Green can with red bands.	
1600	- Buoy 3	44-31-15.980N 067-48-59.686W				Green can.	
1605	- Buoy 5	44-31-04.271N 067-49-06.987W				Green can.	
1610	- Buoy 7	44-30-51.964N 067-49-37.062W				Green can.	
	Flint Island Narrows						
1615	Flint Island North Point Buoy 1	44-28-56.459N 067-47-25.655W				Green can.	
1620	Western Reef Buoy 2	44-28-33.167N 067-48-50.286W				Red nun.	
	Narraguagus Bay						
1625	Jerry Ledge Buoy 1	44-24-55.805N 067-50-53.825W				Green can.	
1630	Jordans Delight Ledge Buoy 2	44-25-23.324N 067-48-54.002W				Red nun.	
1635	*Pond Island Lighted Bell Buoy 1*	44-27-26.401N 067-49-26.604W	Fl G 6s		5	Green.	
1640	Pond Island Ledge Buoy 3	44-28-12.506N 067-50-19.615W				Green can.	
1645	Lower Middle Ground Buoy 5	44-29-44.874N 067-50-38.131W				Green can.	
1650	Trafton Halftide Ledge Daybeacon 6	44-29-56.605N 067-50-06.981W				TR on spindle.	
1655	- Buoy NB	44-30-06.569N 067-50-24.108W				Red and white stripes; can.	
	Narraguagus River						
1660	- Buoy 1	44-30-21.099N 067-50-49.478W				Green can.	
1665	- Buoy 2	44-30-36.464N 067-51-12.208W				Red nun.	
1675	- Buoy 4	44-31-03.891N 067-51-25.831W				Red nun.	
1680	- Buoy 5	44-31-15.608N 067-51-28.310W				Green can.	
1685	- Buoy 7	44-31-33.879N 067-51-35.907W				Green can.	Maintained from April 1 to December 1.
1690	- Buoy 8	44-31-43.188N 067-51-46.621W				Red nun.	Maintained from April 1 to December 1.

(1) No.	(2) Name and Location	(3) Position	(4) Characteristic	(5) Height	(6) Range	(7) Structure	(8) Remarks

MAINE - First District

TIBBETT NARROWS TO SCHOODIC ISLAND

Narraguagus River

(1) No.	(2) Name and Location	(3) Position	(4) Characteristic	(5) Height	(6) Range	(7) Structure	(8) Remarks
1700	- Buoy 9	44-31-51.783N 067-52-02.419W				Green can.	Maintained from April 1 to December 1.
1705	- Buoy 10	44-31-57.403N 067-52-08.964W				Red nun.	Maintained from April 1 to December 1.
1710	- Buoy 12	44-32-06.051N 067-52-22.370W				Red nun.	Maintained from April 1 to December 1.
1715	- Buoy 13	44-32-09.678N 067-52-28.872W				Green can.	Maintained from April 1 to December 1.
1720	- Buoy 15	44-32-21.800N 067-52-35.371W				Green can.	Maintained from April 1 to December 1.
1725	- Buoy 17	44-32-32.869N 067-52-41.315W				Green can.	Maintained from April 1 to December 1.
	Petit Manan Approach						
1730	*Southeast Rock Lighted Whistle Buoy 6A* South of rock.	44-19-46.009N 067-48-37.047W	Fl R 4s		3	Red.	
1735	**Petit Manan Light**	44-22-03.327N 067-51-51.704W	Fl W 10s	123	19	Gray granite tower. 109	Emergency light of reduced intensity when main light is extinguished. HORN: 1 blast ev 30s (3s bl). MRASS-Fog signal is radio activated, during times of reduced visibility, turn marine VHF-FM radio to channel 83A/157.175Mhz. Key microphone 5 times consecutively, to activate fog signal for 60 minutes.
1740	Simms Rock Bell Buoy 1 Northwest of rock.	44-20-31.329N 067-51-13.252W				Green.	
1745	Petit Manan Reef Buoy 2	44-21-35.667N 067-51-45.208W				Red nun.	
1750	Tibbett Rock Isolated Danger Buoy DT South-southwest of rock.	44-23-04.326N 067-47-10.497W				Black and red bands with two black spherical topmarks; can.	
1755	Tibbett Rock South Isolated Danger Buoy DTS	44-22-29.377N 067-46-27.545W				Black and red bands with two black spherical topmarks; can.	
1760	Whale Ledge Buoy 4	44-23-40.506N 067-51-54.286W				Red nun.	
	Prospect Harbor						
1775	*Moulton Ledge Lighted Bell Buoy ML* West of ledge.	44-21-50.431N 067-56-18.909W	Fl (2+1)R 6s		3	Red and green bands.	
1777	Little Black Ledge Buoy 1LB	44-22-05.537N 067-58-21.609W				Green can.	
1780	Cranberry Point Bell Buoy 2CP	44-22-46.326N 067-58-58.017W				Red.	
1785	- POINT LIGHT	44-24-12.125N 068-00-46.822W	Fl R 6s (2 W sectors)	42	W 9 W 9 R 7	White conical tower.	White from 317° to 323° and from 348° to 356°, covers fairway. Lighted throughout 24 hours.
1790	Old Woman Ledge Bell Buoy 2	44-22-12.096N 068-00-14.249W				Red.	
1795	*Brown Cow Lighted Whistle Buoy BC*	44-20-57.327N 068-01-25.302W	Fl (2+1)G 6s		4	Green and red bands.	
1800	Washrock Ledge Gong Buoy 2	44-23-08.992N 067-57-41.683W				Red.	

(1) No.	(2) Name and Location	(3) Position	(4) Characteristic	(5) Height	(6) Range	(7) Structure	(8) Remarks
			MAINE - First District				
	TIBBETT NARROWS TO SCHOODIC ISLAND						
	Prospect Harbor						
1805	Bunker Harbor Ledge Buoy 1 East of ledge.	44-22-04.226N 068-01-05.212W				Green can.	
1810	Clark Ledges Gong Buoy 3	44-23-44.885N 068-00-42.701W				Green.	
1815	Clark Ledges Daybeacon 5	44-23-53.185N 068-00-53.661W				SG on spindle.	
	Schoodic Harbor						
1820	*Schoodic Lighted Bell Buoy 2S*	44-19-07.138N 068-02-06.783W	Fl R 4s		4	Red.	
1825	Schoodic Island Buoy 1	44-20-15.485N 068-02-06.749W				Green can.	
1830	Schoodic Ledge Buoy 2 Off south end of ledge.	44-20-26.418N 068-02-04.174W				Red nun.	
	FRENCHMAN AND BLUEHILL BAYS AND APPROACHES						
	Frenchman Bay						
1840	Otter Cliff Ledge Bell Buoy 1 0.1 mile southeast of ledge.	44-18-30.856N 068-10-54.620W				Green.	
1845	*Schooner Head Lighted Gong Buoy 3*	44-20-05.655N 068-10-03.308W	Fl G 4s		4	Green.	
1850	*Egg Rock Lighted Bell Buoy 4*	44-20-15.675N 068-08-35.133W	Fl R 2.5s		3	Red.	
1855	Turtle Island Ledge Gong Buoy 2	44-20-50.763N 068-06-08.457W				Red.	
1860	*- Lighted Buoy FB*	44-19-21.326N 068-07-24.039W	Fl (2+1)R 6s		4	Red and green bands.	RACON: B (- . . .)
1865	**Egg Rock Light**	44-21-14.224N 068-08-18.042W	Fl R 5s	64	18	White tower. 40	Emergency light of reduced intensity Fl R 5s when main light is extinguished. HORN: 2 blasts ev 30s (2s bl-2s si-2s bl-24s si). MRASS-Fog signal is radio activated, during times of reduced visibility, turn marine VHF-FM radio to channel 83A/157.175Mhz. Key microphone 5 times consecutively, to activate fog signal for 60 minutes.
1870	Newport Ledge Buoy 5	44-21-16.324N 068-10-34.050W				Green can.	
1875	BALD PORCUPINE ISLAND BREAKWATER LIGHT	44-22-57.972N 068-11-33.939W	Q W	20	3	NW on spindle worded DANGER SUBMERGED BREAKWATER.	
1876	Bar Harbor Entrance Buoy 2	44-23-34.850N 068-11-55.360W				Red nun.	Maintained from 1 May to 15 Nov. Private aid.
1877	Bar Harbor CG Mooring Buoy	44-23-43.164N 068-11-51.744W				White with blue band.	Marked CG.
1878	Bar Island Buoy 1	44-24-01.690N 068-11-56.210W				Green can.	Maintained from May 1 to Oct. 31. Private aid.
1879	*Bar Island Lighted Buoy 2*	44-24-01.680N 068-11-54.260W	Fl R 4s			Red	Maintained from May 1 to Oct. 31. Private aid.
1880	Sheep Porcupine Bell Buoy 7	44-24-05.051N 068-11-24.723W				Green.	
1885	Bald Rock Ledge Buoy 2	44-24-52.165N 068-13-26.540W				Red nun.	
1890	Bald Rock Buoy 9	44-25-22.400N 068-12-35.866W				Green can.	
1895	Hulls Cove Buoy 4	44-24-42.820N 068-14-19.061W				Red nun.	
1900	Halftide Ledge Buoy 11	44-25-39.029N 068-13-55.420W				Green can.	
1905	Sunken Ledge Buoy 13	44-26-19.063N 068-14-58.921W				Green can.	

(1) No.	(2) Name and Location	(3) Position	(4) Characteristic	(5) Height	(6) Range	(7) Structure	(8) Remarks
			MAINE - First District				
	FRENCHMAN AND BLUEHILL BAYS AND APPROACHES						
	Eastern Bay						
1910	Googins Ledge Buoy 14	44-26-36.318N 068-17-22.067W					Red nun.
	FRENCHMAN BAY AND MOUNT DESERT ISLAND						
	Winter Harbor						
1915	*Mark Island Junction Lighted Gong Buoy MI*	44-21-29.325N 068-05-07.033W	Fl (2+1)G 6s		4		Green and red bands.
1920	Grindstone Ledge Junction Buoy GL	44-22-06.172N 068-05-13.165W					Green can with red bands.
1925	Grindstone Ledge Daybeacon	44-22-10.624N 068-05-16.834W					NG on iron spindle.
1930	Abijah Ledge Buoy 2	44-23-03.624N 068-04-50.533W					Red nun.
1935	Harbor Point Buoy 3	44-23-07.054N 068-05-02.784W					Green can.
1940	Guptill Point Buoy 4	44-23-14.384N 068-05-03.024W					Red nun.
1945	Guptill Ledge Daybeacon 6	44-23-18.354N 068-05-07.791W					TR on spindle.
	Passage West of Grindstone Neck						
1950	Roaring Bull Junction Buoy RB Off north end of shoal.	44-22-05.265N 068-05-41.205W					Red nun with green bands.
1955	Pulpit Ledge Daybeacon 3	44-22-22.902N 068-05-48.891W					SG on iron spindle.
1960	Crow Island Buoy 5	44-23-00.894N 068-06-26.118W					Green can.
1965	Cod Ledges Buoy 7	44-23-44.323N 068-07-05.540W					Green can.
1970	Halibut Hole Buoy 9	44-24-30.322N 068-07-58.043W					Green can.
	Flanders Bay						
1975	Calf Island Point Buoy 1	44-27-17.370N 068-08-30.035W					Green can.
1980	Halftide Ledge Buoy 3	44-27-40.420N 068-07-53.543W					Green can.
1985	Sunken Ledge Buoy 5	44-28-21.879N 068-08-20.585W					Green can.
	Sullivan Harbor						
1995	Dram Island Ledge Buoy 2	44-28-04.169N 068-11-55.255W					Red nun.
2000	Crabtree Ledge Bell Buoy 1	44-28-18.589N 068-13-10.829W					Green.
2005	Bean Island Ledge Buoy 3	44-28-50.628N 068-12-19.236W					Green can.
2010	Bean Island Ledge Buoy 4	44-28-50.888N 068-12-12.536W					Red nun.
2015	Ingalls Ledge Buoy 6	44-29-23.478N 068-12-46.568W					Red nun.
2020	Grant Cove Rock Buoy 7	44-29-47.607N 068-12-49.648W					Green can.
2025	Low Water Rock Daybeacon 8 On rock.	44-29-52.107N 068-12-31.617W					TR on iron spindle.
2030	Moon Ledge Buoy 9	44-30-41.367N 068-12-20.677W					Green can.
	Somes Sound Approach						
	Baker Island						
2040	- Buoy 1	44-14-17.331N 068-11-17.809W					Green can.
2045	- LIGHT	44-14-28.387N 068-11-56.451W	Fl W 10s	105	10		White stone tower.
2050	- Ledge Buoy 3	44-14-55.328N 068-11-35.051W					Green can.
	Somes Sound Approach						
2055	Gilley Ledge Buoy 5	44-15-19.798N 068-11-58.052W					Green can.

(1) No.	(2) Name and Location	(3) Position	(4) Characteristic	(5) Height	(6) Range	(7) Structure	(8) Remarks
			MAINE - First District				
	FRENCHMAN BAY AND MOUNT DESERT ISLAND						
	Somes Sound Approach						
2060	Harding Ledge Buoy 7	44-15-39.588N 068-12-23.844W				Green can.	
2065	*East Bunker Lighted Gong Buoy 2*	44-16-32.327N 068-13-02.056W	Fl R 4s		4	Red.	
2070	East Bunker Ledge Daybeacon On rock.	44-16-47.856N 068-13-23.017W				White pyramidal stone structure.	
2075	Lewis Rock Buoy 3A	44-17-01.249N 068-13-28.885W				Green can.	
2080	*Seal Harbor Lighted Bell Buoy 4*	44-17-10.015N 068-13-49.368W	Fl R 4s		4	Red.	
2085	Crowninshield Point Buoy 1	44-17-17.399N 068-14-19.507W				Green can.	
2090	Bowden Ledge Buoy 6 Southerly of ledge.	44-17-03.606N 068-14-33.661W				Red nun.	
2095	Long Pond Shoal Buoy 8	44-16-57.975N 068-15-15.409W				Red nun.	
	Northeast Harbor						
2100	Bear Island Buoy 2A	44-17-04.685N 068-16-19.214W				Red nun.	
2105	BEAR ISLAND LIGHT	44-17-00.000N 068-16-11.000W	Fl W 5s	33		White tower.	Private aid.
2110	*Bear Island Lighted Bell Buoy 10*	44-16-52.325N 068-16-09.914W	Fl R 4s		4	Red.	
2115	- Buoy 1	44-17-08.895N 068-16-25.254W				Green can.	
2120	*- Lighted Bell Buoy 2*	44-17-06.625N 068-16-34.585W	Fl R 2.5s		4	Red.	
2125	- Buoy 4	44-17-16.715N 068-16-27.064W				Red nun.	
	Cranberry Harbor						
2165	- Buoy 1	44-15-45.366N 068-14-48.151W				Green can.	
2170	- Buoy 3	44-15-39.652N 068-14-35.444W				Green can.	
2171	Eagle Point Inner Buoy 5	44-15-37.920N 068-14-29.460W				Green can.	Private aid.
2175	*Spurling Rock Lighted Bell Buoy 2*	44-15-56.866N 068-15-20.233W	Fl R 2.5s		4	Red.	
2180	Long Ledge Daybeacon 2A	44-15-43.074N 068-15-39.093W				TR on spindle.	
	Somes Sound						
2185	Gilpatrick Ledge Daybeacon 2	44-17-03.947N 068-17-23.387W				TR on iron spindle.	
2190	Gilpatrick Cove Daybeacon 4	44-17-05.524N 068-17-26.366W				TR on iron spindle.	
2195	*Middle Rock Lighted Buoy 5*	44-17-36.784N 068-18-24.968W	Fl G 2.5s		3	Green.	Replaced by can when endangered by ice.
2197	Valley Cove Mooring Buoy CG	44-18-36.736N 068-18-57.009W				White with blue band.	
2200	Myrtle Ledge Buoy 6	44-21-02.841N 068-19-17.106W				Red nun.	Maintained from May 15 to Nov. 1.
2205	Sargents Point Buoy 2SP	44-21-12.280N 068-18-45.160W				Red nun.	Maintained from May 15 to Nov. 1.
2210	Bar Ledge Buoy 7	44-21-17.025N 068-19-26.835W				Green can.	Maintained from May 15 to Nov. 1.
	Southwest Harbor						
2220	Greening Island Buoy 6	44-16-26.605N 068-17-27.066W				Red nun.	
2225	*Greening Island Lighted Buoy 8*	44-16-28.846N 068-18-23.489W	Fl R 2.5s		4	Red.	

(1) No.	(2) Name and Location	(3) Position	(4) Characteristic	(5) Height	(6) Range	(7) Structure	(8) Remarks
			MAINE - First District				
	FRENCHMAN BAY AND MOUNT DESERT ISLAND						
	Southwest Harbor						
2230	- Daybeacon S	44-16-25.458N 068-19-10.575W				NR on spindle.	
2235	- Inner Harbor Buoy 1	44-16-31.612N 068-19-04.573W				Green can.	Removed when endangered by ice.
2240	- Inner Harbor Buoy 3	44-16-36.074N 068-19-05.019W				Green can.	Removed when endangered by ice.
2245	Clark Point Daybeacon 1 On ledge.	44-16-41.352N 068-18-33.567W				SG on iron spindle.	
	Western Way						
2250	*Long Ledge Lighted Gong Buoy 1*	44-13-15.928N 068-17-46.995W	Fl G 4s		5	Green.	
2255	South Bunker Ledge Daybeacon 2	44-13-35.784N 068-16-58.167W				TR on iron spindle.	
2265	*Cranberry Island Ledge Lighted Bell Buoy 4*	44-14-12.600N 068-16-57.903W	Q R		3	Red.	
2270	Flynns Ledge Buoy 5	44-14-27.336N 068-16-59.909W				Green can.	
2275	Cow Ledge Buoy 6	44-15-21.666N 068-16-45.565W				Red nun.	
2285	*Spurling Point Lighted Gong Buoy 8*	44-15-46.632N 068-16-47.979W	Fl R 4s		4	Red.	
	APPROACHES TO BLUE HILL BAY						
	Blue Hill Bay Approach						
2290 5	**Mount Desert Light**	43-58-07.046N 068-07-42.021W	Fl W 15s	75	14	Granite conical tower. 65	HORN: 2 blasts ev 30s (2s bl-2s si-2s bl-24s si). MRASS-Fog signal is radio activated, during times of reduced visibility, turn marine VHF-FM radio to channel 83A/157.175Mhz. Key microphone 5 times consecutively, to activate fog signal for 60 minutes.
2295	**Great Duck Island Light**	44-08-31.333N 068-14-44.956W	Fl R 5s	67	14	White tower. 36	Light partially obscured by trees from about 143° to 206.5°. Emergency light of reduced intensity when main light is extinguished. HORN: 1 blast ev 15s (2s bl). MRASS-Fog signal is radio activated, during times of reduced visibility, turn marine VHF-FM radio to channel 83A/157.175Mhz. Key microphone 5 times consecutively, to activate fog signal for 60 minutes.
2310	The Drums Junction Bell Buoy D	44-08-30.563N 068-18-33.464W				Green and red bands.	
2315	*Long Island Lighted Gong Buoy LI*	44-08-20.663N 068-20-31.247W	Mo (A) W		6	Red and white stripes with red spherical topmark.	
2320	Horseshoe Ledge Buoy 1	44-09-33.133N 068-18-41.909W				Green can.	
2325	Black Island Buoy 2	44-10-10.021N 068-20-09.027W				Red nun.	
2330	Placentia Island Buoy 1P	44-11-43.143N 068-20-45.028W				Green can.	
	Bass Harbor						
2335	- **Head Light**	44-13-18.536N 068-20-14.209W	Oc R 4s	56	13	White tower connected to dwelling. 33	
2340	- Head Bell Buoy EB	44-13-14.216N 068-20-00.882W				Red and white stripes.	

(1) No.	(2) Name and Location	(3) Position	(4) Characteristic	(5) Height	(6) Range	(7) Structure	(8) Remarks

MAINE - First District

APPROACHES TO BLUE HILL BAY

Bass Harbor

2345	- Head Gong Buoy WB	44-13-04.938N 068-20-28.510W				Red and white stripes with red spherical topmark.	
2350	Weaver Ledge Buoy 1 Southeast end of ledge.	44-13-33.757N 068-21-10.431W				Green can.	
2355	Weaver Ledge Buoy 2 Northwest edge of ledge.	44-13-39.807N 068-21-22.171W				Red nun.	
2360	- Buoy 5 Marks ledge.	44-14-15.676N 068-20-58.151W				Green can.	
2365	- Buoy 6 Marks ledge.	44-14-29.417N 068-21-04.471W				Red nun.	

Southwest Approach

| 2370 | Beach Ledge Bell Buoy 2 | 44-06-18.785N 068-23-03.601W | | | | Red. | |
| 2375 | Harbor Island Bell Buoy 1 | 44-07-18.252N 068-22-32.342W | | | | Green. | |

Black Island

2397.1	- *Aquaculture Lighted Buoy A*	44-10-53.000N 068-21-11.000W	Fl Y 2.5s			Yellow.	Private aid.
2397.2	- *Aquaculture Lighted Buoy B*	44-10-54.000N 068-21-17.000W	Fl Y 2.5s			Yellow.	Private aid.
2397.3	- *Aquaculture Lighted Buoy C*	44-11-08.000N 068-21-10.000W	Fl Y 2.5s			Yellow.	Private aid.
2397.4	- *Aquaculture Lighted Buoy D*	44-11-06.000N 068-21-04.000W	Fl Y 2.5s			Yellow.	Private aid.
2398	*Cooke Aquaculture Lighted Buoy BIS A*	44-10-44.439N 068-21-18.543W	Fl Y 4s			Yellow	Private aid.
2398.1	*Cooke Aquaculture Lighted Buoy BIS B*	44-10-44.440N 068-21-26.800W	Fl Y 4s			Yellow	Private aid.
2398.2	*Cooke Aquaculture Lighted Buoy BIS C*	44-10-36.767N 068-21-29.273W	Fl Y 4s			Yellow	Private aid.
2398.3	*Cooke Aquaculture Lighted Buoy BIS D*	44-10-35.300N 068-21-20.470W	Fl Y 4s			Yellow	Private aid.

BLUE HILL BAY

Eastern Passage

2400	Staple Ledge Buoy 1	44-11-20.009N 068-23-51.354W				Green can.	
2405	Ship and Barges Bell Buoy 3	44-13-36.326N 068-25-40.078W				Green.	
2410	Ship and Barges Ledge Junction Daybeacon SB South end of ledge.	44-13-32.526N 068-25-52.035W				JG on spindle.	
2412	Ship Island Fish & Wildlife Mooring Buoy	44-14-08.294N 068-26-31.948W				White with blue band.	
2415	Trumpet Island Bar Buoy TI	44-14-51.830N 068-26-54.069W				Red and white stripes; can.	
2420	Bar Island Buoy 5	44-15-48.614N 068-27-13.442W				Green can.	
2425	Hardwood Island Buoy 6	44-17-41.962N 068-27-36.164W				Red nun.	
2426	Hardwood Island Aquaculture Buoy A	44-18-21.700N 068-26-48.400W				Yellow.	Private aid.
2427	Hardwood Island Aquaculture Buoy B	44-18-34.600N 068-26-47.600W				Yellow.	Private aid.
2428	Hardwood Island Aquaculture Buoy C	44-18-34.300N 068-26-40.700W				Yellow.	Private aid.
2429	Hardwood Island Aquaculture Buoy D	44-18-21.400N 068-26-41.600W				Yellow.	Private aid.
2430	Long Island Buoy 7	44-19-02.671N 068-28-28.334W				Green can.	
2435	Darling Ledge Buoy 8	44-23-40.057N 068-30-47.837W				Red nun.	
2436	*Grays Mussel Farm Aquaculture Lighted Buoy*	44-22-44.040N 068-29-45.480W	Fl W 30s			White with orange bands.	Private aid.

(1) No.	(2) Name and Location	(3) Position	(4) Characteristic	(5) Height	(6) Range	(7) Structure	(8) Remarks
			MAINE - First District				
	BLUE HILL BAY						
	Union River Bay						
2440	Tupper Ledge Buoy TL	44-28-20.392N 068-26-21.056W					Green can with red bands.
	Union River Channel *Aids maintained from May 1 to Nov. 1.*						
2445	- Buoy 2 Marks rock.	44-28-41.772N 068-25-39.880W					Red nun.
2450	- Buoy 4	44-29-17.118N 068-25-28.678W					Red nun.
2455	- *Lighted Buoy 6*	44-29-48.498N 068-25-43.312W	Fl R 4s		3		Red.
2460	- Buoy 7	44-31-29.742N 068-25-37.738W					Green can.
2465	- Buoy 9	44-31-45.372N 068-25-26.932W					Green can.
2470	- Buoy 11	44-31-57.150N 068-25-23.842W					Green can.
	Patten Bay						
2475	- Buoy 2	44-28-54.913N 068-27-19.981W					Red nun.
	APPROACHES TO BLUE HILL BAY						
	Mackerel Cove						
2480	*North Point Lighted Gong Buoy 1* Northwest from 1-foot ledge.	44-11-34.918N 068-25-47.518W	Fl G 4s		5		Green.
2485	Crow Island Ledge Buoy 2	44-11-12.992N 068-25-58.046W					Red nun.
2487	*Fir Point Ledge Lighted Buoy 5*	44-10-50.596N 068-25-35.072W	Q G		3		Green.
2490	*Fir Point Ledge Lighted Buoy 3*	44-10-47.479N 068-25-45.347W	Fl G 4s		3		Green.
2495	Round Island Ledge Buoy 4	44-10-47.329N 068-26-48.079W					Red nun.
	Casco Passage						
2500	- Bell Buoy CP	44-11-48.214N 068-26-30.774W					Red and white stripes with red spherical topmark.
2505	- Buoy 1	44-11-36.148N 068-27-40.991W					Green can.
2510	- Buoy 3	44-11-38.136N 068-28-03.156W					Green can.
2515	- Buoy 4	44-11-43.248N 068-28-15.862W					Red nun.
2520	- Buoy 5	44-11-40.938N 068-28-18.962W					Green can.
2525	- Buoy 7	44-11-40.248N 068-28-38.464W					Green can.
2530	- Buoy 9	44-11-36.148N 068-29-03.134W					Green can.
2535	- Buoy 10	44-11-37.368N 068-29-38.615W					Red nun.
	Long Ledge						
2540	Orono Point Daybeacon 1A	44-11-27.508N 068-27-42.651W					SG on iron spindle.
2545	- Buoy 2 At east point of ledge.	44-11-25.028N 068-27-52.831W					Red nun.
2550	- Buoy 4 At southeastern end of ledge.	44-11-14.438N 068-28-11.042W					Red nun.
2555	Hawley Ledge Buoy 5	44-11-11.365N 068-28-20.643W					Green can.
2560	- Buoy 6	44-11-13.567N 068-28-32.956W					Red nun.
2565	Hawley Ledge Buoy 7	44-11-10.502N 068-28-43.324W					Green can.

(1) No.	(2) Name and Location	(3) Position	(4) Characteristic	(5) Height	(6) Range	(7) Structure	(8) Remarks
			MAINE - First District				
	APPROACHES TO BLUE HILL BAY						
	Long Ledge						
2570	- *Lighted Bell Buoy 8*	44-11-12.528N 068-28-53.084W	Fl R 4s		4	Red.	
	BLUE HILL BAY						
	Pond Island Passage						
2575	- Buoy 1 Northeasterly of shoal.	44-14-20.235N 068-28-44.945W				Green can.	
2580	- Buoy 2 On south end of shoal.	44-14-19.965N 068-29-03.845W				Red nun.	
2585	- Buoy 3 Northwesterly of rock.	44-14-07.147N 068-29-30.363W				Green can.	
	Western Passage						
2590	Flye Island Channel Buoy 1	44-14-34.064N 068-29-46.436W				Green can.	
2595	BLUE HILL BAY LIGHT 3	44-14-55.424N 068-29-51.696W	Fl G 4s	21	5	SG on skeleton tower.	
2600	Flye Island Channel Bell Buoy FI	44-14-56.454N 068-29-38.346W				Red and white stripes with red spherical topmark.	
2605	Flye Island Channel Buoy 4	44-15-07.804N 068-29-48.957W				Red nun.	
2610	Tinker Island Ledge Buoy 6	44-16-58.862N 068-29-58.477W				Red nun.	
2615	Cow and Calf Buoy 8 Northwest of ledge.	44-17-18.582N 068-29-48.666W				Red nun.	
	Maine Cultured Mussels Long Island East Aquaculture						
2616	- Buoy A	44-20-46.410N 068-28-50.360W				Yellow can.	Private aid.
2616.1	- Buoy B	44-20-40.210N 068-28-48.680W				Yellow can.	Private aid.
2616.2	- Buoy C	44-20-39.610N 068-28-53.000W				Yellow.	Private aid.
2616.3	- Buoy D	44-20-45.810N 068-28-54.680W				Yellow.	Private aid.
	Western Passage						
2620	Harriman Ledge Buoy 9	44-18-02.155N 068-31-20.719W				Green can.	
2625	Jims Point Buoy 10	44-19-45.839N 068-32-08.690W				Red nun.	
	Morgan Bay						
2630	- Entrance Buoy 2 West of 4-foot rock.	44-24-04.067N 068-29-40.835W				Red nun.	
	Blue Hill Harbor						
2635	- Buoy 1 At eastern point of middle ground.	44-24-04.806N 068-33-17.452W				Green can	
2640	- Buoy 3	44-24-08.635N 068-33-18.512W				Green can.	
2645	- Buoy 5	44-24-11.412N 068-33-39.727W				Green can.	
2650	- Buoy 6	44-24-13.150N 068-33-43.767W				Red nun.	
2655	- Buoy 7	44-24-25.503N 068-34-05.593W				Green can.	
2660	- Buoy 8	44-24-22.509N 068-34-15.670W				Red nun.	
	APPROACHES TO BLUE HILL BAY						
	Toothacher Bay						
	Burnt Coat Harbor						
2670	Seal Ledge Buoy 1	44-05-01.565N 068-28-28.022W				Green can.	
2675	Johns Island Sunken Ledge Buoy J South of ledge.	44-05-44.515N 068-24-27.643W				Red nun with green bands.	

(1) No.	(2) Name and Location	(3) Position	(4) Characteristic	(5) Height	(6) Range	(7) Structure	(8) Remarks

MAINE - First District

APPROACHES TO BLUE HILL BAY
Toothacher Bay
Burnt Coat Harbor

(1) No.	(2) Name and Location	(3) Position	(4) Characteristic	(5) Height	(6) Range	(7) Structure	(8) Remarks
2685	Gooseberry Island Ledge Buoy 3	44-07-47.114N 068-27-14.577W				Green can.	
2690	Harbor Island Ledge Daybeacon 4	44-07-55.590N 068-26-43.773W				TR on iron spindle.	
2695	- Gong Buoy 5	44-08-02.052N 068-26-43.428W				Green.	
2700	- LIGHT	44-08-02.836N 068-26-49.809W	Oc W 4s	75	9	White square tower.	
2705	Swans Island Gong Buoy 2 Southerly of shoal.	44-07-27.133N 068-24-46.274W				Red.	
2710	Baker Island Ledge Buoy 3	44-07-42.507N 068-25-52.828W				Green can.	
2711.1	*Scrag Island Aquaculture Lighted Buoy SI-A*	44-07-18.300N 068-26-28.070W	Fl Y 2.5s			Yellow.	Private aid.
2711.2	*Scrag Island Aquaculture Lighted Buoy SI-B*	44-07-14.700N 068-26-29.570W	Fl Y 2.5s			Yellow.	Private aid.
2711.3	*Scrag Island Aquaculture Lighted Buoy SI-C*	44-07-09.800N 068-26-10.570W	Fl Y 2.5s			Yellow.	Private aid.
2711.4	*Scrag Island Aquaculture Lighted Buoy SI-D*	44-07-12.790N 068-26-07.870W	Fl Y 2.5s			Yellow.	Private aid.
2715	Harbor Island Ledge Buoy 5	44-07-56.251N 068-26-04.964W				Green can.	
2720	Marshall Island Buoy 3	44-08-04.461N 068-30-39.926W				Green can.	
2725	Hat Island Ledge Buoy 4	44-08-23.951N 068-30-53.157W				Red nun.	
2730	Sheriff Ledges Buoy 2	44-07-47.262N 068-28-34.211W				Red nun.	

Jericho Bay

(1) No.	(2) Name and Location	(3) Position	(4) Characteristic	(5) Height	(6) Range	(7) Structure	(8) Remarks
2735	Drunkard Ledge Buoy 1	44-04-39.884N 068-32-30.729W				Green can.	
2740	Blue Hill Rock Buoy 3	44-05-30.793N 068-32-11.088W				Green can.	
2745	West Halibut Rock Buoy 4WH North of 2 foot shoal.	44-07-58.331N 068-32-59.090W				Red nun.	
2750	HALIBUT ROCKS LIGHT On northerly rock.	44-08-02.442N 068-31-31.482W	Fl W 6s	25	6	NR on skeleton tower.	HORN: 1 blast ev 10s (1s bl). Operates continuously.
2755	Whaleback Ledge Isolated Danger Buoy DW	44-09-14.943N 068-33-10.309W				Black and red bands with two black spherical topmarks; can.	
2760	Saddleback Island Bell Buoy SI	44-09-02.029N 068-34-16.332W				Red and white stripes with red spherical topmark.	
2765	Shingle Island Sunken Ledge Buoy 2	44-09-07.959N 068-35-31.055W				Red nun.	
2770	The Woodbury Buoy 6	44-09-25.362N 068-31-27.127W				Red nun.	
2775	Hanus Ledge Buoy HL	44-09-48.166N 068-30-23.839W				Red nun with green bands.	
2780	Sunken Egg Rock Buoy 1	44-10-51.658N 068-30-46.687W				Green can.	
2785	Long Ledge Bell Buoy 2	44-10-40.268N 068-32-47.691W				Red.	
2790	Long Ledge Daybeacon LL On southwest end of ledge.	44-10-46.962N 068-32-50.566W				NR on spindle.	
2795	- Buoy 2	44-10-53.038N 068-31-58.059W				Red nun.	
2805	Egg Rock Daybeacon 8A	44-11-06.555N 068-30-32.324W				TR on spindle.	
2810	Green Ledge Buoy 9	44-11-32.627N 068-32-05.169W				Green can.	

MAINE - First District

(1) No.	(2) Name and Location	(3) Position	(4) Characteristic	(5) Height	(6) Range	(7) Structure	(8) Remarks
			MAINE - First District				
	APPROACHES TO BLUE HILL BAY						
	Jericho Bay						
2815	Mahoney Island Ledge Buoy 2	44-12-37.556N 068-31-18.888W				Red nun.	
2820	Mahoney Island Buoy 11	44-12-51.926N 068-30-26.887W				Green can.	
	BLUE HILL BAY						
	Eggemoggin Reach						
2825	Eggemoggin Eastern Bell Buoy EE	44-12-45.016N 068-32-18.350W				Red and white stripes with red spherical topmark.	
2830	Hay Island Ledge Buoy 4 West of ledge.	44-12-52.576N 068-32-10.375W				Red nun.	
2835	Devils Head Ledge Buoy 6	44-13-03.466N 068-32-26.560W				Red nun.	
2840	Channel Rock Buoy 5	44-12-49.656N 068-32-47.551W				Green can.	
2845	Conary Ledge Buoy 7 Northeast of ledge.	44-14-18.764N 068-35-10.295W				Green can.	
2850	Torrey Island Buoy 8	44-14-54.533N 068-36-06.797W				Red nun.	
2855	Torrey Castle Daybeacon 10	44-15-05.811N 068-36-07.800W				TR on spindle.	
2860	Torrey Ledge Buoy 12	44-15-27.512N 068-36-11.937W				Red nun.	
	Center Harbor						
2865	Chatto Island Ledge Buoy 2	44-15-39.942N 068-35-17.635W				Red nun.	
2870	- Ledge Daybeacon 3	44-15-44.452N 068-35-03.004W				SG on iron spindle.	
	Eggemoggin Reach						
2875	Bridges Point Shoal Buoy 14	44-16-09.482N 068-37-26.879W				Red nun.	
2880	Benjamin River Buoy 2	44-17-10.421N 068-37-39.299W				Red nun.	Maintained from May 15 to Nov. 15.
2885	Benjamin River Buoy 3	44-17-18.419N 068-37-40.398W				Green can.	Maintained from May 15 to Nov. 15.
2890	Benjamin River Buoy 4	44-17-28.456N 068-37-40.378W				Red nun.	Maintained from May 15 to Nov. 15.
2895	Stump Cove Ledge Buoy 16	44-16-53.181N 068-38-24.630W				Red nun.	
2900	Tinker Ledges Buoy 17	44-16-53.081N 068-39-24.592W				Green can.	
2905	Billings Cove Buoy 18	44-17-35.210N 068-40-17.634W				Red nun.	
	PENOBSCOT RIVER						
	Eggemoggin Reach						
2910	Howard Ledges Buoy 21	44-18-24.478N 068-43-02.259W				Green can.	
2915	The Triangles Buoy 23 North of 2 foot shoal.	44-18-50.668N 068-44-05.771W				Green can.	
2920	The Triangles Buoy 25 At western edge of ledge.	44-18-47.588N 068-44-18.361W				Green can.	
2925	*Eggemoggin Lighted Bell Buoy EG*	44-19-13.257N 068-44-34.292W	Mo (A) W		4	Red and white stripes with red spherical topmark.	
2930	*Buck Harbor Ledge Lighted Buoy* On north side of ledge.	44-20-16.316N 068-44-11.111W	Fl W 2s		3	White and orange bands.	Marked DANGER.
2931	Buck's Harbor East Channel Buoy 1	44-20-02.880N 068-44-03.060W				Green can.	Private aid.
2932	Buck's Harbor East Channel Buoy 2	44-20-02.700N 068-44-01.860W				Red nun.	Private aid.

(1) No.	(2) Name and Location	(3) Position	(4) Characteristic	(5) Height	(6) Range	(7) Structure	(8) Remarks

PENOBSCOT RIVER

Eggemoggin Reach

2935	Horseshoe Ledge Daybeacon 2	44-19-22.260N 068-46-00.660W				TR on spindle.	Maintained from May 1 to Nov. 1. Private aid.
2940	Horseshoe Cove Buoy 3	44-19-54.720N 068-46-07.500W				Green can.	Maintained from May 1 to Nov. 1. Private aid.
2945	Horseshoe Cove Daybeacon 5	44-19-57.960N 068-46-07.920W				SG on spindle.	Maintained from May 1 to Nov. 1. Private aid.
2950	Cowpens Ledge Daybeacon 6	44-19-58.920N 068-46-06.420W				TR on spindle.	Maintained from May 1 to Nov. 1. Private aid.
2960	Pumpkin Island Ledge Buoy 27	44-18-41.453N 068-45-05.024W				Green can.	
2965	Thrumcap Ledge Buoy 28	44-18-52.369N 068-45-24.926W				Red nun.	
2970	Merriman Ledge Buoy 29	44-18-29.728N 068-45-07.842W				Green can.	
2975	- Buoy 31	44-18-24.858N 068-45-40.961W				Green can.	
2980	Spectacle Island Ledge Buoy 32	44-18-24.303N 068-46-10.231W				Red nun.	
2985	Two Bush Ledge Buoy 33	44-18-04.268N 068-45-49.873W				Green can.	
2990	- Bell Buoy ER	44-18-00.148N 068-46-28.814W				Red and white stripes with red spherical topmark.	

APPROACHES TO BLUE HILL BAY

Deer Island Thorofare

2995	Potato Ledge Buoy 5	44-10-35.418N 068-33-02.591W				Green can.	
3000	Lazygut Ledge Buoy 6	44-10-34.988N 068-33-48.832W				Red nun.	
3005	Eastern Mark Island Ledge Buoy 7	44-10-22.078N 068-34-58.194W				Green can.	
3010	Haycock Rock Daybeacon 9	44-10-08.027N 068-35-19.454W				SG on iron spindle.	
3015	White Rock Buoy 10	44-10-04.548N 068-35-56.426W				Red nun.	
3020	Haskell Ledge Buoy 12	44-09-57.408N 068-36-27.817W				Red nun.	

Bold Island

3025	- East Ledge Buoy 11	44-09-45.388N 068-36-33.737W				Green can.	
3030	- Buoy 1	44-09-23.768N 068-36-31.057W				Green can.	
3032	- Ledges Warning Buoy	44-09-35.142N 068-36-54.058W				White can with orange bands worded ROCK.	
3035	- Western Buoy 3	44-09-29.276N 068-36-59.563W				Green can.	
3040	- Western Ledge Buoy 13 North end of shoal.	44-09-41.418N 068-37-10.098W				Green can.	

Deer Island Thorofare

3045	Humpkins Islet Shoal Buoy 14	44-09-22.678N 068-38-01.060W				Red nun.	
3050	Roebuck Ledge Buoy 15	44-09-11.062N 068-38-45.123W				Green can.	
3055	Dow Ledges Buoy 16	44-09-11.328N 068-39-00.102W				Red nun.	
3060	Staple Point Ledge Buoy 18	44-09-08.718N 068-39-33.023W				Red nun.	
3065	Peggy's Island Ledge Buoy 19	44-08-57.492N 068-40-12.364W				Green can.	

(1) No.	(2) Name and Location	(3) Position	(4) Characteristic	(5) Height	(6) Range	(7) Structure	(8) Remarks
			MAINE - First District				
	APPROACHES TO BLUE HILL BAY						
	Deer Island Thorofare						
3070	CROTCH ISLAND LIGHT 21	44-08-46.446N 068-40-39.076W	Fl G 4s	20	5	SG on skeleton tower.	
3075	Crotch Island Buoy 23	44-08-47.529N 068-40-40.785W				Green can.	
3080	Moose Island Rock Buoy 24	44-08-45.109N 068-40-51.066W				Red nun.	
3085	Crotch Island Daybeacon 25	44-08-30.732N 068-41-04.996W				SG on spindle.	
3090	Field Ledge Buoy 27	44-08-24.958N 068-41-34.126W				Green can.	
3095	- LIGHT	44-08-03.757N 068-42-11.795W	Fl W 6s	52	8	White and black tower.	Obscured from 240° to 335°. HORN: 1 blast ev 15s (2s bl). Operates continuously.
3100	West Mark Island Ledge Buoy 2	44-08-12.037N 068-43-05.829W				Red nun.	
	Oceanville Approach						
3105	Boat Rock Buoy East of ledge.	44-10-45.887N 068-35-15.595W				Red nun with green bands.	
3110	Whaleback Ledge Buoy 1	44-11-17.305N 068-36-24.858W				Green can.	
	Crotch Island Passage						
3115	Green Island Buoy 4	44-08-17.000N 068-38-41.054W				Red nun.	
3120	- Buoy 2	44-08-41.148N 068-39-54.603W				Red nun.	
3125	Two Bush Island Point Buoy 3	44-08-57.278N 068-39-44.523W				Green can.	
	Merchant Row						
3130	Colby Ledge Daybeacon 2	44-07-24.899N 068-35-34.101W				TR on spindle.	
3135	Colby Pup Buoy 1	44-06-56.661N 068-35-34.365W				Green can.	
3140	Barter Island Ledges Daybeacon 8	44-07-08.088N 068-38-07.366W				TR on spindle.	
3145	- Buoy 9 North of ledge.	44-06-56.875N 068-38-54.999W				Green can.	
3150	Midchannel Ledge Buoy 10 South of ledge.	44-07-06.589N 068-39-42.533W				Red nun.	
3155	York Island Rock Buoy 1	44-04-08.214N 068-34-47.333W				Green can.	
3160	Seven Foot Shoal Buoy 2	44-04-55.074N 068-34-47.980W				Red nun.	
3165	Airy Ledge Buoy 3	44-05-08.083N 068-35-15.194W				Green can.	
3170	Burnt Ledge Buoy 5	44-05-59.032N 068-36-12.296W				Green can.	
3175	Leach Rock Buoy 7	44-06-36.071N 068-37-28.099W				Green can.	
	Jericho Bay						
3180	Colt Ledge Buoy 2A	44-01-04.554N 068-33-54.358W				Red nun.	
3185	Eastern Ear Ledge Buoy 2	44-00-10.187N 068-35-41.345W				Red nun.	
3190	*Roaring Bull Lighted Bell Buoy 2*	43-59-24.945N 068-37-55.948W	Fl R 6s		4	Red.	

(1) No.	(2) Name and Location	(3) Position	(4) Characteristic	(5) Height	(6) Range	(7) Structure	(8) Remarks
			MAINE - First District				
	PENOBSCOT BAY AND APPROACHES						
	Penobscot Bay Approaches						
3195 10	**Matinicus Rock Light**	43-47-00.538N 068-51-18.129W	Fl W 10s	90	20	Cylindrical gray granite tower. 41	Emergency light of reduced intensity when main light is extinguished. HORN: 1 blast ev 15s (2s bl). MRASS-Fog signal is radio activated, during times of reduced visibility, turn marine VHF-FM radio to channel 83A/157.175Mhz. Key microphone 5 times consecutively, to activate fog signal for 60 minutes.
3210	Matinicus South Breaker Buoy DMSB	43-47-25.339N 068-53-24.134W				Black and red bands with two black spherical topmarks.	
3215	Matinicus Inner Breaker Buoy 2 Off south end of shoal.	43-48-21.168N 068-53-48.030W				Red nun.	
3220	Southwest Ledge Bell Buoy 4	43-49-08.128N 068-54-31.257W				Red.	
3225	Bantam Ledge Buoy DBL South of ledge.	43-49-32.745N 068-57-02.579W				Black and red bands with two black spherical topmarks.	
3230	Ragged Island Harbor Ledges Buoy 6 Marks ledges west of island.	43-50-08.017N 068-54-02.556W				Red nun.	
3235	CRIEHAVEN BREAKWATER LIGHT 8	43-50-05.037N 068-53-33.444W	Fl R 6s	32	5	TR on skeleton tower.	
3240	*Wooden Ball Island Lighted Bell Buoy 2WB*	43-50-24.517N 068-49-56.876W	Fl R 4s		4	Red.	
3243	Malcolm Ledge Danger VAIS DML	43-52-02.780N 068-46-31.910W					Virtual AIS.MMSI: 993672370
3245	Harbor Ledge Bell Buoy	43-51-54.766N 068-52-44.673W				Red and green bands.	
3250	MATINICUS HARBOR LIGHT 2	43-51-53.682N 068-52-54.618W	Fl R 4s		4	TR on skeleton tower.	
3255	Mackerel Ledge Buoy 5 North of northerly ledge.	43-52-06.718N 068-51-39.116W				Green can.	
3265	*Zephyr Rock Lighted Buoy 5*	43-53-46.335N 068-51-47.130W	Fl G 4s		3	Green.	
3275	Beach Ledges Buoy	43-52-19.866N 068-52-47.893W				Red nun with green bands.	
3280	*Matinicus Island Lighted Bell Buoy 9MI*	43-53-06.336N 068-52-52.133W	Fl G 4s		4	Green.	
3285	Foster Ledges Buoy 10 West of ledge.	43-52-05.766N 068-56-54.202W				Red nun.	
3295	Southern Triangles Buoy 1T South of rock.	43-53-45.935N 069-03-50.857W				Green can.	
3300	Penobscot Bay East Approach (VAIS) PBA	43-55-36.642N 068-39-37.087W					AIS: MMSI 993672149 (21)
3302	*Penobscot Bay Lighted Buoy WP*	43-55-50.660N 068-53-08.919W	Mo (A) W		4	Red and white stripes with red spherical topmark.	
3305	Bay Ledge Isolated Danger Gong Buoy DBL West of ledge.	43-57-57.293N 068-51-45.350W				Black and red bands with two black spherical topmarks.	
3307	*Three Fathom Ledge Isolated Danger Lighted Buoy DTF* East of 16 foot ledge.	43-54-17.949N 068-42-04.751W	Fl (2)W 5s		4	Black and red bands with two black spherical topmarks.	
3308	28 Foot Spot Danger VAIS TE	43-59-01.030N 068-50-35.880W					VAIS MMSI: 993672369
3309	Snippershan Ledge Danger VAIS SL	43-57-01.220N 068-45-39.530W					VAIS MMSI: 993672684

(1) No.	(2) Name and Location	(3) Position	(4) Characteristic	(5) Height	(6) Range	(7) Structure	(8) Remarks
			MAINE - First District				
	PENOBSCOT BAY AND APPROACHES						
	Penobscot Bay Approaches						
3310	*Old Horse Ledge Lighted Bell Buoy 2A*	43-59-55.963N 068-50-04.337W	Fl R 2.5s		4	Red.	
	PENOBSCOT BAY						
	Isle Au Haut Bay						
3320	The Washers Buoy 2	44-00-20.041N 068-40-29.592W				Red nun.	
3325	SADDLEBACK LEDGE LIGHT	44-00-51.733N 068-43-35.227W	Fl W 6s	52	9	Gray conical tower.	HORN: 1 blast ev 10s (1s bl). operates continuously.
3330	Saddleback Ledge Shoal Isolated Danger Buoy DSL Southwest of ledge.	44-01-24.622N 068-44-23.753W				Black and red bands with two black spherical topmarks; can.	
3335	Diamond Rock Ledge Buoy 1	44-01-35.342N 068-45-59.007W				Green can.	
3340	Triangle Ledge Buoy 5	44-03-12.834N 068-45-51.700W				Green can.	
3345	Marsh Cove Ledges Buoy 1	44-04-03.892N 068-40-33.555W				Green can.	
3350	The Brandies Buoy 4	44-01-30.201N 068-41-09.363W				Red nun.	
3355	Rock T Buoy 6 Northwest of rock.	44-02-20.333N 068-40-16.105W				Red nun.	
3360	ISLE AU HAUT LIGHT	44-03-53.112N 068-39-04.962W	Fl R 4s (W sector)	48	W 8 R 6	Tower, lower part conical, gray: upper part cylindrical, white brick; white bridge to shore.	White from 034° to 060°, covers fairway to Isle au Haut Thorofare.
3365	Sawyer Ledge Buoy 1	44-04-01.482N 068-39-15.702W				Green can.	
3370	Inner Ledge Daybeacon 3	44-04-09.762N 068-38-49.011W				SG on spindle.	
	Isle Au Haut Thorofare						
3375	- Buoy 4	44-04-31.944N 068-38-13.236W				Red nun.	Removed when endangered by ice.
3380	- Buoy 6	44-04-35.250N 068-38-09.238W				Red nun.	Removed when endangered by ice.
3385	- Buoy 5	44-04-36.396N 068-38-09.342W				Green can.	Removed when endangered by ice.
3390	- Buoy 7	44-04-42.449N 068-38-02.124W				Green can.	Removed when endangered by ice.
3395	- Buoy 8	44-04-47.018N 068-37-56.463W				Red nun.	Removed when endangered by ice.
3400	- Buoy 9	44-04-46.891N 068-37-57.960W				Green can.	Removed when endangered by ice.
3405	Ram Island Ledge Buoy 2 North side of ledge.	44-05-52.270N 068-40-14.164W				Red nun.	
3410	Merchant Island Ledge Buoy 1	44-06-03.816N 068-39-30.370W				Green can.	
3415	North Bay Ledge Buoy 2	44-05-41.804N 068-39-16.717W				Red nun.	
3425	Birch Point Shoal Buoy 3	44-05-19.761N 068-38-33.141W				Green can.	
3430	Flake Island Buoy 5	44-05-04.612N 068-38-20.561W				Green can.	
3435	Birch Point Daybeacon On ledge.	44-05-27.054N 068-37-54.196W				NG on iron spindle.	

(1) No.	(2) Name and Location	(3) Position	(4) Characteristic	(5) Height	(6) Range	(7) Structure	(8) Remarks
			MAINE - First District				
	PENOBSCOT BAY						
	East Penobscot Bay						
3440	Brown Cow Ledge Whistle Buoy 2BC Southwest of ledge.	44-06-43.978N 068-43-50.981W				Red.	
3445	Sellers Rock Buoy 2 Southwest of rock.	44-10-23.285N 068-43-46.660W				Red nun.	
3450	Porcupine Ledge Bell Buoy 3	44-12-22.224N 068-45-44.776W				Green.	
3455	EAGLE ISLAND LIGHT	44-13-03.564N 068-46-03.994W	Fl W 4s	106	9	White conical tower.	
3460	Eagle Island Gong Buoy 3A	44-13-06.753N 068-45-52.162W				Green.	
3465	Slyvester Cove Buoy 2	44-12-45.504N 068-43-31.819W				Red nun.	
3470	Middle Rock Buoy 4 Westerly of ledge.	44-13-39.222N 068-45-51.932W				Red nun.	
3475	Fling Island Ledge Buoy 1	44-12-29.333N 068-48-17.126W				Green can.	
3480	Channel Rock Buoy 2	44-12-53.732N 068-48-28.116W				Red nun.	
3485	Great Spruce Head Ledge Buoy 3	44-14-28.403N 068-48-38.635W				Green can.	
3490	Gull Ledge Buoy 1	44-14-01.872N 068-43-25.420W				Green can.	
3495	Pressey Ledge Buoy 2	44-14-08.322N 068-42-37.037W				Red nun.	
	PENOBSCOT RIVER						
	East Penobscot Bay						
3500	Swains Ledge Buoy 1	44-17-17.649N 068-44-11.450W				Green can.	
3505	Green Ledge Bell Buoy 2	44-17-13.518N 068-49-59.888W				Red.	Removed when endangered by ice.
3510	GREEN LEDGE LIGHT 4 On ledge west of western island.	44-17-24.648N 068-49-42.357W	Fl R 6s	31	5	TR on skeleton tower.	
3515	Hewes Ledge Buoy 1 At northeast end of ledge.	44-18-33.467N 068-53-08.543W				Green can.	
3520	Hewes Ledge Buoy 2 At southwest end of ledge	44-18-25.707N 068-53-14.499W				Red nun.	
3525	Isleboro Ledge Buoy 9 East of ledge.	44-20-59.925N 068-51-21.591W				Green can.	
	Castine Harbor						
3530	**Dice Head Light**	44-22-57.636N 068-49-07.870W	Fl W 6s	134	11	White tower. 51	
3531	*Castine DeepC Wind Anchor Lighted Buoy NE*	44-23-10.800N 068-49-18.600W	Fl W 4s			White with Orange bands.	Private aid.
3531.1	*Castine DeepC Wind Anchor Lighted Buoy SE*	44-22-55.400N 068-49-24.700W	Fl W 4s			White with Orange bands.	Private aid.
3531.2	*Castine DeepC Wind Anchor Lighted Buoy W*	44-23-03.200N 068-49-35.580W	Fl W 4s			White with Orange bands.	Private aid.
3535	Nautilus Rock Buoy 1A	44-22-19.920N 068-48-37.747W				Green can.	
3540	- Entrance Bell Buoy CH	44-22-29.813N 068-49-03.319W				Red and white stripes with red spherical topmark.	
3545	- Buoy 1	44-22-41.853N 068-48-49.908W				Green can.	
3550	Hosmer Ledge Daybeacon 2	44-22-52.753N 068-47-51.777W				TR on iron spindle on stone monument.	
3555	Smith Cove Buoy 2	44-22-30.314N 068-46-38.216W				Red nun.	
3560	- Buoy 2	44-23-18.673N 068-47-28.247W				Red nun.	35 yards from old monument, awash at half tide.

(1) No.	(2) Name and Location	(3) Position	(4) Characteristic	(5) Height	(6) Range	(7) Structure	(8) Remarks
			MAINE - First District				
	PENOBSCOT RIVER						
	East Penobscot Bay						
	Castine Harbor						
3565	- Buoy 3	44-23-37.540N 068-46-54.861W				Green can.	
	Bagaduce River						
3570	- Shoal Buoy 5	44-24-10.242N 068-46-00.796W				Green can.	Maintained from May 1 to Nov. 15.
3575	- Ledge Buoy 7	44-25-42.123N 068-44-53.662W				Green can.	Maintained from May 1 to Nov. 15.
	Penobscot River						
3580	FORT POINT LEDGE LIGHT 2	44-27-39.797N 068-48-36.332W	Fl R 4s	23	4	TR on spindle on stone monument.	
3585	**Fort Point Light**	44-28-01.718N 068-48-42.068W	F W	88	15	White house. 31	Lighted throughout 24 hours. HORN: 1 blast ev 10s (1s bl). MRASS-Fog signal is radio activated, during times of reduced visibility, turn marine VHF-FM radio to channel 83A/157.175Mhz. Key microphone 5 times consecutively, to activate fog signal for 60 minutes.
3590	- Buoy 1	44-28-07.388N 068-48-24.320W				Green can.	
3595	- Buoy 3	44-29-36.037N 068-48-03.610W				Green can.	
3600	- Buoy 4	44-29-49.817N 068-47-33.610W				Red nun.	
3605	- Buoy 5	44-30-06.636N 068-48-03.241W				Green can.	
3610	- *Lighted Buoy 6*	44-30-48.876N 068-48-09.152W	Q R		3	Red.	
3615	Odom Ledge Daybeacon 6A On highest point of ledge.	44-30-55.874N 068-48-02.772W				TR on post on square stone base.	Ra ref.
3616	WALDO HANCOCK WEST LIGHTS (2)	44-33-39.265N 068-48-10.472W	Fl W 2.5s	15		White.	Marks end of bridge abutment. Private aid.
3617	WALDO HANCOCK EAST LIGHTS (2)	44-33-35.518N 068-48-00.744W	Fl W 2.5s	15		White.	Marks end of bridge abutment. Private aid.
3620	- Buoy 7	44-34-52.356N 068-48-54.054W				Green can.	
3625	- Buoy 9	44-35-17.882N 068-48-55.929W				Green can.	
3630	- Buoy 11	44-36-03.111N 068-49-29.431W				Green can.	
3635	- Buoy 13	44-36-14.520N 068-50-08.905W				Green can.	
3640	- *Lighted Buoy 14*	44-36-23.122N 068-50-38.960W	Fl R 4s		4	Red.	
3645	- Buoy 16	44-36-45.807N 068-51-00.419W				Red nun.	Removed when endangered by ice.
3650	- Buoy 19	44-40-06.996N 068-48-51.850W				Green can.	
3655	- Buoy 18	44-37-12.156N 068-51-00.024W				Red nun.	Removed when endangered by ice.
3660	Bucks Ledge Daybeacon 20 On ledge.	44-40-54.297N 068-48-52.137W				TR on spindle.	
3665	- Buoy 22	44-41-24.156N 068-49-55.210W				Red nun.	
3670	- Buoy 24	44-43-41.439N 068-49-56.272W				Red nun.	
3675	- Buoy 26	44-45-02.794N 068-48-57.299W				Red nun.	

(1) No.	(2) Name and Location	(3) Position	(4) Characteristic	(5) Height	(6) Range	(7) Structure	(8) Remarks
			MAINE - First District				
	PENOBSCOT RIVER						
	Penobscot River						
3680	- Buoy 28	44-45-15.399N 068-48-48.373W				Red nun.	
3681	CIANBRO HAZARD LIGHT A	44-46-16.650N 068-47-08.330W	Q W			On wood pile.	Private aid.
3682	CIANBRO HAZARD LIGHT B	44-46-15.950N 068-47-08.570W	Q W			On wood pile.	Private aid.
	PENOBSCOT BAY						
	Carvers Harbor (Vinal Haven)						
	Carvers Harbor From Eastward						
3685	Halibut Ledge Buoy 2	44-02-40.306N 068-46-23.018W				Red nun.	
3690	Crosby Ledge Buoy 4	44-02-16.721N 068-47-01.239W				Red nun.	
3695	Sheep Island Ledge Buoy 2	44-01-38.962N 068-47-25.100W				Red nun.	
3700	Old Duke Ledges Buoy 6	44-01-53.242N 068-47-48.931W				Red nun.	
3705	Bunker Ledge Buoy 8	44-01-29.962N 068-48-51.603W				Red nun.	
3710	Point Ledge Buoy 10	44-01-40.226N 068-49-43.598W				Red nun.	
	Carvers Harbor From South						
3715	CARVERS HARBOR ENTRANCE LIGHT 2	44-02-03.030N 068-50-37.226W	Fl R 4s	19	4	TR on spindle.	
3720	*Green Ledge Lighted Buoy 4*	44-02-14.831N 068-50-38.126W	Fl R 2.5s		4	Red.	
3725	*Norton Point Ledge Lighted Buoy 5*	44-02-19.531N 068-50-35.426W	Fl G 2.5s		4	Green.	
3730	Colt Ledge Buoy 2	44-00-44.427N 068-50-13.207W				Red nun.	
3735	The Breakers Ledge Buoy 1	44-01-04.252N 068-50-33.290W				Green can.	
3740	Arey Ledges Buoy 4	44-01-07.248N 068-50-21.568W				Red nun.	
	Carvers Harbor From Westward						
3745	James and Willies Ledge Buoy 1	44-01-04.271N 068-52-43.792W				Green can.	
3750	The Breakers Sunken Ledge Buoy 2	44-01-04.502N 068-51-32.521W				Red nun.	
3755	Heron Channel Ledge Buoy 4 North of shoal.	44-01-24.451N 068-51-20.159W				Red nun.	
3760	HERON NECK LIGHT	44-01-30.436N 068-51-43.810W	F R (W sector)	92	W 9 7	White conical tower.	White sector from 030° to 063°.Emergency light of reduced intensity when main light is extinguished. HORN: 1 blast ev 30s (3s bl). MRASS-Fog signal is radio activated, during times of reduced visibility, turn marine VHF-FM radio to channel 83A/157.175Mhz. Key microphone 5 times consecutively, to activate fog signal for 60 minutes.
	The Reach						
3765	- *Rock Lighted Buoy 2*	44-02-18.531N 068-50-57.127W	Q R		3	Red.	
3770	WRECK POINT LIGHT 3	44-02-26.400N 068-51-08.527W	Fl G 2.5s		3	SG on spindle.	
3775	- *Lighted Buoy 5*	44-02-31.895N 068-51-13.936W	Fl G 4s		3	Green.	
3780	- Buoy 7	44-02-34.130N 068-51-27.628W				Green can.	
3785	- *Lighted Buoy 8*	44-02-40.330N 068-51-40.128W	Fl R 2.5s		3	Red.	

(1) No.	(2) Name and Location	(3) Position	(4) Characteristic	(5) Height	(6) Range	(7) Structure	(8) Remarks
			MAINE - First District				
	PENOBSCOT BAY						
	Carvers Harbor (Vinal Haven)						
	The Reach						
3790	- *Ledge Lighted Buoy 9*	44-02-46.030N 068-51-49.129W	Fl G 4s		3	Green.	
3795	*Dog Point Ledge Lighted Buoy 10*	44-02-59.330N 068-52-20.130W	Fl R 2.5s		3	Red.	
3800	Green Island Sunken Ledge Buoy 11	44-02-56.200N 068-52-34.450W				Green can.	
	Hurricane Sound						
3805	- Buoy 15	44-02-30.795N 068-54-03.297W				Green can.	
3810	- Buoy 13	44-02-39.780N 068-53-29.242W				Green can.	
3815	- Buoy 12 South of ledge.	44-02-51.036N 068-53-19.030W				Red nun.	
	Lawrys Narrows						
3820	- *East Entrance Lighted Buoy 1* East of ledge.	44-03-58.162N 068-53-38.999W	Fl G 2.5s		4	Green.	
3825	- *Rocks Lighted Buoy 2A*	44-04-06.148N 068-54-13.132W	Fl R 4s		4	Red.	
3830	- West Entrance Ledge Buoy 1	44-04-02.049N 068-54-27.143W				Green can.	
3835	*Green Island Lighted Bell Buoy 3*	44-04-10.836N 068-55-25.210W	Fl G 4s		4	Green.	
3840	*Green Island Ledge Lighted Buoy 2*	44-04-21.063N 068-55-06.665W	Fl R 2.5s		3	Red nun.	
3845	Seal Ledge Buoy 5	44-04-42.768N 068-56-20.306W				Green can.	
3850	Inner Bay Ledges Buoy 7	44-04-54.328N 068-56-50.137W				Green can.	
	Leadbetter Narrows						
3855	- Buoy 1 On east side of shoal.	44-05-03.028N 068-54-03.531W				Green can.	
	Fox Island Thorofare						
3860	- Buoy 2A	44-07-54.837N 068-46-41.116W				Red nun.	
3865	- Buoy 2 South of shoal.	44-07-50.942N 068-48-06.586W				Red nun.	
3875	Channel Rock Daybeacon 4A	44-07-48.036N 068-48-30.010W				TR on iron spindle.	
3880	- Buoy 5 East of shoal.	44-07-52.937N 068-49-27.155W				Green can.	
3885	GOOSE ROCKS LIGHT On ledge.	44-08-07.536N 068-49-50.410W	Fl R 6s	51	7 W 12	White conical tower, black cylindrical foundation.	White sector from 301° to 304°. HORN: 1 blast ev 10s (1s bl). Fog signal is radio activated, during times of reduced visibility, turn marine VHF-FM radio to channel 83A/157.175Mhz. Key microphone 5 times consecutively, to activate fog signal for 60 minutes.
3887	Carvers Cove CG Mooring Buoy	44-07-27.027N 068-49-37.857W				White with blue band.	
3890	- Buoy 7	44-07-59.306N 068-50-26.692W				Green can.	
3895	- Buoy 6	44-08-03.446N 068-50-43.602W				Red nun.	
3900	- Buoy 8	44-07-52.026N 068-51-09.334W				Red nun.	
3905	- Buoy 10 East of shoal.	44-07-35.046N 068-51-19.584W				Red nun.	
3910	Iron Point Ledge Daybeacon 11 On ledge.	44-07-29.366N 068-51-21.594W				SG on iron spindle.	

(1) No.	(2) Name and Location	(3) Position	(4) Characteristic	(5) Height	(6) Range	(7) Structure	(8) Remarks

MAINE - First District

PENOBSCOT BAY

Fox Island Thorofare

(1) No.	(2) Name and Location	(3) Position	(4) Characteristic	(5) Height	(6) Range	(7) Structure	(8) Remarks
3915	- Buoy 12 South of shoal.	44-07-26.436N 068-51-37.330W				Red nun.	
3925	- Buoy 14	44-07-28.706N 068-52-11.906W				Red nun.	
3930	- Lighted Buoy 16 Southwest of ledge	44-07-29.496N 068-52-27.430W	Fl R 2.5s		3	Red.	
3935	- Lighted Buoy 17	44-07-34.503N 068-53-11.425W	Fl G 2.5s		3	Green.	
3940	- Lighted Buoy 18	44-07-30.886N 068-53-59.489W	Fl R 4s		3	Red.	
3945	Young Point Daybeacon 19	44-07-26.746N 068-53-54.249W				SG on iron spindle.	Ra ref.
3950	- Buoy 20 South of shoal.	44-07-17.346N 068-54-29.160W				Red nun.	
3955	Fox Ears Daybeacon 22 On ledge.	44-07-02.106N 068-54-46.206W				TR on iron spindle.	
3960	- Gong Buoy 23	44-06-49.926N 068-54-38.601W				Green.	
3965	**Browns Head Light**	44-06-42.388N 068-54-34.196W	F W (2R sectors)	39	W 14 R 11 R 11	White cylindrical tower. 24	Red from 001° to 050°, and from 061° to 091°, fairway between. Lighted throughout 24 hours. Emergency light of reduced intensity when main light is extinguished. HORN: 1 blast ev 10s (1s bl). MRASS-Fog signal is radio activated, during times of reduced visibility, turn marine VHF-FM radio to channel 83A/157.175Mhz. Key microphone 5 times consecutively, to activate fog signal for 60 minutes.
3970	- Buoy 24	44-06-31.007N 068-55-45.273W				Red nun.	
3975	- Junction Buoy	44-06-02.516N 068-55-39.593W				Green can with red bands.	
3985	Fiddler Ledge Daybeacon	44-06-05.772N 068-56-22.114W				Gray stone square shaft pyramidal top.	
3990	- Lighted Gong Buoy 26	44-05-48.497N 068-56-48.786W	Fl R 2.5s		3	Red.	
3995	- Buoy 27 North of 14-foot spot.	44-05-16.967N 068-56-55.477W				Green can.	
4000	- Lighted Bell Buoy FT	44-05-17.587N 068-57-16.937W	Mo (A) W		3	Red and white stripes.	
4005	Mcintosh Ledge Buoy 1	44-09-21.024N 068-57-39.674W				Green can.	
4010	Mouse Island Reef Buoy 3	44-10-56.322N 068-56-25.130W				Green can.	
4015	Mouse Island Ledge Buoy 5	44-12-15.321N 068-56-21.128W				Green can.	
4020	Egg Rock Ledge Buoy North-northeast of ledge.	44-11-10.543N 068-53-14.765W				Red nun with green bands.	
4025	Compass Island Ledge Isolated Danger Buoy DCL East of ledge.	44-12-03.453N 068-51-23.541W				Black and red bands with two black spherical topmarks; can.	

PENOBSCOT BAY AND APPROACHES

West Penobscot Bay

(1) No.	(2) Name and Location	(3) Position	(4) Characteristic	(5) Height	(6) Range	(7) Structure	(8) Remarks
4035	Two Bush Island Lighted Whistle Buoy TBI	43-58-16.792N 069-00-16.090W	Mo (A) W		6	Red and white stripes.	
4040	Junken Ledge Isolated Danger Buoy DJ Marks three-fathom ledge.	43-59-26.152N 068-59-29.378W				Black and red bands with two black spherical topmarks; can.	

38

(1) No.	(2) Name and Location	(3) Position	(4) Characteristic	(5) Height	(6) Range	(7) Structure	(8) Remarks

MAINE - First District

PENOBSCOT BAY AND APPROACHES
West Penobscot Bay

4050	*- Entrance Lighted Gong Buoy PA*	44-01-08.450N 069-00-19.278W	Mo (A) W		6	Red and white stripes with red spherical topmark.	AIS: MMSI 993672150 (21)
4052	*University of Maine Oceanographic Lighted Buoy F*	44-03-18.600N 068-59-48.600W	Fl Y 4s			Yellow.	Private aid.
4055	Twenty Five Foot Rock Buoy 9 Southeast of shoal.	44-01-40.467N 069-01-18.459W				Green can.	
4075	*Monroe Island Lighted Bell Buoy 11*	44-04-45.343N 069-01-40.934W	Fl G 4s		3	Green.	

Inner Bay Ledges

4090	- Buoy 4 At south end of ledges.	44-04-21.258N 068-57-20.038W				Red nun.	
4095	- Buoy 6	44-04-50.228N 068-57-37.749W				Red nun.	
4100	Drunkard Ledge Daybeacon	44-06-08.346N 068-57-08.086W				NW on spindle.	Danger rocks.
4105	**Owls Head Light**	44-05-32.094N 069-02-38.500W	F W	100	16	White tower. 26	Obscured from 324° to 354° by Monroe Island.Lighted throughout 24 hours. HORN: 2 blast ev 20s (2s bl-2s si-2s bl-14s si). MRASS-Fog signal is radio activated, during times of reduced visibility, turn marine VHF-FM radio to channel 83A/157.175Mhz. Key microphone 5 times consecutively, to activate fog signal for 60 minutes.
4110	Owls Head Ledge Buoy 7 East of rock.	44-05-25.040N 069-02-31.801W				Green can.	
4115	Shag Rock Daybeacon 9 On northeast end of rock.	44-05-43.666N 069-02-56.548W				SG on tripod.	
4120	*West Penobscot Bay Entrance Lighted Gong Buoy PB*	44-05-53.606N 069-00-11.922W	Mo (A) W		5	Red and white stripes with red spherical topmark.	

CAMDEN, ROCKPORT AND ROCKLAND HARBORS
Rockland Harbor

4125	Spears Rock Buoy 1 North of 5 foot shoal.	44-05-42.396N 069-04-33.472W				Green can.	
4130	**- Breakwater Light**	44-06-14.582N 069-04-39.171W	Fl W 5s	39	14	Red brick tower. 25	HORN: 1 blast ev 15s (2s bl). MRASS-Fog signal is radio activated, during times of reduced visibility, turn marine VHF-FM radio to channel 83A/157.175Mhz. Key microphone 5 times consecutively, to activate fog signal for 60 minutes.
4140	- SOUTHWEST LIGHT	44-04-54.000N 069-05-52.000W	F Y	44		Tower on white house.	Private aid.
4145	Seals Ledge Daybeacon 3	44-05-18.996N 069-05-54.370W				SG on spindle.	
4150	Railway Ledge Buoy 5	44-05-34.966N 069-06-02.650W				Green can.	
4155	*- Main Channel Lighted Buoy 2* Marks 14-foot shoal.	44-06-11.476N 069-05-37.284W	Fl R 4s		3	Red.	
4160	*- Main Channel Lighted Buoy 4*	44-06-14.785N 069-05-57.024W	Fl R 2.5s		3	Red.	

Rockland Harbor Bypass Channel

4165	- Buoy 2	44-06-20.837N 069-05-58.334W				Red nun.	
4170	- Buoy 3	44-06-24.996N 069-06-02.772W				Green can.	
4173	*Rockland Harbor Bypass Lighted Buoy 4*	44-06-27.156N 069-06-02.050W	Fl R 2.5s		3	Red.	

(1) No.	(2) Name and Location	(3) Position	(4) Characteristic	(5) Height	(6) Range	(7) Structure	(8) Remarks
			MAINE - First District				

CAMDEN, ROCKPORT AND ROCKLAND HARBORS
Rockland Harbor
Rockland Harbor Bypass Channel

4175	- Buoy 5	44-06-27.290N 069-06-05.978W				Green can.	
4180	- Buoy 7	44-06-28.122N 069-06-11.890W				Green can.	
4185	- Buoy 8	44-06-29.935N 069-06-11.375W				Red nun.	
	Rockland Harbor						
4190	- Channel Junction Buoy	44-06-31.555N 069-06-13.915W				Green can with red bands.	
	Rockland Harbor Bypass Channel						
4195	- Buoy 9	44-06-37.575N 069-06-14.254W				Green can.	
4200	- Buoy 10	44-06-37.203N 069-06-12.443W				Red nun.	
4205	- Buoy 12	44-06-41.235N 069-06-07.695W				Red nun.	
	Rockland Harbor						
4210	- North Channel Buoy 1	44-06-35.715N 069-05-45.423W				Green can.	
4215	- North Channel Buoy 3	44-06-39.875N 069-05-57.494W				Green can.	
4220	- North Channel Buoy 5	44-06-41.225N 069-06-03.284W				Green can.	
4225	Lermond Cove Channel Buoy 2	44-06-29.211N 069-06-21.740W				Red nun.	
4230	Lermond Cove Channel Buoy 3	44-06-27.571N 069-06-22.749W				Green can.	
4235	- Town Channel Buoy 1	44-06-12.225N 069-06-01.491W				Green can.	
4240	- Town Channel Buoy 3	44-06-07.455N 069-06-11.305W				Green can.	
4245	Red City Channel Buoy 1	44-05-59.160N 069-05-47.100W				Green can.	Private aid.
4245.1	Red City Channel Buoy 2	44-06-00.660N 069-05-47.100W				Red nun.	Private aid.
4245.2	Red City Channel Buoy 3	44-05-59.880N 069-06-03.600W				Green can.	Private aid.
4245.3	Red City Channel Buoy 4	44-06-01.140N 069-06-03.600W				Red nun.	Private aid.
4245.4	Red City Channel Buoy 5	44-06-00.900N 069-06-15.900W				Green can.	Private aid.
4245.5	Red City Channel Buoy 6	44-06-01.980N 069-06-17.820W				Red nun.	Private aid.

PENOBSCOT BAY
West Penobscot Bay

4250	Robinson Rock Bell Buoy 12 Off southerly end of reef.	44-09-00.036N 068-59-05.010W				Red.	
4260	Brewster Point Ledge Buoy 1	44-07-51.104N 069-04-09.389W				Green can.	
4265	Ram Island Ledge Buoy 3	44-08-23.034N 069-04-15.159W				Green can.	
4270	Porterfield Ledge Daybeacon	44-09-14.629N 069-03-41.297W				NG on spindle on square stone pyramid.	
4275	Rockport Outer Bell Buoy RO	44-09-29.223N 069-03-11.975W				Red and white stripes.	
	Rockport Harbor						
4280	LOWELL ROCK LIGHT 2 On south end of rock.	44-09-46.262N 069-03-36.895W	Fl R 6s	25	5	TR on spindle.	
4285	Seal Ledge Daybeacon 4	44-10-29.036N 069-03-53.010W				TR on spindle.	

40

(1) No.	(2) Name and Location	(3) Position	(4) Characteristic	(5) Height	(6) Range	(7) Structure	(8) Remarks
	**MAINE - First District**						

PENOBSCOT BAY

West Penobscot Bay

(1) No.	(2) Name and Location	(3) Position	(4) Characteristic	(5) Height	(6) Range	(7) Structure	(8) Remarks
4295	Deadman Point Buoy 3	44-10-35.962N 069-02-44.083W				Green can.	
4305	*The Graves Lighted Gong Buoy 13*	44-10-55.751N 069-02-00.710W	Fl G 6s		5	Green.	

Camden Harbor
Private aids maintained from May 15 to Oct. 15.

(1) No.	(2) Name and Location	(3) Position	(4) Characteristic	(5) Height	(6) Range	(7) Structure	(8) Remarks
4310	CURTIS ISLAND LIGHT	44-12-04.954N 069-02-55.901W	Oc G 4s	52	6	White tower.	
4315	- Entrance Bell Buoy 2	44-12-00.221N 069-02-25.040W				Red.	
4320	Outer Ledge Buoy 4	44-12-10.841N 069-02-38.421W				Red nun.	
4325	Inner Ledges Buoy 6 At southwest point of ledges.	44-12-23.060N 069-02-52.641W				Red nun.	
4330	- Buoy 7	44-12-19.760N 069-03-07.121W				Green can.	
4335	- Bell Buoy CH	44-12-41.000N 069-02-16.189W				Red and white stripes.	
4340	NORTHEAST POINT LIGHT 2	44-12-30.720N 069-02-47.470W	Fl R 4s	20	5	TR on white skeleton tower, small white house.	
4345	Northeast Passage Ledge Buoy 1 Northeast of outer ledges.	44-12-27.310N 069-02-36.080W				Green can.	
4350	Inner Ledges Daybeacon 3	44-12-25.960N 069-02-46.958W				SG on iron spindle.	

West Penobscot Bay

(1) No.	(2) Name and Location	(3) Position	(4) Characteristic	(5) Height	(6) Range	(7) Structure	(8) Remarks
4355	Dillingham Ledge Buoy 1 East of Ledge	44-13-38.070N 069-01-48.967W				Green can.	
4360	*Ensign Island Lighted Bell Buoy 1*	44-13-31.641N 068-57-49.530W	Fl G 4s		4	Green.	
4365	Ensign Island Buoy 14	44-14-02.786N 068-58-08.369W				Red nun.	

PENOBSCOT RIVER

West Penobscot Bay

(1) No.	(2) Name and Location	(3) Position	(4) Characteristic	(5) Height	(6) Range	(7) Structure	(8) Remarks
4370	Lincolnville Bell Buoy 7	44-16-41.108N 068-59-42.881W				Green.	
4375	LINCOLNVILLE FERRY TERMINAL LIGHT N	44-16-50.400N 069-00-18.790W	F W	20		On pile.	Private aid.
4380	LINCOLNVILLE FERRY TERMINAL LIGHT S	44-16-49.620N 069-00-19.150W	F W	20		On pile.	Private aid.
4385	Haddock Ledge Buoy 2 25 yards southwest of ledge.	44-17-07.777N 068-59-24.231W				Red nun.	

Gilkey Harbor

(1) No.	(2) Name and Location	(3) Position	(4) Characteristic	(5) Height	(6) Range	(7) Structure	(8) Remarks
4390	*Grindel Point Lighted Bell Buoy 2*	44-16-46.998N 068-57-05.698W	Fl R 4s		4	Red.	
4395	ISLEBORO FERRY TERMINAL WEST LIGHT	44-16-49.700N 068-56-34.900W	F W	20		On pile.	Private aid.
4400	ISLEBORO FERRY TERMINAL EAST LIGHT	44-16-48.900N 068-56-36.960W	F W	20		On pile.	Private aid.
4405	GRINDEL POINT LIGHT	44-16-53.187N 068-56-35.007W	Fl W 4s	39	7		
4410	Spruce Island Point Buoy 7	44-16-39.356N 068-56-23.939W				Green can.	
4415	Lobster Rock Buoy 6	44-16-38.426N 068-55-52.432W				Red nun.	

PENOBSCOT BAY

West Penobscot Bay

Gilkey Harbor

(1) No.	(2) Name and Location	(3) Position	(4) Characteristic	(5) Height	(6) Range	(7) Structure	(8) Remarks
4420	Thrumcap Ledge Buoy 4	44-15-51.997N 068-55-45.675W				Red nun.	
4425	Minot Ledge Buoy 2	44-14-45.141N 068-56-28.966W				Red nun.	

(1) No.	(2) Name and Location	(3) Position	(4) Characteristic	(5) Height	(6) Range	(7) Structure	(8) Remarks
			MAINE - First District				

PENOBSCOT RIVER
West Penobscot Bay

| 4435 | *Isleboro Island Lighted Bell Buoy II* | 44-23-12.322N 068-54-54.500W | Mo (A) W | | 4 | Red and white stripes with red spherical topmark. | |

Belfast Harbor

4445	*Steels Ledge Lighted Bell Buoy 2* South of 14 foot spot.	44-25-02.580N 068-58-17.281W	Fl R 4s		4	Red.	
4446	- *Lighted Buoy 2A*	44-25-22.838N 068-58-58.804W	Fl R 6s		3	Red.	Replaced by nun from Oct 1 to May 1.
4447	- Buoy 4	44-25-33.036N 068-59-24.010W				Red nun.	
4448	- *Lighted Buoy 3*	44-25-19.239N 068-59-02.418W	Fl G 6s		3	Green.	Replaced by can from Oct 1 to May 1.
4450	- Buoy 6	44-25-46.226N 069-00-08.457W				Red nun.	

West Penobscot Bay

| 4452 | *Moose Point Isolated Danger Lighted Buoy DMP* | 44-24-51.216N 068-55-04.510W | Fl (2)W 5s | | 4 | Black and red bands with two black spherical topmarks. | |
| 4454 | *University of Maine Belfast Bay Lighted Research Buoy* | 44-23-31.620N 068-57-57.060W | Fl Y 20s | | | Yellow. | Property of The University of Maine. Private aid. |

Searsport Harbor

4455	Sears Island Bell Buoy 2 On south end of shoal.	44-25-21.630N 068-53-32.415W				Red.	
4460	Sears Island Buoy 4	44-26-09.769N 068-53-51.386W				Red nun.	
4465	*Mack Point Channel Lighted Bell Buoy 5*	44-26-34.579N 068-54-07.557W	Fl G 4s		5	Green.	
4470	*Mack Point Channel Lighted Buoy 6*	44-26-42.715N 068-53-41.240W	Fl R 4s		4	Red.	
4475	Long Cove Ledge Buoy 7	44-26-44.854N 068-54-11.227W				Green can.	
4480	Long Cove Ledge Isolated Danger Buoy DLC West of Ledge	44-26-43.612N 068-54-32.481W				Black and red bands with two black spherical topmarks; can.	

Stockton Harbor

4485	- *Entrance Shoal Lighted Gong Buoy 1* South of 23-foot spot.	44-25-03.741N 068-52-27.004W	Fl G 4s		4	Green.	
4495	- Entrance Buoy 4 South of Defence Head.	44-26-15.490N 068-51-39.103W				Red nun.	
4500	- Entrance Buoy 5	44-26-26.499N 068-51-58.264W				Green can.	
4505	- Entrance Buoy 6	44-27-01.759N 068-51-57.374W				Red nun.	

PENOBSCOT BAY AND APPROACHES
Two Bush Channel

4520	Rockweed Shoal Buoy 7 Marks 32-foot shoal.	43-58-31.960N 069-01-21.848W				Green can.	
4525	Halibut Rock Buoy 2B	43-59-00.722N 069-02-58.953W				Red nun.	
4530	- Shoal Isolated Danger Buoy DTBS Northeast of 15-foot shoal.	43-57-01.003N 069-01-57.183W				Black and red bands with two black spherical topmarks; can.	
4535	Northern Triangles Buoy 2	43-56-10.126N 069-02-34.180W				Red nun.	

(1) No.	(2) Name and Location	(3) Position	(4) Characteristic	(5) Height	(6) Range	(7) Structure	(8) Remarks
			MAINE - First District				

PENOBSCOT BAY AND APPROACHES

Two Bush Channel

(1) No.	(2) Name and Location	(3) Position	(4) Characteristic	(5) Height	(6) Range	(7) Structure	(8) Remarks
4540	**Two Bush Island Light**	43-57-51.291N 069-04-26.067W	Fl W 5s	65	W 21 R 15	White tower. 42	Red from 061° to 247°. Emergency light of reduced intensity when main light is extinguished. HORN: 1 blast ev 15s (2s bl). MRASS -Fog signal is radio activated, during times of reduced visibility, turn marine VHF-FM radio to channel 83A/157.175Mhz. Key microphone 5 times consecutively, to activate fog signal for 60 minutes.
4550	- Buoy 6	43-56-41.787N 069-04-03.861W				Red nun.	
4555	*Two Bush Ledge Lighted Bell Buoy 5TB* Marks south side of 28-foot shoal.	43-56-47.460N 069-04-54.922W	Fl G 4s		4	Green.	
4560	Alden Rock Isolated Danger Buoy DAR 35 yards, 212° from 4-foot spot.	43-55-21.442N 069-04-00.757W				Black and red bands with two black spherical topmarks; can.	
4565	Crow Island Ledge Buoy 2CI	43-57-22.865N 069-06-05.138W				Red nun.	
4570	Devils Half Acre Buoy 4	43-55-36.289N 069-08-52.179W				Red nun.	

Muscle Ridge Channel

(1) No.	(2) Name and Location	(3) Position	(4) Characteristic	(5) Height	(6) Range	(7) Structure	(8) Remarks
4575	South Breaker Bell Buoy 2SB	43-58-17.122N 069-07-31.734W				Red.	
4580	WHITEHEAD LIGHT	43-58-43.405N 069-07-27.407W	Oc G 4s	75	6	Gray Granite tower.	Emergency light of reduced intensity when main light is extinguished. HORN: 2 blasts ev 30s (2s bl-2s si-2s bl-24s si). MRASS-Fog signal is radio activated, during times of reduced visibility, turn marine VHF-FM radio to channel 83A/157.175Mhz. Key microphone 5 times consecutively, to activate fog signal for 60 minutes.
4585	Yellow Ledge Daybeacon 2 On southwest end of ledge.	43-58-49.692N 069-06-51.253W				TR on spindle.	
4590	Seal Island Ledge Buoy 3	43-59-05.103N 069-07-05.376W				Green can.	
4595	Lower Gangway Ledge Buoy 4	43-59-14.712N 069-06-47.803W				Red nun.	
4600	Burnt Island Ledge Buoy Southwest of ledge.	43-59-20.592N 069-06-59.703W				Green and red bands; can.	
4605	Hurricane Ledge Buoy 6	43-59-38.842N 069-06-08.262W				Red nun.	
4610	Sunken Ledge Buoy 7	44-00-17.551N 069-06-03.381W				Green can.	
4615	Garden Island Ledge Daybeacon 9	44-00-47.020N 069-05-44.920W				SG on spindle.	
4620	Oak Island Ledge Buoy 10	44-00-55.581N 069-04-52.488W				Red nun.	
4625	Otter Island Ledge Daybeacon 11	44-01-30.390N 069-04-50.367W				SG on spindle.	
4630	Otter Island Daybeacon 12	44-01-21.190N 069-04-24.186W				TR on spindle.	
4635	Ash Island Ledge Buoy 13 Close to south end of ledge.	44-01-51.713N 069-04-21.334W				Green can.	
4640	Upper Gangway Ledge Buoy Close to southwest end of ledge.	44-01-55.070N 069-04-04.475W				Red nun with green bands.	

(1) No.	(2) Name and Location	(3) Position	(4) Characteristic	(5) Height	(6) Range	(7) Structure	(8) Remarks

MAINE - First District

PENOBSCOT BAY AND APPROACHES

Muscle Ridge Channel

4645	Ash Island Rock Buoy 15 SE of rocks	44-02-06.830N 069-04-08.685W				Green can.	
4650	Inner Grindstone Ledge Buoy 16 NW of 8 foot spot	44-02-02.190N 069-03-39.554W				Red nun.	
4655	Ash Island Bell Buoy 17 SE of shoal	44-02-22.109N 069-03-55.985W				Green.	
4660	Emery Ledge Buoy Southeast of ledge.	44-02-48.179N 069-03-11.222W				Green can with red bands.	
4665	Northwest Ledge Buoy 21 South of 4 foot spot	44-02-52.849N 069-02-53.012W				Green can.	
4670	Grindstone Ledge Buoy 22 NW of 2 foot spot	44-02-52.325N 069-02-38.580W				Red nun.	
4675	Sheep Island Shoals Buoy 23 South of shoals	44-03-17.829N 069-02-44.151W				Green can.	

Owls Head Bay

4680	Emery Island Daybeacon 1	44-03-47.858N 069-03-50.434W				SG on iron spindle.	
4685	Hendrickson Point Buoy 3	44-04-02.870N 069-03-30.869W				Green can.	
4690	Sheep Island Bar Buoy 4	44-04-02.538N 069-03-20.521W				Red nun.	
4695	Dodge Point Ledge Daybeacon 5	44-05-08.196N 069-02-45.168W				SG on spindle.	
4700	Sprucehead Island Ledge Buoy 4	43-59-37.049N 069-07-30.929W				Red nun.	

Wheeler Bay

4705	- Buoy 1 South of Norton Island Ledges	43-58-11.833N 069-09-21.368W				Green can.	
4710	- Buoy 3 Off ledge.	43-58-45.532N 069-09-54.769W				Green can.	
4715	- Junction Buoy	43-59-20.393N 069-09-59.120W				Green can with red bands.	

MUSCONGUS BAY

Tenants Harbor Approach
Aids maintained from May 15 to Oct. 15.

4720	Long Cove Buoy 2	43-58-00.606N 069-11-30.304W				Red nun.	
4725	- *Lighted Bell Buoy 1*	43-57-42.553N 069-10-52.551W	Fl G 6s		3	Green.	
4727	Tenants Harbor Channel Buoy 1	43-57-50.160N 069-12-00.660W				Green can.	Private aid.
4727.1	Tenants Harbor Channel Buoy 2	43-57-51.240N 069-12-00.420W				Red nun.	Private aid.
4727.2	Tenants Harbor Channel Buoy 3	43-57-50.160N 069-12-05.100W				Green can.	Private aid.
4727.3	Tenants Harbor Channel Buoy 4	43-57-51.120N 069-12-04.920W				Red nun.	Private aid.
4727.4	Tenants Harbor Channel Buoy 5	43-57-50.100N 069-12-09.900W				Green can.	Private aid.
4727.5	Tenants Harbor Channel Buoy 6	43-57-51.060N 069-12-10.320W				Red nun.	Private aid.
4727.6	Tenants Harbor Channel Buoy 7	43-57-49.920N 069-12-15.360W				Green can.	Private aid.
4727.7	Tenants Harbor Channel Buoy 8	43-57-51.060N 069-12-16.140W				Red nun.	Private aid.
4727.8	Tenants Harbor Channel Buoy 9	43-57-50.450N 069-12-21.360W				Green can.	Private aid.
4727.9	Tenants Harbor Channel Buoy 10	43-57-51.660N 069-12-21.300W				Red nun.	Private aid.

PENOBSCOT BAY AND APPROACHES

4730	Hart Ledge Buoy 1 East of ledge	43-56-57.743N 069-11-24.242W				Green can.	

(1) No.	(2) Name and Location	(3) Position	(4) Characteristic	(5) Height	(6) Range	(7) Structure	(8) Remarks
			MAINE - First District				
	PENOBSCOT BAY AND APPROACHES						
4735	Wheeler Rocks Bell Buoy 1W	43-54-31.824N 069-06-51.272W				Green.	
4740	*Marshall Point Lighted Buoy MP*	43-55-18.334N 069-10-52.171W	Mo (A) W		4	Red and white stripes with red spherical topmark.	
4745	Metinic Island Ledge Buoy MI Southwest of ledge.	43-53-40.335N 069-10-08.169W				Green can with red bands.	
4750	Black Ledges Buoy 3 NW of 6 foot spot	43-51-42.186N 069-12-00.962W				Green can.	
4755	Old Cilley Ledge Bell Buoy 2 OC	43-53-12.456N 069-14-32.938W				Red.	
	MUSCONGUS BAY						
	Port Clyde Approach						
4760	Mosquito Island Bell Buoy 2	43-54-43.152N 069-13-04.692W				Red.	
4765	Mosquito Island Ledge Buoy 4 South of 3 foot spot	43-55-04.836N 069-14-33.250W				Red nun.	
4770	Gunning Rocks Buoy 5 North of 4 foot spot	43-54-53.654N 069-14-46.718W				Green can.	
4775	Marshall Ledge Buoy 6	43-54-51.784N 069-15-35.228W				Red nun.	
4780	**Marshall Point Light**	43-55-02.754N 069-15-40.578W	F W	30	13	White cylindrical tower. 31	Lighted throughout 24 hours. HORN: 1 blast ev 10s (1s bl). MRASS-Fog signal is radio activated, during times of reduced visibility, turn marine VHF-FM radio to channel 83A/157.175Mhz. Key microphone 5 times consecutively, to activate fog signal for 60 minutes.
4785	Allen Ledge Buoy 7 North of rock	43-54-51.394N 069-16-06.488W				Green can.	
4790	Marshall Point Ledge Buoy 2	43-55-06.434N 069-15-48.768W				Red nun.	
4795	Hupper Island Ledge Buoy 3	43-55-21.536N 069-15-48.010W				Green can.	
4796	Port Clyde Channel Buoy 1	43-55-42.840N 069-15-51.480W				Green can.	Private aid.
4797	Port Clyde Channel Buoy 2	43-55-44.160N 069-15-50.580W				Red nun.	Private aid.
4798	Port Clyde Channel Buoy 3	43-55-47.580N 069-15-55.320W				Green can.	Private aid.
4799	Port Clyde Channel Buoy 4	43-55-49.380N 069-15-53.520W				Red nun.	Private aid.
4800	Channel Rock Isolated Danger Buoy DCR	43-56-08.936N 069-16-49.010W				Black and red bands with two black spherical topmarks; can.	
4803	Kelp Ledges Buoy 2	43-55-02.043N 069-17-06.983W				Red nun.	
4805	Hupper Rocks Buoy 8 SE of 6 foot spot	43-54-39.724N 069-16-44.738W				Red nun.	
4810	The Sisters Buoy 9 NW of rocks	43-54-16.004N 069-17-03.128W				Green can.	
4820	Gig Rock Bell Buoy 11 Northwest of rock.	43-53-52.404N 069-17-40.658W				Green.	
4825	Griffen Ledge Buoy 12	43-53-27.336N 069-18-24.910W				Red nun.	
	Muscongus Bay						
4830	Two Bush Island Rock Buoy 1	43-55-18.333N 069-18-46.279W				Green can.	
4835	Seavey Island Ledge Buoy 2	43-55-28.533N 069-18-50.739W				Red nun.	

(1) No.	(2) Name and Location	(3) Position	(4) Characteristic	(5) Height	(6) Range	(7) Structure	(8) Remarks
			MAINE - First District				
MUSCONGUS BAY							
St. George River							
4840	Jenks Ledge Buoy 2JL West of rock.	43-55-25.513N 069-19-23.179W				Red nun.	
4845	Goose Rock Ledge Buoy 1 South of 9 foot spot	43-56-08.573N 069-18-38.819W				Green can.	
4850	Gay Cove Ledge Buoy 3 South of 5 foot spot	43-56-38.078N 069-17-57.271W				Green can.	
4855	St.George River Buoy 4 Buoy marks rock.	43-56-55.013N 069-16-49.409W				Red nun.	
4860	- Buoy 5 South of 5 foot spot	43-57-21.243N 069-17-08.809W				Green can.	
4865	- Buoy 7	43-58-24.332N 069-16-16.179W				Green can.	
4870	- Buoy 9 East of 9 foot spot	43-59-53.725N 069-14-15.606W				Green can.	
4875	- Buoy 11	44-00-56.832N 069-13-03.041W				Green can.	
4880	- Buoy 13	44-02-14.437N 069-12-01.455W				Green can.	
4885	- Buoy 14	44-02-50.518N 069-11-41.100W				Red nun.	
4890	- Buoy 15	44-03-24.566N 069-11-19.963W				Green can.	
4895	- Buoy 16	44-03-52.777N 069-10-59.298W				Red nun.	
4900	- Buoy 17	44-03-59.779N 069-10-55.568W				Green can.	Maintained from Apr .15 to Oct. 1.
4910	- Buoy 19	44-04-07.037N 069-10-46.993W				Green can.	Maintained from Apr .15 to Oct. 1.
4915	- LIGHT 21	44-04-11.196N 069-10-46.764W	Fl W 6s	14	4	SG on white skeleton tower.	
4916	- Buoy 21A	44-04-10.221N 069-10-44.289W				Green can.	Maintained from Apr .15 to Oct. 1.
4917	- Buoy 22	44-04-11.670N 069-10-42.994W				Red nun.	Maintained from Apr .15 to Oct. 1.
4918	- Buoy 22A	44-04-13.347N 069-10-43.423W				Red nun.	Maintained from May 15 to Oct. 15.
4920	- Buoy 23	44-04-12.297N 069-10-44.277W				Green can.	Maintained from Apr .15 to Oct. 1.
	Monhegan Island Approach						
4925 20	**Monhegan Island Light**	43-45-53.318N 069-18-56.991W	Fl W 15s	178	20	White tower. 47	Within 3 miles of island the light is obscured between west and southwest. Emergency light of reduced intensity when main light is extinguished.
PENOBSCOT BAY AND APPROACHES							
4940	Manana Island VAIS 14M	43-46-35.650N 069-22-35.720W					AIS: MMSI 993672353
MUSCONGUS BAY							
Monhegan Island Approach							
4945	Monhegan Island Gong Buoy 3 Northerly of Eastern Duck Rock.	43-46-50.859N 069-18-43.196W				Green.	
4950	*Duck Rocks Lighted Bell Buoy 5* Northerly of 28-foot shoal.	43-46-55.209N 069-19-49.386W	Fl G 2.5s		3	Green.	
4955	Manana Island Northwest Rock Buoy 7	43-46-02.371N 069-19-44.822W				Green can.	

(1) No.	(2) Name and Location	(3) Position	(4) Characteristic	(5) Height	(6) Range	(7) Structure	(8) Remarks
			MAINE - First District				
	MUSCONGUS BAY						
	Muscongus Bay Approach						
4960	Moser Ledge Isolated Danger Buoy DM South of ledge.	43-48-40.145N 069-25-43.794W				Black and red bands with two black spherical topmarks; can.	
4965	*Old Man Ledge Lighted Whistle Buoy 2 OM* South of ledge.	43-50-16.663N 069-18-50.266W	Fl R 4s		4	Red.	
	Muscongus Bay						
4970	New Harbor Sunken Ledge Buoy 16	43-51-23.986N 069-26-50.129W				Red nun.	
4975	Western Egg Rock Breakers Buoy 1 South of 4 foot spot	43-52-47.439N 069-24-23.899W				Green can.	
4980	FRANKLIN ISLAND LIGHT	43-53-31.436N 069-22-28.610W	Fl W 6s	57	8	White tower.	Obscured by trees from 253° to 352°.
4990	Eastern Egg Rock Daybeacon 15 On north end of rock.	43-51-43.154N 069-22-54.584W				SG on pile.	
4995	Egg Rock North Ledge Buoy 14 South eastern most rock	43-51-52.426N 069-22-49.818W				Red nun.	
5000	Seal Ledges Buoy 13 North of 7 foot shoal.	43-52-34.895N 069-20-28.558W				Green can.	
5005	The Kegs Daybeacon TK	43-53-35.463N 069-20-33.043W				NB on pile.	
5011	Devils Back Buoy 3 South of rock	43-53-45.036N 069-24-09.011W				Green can.	
5016	Wreck Island Ledge Buoy 4 SW of southern 3 foot spot	43-54-45.036N 069-24-18.011W				Red nun.	
5021	Round Rock Buoy 5 East of 4 foot spot	43-55-17.036N 069-24-35.011W				Green can.	
5026	Jones Garden Buoy 6	43-55-55.314N 069-23-30.062W				Red nun.	
5030	Cow Island Sunken Ledges Buoy 8 South of 2 foot spot	43-56-44.551N 069-23-59.241W				Red nun.	
	Friendship Harbor						
5035	Morse Ledge Daybeacon 1 On rock.	43-56-28.920N 069-20-20.508W				SG on pile.	
5040	Gay Island Buoy 2 SW of 3 foot spot	43-56-43.992N 069-19-21.739W				Red nun.	
5045	Northeast Point Reef Buoy 3 Marks Northeastern most corner of shoal	43-57-21.882N 069-18-55.170W				Green can.	
5050	Crotch Island Ledges Buoy 4 On south end of ledges.	43-57-33.782N 069-19-26.640W				Red nun.	
5055	Garrison Island Rock Buoy 6	43-57-54.861N 069-19-57.410W				Red nun.	
5060	Garrison Island Buoy 7	43-58-12.211N 069-20-00.440W				Green can.	
5065	Murphy Ledge Daybeacon 9	43-57-59.664N 069-20-24.816W				SG on pile.	
5070	Jameson Point Ledge Daybeacon 10	43-58-02.721N 069-20-41.051W				TR on pile.	
5075	Martin Point Buoy 12 Marks southern of shoal	43-57-45.798N 069-21-58.933W				Red nun.	
	Muscongus Bay						
5080	Cow Island Buoy 1	43-58-06.820N 069-23-22.592W				Green can.	
5085	Cow Island Buoy 3	43-58-07.590N 069-23-32.792W				Green can.	
5090	Palmer Island Buoy 4	43-58-10.560N 069-24-00.192W				Red nun.	

(1) No.	(2) Name and Location	(3) Position	(4) Characteristic	(5) Height	(6) Range	(7) Structure	(8) Remarks
			MAINE - First District				
MUSCONGUS BAY							
Hockomock Channel							
5100	Oar Island Ledge Buoy 9	43-59-20.869N 069-24-11.692W				Green can.	
5105	Northeast Point Ledges Buoy 10	44-00-44.328N 069-23-08.322W				Red nun.	
Flying Passage							
5110	Bremen Long Island Daybeacon 1	44-00-23.880N 069-22-37.956W				SG on pile.	
Medomak River							
5115	- Buoy 12	44-01-34.327N 069-22-27.171W				Red nun.	
5120	- Buoy 13	44-01-36.917N 069-22-24.931W				Green can.	
5125	- Buoy 15	44-02-19.176N 069-21-42.970W				Green can.	
5130	- Buoy 17	44-03-04.156N 069-21-33.409W				Green can.	
5130.1	- Buoy 18	44-03-32.731N 069-21-43.901W				Red nun.	Maintained from Apr. 15 to Oct. 1.
5130.2	- Buoy 20	44-04-02.178N 069-22-40.779W				Red nun.	Maintained from Apr. 15 to Oct. 1.
5130.3	- Buoy 22	44-04-21.438N 069-23-13.524W				Red nun.	Maintained from Apr. 15 to Oct. 1.
5130.4	- Buoy 24	44-04-28.036N 069-23-15.011W				Red nun.	Maintained from Apr. 15 to Oct. 1.
5130.5	- Buoy 25	44-04-56.640N 069-23-00.779W				Green can.	Maintained from Apr. 15 to Oct. 1.
5130.6	- Buoy 26	44-05-13.686N 069-22-51.935W				Red nun.	Maintained from Apr. 15 to Oct. 1.
5130.7	- Buoy 27	44-05-28.590N 069-22-35.177W				Green can.	Maintained from Apr. 15 to Oct. 1.
Muscongus Bay							
Southwest Approach							
5135	Pemaquid Ledge Buoy PL Southeast of ledge.	43-48-53.451N 069-31-13.984W				Green and red bands; can.	
5140	Pemaquid Point Gong Buoy 2	43-49-42.517N 069-30-54.057W				Red.	
5145	**Pemaquid Point Light**	43-50-12.336N 069-30-21.011W	Fl W 6s	79	14	White conical tower. 79	
5150	*New Harbor Lighted Bell Buoy NH*	43-52-25.995N 069-28-43.189W	Mo (A) W		4	Red and white stripes with red spherical topmark.	
5155	New Harbor Buoy 4	43-52-27.864N 069-29-09.509W				Red nun.	
5160	New Harbor Daybeacon 5 On ledge.	43-52-28.284N 069-29-16.968W				SG on pile.	
Muscongus Sound							
5165	Webber Sunken Ledge Buoy 2 SW of rock	43-53-19.604N 069-27-00.460W				Red nun.	
5170	Browns Head Buoy 4 West of 13 foot spot	43-53-53.033N 069-27-19.980W				Red nun.	
5175	Bar Island Ledge Buoy 6	43-54-28.095N 069-26-59.241W				Red nun.	
5180	Poland South Ledge Buoy 7	43-55-27.082N 069-26-50.581W				Green can.	
5185	Poland North Ledge Buoy 9	43-55-47.034N 069-26-58.996W				Green can.	
5190	Round Pond Entrance Buoy 1	43-56-36.291N 069-27-04.561W				Green can.	

(1) No.	(2) Name and Location	(3) Position	(4) Characteristic	(5) Height	(6) Range	(7) Structure	(8) Remarks
			MAINE - First District				
	MUSCONGUS BAY						
	Muscongus Sound						
5195	Ram Ledges Halftide Buoy 11 Off south end of ledge.	43-58-13.669N 069-26-00.582W				Green can.	
5200	Hockomock Point Buoy 13	43-58-36.319N 069-25-34.032W				Green can.	
5205	Hockomock Point Buoy 15 Marks rock off point.	43-58-40.329N 069-25-24.712W				Green can.	
5207	Crow Island North Ledge Buoy 16	43-58-51.087N 069-24-42.120W				Red nun.	
	DAMARISCOTTA, SHEEPSCOT AND KENNEBEC RIVERS						
	Johns Bay						
5210	Corvette Ledge Buoy 1	43-52-18.993N 069-32-46.628W				Green can.	
5215	McFarlands Ledges Buoy 2	43-52-29.033N 069-32-51.368W				Red nun.	
	Pemaquid River						
5235	Johns River Ledge Buoy 4	43-53-39.941N 069-32-35.658W				Red nun.	
	Thread of Life						
5240	- Buoy 1	43-49-42.036N 069-33-15.011W				Green can.	Leave on starboard hand when upbound Damariscotta River.
5245	- Buoy 2	43-50-21.743N 069-32-56.798W				Red nun.	
5250	- Buoy 3 Marks end of reef.	43-50-29.625N 069-32-55.917W				Green can.	
	Damariscotta River						
5255	- Approach Buoy 1	43-46-12.341N 069-33-40.175W				Green can.	
5260	Hypocrite Ledge Daybeacon H	43-47-24.978N 069-35-27.365W				NR on pile.	
5265	Hypocrite Ledge Buoy 1	43-48-15.538N 069-35-08.505W				Green can.	
5270	*Hypocrite Ledge Lighted Bell Buoy HL*	43-48-23.948N 069-34-47.756W	Mo (A) W		4	Red and white stripes with red spherical topmark.	
5275	- Junction Gong Buoy DR	43-49-09.396N 069-34-49.297W				Green and red bands.	
5280	Little River Daybeacon 1	43-49-17.226N 069-34-57.030W				Green cylinder on monopile.	
5285	Little River Buoy 2	43-49-19.922N 069-34-57.317W				Red nun.	
5290	- Buoy 2 West of ledge, dry at low water.	43-49-17.475N 069-34-12.009W				Red nun.	
5295	- Buoy 4	43-50-06.965N 069-34-00.036W				Red nun.	
	Christmas Cove						
5300	Foster Point Shoal Buoy FP Marks 8 foot spot	43-50-27.635N 069-34-00.407W				Red nun with green bands.	
5305	Middle Ledge Daybeacon 2	43-50-43.136N 069-33-26.711W				TR on pile.	
5310	North Ledge Daybeacon 3	43-50-46.260N 069-33-25.878W				SG on pile.	
5315	Steamboat Wharf Daybeacon 4 On point of rock.	43-50-42.972N 069-33-17.022W				TR on pile.	
	Damariscotta River						
5320	- Buoy 6	43-51-25.614N 069-34-01.507W				Red nun.	
5325	The Gut Daybeacon 2 On ledge.	43-51-38.976N 069-33-39.978W				TR on pile.	
5330	The Gut Daybeacon 3	43-51-43.260N 069-33-33.228W				SG on pile.	

(1) No.	(2) Name and Location	(3) Position	(4) Characteristic	(5) Height	(6) Range	(7) Structure	(8) Remarks

MAINE - First District

DAMARISCOTTA, SHEEPSCOT AND KENNEBEC RIVERS

Damariscotta River

(1) No.	(2) Name and Location	(3) Position	(4) Characteristic	(5) Height	(6) Range	(7) Structure	(8) Remarks
5335	- Buoy 7 Off east side of Kelp Ledge.	43-51-51.072N 069-34-43.227W				Green can.	
5340	- Buoy 9	43-52-10.962N 069-34-57.517W				Green can.	
5345	- Buoy 11	43-53-01.431N 069-34-59.208W				Green can.	Buoy may partially or fully submerge during maximum currents or flood waters.
5350	- Buoy 12	43-53-12.843N 069-34-56.678W				Red nun.	
5353	UM Lowe's Cove LOBO Lighted Research Buoy	43-55-50.700N 069-34-46.500W	Fl Y 20s			Yellow.	Property of the University of Maine. Seasonal Mar 25 - Dec 31. Private aid.
5355	- Buoy 13	43-55-54.607N 069-35-08.078W				Green can.	
5360	- Buoy 14	43-57-08.686N 069-34-40.289W				Red nun.	
5365	Merry Island Daybeacon 15	43-57-21.114N 069-34-32.802W				SG on pile.	
5370	Glidden Ledge Daybeacon 16	43-58-11.725N 069-34-23.580W				TR on iron spindle.	
5373	UM UDRE LOBO Lighted Research Buoy	43-59-58.740N 069-32-18.906W	Fl Y 20s			Yellow.	Property of the University of Maine. Seasonal Mar 03 - Dec 31. Private aid.
5375	- Buoy 17	44-00-04.894N 069-32-32.812W				Green can.	
5380	Perkins Point Daybeacon 19 On ledge.	44-00-25.212N 069-32-44.087W				SG on pile.	
5385	- Buoy 20	44-00-43.002N 069-32-49.621W				Red nun.	
5390	- Buoy 21	44-01-19.077N 069-32-24.411W				Green can.	
5395	- Buoy 23	44-01-29.319N 069-32-16.242W				Green can.	
5400	- Buoy 24	44-01-48.318N 069-32-13.301W				Red nun.	
5401	- Buoy 26	44-01-51.746N 069-32-08.368W				Red nun.	Private aid.
5402	- Buoy 28	44-01-55.540N 069-32-05.380W				Red nun.	Private aid.
	Damariscove Island Approach						
5405	Bantam Rock Lighted Buoy 2BR	43-43-40.571N 069-37-33.920W	Fl R 4s		4	Red.	
5410	The Motions Gong Buoy TM	43-44-46.162N 069-37-06.314W				Red and white stripes.	
	Fisherman Island Passage						
5415	Ram Island Ledge Buoy 3 North of 12 foot spot	43-48-22.407N 069-35-47.235W				Green can.	
5420	RAM ISLAND LIGHT	43-48-13.536N 069-35-57.111W	Iso R 6s (2W sectors)	36	W 11 R 9 W 9	White tower.	White from 258° to 261° and from 030° to 046°, covers fairways. HORN: 1 blast ev 30s (3s bl). Fog signal is radio activated, during times of reduced visibility, turn marine VHF-FM radio to channel 83A/157.175Mhz. Key microphone 5 times consecutively, to activate fog signal for 45 minutes.
5425	Gangway Ledge Buoy 4	43-48-28.613N 069-36-10.520W				Red nun.	
5430	Dictator Ledge Buoy 6	43-48-27.467N 069-36-24.015W				Red nun.	

(1) No.	(2) Name and Location	(3) Position	(4) Characteristic	(5) Height	(6) Range	(7) Structure	(8) Remarks
			MAINE - First District				
	DAMARISCOTTA, SHEEPSCOT AND KENNEBEC RIVERS						
	Fisherman Island Passage						
5435	Card Ledge Buoy 8	43-48-38.337N 069-36-32.315W				Red nun.	
	Linekin Bay						
5440	Spruce Point Ledges Buoy 1 At south point of ledges.	43-49-20.206N 069-37-01.386W				Green can.	
5445	Spruce Point Ledges Buoy 2 At north point of ledges.	43-49-30.735N 069-37-12.335W				Red nun.	
5450	- Buoy 2	43-50-06.504N 069-35-58.016W				Red nun.	
5455	Cabbage Island Buoy 3	43-50-14.401N 069-36-24.299W				Green can.	
5460	- Buoy 4	43-50-32.764N 069-35-58.365W				Red nun.	
5465	- Buoy 6	43-50-58.123N 069-35-38.056W				Red nun.	
5470	Seal Rock Buoy 5	43-50-51.283N 069-36-03.766W				Green can.	
5475	Fish Hawk Island Buoy 7	43-51-22.333N 069-35-40.176W				Green can.	
	Booth Bay						
5480	Cuckolds Bell Buoy 1C	43-46-22.910N 069-39-00.644W				Green.	
5485	**The Cuckolds Light**	43-46-46.236N 069-39-00.028W	Fl (2)W 6s 1s fl 1s ec. 1s fl 3s ec.	59	12	White octagonal tower on dwelling. 59	HORN: 1 blast ev 15s (2s bl). MRASS Fog signal is radio activated, during times of reduced visibility, turn marine VHF-FM radio to channel 83A/157.175Mhz. Key microphone 5 times consecutively, to activate fog signal for 45 minutes.
5495	Squirrel Cove Daybeacon 2 Marks rock.	43-48-17.096N 069-38-10.604W				TR on pile.	
5500	*Squirrel Island Ledge Lighted Buoy 4* Northwest of ledge.	43-48-58.420N 069-38-16.355W	Fl R 2.5s		3	Red.	
5505	Pig Cove Daybeacon 5	43-49-03.265N 069-38-43.585W				SG on pile.	
5510	Burnt Island Ledge Buoy BL	43-49-17.012N 069-38-24.001W				Green and red bands; can.	
5515	Capitol Island Daybeacon 1 On ledge.	43-49-25.836N 069-38-43.311W				SG on pile.	
5520	BURNT ISLAND LIGHT	43-49-30.736N 069-38-24.811W	Fl R 6s (2W sectors)	61	W 8 W 8 R 6 R 6	White conical tower.	White from 307° to 316°, and from 355° to 008°, covers fairways. Emergency light of reduced intensity when main light is extinguished. HORN: 1 blast ev 10s (1s bl). MRASS-Fog signal is radio activated, during times of reduced visibility, turn marine VHF-FM radio to channel 83A/157.175Mhz. Key microphone 5 times consecutively, to activate fog signal for 60 minutes.
5525	Tumbler Island Ledge Buoy 6	43-49-41.587N 069-37-46.980W				Red nun.	
5530	*Tumbler Island Lighted Buoy 8*	43-50-17.634N 069-38-13.196W	Fl R 4s		3	Red.	
5531	Tumbler Island East Daybeacon 2	43-50-17.580N 069-37-56.100W				Private aid.	
5535	*- Lighted Buoy 9*	43-50-46.584N 069-37-44.454W	Fl G 4s		3	Green.	Remove when endangered by ice.

(1) No.	(2) Name and Location	(3) Position	(4) Characteristic	(5) Height	(6) Range	(7) Structure	(8) Remarks
			MAINE - First District				
	DAMARISCOTTA, SHEEPSCOT AND KENNEBEC RIVERS						
	Booth Bay						
5535.1	McFarland Island Daybeacon 11	43-50-52.380N 069-37-42.600W				SG on pile.	Private aid.
5536	Signal Point Marina Daybeacon 2	43-50-59.480N 069-38-06.100W				TR on pile.	Private aid.
5540	Boothbay Harbor Mooring Buoy C	43-50-46.999N 069-38-14.312W				White with blue band.	
5545	McFarland Island Daybeacon	43-50-54.690N 069-37-49.800W				TR on spindle.	Private aid.
	Townsend Gut						
5555	- Buoy 2	43-50-07.293N 069-38-57.735W				Red nun.	
5560	- Buoy 4	43-50-31.392N 069-39-11.505W				Red nun.	
5565	CAMERON POINT LIGHT 7 On ledge.	43-51-05.531N 069-40-06.175W	Fl G 4s	24	4	SG on skeleton tower.	
5570	Cameron Point Buoy 6	43-51-04.321N 069-40-02.145W				Red nun.	
	Sheepscot Bay Approach						
5585	*Mile Ledge Lighted Bell Buoy 20ML* South side of ledge.	43-41-24.336N 069-45-17.911W	Q R		3	Red.	
5590 35	**Seguin Light**	43-42-26.936N 069-45-28.911W	F W	180	14	53	HORN: 2 blasts ev 20s (2s bl-2s si-2s bl-14s si). MRASS-Fog signal is radio activated, during times of reduced visibility, turn marine VHF-FM radio to channel 83A/157.175Mhz. Key microphone 5 times consecutively, to activate fog signal for 60 minutes.
5592	Seguin Island Light Station Mooring Buoy B	43-42-35.229N 069-45-24.097W				White with blue band.	
	Sheepscot Bay						
5595	Tom Rock Buoy 2TR South-southwest of outer rock.	43-43-47.707N 069-43-01.619W				Red nun.	
5600	The Sisters Buoy 4S	43-44-33.382N 069-43-35.414W				Red nun.	
5605	Sloop Ledge Buoy 5 35 yards south of ledge.	43-45-54.410N 069-43-39.564W				Green can.	
	Cape Harbor						
5610	- Buoy 2	43-46-53.859N 069-39-50.003W				Red nun.	
5615	Hunting Island Daybeacon 4 On ledge.	43-47-07.708N 069-39-34.424W				TR on pile.	
	Sheepscot River						
5620	- *Entrance Lighted Buoy 2SR*	43-45-38.241N 069-41-09.114W	Fl R 4s		4	Red.	
5625	Griffith Head Ledge Buoy 3 Southeast of ledge.	43-46-55.008N 069-42-30.134W				Green can.	
5630	Cat Ledges Gong Buoy 4CL West side of shoal.	43-47-48.137N 069-41-19.874W				Red.	
5635	Harmon Harbor Buoy 2	43-48-23.125N 069-43-07.834W				Red nun.	
	Hendricks Harbor						
5640	Nick Ledge Daybeacon 2	43-49-01.564N 069-41-08.914W				TR on pile.	
5645	Petes Rock Buoy 3	43-49-01.574N 069-41-05.540W				Green can.	
	Sheepscot River						
5650	Marrs Ledge Daybeacon 5	43-49-02.302N 069-40-59.939W				SG on pile.	
5655	Cedar Bush Ledge Buoy 6 South of ledge.	43-49-05.275N 069-41-22.615W				Red nun.	

(1) No.	(2) Name and Location	(3) Position	(4) Characteristic	(5) Height	(6) Range	(7) Structure	(8) Remarks
			MAINE - First District				
	DAMARISCOTTA, SHEEPSCOT AND KENNEBEC RIVERS						
	Sheepscot River						
5665	HENDRICKS HEAD LIGHT	43-49-21.318N 069-41-23.022W	F W (R sector)	43	W 9 R 7	White house.	Red from 180° to 000°.
5670	Five Islands Ledge Buoy 1	43-49-22.856N 069-42-21.546W				Green can.	
5675	Five Islands Ledge Daybeacon 2	43-49-36.303N 069-42-25.254W				TR on pile.	
5680	Bull Ledge Buoy 9 South of ledge.	43-50-01.112N 069-41-57.494W				Green can.	
	Little Sheepscot River						
5685	MacMahan Ledge Buoy 2	43-50-28.611N 069-42-48.884W				Red nun.	
5690	Six Foot Rock Buoy 3	43-50-59.020N 069-42-51.974W				Green can.	
	Goose Rock Passage						
5695	MacMahan Island Ledge Daybeacon 1	43-51-12.970N 069-42-08.474W				SG on pile.	
5700	Boiler Rock Buoy 4	43-50-59.655N 069-43-07.129W				Red nun.	
5705	- LIGHT 5	43-50-56.230N 069-43-15.074W	Fl G 2.5s	16	5	SG on skeleton tower on caisson.	Higher intensity beam up Knubble Bay and down Goose Rock Passage.
5710	Ebenecook Harbor Buoy 2 On north end of shoal.	43-50-17.602N 069-40-43.474W				Red nun.	
5715	Ebenecook Harbor Buoy 3	43-50-40.882N 069-40-32.155W				Green can.	
	Sheepscot River						
5720	Harding Ledge Buoy 10	43-50-52.892N 069-41-12.155W				Red nun.	
5725	South Powderhorn Buoy 12 At end of ledge.	43-51-06.341N 069-41-10.174W				Red nun.	
5730	Middle Ledge Buoy 13	43-51-16.040N 069-41-46.894W				Green can.	
5735	Clous Ledge Daybeacon 15	43-51-28.066N 069-41-48.313W				SG on pile.	
5740	Clous Ledge Bell Buoy 17	43-51-38.780N 069-41-44.464W				Green.	Removed when endangered by ice.
5750	*Powderhorn Ledge Lighted Buoy 16* Marks westerly edge of ledge.	43-51-34.765N 069-41-27.637W	Fl R 4s		4	Red.	Removed when endangered by ice.
5755	Isle of Springs Daybeacon 1 On ledge.	43-51-59.269N 069-40-58.175W				SG on pile.	
5760	Ram Islands Daybeacon On ledge.	43-52-20.936N 069-41-00.175W				NR on pile.	
5765	Sawyer Island Buoy 1	43-52-25.298N 069-41-00.835W				Green can.	
5770	Barter Island Buoy 18	43-52-33.358N 069-41-12.725W				Red nun.	
5775	Hodgdon Ledge Buoy 19	43-52-49.004N 069-41-39.013W				Green can.	
5780	Stover Ledge Buoy 20	43-52-58.578N 069-41-19.755W				Red nun.	
5783	- Buoy 20A	43-54-11.302N 069-41-03.359W				Red nun.	
5785	Greenleaf Ledge Buoy 21	43-55-07.324N 069-40-59.576W				Green can.	
5790	*Cross Point Lighted Buoy CP*	43-55-32.974N 069-40-22.426W	Fl (2+1)R 6s		4	Red and green bands.	Replaced by nun when endangered by ice.
5795	*Merrill Ledge Lighted Buoy 22*	43-58-02.300N 069-39-59.287W	Fl R 4s		4	Red.	Replaced by nun when endangered by ice.

(1) No.	(2) Name and Location	(3) Position	(4) Characteristic	(5) Height	(6) Range	(7) Structure	(8) Remarks
		MAINE - First District					
DAMARISCOTTA, SHEEPSCOT AND KENNEBEC RIVERS							
Sheepscot River							
5800	Merrill Ledge Daybeacon 22A On south point of ledge.	43-57-57.030N 069-39-56.526W				TR on spindle.	
5805	Hilton Point Buoy 23 On point of shoal extending north from point.	43-58-43.769N 069-39-37.817W				Green can.	
5810	Clough Point Buoy 25	43-59-22.648N 069-39-19.128W				Green can.	
5815	Seal Rock Junction Buoy SR	43-59-27.827N 069-39-46.717W				Green and red bands; can.	
5820	Davis Island Buoy 28	43-59-41.377N 069-39-41.707W				Red nun.	
Back River Channel							
5825	- Buoy 1	43-52-41.448N 069-40-39.895W				Green can.	
5830	- Daybeacon 3	43-52-58.722N 069-40-14.245W				SG on spindle.	
5835	- Buoy 2	43-52-57.638N 069-40-12.335W				Red nun.	
5840	- Buoy 4	43-53-01.518N 069-40-03.465W				Red nun.	
5845	- Buoy 5	43-53-02.468N 069-40-02.625W				Green can.	
Montsweag Bay							
Aids maintained from May 15 to Oct. 15.							
5850	- Buoy 2	43-53-44.312N 069-44-26.980W				Red nun.	
5855	- Buoy 3	43-54-04.404N 069-44-10.104W				Green can.	
5860	- Buoy 4	43-54-40.056N 069-43-41.958W				Red nun.	
5865	- Buoy 6	43-55-00.312N 069-43-20.819W				Red nun.	
5870	- Buoy 7	43-55-10.686N 069-42-44.404W				Green can.	
5875	- Buoy 8	43-55-09.642N 069-42-42.340W				Red nun.	
5880	- Buoy 10	43-55-46.254N 069-42-15.934W				Red nun.	
5881	- Buoy 11	43-55-49.722N 069-42-19.566W				Green can.	
5882	- Buoy 13	43-56-25.902N 069-41-45.556W				Green can.	
Cowseagan Narrows							
Aids maintained from May 15 to Oct. 15.							
5883	- Buoy 15	43-57-35.920N 069-41-08.076W				Green can.	
5884	- Buoy 16	43-57-35.934N 069-41-05.520W				Red nun.	
5885	- Buoy 17	43-57-53.348N 069-40-45.389W				Green can.	
5886	- Buoy 18	43-57-59.424N 069-40-38.977W				Red nun.	
Sasanoa River							
Aids maintained from May 15 to Oct. 15 unless otherwise noted.							
5890	Blacksmithshop Ledge Daybeacon 1	43-51-09.036N 069-43-55.011W				SG on pile.	
5895	The Boilers Buoy 2	43-53-00.326N 069-44-07.174W				Red nun.	
5900	Bareneck Island Ledge Buoy 5	43-53-14.919N 069-44-11.760W				Green can.	Aid is maintained year round.
5905	- Buoy 7	43-53-24.625N 069-44-33.194W				Green can.	Aid is maintained year round.
5910	- Buoy 9	43-53-22.105N 069-44-43.973W				Green can.	Aid is maintained year round.

(1) No.	(2) Name and Location	(3) Position	(4) Characteristic	(5) Height	(6) Range	(7) Structure	(8) Remarks
			MAINE - First District				

DAMARISCOTTA, SHEEPSCOT AND KENNEBEC RIVERS

Sasanoa River
Aids maintained from May 15 to Oct. 15 unless otherwise noted.

(1) No.	(2) Name and Location	(3) Position	(4) Characteristic	(5) Height	(6) Range	(7) Structure	(8) Remarks
5915	- Buoy 12	43-53-17.425N 069-44-59.273W				Red nun.	Aid is maintained year round.
5920	- Buoy 13	43-53-07.536N 069-45-24.011W				Green can.	Aid is maintained year round.
5925	- Buoy 17	43-53-12.955N 069-45-43.324W				Green can.	
5930	- Buoy 20	43-53-20.490N 069-45-54.953W				Red nun.	
5935	Swett Point Daybeacon 21 On ledge.	43-53-31.136N 069-46-04.511W				SG on pile.	
5940	Sassanoa River Daybeacon 22	43-53-43.482N 069-46-24.822W				TR on pile.	Maintained from Apr. 15 to Oct. 15.
5945	Lime Rock Daybeacon 23 Marks ledge.	43-53-50.314N 069-46-30.285W				SG on pile.	
5950	- Buoy 27	43-54-01.677N 069-46-45.159W				Green can.	
5955	- Buoy 29	43-54-03.723N 069-46-50.646W				Green can.	
5958	- Buoy 30	43-54-05.002N 069-46-54.206W				Red nun.	
5960	- Buoy 31	43-54-05.623N 069-47-01.466W				Green can.	
5965	- Buoy 32	43-54-06.936N 069-47-02.911W				Red nun.	
5970	- Buoy 33	43-54-07.284N 069-47-13.676W					
5975	- Buoy 34	43-54-08.163N 069-47-11.576W				Red nun.	
5980	- Buoy 35	43-54-20.323N 069-47-19.176W				Green can.	
5985	- Buoy 37	43-54-29.692N 069-47-21.136W				Green can.	
5990	- Buoy 39	43-54-36.472N 069-47-26.897W				Green can.	
5995	- Buoy 41	43-54-39.112N 069-47-40.937W				Green can.	
6000	- Buoy 42	43-54-40.536N 069-47-44.411W				Red nun.	

Kennebec River Approach

(1) No.	(2) Name and Location	(3) Position	(4) Characteristic	(5) Height	(6) Range	(7) Structure	(8) Remarks
6005	Jackknife Ledge Buoy 1	43-43-13.303N 069-46-41.954W				Green can.	
6010	Pond Island Shoal Gong Buoy 3	43-43-44.992N 069-45-52.573W				Green.	Removed when endangered by ice.
6015	*White Ledge Lighted Bell Buoy 1* Northeast of ledge.	43-43-49.236N 069-44-54.011W	Fl G 4s		5	Green.	
6020	Kennebec River Entrance Buoy KR	43-43-57.895N 069-45-12.048W				Green and red bands; can.	

Kennebec River

(1) No.	(2) Name and Location	(3) Position	(4) Characteristic	(5) Height	(6) Range	(7) Structure	(8) Remarks
6025	POND ISLAND LIGHT	43-44-24.165N 069-46-13.099W	Iso W 6s	52	9	White tower.	HORN: 2 blasts ev 30s (2s bl-2s si-2s bl-24s si). Fog signal is radio activated, during times of reduced visibility, turn marine VHF-FM radio to channel 83A/157.175Mhz. Key microphone 5 times consecutively, to activate fog signal for 45 minutes.
6030	- Buoy 4 On south side of rock.	43-44-27.322N 069-45-52.934W				Red nun.	
6035	Jack Rock Daybeacon 5A Near top of ledge.	43-44-59.541N 069-46-17.084W				SG on pile.	

(1) No.	(2) Name and Location	(3) Position	(4) Characteristic	(5) Height	(6) Range	(7) Structure	(8) Remarks
			MAINE - First District				
DAMARISCOTTA, SHEEPSCOT AND KENNEBEC RIVERS							
Kennebec River							
6040	- Buoy 5	43-44-49.541N 069-46-36.994W				Green can.	
6045	- Buoy 6	43-45-01.952N 069-46-39.767W				Red nun.	
6050	FORT POPHAM LIGHT	43-45-18.040N 069-47-00.211W	Fl G 4s	27	4	On spindle.	
6055	- *Lighted Buoy 8*	43-45-51.829N 069-47-00.044W	Fl R 4s		4	Red.	
6060	- Buoy 11	43-46-32.838N 069-47-19.175W				Green can.	
6065	- Buoy 12 On west side of Perkins Island Ledge.	43-46-44.158N 069-47-18.245W				Red nun.	
6070	PERKINS ISLAND LIGHT	43-47-12.395N 069-47-06.900W	Fl R 2.5s (2W sectors)	41	W 6 W 6 R 5	White conical tower.	White from 018° to 038° and from 172° to 188°, covers fairways.
6075	- Buoy 13 Southeast of ledge.	43-47-12.817N 069-47-17.225W				Green can.	
6080	- Buoy 15 On shoal.	43-47-51.615N 069-47-13.535W				Green can.	
6090	- Buoy 16	43-48-10.125N 069-47-10.816W				Red nun.	
6095	- Buoy 17	43-48-34.044N 069-47-59.876W				Green can.	
6100	SQUIRREL POINT LIGHT	43-48-59.519N 069-48-08.583W	Iso R 6s (W sector)	25	7 W 9	White conical tower.	White from 321° to 324°, covers fairway.
6105	- Buoy 19	43-49-09.880N 069-48-20.047W				Green can.	
6110	- Buoy 21	43-49-37.682N 069-48-11.977W				Green can.	
6120	PETTIS ROCKS LIGHT 23 Off south end of rocks.	43-49-48.711N 069-47-56.676W	Fl G 2.5s	20	4	SG on skeleton tower.	
6125	- LIGHT 25	43-50-10.736N 069-47-50.911W	Fl G 4s	22	4	SG on skeleton tower, small white house.	Ra ref.
6130	- Buoy 27	43-50-50.489N 069-47-46.676W				Green can.	
6135	DOUBLING POINT FRONT RANGE LIGHT	43-52-58.344N 069-47-44.357W	Q W	18		White conical tower.	Visible all around; higher intensity on range line.
6140	DOUBLING POINT REAR RANGE LIGHT 232 yards, 359.6° from front light.	43-53-05.210N 069-47-44.429W	Iso W 6s	32		White conical tower.	Visible all around; higher intensity on range line.
6145	DOUBLING POINT LIGHT	43-52-57.065N 069-48-24.387W	Fl W 4s	23	9	Conical tower.	
6150	- Buoy 28	43-53-00.961N 069-48-29.436W				Red nun.	
6155	- Buoy 29	43-53-04.176N 069-48-41.778W				Green can.	
6160	- Buoy 31	43-53-18.869N 069-48-45.610W				Green can.	
6165	- Buoy 33	43-53-48.874N 069-48-39.848W				Green can.	
6170	- Buoy 34	43-54-12.464N 069-48-32.598W				Red nun.	
Upper Kennebec River							
6185	- Buoy 1 South of rock.	43-55-57.746N 069-48-24.413W				Green can.	
6190	- Buoy 3	43-56-06.560N 069-48-23.709W				Green can.	

(1) No.	(2) Name and Location	(3) Position	(4) Characteristic	(5) Height	(6) Range	(7) Structure	(8) Remarks

MAINE - First District

DAMARISCOTTA, SHEEPSCOT AND KENNEBEC RIVERS
Kennebec River
Upper Kennebec River

6195	- Buoy 5 Off southeasterly side of rocks.	43-56-26.756N 069-48-26.660W				Green can.	
6200	- Buoy 7	43-56-32.930N 069-48-31.878W				Green can.	
6205	- Buoy 8	43-56-42.619N 069-48-31.719W				Red nun.	
6210	- Buoy 10	43-57-06.319N 069-49-16.180W				Red nun.	
6215	- Buoy 11	43-57-09.319N 069-49-28.181W				Green can.	
6220	- Buoy 12	43-58-13.777N 069-49-44.632W				Red nun.	
6225	- Buoy 13	43-58-33.616N 069-49-41.081W				Green can.	

Upper Kennebec River
Merrymeeting Bay
Merrymeeting Bay Buoy positions frequently shifted with changing conditions. Aids maintained May 25 to Oct. 1.

6226.1	- Buoy 1	43-58-58.190N 069-51-17.000W				Green can.	Private aid.
6226.4	- Buoy 2	43-58-52.310N 069-52-15.400W				Red nun.	Private aid.
6226.6	- Buoy 4	43-59-05.400N 069-52-33.720W				Red nun.	Private aid.
6226.7	- Buoy 3	43-59-04.740N 069-52-31.740W				Green nun.	Private aid.

Kennebec River
Upper Kennebec River

6230	- Buoy 15 At south point of flats.	43-59-05.086N 069-49-53.285W				Green can.	
6235	- Buoy 16	43-59-20.781N 069-49-44.189W				Red nun.	
6240	- Buoy 17 Marks rock.	44-00-27.512N 069-49-16.181W				Green can.	
6245	- Buoy 19	44-01-02.511N 069-49-13.181W				Green can.	
6250	- Buoy 20	44-01-16.346N 069-48-55.450W				Red nun.	
6255	- Buoy 21	44-01-32.110N 069-48-46.480W				Green can.	
6260	- Channel Buoy 23	44-02-09.143N 069-48-03.327W				Green can.	
6265	- Channel Buoy 22	44-02-06.919N 069-48-02.512W				Red nun.	
6270	- Channel Buoy 24	44-02-31.422N 069-47-41.754W				Red nun.	
6275	- Channel Daybeacon 26	44-02-50.136N 069-47-29.711W				TR on wooden spindle.	Maintained from Apr. 1 to Nov. 1.
6280	- Buoy 27	44-03-39.206N 069-47-16.376W				Green can.	
6285	- Buoy 29	44-04-13.154N 069-46-58.465W				Green can.	
6290	- Buoy 31	44-05-07.313N 069-47-09.215W				Green can.	
6295	- Buoy 33	44-05-20.274N 069-47-09.136W				Green can.	
6300	Hathorn Rock Buoy	44-08-03.367N 069-45-33.921W				Green can with red bands.	
6305	- Channel Buoy 34	44-08-49.116N 069-45-36.991W				Red nun.	
6310	- Channel Buoy 36	44-09-37.844N 069-45-53.551W				Red nun.	

(1) No.	(2) Name and Location	(3) Position	(4) Characteristic	(5) Height	(6) Range	(7) Structure	(8) Remarks
		MAINE - First District					
	DAMARISCOTTA, SHEEPSCOT AND KENNEBEC RIVERS **Kennebec River** **Upper Kennebec River**						
6315	- Buoy 38	44-09-58.983N 069-45-37.240W				Red nun.	
6320	- Channel Buoy 40	44-10-45.112N 069-45-13.429W				Red nun.	
6325	- Buoy 42	44-11-54.750N 069-45-34.030W				Red nun.	
6330	- Buoy 44	44-12-51.608N 069-45-36.639W				Red nun.	
6335	- Channel Buoy 45	44-13-05.668N 069-45-33.499W				Green can.	
6340	- Channel Buoy 47	44-13-18.517N 069-45-36.799W				Green can.	
6345	- Buoy 47A	44-13-49.287N 069-46-10.170W				Green can.	Maintained from May 15 to Oct. 15.
6350	- Buoy 47B	44-14-35.433N 069-46-02.506W				Green can.	Maintained from May 15 to Oct. 15.
6355	- Buoy 48 On north end of shoal.	44-14-47.675N 069-46-04.799W				Red nun.	Maintained from May 15 to Oct. 15.
6357	- Buoy 48A	44-14-56.310N 069-46-05.336W				Red nun.	Maintained from May 15 to Oct. 15.
6360	- Buoy 49	44-15-15.724N 069-46-02.249W				Green can.	Maintained from May 15 to Oct. 15.
6365	- Buoy 51	44-15-35.474N 069-46-15.240W				Green can.	Maintained from May 15 to Oct. 15.
6370	- Buoy 53	44-15-54.844N 069-46-45.181W				Green can.	Maintained from May 15 to Oct. 15.
6375	- Channel Buoy 54 North of Hinkley Shoal.	44-16-11.854N 069-47-08.052W				Red nun.	Maintained from May 15 to Oct. 15.
6380	- Channel Buoy 55	44-16-15.114N 069-47-11.812W				Green can.	Maintained from May 15 to Oct. 15.
6385	- Channel Buoy 61	44-16-28.964N 069-47-18.553W				Green can.	Maintained from May 15 to Oct. 15.
6390	- Channel Buoy 63	44-16-42.284N 069-47-24.963W				Green can.	Maintained from May 15 to Oct. 15.
6395	- Channel Buoy 64 On west edge of shoal.	44-16-43.464N 069-47-23.913W				Red nun.	Maintained from May 15 to Oct. 15.
6400	- Channel Buoy 68	44-16-51.204N 069-47-24.433W				Red nun.	Maintained from May 15 to Oct. 15.
6403	- Channel Buoy 68A	44-17-09.382N 069-47-18.117W				Red nun.	Maintained from May 15 to Oct. 15.
6405	- Channel Buoy 68B Marks pinnacle rock.	44-17-17.493N 069-47-12.973W				Red nun	Maintained from May 15 to Oct. 15.
6410	- Channel Buoy 70	44-17-22.173N 069-47-04.653W				Red nun.	Maintained from May 15 to Oct. 15.
6415	- Channel Buoy 72 West of shoal.	44-17-37.633N 069-46-54.553W				Red nun.	Maintained from May 15 to Oct. 15.
6420	- Channel Buoy 74	44-17-43.413N 069-46-51.603W				Red nun.	Maintained from May 15 to Oct. 15.

(1) No.	(2) Name and Location	(3) Position	(4) Characteristic	(5) Height	(6) Range	(7) Structure	(8) Remarks

MAINE - First District

DAMARISCOTTA, SHEEPSCOT AND KENNEBEC RIVERS
Kennebec River
Upper Kennebec River

(1) No.	(2) Name and Location	(3) Position	(4) Characteristic	(5) Height	(6) Range	(7) Structure	(8) Remarks
6425	- Channel Buoy 75	44-17-52.153N 069-46-45.053W				Green can.	Maintained from May 15 to Oct. 15.
6430	- Channel Buoy 79	44-17-59.093N 069-46-38.403W				Green can.	Maintained from May 15 to Oct. 15.
6435	- Channel Buoy 82	44-18-28.132N 069-46-25.643W				Red nun.	Maintained from May 15 to Oct. 15.

CASCO BAY
New Meadows River Approach

6440	FULLER ROCK LIGHT	43-41-45.120N 069-50-01.311W	Fl W 4s	17	6	NR on white skeleton tower.	
6445	Bald Head Ledge Bell Buoy 2BH	43-41-47.063N 069-51-19.145W				Red.	
6450	White Bull Lighted Gong Buoy WB	43-42-48.650N 069-55-12.807W	Mo (A) W		6	Red and white stripes.	
6455	Mark Island Ledge Buoy 2	43-43-04.386N 069-54-27.155W				Red nun.	
6460	Small Point Harbor Buoy 2	43-43-11.992N 069-51-52.597W				Red nun.	
6465	Wyman Ledge Buoy 3	43-43-10.401N 069-53-03.296W				Green can.	
6475	Wood Island South Ledge Lighted Bell Buoy 4	43-43-34.065N 069-52-23.626W	Fl R 4s		4	Red.	Replaced by nun when endangered by ice.
6480	Small Point Harbor Ledge Buoy 3 Southwest of ledge.	43-44-06.642N 069-51-35.412W				Green can.	
6495	Pitchpine Ledges Buoy 4	43-44-32.979N 069-51-09.786W				Red nun.	
6500	Carrying Place Head Buoy 6	43-44-23.339N 069-52-21.677W				Red nun.	
6505	Jamison Ledge Buoy 7	43-44-43.339N 069-52-46.677W				Green can.	
6510	Burnt Coat Island Buoy 1	43-44-58.778N 069-52-12.567W				Green can.	
6515	Burnt Coat Island Buoy 2	43-45-08.808N 069-51-59.187W				Red nun.	
6520	Burnt Coat Island Buoy 3	43-45-23.888N 069-51-59.847W				Green can.	
6525	Harbor Island Lighted Buoy 8	43-45-40.397N 069-52-29.047W	Fl R 4s		4	Red.	Replaced by nun when endangered by ice.
6530	Harbor Island Point Buoy 1	43-45-45.741N 069-52-09.306W				Green can.	
6535	Goudy Ledge Daybeacon South of ledge.	43-45-53.680N 069-53-32.178W				NR on pile.	
6540	Rouge Island South Buoy 9	43-46-06.767N 069-53-46.219W				Green can.	
6550	Malaga Island Buoy 1	43-46-29.096N 069-52-29.048W				Green can.	
6555	Malaga Island Buoy 3	43-46-41.476N 069-52-12.498W				Green can.	
6557	Fort Point Lighted Buoy 1	43-46-41.796N 069-53-25.809W	Fl G 4s		4	Green.	Replaced by can when endangered by ice.

New Meadows River

6560	Cedar Ledges Buoy 3	43-47-23.935N 069-53-11.562W				Green can.	
6565	Bear Island Ledges Buoy 4	43-47-28.534N 069-52-41.919W				Red nun.	
6570	Sheep Island Ledge Buoy 5	43-48-02.573N 069-52-42.669W				Green can.	

(1) No.	(2) Name and Location	(3) Position	(4) Characteristic	(5) Height	(6) Range	(7) Structure	(8) Remarks
			MAINE - First District				
CASCO BAY							
New Meadows River							
6575	Hen Island Ledge Daybeacon 6 On west part of ledge.	43-48-56.936N 069-51-51.811W				TR on pile.	
6580	BIRCH POINT LIGHT 8	43-49-32.939N 069-52-10.823W	Fl R 4s	25	5	TR on white structure with small white house.	Higher intensity beam downstream.
6585	Bragdon Rock Daybeacon 10 On rock.	43-51-01.436N 069-52-22.511W				TR on pile.	
6590	- Buoy 11	43-51-50.278N 069-53-50.393W				Green can.	
6595	- Buoy 12 At south end of middle ground.	43-52-01.567N 069-53-45.203W				Red nun.	
6600	- Buoy 13	43-52-28.136N 069-53-45.443W				Green can.	
6605	- Buoy 14 At north end of middle ground.	43-52-54.246N 069-53-32.673W				Red nun.	Maintained from 15 May to 1 October.
6610	- Buoy 15	43-53-08.301N 069-53-12.392W				Green can.	Maintained from 15 May to 1 October.
6615	- Buoy 16	43-54-02.184N 069-52-33.959W				Red nun.	Maintained from 15 May to 1 October.
6617	- Buoy 17	43-54-13.034N 069-52-25.648W				Green can.	Maintained from May 15 to Oct. 1.
6619	- Buoy 19	43-54-21.138N 069-52-20.292W				Green can.	Maintained from May 15 to Oct. 1.
Western Passage							
6620	North Jenny Ledge Buoy 2	43-45-51.367N 069-54-07.929W				Red nun.	
6625	Elm Island Buoy 4 At south end of reef.	43-45-35.336N 069-55-26.179W				Red nun.	
6630	Elm Island Buoy 6	43-45-36.647N 069-55-53.660W				Red nun.	
6635	Oak Island Buoy 8	43-45-38.226N 069-56-59.950W				Red nun.	
6640	Quahog Bay Bell Buoy 2Q South of ledge.	43-40-48.232N 069-56-04.672W				Red.	
6645	*Quahog Bay Lighted Buoy 3*	43-43-01.455N 069-57-31.421W	Fl G 2.5s		3	Green.	
6650	Quahog Bay Buoy 4	43-47-16.286N 069-55-43.186W				Red nun.	
Orr`s Island Approach							
6655	Orr's Island Approach Bell Buoy 1J	43-42-24.336N 069-59-39.511W				Green.	
6660	Orr's Island Approach Buoy 1	43-42-54.036N 069-59-15.011W				Green can.	
6665	Orr's Island Approach Buoy 4	43-44-28.337N 069-58-49.180W				Red nun.	
6670	Orr's Island Approach Buoy 6	43-44-57.866N 069-58-25.560W				Red nun.	
6671	Cribstone Bridge Daybeacon 1	43-44-53.000N 069-59-15.700W				SG on pile.	Private aid.
6672	Cribstone Bridge Daybeacon 2	43-44-52.800N 069-59-14.600W				TR on pile.	Private aid.

(1) No.	(2) Name and Location	(3) Position	(4) Characteristic	(5) Height	(6) Range	(7) Structure	(8) Remarks

CASCO BAY

Merriconeag Sound Approach

(1) No.	(2) Name and Location	(3) Position	(4) Characteristic	(5) Height	(6) Range	(7) Structure	(8) Remarks
6675 40	**Halfway Rock Light**	43-39-20.835N 070-02-12.437W	Fl R 5s	76	14	White tower attached to dwelling. 77	HORN: 2 blasts ev 30s (2s bl-2s si-2s bl-24s si). MRASS-Fog signal is radio activated, during times of reduced visibility, turn marine VHF-FM radio to channel 83A/157.175Mhz. Key microphone 5 times consecutively, to activate fog signal for 60 minutes.
6680	Webster Rock Buoy 1	43-39-37.889N 070-02-19.218W				Green can.	
6685	Eastern Drunkers Ledges Buoy 2 West-southwest of ledge.	43-41-05.088N 070-01-21.038W				Red nun.	
6690	Western Drunkers Ledges Buoy 4	43-41-14.337N 070-01-50.179W				Red nun.	
6695	- Buoy 6	43-42-11.036N 070-01-12.011W				Red nun.	
6705	- *Lighted Gong Buoy 8*	43-42-43.118N 070-00-57.560W	Fl R 4s		3	Red.	
6710	*Mackerel Cove Lighted Buoy 1*	43-43-24.646N 070-00-19.974W	Fl G 4s		4	Green.	Replaced by can when endangered by ice.
6715	- Buoy 9	43-44-24.556N 070-00-16.021W				Green can.	
6716	Rheubins Ledge Buoy 1	43-44-58.140N 069-59-21.960W				Green can.	Maintained May 1 to Nov 1. Private aid.
6717	Rheubins Ledge Buoy 2	43-44-58.800N 069-59-21.180W				Red nun.	Maintained May1 to Nov 1. Private aid.
6720	- Daybeacon 10	43-45-12.136N 069-59-20.911W				TR on pile.	
6725	Merriconeag Sound Buoy 12	43-45-16.766N 069-59-20.621W				Red nun.	
6730	Merriconeag Sound Buoy 13	43-45-30.655N 069-59-42.182W				Green can.	
6733	*Bowdoin College Harpswell Cove Research Lighted Buoy R*	43-45-38.280N 069-59-18.720W	Fl Y 6s			Yellow.	Private aid.
6735	Merriconeag Sound Buoy 15	43-46-22.724N 069-59-12.242W				Green can.	
6740	Merriconeag Sound Buoy 17	43-46-35.154N 069-59-01.493W				Green can.	

Haskell Island

(1) No.	(2) Name and Location	(3) Position	(4) Characteristic	(5) Height	(6) Range	(7) Structure	(8) Remarks
6745	- Buoy 2	43-42-43.137N 070-02-13.540W				Red nun.	
6750	Haddock Rock Buoy 3	43-42-49.056N 070-02-27.800W				Green can.	

Potts Harbor

(1) No.	(2) Name and Location	(3) Position	(4) Characteristic	(5) Height	(6) Range	(7) Structure	(8) Remarks
6755	Pinkham Island Point Buoy 2	43-43-39.866N 070-01-10.420W				Red nun.	
6760	Haskell Island Reef Buoy 3	43-43-43.116N 070-01-28.520W				Green can.	
6765	Potts Point Ledge Buoy 4	43-43-42.018N 070-01-38.339W				Red nun.	
6770	Potts Point Ledge Buoy 5	43-43-43.246N 070-01-40.471W				Green can.	
6775	Northwest Ledge Daybeacon 7 On easterly edge of ledge.	43-43-46.136N 070-01-41.611W				SG on pile.	
6780	Northwest Ledge Buoy 9	43-43-48.576N 070-01-41.361W				Green can.	
6785	Torry Rock Buoy 11	43-43-53.375N 070-01-49.561W				Green can.	
6790	South Harpswell Buoy 12	43-43-58.705N 070-01-40.901W				Red nun.	

(1) No.	(2) Name and Location	(3) Position	(4) Characteristic	(5) Height	(6) Range	(7) Structure	(8) Remarks
			MAINE - First District				

CASCO BAY
Merriconeag Sound Approach
Potts Harbor

6795	Thrumcap Ledge Buoy 13	43-44-09.615N 070-01-51.321W				Green can.	
	Broad Sound						
6800	- Entrance Bell Buoy BS	43-41-43.835N 070-03-26.580W				Red and white stripes with red spherical topmark.	
6805	- Gong Buoy 1	43-42-19.045N 070-03-49.521W				Green.	
6810	- Buoy 2	43-42-31.396N 070-03-29.891W				Red nun.	
6820	Stockman Island Daybeacon 2 On ledge.	43-43-59.633N 070-04-58.330W				TR on pile.	
6825	Upper Flag Shoal Buoy 4 Southwest of shoal.	43-43-27.785N 070-03-10.201W				Red nun.	
6830	Little Birch Island Point Bell Buoy 6	43-43-44.348N 070-03-11.666W				Red.	
6835	Birch Island Ledge Buoy 8	43-44-15.986N 070-03-15.502W				Red nun.	
6840	Whaleboat Island Shoal Buoy WS South of shoal.	43-44-16.114N 070-03-44.392W				Green and red bands.	
6845	WHALEBOAT ISLAND LIGHT	43-44-31.136N 070-03-40.411W	Fl W 6s	47	4	NR on white square skeleton tower.	
6850	Whaleboat Island Buoy 10	43-44-33.253N 070-03-19.042W				Red nun.	
6855	Whaleboat Ledge Buoy 6	43-45-02.812N 070-04-23.653W				Red nun.	
6860	Little Whaleboat Ledge Danger Buoy	43-45-20.252N 070-04-09.083W				White with orange bands worded DANGER.	
	Little Whaleboat Island						
6880	- Buoy 1	43-45-37.992N 070-03-17.663W				Green can.	
6885	- Buoy 2	43-45-33.902N 070-03-05.532W				Red nun.	
6890	- Buoy 3	43-45-56.512N 070-03-03.453W				Green can.	
6895	- Buoy 4	43-45-55.872N 070-02-48.013W				Red nun.	
6904	- Buoy 5	43-46-36.052N 070-02-45.634W				Green can.	
6910	*Goose Island Aquaculture Hazard Lighted Buoy A*	43-48-08.974N 070-02-37.316W	F W			White and orange can.	Private aid.
6925	Lookout Point Buoy 10	43-48-41.041N 069-59-47.475W				Red nun.	
6930	Wilson Ledges Buoy 12	43-49-14.041N 069-59-07.196W				Red nun.	
6932	*Running Tide Aquaculture Hazard Lighted Buoy*	43-49-11.640N 069-59-04.949W	F W			White with Orange bands.	Seasonal 01 Apr - 01 Nov. Private aid.
6933	Branning Ledge Buoy 1	43-48-08.860N 070-01-31.475W				Green can.	
6934	Merepoint Buoy 2	43-49-20.329N 070-01-43.187W				Red nun.	
	Mere Point Brunswick PD Boat Launch						
6935.1	- Buoy 1	43-49-38.040N 070-00-56.880W				Green can.	Private aid.
6935.2	- Buoy 2	43-49-38.820N 070-00-55.980W				Red nun.	Private aid.
6935.3	- Buoy 3	43-49-39.540N 070-00-58.440W				Green can.	Private aid.
6935.4	- Buoy 4	43-49-40.200N 070-00-57.840W				Red nun.	Private aid.

(1) No.	(2) Name and Location	(3) Position	(4) Characteristic	(5) Height	(6) Range	(7) Structure	(8) Remarks
			MAINE - First District				

CASCO BAY

Harraseeket River

(1) No.	(2) Name and Location	(3) Position	(4) Characteristic	(5) Height	(6) Range	(7) Structure	(8) Remarks
6940	Crab Ledge Buoy 1	43-47-29.036N 070-05-10.011W				Green can.	
6945	- Buoy 2	43-48-02.243N 070-05-17.639W				Red nun.	
6950	*- Lighted Buoy 4*	43-48-20.028N 070-06-08.531W	Fl R 4s		3	Red.	Replaced by nun when endangered by ice
6955	- Buoy 5	43-48-22.297N 070-06-13.282W				Green can.	
6960	- Buoy 7	43-48-26.889N 070-06-18.719W				Green can.	
6965	- Buoy 9	43-48-36.377N 070-06-20.597W				Green can.	

Green Island Passage

6990	Green Island Reef Buoy 2	43-39-16.287N 070-06-54.240W				Red nun.	
6995	- Buoy 3	43-39-15.566N 070-07-11.260W				Green can.	

Luckse Sound

7000	- East Buoy 4	43-39-30.505N 070-08-45.981W				Red nun.	
7005	- East Bell Buoy 6	43-40-35.935N 070-07-28.081W				Red.	
7010	*Hope Island Lighted Bell Buoy 2*	43-41-54.203N 070-07-27.872W	Fl R 4s		4	Red.	

Cliff Island

7015	- Buoy 1	43-41-04.695N 070-06-25.321W				Green can.	
7016	- Harbor Buoy 2	43-41-16.035N 070-06-25.011W				Red nun.	
7020	- Harbor Buoy 6	43-41-35.341N 070-06-12.608W				Red nun.	
7025	- Harbor Buoy 4	43-41-29.542N 070-06-16.246W				Red nun.	
7030	- Buoy 4	43-41-28.335N 070-05-24.180W				Red nun.	
7035	- Buoy 3	43-41-29.335N 070-05-29.181W				Green can.	
7040	- Buoy 5	43-42-04.709N 070-05-08.177W				Green can.	

Luckse Sound

7055	Rogues Island Buoy 1	43-42-34.191N 070-06-28.804W				Green can.	
7060	Sand Island Buoy 2	43-42-39.808N 070-06-33.359W				Red nun.	
7065	- West Buoy 3	43-42-57.882N 070-06-49.032W				Green can.	
7070	Sand Island Ledge Buoy 7	43-43-07.682N 070-06-10.502W				Green can.	
7071	Stave Island Ledge Buoy 8	43-43-28.044N 070-04-43.492W				Red nun.	
7075	- West Buoy 5	43-43-54.032N 070-06-03.723W				Green can.	
7080	- West Buoy 6	43-44-03.753N 070-05-26.043W				Red nun.	
7081	- West Buoy 7	43-45-19.250N 070-05-39.973W				Green can.	
7081.1	- West Buoy 8	43-44-39.054N 070-05-24.928W				Red nun.	
7082	- West Buoy 9	43-45-45.330N 070-05-38.864W				Green can.	
7083	- West Buoy 10	43-46-02.160N 070-05-15.804W				Red nun.	

(1) No.	(2) Name and Location	(3) Position	(4) Characteristic	(5) Height	(6) Range	(7) Structure	(8) Remarks
			MAINE - First District				
	CASCO BAY						
	Chandler Cove						
7084	- *Lighted Buoy 2*	43-42-23.171N 070-07-51.987W	Fl R 2.5s		3	Red.	
7085	- Buoy 3	43-42-37.452N 070-08-04.923W				Green can.	
7090	- *Lighted Buoy 5*	43-42-29.661N 070-08-27.973W	Fl G 4s		4	Green.	
7095	- Buoy 6	43-42-27.801N 070-08-42.063W				Red nun.	
7100	- Buoy 8	43-42-13.031N 070-08-58.983W				Red nun.	
7105	- Buoy 9 On north side of ledge.	43-41-49.091N 070-09-39.503W				Green can.	
	Hussey Sound						
7110	- *Approach Lighted Buoy 2*	43-39-05.335N 070-09-07.931W	Fl R 6s		3	Red.	
7115	- *Lighted Buoy 3*	43-39-49.604N 070-10-03.832W	Fl G 4s		4	Green.	
7120	- *Lighted Buoy 4*	43-40-03.313N 070-09-50.961W	Fl R 4s		3	Red.	
7125	- Buoy 5	43-39-55.773N 070-10-26.532W				Green can.	
7130	- *Lighted Buoy 6*	43-40-20.162N 070-10-33.772W	Q R		3	Red.	
7135	- *Lighted Bell Buoy 7*	43-40-29.462N 070-10-48.522W	Fl G 4s		4	Green.	
7140	Diamond Cove Buoy 1	43-41-04.201N 070-11-12.313W				Green can.	
7145	CROW ISLAND LIGHT 9	43-41-10.635N 070-11-11.811W	Fl G 2.5s	41	5	SG on skeleton tower.	Higher intensity beam toward Hussey Sound.
7150	- *Lighted Bell Buoy 10*	43-41-31.971N 070-10-13.563W	Fl R 4s		3	Red.	
7155	- *Lighted Buoy 11*	43-42-10.650N 070-10-25.973W	Fl G 4s		3	Green.	
7160	- Buoy 12	43-42-10.171N 070-09-42.983W				Red nun.	
7165	- *Lighted Buoy 14* Marks shoal.	43-43-19.940N 070-09-10.724W	Fl R 4s		3	Red.	
7170	- Buoy 16	43-43-59.619N 070-08-31.513W				Red nun.	
	Diamond Island Pass						
7175	- *Lighted Buoy 1*	43-40-33.772N 070-11-11.363W	Fl G 2.5s		3	Green.	
7180	- Buoy 3	43-40-20.682N 070-11-28.232W				Green can.	
7185	- *Lighted Buoy 5*	43-40-00.035N 070-12-05.011W	Fl G 4s		3	Green.	Replaced by can when endangered by ice.
7190	- Buoy 6	43-39-40.812N 070-12-44.753W				Red nun.	
	Whitehead Passage						
7195	Ram Island Shoal Buoy 1	43-38-23.585N 070-10-45.911W				Green can.	
7200	Whitehead Ledge Daybeacon 3	43-38-51.019N 070-11-33.938W				SG on pile.	
7210	- Buoy 6	43-38-53.244N 070-11-37.462W				Red nun.	
7215	- *Lighted Bell Buoy 8*	43-38-54.614N 070-12-07.202W	Fl R 4s		4	Red.	Replaced by nun when endangered by ice.
7216	- Buoy 9	43-38-52.043N 070-12-30.592W				Green can.	
7220	House Island Buoy 1	43-39-22.443N 070-12-20.232W				Green can.	

(1) No.	(2) Name and Location	(3) Position	(4) Characteristic	(5) Height	(6) Range	(7) Structure	(8) Remarks
			MAINE - First District				
	CASCO BAY						
	Whitehead Passage						
7225	HOUSE ISLAND LIGHT 3	43-39-21.147N 070-12-27.514W	Fl G 4s	20	4	SG on skeleton tower.	
	Casco Bay Channel						
7230	- Buoy 1	43-39-49.342N 070-12-58.633W				Green can.	
7235	- Buoy 2	43-39-49.242N 070-12-51.933W				Red nun.	
7240	- Buoy 3	43-40-07.585N 070-12-54.744W				Green can.	
7245	- Buoy 4	43-40-20.261N 070-12-44.723W				Red nun.	
7250	- Buoy 6	43-40-46.880N 070-12-40.223W				Red nun.	
7255	- Buoy 8	43-41-05.190N 070-12-36.473W				Red nun.	
7260	- Buoy 9	43-41-05.710N 070-12-42.094W				Green can.	
	Portland To Merepoint						
7265	Brimstone Point Ledge Buoy 10	43-41-31.170N 070-11-57.554W				Red nun.	
7270	Diamond Cove Ledge Buoy 2	43-41-26.540N 070-11-33.053W				Red nun.	
7275	Cow Island Shoal Buoy 4	43-41-45.910N 070-11-14.453W				Red nun.	
7280	COW ISLAND LEDGE LIGHT	43-42-10.635N 070-11-18.611W	Fl W 6s	23	8	NR on spindle on red caisson.	Ra ref.
7285	Cow Island Ledge Buoy CIL	43-42-23.620N 070-11-06.554W				Green can with red bands.	
7290	Clapboard Island South Ledge Buoy CI	43-42-17.358N 070-11-47.883W				Red nun with green bands.	
7295	Lower Basket Ledge Daybeacon 15	43-43-49.434N 070-09-23.960W				SG on iron spindle.	Ra ref.
7300	Basket Island Shoal Buoy 2	43-43-44.419N 070-09-55.034W				Red nun.	
7305	Upper Basket Ledge Daybeacon	43-44-24.435N 070-09-32.311W				NR on pile.	
7320	*Hussey Sound Lighted Buoy 18*	43-45-16.275N 070-07-35.462W	Fl R 2.5s		3	Red.	
	Portland To Yarmouth						
7330	The Brothers Buoy 11	43-42-03.438N 070-12-39.344W				Green can.	
7335	Lower Clapboard Island Ledge Buoy 12 Southwest of ledge.	43-42-41.248N 070-12-01.604W				Red nun.	
7336	*Town Landing Lighted Buoy 1*	43-43-36.300N 070-11-40.620W	Fl G 4s			Green.	Private aid.
7336.1	*Town Landing Lighted Buoy 2*	43-43-39.300N 070-11-37.800W	Fl R 4s			Red.	Private aid.
7337	*Portland Yacht Club Lighted Buoy 1*	43-43-28.080N 070-11-47.880W	Fl G 4s			Green.	Private aid.
7337.1	*Portland Yacht Club Lighted Buoy 2*	43-43-30.720N 070-11-47.940W	Fl R 4s			Red.	Private aid.
7337.2	*HBS Lighted Buoy 1*	43-43-23.940N 070-11-54.780W	Fl G 4s			Green.	Private aid.
7338	*HBS Lighted Buoy 2*	43-43-25.680N 070-11-52.920W	Fl R 4s			Red.	Private aid.
7340	Jones Ledge Buoy 14 South of ledge.	43-42-56.888N 070-12-03.884W				Red nun.	
7345	Prince Point Ledge Buoy 15 Off northeast end of ledge.	43-43-11.754N 070-12-22.382W				Green can.	
7350	York Ledge Daybeacon YL	43-43-31.923N 070-12-14.904W				SG on pile.	
7355	York Ledge Buoy 17 East of ledge.	43-43-32.077N 070-12-10.635W				Green can.	

(1) No.	(2) Name and Location	(3) Position	(4) Characteristic	(5) Height	(6) Range	(7) Structure	(8) Remarks
			MAINE - First District				
	CASCO BAY						
	Portland To Yarmouth						
7360	Clapboard Island North Ledge Daybeacon 18	43-43-27.035N 070-11-25.911W				TR on spindle.	
7365	Sturdivant Island Ledges Buoy SI	43-43-45.318N 070-11-26.105W				Green can with red bands.	
7370	Underwood Ledge Buoy 19 Northeast of ledge.	43-44-00.457N 070-11-43.255W				Green can.	
7375	Underwood Ledge Buoy 20	43-44-01.687N 070-11-32.965W				Red nun.	
7380	Sturdivant Island Ledges Danger Buoy	43-43-50.688N 070-11-06.435W				White with orange bands worded DANGER.	
7385	*Upper Clapboard Island Ledge Lighted Buoy 3*	43-43-56.082N 070-10-31.008W	Fl G 2.5s		3	Green.	
7386	*Basket Island Lighted Buoy 4*	43-44-06.035N 070-10-14.011W	Fl R 2.5s		3	Red.	
7387	*Basket Island Lighted Shellfish Raft A*	43-43-58.000N 070-09-52.000W	Q Y			Shellfish raft.	Private aid.
7390	Birch Point Buoy 6	43-44-57.836N 070-09-52.418W				Red nun.	
7395	Sandy Point Ledges Buoy 22 West of ledge.	43-45-57.367N 070-09-21.856W				Red nun.	
	Royal River						
7400	- *Channel Lighted Buoy 1*	43-47-06.387N 070-07-24.557W	Fl G 4s		3	Green.	Replaced by can when endangered by ice.
7405	- Channel Buoy 2	43-47-09.493N 070-07-39.472W				Red nun.	Maintained from Apr. 1 to Dec. 1.
7410	- Channel Buoy 3	43-47-13.447N 070-07-57.597W				Green can.	Maintained from Apr. 1 to Dec. 1.
7415	- Channel Buoy 4	43-47-21.515N 070-08-17.543W				Red nun.	Maintained from Apr. 1 to Dec. 1.
7418	- Channel Buoy 4A	43-47-31.559N 070-08-26.904W				Red nun.	Maintained from Apr. 1 to Dec 1.
7425	- Channel Buoy 5	43-47-39.131N 070-08-29.234W				Green can.	Maintained from Apr. 1 to Dec. 1.
7430	- Channel Buoy 7	43-47-43.424N 070-08-34.205W				Green can.	Maintained from Apr. 1 to Dec. 1.
7435	- Channel Buoy 8	43-47-45.514N 070-08-37.462W				Red nun.	Maintained from Apr. 1 to Dec. 1.
7440	- Channel Buoy 9	43-47-44.312N 070-08-42.238W				Green can.	Maintained from Apr. 1 to Dec. 1.
7442	- Channel Buoy 11	43-47-34.312N 070-08-57.316W				Green can.	Maintained from Apr. 1 to Dec. 1.
7445	- Channel Buoy 12	43-47-33.947N 070-09-00.776W				Red nun.	Maintained from Apr. 1 to Dec. 1.
7450	- Channel Buoy 13	43-47-29.325N 070-09-12.187W				Green can.	Maintained from Apr. 1 to Dec. 1.
7455	- Channel Buoy 14	43-47-22.711N 070-09-29.470W				Red nun.	Maintained from Apr. 1 to Dec. 1.
7460	- Channel Buoy 15	43-47-21.636N 070-09-31.711W				Green can.	Maintained from Apr. 1 to Dec. 1.
7462	- Channel Buoy 16	43-47-22.333N 070-09-37.472W				Red Nun.	Maintained from Apr. 1 to Dec 1.

(1) No.	(2) Name and Location	(3) Position	(4) Characteristic	(5) Height	(6) Range	(7) Structure	(8) Remarks
			MAINE - First District				

CASCO BAY

Royal River

(1) No.	(2) Name and Location	(3) Position	(4) Characteristic	(5) Height	(6) Range	(7) Structure	(8) Remarks
7465	- Channel Buoy 16A	43-47-32.245N 070-09-53.359W				Red nun.	Maintained from Apr. 1 to Dec. 1.
7470	- Channel Buoy 17	43-47-38.555N 070-10-01.894W				Green can.	Maintained from Apr. 1 to Dec. 1.
7475	- Channel Buoy 18	43-47-44.488N 070-10-19.645W				Red nun.	Maintained from Apr. 1 to Dec. 1.

Portland Harbor Approach

(1) No.	(2) Name and Location	(3) Position	(4) Characteristic	(5) Height	(6) Range	(7) Structure	(8) Remarks
7480 45	*Portland Lighted Whistle Buoy P*	43-31-36.347N 070-05-28.174W	Mo (A) W		6	Red and white stripes with red spherical topmark.	RACON: M (- -) AIS: MMSI 993672144 (21)
7495	Bulwark Shoal Buoy BS 400 yards east of ledge.	43-36-01.802N 070-04-01.206W				Red nun with green bands.	
7500 75	*East Hue and Cry Rock Lighted Buoy 1 (NOAA 44007)* East-southeast of ledge.	43-31-30.397N 070-08-25.576W	Fl G 4s		4	Green.	3 meter discus buoy marked with 44007 on fin. Aid maintained by National Oceanic and Atmospheric Administration.
7505	*Portland Harbor Main Approach Lighted Whistle Buoy 4*	43-33-55.635N 070-08-04.811W	Fl R 4s		4	Red.	
7510	West Cod Ledge Rock Buoy 4WC	43-34-18.845N 070-07-47.479W				Red nun.	
7515	*Corwin Rock Lighted Bell Buoy 3*	43-33-31.813N 070-08-31.587W	Fl G 4s		4	Green.	
7520 60	**Cape Elizabeth Light**	43-33-57.899N 070-12-00.220W	Fl (4)W 15s 0.3s fl 2.2s ec. 0.3s fl 2.2s ec. 0.3s fl 2.2s ec. 0.3s fl 7.2s ec.	129	15	White conical tower. 67	Lighted throughout 24 hours.Emergency light of reduced intensity when main light is extinguished. HORN: 2 blasts ev 60s (3s bl-3s si-3s bl-51s si). Horn located 266 yards, 146° from light tower. MRASS-Fog signal is radio activated, during times of reduced visibility, turn marine VHF-FM radio to channel 83A/157.175Mhz. Key microphone 5 times consecutively, to activate fog signal for 60 minutes.
7525	Broad Cove Rock Buoy 5 Off southeast side of shoal.	43-35-02.019N 070-11-12.379W				Green can.	
7530	*Willard Rock Lighted Gong Buoy 7* On east side of rock.	43-36-05.498N 070-10-57.690W	Fl G 4s		4	Green.	
7533	*East Cod Ledge Lighted Buoy 1EC*	43-36-30.135N 070-02-06.011W	Fl G 6s		4	Green.	
7535	*Portland Harbor Eastern Approach Lighted Gong Buoy 1*	43-37-05.217N 070-09-46.099W	Fl G 2.5s		3	Green.	
7540	*Portland Harbor Eastern Approach Lighted Buoy 3*	43-37-16.836N 070-11-03.181W	Fl G 4s		4	Green.	
7545	*Pine Tree Ledge Lighted Whistle Buoy 8*	43-36-36.315N 070-10-51.393W	Q R		3	Red.	
7550	Jordan Reef Buoy 10	43-37-00.587N 070-11-18.191W				Red nun.	
7555	*Witch Rock Lighted Bell Buoy 2* South of rock.	43-37-20.387N 070-10-31.720W	Fl R 4s		4	Red.	
7560	*Thirty-One Foot Spot Lighted Bell Buoy D*	43-37-12.736N 070-11-55.271W	Fl (2)W 5s		4	Black and red bands with two black spherical topmarks.	

(1) No.	(2) Name and Location	(3) Position	(4) Characteristic	(5) Height	(6) Range	(7) Structure	(8) Remarks
			MAINE - First District				
	PORTLAND HARBOR						
	Portland Harbor						
7565	**Portland Head Light**	43-37-23.209N 070-12-28.323W	Fl W 4s	101	19	White tower. 80	Lighted throughout 24 hours.Emergency light of reduced intensity when main light is extinguished. HORN: 1 blast ev 15s (2s bl). MRASS -Fog signal is radio activated, during times of reduced visibility, turn marine VHF-FM radio to channel 83A/157.175Mhz. Key microphone 5 times consecutively, to activate fog signal for 60 minutes.
7570	PORTLAND HEAD DIRECTIONAL LIGHT	43-37-23.185N 070-12-27.576W	F R W G (RWG sectors)	34	W 15 G 12 R 12	At base of Portland Head Light.	Shows red from 271.3° to 274.3°; white from 274.3° to 275.8°, green from 275.8° to 279.3°.
7575	RAM ISLAND LEDGE LIGHT	43-37-53.325N 070-11-14.573W	Fl (2)W 6s	77	9	Light-gray, conical, granite tower.	HORN: 1 blast ev 10s (1s bl). MRASS-Fog signal is radio activated, during times of reduced visibility, turn marine VHF-FM radio to channel 83A/157.175Mhz. Key microphone 5 times consecutively, to activate fog signal for 60 minutes.
7578	- *Main Approach Lighted Buoy 11*	43-37-44.283N 070-12-37.671W	Q G		3	Green.	
7580	- *Main Approach Lighted Bell Buoy 12*	43-37-55.053N 070-12-31.487W	Q R		3	Red.	
7585	- *Main Approach Lighted Buoy 13*	43-38-06.017N 070-12-58.980W	Fl G 2.5s		3	Green.	
7590	- *Main Approach Lighted Buoy 14*	43-38-11.395N 070-12-43.517W	Fl R 2.5s		3	Red.	
7595	- *Main Approach Lighted Buoy 17*	43-38-47.460N 070-13-11.003W	Fl G 4s		3	Green.	
7600	- *Main Approach Lighted Buoy 16*	43-38-41.019N 070-12-53.970W	Fl R 4s		3	Red.	
7605	FORT SCAMMEL POINT LIGHT 2	43-38-56.583N 070-12-49.752W	Fl R 4s	35	5	TR on tower.	Higher intensity beam up channel.
7610	SPRING POINT LEDGE LIGHT	43-39-07.647N 070-13-26.068W	Fl W 6s (2R sectors)	54	W 12 R 10 R 10	White tower.	White from 331° to 337° covers fairway entrance, white from 074° to 288°; red in intervening sectors.Lighted throughout 24 hours.Emergency light of reduced intensity when main light is extinguished. HORN: 1 blast ev 10s (1s bl). MRASS-Fog signal is radio activated, during times of reduced visibility, turn marine VHF-FM radio to channel 83A/157.175Mhz. Key microphone 5 times consecutively, to activate fog signal for 60 minutes.
7615	- *Channel Lighted Buoy 1*	43-39-17.392N 070-13-31.042W	Fl G 2.5s		3	Green.	
7620	SPRING POINT PIER LIGHT	43-39-19.146N 070-13-41.381W	F W			On pile.	Private aid.
7645	- *Anchorage Lighted Buoy A*	43-39-04.166N 070-13-00.045W	Fl Y 4s		3	Yellow.	
7665	- *Anchorage Lighted Bell Buoy B*	43-39-35.092N 070-12-34.663W	Fl Y 4s		3	Yellow.	
7675	*Seventeen-Foot Shoal Lighted Buoy 3*	43-39-27.232N 070-13-44.433W	Fl G 4s		3	Green.	
7685	*Fort Georges Island Ledge Lighted Buoy 4*	43-39-33.399N 070-13-24.202W	Fl R 2.5s		3	Red.	

(1) No.	(2) Name and Location	(3) Position	(4) Characteristic	(5) Height	(6) Range	(7) Structure	(8) Remarks
			MAINE - First District				
	PORTLAND HARBOR						
	Portland Harbor						
7690	DIAMOND ISLAND LEDGE LIGHT On west side of ledge.	43-39-47.035N 070-13-29.811W	Fl W 2.5s	24	5	NR on skeleton tower.	
7695	*Dredged Channel Lighted Buoy 5* On edge of shoal.	43-39-27.641N 070-14-09.183W	Fl G 4s		3	Green.	
7697	- CG Mooring Buoy	43-39-10.890N 070-12-54.010W				White with blue band.	
7699	SOUTH PORTLAND BREAKWATER LIGHT	43-39-19.872N 070-14-05.471W	Fl W 4s	30		White.	Private aid.
7700.1	South Portland Boat Ramp Buoy 1	43-39-20.820N 070-14-14.040W				Green can.	Private aid.
7700.2	South Portland Boat Ramp Buoy 3	43-39-19.680N 070-14-13.500W				Green can.	Private aid.
7700.3	South Portland Boat Ramp Buoy 5	43-39-18.120N 070-14-12.780W				Green can.	Private aid.
7700.4	South Portland Boat Ramp Buoy 6	43-39-17.460N 070-14-13.620W				Red nun.	Private aid.
7700.5	South Portland Boat Ramp Buoy 8	43-39-17.220N 070-14-13.200W				Red nun.	Private aid.
7701	SOUTH PORTLAND PIER LIGHT	43-39-11.179N 070-14-35.223W	F W			On pile.	Private aid.
7705	COAST GUARD PIERHEAD LIGHT	43-38-59.931N 070-15-12.883W	Fl Y 4s	18	4	On dolphin.	
	Lighthouse Channel						
7710	- *Lighted Buoy 1*	43-38-55.400N 070-15-02.996W	Fl G 6s		3	Green.	
7715	- *Lighted Buoy 2*	43-38-54.131N 070-15-04.533W	Fl R 2.5s		3	Red.	
7720	- LIGHT 3	43-38-49.986N 070-14-56.311W	Fl G 4s		3	SG on dolphin.	
7725	- *Lighted Buoy 4*	43-38-48.935N 070-14-58.747W	Fl R 2.5s		3	Red.	
7730	- Daybeacon 5	43-38-49.135N 070-14-54.182W				SG on dolphin.	
7735	- Buoy 6	43-38-45.277N 070-14-57.804W				Red nun.	Removed when endangered by ice.
	Mill Cove						
7740	- Daybeacon 1	43-38-48.460N 070-15-11.719W				SG on pile.	Private aid.
7745	- Daybeacon 2	43-38-48.107N 070-15-12.489W				TR on pile.	Private aid.
7750	- Buoy 3	43-38-44.980N 070-15-09.090W				Green can.	Maintained from Apr. 1 to Oct. 30. Private aid.
7755	- Daybeacon 4	43-38-44.426N 070-15-10.213W				TR on pile.	Private aid.
7760	- Buoy 5	43-38-42.040N 070-15-07.780W				Green can.	Maintained from Apr. 1 to Oct. 30. Private aid.
7765	- Daybeacon 6	43-38-41.608N 070-15-08.487W				TR on pile.	Private aid.
7770	- Buoy 7	43-38-39.820N 070-15-06.660W				Green can.	Maintained from Apr. 1 to Oct. 30. Private aid.
7775	- Daybeacon 8	43-38-39.356N 070-15-07.134W				TR on pile.	Private aid.
7780	- Daybeacon 9	43-38-36.692N 070-15-06.168W				SG on pile.	Private aid.
7790	- Daybeacon 11	43-38-32.893N 070-15-02.880W				SG on pile.	Private aid.
	Fore River						
7810	- Outfall Daybeacon	43-38-32.466N 070-15-35.280W				NY on pile.	Private aid.

(1) No.	(2) Name and Location	(3) Position	(4) Characteristic	(5) Height	(6) Range	(7) Structure	(8) Remarks
			MAINE - First District				
PORTLAND HARBOR							
Portland Harbor							
Fore River							
7815	- Lighted Buoy 1	43-38-30.021N 070-15-56.124W	Fl G 2.5s		4	Green.	Replaced by can when endangered by ice.
7820	- Buoy 3	43-38-29.001N 070-16-08.504W				Green can.	
7825	- Lighted Buoy 5	43-38-27.831N 070-16-22.474W	Fl G 4s		4	Green.	Replaced by can when endangered by ice.
7827	- Daybeacon 5A	43-38-15.413N 070-16-46.638W				SG on pile.	
7830	- Lighted Buoy 6	43-38-24.807N 070-16-53.996W	Fl R 2.5s		3	Red.	Replaced by nun when endangered by ice.
Back Cove Approach							
7835	Fish Point Lighted Buoy 1	43-39-53.691N 070-14-08.684W	Fl G 4s		3	Green.	Replaced by can when endangered by ice.
7840	- Buoy C	43-40-09.036N 070-13-19.530W				Yellow nun.	
7845	- Buoy 3	43-40-17.030N 070-14-04.964W				Green can.	
7850	- Buoy 4	43-40-20.850N 070-13-42.163W				Red nun.	
7855	- Lighted Buoy 5	43-40-30.939N 070-14-26.684W	Fl G 2.5s		4	Green.	
7860	- Buoy 6	43-40-37.249N 070-14-28.914W				Red nun.	
7865	- Lighted Buoy 8	43-40-31.900N 070-14-53.965W	Fl R 2.5s		3	Red.	
SACO BAY AND VICINITY							
7870	Seal Rocks Buoy 1	43-33-24.918N 070-13-15.016W				Green can.	
Richmond Island Harbor							
7875	Old Proprietor Buoy 1	43-32-07.980N 070-17-11.293W				Green can.	
7880	Chimney Rock Buoy 3	43-32-48.865N 070-15-17.024W				Green can.	
Scarborough River							
	Positions of buoys frequently shifted with changing conditions.						
7886	- Buoy 1	43-31-46.496N 070-19-30.506W				Green can.	
7890	- Buoy 2	43-31-46.480N 070-19-28.587W				Red nun.	
7892	- Buoy 3	43-31-56.409N 070-19-27.303W				Green can.	
7895	- Buoy 4	43-32-01.163N 070-19-23.641W				Red nun.	
7900	- Buoy 5	43-32-22.518N 070-19-39.454W				Green can.	
7915	- Buoy 8	43-32-29.902N 070-19-38.349W				Red nun.	
7920	- Buoy 9	43-32-34.113N 070-19-39.751W				Green can.	
7925	- Buoy 10	43-32-38.899N 070-19-41.692W				Red nun.	
7935	Bar Ledge Buoy 2	43-31-15.945N 070-20-35.309W				Red nun.	
Saco River							
7940	- Approach Bell Buoy SA	43-27-55.063N 070-20-18.245W				Red and white stripes with red spherical topmark.	
7945	- Approach Buoy 1	43-27-44.055N 070-20-13.678W				Green can.	

(1) No.	(2) Name and Location	(3) Position	(4) Characteristic	(5) Height	(6) Range	(7) Structure	(8) Remarks
			MAINE - First District				
	SACO BAY AND VICINITY						
	Saco River						
7950	- Approach Buoy 2	43-27-59.073N 070-20-41.446W				Red nun.	
7955	Stage Island Junction Buoy SI	43-27-30.834N 070-20-50.976W				Green and red bands; can.	
7960	Stage Island Daybeacon	43-27-24.535N 070-21-05.311W				Conical stone tower.	
7965	- North Breakwater Danger Buoy	43-27-50.343N 070-21-35.187W				White can with orange bands worded DANGER SUBMERGED BREAKWATER.	
7970	- *Approach Lighted Buoy 4*	43-27-43.413N 070-21-10.246W	Fl R 4s		4	Red.	
7975	Sharps Rock Daybeacon 4A	43-27-45.943N 070-21-21.186W				TR on spindle.	
7980	- South Jetty Buoy 5	43-27-41.023N 070-21-22.836W				Green can.	
7985	- Buoy 5A	43-27-41.102N 070-21-29.320W				Green can.	
7990	- Daybeacon 5B	43-27-36.942N 070-21-50.727W				SG on spindle.	
7995	- Buoy 6	43-27-43.343N 070-21-33.187W				Red nun.	
8000	- Middle Bar Buoy 6B	43-27-42.392N 070-21-49.017W				Red nun.	
8005	- Buoy 7	43-27-40.342N 070-22-35.189W				Green can.	
8010	- Buoy 8	43-27-42.037N 070-23-19.284W				Red nun	
8015	Jordan Point Daybeacon 9	43-27-41.635N 070-23-18.190W				SG on spindle.	
8020	- Buoy 10	43-27-46.130N 070-23-32.083W				Red nun.	
8025	- Buoy 10A	43-27-53.341N 070-23-38.190W				Red nun.	
8030	- Buoy 11	43-28-18.516N 070-23-51.498W				Green can.	
8035	- Buoy 12	43-28-24.619N 070-24-04.761W				Red nun.	
8040	- Jetty Buoy 14	43-28-26.285N 070-24-19.152W				Red nun.	
8043	- Buoy 14A	43-28-34.030N 070-24-37.983W				Red nun.	
8045	- Buoy 15	43-28-43.812N 070-24-39.066W				Green can.	
8047	- Buoy 16	43-29-06.044N 070-26-01.011W				Red nun.	
8050	Cow Island Ledge Daybeacon 17	43-29-20.735N 070-26-02.812W				SG on spindle.	
8051	Factory Island Channel Buoy 1	43-29-32.250N 070-26-25.600W				Green can.	Private aid.
8051.1	Factory Island Channel Buoy 2	43-29-32.900N 070-26-24.900W				Red nun.	Private aid.
8051.2	Factory Island Channel Buoy 3	43-29-38.400N 070-26-41.000W				Green can.	Private aid.
8051.3	Factory Island Channel Buoy 4	43-29-38.700N 070-26-39.900W				Red nun.	Private aid.
8051.4	Factory Island Channel Buoy 5	43-29-34.800N 070-26-46.300W				Green can.	Private aid.
8051.5	Factory Island Channel Buoy 6	43-29-34.900N 070-26-47.800W				Red nun.	Private aid.
	Wood Island Harbor						
8055	Dansbury Reef Buoy 2	43-26-48.794N 070-19-24.594W				Red nun.	

(1) No.	(2) Name and Location	(3) Position	(4) Characteristic	(5) Height	(6) Range	(7) Structure	(8) Remarks

SACO BAY AND VICINITY

Wood Island Harbor

8060	Washman Rock Buoy 3A	43-26-42.236N 070-19-31.951W				Green can.	
8065	Phillip Rock Daybeacon 5	43-27-08.704N 070-20-29.855W				SG on spindle.	
8070	Negro Island Bar Buoy 6 On point of bar.	43-27-17.483N 070-20-38.955W				Red nun.	
8075	- Buoy 8	43-27-16.526N 070-20-57.820W				Red nun.	
8080	Halftide Rock Daybeacon 9	43-27-00.093N 070-21-06.431W				SG on spindle.	
8085	Biddeford Pool Channel Buoy 10	43-26-44.463N 070-21-27.906W				Red nun.	

CAPE ELIZABETH TO PORTSMOUTH

Cape Porpoise Harbor

8090	Old Prince Bell Buoy 2 South-southeast of ledge.	43-21-07.347N 070-25-06.392W				Red.	
8100 105	**Goat Island Light**	43-21-28.335N 070-25-30.312W	Fl W 6s	38	12	25	HORN: 1 blast ev 15s (2s bl). MRASS-Fog signal is radio activated, during times of reduced visibility, turn marine VHF-FM radio to channel 83A/157.175Mhz. Key microphone 5 times consecutively, to activate fog signal for 60 minutes.
8105	- Buoy 7	43-21-24.440N 070-25-37.010W				Green can.	
8110	Folly Island Daybeacon On ledge.	43-21-23.226N 070-25-38.552W				NW on pile worded DANGER.	
8115	- Buoy 6	43-21-21.040N 070-25-28.810W				Red nun.	
8120	Goat Island Daybeacon 8 On ledge.	43-21-25.656N 070-25-34.072W				TR on pile.	
8125	- Channel Buoy 9	43-21-30.537N 070-25-45.355W				Green can.	
8130	- Channel Buoy 10	43-21-32.146N 070-25-43.193W				Red nun.	
8141	Presidential Security Zone East Buoy	43-20-24.013N 070-27-11.881W				White and orange nun.	
8142	Presidential Security Zone South Buoy	43-20-06.036N 070-27-35.882W				White and orange nun.	
8143	Presidential Security Zone West Buoy	43-20-12.032N 070-27-53.980W				White and orange nun.	

Kennebunkport

8145	- *Approach Lighted Bell Buoy 1*	43-19-30.366N 070-28-02.976W	Fl G 4s		4	Green.	
8150	- Approach Buoy 3	43-20-14.068N 070-28-26.058W				Green can.	
8155	Fishing Rock Daybeacon F	43-20-11.165N 070-28-45.387W				NB on pile.	Ra ref.
8160	Oaks Reef Outer Rock Daybeacon O South side of shoal.	43-20-17.585N 070-29-24.838W				NG on pile.	
8165	- BREAKWATER LIGHT 6	43-20-45.737N 070-28-33.611W	Iso R 6s	18	5	TR on spindle.	

Kennebunk River

8175	- Entrance Buoy 5	43-20-43.775N 070-28-37.567W				Green can.	
8180	- Buoy 8	43-20-50.189N 070-28-31.274W				Red nun.	
8185	- Buoy 9	43-20-51.599N 070-28-30.936W				Green can.	
8190	- Buoy 10	43-20-59.972N 070-28-24.883W				Red nun.	

(1) No.	(2) Name and Location	(3) Position	(4) Characteristic	(5) Height	(6) Range	(7) Structure	(8) Remarks
			MAINE - First District				
	CAPE ELIZABETH TO PORTSMOUTH						
	Kennebunkport						
	Kennebunk River						
8195	- Daybeacon 12	43-21-04.415N 070-28-26.265W				TR on spindle.	
8196	- Buoy 12A	43-21-04.889N 070-28-27.486W				Red nun.	
8205	- Buoy 15	43-21-25.144N 070-28-33.427W				Green can.	
	Wells Harbor						
8208	- *Entrance Lighted Bell Buoy WH*	43-18-50.035N 070-32-52.012W	Mo (A) W		4	Red and white stripes with red spherical topmark.	
8210	- NORTH JETTY LIGHT 2	43-19-02.244N 070-33-10.702W	Fl R 4s	29	5	TR on skeleton tower.	
8215	- SOUTH JETTY LIGHT 1	43-18-58.335N 070-33-13.202W	Fl G 4s	22	5	SG on skeleton tower.	
8220	- Daybeacon 3	43-19-14.644N 070-33-30.902W				SG on dolphin.	
8225	- Buoy 4	43-19-18.944N 070-33-37.602W				Red nun.	
8230	- Daybeacon 5	43-19-17.444N 070-33-37.902W				SG on dolphin.	
	Perkins Cove						
8240	- Buoy 1	43-14-05.309N 070-35-05.417W				Green can.	
8245	- Buoy 2	43-14-06.902N 070-35-05.522W				Red nun.	
	CAPE NEDDICK HARBOR TO ISLES OF SHOALS						
	Cape Neddick Harbor						
8250	Weare Point Bell Buoy 2 Marks end of shoal off point.	43-10-55.035N 070-35-47.012W				Red.	
8255	Barn Point Buoy 1 Marks end of shoal off point.	43-10-59.491N 070-35-58.200W				Green can.	
	York Harbor						
8258 160	- *Lighted Bell Buoy YH*	43-07-45.395N 070-37-01.328W	Mo (A) W		5	Red and white stripes with red spherical topmark.	
8260	- Entrance Buoy 2	43-07-53.255N 070-37-06.388W				Red nun.	
8265	- Buoy 3	43-07-43.284N 070-37-55.709W				Green can.	
8270	- Buoy 4 Southeast of rock.	43-07-48.864N 070-37-55.709W				Red nun.	
8275	- Buoy 6	43-07-46.644N 070-38-13.599W				Red nun.	
8280	- Buoy 7	43-07-44.360N 070-38-25.407W				Green can.	
8290	- Buoy 8	43-07-41.063N 070-38-36.834W				Red nun.	
8295	- Daybeacon 9	43-07-44.461N 070-38-41.892W				SG on pile.	
8300	- Buoy 11	43-07-58.047N 070-38-36.889W				Green can.	
			MAINE AND NEW HAMPSHIRE - First District				
	CAPE NEDDICK HARBOR TO ISLES OF SHOALS						
	Portsmouth Harbor						
8305	- CHANNEL RANGE FRONT LIGHT	43-04-57.401N 070-42-26.850W	Iso R 6s	59		KRW on skeleton tower.	Visible 4° each side of range line.
8310	- CHANNEL RANGE REAR LIGHT 154 yards, 352.9° from front light.	43-05-01.921N 070-42-27.624W	F R	79		KRW on skeleton tower.	Visible 4° each side of range line.
8315	*Wood Island Lighted Buoy 2*	43-03-39.787N 070-42-03.939W	Fl R 4s		3	Red.	
8320	Stielman Rocks Buoy 3	43-04-01.716N 070-42-25.360W				Green can.	

73

(1) No.	(2) Name and Location	(3) Position	(4) Characteristic	(5) Height	(6) Range	(7) Structure	(8) Remarks
MAINE AND NEW HAMPSHIRE - First District							
CAPE NEDDICK HARBOR TO ISLES OF SHOALS							
Portsmouth Harbor							
8325	*UM AquaFort LOBO Temporary Lighted Research Buoy*	43-04-04.732N 070-42-30.833W	Fl Y 20s			Yellow.	Property of the University of Maine. Private aid.
8330	**- (New Castle) Light**	43-04-15.875N 070-42-31.075W	F G	52	12	White conical tower, fog signal house attached. 52	HORN: 1 blast ev 10s (1s bl). Fog signal is radio activated, during times of reduced visibility, turn marine VHF-FM radio to channel 83A/157.175Mhz. Key microphone 5 times consecutively, to activate fog signal for 45 minutes.
8340	*Cod Rock Lighted Buoy 5*	43-04-28.425N 070-42-40.380W	Fl G 4s		3	Green.	
8345	CLARK ISLAND LIGHT 8	43-04-33.854N 070-43-26.701W	Fl R 2.5s	20	4	TR on sectional spindle.	
8350	Fishing Island Ledge Lighted Buoy 4	43-04-39.855N 070-42-18.300W	Q R		3	Red.	
8351	Pepperrell Cove Buoy 2	43-04-46.000N 070-42-16.000W				Red nun.	Private aid.
8352	Pepperrell Cove Buoy 3	43-04-48.700N 070-42-15.700W				Green can.	Private aid.
8353	Pepperrell Cove Buoy 5	43-04-51.600N 070-42-15.300W				Green can.	Private aid.
8354	- CG Mooring Buoy	43-04-44.281N 070-42-23.101W				White with blue band.	
8355	PIERCE ISLAND RANGE FRONT LIGHT	43-04-25.427N 070-44-25.194W	Q G	51		KRW on skeleton tower.	Visible 4° each side of range line.
8360	PIERCE ISLAND RANGE REAR LIGHT 88 yards, 266.6° from front light.	43-04-25.272N 070-44-28.749W	Iso G 6s	63		KRW on skeleton tower.	Visible 4° each side of range line.
8365	Hick Rocks Buoy 6	43-04-40.245N 070-43-09.211W				Red nun.	
8370	*Goat Island Ledge Lighted Buoy 9*	43-04-23.460N 070-43-59.255W	Fl G 4s		3	Green.	
8375	HENDERSON POINT LIGHT 10	43-04-29.354N 070-44-10.201W	Q R	40	5	TR on skeleton tower.	
8385	*South Beacon Shoal Lighted Buoy 11*	43-04-40.112N 070-44-34.926W	Q G		3	Green.	
8386	Seavey Island Daybeacon 12A	43-04-45.672N 070-44-25.986W				TR on pile.	Marks remains of submerged quaywall. Private aid.
8387	Seavey Island Daybeacon 12B	43-04-46.068N 070-44-28.152W				TR on pile.	Marks remains of submerged quaywall. Private aid.
8390	South Beacon Shoal Daybeacon SBS	43-04-39.035N 070-44-43.612W				NG on mast, on granite pier.	
8395	*Gangway Rocks Lighted Buoy 13*	43-04-42.244N 070-44-48.202W	Fl G 2.5s		4	Green.	
8405	*Badgers Island Lighted Buoy 14*	43-04-51.986N 070-45-21.530W	Fl R 2.5s		3	Red.	
8406	Kittery Flats Turning Basin Buoy A	43-04-56.778N 070-45-24.940W				Yellow nun.	
8407	Kittery Flats Turning Basin Buoy B	43-05-01.381N 070-45-23.480W				Yellow nun.	
8408	Kittery Flats Turning Basin Buoy C	43-05-05.001N 070-45-24.615W				Yellow nun.	
8409	Kittery Flats Turning Basin Buoy D	43-05-10.142N 070-45-32.790W				Yellow nun.	
8430	Pierce Island Buoy 3	43-04-40.951N 070-44-59.886W				Green can.	
8435	Pierce Island Buoy 5	43-04-37.304N 070-44-59.658W				Green can.	

(1) No.	(2) Name and Location	(3) Position	(4) Characteristic	(5) Height	(6) Range	(7) Structure	(8) Remarks
		MAINE AND NEW HAMPSHIRE - First District					
	PORTSMOUTH TO DOVER AND EXETER						
	Piscataqua River						
8455	- Lighted Buoy 2	43-05-38.350N 070-46-01.101W	Fl R 4s		4	Red.	Replaced by nun when endangered by ice.
8460	- LIGHT 4	43-05-48.235N 070-46-42.812W	Fl R 4s	18	5	TR on spindle.	
8465	- (VAIS) 4A	43-06-06.590N 070-46-54.590W					Virtual AIS, MMSI 993672944
8470	CABLE PIER WEST LIGHT	43-06-13.200N 070-47-31.500W	F G	18		Square concrete platform.	Private aid.
8485	- Lighted Buoy 6	43-06-12.891N 070-47-06.308W	Fl R 4s		4	Red.	
8490	- Lighted Buoy 7	43-06-21.566N 070-47-33.355W	Fl G 4s		4	Green.	
8495	- Lighted Buoy 8	43-06-25.061N 070-47-30.312W	Fl R 4s		3	Red.	
8500	- Lighted Buoy 9	43-06-47.179N 070-48-15.440W	Fl G 4s		4	Green.	
8505	- Lighted Buoy 10	43-06-50.009N 070-48-11.790W	Fl R 4s		4	Red.	Replaced by nun when endangered by ice.
8510	- Lighted Buoy 11	43-06-53.989N 070-48-26.691W	Fl G 2.5s		4	Green.	
8515	- Buoy 12	43-07-11.535N 070-48-38.212W				Red nun.	
8520	SPRAGUE FUEL TERMINAL LOWER DOCK LIGHT	43-06-57.000N 070-48-36.000W	F G	6		On square concrete platform.	Private aid.
8525	SPRAGUE FUEL TERMINAL CENTER DOCK LIGHT	43-06-59.340N 070-48-37.500W	F G	11		On dolphin.	Private aid.
8530	SPRAGUE FUEL TERMINAL UPPER DOCK LIGHT	43-07-03.000N 070-48-44.000W	F G	8		On square concrete platform.	Private aid.
8535	- Buoy 13 Marks rock.	43-07-10.648N 070-48-46.352W				Green can.	
8540	- Buoy 15	43-07-19.227N 070-49-31.122W				Green can.	
8545	- Buoy 16	43-07-23.437N 070-49-26.002W				Red nun.	
8550	- Buoy 17	43-07-34.857N 070-49-38.313W				Green can.	
8555	- Buoy 18	43-07-59.516N 070-49-46.464W				Red nun.	
8560	- Buoy 20	43-09-17.754N 070-49-51.655W				Red nun.	
8565	- Buoy 21	43-09-38.797N 070-49-40.578W				Green can.	
8566	New Hampshire DES Oil Boom Deployment Lighted Buoy A	43-06-22.320N 070-51-20.880W	Fl W 2.5s			White with orange bands worded NH DES.	Replaced by unlighted buoy Dec. 1 to Apr. 1. Private aid.
8566.2	New Hampshire DES Oil Boom Deployment Lighted Buoy C	43-06-22.800N 070-51-23.280W	Fl W 4s			White with orange bands worded NH DES.	Replaced by unlighted buoy Dec 1 to Apr. 1. Private aid.
8566.3	New Hampshire DES Oil Boom Deployment Lighted Buoy D	43-06-47.580N 070-51-43.620W	Fl W 4s			White with orange bands worded NH DES.	Replaced by unlighted buoy Dec. 1 to Apr. 1. Private aid.
8566.4	New Hampshire DES Oil Boom Deployment Lighted Buoy E	43-06-48.000N 070-51-45.900W	Fl W 4s			White with orange bands worded NH DES.	Replaced by unlighted buoy Dec. 1 to Apr. 1. Private aid.
8566.5	New Hampshire DES Oil Boom Deployment Lighted Buoy F	43-06-40.680N 070-51-37.260W	Fl W 4s			White with orange bands worded NH DES.	Replaced by unlighted buoy Dec. 1 to Apr. 1. Private aid.
8566.6	New Hampshire DES Oil Boom Deployment Lighted Buoy G	43-06-41.280N 070-51-39.600W	Fl W 4s			White with orange bands worded NH DES.	Replaced by unlighted buoy Dec.1 to Apr. 1. Private aid.
8566.7	New Hampshire DES Oil Boom Deployment Lighted Buoy H	43-06-34.320N 070-51-31.500W	Fl W 4s			White with orange bands worded NH DES.	Replaced by unlighted buoy Dec1 to Apr. 1. Private aid.

(1) No.	(2) Name and Location	(3) Position	(4) Characteristic	(5) Height	(6) Range	(7) Structure	(8) Remarks
			MAINE AND NEW HAMPSHIRE - First District				

PORTSMOUTH TO DOVER AND EXETER

Piscataqua River

(1) No.	(2) Name and Location	(3) Position	(4) Characteristic	(5) Height	(6) Range	(7) Structure	(8) Remarks
8566.8	*New Hampshire DES Oil Boom Deployment Lighted Buoy I*	43-06-34.560N 070-51-33.060W	Fl W 2.5s			White with orange bands worded NH DES.	Replaced by unlighted buoy Dec 1. to Apr. 1. Private aid.
8566.9	*New Hampshire DES Oil Boom Deployment Lighted Buoy J*	43-06-25.620N 070-51-23.700W	Fl W 2.5s			White with orange bands worded NH DES.	Replaced by unlighted buoy Dec. 1 to Apr. 1. Private aid.
8566.91	*New Hampshire DES Oil Boom Deployment Lighted Buoy K*	43-06-26.280N 070-51-25.620W	Fl W 4s			White with orange bands worded NH DES.	Replaced by unlighted buoy Dec. 1 to Apr. 1. Private aid.

Little Bay

No.	Name and Location	Position	Characteristic	Height	Range	Structure	Remarks
8570	Hen Island Ledge Buoy 1	43-07-20.867N 070-51-18.836W				Green can.	
8575	Eight-Foot Rock Buoy 2	43-07-20.895N 070-51-45.316W				Red nun.	
8580	Fox Point Rock Buoy 3	43-07-15.255N 070-51-50.516W				Green can.	
8585	The Rocks Buoy 4	43-06-58.016N 070-51-38.116W				Red nun.	
8587	- Buoy 4A	43-06-36.645N 070-51-30.612W				Red nun.	
8590	Great Bay Entrance Buoy 6	43-05-04.298N 070-52-02.464W				Red nun.	
8595	Great Bay Buoy 7	43-04-25.735N 070-52-18.812W				Green can.	

Back Channel

No.	Name and Location	Position	Characteristic	Height	Range	Structure	Remarks
8755	- Buoy 3	43-04-50.224N 070-43-16.551W				Green can.	
8760	- Buoy 4	43-04-54.594N 070-43-22.001W				Red nun.	
8765	- Buoy 5	43-05-00.427N 070-43-33.777W				Green can.	
8770	- Buoy 7	43-05-02.954N 070-43-40.941W				Green can.	

CAPE NEDDICK HARBOR TO ISLES OF SHOALS

Little Harbor

No.	Name and Location	Position	Characteristic	Height	Range	Structure	Remarks
8775	- Entrance Buoy 1	43-03-06.915N 070-42-46.051W				Green can.	
8780	- Entrance Buoy 2	43-03-12.716N 070-42-40.208W				Red nun.	
8785	JAFFREY POINT LIGHT 4	43-03-17.536N 070-42-48.719W	Fl R 4s	22	4	TR on skeleton tower.	
8790	- Buoy 5	43-03-19.676N 070-42-59.839W				Green can.	
8795	- Buoy 6	43-03-21.836N 070-42-56.539W				Red nun.	
8800	- Buoy 8	43-03-22.506N 070-43-11.833W				Red nun.	
8805	- Buoy 10	43-03-22.716N 070-43-30.499W				Red nun.	
8810	- Buoy 11	43-03-24.975N 070-43-39.268W				Green can.	

Sagamore Creek

No.	Name and Location	Position	Characteristic	Height	Range	Structure	Remarks
8815	- Buoy 13	43-03-33.535N 070-43-51.100W				Green can.	Removed when endangered by ice.
8820	- Buoy 15	43-03-33.955N 070-44-02.500W				Green can.	Removed when endangered by ice.
8825	- Buoy SL	43-03-33.755N 070-44-06.200W				Green and red; can.	Removed when endangered by ice.
8830	- Buoy 16	43-03-26.955N 070-44-17.160W				Red nun.	Removed when endangered by ice.

(1) No.	(2) Name and Location	(3) Position	(4) Characteristic	(5) Height	(6) Range	(7) Structure	(8) Remarks
	MAINE AND NEW HAMPSHIRE - First District						
	CAPE NEDDICK HARBOR TO ISLES OF SHOALS						
	Little Harbor						
	Sagamore Creek						
8840	- Buoy 17	43-03-22.595N 070-44-25.740W				Green can.	Removed when endangered by ice.
8842	- Buoy 18	43-03-18.491N 070-44-30.186W				Red nun.	Removed when endangered by ice.
8845	- Buoy 20	43-03-15.755N 070-44-33.700W				Red nun.	Removed when endangered by ice.
	Northward Channel						
8850	- Buoy 2	43-03-36.635N 070-44-07.220W				Red nun.	Removed when endangered by ice.
8855	- Buoy 3	43-03-43.460N 070-44-13.146W				Green can.	Removed when endangered by ice.
8860	- Buoy 4	43-03-50.853N 070-44-16.860W				Red nun.	Removed when endangered by ice.
8865	- Buoy 5	43-04-04.178N 070-44-17.642W				Green can.	
	NEW HAMPSHIRE - First District						
	PORTSMOUTH TO CAPE ANN						
	Rye Harbor						
8870 215	- *Entrance Lighted Whistle Buoy RH*	42-59-37.550N 070-43-45.177W	Mo (A) W		6	Red and white stripes with red spherical topmark.	
8875	- Buoy 3	42-59-56.517N 070-44-37.677W				Green can.	
8880	- LIGHT 4	42-59-59.035N 070-44-39.312W	Fl R 6s	24	5	TR on skeleton tower.	
8885	- Buoy 5	42-59-58.250N 070-44-42.272W				Green can.	
8890	Seabrook Power Plant Buoy A	42-54-17.000N 070-47-12.000W				White with orange bands.	DANGER POWER PLANT INTAKE SHAFTS. Private aid.
8895	Seabrook Power Plant Buoy B	42-53-43.000N 070-47-25.000W				White with orange bands.	DANGER POWER PLANT INTAKE SHAFTS. Private aid.
8900	Seabrook Power Plant Buoy C	42-53-36.000N 070-47-15.000W				White with orange bands.	DANGER POWER PLANT INTAKE SHAFTS. Private aid.
	Hampton Harbor						
	Positions of aids frequently shifted with changing conditions.						
8905	Outer Sunk Rocks Buoy 2	42-54-05.842N 070-47-01.557W				Red nun.	
8915	Seabrook Station Buoy DS	42-53-41.000N 070-47-12.000W				White with orange bands, can.	Private aid.
8920	- *Channel Approach Lighted Bell Buoy 2*	42-53-01.003N 070-47-16.797W	Fl R 4s		4	Red.	
8923	- Channel Buoy 3	42-53-27.383N 070-48-16.141W				Green can.	Removed when endangered by ice.
8925	- Channel Gong Buoy 4	42-53-20.892N 070-48-04.498W				Red.	
8930	- Channel Buoy 4A	42-53-27.812N 070-48-13.149W				Red nun.	
8935	- Channel Buoy 5	42-53-35.955N 070-48-25.265W				Green can.	
8940	- Channel Buoy 7	42-53-38.915N 070-48-37.656W				Green can.	
8945	- North Jetty Daybeacon 8 125 yards from channel line.	42-53-41.592N 070-48-29.064W				TR on spindle.	
8950	- Channel Buoy 9	42-53-41.573N 070-48-47.862W				Green can.	

(1) No.	(2) Name and Location	(3) Position	(4) Characteristic	(5) Height	(6) Range	(7) Structure	(8) Remarks
		NEW HAMPSHIRE - First District					
	PORTSMOUTH TO CAPE ANN						
	Hampton Harbor						
	Positions of aids frequently shifted with changing conditions.						
8955	- South Daybeacon H 185 yards from channel line.	42-53-33.077N 070-48-38.724W				NG on spindle.	
8960	- Junction Buoy	42-53-46.547N 070-49-02.849W				Green can with red bands.	
		MASSACHUSETTS - First District					
	NEWBURYPORT HARBOR AND PLUM ISLAND SOUND						
	Merrimack River						
8990 265	- *Entrance Lighted Whistle Buoy MR*	42-48-34.367N 070-47-03.193W	Mo (A) W		4	Red and white stripes with red spherical topmark.	
8995	- *Entrance Lighted Buoy 2*	42-49-05.672N 070-47-36.374W	Fl R 4s		4	Red.	
9005	- Entrance Buoy 3	42-48-49.898N 070-47-50.984W				Green can.	
9006	- NORTH JETTY LIGHT 4	42-49-08.285N 070-48-13.974W	Fl R 2.5s	15	4	TR on skeleton tower.	
9010	- ENTRANCE SOUTH JETTY LIGHT 5	42-48-57.819N 070-48-15.978W	Fl G 2.5s	15	4	SG on spindle.	
9020	- *Lighted Buoy 7* On northeast edge of spit.	42-49-11.651N 070-48-47.153W	Fl G 4s		3	Green.	Replaced by can from Oct 15 to May 1.
9035	- *Lighted Buoy 8*	42-49-08.169N 070-49-17.374W	Fl R 4s		3	Red.	Replaced by nun from Oct 15 to May 1.
9040	Black Rocks Daybeacon 10 On outer rock of ledge.	42-49-13.932N 070-49-36.895W				TR on red wooden slat pyramid on granite foundation.	
9045	- Buoy 11	42-49-05.961N 070-49-46.316W				Green can.	
9050	- *Lighted Buoy 13*	42-49-02.465N 070-50-19.690W	Fl G 4s		3	Green.	Replaced by can from Oct 15 to May 1.
9053	*USGS Lighted Research Buoy A*	42-49-10.087N 070-50-18.549W	Fl Y 4s			Yellow.	Property of USGS. Seasonal 15 Apr - 15 Nov. Private aid.
9055	- *Lighted Buoy 15*	42-48-48.504N 070-51-07.400W	Fl G 4s		3	Green.	Replaced by can from Oct 15 to May 1.
9060	- Buoy 16	42-48-49.324N 070-51-16.610W				Red nun.	
9070	NORTH PIER LIGHT 18 On ledge.	42-48-48.875N 070-51-27.384W	Fl R 6s	22	3	TR on skeleton tower on concrete foundation.	
9075	- Buoy 17 Marks shoal.	42-48-46.964N 070-51-31.671W				Green can.	
9080	- Buoy 20	42-48-47.487N 070-51-49.108W				Red nun.	
9085	- Buoy 22	42-48-48.923N 070-51-56.556W				Red nun.	
9090	- Buoy 24	42-49-20.773N 070-52-40.053W				Red nun.	
9095	- Buoy 26	42-49-36.577N 070-53-24.037W				Red nun.	
9099	Carr Island Danger Buoy	42-49-55.000N 070-53-40.000W				White can with orange bands, worded ROCK.	Maintained from May 1 to Oct. 1. Private aid.
9105	Steamboat Channel South Junction Buoy SCS	42-49-57.434N 070-53-53.442W				Green and red bands; can.	
9110	Steamboat Channel Buoy 2A	42-50-00.687N 070-54-08.680W				Red nun.	
9115	Steamboat Channel Buoy 4A	42-50-01.561N 070-54-39.052W				Red nun.	
9120	Steamboat Channel Buoy 6A	42-50-05.531N 070-54-49.566W				Red nun.	

(1) No.	(2) Name and Location	(3) Position	(4) Characteristic	(5) Height	(6) Range	(7) Structure	(8) Remarks

MASSACHUSETTS - First District

NEWBURYPORT HARBOR AND PLUM ISLAND SOUND
  Merrimack River

(1) No.	(2) Name and Location	(3) Position	(7) Structure	(8) Remarks
9125	- Buoy 27	42-50-11.535N 070-54-02.337W	Green can.	
9145	Steamboat Channel North Junction Buoy SCN	42-50-11.015N 070-54-48.943W	Green and red bands; can.	
9155	- Buoy 30	42-50-27.119N 070-54-52.043W	Red nun.	
9160	- Buoy 31	42-50-24.691N 070-54-52.850W	Green can.	
9165	- Buoy 32	42-50-29.979N 070-55-11.056W	Red nun.	
9170	- Buoy 34	42-50-19.331N 070-55-30.348W	Red nun.	Maintained from 1 May to 15 Oct.
9175	- Buoy 35	42-49-52.757N 070-55-54.252W	Green can.	Maintained from 1 May to 15 Oct.
9180	- Buoy 36	42-49-41.508N 070-55-58.973W	Red nun.	Maintained from 1 May to 15 Oct.
9185	- Buoy 38	42-49-22.831N 070-56-16.328W	Red nun.	Maintained from 1 May to 15 Oct.
9190	- Buoy 40	42-49-10.711N 070-56-43.975W	Red nun.	Maintained from 1 May to 15 Oct.
9195	- Buoy 42	42-49-09.730N 070-57-33.437W	Red nun.	Maintained from 1 May to 15 Oct.
9197	- Buoy 42A	42-49-26.785N 070-58-14.686W	Red nun.	Maintained from 1 May to 15 Oct.
9200	- Buoy 43	42-49-24.226N 070-58-14.503W	Green can.	Maintained from 1 May to 15 Oct.
9204	- Buoy 44	42-49-28.779N 070-58-42.038W	Red nun.	Maintained from 1 May to 15 Oct.
9205	- Buoy 45	42-49-28.071N 070-58-59.402W	Green can.	Maintained from 1 May to 15 Oct.
9206	- Buoy 46	42-49-21.507N 070-59-27.234W	Red nun.	Maintained from 1 May to 15 Oct.
9210	- Buoy 47	42-49-22.399N 070-59-38.332W	Green can.	Maintained from 1 May to 15 Oct.
9215	- Buoy 49	42-49-08.509N 071-00-05.887W	Green can.	Maintained from 1 May to 15 Oct.
9220	- Buoy 51	42-48-57.477N 071-00-06.315W	Green can.	Maintained from 1 May to 15 Oct.
9223	- Buoy 52	42-48-48.468N 071-00-05.233W	Red nun.	Maintained from 1 May to 15 Oct.
9225	- Buoy 53	42-48-43.111N 071-00-02.394W	Green can.	Maintained from 1 May to 15 Oct.
9227	Rocks Village Hazard Buoy	42-48-51.783N 071-00-05.947W	White with orange bands marked DANGER ROCKS.	Maintained from May 1 to Nov. 1.
9230	- Buoy 54	42-48-22.248N 070-59-54.797W	Red nun.	Maintained from 1 May to 15 Oct.
9235	- Buoy 55	42-48-12.051N 070-59-58.631W	Green can.	Maintained from 1 May to 15 Oct.

(1) No.	(2) Name and Location	(3) Position	(4) Characteristic	(5) Height	(6) Range	(7) Structure	(8) Remarks
			MASSACHUSETTS - First District				

NEWBURYPORT HARBOR AND PLUM ISLAND SOUND

Merrimack River

(1) No.	(2) Name and Location	(3) Position	(4) Characteristic	(5) Height	(6) Range	(7) Structure	(8) Remarks
9240	- Buoy 57	42-47-56.070N 071-00-35.191W				Green can.	Maintained from 1 May to 15 Oct.
9243	- Buoy 58	42-47-47.675N 071-00-48.372W				Red nun.	Maintained from 1 May to 15 Oct.
9245	- Buoy 59	42-47-31.618N 071-01-10.454W				Green can.	Maintained from 1 May to 15 Oct.
9250	- Buoy 61	42-47-16.916N 071-01-14.396W				Green can.	Maintained from 1 May to 15 Oct.
9252	- Buoy 61A	42-46-54.311N 071-01-19.560W				Green can.	Maintained from 1 May to 15 Oct.
9253	- Buoy 62	42-47-06.006N 071-01-16.865W				Red nun.	Maintained from 1 May to 15 Oct.
9255	- Buoy 63	42-46-25.291N 071-01-32.809W				Green can.	Maintained from 1 May to 15 Oct.
9260	- Buoy 65	42-46-13.330N 071-01-46.910W				Green can.	Maintained from 1 May to 15 Oct.
9265	- Buoy 67	42-45-35.723N 071-02-14.766W				Green can.	Maintained from 1 May to 15 Oct.
9270	- Buoy 68	42-45-26.843N 071-02-24.456W				Red nun.	Maintained from 1 May to 15 Oct.
9275	- Buoy 70	42-45-24.312N 071-02-36.512W				Red nun.	Maintained from 1 May to 15 Oct.
9280	- Buoy 71	42-45-34.331N 071-02-56.910W				Green can.	Maintained from 1 May to 15 Oct.
9285	- Buoy 73	42-46-01.061N 071-03-31.248W				Green can.	Maintained from 1 May to 15 Oct.
9290	- Buoy 75	42-46-10.565N 071-03-53.778W				Green can.	Maintained from 1 May to 15 Oct.
9295	- Buoy 76 Marks submerged cofferdam.	42-46-11.705N 071-03-52.470W				Red nun.	Maintained from 1 May to 15 Oct.
9297	Haverhill Buoy 1	42-46-23.000N 071-04-43.000W				Green can.	Seasonal 01 May - 01 Nov. Private aid.
9297.1	Haverhill Buoy 2	42-46-24.000N 071-04-44.000W				Red nun.	Seasonal 01 May - 01 Nov. Private aid.
9297.2	Haverhill Buoy 3	42-46-21.000N 071-04-52.000W				Green can.	Seasonal 01 May - 01 Nov. Private aid.
9297.3	Haverhill Buoy 4	42-46-22.000N 071-04-53.000W				Red nun.	Seasonal 01 May - 01 Nov. Private aid.
9297.4	Haverhill Buoy 5	42-46-18.000N 071-05-01.000W				Green can.	Seasonal 01 May - 01 Nov. Private aid.
9297.5	Haverhill Buoy 6	42-46-19.000N 071-05-02.000W				Red nun.	Seasonal 01 May - 01 Nov. Private aid.

Plum Island Sound

(1) No.	(2) Name and Location	(3) Position	(4) Characteristic	(5) Height	(6) Range	(7) Structure	(8) Remarks
9300	- *Entrance Lighted Buoy 2*	42-42-10.035N 070-44-24.012W	Fl R 4s		4	Red.	
9305	- Entrance Buoy 3	42-41-29.348N 070-44-13.648W				Green can.	Position frequently shifted with changing conditions.
9310	- Entrance Buoy 4	42-41-18.331N 070-44-41.192W				Red nun.	Position frequently shifted with changing conditions.

(1) No.	(2) Name and Location	(3) Position	(4) Characteristic	(5) Height	(6) Range	(7) Structure	(8) Remarks
		MASSACHUSETTS - First District					
	NEWBURYPORT HARBOR AND PLUM ISLAND SOUND						
	Plum Island Sound						
9315	IPSWICH LIGHT	42-41-06.935N 070-45-58.212W	Oc W 4s	30	5	NR on skeleton tower.	
9320	- Entrance Buoy 6	42-41-21.661N 070-45-01.222W				Red nun.	Position frequently shifted with changing conditions.
9325	- Entrance Buoy 8	42-41-32.389N 070-45-52.441W				Red nun.	Position frequently shifted with changing conditions. Removed when endangered by ice.
9328	- Entrance Buoy 8A	42-41-36.820N 070-46-31.101W				Red nun.	
9330	- Entrance Buoy 10	42-41-41.524N 070-46-56.436W				Red nun.	
9335	- Entrance Buoy 11	42-41-43.198N 070-47-07.836W				Green can.	Maintained from Apr. 15 to Oct. 15.
9336	- Buoy 11A	42-42-07.866N 070-47-21.467W				Green can.	Maintained from Apr. 15 to Oct. 15.
9340	Bass Rock Daybeacon BR On ledge.	42-41-52.283N 070-47-00.834W				NR on iron spindle.	
9345	- Buoy 12	42-42-21.338N 070-47-28.599W				Red nun.	Maintained from Apr 15. to Oct. 15.
9350	- Buoy 13	42-42-40.084N 070-47-45.282W				Green can.	Maintained from Apr 15. to Oct. 15.
9375	- Buoy 14	42-42-42.139N 070-48-34.399W				Red nun.	Maintained from Apr 15. to Oct. 15.
9380	- Buoy 16	42-42-49.268N 070-48-51.261W				Red nun.	Maintained from Apr 15. to Oct. 15.
9385	- Buoy 18	42-42-59.358N 070-48-48.993W				Red nun.	Maintained from Apr 15. to Oct. 15.
9390	- Buoy 19	42-43-13.888N 070-48-46.672W				Green can.	Maintained from Apr 15. to Oct. 15.
9392	- Buoy 21	42-43-31.548N 070-48-47.331W				Green can.	Maintained from Apr 15. to Oct. 15.
9395	- Buoy 22	42-43-36.628N 070-48-39.201W				Red nun.	Maintained from Apr 15. to Oct. 15.
9397	- Buoy 23	42-43-38.088N 070-48-26.577W				Green can.	Maintained from Apr 15. to Oct. 15.
9400	- Buoy 23A	42-43-43.975N 070-48-06.661W				Green can.	Maintained from Apr 15. to Oct. 15.
9405	- Buoy 25	42-44-02.025N 070-48-03.645W				Green can.	Maintained from Apr 15. to Oct. 15.
9410	- Buoy 27	42-44-12.814N 070-48-10.731W				Green can.	Maintained from Apr 15. to Oct. 15.
9413	- Buoy 29	42-44-23.721N 070-48-39.537W				Green can.	Maintained from Apr 15. to Oct. 15.
9415	- Buoy 30	42-44-31.961N 070-49-02.062W				Red nun.	Maintained from Apr 15. to Oct. 15.
	Ipswich River *Maintained from May 1 to Sept. 30.*						
9416	- Buoy 1	42-41-34.440N 070-47-34.800W				Green can.	Private aid.

(1) No.	(2) Name and Location	(3) Position	(4) Characteristic	(5) Height	(6) Range	(7) Structure	(8) Remarks

MASSACHUSETTS - First District

NEWBURYPORT HARBOR AND PLUM ISLAND SOUND

Ipswich River
Maintained from May 1 to Sept. 30.

9416.1	- Buoy 2	42-41-38.220N 070-47-42.360W				Red nun.	Private aid.
9416.2	- Buoy 3	42-41-42.900N 070-47-47.520W				Green can.	Private aid.
9416.3	- Buoy 5	42-41-47.400N 070-48-06.840W				Green can.	Private aid.
9416.4	- Buoy 6	42-41-46.140N 070-47-48.960W				Red nun.	Private aid.
9416.5	- Buoy 7	42-41-38.160N 070-48-17.280W				Green can.	Private aid.
9416.6	- Buoy 8	42-41-35.580N 070-48-18.060W				Red nun.	Private aid.
9416.7	- Buoy 10	42-41-29.580N 070-48-22.800W				Red nun.	Private aid.
9416.8	- Buoy 11	42-41-26.040N 070-48-27.180W				Green can.	Private aid.
9416.9	- Buoy 12	42-41-22.200N 070-48-26.880W				Red nun.	Private aid.
9417	- Buoy 14	42-41-18.480N 070-48-29.040W				Red nun.	Private aid.
9417.1	- Buoy 15	42-41-18.720N 070-48-28.660W				Green can.	Private aid.
9417.2	- Buoy 16	42-41-17.340N 070-48-27.360W				Red nun.	Private aid.
9417.3	- Buoy 17	42-41-16.680N 070-48-41.400W				Green can.	Private aid.
9417.4	- Buoy 19	42-41-15.720N 070-48-45.720W				Green can.	Private aid.
9417.5	- Buoy 20	42-41-10.860N 070-48-52.920W				Red nun.	Private aid.
9417.6	- Buoy 22	42-41-07.560N 070-48-56.580W				Red nun.	Private aid.
9417.7	- Buoy 23	42-41-03.900N 070-49-01.080W				Green can.	Private aid.

Parker River
Position of buoys are frequently shifted due to changing conditions.

9420	- Buoy 32	42-44-40.200N 070-49-09.900W				Red nun.	Private aid.
9425	- Buoy 33	42-44-47.400N 070-49-13.200W				Green can.	Private aid.
9426	- Buoy 34	42-44-59.700N 070-49-11.400W				Red nun.	Private aid.
9430	- Buoy 35	42-45-06.000N 070-49-18.700W				Green can.	Private aid.
9436	- Buoy 37	42-45-12.600N 070-49-24.000W				Green can.	Private aid.
9440	- Buoy 38	42-45-17.100N 070-49-20.400W				Red nun.	Private aid.
9445	- Buoy 39	42-45-20.500N 070-49-24.000W				Green can.	Private aid.
9450	- Buoy 40	42-45-22.800N 070-49-20.400W				Red nun.	Private aid.
9455	- Buoy 42	42-45-26.400N 070-49-27.900W				Red nun.	Private aid.
9460	- Buoy 43	42-45-25.800N 070-49-28.800W				Green can.	Private aid.
9465	- Buoy 44	42-45-27.600N 070-49-37.800W				Red nun.	Private aid.
9475	- Buoy 46	42-45-30.100N 070-49-41.100W				Red nun.	Private aid.
9476	- Buoy 47	42-45-33.600N 070-49-45.000W				Green can.	Private aid.

(1) No.	(2) Name and Location	(3) Position	(4) Characteristic	(5) Height	(6) Range	(7) Structure	(8) Remarks
			MASSACHUSETTS - First District				

NEWBURYPORT HARBOR AND PLUM ISLAND SOUND

Parker River

Position of buoys are frequently shifted due to changing conditions.

| 9477 | - Buoy 48 | 42-45-37.200N
070-49-51.000W | | | | Red nun. | Private aid. |

IPSWICH BAY TO GLOUCESTER HARBOR

Essex Bay

Positions of buoys frequently shifted with changing conditions. Aids maintained from Apr. 15 to Oct. 15 unless otherwise noted.

9480	- *Entrance Lighted Bell Buoy 1*	42-40-48.216N 070-42-17.347W	Fl G 4s		4	Green.	Removed when endangered by ice.
9483	- Entrance Buoy 3	42-40-32.571N 070-42-52.663W				Green can.	Removed when endangered by ice.
9484	- Channel Buoy 3A Marks edge of shoal. Do not pass outside of marked channel.	42-40-16.581N 070-43-15.032W				Green can.	
9485	- Channel Buoy 4	42-39-39.461N 070-43-24.738W				Red nun.	
9490	- Channel Buoy 6	42-39-25.864N 070-43-21.225W				Red nun.	
9495	- Danger Daybeacon On ledge.	42-39-31.846N 070-43-23.740W				NW on spindle.	DANGER - SHOALING.
9500	- Channel Buoy 8 At northeast end of middle ground.	42-39-23.249N 070-43-20.646W				Red nun.	
9505	- Channel Buoy 10	42-39-13.295N 070-43-21.822W				Red nun.	
9510	- Channel Buoy 11	42-39-03.713N 070-43-25.542W				Green can.	
9515	- Channel Buoy 12 At east side of middle ground.	42-38-58.373N 070-43-42.894W				Red nun.	
9520	- Channel Buoy 14	42-38-57.393N 070-43-57.370W				Red nun.	
9525	- Channel Buoy 15	42-38-59.597N 070-44-10.304W				Green can.	
9530	- Channel Buoy 16	42-39-05.051N 070-44-17.023W				Red nun.	
9535	- Channel Buoy 17	42-39-07.739N 070-44-25.434W				Green can.	

Essex River

Aids maintained from May. 1 to Oct. 1 unless otherwise noted.

9540	- Channel Buoy 18	42-39-09.126N 070-45-01.242W				Red nun.	Private aid.
9545	- Channel Buoy 19	42-39-14.000N 070-45-04.000W				Green can.	Private aid.
9550	- Midchannel Buoy A	42-39-16.400N 070-45-16.500W				Red and white stripes; spar.	Private aid.
9555	- Midchannel Buoy B	42-39-11.400N 070-45-28.900W				Red and white stripes; spar.	Private aid.
9560	- Midchannel Buoy C	42-39-07.300N 070-45-31.100W				Red and white stripes; spar.	Private aid.
9565	- Midchannel Buoy D	42-39-02.200N 070-45-32.400W				Red and white stripes; spar.	Private aid.
9570	- Midchannel Buoy E	42-38-55.900N 070-45-37.000W				Red and white stripes; spar.	Private aid.
9575	- Midchannel Buoy F	42-38-50.000N 070-45-41.000W				Red and white stripes; spar.	Private aid.
9578	- Midchannel Buoy J	42-38-28.200N 070-45-39.700W				Red with white stripes; spar.	Private aid.
9580	- Midchannel Buoy G	42-38-50.200N 070-45-41.300W				Red and white stripes; spar.	Private aid.
9585	- Midchannel Buoy H	42-38-41.700N 070-45-39.900W				Red and white stripes; spar.	Private aid.

(1) No.	(2) Name and Location	(3) Position	(4) Characteristic	(5) Height	(6) Range	(7) Structure	(8) Remarks

MASSACHUSETTS - First District

IPSWICH BAY TO GLOUCESTER HARBOR

Essex River
Aids maintained from May. 1 to Oct. 1 unless otherwise noted.

(1) No.	(2) Name and Location	(3) Position	(4) Characteristic	(5) Height	(6) Range	(7) Structure	(8) Remarks
9588	- Midchannel Buoy K	42-38-26.600N 070-45-48.101W				Red and white stripes; spar.	Private aid.
9589.1	- Midchannel Buoy L	42-38-24.100N 070-45-53.400W				Red and white stripes; spar.	Private aid.

Annisquam River

(1) No.	(2) Name and Location	(3) Position	(4) Characteristic	(5) Height	(6) Range	(7) Structure	(8) Remarks
9590	Plum Cove Ledge Buoy 1	42-40-44.604N 070-40-06.136W				Green can.	
9595	- *Entrance Lighted Bell Buoy AR*	42-40-23.025N 070-40-58.366W	Mo (A) W		3	Red and white stripes with red spherical topmark.	Removed when endangered by ice.
9600	- Entrance Buoy 3	42-40-06.906N 070-40-52.795W				Green can.	
9605	- Channel Buoy 4	42-39-57.561N 070-40-57.811W				Red nun.	
9610	- Channel Buoy 5	42-39-47.411N 070-40-56.449W				Green can.	
9615	**Annisquam Harbor Light**	42-39-42.816N 070-40-53.451W	Fl W 7.5s (R sector)	45	W 14 R 11	White cylindrical tower; elevated walk to dwelling.	Red from 180° to 217°. HORN: 2 blasts ev 60s (3s bl-3s si-3s bl-51s si). MRASS-Fog signal is radio activated, during times of reduced visibility, turn marine VHF-FM radio to channel 83A/157.175Mhz. Key microphone 5 times consecutively, to activate fog signal for 45 minutes.
9620	- Channel Buoy 6	42-39-39.408N 070-40-59.449W				Red nun.	
9625	- Channel Daybeacon 7	42-39-29.897N 070-40-59.705W				SG on spindle on mound.	
9630	- Channel Buoy 8	42-39-22.521N 070-41-04.413W				Red nun.	
9635	Barn Rocks Daybeacon BN North of rocks.	42-39-16.967N 070-41-08.753W				NR on spindle.	
9640	- Channel Buoy 9	42-39-13.190N 070-40-59.545W				Green can.	
9645	- Channel Buoy 11	42-39-03.316N 070-40-46.494W				Green can.	
9647	- Channel Buoy 12	42-38-59.681N 070-40-44.833W				Red nun.	
9650	Lobster Cove Daybeacon LC	42-39-05.676N 070-40-43.294W				NG on stone crib.	
9655	- Channel Buoy 14	42-38-55.735N 070-40-43.811W				Red nun.	
9660	- CHANNEL LIGHT 15	42-38-55.901N 070-40-40.163W	Fl G 2.5s	10	3	SG on black cylindrical structure.	
9665	- Channel Buoy 16	42-38-44.196N 070-40-48.930W				Red nun.	
9670	- Channel Buoy 17	42-38-29.713N 070-40-56.326W				Green can.	
9675	- CHANNEL LIGHT 19	42-38-21.467N 070-41-04.583W	Fl G 4s	10	4	SG on black cylindrical structure.	
9680	- Channel Buoy 21	42-38-18.660N 070-41-06.926W				Green can.	
9685	- Channel Buoy 23 Close to rock.	42-38-11.249N 070-41-08.207W				Green can.	
9690	- Channel Buoy 24	42-38-08.822N 070-41-09.281W				Red nun.	
9695	- CHANNEL LIGHT 25	42-38-07.763N 070-41-06.617W	Fl G 2.5s	11	3	SG on black cylindrical structure.	

(1) No.	(2) Name and Location	(3) Position	(4) Characteristic	(5) Height	(6) Range	(7) Structure	(8) Remarks
			MASSACHUSETTS - First District				
	IPSWICH BAY TO GLOUCESTER HARBOR						
	Annisquam River						
9700	- Channel Buoy 26	42-38-02.586N 070-41-13.984W				Red nun.	
9705	- Channel Buoy 28	42-37-53.345N 070-41-26.388W				Red nun.	
9710	- Channel Buoy 29	42-37-44.945N 070-41-28.470W				Green can.	
9715	- CHANNEL LIGHT 30	42-37-46.253N 070-41-31.181W	Fl R 4s	12	4	TR on red cylindrical structure.	
9720	- Channel Buoy 31	42-37-41.752N 070-41-25.814W				Green can.	
9725	- Channel Buoy 32	42-37-33.177N 070-41-21.759W				Red nun.	
9730	- Channel Buoy 33	42-37-25.984N 070-41-17.932W				Green can.	
9735	- Channel Buoy 34 On end of shoal.	42-37-24.024N 070-41-19.394W				Red nun.	
9740	- CHANNEL LIGHT 35	42-37-19.955N 070-41-19.751W	Fl G 2.5s	10	3	SG on black cylindrical structure.	
9745	- Channel Buoy 36	42-37-19.279N 070-41-21.215W				Red nun.	
9750	- Channel Buoy 38	42-37-14.029N 070-41-15.927W				Red nun.	
9755	- Channel Buoy 39	42-37-13.796N 070-41-13.829W				Green can.	
9760	- Channel Buoy 40	42-37-11.730N 070-41-12.078W				Red nun.	
9765	- CHANNEL LIGHT 41	42-37-11.783N 070-41-07.439W	Fl G 4s	10	4	SG on black cylindrical structure.	
9770	- Channel Buoy 43	42-37-09.262N 070-40-56.589W				Green can.	
9775	- Channel Buoy 44	42-37-06.510N 070-40-46.126W				Red nun.	
9785	- Channel Buoy 46	42-36-56.085N 070-40-45.183W				Red nun.	
9787	- Channel Buoy 47	42-36-51.746N 070-40-44.117W				Green can.	
9790	- Channel Buoy 49	42-36-46.507N 070-40-42.648W				Green can.	
9795	- CHANNEL LIGHT 48	42-36-47.393N 070-40-44.825W	Fl R 4s	10	4	TR on box on black cylindrical structure.	
9800	- Channel Buoy 50	42-36-45.121N 070-40-42.354W				Red nun.	
9805	- *South Entrance Danger Lighted Buoy*	42-36-32.659N 070-40-19.219W	Q W		3	White with orange bands marked DANGER.	Removed when endangered by ice.
9810	- South Entrance Buoy BC	42-36-31.358N 070-40-15.411W				Red and white stripes; can.	
	Sandy Bay						
9815	- *Breakwater Lighted Gong Buoy 3*	42-40-48.817N 070-36-05.378W	Q G		4	Green.	Replaced by can when endangered by ice. Do not pass to eastward of buoy.
9820	*Avery Ledge Lighted Buoy 2*	42-40-02.803N 070-35-16.725W	Fl R 4s		3	Red.	
9825	Nine Foot Rock Buoy 3	42-39-50.377N 070-36-02.917W				Green can.	
9830	Harbor Rock Buoy 4 Marks granite block.	42-39-43.256N 070-36-34.651W				Red nun.	
9835	ROCKPORT BREAKWATER LIGHT 6	42-39-38.741N 070-36-42.863W	Fl R 4s	32	4	TR on Spindle.	
9840	Dodge Rock Daybeacon 2 Off southwest side of ledge.	42-40-03.811N 070-37-05.706W				TR on spindle.	

(1) No.	(2) Name and Location	(3) Position	(4) Characteristic	(5) Height	(6) Range	(7) Structure	(8) Remarks
			MASSACHUSETTS - First District				
	IPSWICH BAY TO GLOUCESTER HARBOR						
	Sandy Bay						
9845	Pigeon Cove Rock Buoy 2	42-40-27.099N 070-37-11.310W					
	Gloucester Harbor						
9850	Eastern Point Ledge Buoy 4 Off southwest point of ledge.	42-34-36.600N 070-39-58.732W				Red nun.	
9855	GLOUCESTER BREAKWATER LIGHT	42-34-57.420N 070-40-20.475W	Oc R 4s	45	6	White house and tower on brown square skeleton framework.	HORN: 1 blast ev 10s (1s bl). Fog signal is radio activated, during times of reduced visibility, turn marine VHF-FM radio to channel 83A/157.175Mhz. Key microphone 5 times consecutively, to activate fog signal for 60 minutes.
9860	Dog Bar Buoy 2DB	42-34-58.569N 070-40-24.370W				Red nun.	
9865	Normans Woe Rock Bell Buoy 3	42-34-40.100N 070-41-19.157W				Green.	
9870	*Round Rock Shoal Lighted Buoy RR* Southwest of shoal.	42-34-53.789N 070-40-46.900W	Fl (2+1)R 6s		4	Red and green bands.	
9875	Dog Bar Channel Buoy 1DB Northeast of shoal.	42-35-00.271N 070-40-31.025W				Green can.	
9877	- CG Mooring Buoy	42-35-31.595N 070-39-52.091W					
9880	*Tenpound Island Ledge Lighted Buoy 6*	42-35-45.969N 070-40-19.760W	Fl R 4s		3	Red.	
9885	*Praire Ledge Lighted Buoy 7*	42-35-53.919N 070-40-34.581W	Fl G 4s		4	Green.	
9890	Mayflower Ledge Buoy 8	42-36-02.779N 070-40-06.110W				Red nun.	
9895	TEN POUND ISLAND LIGHT	42-36-06.735N 070-39-56.011W	Iso R 6s	57	5	White conical tower.	HORN: 2 blasts ev 20s (2s bl-2s si-2s bl-14s si). Fog signal is radio activated, during times of reduced visibility, turn marine VHF-FM radio to channel 83A/157.175Mhz. Key microphone 5 times consecutively, to activate fog signal for 60 minutes.
	Gloucester Inner Harbor						
9900	- *Channel Lighted Buoy 9*	42-36-20.482N 070-39-59.955W	Fl G 4s		3	Green.	
	Gloucester Harbor						
9905	Black Rock Danger Daybeacon	42-36-21.738N 070-39-42.960W				NW on spindle on ledge.	DANGER ROCKS
	Gloucester Inner Harbor						
9912	- *Channel Lighted Buoy 10*	42-36-18.335N 070-39-50.080W	Fl R 2.5s		3	Red.	
9915	- *Channel Lighted Buoy 12*	42-36-28.743N 070-39-32.154W	Fl R 4s		3	Red.	
9920	- *Junction Lighted Buoy GH*	42-36-34.469N 070-39-27.230W	Fl (2+1)R 6s		4	Red with green bands.	
9935	- North Channel Buoy 2	42-36-43.919N 070-39-22.850W				Red nun.	
9940	- North Channel Buoy 4	42-36-47.468N 070-39-19.630W				Red nun.	
9942	- Danger Daybeacon	42-36-47.231N 070-39-17.075W				NW on spindle.	
9945	- South Channel Buoy 2S	42-36-34.289N 070-39-21.320W				Red nun.	
9950	- South Channel Buoy 3	42-36-38.830N 070-39-14.925W				Green can.	

(1) No.	(2) Name and Location	(3) Position	(4) Characteristic	(5) Height	(6) Range	(7) Structure	(8) Remarks

MASSACHUSETTS - First District

IPSWICH BAY TO GLOUCESTER HARBOR
Gloucester Harbor

(1) No.	(2) Name and Location	(3) Position	(4) Characteristic	(5) Height	(6) Range	(7) Structure	(8) Remarks
9960	Green Rock Danger Daybeacon On outer rock of ledge.	42-36-09.518N 070-39-43.569W				NW on iron spindle.	DANGER ROCKS.

SALEM AND LYNN HARBORS
Salem Channel

(1) No.	(2) Name and Location	(3) Position	(4) Characteristic	(5) Height	(6) Range	(7) Structure	(8) Remarks
9965	- Buoy 3	42-31-08.891N 070-45-04.383W				Green can.	
9970	- Buoy 5	42-31-46.040N 070-45-43.095W				Green can.	
9975 350	**Bakers Island Light**	42-32-11.235N 070-47-09.312W	Al WR 20s	111	W 16 R 14	White conical tower. 111	Emergency light, Fl W 10s when main light extinguished. Light and Horn is reduced intensity when main light or horn is extinguished. HORN: 1 blast ev 30s (3s bl). MRASS-Fog signal is radio activated, during times of reduced visibility, turn marine VHF-FM radio to channel 83A/157.175Mhz. Key microphone 5 times consecutively, to activate fog signal for 60 minutes.
9980	- Buoy 6	42-32-49.699N 070-45-53.467W				Red nun.	
9985	- Buoy 7	42-32-05.750N 070-46-29.068W				Green can.	
9990	Whaleback Daybeacon 8 On rock.	42-32-54.760N 070-47-04.641W				TR on spindle.	
9995	- Lighted Bell Buoy 9	42-32-23.599N 070-47-17.379W	Q G		4	Green.	
10000	HOSPITAL POINT RANGE FRONT LIGHT	42-32-47.396N 070-51-21.490W	F W	69		White pyramidal tower.	Visible all around; higher intensity on range line. Floodlighted sunset to sunrise.
10005	HOSPITAL POINT RANGE REAR LIGHT 2,032 yards, 276.3° from front light.	42-32-53.976N 070-52-42.444W	F W	161		White church spire.	Visible 2° each side of range line.
10010	Salem-Eagle Island Channel Junction Buoy SE	42-32-21.446N 070-47-45.247W				Green can with red bands.	
10015	- Lighted Buoy 10 Off southwest edge of shoal.	42-32-34.689N 070-48-01.850W	Fl R 2.5s		4	Red.	
10020	- Lighted Buoy 11	42-32-32.935N 070-48-33.312W	Fl G 4s		4	Green.	
10025	Bowditch Ledge Daybeacon	42-32-25.179N 070-48-41.382W				NR on conical granite monument.	
10026	Bowditch Ledge North Danger Buoy	42-32-25.908N 070-48-40.581W				White with orange bands, can marked DANGER ROCKS	Removed when endangered by ice.
10027	Bowditch Ledge South Danger Buoy	42-32-23.934N 070-48-41.022W				White with orange bands, can marked DANGER ROCKS.	Removed when endangered by ice.
10030	- Lighted Buoy 12 South of ledge.	42-32-37.861N 070-48-52.917W	Fl R 4s		4	Red.	
10035	- Lighted Buoy 13	42-32-34.719N 070-50-21.214W	Fl G 4s		3	Green.	
10040	- Buoy 14	42-32-43.798N 070-50-11.964W				Red nun	
10045	- Lighted Buoy 15	42-32-28.779N 070-50-44.004W	Q G		3	Green.	
10050	- Lighted Buoy 16	42-32-14.158N 070-51-08.185W	Fl R 4s		4	Red.	
10055	- Lighted Buoy 17	42-31-56.278N 070-51-21.285W	Fl G 2.5s		4	Green.	
10060	- Buoy 18	42-31-58.658N 070-51-26.135W				Red nun.	

(1) No.	(2) Name and Location	(3) Position	(4) Characteristic	(5) Height	(6) Range	(7) Structure	(8) Remarks
			MASSACHUSETTS - First District				
	SALEM AND LYNN HARBORS						
	Salem Channel						
10065	Abbot Rock Daybeacon	42-31-49.312N 070-51-44.634W				NR on staff on pyramidal granite base.	
10070	Great Aquavitae Daybeacon	42-31-34.594N 070-51-26.016W				NR on spindle.	
10075	Little Aquavitae Daybeacon	42-31-34.596N 070-51-11.303W				NR on spindle.	
10080	- Buoy 20	42-31-48.394N 070-51-36.012W				Red nun.	
10085	- *Lighted Buoy 21*	42-31-18.794N 070-52-01.092W	Fl G 4s		3	Green.	Replaced by can when endangered by ice.
10090	FORT PICKERING LIGHT	42-31-35.200N 070-51-59.000W	Fl W 4s	28		Atop of white conical tower on concrete base.	Private aid.
10095	- *Lighted Buoy 22*	42-31-28.319N 070-51-56.523W	Q R		3	Red	Replaced by nun when endangered by ice.
10100	SALEM LIGHT 23	42-31-13.252N 070-52-22.878W	Q G	20	4	SG on gray skeleton tower on pile structure.	
10105	- Buoy 24	42-31-18.378N 070-52-21.586W				Red nun.	
10110	- Buoy 25	42-31-15.018N 070-52-30.706W				Green can.	
	Derby Channel						
10115	- Daybeacon 2	42-30-54.434N 070-52-28.312W				TR on pile.	
10120	- Daybeacon 3	42-30-49.546N 070-52-41.166W				SG on pile structure.	
10125	- *Lighted Buoy 4*	42-30-55.808N 070-52-55.056W	Fl R 2.5s		4	Red.	
10129	DERBY WHARF LIGHT	42-30-59.548N 070-53-00.768W	Fl R 6s	25	4	White square tower.	Maintained by the U.S.Park Service.
10130	- Daybeacon 5	42-30-57.234N 070-53-02.112W				SG on spindle.	
	Palmer Cove Channel *Maintained from May 1 to Dec. 1.*						
10131	- Buoy 1	42-30-52.020N 070-52-57.362W				Green can.	Private aid.
10131.5	- Buoy 2PC	42-30-52.800N 070-52-57.800W				Red nun.	Private aid.
10131.6	- Buoy 3	42-30-50.940N 070-53-00.360W				Green can.	Private aid.
10132	- Buoy 4	42-30-52.380N 070-53-00.300W				Red nun.	Private aid.
10132.5	- Buoy 5	42-30-50.040N 070-53-03.660W				Green can.	Private aid.
10133	- Buoy 6	42-30-51.700N 070-53-03.000W				Red nun.	Private aid.
10133.5	- Buoy 7	42-30-49.560N 070-53-08.220W				Green can.	Private aid.
10134	- Buoy 8	42-30-51.000N 070-53-06.100W				Red nun.	Private aid.
10134.1	- Daybeacon 9	42-30-48.900N 070-53-09.200W				SG on pile.	Private aid.
10134.2	- Daybeacon 10	42-30-49.980N 070-53-09.120W				TR on pile.	Private aid.
	Dion Yacht Yard						
10135	- Channel Daybeacon 1	42-30-45.900N 070-52-45.700W				SG on pile.	Private aid.
10135.1	- Channel Daybeacon 2	42-30-47.200N 070-52-46.300W				TR on pile.	Private aid.
10136	- Channel Daybeacon 3	42-30-43.600N 070-52-50.000W				SG on pile.	Private aid.

(1) No.	(2) Name and Location	(3) Position	(4) Characteristic	(5) Height	(6) Range	(7) Structure	(8) Remarks
			MASSACHUSETTS - First District				
	SALEM AND LYNN HARBORS						
	Dion Yacht Yard						
10136.1	- Channel Daybeacon 4	42-30-44.400N 070-52-51.500W				TR on pile.	Private aid.
10137	- Channel Daybeacon 5	42-30-41.500N 070-52-54.600W				SG on pile.	Private aid.
10137.1	- Channel Daybeacon 6	42-30-42.500N 070-52-55.700W				TR on pile.	Private aid.
10138	- Channel Daybeacon 7	42-30-39.000N 070-52-59.900W				SG on pile.	Private aid.
10138.1	- Channel Daybeacon 8	42-30-40.200N 070-53-00.500W				TR on pile.	Private aid.
10139	- Channel Daybeacon 9	42-30-37.700N 070-53-02.900W				SG on pile.	Private aid.
10139.1	- Channel Daybeacon 10	42-30-38.900N 070-53-03.400W				TR on pile.	Private aid.
	Salem Channel						
10143	Forest River Rock Daybeacon 2	42-30-13.834N 070-52-49.512W				TR on spindle.	
	Salem South Channel						
10144	- Buoy 2	42-31-14.934N 070-50-00.796W				Red nun.	
10145	- Buoy 3	42-31-23.739N 070-50-36.873W				Green can.	
10150	- Buoy 4	42-31-25.639N 070-50-34.683W				Red nun.	
10152	Endeavors Rock Daybeacon	42-31-17.152N 070-50-36.786W				NR on spindle.	
10155	- Buoy 6	42-31-29.388N 070-51-15.164W				Red nun.	
	Manchester Channel						
10160	Sauli Rock Daybeacon 1	42-33-07.325N 070-47-28.032W				SG on spindle.	
10165	- Buoy 2 Off southwest end of ledge.	42-33-16.933N 070-47-08.787W				Red nun.	
10170	- Buoy 4	42-33-24.099N 070-47-09.720W				Red nun.	
10175	- Buoy 5	42-33-35.788N 070-47-11.350W				Green can.	
10180	- Buoy 6	42-33-45.573N 070-46-57.342W				Red nun.	
10185	- Buoy 7	42-33-46.167N 070-46-58.351W				Green can.	
10190	- Buoy 8	42-33-51.796N 070-46-49.556W				Red nun.	
10195	- Buoy 9	42-33-52.326N 070-46-50.319W				Green can.	
10200	- Buoy 10	42-33-57.697N 070-46-42.183W				Red nun.	
10205	- Buoy 12	42-34-00.509N 070-46-38.549W				Red nun.	
10210	- Buoy 13	42-34-07.109N 070-46-29.362W				Green can.	
	Beverly Channel						
10215	- Buoy 2	42-32-22.558N 070-51-31.346W				Red nun.	
10220	- Buoy 3	42-32-19.917N 070-51-45.146W				Green can.	
10225	- Buoy 4	42-32-30.397N 070-51-59.926W				Red nun.	
10230	- Buoy 5	42-32-28.317N 070-52-02.606W				Green can.	
10235	- Buoy 7	42-32-30.007N 070-52-13.607W				Green can.	
10240	- Buoy 8	42-32-27.940N 070-52-25.130W				Red nun.	

(1) No.	(2) Name and Location	(3) Position	(4) Characteristic	(5) Height	(6) Range	(7) Structure	(8) Remarks

MASSACHUSETTS - First District

SALEM AND LYNN HARBORS

Beverly Channel

10245	- Buoy 9	42-32-23.867N 070-52-27.727W					Green can.
10250	- Buoy 10	42-32-22.497N 070-52-37.147W					Red nun.
10255	- Buoy 11	42-32-17.957N 070-52-39.797W					Green can.
10260	- Buoy 13	42-32-19.497N 070-52-52.838W					Green can.
10265	Lobster Rocks Daybeacon 13A	42-32-18.222N 070-52-53.373W					SG on staff on square, granite cribwork.
10268	- Buoy 15	42-32-20.766N 070-53-10.273W					Green can.

Rams Horn Channel

10270	Monument Bar Daybeacon 1	42-32-22.671N 070-52-23.744W					SG on spindle on cribwork base.
10275	Rams Horn Rock Daybeacon 3	42-32-09.468N 070-52-30.523W					SG on pile on granite cribwork.

Danvers River

10280	- Buoy 1	42-32-16.177N 070-53-28.188W					Green can.
10285	- Buoy 2	42-32-19.081N 070-53-41.766W					Red nun.
10290	- Buoy 3	42-32-23.888N 070-53-49.775W					Green can.
10295	- Buoy 4	42-32-39.033N 070-54-05.153W					Red nun.
10300	- Buoy 5	42-32-47.699N 070-54-25.301W					Green can.
10305	- Buoy 6	42-32-42.196N 070-54-38.983W					Red nun.
10310	- Buoy 8	42-32-43.600N 070-54-48.895W					Red nun.

Bass River

10320	- Channel Junction Buoy	42-32-18.349N 070-53-33.962W					Green can with red bands.
10325	- Channel Buoy 2	42-32-20.203N 070-53-31.784W					Red nun.
10330	- Channel Buoy 3	42-32-28.277N 070-53-37.989W					Green can.
10335	- Channel Buoy 4	42-32-30.421N 070-53-37.267W					Red nun.
10340	- Channel Buoy 5	42-32-31.051N 070-53-39.323W					Green can.
10345	- Channel Buoy 6	42-32-38.592N 070-53-29.615W					Red nun.
10350	- Channel Buoy 7	42-32-42.947N 070-53-22.772W					Green can.
10355	- Channel Buoy 9	42-32-45.173N 070-53-19.276W					Green can.

Eagle Island Channel

10360	Hardy Rock Daybeacon HR	42-32-10.229N 070-47-59.622W					NR on spindle.
10365	- Buoy 3	42-32-01.180N 070-47-42.579W					Green can
10370	- Buoy 4	42-31-56.290N 070-48-01.030W					Red nun.
10375	- Buoy 5	42-31-41.240N 070-47-57.899W					Green can.
10380	- Buoy 6	42-31-41.440N 070-48-13.860W					Red nun.

Childrens Island Channel

10383 355	*Newcomb Ledge Lighted Whistle Buoy 1*	42-30-27.872N 070-44-23.262W	Fl G 4s		4		Green.

(1) No.	(2) Name and Location	(3) Position	(4) Characteristic	(5) Height	(6) Range	(7) Structure	(8) Remarks
			MASSACHUSETTS - First District				
	SALEM AND LYNN HARBORS						
	Childrens Island Channel						
10385	- Buoy 2	42-30-28.681N 070-45-36.174W				Red nun.	
10390	- Buoy 4	42-30-29.200N 070-46-50.357W				Red nun.	
10395	Satan Rock Daybeacon 6	42-30-36.898N 070-48-01.536W				TR on spindle.	
10400	- Buoy 7	42-30-59.269N 070-48-46.640W				Green can.	
10405	Brimbles Daybeacon On rock.	42-31-16.576N 070-48-28.608W				NR on spindle.	
	Marblehead Channel						
10410	Tinkers Rock Gong Buoy TR South of shoal.	42-28-54.771N 070-48-51.988W				Green with red bands.	
10420	Tom Moore Rock Buoy 1A	42-29-42.034N 070-49-39.512W				Green can.	
10425	*Fifteen-Foot Rock Lighted Bell Buoy FR*	42-30-14.590N 070-49-04.650W	Fl (2+1)R 6s		3	Red and green bands.	
10430	- Buoy 1	42-30-26.860N 070-49-48.081W				Green can.	
10435	- Buoy 2	42-30-43.449N 070-49-25.251W				Red nun.	
	Marblehead Harbor						
10440	- Buoy 1MH	42-30-29.619N 070-50-01.541W				Green can.	
10445	- Buoy 2MH	42-30-39.039N 070-50-14.742W				Red nun.	
10450	MARBLEHEAD LIGHT	42-30-19.479N 070-50-01.481W	F G	130	7	Square skeleton tower, brown to gallery, black above..	
10451.1	- Fairway Buoy 3	42-30-30.200N 070-50-22.800W				Green can.	Private aid.
10451.12	- Fairway Buoy 4	42-30-32.700N 070-50-22.500W				Red nun.	Private aid.
10451.13	- Fairway Buoy 5	42-30-27.000N 070-50-27.700W				Green can.	Private aid.
10451.14	- Fairway Buoy 6	42-30-28.800N 070-50-27.200W				Red nun.	Private aid.
10451.15	- Fairway Buoy 7	42-30-24.600N 070-50-30.100W				Green can.	Private aid.
10451.16	- Fairway Buoy 8	42-30-26.000N 070-50-30.000W				Red nun.	Private aid.
10451.17	- Fairway Buoy 9	42-30-20.900N 070-50-34.700W				Green can.	Private aid.
10451.18	- Fairway Buoy 10	42-30-23.700N 070-50-33.100W				Red nun.	Private aid.
10451.19	- Fairway Buoy 11	42-30-18.100N 070-50-37.600W				Green can.	Private aid.
10451.2	- Fairway Buoy 12	42-30-20.500N 070-50-36.800W				Red nun.	Private aid.
10451.21	- Fairway Buoy 13	42-30-16.500N 070-50-40.200W				Green can.	Private aid.
10451.22	- Fairway Buoy 14	42-30-18.200N 070-50-39.700W				Red nun.	Private aid.
	Marblehead Channel						
10455	Kettle Bottom Ledge Daybeacon 1	42-31-08.872N 070-50-10.800W				SG on monopole.	
10465	- *Lighted Buoy 3*	42-31-07.869N 070-49-28.201W	Fl G 4s		4	Green.	
10470	- *Lighted Buoy 4*	42-31-17.439N 070-49-05.961W	Fl R 4s		3	Red.	
10475	- Buoy 5	42-31-39.758N 070-49-46.542W				Green can.	

91

(1) No.	(2) Name and Location	(3) Position	(4) Characteristic	(5) Height	(6) Range	(7) Structure	(8) Remarks
			MASSACHUSETTS - First District				

SALEM AND LYNN HARBORS
Marblehead Channel

(1) No.	(2) Name and Location	(3) Position	(4) Characteristic	(5) Height	(6) Range	(7) Structure	(8) Remarks
10480	- Buoy 6	42-31-47.749N 070-49-16.902W				Red nun.	
10485	Little Haste Daybeacon On rock.	42-32-07.518N 070-50-34.147W				NR on spindle.	
10490	- Buoy 7	42-32-09.759N 070-50-01.033W				Green can.	
	Nahant Bay Approach						
10495	Roaring Bull Daybeacon 2 On rock.	42-28-46.654N 070-50-12.822W				TR on spindle.	
10500	Pitchers Shoal Buoy PS	42-28-03.615N 070-51-19.886W				Green can with red bands.	
10505	Middle Ground Buoy 4	42-28-08.048N 070-51-26.368W				Red nun.	
10510	Sammy Rock Buoy 6	42-28-16.161N 070-51-58.183W				Red nun.	
10520	Great Pig Rocks Buoy 6	42-27-29.082N 070-51-28.181W				Red nun.	
10525	Dolphin Rock Buoy 10	42-27-58.432N 070-51-59.783W				Red nun.	
10530	Dread Ledge Daybeacon 2	42-27-22.864N 070-53-41.776W				TR on spindle.	
10535	Fishing Point Rock Buoy 2	42-27-40.381N 070-54-27.186W				Red nun.	
	Nahant Harbor						
10540	Shag Rocks Lighted Buoy 2 Marks south side of shoal.	42-24-43.284N 070-54-21.564W	Fl R 4s		4	Red.	Replaced by nun when endangered by ice.
10545	Joe Beach Isolated Danger Buoy DJB	42-24-53.624N 070-54-54.945W				Black and red bands with two black spherical topmarks; can.	
10550	Bass Rock Isolated Danger Buoy DBR	42-24-43.384N 070-55-22.685W				Black and red bands with two black spherical topmarks; can.	
10555	Flip Rock Gong Buoy FR	42-24-08.571N 070-55-27.257W				Red with green bands.	
10560	Nahant Rock Buoy 1	42-24-22.034N 070-56-46.512W				Green can.	
	Lynn Harbor						
10565	- Channel Lighted Bell Buoy 2	42-25-11.633N 070-57-10.488W	Fl R 2.5s		4	Red.	Replaced by nun when endangered by ice.
10570	- Channel Buoy 4	42-25-30.709N 070-57-10.876W				Red nun.	
10575	- Channel Buoy 6	42-25-47.843N 070-56-56.081W				Red nun.	
10580	WHITE ROCKS LIGHT 7 125 feet outside channel limit.	42-25-33.613N 070-57-14.500W	Fl G 2.5s	49	4	SG on multi-pile.	
10585	BLACK ROCKS LIGHT 9	42-25-59.162N 070-56-52.621W	Fl G 6s	49	4	SG on multi-pile.	
10590	- Channel Lighted Buoy 10	42-26-04.472N 070-56-43.758W	Fl R 6s		3	Red.	Replaced by nun from Oct. 15 to Apr. 15.
10595	SANDY POINT LIGHT 11 75 feet outside channel limit.	42-26-34.276N 070-56-32.673W	Fl G 2.5s	45	4	SG on multi-pile.	
10600	- Channel Buoy 12	42-26-28.961N 070-56-31.742W				Red nun.	
10605	- Channel Buoy 13	42-26-47.206N 070-56-28.530W				Green can.	
10610	- Channel Lighted Buoy 14	42-26-52.382N 070-56-26.188W	Fl R 4s		3	Red.	Replaced by nun from Oct. 15 to Apr. 15.

(1) No.	(2) Name and Location	(3) Position	(4) Characteristic	(5) Height	(6) Range	(7) Structure	(8) Remarks
			MASSACHUSETTS - First District				
	SALEM AND LYNN HARBORS						
	Lynn Harbor						
10615	BLACK MARSH CHANNEL LIGHT 15	42-26-54.370N 070-56-31.509W	Fl G 4s	35	4	SG on multi-pile.	
10620	UPPER TURN LIGHT 16	42-27-10.819N 070-56-31.123W	Fl R 2.5s	28	4	TR on skeleton tower.	
10625	- Channel Lighted Buoy 17	42-27-14.261N 070-56-38.689W	Fl G 2.5s		3	Green.	Replaced by can from Oct.15 to Apr. 15.
10630	- Channel Buoy 18	42-27-18.111N 070-56-41.039W				Red nun.	
10635	- Channel Buoy 19	42-27-15.441N 070-56-44.259W				Green can.	
10640	- Channel Buoy 21	42-27-13.692N 070-56-53.113W				Green can.	
	Saugus River Approach Channel						
10645	- Lighted Buoy 2	42-25-34.913N 070-57-36.879W	Fl R 4s		3	Red.	Replaced by nun from Oct. 15 to Apr. 15.
10650	- Buoy 3	42-25-54.612N 070-57-32.499W				Green can.	
10655	- Lighted Buoy 5	42-26-16.380N 070-57-20.598W	Fl G 4s		4	Green.	Replaced by can from Oct. 15 to Apr. 15.
10657	- Buoy 5A	42-26-26.050N 070-57-25.574W				Green can.	
10660	- Lighted Buoy 6	42-26-26.576N 070-57-24.565W	Fl R 2.5s		3	Red.	Replaced by nun from Oct. 15 to Apr. 15.
10665	- Buoy 7	42-26-29.573N 070-57-30.521W				Green can.	
10670	- Buoy 8	42-26-33.092N 070-57-35.490W				Red nun.	
10675	- Buoy 10	42-26-35.742N 070-57-48.362W				Red nun.	
	BOSTON HARBOR						
	Boston Harbor and Approaches						
10676 410	Boston Lighted Whistle Buoy B	42-22-42.189N 070-46-58.171W	Mo (A) W		6	Red and white stripes with red spherical topmark.	RACON: B (- . . .) AIS: MMSI 993672065
10677 385	Boston Approach Lighted Buoy BG	42-23-26.857N 070-51-29.069W	Mo (A) W		4	Red and white stripes with red spherical topmark.	AIS: MMSI 993672145 (21)
10678 380	The Graves Lighted Whistle Buoy 5	42-22-32.857N 070-51-28.458W	Fl G 4s		4	Green.	
10679 390	**The Graves Light**	42-21-53.634N 070-52-08.712W	Fl (2)W 12s 0.1s fl 1.8s ec. 0.1s fl 10s ec.	98	15	On light gray conical granite tower. 98	Emergency light of reduced intensity when main light is extinguished. HORN: 2 blasts ev 20s (2s bl-2s si-2s bl-14s si). MRASS-Fog signal is radio activated, during times of reduced visibility, turn marine VHF-FM radio to channel 83A/157.175Mhz. Key microphone 5 times consecutively, to activate fog signal for 60 minutes.
	Boston North Channel						
10680	- Entrance Lighted Whistle Buoy NC	42-22-32.117N 070-54-17.842W	Mo (A) W		6	Red and white stripes with red spherical topmark.	RACON: N (- .) AIS: MMSI 993672151
10685	- Lighted Bell Buoy 2	42-22-10.667N 070-55-09.383W	Q R		4	Red.	
10690	- Lighted Buoy 3	42-22-04.898N 070-54-55.519W	Q G		4	Green.	
10695	- Lighted Buoy 4	42-21-38.997N 070-55-46.954W	Fl R 2.5s		4	Red.	

(1) No.	(2) Name and Location	(3) Position	(4) Characteristic	(5) Height	(6) Range	(7) Structure	(8) Remarks
			MASSACHUSETTS - First District				
	BOSTON HARBOR						
	Boston North Channel						
10700	- Lighted Buoy 5	42-21-39.788N 070-55-24.437W	Fl G 2.5s		4	Green.	
10705	- Lighted Buoy 6	42-21-16.797N 070-56-02.444W	Fl R 4s		4	Red.	
10710	Great Faun Bar Buoy 6A	42-21-16.491N 070-56-24.393W				Red nun.	
10712	- Lighted Buoy 7	42-21-10.634N 070-55-44.812W	Fl G 4s		4	Green.	
10715	- Lighted Buoy 8	42-20-56.634N 070-56-17.012W	Fl R 6s		3	Red.	
10720	- Lighted Buoy 9	42-20-48.634N 070-56-00.812W	Fl G 6s		4	Green.	
10730	- Lighted Bell Buoy 10 Off Little Faun Shoal.	42-20-36.721N 070-56-31.688W	Q R		3	Red.	
10735	President Roads Junction Lighted Buoy PR	42-20-29.388N 070-56-13.593W	Fl (2+1)G 6s		4	Green and red bands.	
10736	Boston Pilots Mooring Buoy	42-25-00.384N 070-55-00.685W				White with blue band.	
	Boston South Channel						
10740	- Entrance Lighted Buoy 1	42-21-52.634N 070-53-49.812W	Q G		3	Green.	
10745	- Buoy 3 On northwest side of Commissioners Ledge.	42-21-24.418N 070-54-13.351W				Green can.	
10750	- Lighted Buoy 5	42-21-06.634N 070-54-33.812W	Fl G 4s		4	Green.	
10755	- Lighted Buoy 6	42-21-14.634N 070-54-46.812W	Fl R 4s		4	Red.	
10760	- Buoy 7 On northwest side of Aldridge Ledge.	42-20-47.068N 070-54-51.912W				Green can.	
10765	- Lighted Buoy 9	42-20-39.034N 070-55-01.012W	Q G		4	Green.	
10768	- Lighted Buoy 10	42-20-46.034N 070-55-10.012W	Q R		4	Red.	
10769	Stone Living Lab Harbor Entrance Lighted Research Buoy BC	42-20-27.200N 070-55-11.100W	Fl Y 2.5s			Yellow.	Private aid.
10770	- Buoy 11	42-20-30.134N 070-55-27.812W				Green can.	
10780	- Buoy 13	42-20-21.993N 070-55-55.187W				Green can.	
10785	Halftide Rocks Buoy 2 On south side of ledge.	42-20-48.388N 070-54-04.181W				Red nun.	
	President Roads						
10790	Nixes Mate Lighted Buoy 15	42-20-02.559N 070-56-40.514W	Q G		4	Green.	
10795	DEER ISLAND LIGHT Southwest of old stone foundation.	42-20-22.462N 070-57-16.302W	Al WR 10s	53	9		HORN: 1 blast ev 10s (1s bl). MRASS-Fog signal is radio activated, during times of reduced visibility, turn marine VHF-FM radio to channel 83A/157.175Mhz. Key microphone 5 times consecutively, to activate fog signal for 60 minutes.
10800	LONG ISLAND HEAD LIGHT	42-19-48.813N 070-57-27.636W	Fl W 2.5s	120	6	White cylindrical tower.	
10805	Long Island Head Lighted Buoy 17	42-19-57.368N 070-57-31.445W	Fl G 2.5s		4	Green.	
10815	- Anchorage Gong Buoy A	42-20-35.533N 070-57-33.798W				Yellow.	AIS: MMSI 993672071 (21)
10820	- Anchorage Lighted Buoy B	42-20-42.972N 070-57-50.393W	Fl Y 4s		3	Yellow.	AIS: MMSI 993672072 (21)

(1) No.	(2) Name and Location	(3) Position	(4) Characteristic	(5) Height	(6) Range	(7) Structure	(8) Remarks

BOSTON HARBOR
President Roads
Deer Island

10830	- PIER OUTER LIGHT	42-20-48.000N 070-57-35.300W	F Y	13		On pier.	Private aid.
10840	- PIER INNER LIGHT	42-20-48.550N 070-57-35.850W	F Y	13		On pier.	Private aid.

President Roads

10852	- Anchorage Buoy C	42-20-38.911N 070-58-18.868W				Yellow can.	AIS: MMSI 993672073 (21). Removed when endangered by ice.
10855	- Anchorage Lighted Buoy D	42-20-32.863N 070-58-51.017W	Fl Y 4s		3	Yellow.	AIS: MMSI 993672074 (21). Removed when endangered by ice.
10860	- Anchorage Buoy E	42-20-12.808N 070-58-46.737W				Yellow nun.	AIS: MMSI 993672075 (21)

BOSTON INNER HARBOR
President Roads

10865	Boston Main Channel Lighted Buoy 1	42-19-52.662N 070-58-44.147W	Fl G 4s		3	Green.	
10870	Boston Main Channel Lighted Buoy 2	42-20-04.738N 070-58-57.167W	Fl R 4s		3	Red.	Replaced by nun when endangered by ice.
10875	Boston Main Channel Lighted Buoy 3	42-19-51.692N 070-59-27.436W	Q G		3	Green.	Replaced by can when endangered by ice.
10885	Boston Main Channel Lighted Bell Buoy 4	42-20-04.134N 070-59-27.512W	Q R		3	Red.	Replaced by nun when endangered by ice.
10890	BOSTON MAIN CHANNEL LIGHT 5	42-20-00.196N 071-00-03.744W	Fl G 2.5s	32	5	SG on pile.	
10895	Boston Main Channel Lighted Buoy 6	42-20-12.117N 070-59-54.038W	Fl R 2.5s		3	Red.	Replaced by nun when endangered by ice.
10897	Boston Main Channel Lighted Buoy 5A	42-20-12.830N 071-00-19.628W	Q G		3	Green.	Replaced by can when endangered by ice.
10900	BOSTON MAIN CHANNEL LIGHT 7	42-20-17.234N 071-00-29.012W	Fl G 4s	26	5	SG on pile.	
10905	Boston Main Channel Lighted Buoy 8	42-20-26.834N 071-00-17.512W	Fl R 4s		3	Red.	

Logan Airport Security Zone

10909	- Lighted Buoy 24	42-20-45.060N 071-00-28.860W	Fl W 4s			White and orange .	Marked RESTRICTED AREA. Private aid.

President Roads

10910	Boston Main Channel Lighted Buoy 10	42-20-42.018N 071-00-41.497W	Fl R 6s		3	Red.	Replaced by nun when endangered by ice. AIS: MMSI 993672067

Logan Airport Security Zone

10912	- Buoy 25	42-20-49.200N 071-00-35.400W				White and orange.	Marked RESTRICTED AREA. Private aid.
10919	- Buoy 26	42-21-02.880N 071-00-56.880W				White and orange.	Marked RESTRICTED AREA. Private aid.

President Roads

10920	Boston Main Channel Lighted Buoy 12	42-20-57.934N 071-01-08.012W	Fl R 2.5s		3	Red.	Replaced by nun when endangered by ice.

Logan Airport Security Zone

10921	- Buoy 27	42-21-06.960N 071-01-07.920W				White and orange.	Marked RESTRICTED AREA. Private aid.
10922	- Buoy 28	42-21-15.360N 071-01-19.320W				White and orange.	Marked RESTRICTED AREA. Private aid.
10923	- Buoy 29	42-21-19.400N 071-01-27.800W				White and orange.	Marked RESTRICTED AREA. Private aid.

(1) No.	(2) Name and Location	(3) Position	(4) Characteristic	(5) Height	(6) Range	(7) Structure	(8) Remarks

MASSACHUSETTS - First District

BOSTON INNER HARBOR

Logan Airport Security Zone

10923.1	- Lighted Buoy 30	42-21-26.040N 071-01-42.060W	Fl W 4s			White and Orange.	Marked RESTRICTED AREA. Private aid.
10924	Boston Anchorage One CG Mooring Buoy	42-21-08.379N 071-01-16.091W				White with blue band.	Marked "CG"

President Roads

10925	Boston Main Channel Lighted Buoy 13	42-21-11.186N 071-02-07.363W	Fl G 4s		3	Green.	Replaced by can when endangered by ice.
10926	Fan Pier South Hazard Lighted Buoy	42-21-16.900N 071-02-29.700W	Fl W 2.5s			White and orange buoy.	Marks south end of mooring field. Private aid.
10927	Fan Pier North Hazard Lighted Buoy	42-21-20.100N 071-02-39.000W	Fl W 4s			White and orange buoys.	Marks north end of mooring field. Private aid.
10950	New England Aquarium Intake Buoy	42-21-32.000N 071-02-54.000W				White with orange bands.	Private aid.

Charles River

10951	CBI Lighted No Wake Buoy	42-21-37.141N 071-04-25.172W	Fl W 15s				Private aid.
10952	Community Boating Entrance Lighted Buoy 2	42-21-35.752N 071-04-26.000W	Fl R 6s				Private aid.
10953	Commissioner's Landing Lighted Buoy 1	42-21-31.601N 071-04-29.261W	Fl G 4s				Private aid.
10954	Commissioner's Landing Lighted Buoy 2	42-21-31.085N 071-04-29.384W	Fl R 4s				Private aid.

President Roads

10957	BOSTON MAIN CHANNEL LIGHT 14	42-22-17.344N 071-02-44.632W	Q R	26	4	TR on skeleton tower.	
10960	Boston Main Channel Lighted Buoy 16	42-23-03.217N 071-02-31.917W	Q R		3	Red.	

Chelsea River

10965	- LIGHT 1	42-23-09.730N 071-01-24.942W	Fl G 2.5s	20	3	SG on wood multi- pile.	
10967	- LIGHT 2	42-23-07.920N 071-01-23.200W	Fl R 2.5s	20	3	TR on wood multi- pile.	
10969	- LIGHT 3	42-23-10.617N 071-01-23.363W	Q G	20	3	SG on wood multi- pile.	
10970	- LIGHT 4	42-23-09.758N 071-01-20.460W	Q R	20	3	TR on wood multi- pile.	
10971	- LIGHT 5	42-23-11.776N 071-01-21.156W	Oc G 4s	20	3	SG on wood multi- pile.	
10972	- LIGHT 6	42-23-10.850N 071-01-18.546W	Oc R 4s	20	3	TR on wood multi- pile.	
10973	CHELSEA STREET BRIDGE NORTHSIDE BULKHEAD LIGHT	42-23-10.000N 071-01-25.000W	Q Y				Private aid.
10973.1	CHELSEA STREET BRIDGE SOUTHSIDE BULKHEAD LIGHT	42-23-08.000N 071-01-23.000W	Q Y				Private aid.
10975	- Channel Lighted Buoy 8	42-23-19.365N 071-01-06.853W	Fl R 2.5s		3	Red.	
10980	- Channel Lighted Buoy 10	42-23-28.930N 071-01-00.001W	Fl R 4s		3	Red.	
10985	- Channel Lighted Buoy 12	42-23-39.371N 071-00-58.283W	Fl R 6s		3	Red.	
10990	- Channel Lighted Buoy 13	42-23-54.643N 071-00-52.213W	Fl G 2.5s		3	Green.	

Mystic River

10995	Island End Flats Lighted Buoy 2	42-23-11.629N 071-03-09.492W	Fl R 4s		3	Red.	
11000	Island End Point Buoy 4	42-23-14.882N 071-03-17.195W				Red nun.	
11005	- Buoy 5	42-23-31.894N 071-04-25.198W				Green can.	
11010	Encore Casino Channel Lighted Buoy 2	42-23-30.336N 071-04-19.956W	Fl R 2.5s			Red.	Private aid.

96

(1) No.	(2) Name and Location	(3) Position	(4) Characteristic	(5) Height	(6) Range	(7) Structure	(8) Remarks
			MASSACHUSETTS - First District				
	BOSTON INNER HARBOR						
	Mystic River						
11010.1	*Encore Casino Channel Lighted Buoy 3*	42-23-31.674N 071-04-21.036W	Fl G 2.5s			Green.	Private aid.
11010.2	*Encore Casino Channel Lighted Buoy 4*	42-23-30.806N 071-04-19.642W	Fl R 2.5s			Red.	Private aid.
11010.3	*Encore Casino Channel Lighted Buoy 5*	42-23-34.044N 071-04-18.186W	Fl G 2.5s			Green.	Private aid.
11010.4	*Encore Casino Channel Lighted Buoy 6*	42-23-35.754N 071-04-14.190W	Fl R 2.5s			Red.	Private aid.
11010.5	*Encore Casino Channel Lighted Buoy 8*	42-23-37.500N 071-04-12.768W	Fl R 2.5s			Red.	Private aid.
11011	*Encore Casino Outer Channel Lighted Buoy*	42-23-30.270N 071-04-21.294W	Fl W 3s			White with Orange bands.	Private aid.
11012	*Encore Casino Inner Channel Lighted Buoy*	42-23-34.044N 071-04-16.530W	Fl W 3s			White with Orange bands.	Private aid.
	Island End River						
11015	- Daybeacon 4	42-23-25.000N 071-03-10.300W				TR on pile.	Private aid.
11020	- Daybeacon 6	42-23-29.200N 071-03-04.100W				TR on pile.	Private aid.
	Logan Airport Security Zone						
11033	- Buoy 16	42-21-37.200N 070-59-08.400W				White and orange.	Marked RESTRICTED AREA. Private aid.
11034	- Buoy 15	42-21-46.500N 070-59-13.920W				White and orange.	Marked RESTRICTED AREA. Private aid.
	Winthrop Harbor Approach						
11035	- Buoy 1	42-20-34.837N 070-58-55.838W				Green can.	
11040	- Buoy 3	42-20-57.046N 070-58-44.995W				Green can.	
11045	- Buoy 4	42-21-01.127N 070-58-42.208W				Red nun.	
11050	- Lighted Buoy 5	42-21-15.996N 070-58-42.156W	Fl G 4s		4	Green.	Replaced by can when endangered by ice.
11055	- Buoy 6	42-21-25.478N 070-58-44.982W				Red nun.	
	Logan Airport Security Zone						
11056	- Lighted Buoy 17	42-21-27.540N 070-59-06.660W	Fl W 5s			White and orange.	Marked RESTRICTED AREA. Private aid.
	Winthrop Harbor Approach						
11060	- Buoy 7	42-21-24.315N 070-58-49.059W				Green can.	
11065	WINTHROP LIGHT 1	42-21-42.400N 070-58-46.920W	Fl G 6s	24	5	SG on skeleton tower on piles.	
	Winthrop Channel						
11067	- Buoy 1A	42-21-49.425N 070-58-38.844W				Green can.	Removed when endangered by ice.
11070	- Buoy 2	42-21-47.422N 070-58-36.621W				Red nun.	
11075	- Buoy 3	42-21-58.766N 070-58-29.751W				Green can.	
11077	Cottage Park Buoy 2	42-21-52.990N 070-59-17.028W				Red nun.	
11080	Cottage Park Buoy 4	42-21-58.071N 070-59-14.009W				Red nun.	
	Chelsea Point Channel						
11085	- Buoy 1	42-21-48.666N 070-59-15.089W				Green can.	
	Logan Airport Security Zone						
11094	- Buoy 14	42-21-51.600N 070-59-30.300W				White and orange.	Marked RESTRICTED AREA. Private aid.

(1) No.	(2) Name and Location	(3) Position	(4) Characteristic	(5) Height	(6) Range	(7) Structure	(8) Remarks
			MASSACHUSETTS - First District				
	BOSTON INNER HARBOR						
	Chelsea Point Channel						
11095	- Buoy 4	42-21-55.090N 070-59-31.050W				Red nun.	
	Logan Airport Security Zone						
11099	- Buoy 13	42-21-57.600N 070-59-42.960W				White and orange.	Marked RESTRICTED AREA. Private aid.
	Chelsea Point Channel						
11100	- Buoy 5	42-21-59.477N 070-59-42.910W				Green can.	
	Logan Airport Security Zone						
11106	- Buoy 12	42-22-04.560N 070-59-51.840W				White and orange.	Marked RESTRICTED AREA. Private aid.
11109	- Buoy 11	42-22-12.060N 070-59-57.360W				White and orange.	Marked RESTRICTED AREA. Private aid.
	Chelsea Point Channel						
11110	- Buoy 7	42-22-15.515N 070-59-56.770W				Green can.	
11115	- Buoy 8	42-22-16.565N 070-59-55.050W				Red nun.	
	Logan Airport Security Zone						
11116	- Buoy 10	42-22-22.500N 070-59-56.100W				White and orange.	Marked RESTRICTED AREA. Private aid.
11119	- Buoy 9	42-22-30.600N 070-59-53.160W				White and orange.	Marked RESTRICTED AREA. Private aid.
	Chelsea Point Channel						
11120	- Buoy 9	42-22-37.855N 070-59-48.690W				Green can.	
11125	- Buoy 10	42-22-36.405N 070-59-46.190W				Red nun.	
	Logan Airport Security Zone						
11125.1	- *Lighted Buoy 8*	42-22-39.840N 070-59-50.041W	Fl W 5s			White and orange.	Marked RESTRICTED AREA. Private aid.
11126	- Buoy 1	42-22-27.780N 071-00-44.640W				White and orange.	Marked RESTRICTED AREA. Private aid.
11126.1	- Buoy 2	42-22-26.220N 071-00-39.120W				White and orange.	Marked RESTRICTED AREA. Private aid.
11127	- Buoy 3	42-22-33.540N 071-00-34.560W				White and orange.	Marked RESTRICTED AREA. Private aid.
11127.1	- Buoy 4	42-22-41.220N 071-00-30.840W				White and orange.	Marked RESTRICTED AREA. Private aid.
11128	- Buoy 5	42-22-49.800N 071-00-22.860W				White and orange.	Marked RESTRICTED AREA. Private aid.
11128.1	- Buoy 6	42-22-47.160N 071-00-14.580W				White and orange.	Marked RESTRICTED AREA. Private aid.
11129	- Buoy 7	42-22-42.660N 071-00-01.560W				White and orange.	Marked RESTRICTED AREA. Private aid.
	Lower Middle Channel						
11130	- Buoy 1	42-20-18.897N 070-59-14.708W				Green can.	
11135	- Buoy 4	42-20-28.451N 070-59-36.769W				Red nun.	
11140	- *Lighted Buoy 3*	42-20-23.725N 070-59-40.458W	Fl G 2.5s		3	Green.	
11145	- Buoy 5	42-20-29.547N 070-59-57.309W				Green can.	
	Logan Airport Security Zone						
11146	- Buoy 18	42-21-22.200N 070-59-13.620W				White and orange.	Marked RESTRICTED AREA. Private aid.
11146.1	- Buoy 19	42-21-09.360N 070-59-32.160W				White and orange.	Marked RESTRICTED AREA. Private aid.
11147	- Buoy 20	42-21-02.040N 070-59-44.640W				White and orange.	Marked RESTRICTED AREA. Private aid.
11148	- Buoy 21	42-20-59.400N 070-59-55.380W				White and orange.	Marked RESTRICTED AREA. Private aid.

(1) No.	(2) Name and Location	(3) Position	(4) Characteristic	(5) Height	(6) Range	(7) Structure	(8) Remarks
			MASSACHUSETTS - First District				
BOSTON INNER HARBOR							
Logan Airport Security Zone							
11149	- Buoy 22	42-20-52.500N 071-00-05.820W				White and orange.	Marked RESTRICTED AREA. Private aid.
11149.1	- Buoy 23	42-20-46.140N 071-00-18.300W				White and orange.	Marked RESTRICTED AREA. Private aid.
Bird Island Flats							
11150	- Anchorage Buoy A	42-21-12.266N 071-01-12.612W				Yellow can.	
11170	- Buoy 2	42-21-30.035N 071-01-45.831W				Red nun.	
11175	- Buoy 3	42-21-37.535N 071-01-45.453W				Green can.	
BOSTON HARBOR							
Dorchester Bay							
11195	- Buoy 2	42-19-38.538N 071-00-01.899W				Red nun.	
11200	- Buoy 3	42-19-28.018N 071-00-08.129W				Green can.	
11205	- Buoy 4	42-19-17.688N 071-00-48.030W				Red nun.	
11210	- *Lighted Buoy 5*	42-19-02.568N 071-01-15.640W	Fl G 4s		4	Green.	Replaced by can when endangered by ice.
11215	- Buoy 6	42-19-01.758N 071-01-21.430W				Red nun.	
11220	- Buoy 8	42-18-48.048N 071-01-33.901W				Red nun.	
11225	- Buoy 10	42-18-37.928N 071-01-44.991W				Red nun.	
11230	- *Lighted Buoy 12*	42-18-28.428N 071-01-57.650W	Fl R 4s		3	Red.	Replaced by nun when endangered by ice.
11235	PLEASURE BAY LIGHT	42-19-50.600N 071-00-54.500W	Fl W 2.5s			On top of cupola.	Private aid.
11236	Columbia Point Channel Buoy 1C	42-18-59.181N 071-01-28.316W				Green can.	
11237	Columbia Point Channel Buoy 2C	42-19-00.386N 071-01-28.427W				Red nun.	
11238	Columbia Point Channel Buoy 3	42-18-57.663N 071-01-50.956W				Green can.	
11239	Columbia Point Channel Buoy 4	42-18-58.840N 071-01-51.200W				Red nun.	
11240	UMass Buoy 1	42-18-24.402N 071-02-32.082W				Green can.	Private aid.
11240.1	UMass Buoy 2	42-18-25.494N 071-02-31.542W				Red nun.	Private aid.
11240.2	UMass Buoy 3	42-18-28.134N 071-02-34.644W				Green can.	Private aid.
11240.3	UMass Buoy 4	42-18-28.806N 071-02-33.654W				Red nun.	Private aid.
11240.4	UMass Buoy 5	42-18-30.966N 071-02-33.282W				Green can.	Private aid.
11240.5	UMass Buoy 6	42-18-32.820N 071-02-30.396W				Red nun.	Private aid.
11240.6	UMass Buoy 7	42-18-35.070N 071-02-29.268W				Green can.	Private aid.
11240.7	UMass Buoy 8	42-18-35.202N 071-02-27.798W				Red nun.	Private aid.
11240.8	UMass Buoy 9	42-18-38.220N 071-02-25.704W				Green can.	Private aid.
11240.9	UMass Buoy 10	42-18-38.500N 071-02-24.000W				Red nun.	Private aid.
Squantum Channel							
11245	- Buoy 1SC	42-18-27.668N 071-01-54.420W				Green can.	

(1) No.	(2) Name and Location	(3) Position	(4) Characteristic	(5) Height	(6) Range	(7) Structure	(8) Remarks

MASSACHUSETTS - First District

BOSTON HARBOR
Dorchester Bay
Squantum Channel

(1)	(2)	(3)	(4)	(5)	(6)	(7)	(8)
11250	- Buoy 2	42-18-17.034N 071-01-55.012W				Red nun.	
11252	- Buoy 3	42-18-11.054N 071-01-52.010W				Green can.	

Dorchester Bay Basin
Aids maintained from May 1 to Dec. 1.

(1)	(2)	(3)	(4)	(5)	(6)	(7)	(8)
11260	- Channel Buoy 1	42-18-15.000N 071-02-59.200W				Green can.	Private aid.
11265	- Channel Buoy 2	42-18-16.300N 071-02-58.100W				Red nun.	Private aid.
11275	- Channel Buoy 4	42-18-17.300N 071-03-01.900W				Red nun.	Private aid.
11280	- Channel Buoy 5	42-18-17.400N 071-03-05.200W				Green can.	Private aid.
11285	- Channel Buoy 6	42-18-18.700N 071-03-05.600W				Red nun.	Private aid.

Neponset River

(1)	(2)	(3)	(4)	(5)	(6)	(7)	(8)
11290	- Buoy 1	42-18-21.911N 071-02-18.501W				Green can.	
11292	- Buoy 2	42-18-24.178N 071-02-19.531W				Red nun.	
11295	- Buoy 3	42-18-17.138N 071-02-29.061W				Green can.	
11300	- Buoy 5	42-18-12.938N 071-02-31.351W				Green can.	
11305	- *Lighted Buoy 7*	42-17-49.089N 071-02-35.282W	Fl G 4s		4	Green.	Replaced by can from Nov. 1 to June 1.
11310	- Buoy 9	42-17-41.918N 071-02-30.471W				Green can.	
11315	- Buoy 11	42-17-32.123N 071-02-11.053W				Green can.	
11320	- Buoy 13	42-17-25.309N 071-02-05.780W				Green can.	
11325	- Buoy 14	42-17-21.259N 071-02-06.247W				Red nun.	
11330	- Buoy 16	42-17-15.569N 071-02-08.508W				Red nun.	

Nantasket Roads (Southern Approach)

(1)	(2)	(3)	(4)	(5)	(6)	(7)	(8)
11333 430	*Thieves Ledge Lighted Whistle Buoy 1*	42-19-34.101N 070-49-49.343W	Q G		3	Green.	
11334 395	*Three and One-Half Fathom Ledge Lighted Bell Buoy 2*	42-21-05.009N 070-50-29.796W	Fl R 4s		4	Red.	
11335 400	Martin Ledge Buoy 4	42-20-45.739N 070-51-12.086W				Red nun.	
11336 405	Boston Ledge Buoy 6	42-20-04.679N 070-51-49.706W				Red nun.	
11337 435	*Harding Ledge Lighted Bell Buoy 1HL*	42-18-34.222N 070-50-37.883W	Fl G 4s		4	Green.	
11340 425	**Boston Light**	42-19-40.889N 070-53-24.278W	Fl W 10s	102	27	On white conical tower. 89	Emergency light of reduced intensity when main light is extinguished. Two emergency lights may be visable from 336° to 001° and from 156° to 181°. HORN: 1 blast ev 30s (3s bl). MRASS-Fog signal is radio activated, during times of reduced visibility, turn marine VHF-FM radio to channel 83A/157.175Mhz. Key microphone 5 times consecutively, to activate fog signal for 60 minutes.
11348	LITTLE BREWSTER ISLAND DOCK LIGHT	42-19-40.034N 070-53-34.012W	Fl Y 2.5s	15	3	Spindle on dock.	

(1) No.	(2) Name and Location	(3) Position	(4) Characteristic	(5) Height	(6) Range	(7) Structure	(8) Remarks
			MASSACHUSETTS - First District				
	BOSTON HARBOR						
	Nantasket Roads (Southern Approach)						
11350	*Nantasket Roads Channel Lighted Buoy 4*	42-19-10.480N 070-53-18.118W	Fl R 4s		4	Red.	
11355	*Nantasket Roads Channel Lighted Bell Buoy 3*	42-19-07.161N 070-52-47.008W	Fl G 4s		4	Green.	Replaced by can when endangered by ice.
11360	*Nantasket Roads Channel Lighted Buoy 6*	42-19-09.700N 070-53-56.209W	Fl R 2.5s		4	Red.	Replaced by nun when endangered by ice.
11365	*Nantasket Roads Channel Lighted Buoy 7*	42-19-04.190N 070-54-07.369W	Fl G 2.5s		4	Green.	Replaced by can when endangered by ice.
11370	*Nantasket Roads Channel Lighted Buoy 9*	42-19-00.867N 070-54-30.650W	Fl G 4s		4	Green.	Replaced by can when endangered by ice.
11380	Toddy Rocks Buoy 9A	42-18-48.919N 070-54-35.089W				Green can.	
11385	*Nantasket Roads Channel Lighted Buoy TN*	42-18-59.138N 070-54-47.144W	Fl (2+1)R 6s		4	Red and green bands.	Replaced by nun when endangered by ice.
11390	Nantasket Roads Channel Buoy 10 On south side of shoal spots.	42-18-52.970N 070-55-14.211W				Red nun.	
11395	*Nantasket Roads Channel Lighted Buoy 11*	42-18-40.410N 070-55-15.961W	Fl G 2.5s		4	Green.	Replaced by can when endangered by ice.
11397	Nantasket Roads Bell Buoy 10A	42-18-44.079N 070-55-41.935W				Red.	
11410	*Nantasket Roads Channel Lighted Buoy 14*	42-18-15.130N 070-55-33.791W	Fl R 2.5s		4	Red.	Replaced by nun when endangered by ice.
11411	*Nantasket Roads DRC Lighted Hazard Buoy A*	42-18-56.700N 070-55-38.500W	Fl W 4s			White with orange bands.	Private aid.
11411.1	*Nantasket Roads DRC Lighted Hazard Buoy B*	42-18-52.300N 070-55-34.500W	Fl W 4s			White with orange bands.	Private aid.
11411.2	*Nantasket Roads DRC Lighted Hazard Buoy C*	42-18-32.940N 070-55-19.140W	Fl W 4s			White with orange bands.	Private aid.
11411.3	*Nantasket Roads DRC Lighted Hazard Buoy D*	42-18-29.900N 070-55-18.300W	Fl W 4s			White with orange bands.	Private aid.
	The Narrows						
11415	Kelly Rock Bell Buoy 2	42-19-14.190N 070-54-42.151W				Red.	
11420	- Daybeacon 2A	42-19-22.576N 070-54-46.182W				TR on dolphin.	
11425	*Georges Island Rocks Lighted Buoy 3*	42-19-07.390N 070-55-02.061W	Q G		3	Green.	Replaced by can when endangered by ice.
11430	- LIGHT 4	42-19-20.535N 070-55-10.876W	Fl R 4s	35	6	TR on pile structure.	
11435	- Bell Buoy 5	42-19-17.162N 070-55-24.320W				Green.	
11437	- Buoy 6	42-19-25.533N 070-55-27.932W				Red nun.	
11440	GALLOPS ISLAND LIGHT 7	42-19-32.234N 070-55-57.112W	Fl G 4s	29	5	SG on skeleton tower.	HORN: 2 blasts ev 20s (2s bl-2s si-2s bl-14s si). MRASS-Fog signal is radio activated, during times of reduced visibility, turn marine VHF-FM radio to channel 83A/157.175Mhz. Key microphone 5 times consecutively, to activate fog signal for 60 minutes.
11441	*Georges Island Lighted Hazard Buoy A*	42-19-25.968N 070-55-48.738W	Fl W 4s			White with orange bands.	Seasonal May 1 - Oct 31. Private aid.
11442	*Georges Island Lighted Hazard Buoy B*	42-19-16.277N 070-56-02.458W	Fl W 4s			White with orange bands.	Seasonal May 1 - Oct 31. Private aid.

(1) No.	(2) Name and Location	(3) Position	(4) Characteristic	(5) Height	(6) Range	(7) Structure	(8) Remarks
			MASSACHUSETTS - First District				
	BOSTON HARBOR						
	The Narrows						
11443	*Georges Island Lighted Hazard Buoy C*	42-19-10.816N 070-55-54.480W	Fl W 4s			White with orange bands.	Seasonal May 1 - Oct 31. Private aid.
11445	- Buoy 10	42-19-58.519N 070-56-14.463W				Red nun.	
11450	Nixes Mate Daybeacon Marks foul area between Nubble Channel and The Narrows.	42-19-53.266N 070-56-39.288W				Black, white band midway of height; octagonal pyramid on square granite base.	
11455	Black Rocks Channel Buoy 2B	42-19-38.042N 070-55-10.161W				Red nun.	
	Quincy Bay Approach						
11470	- Buoy 1	42-19-01.380N 070-56-17.313W				Green can.	
11475	- Buoy 3	42-18-53.034N 070-57-18.012W				Green can.	
11477	- Buoy 4	42-18-47.034N 070-57-48.012W				Red nun.	
11480	*Stone Living Lab Rainsford Island Lighted Research Buoy A*	42-19-00.591N 070-56-58.135W	Fl Y 2.5s			Yellow.	Private aid.
	Nubble Channel						
11485	- Buoy 1	42-19-31.439N 070-56-50.534W				Green can.	
11490	- Buoy 2	42-19-33.578N 070-56-45.307W				Red nun.	
11492	- Buoy 3	42-19-43.928N 070-56-56.566W				Green can.	
11495	- Buoy 4	42-19-45.255N 070-56-52.556W				Red nun.	
11500	- Buoy 5	42-19-51.011N 070-57-02.350W				Green can.	
11502	- Buoy 6	42-19-53.197N 070-56-57.424W				Red nun.	
	Peddocks Island Channel						
11504	- Hospital Shoal Buoy HS	42-18-44.034N 070-56-15.012W				Green and red bands; can.	
11507	Rainsford Island Shoal Danger Buoy	42-18-37.670N 070-56-43.323W				White can with orange bands.	
11514	- Buoy 2P	42-17-58.034N 070-57-12.012W				Red nun.	
11519	- *Lighted Buoy 4P*	42-17-36.863N 070-57-26.520W	Fl R 6s		4	Red.	Removed when endangered by ice.
11524	- Buoy 5P	42-17-27.034N 070-57-11.012W				Green can.	
	Western Way						
11529	- LIGHT 1	42-16-47.470N 070-56-20.970W	Fl G 4s	31	5	SG on pile.	
11533	NUT ISLAND PIER LIGHT	42-16-53.200N 070-57-13.100W	STROBE			On pier.	Private aid.
11537	- *Lighted Buoy 2*	42-17-00.321N 070-56-59.692W	Fl R 2.5s		3	Red.	Replaced by nun when endangered by ice.
11539	- *Lighted Buoy 3*	42-17-12.034N 070-57-28.012W	Fl G 2.5s		3	Green.	Replaced by can when endangered by ice.
11544	Hangman Island Ledge Daybeacon HM	42-17-19.493N 070-58-32.697W				NG on spindle.	
11549	Sunken Ledge Daybeacon SL	42-17-44.570N 070-57-37.425W				NB on spindle.	
11554	- *Lighted Buoy 4*	42-17-48.034N 070-57-56.512W	Fl R 4s		3	Red.	Replaced by nun when endangered by ice.
11564	- Buoy 6	42-18-23.632N 070-58-33.283W				Red nun.	

(1) No.	(2) Name and Location	(3) Position	(4) Characteristic	(5) Height	(6) Range	(7) Structure	(8) Remarks
			MASSACHUSETTS - First District				
	BOSTON HARBOR						
	Peddocks Island Channel						
	Western Way						
11564.1	- CHANNEL OBSTRUCTION LIGHT 6A	42-18-34.017N 070-58-45.200W	F R			On pole.	Private aid.
11564.2	- CHANNEL OBSTRUCTION LIGHT 6B	42-18-34.431N 070-58-45.501W	F R			On pole.	Private aid.
11566	- Buoy 5	42-18-21.034N 070-58-40.012W				Green can.	
11566.1	- CHANNEL OBSTRUCTION LIGHT 5A	42-18-32.841N 070-58-48.125W	F G			On pole.	Private aid.
11566.2	- CHANNEL OBSTRUCTION LIGHT 5B	42-18-33.254N 070-58-48.430W	F G			On pole.	Private aid.
11567	- OBSTRUCTION LIGHT A1	42-18-23.474N 070-59-11.564W	F W				Private aid.
11567.1	- OBSTRUCTION LIGHT A2	42-18-23.808N 070-59-11.806W	F W				Private aid.
11567.2	- OBSTRUCTION LIGHT B1	42-18-24.650N 070-59-08.641W	F W				Private aid.
11567.3	- OBSTRUCTION LIGHT B2	42-18-24.985N 070-59-08.880W	F W				Private aid.
11567.4	- OBSTRUCTION LIGHT C1	42-18-25.796N 070-59-05.691W	F W				Private aid.
11567.5	- OBSTRUCTION LIGHT C2	42-18-26.189N 070-59-05.979W	F W				Private aid.
11567.6	- OBSTRUCTION LIGHT D1	42-18-27.003N 070-59-02.787W	F W				Private aid.
11567.7	- OBSTRUCTION LIGHT D2	42-18-27.335N 070-59-03.027W	F W				Private aid.
11567.8	- OBSTRUCTION LIGHT E1	42-18-28.179N 070-58-59.860W	F W				Private aid.
11567.9	- OBSTRUCTION LIGHT E2	42-18-28.510N 070-59-00.101W	F W				Private aid.
11568	- Buoy 7	42-18-40.563N 070-58-58.872W				Green can.	
11569	- OBSTRUCTION LIGHT F1	42-18-29.322N 070-58-56.913W	F W				Private aid.
11569.1	- OBSTRUCTION LIGHT F2	42-18-29.719N 070-58-57.201W	F W				Private aid.
11569.2	- OBSTRUCTION LIGHT G1	42-18-30.541N 070-58-54.017W	F W				Private aid.
11569.3	- OBSTRUCTION LIGHT G2	42-18-30.861N 070-58-54.250W	F W				Private aid.
11569.4	- OBSTRUCTION LIGHT H1	42-18-31.710N 070-58-51.085W	F W				Private aid.
11569.5	- OBSTRUCTION LIGHT H2	42-18-32.038N 070-58-51.324W	F W				Private aid.
11569.6	- OBSTRUCTION LIGHT K1	42-18-35.235N 070-58-42.304W	F W				Private aid.
11569.7	- OBSTRUCTION LIGHT K2	42-18-35.566N 070-58-42.546W	F W				Private aid.
11569.8	- OBSTRUCTION LIGHT L1	42-18-36.409N 070-58-39.375W	F W				Private aid.
11569.9	- OBSTRUCTION LIGHT L2	42-18-36.747N 070-58-39.612W	F W				Private aid.
11574	- Buoy 8	42-19-04.249N 070-59-12.261W				Red nun.	
11575	- Buoy 8A	42-18-54.389N 070-58-51.186W				Red nun.	
11579	- Buoy 9	42-19-15.388N 070-59-42.188W				Green can.	
11580	*Spectacle Island Lighted No Wake Buoy A*	42-19-25.440N 070-59-29.220W	Fl W 5s			White with orange bands.	Private aid.
11581	*Spectacle Island Lighted No Wake Buoy B*	42-19-16.620N 070-59-25.020W	Fl W 5s			White with orange bands.	Private aid.

(1) No.	(2) Name and Location	(3) Position	(4) Characteristic	(5) Height	(6) Range	(7) Structure	(8) Remarks
			MASSACHUSETTS - First District				
	BOSTON HARBOR						
	Peddocks Island Channel						
	Western Way						
11582	*Spectacle Island Lighted No Wake Buoy C*	42-19-09.120N 070-59-18.600W	Fl W 5s			White with orange bands.	Private aid.
11583	*Spectacle Island Lighted No Wake Buoy D*	42-19-03.780N 070-59-07.380W	Fl W 5s			White with orange bands.	Private aid.
11584	*Spectacle Island Lighted Danger Buoy A*	42-19-11.580N 070-59-18.600W	Fl W 5s			White with orange bands.	Marks rocks. Private aid.
11585	*Spectacle Island Lighted Hazard Buoy A*	42-19-28.520N 070-59-30.397W	Fl W 4s			White with orange bands.	Seasonal May 1 - Oct 31. Private aid.
11586	*Spectacle Island Lighted Hazard Buoy B*	42-19-24.488N 070-59-30.415W	Fl W 4s			White with orange bands.	Seasonal May 1 - Oct 31. Private aid.
11587	*Spectacle Island Lighted Hazard Buoy C*	42-19-19.492N 070-59-23.586W	Fl W 4s			White with orange bands.	Seasonal May 1 - Oct 31. Private aid.
	Wollaston Channel						
11599	- Buoy 2	42-17-17.850N 071-00-11.107W				Red nun.	
11601	- Buoy 4	42-16-56.018N 071-00-34.150W				Red nun.	Maintained from Apr. 1 to Nov. 1.
	Houghs Neck Channel						
11620	- Buoy 1	42-16-31.222N 070-56-37.922W				Green can.	
11625	- Buoy 2	42-16-32.092N 070-56-39.492W				Red nun.	
	Spiers Stand						
11635	- Daybeacon	42-16-17.290N 070-56-36.582W				NW on pile worded DANGER ROCKS.	
	Hingham Bay						
	Weymouth Fore River *Aids maintained from Apr. 15 to Oct. 30.*						
11645	- *Channel Lighted Buoy 2*	42-18-08.446N 070-55-30.563W	Fl R 4s		3	Red.	Replace by nun when endangered by ice. AIS: MMSI 993672282 (21)
11650	WINDMILL POINT LIGHT WP	42-18-11.015N 070-55-19.267W	Q W	20	6	NR on gray skeleton tower.	Horn: 1 Blast ev 10s. MRASS-Fog signal is radio activated, during times of reduced visibility, turn marine VHF-FM radio to channel 83A/157.175Mhz. Key microphone 5 times consecutively, to activate fog signal for 45 minutes.
11655	- *Channel Lighted Buoy 4*	42-17-51.674N 070-55-24.457W	Q R		3	Red.	Replaced by nun when endangered by ice. AIS: MMSI 993672102 (21)
11660	- *Channel Lighted Buoy 5*	42-17-37.991N 070-55-24.271W	Fl G 4s		3	Green.	Replaced by can when endangered by ice.
11665	- *Channel Lighted Buoy 6*	42-17-39.143N 070-55-30.189W	Fl R 4s		3	Red.	Replaced by nun when endangered by ice. AIS: MMSI 993672283 (21)
11670	- *Channel Lighted Buoy 8*	42-17-12.939N 070-55-48.004W	Fl R 2.5s		3	Red.	Replaced by nun when endangered by ice.
11675	HARRY'S ROCK LIGHT HR East of rock.	42-17-13.291N 070-55-54.280W	Fl W 4s	26	4	NR on gray skeleton tower on pile structure.	
11685	- *Channel Lighted Buoy 9*	42-17-03.098N 070-55-47.249W	Fl G 2.5s		3	Green.	Replaced by can when endangered by ice. AIS: MMSI 993672284 (21)
11690	- *Channel Lighted Buoy 10*	42-16-51.392N 070-55-57.181W	Q R		3	Red.	Replaced by nun when endangered by ice.

104

(1) No.	(2) Name and Location	(3) Position	(4) Characteristic	(5) Height	(6) Range	(7) Structure	(8) Remarks
			MASSACHUSETTS - First District				

BOSTON HARBOR

Hingham Bay

Weymouth Fore River
Aids maintained from Apr. 15 to Oct. 30.

(1) No.	(2) Name and Location	(3) Position	(4) Characteristic	(5) Height	(6) Range	(7) Structure	(8) Remarks
11695	*Western Way Lighted Buoy WW*	42-16-38.850N 070-55-55.829W	Fl (2+1)R 6s		3	Red and green bands.	Replaced by nun when endangered by ice. AIS: MMSI 993672281 (21)
11700	*- Channel Lighted Buoy 11*	42-16-49.392N 070-55-51.181W	Fl G 4s		3	Green.	Replaced by can when endangered by ice.
11706	*- Channel Lighted Buoy 12*	42-16-23.499N 070-55-54.127W	Fl R 2.5s		3	Red.	Replaced by nun when endangered by ice. AIS: MMSI 993672285 (21)
11710	*- CHANNEL LIGHT 13*	42-16-16.270N 070-55-47.010W	Q G	28	4	SG on black skeleton tower on pile structure.	
11712	*- Channel Lighted Buoy 14*	42-16-11.771N 070-55-58.465W	Fl R 4s		3	Red.	Replaced by nun when endangered by ice. AIS: MMSI 993672286 (21)
11715	*- CHANNEL LIGHT 16*	42-16-03.129N 070-56-06.484W	Fl R 2.5s	28	4	TR on skeleton tower on a pile structure.	
11720	*Weymouth Back River Lighted Buoy BR*	42-16-00.192N 070-56-00.150W	Fl (2+1)G 6s		3	Green and red bands.	Replaced by can when endangered by ice.
11725	*- Channel Lighted Buoy 17*	42-15-44.213N 070-56-14.250W	Fl G 6s		3	Green.	Replaced by can when endangered by ice.
11730	*- Channel Lighted Buoy 18*	42-15-43.417N 070-56-20.875W	Fl R 6s		3	Red.	Replaced by nun when endangered by ice. AIS: MMSI 993672287 (21)
11735	*- Channel Lighted Buoy 19*	42-15-24.066N 070-56-29.431W	Fl G 2.5s		3	Green.	Replaced by can when endangered by ice. AIS: MMSI 993672288 (21)
11737	- Channel Buoy 21	42-15-15.369N 070-56-34.923W				Green can.	Replaced by can when endangered by ice.
11740	*- Channel Lighted Buoy 22*	42-15-18.047N 070-56-41.993W	Q R		3	Red.	Replaced by nun when endangered by ice. AIS: MMSI 993672289 (21)
11746	- Channel Buoy 23	42-15-08.975N 070-56-47.070W				Green can.	
11750	*- Channel Lighted Buoy 25*	42-15-06.172N 070-56-59.557W	Fl G 4s		3	Green.	Replaced by can when endangered by ice.
11755	*- Channel Lighted Buoy 26*	42-15-04.053N 070-57-14.471W	Fl R 4s		3	Red.	Replaced by nun when endangered by ice. AIS: MMSI 993672290 (21)
11757	- Channel Buoy 27	42-14-53.407N 070-57-31.009W				Green can.	Replaced by ice can if endangered by ice.
11760	*- Channel Lighted Buoy 28*	42-14-53.138N 070-57-43.117W	Fl R 2.5s		3	Red.	Replaced by nun when endangered by ice. AIS: MMSI 993672291 (21)
11765	- Channel Buoy 31	42-14-11.197N 070-57-55.859W				Green can.	Aid maintained from May 1 to Oct 15.
11770	- Channel Buoy 33	42-14-09.989N 070-57-41.033W				Green can.	Maintained from 1 Apr to 1 Nov.
11775	- Channel Buoy 32	42-14-09.986N 070-57-44.832W				Red nun.	Maintained from 1 Apr to 1 Nov.

(1) No.	(2) Name and Location	(3) Position	(4) Characteristic	(5) Height	(6) Range	(7) Structure	(8) Remarks
			MASSACHUSETTS - First District				
	BOSTON HARBOR						
	Hingham Bay						
	Weymouth Fore River *Aids maintained from Apr. 15 to Oct. 30.*						
11780	- Channel Buoy 34	42-14-05.733N 070-57-36.669W				Red nun.	Maintained from 1 Apr to 1 Nov.
11785	- Channel Buoy 36	42-14-02.077N 070-57-34.371W				Red nun.	Maintained from 1 Apr to 1 Nov.
11790	- Channel Buoy 38	42-13-57.639N 070-57-34.597W				Red nun.	Maintained from 15 Apr to 30 Nov.
	Braintree Yacht Club Channel *Aids maintained from Apr. 15 to Oct. 30.*						
11794	- *Lighted Buoy 40*	42-13-40.320N 070-57-40.500W	Fl R 4s			Red.	Private aid.
11795	- Buoy 42	42-13-39.900N 070-57-40.020W				Red nun.	Private aid.
11805	- *Lighted Buoy 44*	42-13-36.700N 070-57-41.100W	Fl R 4s			Red.	Private aid.
11810	- Buoy 46	42-13-34.800N 070-57-43.860W				Red nun.	Private aid.
11815	- *Lighted Buoy 48*	42-13-31.860N 070-57-48.180W	Fl R 4s			Red nun.	Private aid.
11820	- Lighted Buoy 50	42-13-28.200N 070-57-54.360W	Fl R 4s			Red nun.	Private aid.
	Town River Bay						
11825	- Channel Buoy 2	42-14-57.098N 070-57-59.906W				Red nun.	AIS: MMSI 993672292 (21)
11830	- Channel Buoy 3	42-14-58.367N 070-58-15.784W				Green can.	
11835	- Channel Buoy 4	42-15-02.289N 070-58-16.909W				Red nun.	AIS: MMSI 993672293 (21)
11840	- Channel Buoy 6	42-15-10.904N 070-58-27.052W				Red nun.	
11845	- Channel Buoy 7	42-15-09.785N 070-58-31.843W				Green can.	AIS: MMSI 993672294 (21)
11850	- Channel Buoy 9	42-15-13.836N 070-58-35.962W				Green can.	AIS: MMSI 993672295 (21)
11855	- Channel Buoy 11	42-15-15.829N 070-58-42.574W				Green can.	AIS: MMSI 993672296 (21)
11860	- Channel Buoy 12	42-15-21.342N 070-58-44.340W				Red nun.	
11865	- Channel Buoy 14	42-15-22.220N 070-58-54.909W				Red nun.	
11870	- Channel Buoy 16	42-15-16.713N 070-59-03.450W				Red nun.	AIS: MMSI 993672297 (21)
11875	Yacht Yard Channel Buoy 2	42-15-21.772N 070-58-40.260W				Red nun.	
11880	Yacht Yard Channel Buoy 3	42-15-22.918N 070-58-40.914W				Green can.	
	Weymouth Back River						
11885	- *Channel Lighted Buoy 1*	42-15-56.253N 070-55-50.850W	Fl G 2.5s		3	Green.	Replaced by can when endangered by ice. AIS: MMSI 993672298 (21)
11890	- Channel Buoy 2	42-15-49.273N 070-55-42.770W				Red nun.	
11895	- Channel Buoy 3	42-15-54.724N 070-55-28.775W				Green can.	AIS: MMSI 993672299 (21)
11900	- *Channel Lighted Buoy 4*	42-15-52.415N 070-55-25.697W	Fl R 2.5s		3	Red.	Replaced by LIB from Dec. 1 to Apr. 15. AIS: MMSI 993672302 (21)
11905	- Channel Buoy 6	42-15-44.331N 070-55-16.507W				Red nun.	AIS: MMSI 993672303 (21)

(1) No.	(2) Name and Location	(3) Position	(4) Characteristic	(5) Height	(6) Range	(7) Structure	(8) Remarks
			MASSACHUSETTS - First District				
	BOSTON HARBOR						
	Hingham Bay						
	Weymouth Back River						
11910	- Channel Buoy 7	42-15-42.263N 070-55-12.249W				Green can.	AIS: MMSI 993672304 (21)
11915	- *Channel Lighted Buoy 8*	42-15-30.587N 070-55-07.091W	Fl R 4s		3	Red.	Replaced by LIB from Dec. 1 to Apr. 15. AIS: MMSI 993672305 (21)
11920	- Channel Buoy 10	42-15-25.084N 070-55-08.329W				Red nun.	AIS: MMSI 993672306 (21)
11925	- Channel Buoy 12	42-15-19.334N 070-55-11.179W				Red nun.	AIS: MMSI 993672307 (21)
11930	- Channel Buoy 13	42-15-06.845N 070-55-57.512W				Green can.	
	Hingham Bay						
11933	POINT ALLERTON NORTH BREAKWATER LIGHT	42-18-06.879N 070-54-59.340W	Fl W 2.5s	20	3	On pile.	
11934	POINT ALLERTON SOUTH BREAKWATER LIGHT	42-18-05.728N 070-54-56.940W	Fl W 2.5s	20	3	On pile.	
11935	Inner Seal Rock Channel Buoy 1	42-17-52.831N 070-54-33.399W				Green can.	
11940	Outer Seal Rock Isolated Danger Buoy DSR	42-17-48.041N 070-54-29.679W				Black and red bands with two black spherical topmarks; can.	
11945	*Bumkin Island Lighted Buoy 1* Off northwest end of shoal.	42-17-25.092N 070-54-51.560W	Fl G 4s		3	Green.	
11970	Crow Point Flats Buoy CF	42-16-55.536N 070-54-35.933W				Red nun with green bands.	
11971	Sheep Island Buoy 1	42-16-40.034N 070-55-04.012W				Green can.	
11973	Sheep Island Buoy 2	42-16-41.034N 070-55-18.012W				Red nun.	
11975	*Bumkin Island Lighted Bell Buoy 3*	42-16-50.959N 070-54-19.026W	Fl G 4s		3	Green.	Replaced by can when endangered by ice.
11980	Crow Flats Middle Buoy 4	42-16-40.130N 070-54-14.599W				Red nun.	
	Hingham Harbor Approach						
11985	- *Lighted Buoy HH*	42-16-27.983N 070-53-51.447W	Fl (2+1)G 6s		3	Green and red bands.	Removed when endangered by ice.
11990	- Buoy 6	42-16-26.363N 070-53-55.918W				Red nun.	
11995	- Buoy 7	42-16-00.047N 070-53-40.652W				Green can.	
12000	- Buoy 8	42-15-58.334N 070-53-45.147W				Red nun.	
12005	- Buoy 9	42-15-36.394N 070-53-24.176W				Green can.	
12010	- Buoy 10	42-15-33.139N 070-53-18.020W				Red nun.	
12015	- Buoy 11	42-15-34.614N 070-53-21.532W				Green can.	
	Hingham Harbor Channel						
12020	- Buoy 12	42-15-33.705N 070-53-03.114W				Red nun.	
12025	- Buoy 13	42-15-32.244N 070-53-00.112W				Green can.	
12030	- Buoy 14	42-15-27.919N 070-52-58.913W				Red nun.	
12035	- Buoy 15	42-15-22.513N 070-52-57.283W				Green can.	
12040	- Buoy 16	42-15-18.941N 070-52-57.997W				Red nun.	

(1) No.	(2) Name and Location	(3) Position	(4) Characteristic	(5) Height	(6) Range	(7) Structure	(8) Remarks

MASSACHUSETTS - First District

BOSTON HARBOR
Hingham Bay
Hingham Harbor Channel

12045	- Buoy 17	42-15-19.182N 070-52-56.199W				Green can.	
12050	- Buoy 18	42-15-16.893N 070-52-42.702W				Red nun.	
12055	- Buoy 19	42-15-17.062N 070-52-41.329W				Green can.	
12060	- Buoy 20	42-15-12.991N 070-52-40.388W				Red nun.	
12065	- Buoy 21	42-15-06.658N 070-52-43.553W				Green can.	
12070	- Buoy 22	42-15-02.534N 070-52-47.712W				Red nun.	

Weir River

12073	- Buoy 1	42-16-29.055N 070-53-41.010W				Green can.	
12075	- Buoy 3	42-16-29.873N 070-53-05.186W				Green can.	
12078	- Buoy 4	42-16-29.607N 070-52-57.031W				Red nun.	
12080	- Buoy 6	42-16-29.773N 070-52-43.186W				Red nun.	
12085	- Buoy 7	42-16-28.972N 070-52-33.114W				Green can.	
12090	- Buoy 8	42-16-19.893N 070-52-28.409W				Red nun.	
12095	- Buoy 9	42-16-14.346N 070-52-14.123W				Green can.	
12100	- Buoy 10	42-16-10.415N 070-52-13.725W				Red nun.	
12105	- Buoy 11	42-16-06.913N 070-52-00.240W				Green can.	
12110	- Buoy 12	42-16-03.446N 070-51-58.862W				Red nun.	

Allerton Harbor
Aids maintained from May 15 to Sep. 30.

12125	- Buoy 1	42-17-55.300N 070-53-19.000W				Green.	Private aid.
12130	- *Buoy 2*	42-17-56.100N 070-53-17.800W				Red.	Private aid.
12135	- Buoy 3	42-18-06.900N 070-53-15.480W				Green can.	Private aid.
12140	- Buoy 4	42-18-07.600N 070-53-14.100W				Red nun.	Private aid.
12145	- Buoy 5	42-18-12.180N 070-53-17.280W				Green can.	Private aid.
12150	- Buoy 6	42-18-12.800N 070-53-17.100W				Red nun.	Private aid.
12151	- Buoy 7	42-18-15.720N 070-53-23.280W				Green can.	Private aid.
12152	- Buoy 8	42-18-16.800N 070-53-23.800W				Red nun.	Private aid.
12153	- Buoy 9	42-18-17.820N 070-53-27.120W				Green can.	Private aid.
12154	- Buoy 10	42-18-18.600N 070-53-28.000W				Red nun.	Private aid.

Cohasset Harbor
Cohasset Western Channel

12155	- Buoy 2W	42-15-47.886N 070-47-42.487W				Red nun.	
12160	- Buoy 3	42-15-41.466N 070-47-10.596W				Green can.	
12165	- Buoy 4	42-15-34.726N 070-47-17.916W				Red nun.	

(1) No.	(2) Name and Location	(3) Position	(4) Characteristic	(5) Height	(6) Range	(7) Structure	(8) Remarks

MASSACHUSETTS - First District

BOSTON HARBOR
Cohasset Harbor
Cohasset Western Channel

12170	- Daybeacon 5 On ledge.	42-15-30.825N 070-47-06.024W				SG on spindle.	
12175	- Buoy 6W	42-15-22.057N 070-47-00.246W				Red nun.	

Cohasset Channel

12185	- LIGHT 8	42-15-05.497N 070-47-00.665W	Fl R 2.5s	29	4	TR on skeleton tower on pile structure.	
12190	- Buoy 9	42-14-56.508N 070-46-59.274W				Green can.	
12195	- LIGHT 10	42-14-56.646N 070-47-00.844W	Fl R 4s	16	3	TR on skeleton tower, on cylindrical base.	
12200	- Buoy 11	42-14-51.022N 070-47-02.981W				Green can.	
12205	- LIGHT 12	42-14-48.155N 070-47-05.846W	Fl R 6s	16	3	TR on skeleton tower, on cylindrical base.	
12210	- Buoy 13	42-14-37.222N 070-47-11.411W				Green can.	
12215	- LIGHT 14	42-14-34.538N 070-47-13.861W	Fl R 2.5s	16	3	TR on skeleton tower, on cylindrical base.	

COHASSET AND SCITUATE HARBORS
Cohasset Harbor

12220	*Cohasset Gangway Lighted Bell Buoy 1G*	42-16-08.081N 070-46-22.646W	Fl G 6s		3	Green.	
12225	Cohasset Gangway Buoy 2 Off northeast side of ledge.	42-16-04.851N 070-46-41.879W				Red nun.	
12227	Cohasset Gangway Buoy 4	42-15-54.562N 070-46-34.586W				Red nun.	
12230	Cohasset Shag Rock Buoy 1S	42-15-50.547N 070-46-05.615W				Green can.	
12235	- Buoy 5	42-15-31.177N 070-46-25.065W				Green can.	
12240	- Buoy 6	42-15-22.596N 070-46-46.785W				Red nun.	

Cohasset Eastern Channel

12243	- Buoy 1E Off north end of shoal.	42-15-40.164N 070-45-39.763W				Green can.	
12245	- Buoy 2	42-15-48.307N 070-45-48.224W				Red nun.	

Scituate Harbor Approach

12256 455	Tar Pouch Buoy 2	42-13-10.269N 070-42-13.386W				Red nun.	
12258 460	*Scituate Approach Lighted Gong Buoy SA*	42-12-07.579N 070-41-49.355W	Mo (A) W		4	Red and white stripes with red spherical topmark.	AIS: MMSI 993672146 (21)

Scituate Harbor

12260	- Channel Buoy 1	42-12-07.789N 070-42-39.656W				Green can.	
12265	- Channel Buoy 2	42-12-09.579N 070-42-39.546W				Red nun.	
12270 465	SCITUATE NORTH JETTY LIGHT 2A	42-12-11.356N 070-42-47.495W	Fl R 4s	23	4	TR on white skeleton tower.	Higher intensity beam eastward.
12275	OLD SCITUATE LIGHT	42-12-17.200N 070-42-56.700W	Fl W 15s			White tower with dwelling.	Private aid.
12280	- Channel Buoy 3	42-12-08.069N 070-42-51.276W				Green can.	
12285	- Channel Buoy 4	42-12-10.000N 070-42-55.219W				Red nun.	
12290	- Channel Buoy 5	42-12-08.299N 070-43-01.397W				Green can.	

(1) No.	(2) Name and Location	(3) Position	(4) Characteristic	(5) Height	(6) Range	(7) Structure	(8) Remarks
			MASSACHUSETTS - First District				

COHASSET AND SCITUATE HARBORS

Scituate Harbor

(1) No.	(2) Name and Location	(3) Position	(4) Characteristic	(5) Height	(6) Range	(7) Structure	(8) Remarks
12295	- Channel Buoy 6	42-12-09.985N 070-43-02.355W				Red nun.	
12300	- Channel Buoy 7	42-12-06.128N 070-43-08.960W				Green can.	
12305	- Channel Buoy 8	42-12-02.733N 070-43-18.099W				Red nun.	
12310	- Channel Buoy 9	42-12-02.002N 070-43-16.025W				Green can.	
12315	- Channel Buoy 11	42-11-53.910N 070-43-26.009W				Green can.	
12320	- Channel Buoy 13	42-11-51.709N 070-43-25.815W				Green can.	

MASSACHUSETTS BAY

New Inlet
Positions of buoys frequently shifted with changing conditions.

(1) No.	(2) Name and Location	(3) Position	(4) Characteristic	(5) Height	(6) Range	(7) Structure	(8) Remarks
12325	- Lighted Bell Buoy 1	42-10-13.660N 070-41-58.407W	Fl G 2.5s	3		Green.	
12330	- Buoy 2	42-10-04.806N 070-42-17.357W				Red nun.	
12332	- Buoy 3	42-09-56.479N 070-42-18.468W				Green can.	
12335	- Buoy 4	42-09-56.671N 070-42-22.593W				Red nun.	Removed when endangered by ice.
12340	- Buoy 6	42-09-49.855N 070-42-32.825W				Red nun.	
12342	- Buoy 7	42-09-47.136N 070-42-34.199W				Green can.	
12345	- Buoy 8	42-09-41.070N 070-42-47.320W				Red nun.	
12350	- Buoy 9	42-09-39.385N 070-42-46.341W				Green can.	
12355	North River Junction Buoy NR	42-09-38.689N 070-42-49.766W				Green can with red bands.	

South River
Aids maintained from May 1 to Oct. 31.

(1) No.	(2) Name and Location	(3) Position	(4) Characteristic	(5) Height	(6) Range	(7) Structure	(8) Remarks
12360	- Buoy 2	42-09-27.168N 070-42-44.756W				Red nun.	
12361.2	- Buoy 4	42-09-22.980N 070-42-39.000W				Red nun.	Private aid.
12365	- Buoy 6	42-09-20.900N 070-42-23.900W				Red nun.	Private aid.
12369	- Buoy 7	42-09-11.300N 070-42-08.900W				Green can.	Private aid.
12370	- Buoy 8	42-09-06.200N 070-42-02.000W				Red nun.	Private aid.
12374	- Buoy 9	42-09-05.000N 070-42-00.900W				Green can.	Private aid.
12375	- Buoy 10	42-08-54.400N 070-42-07.600W				Red nun.	Private aid.
12380	- Buoy 12	42-08-46.400N 070-42-09.900W				Red nun.	Private aid.
12381	- Buoy 13	42-08-42.000N 070-42-09.000W				Green can.	Private aid.
12385	- Buoy 14	42-08-39.200N 070-42-08.200W				Red nun.	Private aid.
12390	- Buoy 16	42-08-32.000N 070-41-51.000W				Red nun.	Private aid.
12392	- Buoy 18	42-08-20.000N 070-41-39.000W				Red nun.	Private aid.

New Inlet
Positions of buoys frequently shifted with changing conditions.

(1) No.	(2) Name and Location	(3) Position	(4) Characteristic	(5) Height	(6) Range	(7) Structure	(8) Remarks
12395	- Buoy 10	42-09-40.497N 070-42-55.457W				Red nun.	

(1) No.	(2) Name and Location	(3) Position	(4) Characteristic	(5) Height	(6) Range	(7) Structure	(8) Remarks

MASSACHUSETTS - First District

MASSACHUSETTS BAY

New Inlet

Positions of buoys frequently shifted with changing conditions.

12397	- Buoy 11	42-09-40.224N 070-42-58.795W				Green can.	Removed when endangered by ice.
12400	- Buoy 12	42-09-42.654N 070-43-04.236W				Red nun.	

North River

Positions of buoys frequently shifted with changing conditions. Aids maintained from May 1 to Oct. 31.

12403	- Buoy 12A	42-09-43.800N 070-43-09.000W				Red nun.	Private aid.
12405	- Buoy 13	42-09-51.300N 070-43-20.300W				Green can.	Private aid.
12407	- Buoy 14	42-09-53.400N 070-43-23.500W				Red nun.	Private aid.
12410	- Buoy 15	42-09-53.300N 070-43-30.900W				Green can.	Private aid.
12412	- Buoy 16	42-09-54.500N 070-43-28.500W				Red nun.	Private aid.
12415	- Buoy 17	42-09-51.400N 070-43-41.700W				Green can.	Private aid.
12418	- Buoy 18	42-09-52.200N 070-43-42.000W				Red nun.	Private aid.
12424	- Buoy 20	42-09-49.600N 070-43-46.700W				Red nun.	Private aid.
12425	- Buoy 21	42-09-44.500N 070-43-52.400W				Green can.	Private aid.
12430	- Daybeacon 23	42-09-37.600N 070-43-58.000W				SG on pile.	Private aid.
12432	- Daybeacon 24	42-09-38.300N 070-43-58.600W				TR on pile.	Private aid.
12435	- Buoy 25	42-09-40.700N 070-44-03.600W				Green can.	Private aid.
12436	- Buoy 27	42-09-43.000N 070-44-06.900W				Green can.	Private aid.
12438	- Buoy 29	42-09-42.500N 070-44-15.800W				Green can.	Private aid.

Herring River

Aids maintained from May 1 to Oct. 31.

12440	- Buoy 1	42-09-55.800N 070-43-23.800W				Green can.	Private aid.
12445	- Buoy 2	42-09-56.100N 070-43-23.800W				Red nun.	Private aid.
12450	- Buoy 3	42-09-59.500N 070-43-26.800W				Green can.	Private aid.
12455	- Buoy 4	42-09-57.500N 070-43-24.900W				Red nun.	Private aid.
12460	- Buoy 5	42-10-24.800N 070-44-04.200W				Green can.	Private aid.
12465	- Buoy 6	42-10-16.700N 070-43-56.000W				Red Nun.	Private aid.
12470	- Buoy 8	42-10-30.900N 070-44-09.500W				Red nun.	Private aid.
12475	- Buoy 9	42-10-28.400N 070-44-07.800W				Green can.	Private aid.
12480	- Buoy 10	42-10-31.740N 070-44-12.540W				Red nun.	Private aid.
12485	- Buoy 12	42-10-32.300N 070-44-19.500W				Red nun.	Private aid.

PLYMOUTH, KINGSTON AND DUXBURY HARBORS

Green Harbor Approach

12490	*Farnham Rock Lighted Bell Buoy 6*	42-05-35.899N 070-36-23.488W	Fl R 4s		4	Red.	
12495	- Buoy 2GH	42-04-35.034N 070-36-50.011W				Red nun.	

(1) No.	(2) Name and Location	(3) Position	(4) Characteristic	(5) Height	(6) Range	(7) Structure	(8) Remarks

MASSACHUSETTS - First District

MASSACHUSETTS BAY
PLYMOUTH, KINGSTON AND DUXBURY HARBORS
Green Harbor Approach

(1) No.	(2) Name and Location	(3) Position	(4) Characteristic	(5) Height	(6) Range	(7) Structure	(8) Remarks
12500	Bartlett Rock Isolated Danger Buoy BR	42-04-43.989N 070-37-48.912W				Black and red bands with two black spherical topmarks; can.	
12505	- Buoy 4	42-04-28.104N 070-37-42.540W					

PLYMOUTH, KINGSTON AND DUXBURY HARBORS
Green Harbor

12510	- *Entrance Lighted Buoy 3*	42-04-20.903N 070-38-21.141W	Fl G 4s		4	Green.	Replaced by can when endangered by ice.
12515	- Entrance Buoy 6	42-04-33.450N 070-38-32.673W				Red nun.	
12520	- BREAKWATER LIGHT 8	42-04-38.590N 070-38-35.351W	Fl R 2.5s		3	TR on spindle.	
12523	- Channel Buoy 8A	42-04-47.674N 070-38-44.531W				Red nun.	
12525	- Buoy 9	42-04-50.699N 070-38-47.455W				Green can.	
12530	High Pine Ledge Buoy 10	42-02-04.425N 070-36-18.945W				Red nun.	
12531	- Buoy 11	42-05-02.484N 070-38-53.927W				Green can.	Private aid.

Plymouth Bay

12535	- *Entrance Lighted Bell Buoy 1*	41-59-42.869N 070-35-24.319W	Q G		3	Green.	
12540	Gurnet Rock Buoy 2	42-00-05.861N 070-35-39.827W				Red nun.	
12545	**Plymouth Light**	42-00-13.428N 070-36-02.178W	Fl (3)W 30s	102	17 R 15	White, octagonal, pyramidal tower, white dwelling. 102	Red from 323° to 352°, covers Mary Ann Rocks. Emergency light of reduced intensity when main light is extinguished. HORN: 2 blasts ev 15s (3s bl). MRASS-Fog signal is radio activated, during times of reduced visibility, turn marine VHF-FM radio to channel 83A/157.175Mhz. Key microphone 5 times consecutively, to activate fog signal for 45 minutes.
12555	- *Channel Lighted Buoy 3*	41-59-42.014N 070-36-06.007W	Fl G 4s		4	Green.	Replaced by can when endangered by ice.
12560	- Channel Buoy 4	41-59-50.940N 070-35-53.286W				Red nun.	
12565	- *Channel Lighted Buoy 5*	41-59-41.524N 070-36-53.447W	Fl G 2.5s		4	Green.	
12570	- Channel Buoy 6	41-59-20.914N 070-37-55.676W				Red nun.	
12575	- Channel Buoy 7	41-59-22.515N 070-37-24.059W				Green can.	

Duxbury Bay

12580	DUXBURY PIER LIGHT	41-59-14.766N 070-38-54.784W	Fl (2)R 5s	35	6	Brown conical tower; upper half white.	Higher intensity beam seaward. HORN: 1 blast ev 15s (2s bl). MRASS-Fog signal is radio activated, during times of reduced visibility, turn marine VHF-FM radio to channel 83A/157.175Mhz. Key microphone 5 times consecutively, to activate fog signal for 60 minutes.
12585	- Channel Buoy 1	41-59-22.026N 070-39-10.678W				Green can.	

(1) No.	(2) Name and Location	(3) Position	(4) Characteristic	(5) Height	(6) Range	(7) Structure	(8) Remarks
			MASSACHUSETTS - First District				

PLYMOUTH, KINGSTON AND DUXBURY HARBORS
Duxbury Bay

(1) No.	(2) Name and Location	(3) Position	(4) Characteristic	(5) Height	(6) Range	(7) Structure	(8) Remarks
12590	- Channel Buoy 2	41-59-30.356N 070-39-01.558W				Red nun.	
12595	- Channel Buoy 2A	41-59-17.473N 070-39-04.371W				Red nun.	
12600	- Channel Buoy 4	42-00-00.506N 070-38-50.288W				Red nun.	
12605	- Channel Buoy 5	42-00-15.195N 070-38-52.198W				Green can.	
12610	- *Channel Lighted Buoy 6*	42-00-19.265N 070-38-51.058W	Fl R 4s	3		Red.	Replaced by nun from Oct. 15 to Mar. 15.
12615	- Channel Buoy 7	42-00-32.225N 070-39-04.839W				Green can.	
12620	- Channel Buoy 8	42-00-47.437N 070-39-14.720W				Red nun.	
12625	- Channel Buoy 9	42-00-58.125N 070-39-27.540W				Green can.	
12630	- *Channel Lighted Buoy 10*	42-01-08.995N 070-39-28.090W	Fl R 4s	3		Red.	Replaced by nun from Oct. 15 to Mar. 15.
12635	- Channel Buoy 11	42-01-32.553N 070-39-31.182W				Green can.	
12640	- Channel Buoy 12	42-01-33.676N 070-39-28.936W				Red nun.	
12645	- Channel Buoy 13	42-01-35.553N 070-39-35.318W				Green can.	
12650	- Channel Buoy 14	42-01-39.515N 070-39-51.780W				Red nun.	
12655	- Channel Buoy 15	42-01-42.221N 070-39-58.104W				Green can.	
12660	- Channel Buoy 16	42-01-41.720N 070-39-55.713W				Red nun.	
12665	- Channel Buoy 18	42-01-44.190N 070-39-56.762W				Red nun.	
12670	- Channel Buoy 19	42-01-52.194N 070-39-56.208W				Green can.	
12675	- Channel Buoy 20	42-01-52.557N 070-39-54.908W				Red nun.	
12680	- Channel Buoy 21	42-02-11.470N 070-40-00.540W				Green can.	
12685	- Channel Buoy 22	42-02-09.302N 070-39-58.791W				Red nun.	

Duxbury Bay Beach Channel
Positions of buoys frequently shifted with changing conditions. Use only with local knowledge. Aids maintained from June 1 to Dec. 1.

No.	Name and Location	Position	Characteristic	Height	Range	Structure	Remarks
12690	- Buoy 2BC	42-01-02.460N 070-38-17.280W				Red nun.	Private aid.
12695	- Buoy 4	42-01-13.560N 070-38-16.320W				Red nun.	Private aid.
12700	- Buoy 6	42-01-28.800N 070-38-18.180W				Red nun.	Private aid.
12705	- Buoy 8	42-01-39.660N 070-38-14.400W				Red nun.	Private aid.
12710	- Buoy 10	42-01-45.840N 070-38-11.100W				Red nun.	Private aid.
12715	- Buoy 12	42-01-55.080N 070-38-07.560W				Red nun.	Private aid.
12720	- Buoy 14	42-02-10.860N 070-38-15.180W				Red nun.	Private aid.
12725	- Buoy 16	42-02-28.260N 070-38-17.340W				Red nun.	Private aid.
12727	- Buoy 17	42-02-31.100N 070-38-22.900W				Green can.	Private aid.
12730	- Buoy 18	42-02-41.100N 070-38-29.900W				Red nun.	Private aid.

(1) No.	(2) Name and Location	(3) Position	(4) Characteristic	(5) Height	(6) Range	(7) Structure	(8) Remarks
			MASSACHUSETTS - First District				

PLYMOUTH, KINGSTON AND DUXBURY HARBORS
Duxbury Bay
Duxbury Bay Beach Channel
Positions of buoys frequently shifted with changing conditions. Use only with local knowledge. Aids maintained from June 1 to Dec. 1.

(1) No.	(2) Name and Location	(3) Position	(4) Characteristic	(5) Height	(6) Range	(7) Structure	(8) Remarks
12735	- Buoy 20	42-02-42.800N 070-38-44.300W				Red nun.	Private aid.
12740	- Buoy 22	42-02-51.600N 070-38-55.680W				Red nun.	Private aid.
	The Nummet Channel						
12744 12905	- Buoy NC	41-59-03.395N 070-39-19.779W				Red and green bands.	
12745	- Buoy 2	41-59-05.406N 070-39-31.139W				Red nun.	
12750	- Buoy 4	41-59-13.406N 070-39-59.140W				Red nun.	
12755	- Buoy 6	41-59-21.406N 070-40-16.511W				Red nun.	
12760	- Buoy 7	41-59-26.262N 070-40-40.943W				Green can.	
12764	- Buoy 8	41-59-27.760N 070-40-41.464W				Red nun.	
12765	- Buoy 9	41-59-19.515N 070-40-49.797W				Green can.	
	Kingston Channel						

Positions of buoys frequently shifted with changing conditions. Use only with local knowledge. Aids maintained from May 15 to Nov. 1.

(1) No.	(2) Name and Location	(3) Position	(4) Characteristic	(5) Height	(6) Range	(7) Structure	(8) Remarks
12770	- Buoy 2	41-59-34.600N 070-39-38.800W				Red nun.	Private aid.
12775	- Buoy 4	41-59-41.700N 070-39-53.500W				Red nun.	Private aid.
12780	- Buoy 6	41-59-47.400N 070-40-09.900W				Red nun.	Private aid.
12785	Standish Shore Guzzle Buoy 2S	42-00-07.800N 070-40-14.400W				Red nun.	Private aid.
12790	Standish Shore Guzzle Buoy 4	42-00-19.200N 070-40-08.040W				Red nun.	Private aid.
12795	Standish Shore Guzzle Buoy 6	42-00-27.000N 070-39-56.700W				Red nun.	Private aid.
12800	- Buoy 8	41-59-51.800N 070-40-20.900W				Red nun.	Private aid.
12805	- Buoy 10	41-59-55.100N 070-40-29.700W				Red nun.	Private aid.
12815	- Buoy 12	42-00-05.000N 070-40-35.400W				Red nun.	Private aid.
12820	- Buoy 14	42-00-13.500N 070-40-53.100W				Red nun.	Private aid.
12825	- Buoy 16	42-00-16.200N 070-41-00.300W				Red nun.	Private aid.
12830	- Buoy 18	42-00-18.800N 070-41-17.070W				Red nun.	Private aid.
12835	- Buoy 20	42-00-20.800N 070-41-21.200W				Red nun.	Private aid.
12840	- Buoy 22	42-00-26.400N 070-41-31.600W				Red nun.	Private aid.
12845	- Buoy 24	42-00-26.700N 070-41-41.700W				Red nun.	Private aid.
12850	- Buoy 26	42-00-22.800N 070-41-52.300W				Red nun.	Private aid.
12855	- Buoy 28	42-00-20.800N 070-42-02.800W				Red nun.	Private aid.
12860	- Buoy 30	42-00-14.700N 070-42-09.700W				Red nun.	Private aid.
12865	- Buoy 32	42-00-11.200N 070-42-12.900W				Red nun.	Private aid.
12870	- Buoy 34	42-00-09.300N 070-42-17.300W				Red nun.	Private aid.

(1) No.	(2) Name and Location	(3) Position	(4) Characteristic	(5) Height	(6) Range	(7) Structure	(8) Remarks

MASSACHUSETTS - First District

PLYMOUTH, KINGSTON AND DUXBURY HARBORS
The Nummet Channel

Kingston Channel
Positions of buoys frequently shifted with changing conditions. Use only with local knowledge. Aids maintained from May 15 to Nov. 1.

12875	- Buoy 36	42-00-10.600N 070-42-22.000W				Red nun.	Private aid.
12885	- Buoy 38	42-00-11.500N 070-42-24.800W				Red nun.	Private aid.
12890	- Buoy 40	42-00-16.100N 070-42-35.300W				Red nun.	Private aid.
12895	- Buoy 42	42-00-09.700N 070-42-33.000W				Red nun.	Private aid.

Plymouth Harbor
Positions of buoys are frequently shifted with changing conditions. Use only with local knowledge.

12905 12744	The Nummet Channel Buoy NC	41-59-03.395N 070-39-19.779W				Red and green bands.	
12910	- *Channel Lighted Bell Buoy 9*	41-59-06.806N 070-39-15.388W	Fl G 4s		4	Green.	Removed when endangered by ice.
12915	- Channel Buoy 10	41-58-53.986N 070-39-23.238W				Red nun.	
12920	- Channel Buoy 11	41-58-54.086N 070-39-20.318W				Green can.	
12925	- CHANNEL LIGHT 12 50 feet west of channel limit.	41-58-47.304N 070-39-24.426W	Q R	16	3	TR on skeleton tower on black cylindrical pier.	
12930	- Channel Buoy 13	41-58-44.536N 070-39-18.948W				Green can.	
12935	Plymouth Beach Jetty Daybeacon	41-58-46.325N 070-39-11.597W				NW on spindle on granite cribwork worded DANGER SUBMERGED JETTY.	
12940	- Channel Buoy 14	41-58-31.136N 070-39-10.448W				Red nun.	
12945	- Channel Buoy 15	41-58-20.677N 070-38-56.518W				Green can.	
12950	- Channel Buoy 16	41-58-05.986N 070-38-46.767W				Red nun.	
12955	- CHANNEL LIGHT 17 50 feet east of channel limit.	41-58-03.130N 070-38-41.723W	Fl G 4s	16	5	SG on skeleton tower on black cylindrical pier.	
12960	- Channel Buoy 18 Marks end of shoal.	41-57-59.306N 070-38-50.007W				Red nun.	
12965	- Channel Buoy 19	41-57-55.376N 070-38-50.897W				Green can.	
12980	- Channel Buoy 20	41-57-44.926N 070-39-12.057W				Red nun.	
12985	- Channel Buoy 21	41-57-42.846N 070-39-10.807W				Green can.	
12990	- Channel Buoy 22	41-57-41.984N 070-39-19.587W				Red nun.	
13005	- Channel Buoy 23	41-57-34.046N 070-39-31.298W				Green can.	
13010	- Channel Buoy 24	41-57-36.468N 070-39-34.849W				Red nun.	
13015	- Channel Buoy 25	41-57-35.756N 070-39-38.666W				Green can.	
13020	- Channel Buoy 27	41-57-39.120N 070-39-47.421W				Green can.	
13025	- Channel Buoy 29	41-57-41.296N 070-39-53.319W				Green can.	

CAPE COD BAY
Cape Cod Canal Approach

| 13035 | *Mary Ann Rocks Lighted
Whistle Buoy 12* | 41-55-06.651N
070-30-22.138W | Fl R 2.5s | | 4 | Red. | |

(1) No.	(2) Name and Location	(3) Position	(4) Characteristic	(5) Height	(6) Range	(7) Structure	(8) Remarks
			MASSACHUSETTS - First District				
	CAPE COD BAY						
	Cape Cod Canal Approach						
13037	*WHG Research Lighted Buoy W NERACOOS 44090*	41-50-54.600N 070-19-48.000W	Fl (5)Y 20s			Yellow.	Property of Woods Hole Group Research. Private aid.
13040	- *Lighted Bell Buoy CC*	41-48-52.926N 070-27-38.810W	Mo (A) W		4	Red and white stripes with red spherical topmark.	AIS: MMSI 993672152 (21)
13045	- *Lighted Buoy 1*	41-47-05.817N 070-28-06.509W	Fl G 2.5s		4	Green.	
	Cape Cod Canal Eastern Entrance						
13050	CAPE COD CANAL BREAKWATER LIGHT 6	41-46-47.254N 070-29-23.291W	Fl R 5s	43	9	TR on red cylindrical.	HORN: 1 blast ev 15s (2s bl). Fog signal is radio activated, during times of reduced visibility, turn marine VHF-FM radio to channel 83A/157.175Mhz. Key microphone 5 times consecutively, to activate fog signal for 45 minutes.
13060	- *Lighted Bell Buoy 3*	41-46-48.908N 070-28-55.983W	Q G		3	Green.	
13065	- *Lighted Buoy 4*	41-46-49.716N 070-29-17.314W	Q R		3	Red.	
13070	- Buoy 5	41-46-38.853N 070-29-24.514W				Green can.	
13075	- Buoy 7 Off end of submerged breakwater.	41-46-34.811N 070-29-36.385W				Green can.	
13080	- RANGE FRONT LIGHT	41-46-17.748N 070-30-32.526W	Oc G 4s	38		KRW on skeleton tower.	Visible 4° each side of range line.
13085	- RANGE REAR LIGHT 267 yards, 244.9° from front light.	41-46-14.390N 070-30-42.094W	F G	51		KRW on skeleton tower.	Visible 4° each side of range line.
	Barnstable Harbor *Positions of buoys frequently shifted with changing conditions.*						
13090	- *Entrance Lighted Bell Buoy BH*	41-45-16.424N 070-16-25.689W	Mo (A) W		4	Red and white stripes with red spherical topmark.	
13095	- Entrance Buoy 1	41-44-42.710N 070-16-22.476W				Green can.	
13100	- Entrance Buoy 2 Marks easterly side of rock.	41-44-25.415N 070-16-19.947W				Red nun.	
13105	- Entrance Buoy 3	41-44-09.693N 070-16-15.522W				Green can	
13106	- Entrance Buoy 4	41-43-51.700N 070-16-17.370W				Red nun.	
13110	- *Entrance Lighted Buoy 6* Marks outer extremity of shoal.	41-43-26.451N 070-16-12.427W	Fl R 2.5s		3	Red.	Replaced by nun from Oct. 15 to Apr. 15.
13115	- Buoy 7	41-43-16.147N 070-16-44.788W				Green can.	
13117	SANDY NECK LIGHT	41-43-22.000N 070-16-52.000W	Fl W 6s			Brick structure.	Private aid.
13120	- *Lighted Buoy 8*	41-43-15.627N 070-17-04.488W	Fl R 4s		3	Red.	Replaced by can from Oct. 15 to Apr. 15.
13125	- *Lighted Buoy 9* On south-southeast side of shoal.	41-42-56.901N 070-17-25.241W	Fl G 4s		3	Green.	Replaced by nun from Oct. 15 to Apr. 15.
13130	- Buoy 11 Marks north side of Baxter Rock.	41-42-50.217N 070-17-41.910W				Green can.	
13135	*Maraspin Creek Lighted Buoy 1*	41-42-43.500N 070-17-58.900W	Fl G 4s			Green	Maintained from Jun 1 to Nov 1. Private aid.
13135.1	Maraspin Creek Daybeacon 2	41-42-39.300N 070-18-04.400W				TR	Maintained from Jun 1 to Nov 1. Private aid.
13135.2	Maraspin Creek Daybeacon 3	41-42-36.100N 070-18-04.400W				SG	Maintained from Jun 1 to Nov 1. Private aid.

(1) No.	(2) Name and Location	(3) Position	(4) Characteristic	(5) Height	(6) Range	(7) Structure	(8) Remarks
			MASSACHUSETTS - First District				
CAPE COD BAY							
Barnstable Harbor							
Positions of buoys frequently shifted with changing conditions.							
13135.3	Maraspin Creek Daybeacon 4	41-42-34.700N 070-18-06.200W				TR	Maintained from Jun 1 to Nov 1. Private aid.
13135.4	Maraspin Creek Daybeacon 5	41-42-34.400N 070-18-04.800W				SG	Maintained from Jun 1 to Nov 1. Private aid.
13135.5	Maraspin Creek Daybeacon 6	41-42-32.100N 070-18-05.000W				TR	Maintained from Jun 1 to Nov 1. Private aid.
13135.6	Maraspin Creek Daybeacon 7	41-42-31.900N 070-18-03.600W				SG	Maintained from Jun 1 to Nov 1. Private aid.
13135.7	Maraspin Creek Daybeacon 8	41-42-30.100N 070-18-03.900W				TR	Maintained from Jun 1 to Nov 1. Private aid.
13135.8	Maraspin Creek Daybeacon 9	41-42-30.100N 070-18-02.800W				SG	Maintained from Jun 1 to Nov 1. Private aid.
13136	Salten Point Buoy 1	41-42-45.400N 070-18-12.000W				Green can.	Private aid.
13137	Salten Point Buoy 2	41-42-44.900N 070-18-17.900W				Red nun.	Private aid.
13137.5	Salten Point Buoy 4	41-42-44.200N 070-18-28.700W				Red nun.	Private aid.
13138	Salten Point Buoy 5	41-42-41.800N 070-18-43.300W				Green can.	Private aid.
13139	Salten Point Buoy 6	41-42-41.100N 070-19-01.400W				Red nun.	Private aid.
Sesuit Harbor							
13140	*- Approach Lighted Bell Buoy 1S*	41-46-27.134N 070-09-48.910W	Fl G 4s		4	Green.	
13150	*- WEST JETTY LIGHT 2*	41-45-31.554N 070-09-22.390W	Fl R 2.5s	12	5	TR on modular tower.	
13155	*- East Jetty Daybeacon 3*	41-45-30.554N 070-09-18.310W				SG on pile.	
13158	*- Lighted Buoy 4*	41-45-24.300N 070-09-16.300W	Fl R 2s			Red nun.	Private aid.
13159	*- Lighted Buoy 5*	41-45-20.300N 070-09-13.500W	Fl G 2s			Green can.	Private aid.
Wellfleet Harbor							
13160	*Billingsgate Shoal Lighted Bell Buoy 1*	41-48-52.741N 070-10-47.856W	Fl G 4s		3	Green.	
13161	ROCK HARBOR EAST JETTY LIGHT	41-48-02.360N 070-00-32.730W	Fl G 4s			Steel tower.	Private aid.
13162	ROCK HARBOR WEST JETTY LIGHT	41-48-00.540N 070-00-31.620W	Fl R 4s			Steel tower.	Private aid.
13174	*James Longstreet Isolated Danger Lighted Buoy DJ*	41-49-52.611N 070-02-40.465W	Fl (2)W 5s		4	Black and red bands with two black spherical topmarks.	Replaced by can when endangered by ice.
13180	*Billingsgate Flat Lighted Buoy 3*	41-50-48.813N 070-02-53.378W	Fl G 2.5s		4	Green.	Replaced by LIB when endangered by ice.
13185	*Billingsgate Lighted Buoy 5*	41-51-59.955N 070-03-18.560W	Fl G 4s		4	Green.	Replaced by can from Oct. 15 to Apr. 15.
13190	Billingsgate Island Buoy 6 At south end of middle ground.	41-52-18.202N 070-03-37.756W				Red nun.	
13195	*Billingsgate Island Lighted Buoy 8* At north end of middle ground.	41-52-31.772N 070-03-39.418W	Fl R 2.5s		4	Red.	Replaced by nun from Oct. 15 to Apr. 15.
13200	*- Channel Lighted Buoy 10*	41-53-49.870N 070-02-20.977W	Fl R 4s		4	Red.	Replaced by nun from Oct. 15 to Apr. 15.
13205	- Channel Buoy 11	41-54-31.714N 070-02-22.336W				Green can.	
13210	- Channel Buoy 12	41-55-06.360N 070-02-19.360W				Red nun.	

(1) No.	(2) Name and Location	(3) Position	(4) Characteristic	(5) Height	(6) Range	(7) Structure	(8) Remarks
			MASSACHUSETTS - First District				
CAPE COD BAY							
Wellfleet Harbor							
13215	- Channel Buoy 13	41-55-16.613N 070-02-15.557W				Green can.	
13220	- BREAKWATER LIGHT 14	41-55-31.511N 070-02-07.000W	Fl R 2.5s	16	5	TR on spindle.	
13221	- Buoy 14A	41-55-35.000N 070-02-06.000W				Red nun.	Private aid.
13222	- Buoy 14B	41-55-38.800N 070-02-01.300W				Red nun.	Private aid.
13225	- Channel Buoy 15	41-55-36.186N 070-02-08.027W				Green can.	
13226	- Channel Buoy 15A	41-55-41.280N 070-02-01.260W				Green can.	Private aid.
13230	- Channel Buoy 16	41-55-41.008N 070-01-55.120W				Red nun.	
Duck Creek							
Aids maintained from Apr. 15 to Oct. 15.							
13235	- Buoy 1	41-55-42.600N 070-01-38.700W				Green can.	Private aid.
13240	- Buoy 2	41-55-41.600N 070-01-36.600W				Red nun.	Private aid.
13245	- Buoy 3	41-55-43.900N 070-01-30.600W				Green can.	Private aid.
13250	- Buoy 4	41-55-43.200N 070-01-29.600W				Red nun.	Private aid.
13255	- Buoy 5	41-55-47.300N 070-01-26.900W				Green can.	Private aid.
13260	- Buoy 6	41-55-46.900N 070-01-25.700W				Red nun.	Private aid.
13260.1	PAMET RIVER NORTH BREAKWATER LIGHT 1	41-59-32.100N 070-04-48.000W	Fl G 4s				Private aid.
13260.2	*Pamet River Entrance Lighted Buoy 2*	41-59-30.000N 070-04-49.900W	Fl R 4s			Red.	Private aid.
13260.4	Pamet River Buoy 4	41-59-30.600N 070-04-45.700W				Red nun.	Private aid.
13260.7	Pamet River Buoy 7	41-59-31.600N 070-04-34.000W				Green can.	Private aid.
13260.9	Pamet River Buoy 10	41-59-30.300N 070-04-27.300W					Private aid.
Provincetown Harbor Approach							
13265	- *Lighted Bell Buoy 1*	42-00-21.993N 070-11-33.359W	Fl G 4s		4	Green.	
13267	Race Point Coast Guard Station Mooring Buoy C	42-02-00.548N 070-10-39.267W				White with blue band.	
13270	**Wood End Light**	42-01-16.834N 070-11-36.511W	Fl R 10s	45	3	White square tower. 39	Light may also be displayed during daytime when sound signal is in operation. HORN: 1 blast ev 30s (3s bl). Fog signal is radio activated, during times of reduced visibility, turn marine VHF-FM radio to channel 83A/157.175Mhz. Key microphone 5 times consecutively, to activate fog signal for 45 minutes.
13275	LONG POINT LIGHT	42-01-59.264N 070-10-07.161W	Oc G 4s	36	8	White square tower.	HORN: 1 blast ev 15s (2s bl). Fog signal is radio activated, during times of reduced visibility, turn marine VHF-FM radio to channel 83A/157.175Mhz. Key microphone 5 times consecutively, to activate fog signal for 45 minutes.
13280	*Long Point Shoal Lighted Bell Buoy 3*	42-02-02.595N 070-09-40.424W	Q G		3	Green.	

(1) No.	(2) Name and Location	(3) Position	(4) Characteristic	(5) Height	(6) Range	(7) Structure	(8) Remarks
			MASSACHUSETTS - First District				
CAPE COD BAY							
Provincetown Harbor Approach							
13283	Provincetown Harbor Mooring Buoy E	42-02-10.335N 070-10-43.665W				White with blue band.	
13285	PROVINCETOWN HARBOR BREAKWATER WEST END LIGHT 4	42-02-45.567N 070-10-52.036W	Fl R 2.5s	32	5	TR on spindle.	
13290	PROVINCETOWN HARBOR BREAKWATER EAST END LIGHT 5	42-03-05.114N 070-10-32.718W	Fl G 6s	32	5	SG on spindle.	
13301	Provincetown Aquaculture Lighted Buoy A	42-03-01.500N 070-09-31.000W	Fl Y 3s			Yellow.	Private aid.
13301.1	Provincetown Aquaculture Lighted Buoy B	42-03-04.800N 070-09-29.600W	Fl Y 3s			Yellow.	Private aid.
13301.2	Provincetown Aquaculture Lighted Buoy C	42-02-43.000N 070-08-12.000W	Fl Y 3s			Yellow.	Private aid.
13301.3	Provincetown Aquaculture Lighted Buoy D	42-02-47.000N 070-08-12.000W	Fl Y 3s			Yellow.	Private aid.
NANTUCKET SOUND AND APPROACHES							
Chatham Harbor Approach							
13305	CHATHAM INLET BAR GUIDE LIGHT	41-40-17.634N 069-57-00.210W	Fl Y 2.5s	62	11	NW on Pole worded DANGER ROUGH BAR.	Light flashing: bar condition two foot breaking seas or greater. Light extinguished: lesser sea consitions but with no guarantee that bar is safe.
CAPE COD BAY							
Provincetown Harbor Approach							
Southway Mid-Channel							
Aids not charted due to numerous aids in area. Use with local knowledge.							
13306	- Buoy A	41-39-24.300N 069-58-54.200W				Red and white sphere.	Private aid.
13306.1	- Buoy B	41-39-14.400N 069-58-54.800W				Red and white sphere.	Private aid.
13306.2	- Buoy C	41-39-16.700N 069-58-48.800W				Red and white sphere.	Private aid.
13306.3	- Buoy D	41-39-10.400N 069-58-44.900W				Red and white sphere.	Private aid.
13306.4	- Buoy E	41-39-00.600N 069-58-44.500W				Red and white sphere.	Private aid.
13306.5	- Buoy F	41-39-57.000N 069-58-34.100W				Red and white sphere.	Private aid.
13306.6	- Buoy G	41-39-07.600N 069-58-16.100W				Red and white sphere.	Private aid.
13306.7	- Buoy H	41-39-14.500N 069-58-42.700W				Red and white sphere.	Private aid.
13306.8	- Buoy I	41-39-13.400N 069-58-25.300W				Red and white sphere.	Private aid.
13306.9	- Buoy J	41-39-05.700N 069-57-50.400W				Red and white sphere.	Private aid.
13308.51	Outermost Mid-Channel Buoy OMH	41-39-43.100N 069-57-13.700W				Red and white.	Private aid.
Chatham Midchannel							
Aids not charted due to numerous aids in area. Use with local knowledge.							
13308.95	Outermost Harbor Mid Channel Buoy A	41-39-29.000N 069-57-18.000W				Red and white sphere.	Positions of buoys frequently shifted with changing conditions. Private aid.
Chatham Harbor							
Aids maintained Apr. 15 to Oct. 15.							
13309	- Buoy 1	41-39-43.500N 069-56-46.700W				Green can.	Positions of buoys frequently shifted with changing conditions. Private aid.
13310	- Buoy 2	41-39-56.900N 069-56-38.100W				Red nun.	Positions of buoys frequently shifted with changing conditions. Private aid.
13315	- Buoy 3	41-40-13.800N 069-56-40.100W				Green can.	Positions of buoys frequently shifted with changing conditions. Private aid.

(1) No.	(2) Name and Location	(3) Position	(4) Characteristic	(5) Height	(6) Range	(7) Structure	(8) Remarks
			MASSACHUSETTS - First District				

CAPE COD BAY

Chatham Harbor
Aids maintained Apr. 15 to Oct. 15.

No.	Name and Location	Position				Structure	Remarks
13320	- Buoy 4	41-40-23.700N 069-56-41.000W				Red nun.	Positions of buoys frequently shifted with changing conditions. Private aid.
13325	- Buoy 5	41-40-40.100N 069-56-42.100W				Green can.	Private aid.
13330	- Buoy 6	41-40-05.940N 069-56-39.000W				Red nun.	Private aid.

CHATHAM HARBOR AND PLEASANT BAY

Aunt Lydias Cove
Aids maintained Apr. 15 to Oct. 15.

No.	Name and Location	Position				Structure	Remarks
13335	Bassing Harbor Buoy 2	41-42-46.000N 069-57-52.500W				Red nun.	Private aid.
13336	Bassing Harbor Buoy 3	41-42-49.600N 069-57-59.500W				Green can.	Private aid.
13337	Bassing Harbor Buoy 4	41-42-39.660N 069-58-17.460W				Red nun.	Private aid.
13340	- Buoy 1	41-40-49.600N 069-56-48.300W				Green can.	Private aid.
13350	- Buoy 2	41-40-54.000N 069-56-49.500W				Red nun.	Private aid.
13355	- Buoy 3	41-40-58.100N 069-56-52.100W				Green can.	Private aid.
13360	- Buoy 4	41-41-00.200N 069-56-51.900W				Red nun.	Private aid.
13365	- Buoy 5	41-41-05.200N 069-56-54.900W				Green can.	Private aid.
13370	- Buoy 6	41-41-07.700N 069-56-55.300W				Red nun.	Private aid.

Round Cove
Aids maintained May 1 to Nov. 1.

No.	Name and Location	Position				Structure	Remarks
13390	- Channel Buoy 1	41-43-02.700N 069-59-40.600W				Green can.	Private aid.
13391	- Channel Buoy 2	41-43-04.300N 069-59-41.200W				Red nun.	Private aid.
13392	- Channel Buoy 3	41-43-03.500N 069-59-42.400W				Green can.	Private aid.
13393	- Channel Buoy 4	41-43-04.500N 069-59-43.500W				Red nun.	Private aid.
13394	- Channel Buoy 6	41-43-04.140N 069-59-46.500W				Red nun.	Private aid.
13395	- Channel Buoy 7	41-43-10.600N 069-59-49.000W				Green can.	Private aid.

Pleasant Bay
Aids maintained from May 15 to Nov. 1.

No.	Name and Location	Position				Structure	Remarks
13398	Strong Island Rock Buoy	41-43-30.900N 069-56-59.220W					Marked DANGER ROCKS Private aid.
13399	- Junction Buoy	41-42-46.200N 069-57-45.700W				Red green bands: nun.	Private aid.
13400	- Buoy 6	41-40-45.000N 069-56-34.700W				Red nun.	Private aid.
13405	- Buoy 7	41-40-54.200N 069-56-26.900W				Green can.	Private aid.
13410	- Buoy 8	41-41-05.300N 069-56-20.300W				Red nun.	Private aid.
13415	- Buoy 9	41-41-25.600N 069-56-17.900W				Green can.	Private aid.
13420	- Buoy 10	41-41-38.900N 069-56-08.700W				Red nun.	Private aid.
13425	- Buoy 11	41-41-42.800N 069-56-11.300W				Green can.	Private aid.
13430	- Buoy 12	41-41-47.200N 069-56-16.800W				Red nun.	Private aid.
13435	- Buoy 13	41-41-50.800N 069-56-34.600W				Green can.	Private aid.

(1) No.	(2) Name and Location	(3) Position	(4) Characteristic	(5) Height	(6) Range	(7) Structure	(8) Remarks
			MASSACHUSETTS - First District				

CHATHAM HARBOR AND PLEASANT BAY

Pleasant Bay
Aids maintained from May 15 to Nov. 1.

13437	- Buoy 14	41-41-59.900N 069-56-32.400W				Red nun.	Private aid.
13440	- Buoy 15	41-42-08.300N 069-56-34.100W				Green can.	Private aid.
13445	- Buoy 16	41-42-33.200N 069-56-44.800W				Red nun.	Private aid.
13450	- Buoy 17	41-42-35.000N 069-57-51.000W				Green can.	Private aid.
13455	- Buoy 18	41-42-45.900N 069-57-57.600W				Red nun.	Private aid.
13460	- Buoy 19	41-42-33.400N 069-57-06.200W				Green can.	Private aid.
13465	- Buoy 20	41-42-39.600N 069-57-21.300W				Red nun.	Private aid.
13470	- Buoy 21	41-42-41.800N 069-57-38.000W				Green can.	Private aid.
13475	- Buoy 22	41-42-49.500N 069-57-43.600W				Red nun.	Private aid.
13475.1	- Buoy 23	41-42-58.100N 069-57-45.500W				Green can.	Private aid.
13475.2	- Buoy 24	41-43-09.800N 069-57-48.600W				Red nun.	Private aid.
13475.3	- Buoy 25	41-43-27.500N 069-57-55.700W				Green can.	Private aid.
13475.4	- Buoy 26	41-43-26.200N 069-58-02.900W				Red nun.	Private aid.
13475.5	- Buoy 27	41-43-23.400N 069-58-12.000W				Green can.	Private aid.
13475.6	- Buoy 28	41-43-25.700N 069-58-22.100W				Red nun.	Private aid.
13475.7	- Buoy 29	41-43-25.300N 069-58-23.900W				Green can.	Private aid.
13475.8	- Buoy 30	41-43-24.100N 069-58-15.600W				Red nun.	Private aid.
13475.9	- Buoy 31	41-43-23.900N 069-58-24.500W				Green can.	Private aid.
13475.91	Quanset Pond Buoy 2	41-44-10.000N 069-58-53.000W				Red nun.	Private aid.
13475.92	Quanset Pond Buoy 4	41-44-14.800N 069-58-53.700W				Red nun.	Private aid.
13476	- Buoy 32	41-43-25.800N 069-58-25.400W				Red nun.	Private aid.

Little Pleasant Bay
Aids maintained from May 1 to Nov. 1, unless otherwise noted.

13476.1	- Buoy 32A	41-43-39.700N 069-58-23.000W				Red nun.	Private aid.
13476.12	- Buoy 34	41-43-51.200N 069-58-14.100W				Red nun.	Private aid.
13476.13	- Buoy 35	41-44-03.200N 069-57-59.400W				Green can.	Private aid.
13476.14	- Buoy 36	41-44-01.700N 069-57-59.700W				Red nun.	Private aid.
13476.15	- Buoy 37	41-44-06.000N 069-57-55.800W				Green can.	Private aid.
13476.16	- Buoy 38	41-44-06.000N 069-57-54.700W				Red nun.	Private aid.
13476.17	- Buoy 39	41-44-13.100N 069-57-56.900W				Green can.	Private aid.
13476.18	- Buoy 40	41-44-23.100N 069-57-57.000W				Red nun.	Private aid.
13476.19	- Buoy 41	41-44-28.300N 069-57-54.700W				Green can.	Private aid.

(1) No.	(2) Name and Location	(3) Position	(4) Characteristic	(5) Height	(6) Range	(7) Structure	(8) Remarks

MASSACHUSETTS - First District

CHATHAM HARBOR AND PLEASANT BAY
Pleasant Bay
Little Pleasant Bay
Aids maintained from May 1 to Nov. 1, unless otherwise noted.

No.	Name	Position	Structure	Remarks
13476.2	- Buoy 42	41-44-36.200N 069-57-49.200W	Red nun.	Private aid.
13476.21	- Buoy 43	41-44-42.900N 069-57-54.700W	Green can.	Private aid.
13476.22	- Buoy 44	41-44-52.300N 069-58-03.800W	Red nun.	Private aid.
13476.24	- Buoy 46	41-45-01.600N 069-58-00.400W	Red nun.	Private aid.
13476.25	Paw Wah Pond Entrance Buoy 1	41-45-12.000N 069-58-06.000W	Green can.	Private aid.
13476.26	- Buoy 48	41-45-08.400N 069-57-49.000W	Red nun.	Private aid.
13476.27	Paw Wah Pond Entrance Buoy 2	41-45-09.800N 069-58-02.000W	Red nun.	Private aid.
13476.28	- Buoy 50	41-45-12.500N 069-57-38.400W	Red nun.	Private aid.
13476.29	- Buoy 51	41-45-23.000N 069-57-29.200W	Green can.	Private aid.
13476.3	- Buoy 52	41-45-31.400N 069-57-27.500W	Red nun.	Private aid.
13476.31	- Buoy 53	41-45-31.200N 069-57-29.400W	Green can.	Private aid.
13476.32	- Buoy 54	41-45-36.400N 069-57-40.200W	Red nun.	Private aid.
13476.33	- Buoy 55	41-45-43.200N 069-57-43.500W	Green can.	Private aid.
13476.34	- Buoy 56	41-45-49.900N 069-57-44.900W	Red nun.	Private aid.
13476.35	- Buoy 57	41-45-56.200N 069-57-48.900W	Green can.	Private aid.
13476.36	- Buoy 58	41-46-02.800N 069-57-51.600W	Red nun.	Private aid.
13476.37	- Buoy 59	41-46-10.100N 069-57-57.100W	Green can.	Private aid.
13476.38	- Buoy 60	41-46-15.900N 069-57-57.500W	Red nun.	Private aid.
13476.39	- Buoy 61	41-46-20.700N 069-57-52.900W	Green can.	Private aid.
13476.41	- Buoy 63	41-46-25.200N 069-57-57.000W	Green can.	Private aid.
13476.42	- Buoy 64	41-46-45.200N 069-58-05.400W	Red nun.	Private aid.
13476.43	- Buoy 65	41-46-45.700N 069-58-06.100W	Green can.	Private aid.

Ryder Cove
Aids maintained from May 15 to Nov. 1 unless otherwise noted.

No.	Name	Position	Structure	Remarks
13477	- Buoy 1	41-42-45.000N 069-57-47.300W	Green can.	Private aid.
13480	- Buoy 2	41-42-43.700N 069-57-50.900W	Red nun.	Private aid.
13485	- Buoy 3	41-42-33.700N 069-57-54.500W	Green can.	Private aid.
13486	- Buoy 4	41-42-40.700N 069-58-01.100W	Red nun.	Private aid.
13487	- Buoy 5	41-42-32.900N 069-58-06.500W	Green can.	Private aid.
13495	- Buoy 6	41-42-25.200N 069-58-14.200W	Red nun.	Private aid.
13500	- Buoy 7	41-42-25.100N 069-58-21.500W	Green can.	Private aid.
13501	- Buoy 8	41-42-16.700N 069-58-35.900W	Red nun.	Private aid.

(1) No.	(2) Name and Location	(3) Position	(4) Characteristic	(5) Height	(6) Range	(7) Structure	(8) Remarks

MASSACHUSETTS - First District

CHATHAM HARBOR AND PLEASANT BAY

Pleasant Bay

Ryder Cove
Aids maintained from May 15 to Nov. 1 unless otherwise noted.

13505	- Buoy 9	41-42-24.360N 069-58-21.600W				Green can.	Private aid.
13506	- Buoy 10	41-42-17.100N 069-58-36.060W				Red nun.	Private aid.
13510	- Buoy 11	41-42-24.500N 069-58-22.700W				Green can.	Private aid.
13515	- Buoy 12	41-42-17.300N 069-58-35.400W				Red nun.	Private aid.

Town Cove
Aids maintained from May 15 to Nov. 1 unless otherwise noted.

13520	- Buoy 1	41-48-33.800N 069-57-01.300W				Green can.	Private aid.
13520.11	- Buoy 1A	41-48-34.500N 069-57-03.600W				Green can.	Private aid.
13520.5	- Buoy 2	41-48-44.100N 069-57-12.900W				Red nun.	Private aid.
13521	- Buoy 3	41-48-49.200N 069-57-20.600W				Green can.	Private aid.
13521.5	- Buoy 4	41-48-54.800N 069-57-26.900W				Red nun.	Private aid.
13522	- Buoy 5	41-48-52.600N 069-57-39.800W				Green can.	Private aid.
13522.5	- Buoy 6	41-48-45.800N 069-57-51.400W				Red can.	Private aid.
13523	- Buoy 7	41-48-37.900N 069-57-55.700W				Green can.	Private aid.
13523.5	- Buoy 8	41-48-27.500N 069-57-56.900W				Red nun.	Private aid.
13524	- Buoy 9	41-48-24.200N 069-57-56.800W				Green can.	Private aid.
13524.5	- Buoy 10	41-48-18.900N 069-58-00.500W				Red nun.	Private aid.
13524.51	- Buoy 10A	41-48-21.500N 069-58-16.400W				Red nun.	Private aid.
13525	- Buoy 11	41-48-19.000N 069-58-19.500W				Green can.	Private aid.
13525.5	- Buoy 12	41-48-12.200N 069-58-25.700W				Red nun.	Private aid.
13526	- Buoy 13	41-48-06.900N 069-58-27.200W				Green can.	Private aid.
13526.5	- Buoy 14	41-48-03.000N 069-58-31.000W				Red nun.	Private aid.
13527	- Buoy 15	41-47-57.800N 069-58-32.200W				Green can.	Private aid.
13527.5	- Buoy 16	41-47-54.000N 069-58-36.700W				Red nun.	Private aid.
13527.7	- Buoy 17	41-47-51.200N 069-58-36.500W				Green can.	Private aid.

NANTUCKET SOUND AND APPROACHES

Pollock Rip Channel

13535	- *Lighted Gong Buoy 4*	41-33-09.475N 069-55-08.420W	Fl R 4s		3	Red.	Replaced by nun when endangered by ice.
13540	- Buoy 5	41-32-54.520N 069-56-02.700W				Green can.	
13545	- *Lighted Buoy 6*	41-32-59.246N 069-57-11.364W	Fl R 4s		3	Red.	Replaced by nun when endangered by ice.
13550	- *Lighted Buoy 8*	41-32-42.763N 069-58-55.557W	Fl R 6s		3	Red.	
13555	- *Lighted Buoy 9*	41-32-06.568N 069-59-27.223W	Fl G 4s		3	Green.	

(1) No.	(2) Name and Location	(3) Position	(4) Characteristic	(5) Height	(6) Range	(7) Structure	(8) Remarks
			MASSACHUSETTS - First District				
	NANTUCKET SOUND AND APPROACHES						
	Pollock Rip Channel						
13565	- *Lighted Buoy 10*	41-31-51.450N 070-00-31.064W	Fl R 4s		3	Red.	Replaced by nun when endangered by ice.
13570	Stone Horse Shoal Buoy 11	41-30-40.455N 070-00-10.376W				Green can.	
13575	Handkerchief Shoal Buoy 12	41-30-04.620N 070-03-14.702W				Red nun.	
13580	Handkerchief Shoal Buoy 14	41-29-06.555N 070-05-05.029W				Red nun.	
	Great Round Shoal Channel						
13586	- *Lighted Buoy 2*	41-26-11.039N 069-44-33.001W	Fl R 2.5s		3	Red.	
13590	- *Lighted Buoy 3*	41-25-34.501N 069-44-55.432W	Fl G 2.5s		4	Green.	Replaced by can when endangered by ice.
13595	- *Lighted Buoy 4*	41-25-52.538N 069-46-02.400W	Fl R 4s		3	Red.	
13600	- *Lighted Buoy 5*	41-24-58.212N 069-48-26.120W	Fl G 4s		3	Green.	Replaced by can when endangered by ice.
13605	- *Lighted Buoy 6*	41-25-16.085N 069-50-51.997W	Fl R 2.5s		3	Red.	Replaced by nun when endangered by ice.
13610	- *Lighted Buoy 7*	41-24-11.463N 069-52-21.471W	Fl G 2.5s		3	Green.	Replaced by can when endangered by ice.
13615	- *Lighted Buoy 8*	41-24-49.171N 069-52-57.084W	Fl R 4s		3	Red.	
13620	- *Lighted Buoy 10*	41-24-49.349N 069-54-32.497W	Fl R 2.5s		3	Red.	
13625	- Buoy 9 East of north end of shoal.	41-23-51.803N 069-54-57.825W				Green can.	
13635	Point Rip Shoal Buoy 11	41-25-06.098N 069-58-08.269W				Green can.	
13640	- *Lighted Buoy 13* Off shoal.	41-25-55.360N 069-58-54.411W	Fl G 2.5s		3	Green.	Replaced by can when endangered by ice.
13645	Point Rip Buoy 1 On north part of outer shoal.	41-25-13.041N 069-59-49.102W				Green can.	
13650 545	**Nantucket (Great Point) Light**	41-23-24.634N 070-02-53.810W	Fl W 5s (R sector)	71	W 14 R 12	On white tower. 70	Red from 084° to 106°. Covers Cross Rip and Tuckernuck Shoals.
13655	- *Lighted Buoy 15*	41-26-12.139N 070-05-04.617W	Fl G 4s		3	Green.	
	Nantucket Sound Main Channel						
13660	*Tuckernuck Shoal Lighted Bell Buoy 1* Off east end of shoal.	41-24-18.744N 070-09-47.744W	Fl G 4s		4	Green.	Replaced by lighted ice buoy when endangered by ice.
13665	- *Lighted Buoy 17*	41-26-34.842N 070-11-13.597W	Fl G 6s		4	Green.	
13670	Tuckernuck Shoal Buoy 3	41-24-54.592N 070-12-55.141W				Green can.	Removed when endangered by ice.
13675	*Halfmoon Shoal Lighted Bell Buoy 18* On southeast part of shoal.	41-27-14.406N 070-14-04.207W	Fl R 4s		4	Red.	Replaced by nun when endangered by ice.
13680	Cross Rip Shoal South End Buoy 4 Southeasterly of 11-foot shoal.	41-26-05.217N 070-17-04.952W				Red nun.	
13685	*Cross Rip Lighted Gong Buoy 21*	41-26-51.474N 070-17-29.723W	Fl G 2.5s		4	Green.	
13690	*Horseshoe Shoal Lighted Buoy 20* On south side of shoal.	41-27-33.160N 070-16-54.921W	Fl R 4s		4	Red.	Replaced by nun when endangered by ice.

(1) No.	(2) Name and Location	(3) Position	(4) Characteristic	(5) Height	(6) Range	(7) Structure	(8) Remarks

MASSACHUSETTS - First District

NANTUCKET SOUND AND APPROACHES

Nantucket Sound Main Channel

(1) No.	(2) Name and Location	(3) Position	(4) Characteristic	(5) Height	(6) Range	(7) Structure	(8) Remarks
13695	Norton Shoal Northeast Buoy 5	41-26-09.956N 070-19-50.428W				Green can.	
13700	*NOAA Data Lighted Buoy 44020*	41-29-50.000N 070-16-59.000W	Fl Y 4s		3	Yellow.	Marked NOAA 44020. Aid maintained by National Oceanic and Atmospheric Administration.
13705	Horseshoe Shoal West Part South End Buoy 2	41-30-03.101N 070-23-25.078W				Red nun.	
13715	CAPE POGE LIGHT	41-25-10.026N 070-27-08.359W	Fl W 6s	65	9	White conical tower.	
13717	*Nantucket Sound Channel Lighted Buoy 21A*	41-26-54.634N 070-25-12.011W	Fl G 4s		4	Green	Replaced by can when endangered by ice.
13720	*Hedge Fence Lighted Gong Buoy 22*	41-28-21.361N 070-29-00.759W	Fl R 4s		4	Red.	
13725	Squash Meadow East End Bell Buoy	41-27-17.794N 070-30-06.011W				Green and red bands.	Removed when endangered by ice.
13730	Squash Meadow West End Buoy W	41-27-52.569N 070-31-59.281W				Green and red bands; can.	Bouy marked with letter "W".
13735	*East Chop Flats Lighted Bell Buoy 23*	41-28-22.805N 070-33-26.803W	Fl G 4s		4	Green.	Removed when endangered by ice.
13740	East Chop Shoal Buoy 23A	41-28-22.266N 070-34-05.913W				Green can.	
13745	EAST CHOP LIGHT	41-28-12.984N 070-34-02.836W	Iso G 6s	79	9	White tower.	
13755	Hedge Fence West End Buoy	41-30-02.744N 070-33-55.459W				Red and green bands; nun.	
13760	*West Chop Lighted Gong Buoy 2*	41-29-10.563N 070-35-30.885W	Fl R 4s		4	Red.	
13775	**West Chop Light**	41-28-50.899N 070-35-59.221W	Oc W 4s (R sector)	84	W 14 R 10 45	White conical tower.	Red from 281° to 331°, covers Squash Meadow and Norton Shoal. HORN: 1 blast ev 30s (3s bl). MRASS-Fog signal is radio activated, during times of reduced visibility, turn marine VHF-FM radio to channel 83A/157.175Mhz. Key microphone 5 times consecutively, to activate fog signal for 45 minutes.
13780	Alleghany Rock Buoy 25	41-29-11.609N 070-36-02.964W				Green can.	

North Side

(1) No.	(2) Name and Location	(3) Position	(4) Characteristic	(5) Height	(6) Range	(7) Structure	(8) Remarks
13785	Handkerchief Shoal Buoy 2 On northwest point of shoal.	41-33-50.346N 070-03-39.758W				Red nun.	
13790	MONOMOY ISLAND FISH TRAP LIGHT E	41-35-00.000N 070-00-06.000W	Fl Y 6s	10		On pile at inshore end of weir.	Maintained from Mar. 1 to Oct. 1. Private aid.
13790.2	MONOMOY ISLAND WESTERN LIGHT	41-32-24.600N 070-00-35.160W	Fl W 10s			On piling.	Private aid.
13790.3	MONOMOY ISLAND EASTERN LIGHT	41-32-59.820N 070-00-03.600W	Fl W 15s			On piling.	Private aid.
13795	MONOMOY ISLAND FISH TRAP LIGHT W	41-35-06.000N 070-00-30.000W	Fl Y 6s	10		On pile at offshore end of trap.	Maintained from Mar. 1 to Oct. 1. Private aid.

Chatham Roads
Aids maintained from Mar. 1 to Oct. 30 unless otherwise noted.

(1) No.	(2) Name and Location	(3) Position	(4) Characteristic	(5) Height	(6) Range	(7) Structure	(8) Remarks
13800	- Bell Buoy 3	41-38-18.205N 070-02-52.550W				Green.	Removed when endangered by ice.
13835	MONOMOY ISLAND WESTERN TRAP LIGHT NE	41-36-04.000N 070-01-03.000W	Fl Y 6s	10		On pile at inshore end of trap.	Private aid.
13840	MONOMOY ISLAND WESTERN TRAP LIGHT SW	41-36-02.000N 070-01-48.000W	Fl Y 6s	10		On pile at offshore end of trap.	Private aid.

(1) No.	(2) Name and Location	(3) Position	(4) Characteristic	(5) Height	(6) Range	(7) Structure	(8) Remarks
			MASSACHUSETTS - First District				

NANTUCKET SOUND AND APPROACHES

Chatham Roads
Aids maintained from Mar. 1 to Oct. 30 unless otherwise noted.

(1) No.	(2) Name and Location	(3) Position	(4) Characteristic	(5) Height	(6) Range	(7) Structure	(8) Remarks
13845	- Buoy 4	41-38-36.879N 070-01-23.608W				Red nun.	Maintained year round.

Stage Harbor
Positions of buoys frequently shifted with changing conditions. Use only with local knowledge.

(1) No.	(2) Name and Location	(3) Position	(4) Characteristic	(5) Height	(6) Range	(7) Structure	(8) Remarks
13855	- Entrance Lighted Bell Buoy SH	41-39-10.198N 069-59-58.963W	Mo (A) W		4	Red and white stripes with red spherical topmark.	Removed when endangered by ice.
13860	- LIGHT	41-39-30.299N 069-59-04.105W	Fl W 6s	28	7	Modular tower.	
13865	- Lighted Buoy 1	41-39-14.019N 069-59-27.406W	Fl G 4s		4	Green.	Removed when endangered by ice.
13870	- Buoy 2	41-39-11.978N 069-59-26.585W				Red nun.	
13875	- Buoy 4	41-39-13.239N 069-59-22.196W				Red nun.	
13880	- Buoy 5	41-39-15.862N 069-59-18.251W				Green can.	
13885	- Buoy 6	41-39-15.582N 069-59-14.760W				Red nun.	
13890	- Lighted Buoy 7	41-39-20.260N 069-59-10.649W	Fl G 4s		3	Green can.	Removed when endangered by ice.
13895	- Lighted Buoy 8	41-39-27.214N 069-58-54.404W	Fl R 4s		3	Red.	Removed when endangered by ice.
13900	- Buoy 10	41-39-36.910N 069-58-38.723W				Red nun.	Removed when endangered by ice.
13905	- Buoy 11	41-39-43.109N 069-58-33.950W				Green can.	Removed when endangered by ice.
13910	- Buoy 12	41-39-51.898N 069-58-17.895W				Red nun.	Removed when endangered by ice.
13915	- Buoy 13	41-39-53.564N 069-58-18.471W				Green can.	Removed when endangered by ice.
13920	- Buoy 15	41-39-57.200N 069-58-08.500W				Green can.	Maintained from Apr. 15 to Dec.01. Private aid.
13925	- Buoy 14	41-39-56.000N 069-58-08.000W				Red nun.	Maintained from Apr. 15 to Dec. 1. Private aid.
13927	- Buoy 16	41-39-57.200N 069-58-03.080W				Red nun.	Maintained from Apr. 15 to Dec.01. Private aid.
13930	- Buoy 17	41-39-57.000N 069-57-57.000W				Green can.	Maintained from Apr. 15 to Dec. 1. Private aid.
13930.1	- Buoy 18	41-39-57.000N 069-57-49.000W				Red nun.	Maintained from Apr. 15 to Dec.01. Private aid.
13930.2	- Buoy 19	41-40-07.320N 069-57-42.480W				Green can.	Maintained from Apr. 15 to Dec.01. Private aid.
13930.3	- Buoy 20	41-40-07.960N 069-57-42.494W				Red nun.	Maintained from Apr. 15 to Dec.01. Private aid.

Oyster Pond River

(1) No.	(2) Name and Location	(3) Position	(4) Characteristic	(5) Height	(6) Range	(7) Structure	(8) Remarks
13931	- Buoy 1	41-39-40.446N 069-58-38.726W				Green can.	Positions of buoys frequently shifted with changing conditions. Private aid.
13932	- Buoy 2	41-39-41.940N 069-58-38.400W				Red nun.	Positions of buoys frequently shifted with changing conditions. Private aid.

(1) No.	(2) Name and Location	(3) Position	(4) Characteristic	(5) Height	(6) Range	(7) Structure	(8) Remarks

MASSACHUSETTS - First District

NANTUCKET SOUND AND APPROACHES
Oyster Pond River

13933	- Buoy 3	41-39-48.429N 069-58-46.772W				Green can.	Private aid.
13934	- Buoy 4	41-39-58.400N 069-59-04.100W				Red nun.	Private aid.
13935	- Buoy 5	41-40-02.851N 069-59-11.273W				Green can.	Private aid.
13936	- Buoy 6	41-40-08.696N 069-58-22.679W				Red nun.	Private aid.
13937	- Buoy 7	41-40-20.631N 069-59-12.764W				Green can.	Private aid.
13938	- Buoy 8	41-40-40.893N 069-58-44.464W				Red nun.	Private aid.
13939	- Buoy 9	41-40-45.480N 069-58-35.400W				Green can.	Private aid.
13939.1	- Buoy 10	41-40-48.432N 069-58-22.619W				Red nun.	Private aid.

Stage Harbor
Outermost Harbor Channel
Positions of buoys frequently shifted with changing conditions. Use only with local knowledge.

13945.1	- Buoy 1	41-39-42.700N 069-57-13.600W				Green can.	Private aid.
13945.2	- Buoy 2	41-39-43.200N 069-57-13.500W				Red nun.	Private aid.
13945.3	- Buoy 3	41-39-46.100N 069-57-12.000W				Green can.	Private aid.
13945.4	- Buoy 4	41-39-48.800N 069-57-13.400W				Red nun.	Private aid.
13945.5	- Buoy 5	41-39-40.800N 069-57-15.500W				Green can.	Private aid.
13945.6	- Buoy 6	41-39-49.800N 069-57-13.200W				Red nun.	Private aid.
13945.7	- Buoy 7	41-39-51.400N 069-57-18.000W				Green can.	Private aid.

Mitchell River
Mill Pond
Aids maintained from Apr. 1 to Dec. 1.

13960	- Buoy 2	41-40-12.769N 069-57-40.553W				Red nun.	Private aid.
13965	- Buoy 4	41-40-13.860N 069-57-43.860W				Red nun.	Private aid.
13970	- Buoy 6	41-40-15.368N 069-57-44.871W				Red nun.	Private aid.
13975	- Buoy 8	41-40-16.779N 069-57-44.397W				Red nun.	Private aid.
13980	- Buoy 10	41-40-18.000N 069-57-42.720W				Red nun.	Private aid.
13985	- Buoy 11	41-40-19.098N 069-57-42.464W				Green can.	Private aid.
13990	- Buoy 12	41-40-18.141N 069-57-37.281W				Red nun.	Private aid.
13995	- Buoy 14	41-40-20.400N 069-57-33.600W				Red nun.	Private aid.
14000	- Buoy 15	41-40-19.718N 069-57-35.758W				Green can.	Private aid.
14003	- Buoy 16	41-40-21.593N 069-57-32.983W				Red nun.	Private aid.
14005	- Buoy 17	41-40-30.300N 069-57-19.260W				Green can.	Private aid.

Saquatucket Harbor

14030	- Buoy 1	41-39-23.960N 070-03-35.728W				Green can.	
14035	- Buoy 2	41-39-27.372N 070-03-33.749W				Red nun.	Removed when endangered by ice.

MASSACHUSETTS - First District

(1) No.	(2) Name and Location	(3) Position	(4) Characteristic	(5) Height	(6) Range	(7) Structure	(8) Remarks
			MASSACHUSETTS - First District				

NANTUCKET SOUND AND APPROACHES

Saquatucket Harbor

(1)	(2)	(3)	(4)	(5)	(6)	(7)	(8)
14037	- Buoy 3	41-39-29.941N 070-03-37.211W				Green can.	
14040	- Junction Buoy S	41-39-39.254N 070-03-41.090W				Green and red bands.	
14045	- Buoy 4	41-39-43.951N 070-03-39.502W				Red nun.	
14050	- EAST JETTY LIGHT 6	41-39-48.640N 070-03-39.570W	Fl R 4s	20	6	TR on white skeleton tower.	
14055	- Buoy 8	41-39-52.969N 070-03-41.293W				Red nun.	
14060	- Buoy 9	41-39-58.331N 070-03-39.069W				Green can.	Removed when endangered by ice.

Wychmere Harbor

| 14065 | - JETTY LIGHT 1 | 41-39-37.847N
070-03-47.861W | Fl G 4s | 25 | 5 | SG on spindle. | |
| 14070 | - Buoy 2 | 41-39-40.937N
070-03-49.121W | | | | Red nun. | |

Allen Harbor Entrance
Aids maintained from Jun. 15 to Oct. 1.

14085	- BREAKWATER LIGHT	41-39-40.000N 070-05-22.600W	Q G	20		On tower.	Private aid.
14090	- Lighted Buoy 1	41-39-20.100N 070-05-04.100W	Fl G 4s			Green.	Private aid.
14095	- Buoy 2	41-39-23.800N 070-05-06.600W				Red nun.	Private aid.
14100	- Buoy 3	41-39-28.300N 070-05-12.600W				Green can.	Private aid.
14105	- Buoy 4	41-39-32.500N 070-05-14.100W				Red nun.	Private aid.
14110	- Buoy 5	41-39-34.800N 070-05-19.300W				Green can.	Private aid.
14115	- Buoy 6	41-39-39.200N 070-05-19.500W				Red nun.	Private aid.
14120	HERRING RIVER TRAP LIGHT N	41-39-04.600N 070-04-25.000W	Fl Y 6s	10		On pile at inshore end of trap.	Maintained 1 March to 1 October. Private aid.
14125	HERRING RIVER TRAP LIGHT S	41-38-43.400N 070-04-20.500W	Fl Y 6s	10		On pile at offshore end of trap.	Maintained 1 March to 1 October. Private aid.

Herring River
Aids maintained from May 1 to Oct. 30 unless otherwise noted.

14140	- Entrance Buoy 1	41-39-02.520N 070-06-53.880W				Green can.	Private aid.
14145	- Entrance Buoy 2	41-39-05.220N 070-06-53.340W				Red nun.	Private aid.
14150	- Entrance Buoy 3	41-39-07.980N 070-06-55.560W				Green can.	Private aid.
14155	- Entrance Buoy 4	41-39-09.600N 070-06-54.800W				Red nun.	Private aid.
14160	- Entrance Buoy 5	41-39-13.440N 070-06-56.520W				Green can.	Private aid.
14165	- Entrance Buoy 6	41-39-18.720N 070-06-55.560W				Red nun.	Private aid.
14170	- WEST BREAKWATER LIGHT 7	41-39-16.500N 070-06-57.500W	Fl G 4s	14		On skeleton tower.	Private aid.
14175	WEST DENNIS LIGHT	41-39-07.000N 070-10-13.000W	Fl W 6s	44		On white wooden building.	Maintained from May 1 to Oct. 31. Private aid.
14180	*Kill Pond Bar Lighted Whistle Buoy KP* Off southeast end of shoal.	41-37-26.418N 070-06-29.216W	Fl (2+1)R 6s		4	Red and green bands.	Replaced by nun when endangered by ice.
14190	KILL POND BAR FISH TRAP LIGHT S	41-37-00.000N 070-07-38.000W	Fl Y 6s	10		On pile at offshore end of weir.	Maintained from Mar. 1 to Oct. 1. Private aid.

128

(1) No.	(2) Name and Location	(3) Position	(4) Characteristic	(5) Height	(6) Range	(7) Structure	(8) Remarks
			MASSACHUSETTS - First District				

NANTUCKET SOUND AND APPROACHES

Bass River

Aids maintained from May 15 to Nov. 15 unless otherwise noted.

(1) No.	(2) Name and Location	(3) Position	(4) Characteristic	(5) Height	(6) Range	(7) Structure	(8) Remarks
14205	- *Entrance Lighted Buoy 2*	41-37-35.118N 070-11-30.308W	Fl R 2.5s		3	Red.	Replaced by nun when endangered by ice.
14215	- Entrance Buoy 4	41-38-09.300N 070-11-44.400W				Red nun.	Private aid.
14220	- Entrance Buoy 5	41-38-12.900N 070-11-45.700W				Green can.	Private aid.
14225	- Entrance Buoy 6	41-38-13.100N 070-11-41.800W				Red nun.	Private aid.
14230	- Entrance Buoy 7	41-38-19.700N 070-11-46.300W				Green can.	Private aid.
14235	- Entrance Buoy 8	41-38-23.500N 070-11-44.600W				Red nun.	Private aid.
14240	- Entrance Buoy 9	41-38-31.900N 070-11-46.100W				Green can.	Private aid.
14245	- Entrance Buoy 10	41-38-32.300N 070-11-44.900W				Red nun.	Private aid.
14250	- Buoy 12	41-38-54.600N 070-11-49.600W				Red nun.	Private aid.
14255	- Buoy 14	41-39-02.700N 070-11-49.300W				Red nun.	Private aid.
14256	- Buoy 14A	41-39-14.100N 070-11-46.300W				Red nun.	Private aid.
14260	- Buoy 16	41-39-18.400N 070-11-41.000W				Red nun.	Private aid.
14265	- Buoy 16A	41-39-22.100N 070-11-32.200W				Red nun.	Private aid.
14270	- Buoy 18	41-39-26.600N 070-11-23.800W				Red nun.	Private aid.
14275	- Buoy 20	41-39-36.300N 070-11-16.900W				Red nun.	Private aid.
14280	- Buoy 22	41-39-41.100N 070-11-12.600W				Red nun.	Private aid.
14281	- Buoy 22A	41-39-45.400N 070-11-02.900W				Red nun.	Private aid.
14285	- Buoy 24	41-40-03.100N 070-10-50.100W				Red nun.	Private aid.
14290	- Buoy 25	41-40-08.200N 070-10-46.700W				Green can.	Private aid.
14295	- Buoy 26	41-40-11.700N 070-10-30.500W				Red nun.	Private aid.
14300	- Buoy 28	41-40-21.400N 070-10-19.100W				Red nun.	Private aid.
14301	- Buoy 28A	41-40-27.600N 070-10-15.800W				Red nun.	Private aid.
14305	- Buoy 30	41-40-32.900N 070-10-08.600W				Red nun.	Private aid.
14310	- Buoy 32	41-40-49.700N 070-09-44.300W				Red nun.	Private aid.
14315	- Buoy 33	41-40-57.300N 070-09-45.300W				Green can.	Private aid.
14320	- Buoy 34	41-40-57.500N 070-09-43.300W				Red nun.	Private aid.
14325	- Buoy 35	41-41-03.800N 070-09-33.800W				Green can.	Private aid.
14330	- Buoy 36	41-41-09.800N 070-09-38.800W				Red nun.	Private aid.
14335	- Buoy 37	41-41-16.300N 070-09-43.300W				Green can.	Private aid.
14340	- Buoy 38	41-41-16.900N 070-09-44.700W				Red nun.	Private aid.
14345	- Buoy 39	41-41-17.200N 070-09-56.400W				Green can.	Private aid.

(1) No.	(2) Name and Location	(3) Position	(4) Characteristic	(5) Height	(6) Range	(7) Structure	(8) Remarks

MASSACHUSETTS - First District

NANTUCKET SOUND AND APPROACHES

Bass River
Aids maintained from May 15 to Nov. 15 unless otherwise noted.

14346	- Buoy 39A	41-41-20.000N 070-09-58.800W				Green can.	Private aid.
14350	- Buoy 40	41-41-21.700N 070-10-00.600W				Red nun.	Private aid.
14355	- Buoy 41	41-41-29.250N 070-10-01.700W				Green can.	Private aid.
14360	- Buoy 41A	41-41-24.800N 070-10-05.500W				Green can.	Private aid.
14365	- Buoy 42	41-41-15.200N 070-09-52.500W				Red nun.	Private aid.
14370	- Buoy 43	41-41-33.600N 070-10-08.000W				Green can.	Private aid.
14375	- Buoy 44	41-41-41.300N 070-10-11.100W				Red nun.	Private aid.
14380	- Buoy 45	41-41-39.300N 070-10-11.600W				Green can.	Private aid.
14385	- Buoy 46	41-41-43.400N 070-10-11.500W				Red nun.	Private aid.
14390	- Buoy 47	41-41-41.700N 070-10-12.000W				Green can.	Private aid.
14393	- Buoy 48	41-41-45.700N 070-10-11.600W				Red nun.	Private aid.
14395	- Buoy 49	41-41-48.200N 070-10-13.100W				Green can.	Private aid.
14396	- Buoy 50	41-41-49.500N 070-10-10.800W				Red nun.	Private aid.
14400	- Buoy 51	41-41-51.000N 070-10-14.600W				Green can.	Private aid.
14405	- Buoy 52	41-41-52.500N 070-10-21.600W				Red nun.	Private aid.
14410	- Buoy 53	41-42-01.100N 070-10-28.500W				Green can.	Private aid.
14415	- Buoy 54	41-42-02.900N 070-10-33.000W				Red nun.	Private aid.

Weir Creek
Aids maintained from May 15 to Nov. 15 unless otherwise noted.

14416	- Buoy 1	41-39-05.200N 070-11-43.100W				Green can.	Private aid.
14417	- Buoy 2	41-39-04.400N 070-11-43.900W				Red nun.	Private aid.
14417.1	- Buoy 3	41-39-09.500N 070-11-30.000W				Green can.	Private aid.
14417.2	- Buoy 3A	41-39-14.700N 070-11-19.600W				Green can.	Private aid.
14417.3	- Buoy 4	41-39-13.400N 070-11-16.000W				Red nun.	Private aid.
14417.4	- Buoy 5	41-39-11.200N 070-11-05.100W				Green can.	Private aid.
14417.5	- Buoy 6	41-39-10.700N 070-11-09.700W				Red nun.	Private aid.
14417.55	- Buoy 7	41-39-14.000N 070-11-00.100W				Green can.	Private aid.
14417.6	- Buoy 8	41-39-15.400N 070-10-58.700W				Red nun.	Private aid.

Grand Cove
Aids maintained from May 15 to Nov. 15.

14420	- Channel Buoy 2	41-40-22.800N 070-10-13.400W				Red nun.	Private aid.
14420.5	- Channel Buoy 3	41-40-23.700N 070-10-13.800W				Green can.	Private aid.
14421	- Channel Buoy 3A	41-40-19.900N 070-10-03.600W				Green can.	Private aid.
14425	- Buoy 4	41-40-17.700N 070-10-02.400W				Red nun.	Private aid.

(1) No.	(2) Name and Location	(3) Position	(4) Characteristic	(5) Height	(6) Range	(7) Structure	(8) Remarks
			MASSACHUSETTS - First District				

NANTUCKET SOUND AND APPROACHES

Grand Cove
Aids maintained from May 15 to Nov. 15.

(1) No.	(2) Name and Location	(3) Position	(4) Characteristic	(5) Height	(6) Range	(7) Structure	(8) Remarks
14430	- Buoy 5	41-40-15.000N 070-09-57.200W				Green can.	Private aid.

Bass River
Aids maintained from May 15 to Nov. 15 unless otherwise noted.

No.	Name and Location	Position	Characteristic	Height	Range	Structure	Remarks
14450	- WEST JETTY LIGHT 11	41-38-38.236N 070-11-50.969W	Fl G 6s	33	6	SG on skeleton tower.	Maintained year round.
14460	Parkers River Buoy 2	41-37-43.700N 070-12-58.000W				Red nun.	Maintained from Apr. 1 to Nov. 1. Private aid.
14461	Parkers River Buoy 3	41-37-46.300N 070-13-01.500W				Green can.	Private aid.
14462	Parkers River Buoy 4	41-37-52.700N 070-13-02.800W				Red nun.	Private aid.
14463	Parkers River Buoy 5	41-37-57.600N 070-13-08.400W				Green can.	Private aid.
14464	Parkers River Buoy 6	41-38-01.200N 070-13-09.000W				Red nun.	Private aid.
14465	Parkers River Buoy 7	41-38-14.900N 070-13-18.650W				Green can.	Private aid.

Bishop and Clerks

No.	Name and Location	Position	Characteristic	Height	Range	Structure	Remarks
14485	- Lighted Bell Buoy 1 Off northeasterly end of shoal.	41-34-43.999N 070-14-07.037W	Fl G 4s		4	Green.	Replaced by can when endangered by ice.
14490	- Light	41-34-27.470N 070-15-00.425W	Fl W 6s	45	14	White and red cylindrical tower. 30	
14495	- South Approach Lighted Gong Buoy 2	41-33-21.444N 070-14-37.080W	Fl R 4s		4	Red.	
14500	- South Approach Buoy 4	41-34-28.441N 070-15-58.083W				Red nun.	
14510	Gazelle Rock Lighted Buoy 2	41-36-06.269N 070-15-48.503W	Fl R 2.5s		4	Red.	Replaced by nun when endangered by ice.

Hyannis Harbor

No.	Name and Location	Position	Characteristic	Height	Range	Structure	Remarks
14515	- Approach Lighted Bell Buoy HH	41-35-57.438N 070-17-22.086W	Mo (A) W		4	Red and white stripes with red spherical topmark.	
14520	Halftide Rock Buoy HR	41-36-52.000N 070-16-05.000W				White can with orange bands.	Maintained from June 1 to Sept. 30. Private aid.
14525	- Lighted Buoy 4	41-37-03.717N 070-17-25.305W	Fl R 2.5s		3	Red.	Removed when endangered by ice.
14530	Great Rock Daybeacon 4A On edge of flats.	41-37-03.350N 070-17-08.571W				TR on spindle.	
14540	- BREAKWATER LIGHT H	41-37-27.162N 070-17-32.514W	Fl W 6s	31	7	NB on black skeleton tower.	
14541	- Danger Buoy A	41-37-48.547N 070-17-55.415W				White can with orange bands worded ROCKS.	Marks Rocks. Maintained Jun. 1 to Nov. 1 Private aid.
14542	- Danger Buoy B	41-37-48.271N 070-17-53.077W				White can with orange bands worded ROCKS.	Marks Rocks. Maintained Jun. 1 to Nov. 1 Private aid.
14543	- Danger Buoy C	41-37-45.964N 070-17-53.901W				White can with orange bands worded ROCKS	Marks Rocks. Maintained Jun. 1 to Nov. 1 Private aid.
14550	- Wreck Buoy	41-37-50.176N 070-17-26.941W				White can with orange bands.	

Lewis Bay

No.	Name and Location	Position	Characteristic	Height	Range	Structure	Remarks
14553	- Approach Channel Lighted Buoy 5	41-37-14.878N 070-17-22.438W	Fl G 4s		4	Green.	Replaced by can from Dec. 1 to Apr. 1. AIS: MMSI 993672423 (21)
14555	- Approach Channel Lighted Buoy 6 Marks flats.	41-37-12.034N 070-17-19.090W	Fl R 4s		3	Red.	Replaced by nun when endangered by ice.

(1) No.	(2) Name and Location	(3) Position	(4) Characteristic	(5) Height	(6) Range	(7) Structure	(8) Remarks
			MASSACHUSETTS - First District				

NANTUCKET SOUND AND APPROACHES

Lewis Bay

14560	- Approach Channel Buoy 7	41-37-29.350N 070-16-51.166W				Green can.	
14565	- Approach Channel Buoy 8	41-37-28.727N 070-16-43.985W				Red nun.	
14570	*- Approach Channel Lighted Buoy 10*	41-37-39.184N 070-16-24.742W	Fl R 2.5s	4		Red.	Replaced by nun from Dec. 1 to Apr. 1. AIS: MMSI 993672519 (21)
14575	*- Approach Channel Lighted Buoy 9*	41-37-39.343N 070-16-28.384W	Fl G 2.5s	4		Green.	Replaced by can from Dec. 1 Apr. 1. AIS: MMSI 993672520 (21)
14580	*- Approach Channel Lighted Buoy 11*	41-37-52.014N 070-16-19.520W	Fl G 4s	4		Green.	Replaced by can from Dec. 1 to Apr. 1. AIS: MMSI 993672516 (21)
14585	- Approach Channel Buoy 12	41-37-49.165N 070-16-17.445W				Red nun.	
14590	- Approach Channel Buoy 13	41-38-01.335N 070-16-16.075W				Green can.	
14592	*- Approach Channel Lighted Buoy 14*	41-38-05.484N 070-16-11.151W	Fl R 4s	4		Red.	Replaced by nun Dec. 1 to Apr. 1. AIS: MMSI 993672592 (21)
14600	Fiddle Head Rock Danger Buoy	41-38-15.318N 070-15-55.546W					
14601	Fiddle Head Rock Daybeacon	41-38-20.100N 070-15-54.200W				On wood pile.	Private aid.

Hyannis Yacht Club
Aids maintained from May 1 to Nov. 1.

14605	- Channel Buoy 1A	41-38-20.200N 070-16-23.400W				Green can.	Private aid.
14610	- Channel Buoy 2A	41-38-20.800N 070-16-18.400W				Red nun.	Private aid.
14615	- Channel Buoy 3A	41-38-20.900N 070-16-28.000W				Green can.	Private aid.
14620	- Channel Buoy 4A	41-38-21.600N 070-16-27.500W				Red nun.	Private aid.

Lewis Bay

14625	- Approach Channel Buoy 15	41-38-20.975N 070-16-11.425W				Green can.	
14630	- Approach Channel Buoy 19	41-38-31.963N 070-16-09.871W				Green can.	
14635	*- Approach Channel Lighted Buoy 18*	41-38-31.627N 070-16-06.097W	Q R	4		Red.	Replaced by nun from Dec. 1 to Apr. 1. AIS: MMSI 993672589 (21)
14637	- Approach Channel Buoy 20	41-38-40.324N 070-16-14.938W				Red nun.	
14640	- Approach Channel Buoy 21	41-38-41.381N 070-16-20.565W				Green can.	AIS: MMSI 993672536 (21)
14645	- Approach Channel Buoy 22	41-38-51.417N 070-16-29.366W				Red nun.	
14646	Mill Creek Entrance Buoy 1	41-38-40.356N 070-15-29.888W				Green can.	Maintained from May 15 to Nov. 15. Private aid.
14647	Mill Creek Entrance Buoy 2	41-38-42.695N 070-15-28.367W				Red nun.	Maintained from May 15 to Nov. 15. Private aid.

Englewood Channel
Aids maintained from May 15 to Nov. 15.

14650	- Buoy 1	41-38-09.274N 070-15-03.538W				Green can.	Private aid.
14650.1	- Buoy 2	41-38-09.300N 070-15-00.240W				Red nun.	Private aid.
14650.2	- Buoy 3	41-38-10.300N 070-14-58.600W				Green can.	Private aid.

(1) No.	(2) Name and Location	(3) Position	(4) Characteristic	(5) Height	(6) Range	(7) Structure	(8) Remarks

MASSACHUSETTS - First District

NANTUCKET SOUND AND APPROACHES

Lewis Bay

Englewood Channel
Aids maintained from May 15 to Nov. 15.

(1) No.	(2) Name and Location	(3) Position	(4) Characteristic	(5) Height	(6) Range	(7) Structure	(8) Remarks
14650.3	- Buoy 4	41-38-10.600N 070-14-56.200W				Red nun.	Private aid.
14650.4	- Buoy 5	41-38-12.240N 070-14-53.460W				Green can.	Private aid.
14650.5	- Buoy 6	41-38-12.780N 070-14-49.980W				Red nun.	Private aid.
14650.6	- Buoy 7	41-38-13.600N 070-14-48.000W				Green can.	Private aid.

Centerville Harbor Approach

14675	Hodges Rock Buoy 2	41-35-23.337N 070-18-58.438W				Red nun.	
14680	Gallatin Rock Buoy 3 South of rock.	41-35-47.936N 070-20-01.090W				Green can.	
14685	*Collier Ledge Lighted Isolated Danger Buoy DCL*	41-35-44.449N 070-21-08.210W	Fl (2)W 5s	3		Black and red bands with two black spherical topmarks.	Replaced by can when endangered by ice.
14686	Collier Ledge Isolated Danger VAIS	41-35-49.654N 070-21-03.979W					VAIS MMSI: 993672629
14687	Collier Ledge Hazard Buoy	41-35-47.473N 070-20-58.419W				White and orange can marked DANGER ROCKS.	Removed when endangered from ice.
14705	Bearse Rock Buoy 4 West of rock.	41-36-09.965N 070-19-48.140W				Red nun.	
14710	Channel Rock Buoy Southeast of rock.	41-36-05.865N 070-20-13.602W				Green can with red bands.	
14712	*Southwest Rock Lighted Hazard Buoy*	41-36-25.874N 070-19-10.535W	Fl W 2.5s	3		White and orange marked DANGER ROCKS.	Removed when endangered by ice.
14725	Spindle Rock Buoy 8	41-37-48.960N 070-20-16.800W				Red nun.	Private aid.

Centerville River
Aids maintained from Jun. 1 to Nov. 1 unless otherwise noted.
Positions of buoys frequently shifted with changing conditions.

14725.1	- Buoy 1	41-37-32.800N 070-22-04.300W				Green can.	Private aid.
14725.2	- Buoy 2	41-37-33.300N 070-22-05.100W				Red nun.	Private aid.
14726	- Buoy 3	41-37-38.500N 070-22-01.100W				Green can.	Private aid.
14726.1	- Buoy 4	41-37-38.800N 070-22-00.500W				Red nun.	Private aid.
14726.2	- Buoy 6	41-37-43.790N 070-21-57.450W				Red nun.	Private aid.
14726.3	- Buoy 7	41-37-51.400N 070-21-48.200W				Green can.	Private aid.
14726.4	- Buoy 8	41-37-46.845N 070-21-52.758W				Red nun.	Private aid.
14726.5	- Buoy 10	41-37-54.100N 070-21-42.500W				Red nun.	Private aid.
14726.6	- Buoy 11	41-38-01.800N 070-21-30.230W				Green can.	Private aid.
14726.7	- Buoy 12	41-38-02.000N 070-21-29.300W				Red nun.	Private aid.
14726.8	- Buoy 13	41-38-03.000N 070-21-26.100W				Green can.	Private aid.
14726.9	- Buoy 14	41-38-01.697N 070-21-27.789W				Red nun.	Private aid.

East Bay
Aids maintained from Jun. 1 to Nov. 1 unless otherwise noted.
Positions of buoys frequently shifted with changing conditions.

| 14726.91 | - LIGHT | 41-37-23.300N 070-21-48.025W | Fl G 4s | 15 | | On monopole. | Private aid. |

(1) No.	(2) Name and Location	(3) Position	(4) Characteristic	(5) Height	(6) Range	(7) Structure	(8) Remarks
			MASSACHUSETTS - First District				

NANTUCKET SOUND AND APPROACHES

East Bay
Aids maintained from Jun. 1 to Nov. 1 unless otherwise noted.
Positions of buoys frequently shifted with changing conditions.

(1) No.	(2) Name and Location	(3) Position	(4) Characteristic	(5) Height	(6) Range	(7) Structure	(8) Remarks
14727	Dowses Rock Danger Buoy DR	41-37-12.607N 070-21-43.870W				White with Orange bands; can.	Maintained from Jun. 1 to Nov. 1. Private aid.
14727.1	- Buoy 1	41-37-16.100N 070-21-31.700W				Green can.	Private aid.
14727.2	- Buoy 2	41-37-16.300N 070-21-28.500W				Red nun.	Private aid.
14727.3	- Buoy 3	41-37-19.600N 070-21-38.960W				Green can.	Private aid.
14727.4	- Buoy 4	41-37-20.200N 070-21-36.300W				Red nun.	Private aid.
14727.5	- Buoy 6	41-37-30.200N 070-21-59.594W				Red nun.	Private aid.

Cotuit Anchorage

14735	- Shoal Buoy 3 At southend of shoal.	41-35-34.619N 070-23-39.633W				Green can.	

West Bay
Aids maintained from Jun. 1 to Nov. 1 unless otherwise noted.
Positions of buoys frequently shifted with changing conditions.

14741	- Entrance Buoy 5	41-36-00.000N 070-24-06.400W				Green can.	Private aid.
14741.1	- *Entrance Lighted Buoy 6*	41-36-00.960N 070-24-04.440W	Fl R 4s			Red.	Private aid.
14741.13	- Entrance Buoy 7	41-36-06.400N 070-24-06.100W				Green can.	Private aid.
14741.16	- Entrance Buoy 8	41-36-06.720N 070-24-04.020W				Red nun.	Private aid.
14741.19	- Entrance Buoy 9	41-36-13.100N 070-24-05.800W				Green can.	Private aid.
14741.2	- Entrance Buoy 10	41-36-13.400N 070-24-03.300W				Red nun.	Private aid.
14741.21	- ENTRANCE LIGHT	41-36-20.139N 070-24-02.720W	Fl R 2.5s			On monopole.	Private aid.

West Bay Inside
Aids maintained from Jun. 1 to Nov. 1 unless otherwise noted.
Positions of buoys frequently shifted with changing conditions.

14741.23	- Buoy 1	41-36-38.900N 070-24-03.000W				Green can.	Private aid.
14741.28	- Buoy 2	41-36-38.900N 070-24-01.000W				Red nun.	Private aid.
14741.29	- Buoy 3	41-36-46.900N 070-24-01.900W				Green can.	Private aid.
14741.3	- Buoy 4	41-36-46.700N 070-24-00.700W				Red nun.	Private aid.
14741.33	- Buoy 5	41-36-52.100N 070-24-02.000W				Green can.	Private aid.
14741.36	- Buoy 6	41-36-51.800N 070-24-01.200W				Red nun.	Private aid.
14741.39	- Buoy 7	41-36-55.200N 070-24-02.300W				Green can.	Private aid.
14741.4	- Buoy 8	41-36-55.400N 070-24-01.500W				Red nun.	Private aid.
14741.43	- Buoy 9	41-37-01.500N 070-24-03.700W				Green can.	Private aid.
14741.46	- Buoy 10	41-37-01.700N 070-24-02.147W				Red nun.	Private aid.
14741.49	- Buoy 11	41-37-05.300N 070-24-02.400W				Green can.	Private aid.
14741.5	- Buoy 12	41-37-04.600N 070-24-01.600W				Red nun.	Private aid.
14741.53	- Buoy 13	41-37-07.500N 070-24-00.100W				Green can.	Private aid.
14741.56	- Buoy 14	41-37-06.700N 070-23-58.300W				Red nun.	Private aid.

(1) No.	(2) Name and Location	(3) Position	(4) Characteristic	(5) Height	(6) Range	(7) Structure	(8) Remarks

MASSACHUSETTS - First District

NANTUCKET SOUND AND APPROACHES

West Bay Inside
Aids maintained from Jun. 1 to Nov. 1 unless otherwise noted.
Positions of buoys frequently shifted with changing conditions.

14741.59	- Buoy 15	41-37-09.700N 070-23-57.200W				Green can.	Private aid.
14741.6	- Buoy 16	41-37-08.500N 070-23-56.500W				Red nun.	Private aid.
14741.63	- Buoy 17	41-37-09.700N 070-23-51.900W				Green can.	Private aid.
14741.66	- Buoy 18	41-37-09.100N 070-23-51.700W				Red nun.	Private aid.
14741.69	- Buoy 19	41-37-10.000N 070-23-44.400W				Green can.	Private aid.
14741.7	- Buoy 20	41-37-09.500N 070-23-43.000W				Red nun.	Private aid.
14741.73	- Buoy 21	41-37-13.100N 070-23-45.100W				Green can.	Private aid.

North Bay Channel
Aids maintained from Jun. 1 to Nov. 1 unless otherwise noted.
Positions of buoys frequently shifted with changing conditions.

14742	- Buoy 21	41-37-48.700N 070-24-03.000W				Green can.	Private aid.
14742.1	- Buoy 22	41-37-48.100N 070-24-03.500W				Red nun.	Private aid.
14742.3	- Buoy 23	41-37-41.100N 070-23-49.300W				Green can.	Private aid.
14742.5	- Buoy 25	41-37-35.700N 070-23-42.900W				Green can.	Private aid.
14742.7	- Buoy 26	41-37-37.500N 070-23-45.600W				Red nun.	Private aid.

Marston Mills River
Aids maintained from Jun. 1 to Nov. 1 unless otherwise noted.
Positions of buoys frequently shifted with changing conditions.

14743.1	Marstons Mills River Buoy 1	41-38-08.400N 070-24-24.500W				Green can.	Private aid.
14743.2	Marstons Mills River Buoy 2	41-38-08.300N 070-24-23.700W				Red nun.	Private aid.
14743.3	Marstons Mills River Buoy 4	41-38-14.300N 070-24-22.500W				Red nun.	Private aid.
14743.4	Marstons Mills River Buoy 6	41-38-18.500N 070-24-20.869W				Red nun.	Private aid.
14743.5	Marstons Mills River Buoy 7	41-38-22.190N 070-24-18.231W				Green can.	Private aid.
14743.6	Marstons Mills River Buoy 9	41-38-23.437N 070-24-17.809W				Green can.	Private aid.
14743.7	Marstons Mills River Buoy 11	41-38-24.500N 070-24-18.600W				Green can.	Private aid.
14743.8	Marstons Mills River Buoy 12	41-38-28.087N 070-24-21.113W				Red nun.	Private aid.
14743.9	Marstons Mills River Buoy 13	41-38-31.660N 070-24-22.202W				Green can.	Private aid.
14744	Marstons Mills River Buoy 14	41-38-39.064N 070-24-26.823W				Red nun.	Private aid.
14744.1	Marstons Mills River Buoy 15	41-38-40.914N 070-24-32.434W				Green can.	Private aid.
14744.5	Marstons Mills River Buoy 16	41-38-41.678N 070-24-31.806W				Red nun.	Private aid.

Cotuit Anchorage

14755	Lone Rock Buoy	41-35-11.433N 070-24-18.100W				Red and green bands; nun.	
14756	Cotuit Harbor Junction Buoy CS	41-36-43.200N 070-25-41.500W				Red and green bands; nun.	Maintained from Jun. 1 to Dec. 1. Private aid.

(1) No.	(2) Name and Location	(3) Position	(4) Characteristic	(5) Height	(6) Range	(7) Structure	(8) Remarks
		MASSACHUSETTS - First District					

NANTUCKET SOUND AND APPROACHES

Seapuit River
Aids maintained from Jun. 1 to Nov. 1 unless otherwise noted.
Positions of buoys frequently shifted with changing conditions.

(1) No.	(2) Name and Location	(3) Position	(4) Characteristic	(5) Height	(6) Range	(7) Structure	(8) Remarks
14756.2	- Buoy 1	41-36-44.900N 070-25-42.200W				Green can.	Private aid.
14756.4	- Buoy 4	41-36-42.700N 070-25-34.500W				Red nun.	Private aid.
14756.6	- Buoy 3	41-36-43.700N 070-25-34.400W				Green can.	Private aid.
14756.8	- Buoy 5	41-36-43.125N 070-25-23.515W				Green can.	Private aid.
14757	- Buoy 6	41-36-42.176N 070-25-21.389W				Red nun.	Private aid.
14757.2	- Buoy 8	41-36-37.700N 070-25-16.300W				Red nun.	Private aid.
14757.4	- Buoy 9	41-36-31.800N 070-25-04.800W				Green can.	Private aid.
14757.6	- Buoy 10	41-36-32.547N 070-24-52.068W				Red nun.	Private aid.
14757.8	- Buoy 12	41-36-32.500N 070-24-39.100W				Red nun.	Private aid.
14758.2	- Buoy 14	41-36-32.316N 070-24-35.768W				Red nun.	Private aid.
14758.4	- Buoy 15	41-36-32.907N 070-24-34.837W				Green can.	Private aid.
14758.6	- Buoy 16	41-36-31.543N 070-24-32.176W				Red nun.	Private aid.
14758.8	- Buoy 17	41-36-32.165N 070-24-31.884W				Green can.	Private aid.
14759	- Buoy 18	41-36-30.300N 070-24-26.600W				Red nun.	Private aid.
14759.2	- Buoy 19	41-36-31.100N 070-24-26.900W				Green can.	Private aid.
14759.4	- Buoy 21	41-36-30.515N 070-24-23.219W				Green can.	Private aid.
14759.6	- Buoy 23	41-36-30.012N 070-24-09.977W				Green can.	Private aid.
14759.8	- Buoy 24	41-36-28.800N 070-24-07.100W				Red nun.	Private aid.

Cotuit Entrance Channel
Aids maintained from Jun. 1 to Nov. 1 unless otherwise noted.
Positions of buoys frequently shifted with changing conditions.

No.	Name and Location	Position	Characteristic	Height	Range	Structure	Remarks
14760.1	- Buoy 1	41-35-54.200N 070-25-51.800W				Green can.	Private aid.
14760.13	- Buoy 2	41-35-54.700N 070-25-50.700W				Red nun.	Private aid.
14760.16	- Buoy 3	41-36-01.100N 070-25-56.200W				Green can.	Private aid.
14760.19	- Buoy 4	41-36-01.500N 070-25-55.600W				Red nun.	Private aid.
14760.2	- Buoy 5	41-36-08.100N 070-26-01.200W				Green can.	Private aid.
14760.23	- Buoy 6	41-36-08.360N 070-25-58.760W				Red nun.	Private aid.
14760.26	- Buoy 7	41-36-19.100N 070-26-04.700W				Green can.	Private aid.
14760.29	- Buoy 8	41-36-19.700N 070-26-03.500W				Red nun.	Private aid.
14760.3	- Buoy 9	41-36-25.600N 070-26-06.300W				Green can.	Private aid.
14760.33	- Buoy 10	41-36-25.900N 070-26-04.900W				Red nun.	Private aid.

(1) No.	(2) Name and Location	(3) Position	(4) Characteristic	(5) Height	(6) Range	(7) Structure	(8) Remarks
		MASSACHUSETTS - First District					

NANTUCKET SOUND AND APPROACHES

Cotuit Harbor
Aids maintained from Jun. 1 to Nov. 1 unless otherwise noted.
Positions of buoys frequently shifted with changing conditions.

(1) No.	(2) Name and Location	(3) Position	(4) Characteristic	(5) Height	(6) Range	(7) Structure	(8) Remarks
14760.36	- Buoy 1	41-36-33.100N 070-25-56.900W				Green can.	Private aid.
14760.39	- Buoy 2	41-36-32.200N 070-25-59.900W				Red nun.	Private aid.
14760.4	- Buoy 3	41-36-32.600N 070-25-46.900W				Green can.	Private aid.
14760.43	- Buoy 4	41-36-33.140N 070-25-43.310W				Red nun.	Private aid.
14760.46	- Buoy 5	41-36-34.100N 070-25-44.100W				Green can.	Private aid.
14760.49	- Buoy 7	41-36-37.500N 070-25-42.800W				Green can.	Private aid.
14760.5	- Buoy 8	41-36-50.410N 070-25-41.950W				Red nun.	Private aid.
14760.53	- Buoy 10	41-37-22.600N 070-25-17.600W				Red nun.	Private aid.
14760.56	- Buoy 11	41-37-30.900N 070-25-03.800W				Green can.	Private aid.
14760.59	- Buoy 12	41-37-30.120N 070-25-03.800W				Red nun.	Private aid.
14760.6	- Buoy 13	41-37-38.339N 070-24-54.099W				Green can.	Private aid.
14760.63	- Buoy 14	41-37-37.552N 070-24-53.443W				Red nun.	Private aid.
14760.66	- Buoy 15	41-37-44.066N 070-24-44.495W				Green can.	Private aid.
14760.69	- Buoy 16	41-37-43.425N 070-24-43.662W				Red nun.	Private aid.
14760.7	- Buoy 17	41-37-47.906N 070-24-35.410W				Green can.	Private aid.
14760.73	- Buoy 18	41-37-47.476N 070-24-34.657W				Red nun.	Private aid.
14760.76	- Buoy 19	41-37-51.300N 070-24-27.200W				Green can.	Private aid.
14760.79	- Buoy 20	41-37-50.600N 070-24-26.800W				Red nun.	Private aid.

Popponesett Bay
Aids maintained from May 15 to Oct. 15.

(1) No.	(2) Name and Location	(3) Position	(4) Characteristic	(5) Height	(6) Range	(7) Structure	(8) Remarks
14760.8	- Approach Buoy 1	41-35-11.900N 070-26-45.600W				Green can.	Private aid.
14760.81	- *Approach Lighted Buoy 2*	41-35-12.000N 070-26-44.340W	Fl R 2.5s			Red.	Private aid.
14760.82	- Approach Buoy 3	41-35-15.820N 070-26-48.640W				Green can.	Private aid.
14760.83	- Approach Buoy 4	41-35-16.790N 070-26-47.870W				Red nun.	Private aid.
14760.84	- Approach Buoy 5	41-35-18.000N 070-26-50.680W				Green can.	Private aid.
14760.85	- *Approach Lighted Buoy 6*	41-35-18.826N 070-26-49.647W	Fl R 2.5s			Red.	Private aid.
14760.86	- *Approach Lighted Buoy 7*	41-35-19.800N 070-26-58.300W	Fl G 2.5s			Green.	Private aid.
14760.87	- *Approach Lighted Buoy 8*	41-35-19.580N 070-27-06.170W	Fl R 2.5s			Red.	Private aid.
14760.88	- Approach Buoy 9	41-35-13.640N 070-27-14.180W				Green can.	Private aid.
14760.89	- *Approach Lighted Buoy 10*	41-35-14.700N 070-27-14.200W	Fl R 2.5s			Red.	Private aid.
14760.9	- Channel Buoy 11	41-35-15.600N 070-27-19.000W				Green can.	Private aid.
14760.91	- Channel Buoy 12	41-35-16.300N 070-27-19.100W				Red nun.	Private aid.

(1) No.	(2) Name and Location	(3) Position	(4) Characteristic	(5) Height	(6) Range	(7) Structure	(8) Remarks
		MASSACHUSETTS - First District					

NANTUCKET SOUND AND APPROACHES

Cotuit Harbor

Popponesett Bay

Aids maintained from May 15 to Oct. 15.

(1) No.	(2) Name and Location	(3) Position	(4) Characteristic	(5) Height	(6) Range	(7) Structure	(8) Remarks
14760.92	- Channel Lighted Buoy 13	41-35-14.040N 070-27-26.500W	Fl G 2.5s			Green.	Private aid.
14760.93	- Channel Buoy 14	41-35-18.140N 070-27-26.400W				Red nun.	Private aid.

Popponesett Spit Channel

Aids maintained from May 15 to Oct. 15.

(1) No.	(2) Name and Location	(3) Position	(4) Characteristic	(5) Height	(6) Range	(7) Structure	(8) Remarks
14761.1	- Buoy S1	41-35-11.300N 070-27-10.680W				Green can.	Private aid.
14761.2	- Lighted Buoy S2	41-35-12.100N 070-27-11.400W	Fl R 2.5s			Red.	Private aid.
14761.3	- Buoy S3	41-35-05.600N 070-27-14.300W				Green can.	Private aid.
14761.4	- Lighted Buoy S4	41-35-05.000N 070-27-16.600W	Fl R 2.5s			Red.	Private aid.
14761.5	- Buoy S5	41-35-02.980N 070-27-17.410W				Green can.	Private aid.
14761.55	- Buoy S5A	41-35-00.840N 070-27-20.210W				Green can.	Private aid.
14761.6	- Buoy S6	41-35-03.470N 070-27-18.520W				Red nun.	Private aid.
14761.7	- Lighted Buoy S7	41-34-57.400N 070-27-22.700W	Fl G 2.5s			Green.	Private aid.
14761.8	- Buoy S8	41-34-57.800N 070-27-23.700W				Red nun.	Private aid.
14762.5	Popponesett Bay Mid-Channel Buoy A	41-35-17.700N 070-27-28.830W				Red and white sphere.	Private aid.
14762.6	Popponesett Bay Mid-Channel Buoy B	41-35-19.000N 070-27-32.300W				Red and white sphere.	Private aid.
14762.7	Popponesett Bay Mid-Channel Buoy C	41-35-22.750N 070-27-38.200W				Red and white sphere.	Private aid.
14762.8	Popponesett Bay Mid-Channel Buoy D	41-35-33.700N 070-27-47.000W				Red and white sphere.	Private aid.
14762.9	Popponesett Bay Mid-Channel Buoy E	41-35-33.950N 070-27-47.280W				Red and white sphere.	Private aid.

Santuit River Mid-Channel

Aids maintained from May 15 to Oct. 15.

(1) No.	(2) Name and Location	(3) Position	(4) Characteristic	(5) Height	(6) Range	(7) Structure	(8) Remarks
14763	- Buoy F	41-35-41.900N 070-27-49.420W				Red and white sphere.	Private aid.
14763.1	- Buoy G	41-35-48.780N 070-27-52.050W				Red and white sphere.	Private aid.
14763.2	- Buoy H	41-35-52.200N 070-27-56.930W				Red and white sphere.	Private aid.
14763.3	- Buoy I	41-35-57.250N 070-27-56.610W				Red and white sphere.	Private aid.
14763.4	- Buoy J	41-36-02.700N 070-27-53.900W				Red and white sphere.	Private aid.

North Channel

(1) No.	(2) Name and Location	(3) Position	(4) Characteristic	(5) Height	(6) Range	(7) Structure	(8) Remarks
14765	Nantucket Sound North Side Lighted Bell Buoy 5	41-33-05.221N 070-20-48.466W	Fl G 2.5s		4	Green.	
14770	Horseshoe Shoal Buoy 7 At northwest part of shoal.	41-32-18.842N 070-23-06.835W				Green can.	
14775	Horseshoe Shoal Wreck Buoy WR	41-30-52.171N 070-22-24.531W				Green can with red bands.	
14780	Wreck Shoal Lighted Bell Buoy 8 Off east point of shoal.	41-32-26.005N 070-24-01.978W	Fl R 2.5s		4	Red.	
14785	Eldridge Shoal Buoy 9 Off north part of shoal.	41-31-57.917N 070-24-58.841W				Green can.	
14790	Wreck Shoal West Lighted Bell Buoy 10 Off southwest end of shoal.	41-31-58.652N 070-26-24.439W	Fl R 4s		4	Red.	Replaced by nun buoy when endangered by ice.

138

(1) No.	(2) Name and Location	(3) Position	(4) Characteristic	(5) Height	(6) Range	(7) Structure	(8) Remarks

MASSACHUSETTS - First District

NANTUCKET SOUND AND APPROACHES
North Channel

14795	Succonnesset Shoal South Buoy Off north end of shoal.	41-31-50.734N 070-27-58.878W				Green can with red bands.	
14800	*Succonnesset Shoal Lighted Buoy 12*	41-32-24.433N 070-29-26.111W	Fl R 2.5s		4	Red.	
14805	L'Hommedieu Shoal Buoy 11 At east end of shoal.	41-30-59.655N 070-28-24.899W				Green can.	
14810	L'Hommedieu Shoal Buoy 13	41-31-23.433N 070-30-57.113W				Green can.	
14815	L'Hommedieu Shoal Buoy 15 At west end of shoal.	41-31-16.250N 070-34-27.855W				Green can.	
14820	Davis Neck Shoal Buoy 14	41-32-00.066N 070-34-40.054W				Red nun.	

Waquoit Bay
Aids maintained Apr. 15 to Oct. 15. Positions of buoys frequesntly shifted with changing conditions.

14825	- *Entrance Lighted Bell Buoy 2*	41-32-29.480N 070-32-30.294W	Fl R 4s		3	Red.	Removed when endangered by ice.
14830	- EAST JETTY LIGHT	41-32-42.000N 070-31-48.400W	Fl R 6s			Red.	Private aid.
14833	- WEST JETTY LIGHT	41-32-44.300N 070-31-50.200W	Fl G 6s			On wood dolphin.	Private aid.
14834	- *Lighted Buoy 1*	41-33-06.090N 070-31-41.400W	Fl G 4s			Green.	Private aid.
14835	- Buoy 2	41-33-06.500N 070-31-40.100W				Red nun.	Private aid.
14840	- Buoy 3	41-33-24.480N 070-31-35.760W				Green can.	Private aid.
14845	- *Lighted Buoy 4*	41-33-24.200N 070-31-33.100W	Fl R 4s			Red.	Private aid.
14850	- Buoy 5	41-33-36.500N 070-31-31.000W				Green can.	Private aid.
14855	- Buoy 6	41-33-36.000N 070-31-28.000W				Red nun.	Private aid.
14860	- Buoy 7	41-33-49.700N 070-31-28.900W				Green can.	Private aid.
14865	- Buoy 9	41-34-03.360N 070-31-26.700W				Green can.	Private aid.
14870	- Buoy 11	41-34-22.800N 070-31-27.100W				Green can.	Private aid.

Little River Entrance
Aids maintained from May 15 to Oct. 15.

14870.5	- Buoy 1	41-33-30.300N 070-31-09.200W				Green can.	Private aid.
14871	- *Lighted Buoy 2*	41-33-28.690N 070-31-09.210W	Fl R 2.5s			Red.	Private aid.
14871.1	- Buoy 3	41-33-30.700N 070-31-05.800W				Green can.	Private aid.
14871.2	- Buoy 4	41-33-29.600N 070-31-04.100W				Red nun.	Private aid.
14871.3	- Buoy 5	41-33-31.900N 070-31-00.700W				Green can.	Private aid.
14871.4	- *Lighted Buoy 6*	41-33-30.400N 070-31-00.800W	Fl R 2.5s			Red.	Private aid.
14871.6	*Little River Lighted Buoy 8*	41-33-38.800N 070-30-52.400W	Fl R 2.5s			Red.	Private aid.
14871.65	*Little River Lighted Buoy 9*	41-33-42.500N 070-30-49.700W	Fl G 2.5s			Green.	Private aid.
14871.7	Little River Buoy 10	41-33-42.200N 070-30-48.300W				Red nun.	Private aid.

Great River
Aids maintained from May 15 to Oct. 15.

| 14872.1 | - Lighted Buoy G1 | 41-33-39.400N
070-30-44.000W | Fl G 2.5s | | | Green. | Private aid. |

(1) No.	(2) Name and Location	(3) Position	(4) Characteristic	(5) Height	(6) Range	(7) Structure	(8) Remarks
		MASSACHUSETTS - First District					

NANTUCKET SOUND AND APPROACHES

Waquoit Bay

Great River
Aids maintained from May 15 to Oct. 15.

(1) No.	(2) Name and Location	(3) Position	(4) Characteristic	(5) Height	(6) Range	(7) Structure	(8) Remarks
14872.2	- Buoy G2	41-33-38.650N 070-30-43.800W				Red nun.	Private aid.
14872.3	- Buoy G4	41-33-51.500N 070-30-24.500W				Red nun.	Private aid.

Seapit River
Aids Maintained from May 15 to Oct. 15.

14875	- Buoy 1	41-34-22.580N 070-31-45.340W				Green can.	Private aid.
14880	- Buoy 2	41-34-22.100N 070-31-45.500W				Red nun.	Private aid.
14885	- Buoy 3	41-34-25.700N 070-31-43.700W				Green can.	Private aid.
14890	- Buoy 4	41-34-25.100N 070-31-43.700W				Red nun.	Private aid.
14895	- Buoy 6	41-34-26.430N 070-31-41.930W				Red nun.	Private aid.
14900	- Buoy 7	41-34-27.000N 070-31-42.190W				Green can.	Private aid.

Eel Pond
Aids maintained from May 15 to Oct. 15.

14920	- Buoy 2	41-33-02.580N 070-32-51.060W				Red nun.	Private aid.
14925	- WEST JETTY LIGHT 3	41-33-03.000N 070-32-52.000W	Fl G 4s			SG on pile.	Private aid.
14935	- Buoy 6	41-33-07.400N 070-32-53.400W				Red nun.	Private aid.
14950	- Buoy 9	41-33-14.100N 070-32-53.600W				Green can.	Private aid.
14955	- Buoy 11	41-33-17.700N 070-32-36.600W				Green can.	Private aid.
14965	- Buoy 15	41-33-22.760N 070-32-31.690W				Green can.	Private aid.
14966	- Buoy 16	41-33-22.920N 070-32-30.780W				Red nun.	Private aid.

Green Pond
Aids maintained from May 15 to Oct. 15.

15030	- Harbor Approach Lighted Buoy 2	41-32-38.221N 070-34-10.384W	Fl R 2.5s		3	Red.	Removed when endangered by ice.
15035	- HARBOR LIGHT 3	41-32-50.280N 070-34-14.760W	Fl G 4s			SG on pile.	Private aid.
15037	- Buoy 2	41-32-58.400N 070-34-15.700W				Red nun.	Private aid.
15038	- Buoy 3A	41-32-59.460N 070-34-16.200W				Green can.	Private aid.

Great Pond

15065	- WEST JETTY LIGHT	41-32-38.530N 070-34-50.350W	Fl G 3s			On wood pile.	Private aid.
15070	- Buoy 3	41-32-51.200N 070-34-55.600W				Green can.	Private aid.
15075	- Buoy 4	41-32-51.180N 070-34-54.600W				Red nun.	Private aid.
15095	- Buoy 8	41-32-56.300N 070-34-58.700W				Red nun.	Private aid.
15100	- Buoy 9	41-32-56.040N 070-34-59.340W				Green can.	Private aid.

Falmouth Harbor

15105	*Falmouth Lighted Bell Buoy 16*	41-32-02.798N 070-36-28.997W	Fl R 6s		4	Red.	
15110	FALMOUTH INNER HARBOR LIGHT 1	41-32-31.474N 070-36-29.831W	Fl G 2.5s	20	6	SG on white skeleton tower.	
15112	FALMOUTH INNER HARBOR LIGHT 2	41-32-33.000N 070-36-27.000W	Fl R 2.5s	12		TR on pile.	Private aid.

140

(1) No.	(2) Name and Location	(3) Position	(4) Characteristic	(5) Height	(6) Range	(7) Structure	(8) Remarks
		MASSACHUSETTS - First District					
	NANTUCKET SOUND AND APPROACHES						
	Falmouth Harbor						
15115	- East Shoal Buoy 17 On west end of shoal.	41-31-05.179N 070-36-41.800W				Green can.	
15120	- West Shoal Buoy FW	41-31-13.708N 070-37-43.217W				Red nun with green bands.	
15125	Nobska Point Ledge Buoy 18 Off east side of ledge.	41-31-00.567N 070-39-02.518W				Red nun.	
15130	Nobska Point Ledge Buoy 20	41-30-49.850N 070-39-17.529W				Red nun.	
15134	Nantucket Sound Coast Guard Mooring Buoy	41-21-00.034N 070-05-00.010W				White with blue band.	
	Nantucket Harbor						
15135	*Nantucket Bar Lighted Bell Buoy NB*	41-19-01.223N 070-06-13.308W	Mo (A) W		4	Red and white stripes with red spherical topmark.	Removed when endangered by ice.
15140	- Channel Buoy 1	41-18-43.343N 070-06-04.778W				Green can.	
15145	- *Channel Lighted Buoy 2*	41-18-39.294N 070-06-07.458W	Fl R 4s		4	Red.	Removed when endangered by ice.
15150	NANTUCKET EAST BREAKWATER LIGHT 3	41-18-37.092N 070-06-00.122W	Fl G 4s	30	3	SG on skeleton tower.	
15155	- West Breakwater Buoy	41-18-29.862N 070-06-10.271W				White can with orange bands and diamond worded DANGER SUBMERGED JETTY.	
15160	- RANGE FRONT LIGHT	41-17-23.626N 070-05-32.371W	Q W	35		KRW on white wooden skeleton tower.	Higher intensity beam to seaward. Lighted throughout 24 hours.
15165	- RANGE REAR LIGHT 81 yards, 161.9° from front light.	41-17-21.352N 070-05-31.387W	F W	51		KRW on white wooden skeleton tower.	Higher intensity beam to seaward.Lighted throughout 24 hours.
15170	- Channel Buoy 4	41-18-18.374N 070-05-58.298W				Red nun.	
15175	- Channel Buoy 5	41-18-18.704N 070-05-53.998W				Green can.	
15180	- Channel Buoy 6	41-17-55.455N 070-05-48.388W				Red nun.	
15185	- Channel Buoy 7	41-17-57.625N 070-05-44.968W				Green can.	
15190	- Channel Buoy 8	41-17-45.325N 070-05-43.958W				Red nun.	
15195	- Channel Buoy 9	41-17-44.175N 070-05-38.978W				Green can.	
15200	- *Channel Lighted Buoy 10*	41-17-36.584N 070-05-40.447W	Q R		3	Red.	Replaced by Nun from Nov. 1 to May 1.
15205	BRANT POINT LIGHT	41-17-24.094N 070-05-24.970W	Oc R 4s	26	9	White, cylindrical tower, footbridge to shore.	HORN: 1 blast ev 10s (1s bl). MRASS-Fog signal is radio activated, during times of reduced visibility, turn marine VHF-FM radio to channel 83A/157.175Mhz. Key microphone 5 times consecutively, to activate fog signal for 45 minutes.
15213	NANTUCKET FERRY SLIP 1 LIGHT 1	41-17-10.560N 070-05-42.960W	F G	14		Green.	Private aid.
15214	NANTUCKET FERRY SLIP 2 LIGHT 2	41-17-08.880N 070-05-42.240W	F R	14		Red.	Private aid.
15225	- *Channel Lighted Buoy 11* On west part of shoal.	41-17-30.755N 070-05-25.390W	Fl G 2.5s		3	Green.	Replaced by can from Nov. 1 to May 1.
15230	- Channel Buoy 13	41-17-23.534N 070-05-16.110W				Green can.	

(1) No.	(2) Name and Location	(3) Position	(4) Characteristic	(5) Height	(6) Range	(7) Structure	(8) Remarks

NANTUCKET SOUND AND APPROACHES

Nantucket Harbor

15250	- Obstruction Buoy NH Marks stone pier.	41-17-08.564N 070-05-36.591W				Yellow can.	

Nantucket Inner Harbor
Nantucket Head of Harbor
Aids maintained from June 15 to Sept. 15.

15260	Head of Harbor Buoy 2	41-17-27.900N 070-04-43.300W				Red nun.	Private aid.
15261	- Buoy 2A	41-17-49.100N 070-04-27.300W				Red nun.	Private aid.
15262	- Buoy 3	41-17-35.100N 070-04-38.400W				Green can.	Private aid.
15263	- Buoy 3A	41-17-49.900N 070-04-29.100W				Green can.	Private aid.
15264	- Buoy 3B	41-18-01.900N 070-03-42.800W				Green can.	Private aid.
15270	Head of Harbor Buoy 4	41-17-59.000N 070-03-38.200W				Red nun.	Private aid.
15275	Head of Harbor Buoy 5	41-18-06.400N 070-03-14.300W				Green can.	Private aid.
15280	Head of Harbor Buoy 6	41-18-03.900N 070-03-14.200W				Red nun.	Private aid.
15290	Head of Harbor Buoy 8	41-18-47.500N 070-02-02.400W				Red nun.	Private aid.
15290.1	- Buoy 8A	41-19-13.200N 070-02-15.000W				Red nun.	Private aid.
15290.2	- Buoy 8B	41-19-16.900N 070-02-15.400W				Red nun.	Private aid.
15291	Head of Harbor Buoy 9	41-19-23.300N 070-02-15.600W				Green can.	Private aid.
15292	Head of Harbor Buoy 10	41-19-21.700N 070-02-06.700W				Red nun.	Private aid.
15292.1	- Buoy 10A	41-19-07.800N 070-01-45.900W				Red nun.	Private aid.

Polpis Harbor
Aids maintained from June 15 to Sept. 15.

15293.2	- Lighted Buoy 2	41-18-19.500N 070-01-44.800W	Fl R 4s			Red.	Private aid.
15293.3	- Buoy 3	41-18-18.700N 070-01-35.600W				Green can.	Private aid.
15293.4	- Lighted Buoy 4	41-18-18.000N 070-01-37.000W	Fl R 4s			Red	Private aid.
15293.5	- Buoy 5	41-18-18.800N 070-01-35.700W				Green can.	Private aid.
15293.6	- Buoy 6	41-18-20.600N 070-01-30.100W				Red nun.	Private aid.
15293.7	- Buoy 7	41-18-19.900N 070-01-23.800W				Green can.	Private aid.

Madaket Harbor
Aids maintained from June 15 to Sept. 15. unless otherwise noted.

15297	Eel Point Channel Buoy 3	41-18-21.800N 070-11-24.000W				Green can.	Private aid.
15301	Eel Point Channel Lighted Buoy 4	41-18-18.300N 070-11-30.200W	Q R			Red.	Private aid.
15301.1	Eel Point Channel Buoy 4A	41-18-24.200N 070-11-42.600W				Red nun.	Private aid.
15301.5	Eel Point Channel Lighted Buoy 5	41-18-30.500N 070-12-03.600W	Q G			Green.	Private aid.
15302	Eel Point Channel Buoy 6	41-18-34.100N 070-12-03.600W				Red nun.	Private aid.
15302.1	Eel Point Channel Buoy 6A	41-18-13.100N 070-12-17.600W				Red nun.	Private aid.
15302.2	Eel Point Channel Buoy 7	41-18-24.300N 070-12-12.500W				Green can.	Private aid.
15302.3	Eel Point Buoy 7A	41-18-06.700N 070-12-10.600W				Green can.	Private aid.

(1) No.	(2) Name and Location	(3) Position	(4) Characteristic	(5) Height	(6) Range	(7) Structure	(8) Remarks
			MASSACHUSETTS - First District				

NANTUCKET SOUND AND APPROACHES

Madaket Harbor
Aids maintained from June 15 to Sept. 15. unless otherwise noted.

15303	Eel Point Channel Buoy 8	41-17-57.500N 070-12-12.300W				Red nun.	Private aid.
15303.1	Eel Point Buoy 8A	41-17-38.600N 070-12-22.800W				Red nun.	Private aid.
15305	- Lighted Buoy MH	41-17-22.800N 070-14-21.500W	Mo (A) W			Red and white stripes.	Private aid.
15310	- Lighted Buoy 4	41-17-12.900N 070-13-52.200W	Fl R 4s			Red.	Private aid.
15311	- Buoy 6	41-17-07.700N 070-13-30.000W				Red nun.	Private aid.
15312	- Buoy 8	41-17-05.000N 070-12-58.400W				Red nun.	Private aid.
15314	- Lighted Buoy 10	41-17-17.600N 070-12-27.200W	Fl R 4s			Red.	Private aid.
15315	- Buoy 11	41-17-14.700N 070-12-18.700W				Green can.	Private aid.
15316	- Buoy 12	41-17-12.800N 070-12-15.400W				Red nun.	Private aid.
15317	- Buoy 13	41-17-16.400N 070-12-06.400W				Green can.	Private aid.
15318	- Buoy 14	41-17-15.100N 070-12-05.000W				Red nun.	Private aid.
15319	- Buoy 15	41-17-17.770N 070-11-50.520W				Green can.	Private aid.
15320	- Lighted Buoy 16	41-17-16.100N 070-11-50.800W	Fl R 4s			Red.	Private aid.
15321	- Buoy 17	41-17-07.200N 070-11-41.600W				Green can.	Private aid.
15322	- Buoy 18	41-17-05.400N 070-11-44.000W				Red nun.	Private aid.
15323	- Buoy 19	41-16-54.900N 070-11-42.600W				Green can.	Private aid.
15324	- Lighted Buoy 20	41-16-56.200N 070-11-44.100W	Fl R 4s			Red.	Private aid.
15325	- Buoy 21	41-16-47.700N 070-11-52.200W				Green can.	Private aid.
15326	- Buoy 22	41-16-50.200N 070-11-50.800W				Red nun.	Private aid.
15327	- Buoy 23	41-16-42.900N 070-11-58.000W				Green can.	Private aid.
15328	- Lighted Buoy 24	41-16-42.700N 070-11-59.500W	Fl R 4s			Red.	Private aid.
15329	- Buoy 25	41-16-38.000N 070-11-58.000W				Green can.	Private aid.
15330	- Buoy 26	41-16-37.400N 070-11-59.300W				Red nun.	Private aid.

Muskeget Channel

15350	- Lighted Whistle Buoy MC	41-15-00.479N 070-26-10.092W	Mo (A) W		4	Red and white stripes with red spherical topmark.	
15355	- Buoy 1	41-17-30.095N 070-26-41.824W				Green can.	
15360	- Lighted Bell Buoy 2	41-19-31.966N 070-25-22.194W	Fl R 4s		4	Red.	
15365	- Buoy 3	41-19-49.605N 070-25-40.202W				Green can.	
15370	- Buoy 4 At southeast end of shoal.	41-22-57.428N 070-25-04.476W				Red nun.	
15380	- Buoy 6 On northwest part of shoal.	41-26-01.303N 070-25-15.749W				Red nun.	

Edgartown Harbor

15390	Outer Flats Bell Buoy 2	41-26-17.015N 070-29-22.025W				Red.	

143

(1) No.	(2) Name and Location	(3) Position	(4) Characteristic	(5) Height	(6) Range	(7) Structure	(8) Remarks
			MASSACHUSETTS - First District		﹒		

NANTUCKET SOUND AND APPROACHES

Edgartown Harbor

15395	- Channel Buoy 3	41-25-23.399N 070-28-19.704W				Green can.	
15400	- Channel Buoy 4	41-25-19.017N 070-29-18.000W				Red nun.	
15405	- *Channel Lighted Buoy 6* Off Middle Flats.	41-24-26.940N 070-29-13.984W	Fl R 4s		4	Red.	Removed when endangered by ice.
15410	- Channel Buoy 7	41-23-45.403N 070-28-58.344W				Green can.	
15415	- Channel Buoy 8 On spit.	41-23-23.038N 070-29-52.561W				Red nun.	
15420	- LIGHT	41-23-27.150N 070-30-11.024W	Fl R 6s	45	5	White conical tower.	
15425	- Channel Buoy 9 On west edge of shoal.	41-23-11.483N 070-30-39.726W				Green can.	
15426	- Channel Buoy 11	41-23-02.220N 070-30-33.600W				Green can.	Private aid.
15427	- Channel Buoy 13	41-22-25.080N 070-30-16.800W				Green can.	Private aid.

Oak Bluffs Harbor

15447	OAK BLUFFS FERRY SLIP LIGHT 2	41-27-32.820N 070-33-15.900W	F R	14		Wharf end dolphin.	Private aid.
15448	OAK BLUFFS FERRY SLIP LIGHT 1	41-27-32.340N 070-33-14.520W	F G	14		Wharf end dolphin.	Private aid.
15460	OAK BLUFFS NORTH BREAKWATER LIGHT 2	41-27-39.752N 070-33-24.840W	Fl R 4s	30	5	TR on white skeleton tower.	

Vineyard Haven

15465	- Buoy 4	41-28-44.434N 070-35-17.114W				Red nun.	
15470	- Buoy 6	41-27-45.436N 070-35-32.113W				Red nun.	
15475	- LIGHT 7	41-27-38.919N 070-35-19.033W	Fl G 4s	20	4	SG on spindle.	
15480	- BREAKWATER LIGHT 10	41-27-27.043N 070-35-46.893W	Fl R 4s	25	4	TR on spindle.	
15490	- FERRY SLIP 2 LIGHT 1	41-27-19.080N 070-35-58.560W	F G			Wharf end dolphin.	Private aid.
15491	- FERRY SLIP 2 LIGHT 2	41-27-19.980N 070-35-57.840W	F R	14		Wharf end dolphin.	Private aid.
15493	- FERRY SLIP 1 LIGHT 1	41-27-20.640N 070-35-58.080W	F G	14		Wharf end dolphin.	Private aid.
15494	- FERRY SLIP 1 LIGHT 2	41-27-21.540N 070-35-58.920W	F R	14		Wharf end dolphin.	Private aid.

Lagoon Pond
Aids maintained from Apr. 1 to Nov. 1.

15495	- Daybeacon 2	41-27-34.300N 070-35-25.460W				On pile.	Private aid.
15500	- Daybeacon 4	41-27-25.900N 070-35-08.600W				TR on pile.	Private aid.
15505	- Daybeacon 6	41-27-10.560N 070-35-13.140W				TR on pile.	Private aid.
15510	- Daybeacon 8	41-26-35.520N 070-35-43.260W				Red.	Private aid.

Maciel Marine Channel

15521	- Buoy 1	41-27-15.900N 070-35-10.620W				Green can.	Private aid.
15521.2	- Buoy 2	41-27-16.680N 070-35-10.440W				Red nun.	Private aid.
15521.3	- Buoy 3	41-27-15.900N 070-35-16.900W				Green can.	Private aid.
15521.5	- Buoy 4	41-27-16.020N 070-35-17.460W				Red nun.	Private aid.
15521.7	- Buoy 5	41-27-13.500N 070-35-29.100W				Green can.	Private aid.

(1) No.	(2) Name and Location	(3) Position	(4) Characteristic	(5) Height	(6) Range	(7) Structure	(8) Remarks

NANTUCKET SOUND AND APPROACHES
Vineyard Haven
Maciel Marine Channel

15521.8	- Buoy 6	41-27-14.000N 070-35-28.800W				Red nun.	Private aid.
15521.9	- Buoy 7	41-27-10.300N 070-35-33.100W				Green can.	Private aid.
15522	- Buoy 8	41-27-10.800N 070-35-33.200W				Red nun.	Private aid.
15522.1	- Buoy 9	41-27-04.500N 070-35-39.480W				Green can.	Private aid.
15522.3	- Buoy 10	41-27-04.800N 070-35-39.180W				Red nun.	Private aid.
15522.5	- Buoy 11	41-27-03.700N 070-35-51.400W				Green can.	Private aid.
15522.6	- Buoy 12	41-27-03.800N 070-35-51.600W				Red nun.	Private aid.

Lake Tashmoo
Aids maintained from Apr. 1 to Nov. 1 unless otherwise noted.

15525	- EAST JETTY LIGHT Marks end of jetty.	41-28-04.100N 070-37-58.100W	Fl W 3s	13		Single metal post.	Maintained from Apr. 1 to Dec. 1. Private aid.
15530	- Buoy 1	41-27-57.091N 070-37-50.522W				Green can.	Private aid.
15532	- Buoy 2	41-28-04.600N 070-37-58.712W				Red nun.	Private aid.
15535	- Buoy 2A	41-27-56.732N 070-37-52.207W				Red nun.	Private aid.
15540	- Buoy 3	41-27-53.194N 070-37-46.179W				Green can.	Private aid.
15546	- Channel Daybeacon 4A	41-27-51.300N 070-37-44.520W				TR on pile.	Private aid.
15547	- Buoy 5	41-27-51.100N 070-37-42.300W				Green can.	Private aid.
15548	- Buoy 6	41-27-50.100N 070-37-42.000W				Red nun.	Private aid.
15548.1	- Buoy 7	41-27-47.870N 070-37-38.830W				Green can.	Private aid.
15548.2	- Buoy 8	41-27-46.350N 070-37-38.480W				Red nun.	Private aid.
15548.3	- Buoy 9	41-27-46.850N 070-37-37.420W				Green can.	Private aid.
15548.4	- Buoy 10	41-27-44.930N 070-37-37.490W				Red nun.	Private aid.

MARTHA'S VINEYARD TO BLOCK ISLAND
Vineyard Sound
Main Channel

15550	Middle Ground East End Buoy	41-29-07.426N 070-36-26.544W				Green can with red bands.	
15555	*Nobska Point Lighted Bell Buoy 26*	41-30-19.418N 070-38-43.057W	Fl R 4s		4	Red.	Replaced by nun when endangered by ice.
15560	**Nobska Point Light**	41-30-56.850N 070-39-18.409W	Fl W 6s	87	W 13 R 11	White tower. 40	Obscured from 125° to 195°. Red from 263° to 289°, covers Hedge Fence and L`Hommedieu Shoal. Lighted throughout 24 hours. HORN: 2 blasts ev 30s (2s bl-2s si-2s bl-24s si). MRASS-Fog signal is radio activated, during times of reduced visibility, turn marine VHF-FM radio to channel 83A/157.175Mhz. Key microphone 5 times consecutively, to activate fog signal for 45 minutes.
15575	*Middle Ground Lighted Bell Buoy 27*	41-28-28.017N 070-41-07.930W	Fl G 4s		4	Green.	Replaced by can when endangered by ice.

(1) No.	(2) Name and Location	(3) Position	(4) Characteristic	(5) Height	(6) Range	(7) Structure	(8) Remarks
			MASSACHUSETTS - First District				
	MARTHA'S VINEYARD TO BLOCK ISLAND						
	Vineyard Sound						
	Main Channel						
15577	*Vineyard Sound Lighted Buoy 29*	41-25-08.426N 070-48-04.990W	Fl G 4s		4	Green.	Replaced by can when endangered by ice.
15580	TARPAULIN COVE LIGHT	41-28-07.774N 070-45-27.002W	Fl W 6s	78	9	White tower; small white building attached to west side of tower.	
15597	*Vineyard Sound Entrance Lighted Buoy 30*	41-24-00.105N 070-50-11.015W	Fl R 4s		4	Red.	Replaced by nun when endangered by ice.
15605	*Gay Head Lighted Gong Buoy 31*	41-21-49.431N 070-51-47.626W	Fl G 4s		4	Green.	Replaced by can when endangered by ice.
15610 620	**Gay Head Light**	41-20-54.454N 070-50-03.687W	Al WR 15s 0.2s W fl 7.3s ec. 0.2s R fl 7.3s ec.	175	W 24 R 20	Red brick tower. 51	Obscured from 342° to 359° by Nomans Land; light occasionally visible through notches in hilltop.Emergency light (Fl W 6s) of reduced intensity when main is extinguished.Lighted throughout 24 hours.
15613	*Vineyard Sound Entrance Lighted Whistle Buoy 32*	41-22-04.951N 070-57-25.102W	Fl R 2.5s		4	Red.	Replaced by nun when endangered by ice.
15615	*Vineyard Sound Acoustic Lighted Research Buoy*	41-19-47.640N 070-54-38.160W	Fl Y 20s			Yellow.	Private aid.
15617	Sow and Pigs Buoy 34	41-23-45.762N 070-57-46.371W				Red nun.	
15618	*Sow and Pigs Lighted Bell Buoy 36*	41-23-48.420N 070-59-04.143W	Fl R 4s		4	Red.	
	WOODS HOLE						
	Little Harbor						
15650	*Coffin Rock Lighted Buoy 1*	41-30-41.401N 070-39-38.437W	Q G		3	Green.	
15655	- *Channel Lighted Buoy 2*	41-30-46.537N 070-39-30.965W	Fl R 2.5s		3	Red.	
15660	- *Channel Lighted Buoy 4*	41-30-54.644N 070-39-49.263W	Fl R 4s		4	Red.	
15665	- *Channel Lighted Buoy 6*	41-31-00.567N 070-39-54.339W	Fl R 2.5s		4	Red.	
15670	- *Lighted Buoy 7*	41-31-00.357N 070-39-56.819W	Fl G 2.5s		4	Green.	
	Great Harbor						
15695	- Channel Entrance Gong Buoy 1 On south end of shoal.	41-30-31.234N 070-40-13.835W				Green.	
15700	- *Channel Entrance Lighted Bell Buoy 2* On southwest side of shoal.	41-30-34.236N 070-40-05.903W	Fl R 4s		4	Red.	Replaced by nun when endangered by ice.
15705	- Channel Buoy 4 Off west end of ledge.	41-30-42.628N 070-40-09.045W				Red nun	
15710	Great Ledge Buoy	41-30-49.309N 070-40-01.376W				White with orange bands and orange diamond.	Marked ROCKS. Removed when endangered by ice.
15715	- *Channel Lighted Buoy 5*	41-30-56.394N 070-40-19.421W	Fl G 4s		4	Green.	Replaced by can when endangered by ice.
15720	- Channel Buoy 6	41-30-59.514N 070-40-06.573W				Red nun.	
15725	JUNIPER POINT LIGHT 6A	41-31-02.626N 070-40-05.618W	Q R	12	4	TR on spindle.	
15730	- Channel Buoy 8	41-31-15.105N 070-40-19.759W				Red nun.	
15737	- FERRY SLIP 1 LIGHT 2	41-31-22.171N 070-40-17.308W	F R	14		Red. On dolphin.	Marks ferry slip. Private aid.
15740	- FERRY SLIP 1 LIGHT 1	41-31-23.297N 070-40-15.860W	F G	14		Green. On dolphin.	Marks ferry slip. Private aid.

146

(1) No.	(2) Name and Location	(3) Position	(4) Characteristic	(5) Height	(6) Range	(7) Structure	(8) Remarks
		MASSACHUSETTS - First District					
	WOODS HOLE						
	Great Harbor						
15740.3	- FERRY SLIP 2 LIGHT 1	41-31-21.540N 070-40-17.229W	F G	14		Green. On dolphin.	Marks ferry slip. Private aid.
15740.4	- FERRY SLIP 2 LIGHT 2	41-31-20.584N 070-40-17.139W	F R	14		Red. On dolphin.	Marks ferry slip. Private aid.
15740.8	- FERRY SLIP 3 LIGHT 1	41-31-20.029N 070-40-16.724W	F G	14		Green. On dolphin.	Marks ferry slip. Private aid.
15740.9	- FERRY SLIP 3 LIGHT 2	41-31-19.219N 070-40-15.484W	F R	14		Red. On dolphin.	Marks ferry slip. Private aid.
15745	- Channel Buoy 9 On north part of ledge.	41-31-22.125N 070-40-30.959W				Green can.	
15750	TIMBER PIER LIGHT	41-31-28.398N 070-40-23.008W	F R	14			Private aid.
	Broadway						
	During periods of high currents, aids may appear to be sinking or riding low.						
15755	- Buoy 1	41-31-02.230N 070-40-32.853W				Green can.	
15760	- Daybeacon 3	41-31-08.905N 070-40-48.062W				SG on pile.	
15765	- Buoy 2	41-31-04.561N 070-40-30.791W				Red nun.	
15770	- Buoy 4	41-31-08.574N 070-40-39.135W				Red nun.	
	Woods Hole Passage						
15773	WOODS HOLE PASS DIRECTIONAL LIGHT	41-31-17.252N 070-40-16.524W	Oc W 4s	30		NR on dolphin.	Visible on course to steer 077°T.
15775	GRASSY ISLAND LEDGE LIGHT On south end of ledge.	41-31-16.231N 070-40-33.257W	Q W (R sector)	26	4	NR on white skeleton tower.	
15780	- Buoy 1	41-31-13.266N 070-40-30.179W				Green can.	
15783	Woods Hole Pass Buoy 1A	41-31-11.914N 070-40-39.551W				Green can.	
15785	- Buoy 2 On south part of ledge.	41-31-15.946N 070-40-30.154W				Red nun.	
15788	Woods Hole Pass Buoy 2A	41-31-14.347N 070-40-40.280W				Red nun.	
15790	- *Junction Lighted Buoy SB* North of ledge.	41-31-10.856N 070-40-44.008W	Fl (2+1)G 6s		3	Green can with red band.	
15795	- Buoy 7	41-31-07.570N 070-41-04.493W				Green can.	
15800	- Buoy 5	41-31-09.612N 070-40-51.634W				Green can.	
15805	- LIGHT 4	41-31-13.522N 070-40-51.563W	Fl R 2.5s	28	4	TR on skeleton tower.	
15807	- Buoy 4A	41-31-12.646N 070-40-50.840W				Red nun.	
15810	- LIGHT W At west end of ledge.	41-31-06.836N 070-41-01.021W	Fl W 2.5s	34	6	NG on skeleton tower.	
15815	- Buoy 6	41-31-10.495N 070-41-05.190W				Red nun.	
15820	- Buoy 8	41-31-11.825N 070-41-12.720W				Red nun.	
15825	- *Lighted Buoy 10*	41-31-14.521N 070-41-24.805W	Fl R 4s		4	Red.	Replaced by nun when endangered by ice.
15830	- Buoy 11	41-31-26.485N 070-41-38.610W				Green can.	
15835	- *Lighted Bell Buoy 13*	41-31-41.034N 070-41-51.611W	Fl G 4s		5	Green.	Replaced by can when endangered by ice.
	Hadley Harbor						
15840	Hadley Rock Buoy North of rock.	41-31-03.535N 070-41-21.130W				White can with orange bands worded ROCK.	

(1) No.	(2) Name and Location	(3) Position	(4) Characteristic	(5) Height	(6) Range	(7) Structure	(8) Remarks
			MASSACHUSETTS - First District				
	WOODS HOLE						
	Hadley Harbor						
15845	- Bouy 3	41-30-53.401N 070-41-52.514W				Green can.	
15850	- Buoy 2	41-30-54.357N 070-41-52.520W				Red. nun.	
	MARTHA'S VINEYARD TO BLOCK ISLAND						
	Tarpaulin Cove						
15867	- CG Mooring Buoy	41-28-25.938N 070-45-08.542W				White with blue band.	
15870	- Rock Buoy Off east side of rock.	41-28-26.650N 070-45-27.629W				White can with orange bands worded ROCK.	
	Robinsons Hole						
15875	- Buoy 1 On shoal.	41-26-46.526N 070-48-14.124W				Green can.	
15880	- Buoy 3	41-26-57.665N 070-48-23.046W				Green can.	
15885	- Rock Buoy 4	41-27-01.916N 070-48-25.776W				Red nun.	
15890	- Buoy 6 At northwest end of Middle Ground.	41-27-07.632N 070-48-29.725W				Red nun.	
15895	- Rock Buoy 8	41-27-12.845N 070-48-34.265W				Red nun.	
15900	- Buoy 10 At northwest end of Middle Ground.	41-27-18.016N 070-48-35.681W				Red nun.	
15905	- Rock Buoy 11 Off point of flats.	41-27-20.486N 070-48-36.689W				Green can.	
	Quicks Hole						
15910	- *Entrance Lighted Bell Buoy 1*	41-25-48.426N 070-50-22.127W	Fl G 4s		4	Green.	Replaced by can when endangered by ice.
15915	- *Ledge Lighted Buoy 2*	41-26-39.499N 070-50-41.901W	Fl R 4s		3	Red.	Replaced by nun when endangered by ice.
15920	Felix Ledge Buoy 3	41-26-46.944N 070-50-56.719W				Green can.	
	Canapitsit Channel						
15930	- Buoy 1	41-25-13.778N 070-54-24.667W				Green can.	
15935	- Buoy 2	41-25-20.287N 070-54-22.973W				Red nun.	
15940	- Buoy 3	41-25-21.266N 070-54-24.556W				Green can.	
15945	- Buoy 5	41-25-28.814N 070-54-31.690W				Green can.	
15947	Menemsha Bight CG Mooring Buoy	41-21-22.041N 070-47-10.126W				White with blue band.	
	Menemsha Creek						
15950	- *Entrance Lighted Bell Buoy 1*	41-21-21.907N 070-46-15.017W	Fl G 2.5s		3	Green.	
15955	- ENTRANCE JETTY LIGHT 3	41-21-16.198N 070-46-06.953W	Fl G 4s	25	5	SG on spindle.	
15960	- ENTRANCE JETTY LIGHT 2	41-21-15.184N 070-46-08.501W	Fl R 4s	13	4	TR on spindle.	
15965	- Buoy 4	41-21-05.100N 070-45-58.917W				Red nun.	
15966	- Buoy 4A	41-20-53.218N 070-46-04.949W				Red nun.	Maintained from May 1 to Oct. 15.
15967	- Buoy 5	41-20-32.671N 070-46-06.237W				Green can.	Maintained from May 1 to Oct. 15.

(1) No.	(2) Name and Location	(3) Position	(4) Characteristic	(5) Height	(6) Range	(7) Structure	(8) Remarks
			MASSACHUSETTS - First District				
	MARTHA'S VINEYARD TO BLOCK ISLAND						
	Menemsha Creek						
15968	- Buoy 6	41-20-30.880N 070-46-08.322W				Red nun.	Maintained from May 1 to Oct. 15.
15970	- Daybeacon 7	41-20-20.340N 070-46-12.060W				SG on pile.	Private aid.
15975	- Daybeacon 8	41-20-20.860N 070-46-12.990W				TR on pile.	Private aid.
15985 630	**Buzzards Bay Main Channel** **Buzzards Bay Entrance Light**	41-23-49.152N 071-02-04.877W	Fl W 2.5s	67	14	Tower on red square on 3 red piles with large red tube in center, worded BUZZARDS on sides. 68	RACON: B (- . . .) HORN: 2 blasts ev 30s (2s bl-2s si-2s bl-24s si). Fog signal is radio activated, during times of reduced visibility, turn marine VHF-FM radio to channel 83A/157.175Mhz. Key microphone 5 times consecutively, to activate fog signal for 45 minutes.
15990	*Buzzards Bay Wave Lighted Buoy*	41-23-13.200N 071-01-55.200W	Fl (5)Y 20s			Yellow.	Property of Woods Hole Group Inc. Private aid.
16000	*Buzzards Bay Lighted Buoy 1*	41-25-50.525N 071-02-15.881W	Fl G 2.5s		3	Green.	
16005	*Buzzards Bay Lighted Bell Buoy 2*	41-26-08.466N 071-00-39.328W	Fl R 2.5s		3	Red.	
16010	*Buzzards Bay Lighted Gong Buoy 3*	41-27-15.034N 071-00-34.011W	Fl G 4s		4	Green.	
16015	Hen and Chickens Buoy 1 Off south part of ledge.	41-27-33.733N 071-01-48.352W				Green can.	
16025	*Buzzards Bay Lighted Bell Buoy 4* West side of shoal.	41-27-01.916N 070-59-13.646W	Q R		3	Red.	
16030	*Buzzards Bay Lighted Gong Buoy 5* Off southeast side of ledge.	41-28-58.135N 070-57-22.294W	Fl G 6s		4	Green.	Replaced by can when endangered by ice.
16035	*Buzzards Bay Lighted Buoy 6*	41-28-04.063N 070-56-41.063W	Fl R 4s		4	Red.	
16040 16731	DUMPLING ROCKS LIGHT 7 On rock.	41-32-17.834N 070-55-17.111W	Fl G 6s	52	8	SG on skeleton tower.	
16043	*EOM Lighted Research Buoy A*	41-30-48.239N 070-55-22.155W	Fl Y 20s			Yellow.	Private aid.
16045	*Buzzards Bay Lighted Buoy 7*	41-30-25.022N 070-54-18.894W	Fl G 2.5s		3	Green.	Replaced by can when endangered by ice.
16050	*Buzzards Bay Lighted Buoy 8*	41-28-57.526N 070-53-50.038W	Fl R 2.5s		3	Red.	Replaced by LIB when endangered.
16053	*Buzzard's Bay Acoustic Lighted Research Buoy*	41-30-12.600N 070-52-38.280W	Fl Y 20s			Yellow.	Private aid.
16055	*Buzzards Bay Midchannel Lighted Buoy BB*	41-30-33.034N 070-49-54.011W	Mo (A) W		4	Red and white stripes with red spherical topmark.	Removed when endangered by ice.
16058	*Buzzards Bay Lighted Bell Buoy 9*	41-32-52.034N 070-46-27.011W	Fl G 4s		4	Green.	Replaced by LIB when endangered by ice.
16060	*Buzzards Bay Lighted Buoy 10*	41-34-24.020N 070-43-11.954W	Fl R 4s		4	Red.	Replaced by LIB when endangered by ice.
16075	Bird Island Bell Buoy 3	41-39-59.424N 070-42-23.310W				Green.	Removed when endangered by ice.

(1) No.	(2) Name and Location	(3) Position	(4) Characteristic	(5) Height	(6) Range	(7) Structure	(8) Remarks

MASSACHUSETTS - First District

MARTHA'S VINEYARD TO BLOCK ISLAND
Buzzards Bay Main Channel

(1) No.	(2) Name and Location	(3) Position	(4) Characteristic	(5) Height	(6) Range	(7) Structure	(8) Remarks
16080	**Cleveland East Ledge Light**	41-37-51.504N 070-41-39.057W	Fl W 10s	74	14	White cylindrical tower and dwelling on red caisson. 74	HORN: 1 blast ev 15 (2s bl). MRASS-Fog signal is radio activated, during times of reduced visibility, turn marine VHF-FM radio to channel 83A/157.175Mhz. Key microphone 5 times consecutively, to activate fog signal for 45 minutes.

Cleveland Ledge Channel

(1) No.	(2) Name and Location	(3) Position	(4) Characteristic	(5) Height	(6) Range	(7) Structure	(8) Remarks
16085	- PRECISION DIRECTIONAL LIGHT On southern end of Stoney Point Dike.	41-41-32.975N 070-40-27.516W			R G W		Inbound from Cleveland Ledge Light, light shows Fl G from 016.4T to 016.7T, F G from 016.1T to 016.4T, Alternating G W from 015.8T to 016.1T, F W from 015.6T to 015.8T centered on channel centerline, Alternating W R from 015.3T to 015.6T, F R from 015.0T to 015.3T, Fl R from 014.7T to 015.0T. Lighted 24 hours.
16095	- Lighted Buoy 2 West of shoal.	41-36-38.696N 070-42-11.007W	Fl R 4s		3	Red.	Replaced by nun when endangered by ice.
16100	- Lighted Buoy 3	41-37-19.034N 070-42-10.011W	Q G		3	Green.	Replaced by LIB from Nov. 15 to Mar. 15.
16105	- Lighted Buoy 4	41-37-17.625N 070-41-56.564W	Q R		3	Red.	Replaced by nun when endangered by ice.
16120	- Lighted Buoy 7 Marks shoal.	41-39-07.076N 070-41-27.507W	Fl G 4s		3	Green.	Replaced by can when endangered by ice.
16125	- Lighted Buoy 8	41-39-05.657N 070-41-17.192W	Fl R 4s		3	Red.	Replaced by nun when endangered by ice.

Cape Cod Canal Approach
Hog Island Channel
Both banks of the Cape Cod Canal are lighted by alternating sodium vapor and incandescent lights spaced about 500 feet apart, 140 feet from the edge of the channel, 25 feet above water (maintained by Corps of Engineers). Hog Island Channel lights are located 125 feet outside the channel limits and the shoal water, except Light 6 located 174 feet outside the channel limit.

(1) No.	(2) Name and Location	(3) Position	(4) Characteristic	(5) Height	(6) Range	(7) Structure	(8) Remarks
16130	- Lighted Buoy 1	41-40-55.434N 070-40-46.711W	Q G		3	Green.	Replaced by can when endangered by ice.
16135	- Lighted Bell Buoy 2	41-41-03.634N 070-40-30.251W	Q R		3	Red.	Replaced by a nun when endangered by ice.
16140	- Lighted Bell Buoy 3	41-41-16.730N 070-40-26.479W	Fl G 4s		3	Green.	Replaced by a can when endangered by ice.
16145	- LIGHT 5	41-41-24.491N 070-40-20.654W	Fl G 6s	32	5	SG on skeleton tower on cylindrical pier.	
16150	- LIGHT 4	41-41-20.503N 070-40-12.478W	Fl R 6s	24	5	TR on skeleton tower on cylindrical pier.	
16155	- Lighted Buoy 6	41-41-36.034N 070-39-59.611W	Fl R 4s		3	Red.	Replaced by a nun when endangered by ice.
16160	- Lighted Buoy 7	41-41-39.134N 070-40-05.411W	Fl G 4s		3	Green.	Replaced by a can when endangered by ice.
16165	- LIGHT 9	41-41-57.071N 070-39-50.518W	Fl G 6s	24	5	SG on skeleton tower on cylindrical pier.	
16170	- LIGHT 8	41-41-53.097N 070-39-42.462W	Fl R 6s	24	5	TR on skeleton tower on cylindrical pier.	
16175	- Lighted Buoy 10	41-42-09.934N 070-39-28.211W	Fl R 4s		3	Red.	Replaced by a nun when endangered by ice.

(1) No.	(2) Name and Location	(3) Position	(4) Characteristic	(5) Height	(6) Range	(7) Structure	(8) Remarks

MASSACHUSETTS - First District

Cape Cod Canal Approach

Hog Island Channel

Both banks of the Cape Cod Canal are lighted by alternating sodium vapor and incandescent lights spaced about 500 feet apart, 140 feet from the edge of the channel, 25 feet above water (maintained by Corps of Engineers). Hog Island Channel lights are located 125 feet outside the channel limits and the shoal water, except Light 6 located 174 feet outside the channel limit.

(1) No.	(2) Name and Location	(3) Position	(4) Characteristic	(5) Height	(6) Range	(7) Structure	(8) Remarks
16180	- Lighted Buoy 11	41-42-12.834N 070-39-33.811W	Fl G 4s		4	Green.	Replaced by a can when endangered by ice.
16185	- LIGHT 13	41-42-29.542N 070-39-20.123W	Fl G 6s	24	5	SG on skeleton tower on cylindrical pier.	
16195	- Lighted Buoy 12	41-42-26.534N 070-39-13.011W	Fl R 4s		3	Red.	Replaced by a nun when endangered by ice.
16200	- Lighted Bell Buoy 15	41-42-46.434N 070-39-02.511W	Fl G 4s		3	Green.	Replaced by a can when endangered by ice.
16205	- LIGHT 17	41-42-59.343N 070-38-52.116W	Fl G 6s	24	5	SG on skeleton tower on cylindrical tower.	
16210	- Lighted Buoy 16	41-42-43.507N 070-38-56.859W	Fl R 4s		3	Red.	Replaced by nun when endangered by ice.
16215	- Lighted Buoy 19	41-43-16.534N 070-38-34.111W	Fl G 4s		3	Green.	Replaced by can when endangered by ice.
16220	- Lighted Bell Buoy 18	41-43-13.734N 070-38-28.711W	Fl R 4s		3	Red.	Replaced by nun when endangered by ice.
16225	- LIGHT 21	41-43-28.163N 070-38-25.385W	Q G	35	5	SG on skeleton tower.	
16230	- Lighted Buoy 23	41-43-52.689N 070-37-59.908W	Fl G 4s		3	Green.	Replaced by can when endangered by ice.
16240	- Lighted Bell Buoy 26	41-44-00.520N 070-37-39.622W	Fl R 4s		3	Red.	Replaced by nun when endangered by ice.
16245	- Lighted Buoy 27	41-44-03.814N 070-37-45.131W	Fl G 4s		3	Green.	Replaced by can when endangered by ice.
16250	- LIGHT 28	41-44-12.143N 070-37-22.094W	Fl R 6s	15	4	TR on white skeleton tower.	
16251	Gray Gables Buoy 1	41-44-09.660N 070-37-24.120W				Green can.	Private aid.
16252	Gray Gables Buoy 2	41-44-09.000N 070-37-24.660W				Red nun.	Private aid.

MARTHA'S VINEYARD TO BLOCK ISLAND

Cuttyhunk Harbor

(1) No.	(2) Name and Location	(3) Position	(4) Characteristic	(5) Height	(6) Range	(7) Structure	(8) Remarks
16260	Middle Ground Buoy MG	41-26-24.410N 070-55-43.910W				Red and green bands; nun.	
16265	- West Entrance Buoy 1W	41-26-40.420N 070-55-30.138W				Green can.	
16270	Whale Rock Danger Buoy	41-26-02.220N 070-55-12.637W				White with orange bands worded DANGER ROCK.	
16275	- West Entrance Buoy 3W	41-26-25.060N 070-54-51.756W				Green can.	
16280	- West Entrance Buoy 2W	41-26-04.792N 070-55-02.519W				Red nun.	
16285	Pease Ledge Buoy 4	41-25-46.281N 070-54-58.316W				Red nun.	
16290	- North Jetty Bell Buoy 6	41-25-34.482N 070-54-51.676W				Red.	
16295	- NORTH JETTY LIGHT 8	41-25-30.534N 070-55-00.911W	Fl R 6s	29	5	TR on gray skeleton tower on concrete base.	Obscured from 284° to 044°.
16300	- Buoy 9	41-25-29.747N 070-54-57.281W				Green can.	

(1) No.	(2) Name and Location	(3) Position	(4) Characteristic	(5) Height	(6) Range	(7) Structure	(8) Remarks

MASSACHUSETTS - First District

MARTHA'S VINEYARD TO BLOCK ISLAND
Cuttyhunk Harbor
Cuttyhunk Pond Inner Channel

16301.3	- Buoy 1	41-25-28.800N 070-55-27.600W				Green can.	Private aid.
16301.5	- Buoy 3	41-25-29.700N 070-55-36.240W				Green can.	Private aid.

Cuttyhunk Pond Upper Channel

16302.1	- Buoy 1	41-25-31.440N 070-55-24.690W				Green can.	Private aid.
16302.2	- Buoy 2	41-25-31.380N 070-55-22.938W				Red nun.	Private aid.
16302.3	- Buoy 3	41-25-33.600N 070-55-24.660W				Green can.	Private aid.
16302.4	- Buoy 4	41-25-33.254N 070-55-22.450W				Red nun.	Private aid.

Cuttyhunk Harbor

16305	- East Entrance Buoy 1E	41-26-13.133N 070-54-08.137W				Green can.	
16310	- East Entrance Buoy 2E	41-26-26.761N 070-54-12.125W				Red nun.	

Cuttyhunk

16315	- *East Entrance Lighted Bell Buoy CH*	41-26-34.105N 070-53-21.816W	Mo (A) W		4	Red and white stripes with red spherical topmark.	Replaced by can when endangered by ice.

South Side

16320	*Lone Rock Lighted Buoy LR* Southeasterly of rock.	41-27-39.380N 070-51-08.843W	Fl (2+1)G 6s		4	Green and red bands.	Replaced by can when endangered by ice.
16325	*Weepecket Rock Lighted Gong Buoy 8* On northeasterly end of shoal.	41-31-48.493N 070-43-26.402W	Fl R 2.5s		3	Red.	

Quisset Harbor

16330	- *Entrance Lighted Buoy 2*	41-32-31.196N 070-39-56.433W	Fl R 4s		4	Red.	Replaced by nun from Dec. 1 to Apr. 1.
16335	- Buoy 4 Marks rock.	41-32-25.460N 070-39-46.887W				Red nun.	
16340	- Buoy 3	41-32-30.004N 070-39-52.020W				Green can.	
16345	- Buoy 5	41-32-26.762N 070-39-45.887W				Green can.	
16350	- Buoy 6	41-32-24.923N 070-39-40.831W				Red nun.	
16355	- Buoy 7 South side of rock.	41-32-25.793N 070-39-36.658W				Green can.	
16360	- Buoy 8	41-32-32.880N 070-39-19.020W				Red nun.	Private aid.
16365	- Buoy 9	41-32-34.573N 070-39-16.275W				Green can.	Private aid.

East Side

16375	Great Sippewisset Rock Daybeacon	41-35-17.500N 070-39-13.500W				TR on spindle.	Maintained from May 15 to Oct. 15. Private aid.

West Falmouth Harbor
Private aids are maintained from May 15 to Oct. 15 unless otherwise noted.

16380	- Entrance Buoy 1 Marks ledge.	41-36-34.870N 070-39-29.192W				Green can.	
16385	- *Entrance Lighted Bell Buoy 2*	41-36-22.613N 070-39-30.260W	Fl R 4s		3	Red.	Removed when endangered by ice.
16390	- Entrance Buoy 4 Marks ledge.	41-36-24.840N 070-39-09.514W				Red nun.	
16395	- Buoy 6	41-36-24.000N 070-39-00.000W				Red nun.	Private aid.

(1) No.	(2) Name and Location	(3) Position	(4) Characteristic	(5) Height	(6) Range	(7) Structure	(8) Remarks
			MASSACHUSETTS - First District				

MARTHA'S VINEYARD TO BLOCK ISLAND

West Falmouth Harbor

Private aids are maintained from May 15 to Oct. 15 unless otherwise noted.

(1) No.	(2) Name and Location	(3) Position	(4) Characteristic	(5) Height	(6) Range	(7) Structure	(8) Remarks
16400	- Buoy 7	41-36-21.300N 070-39-01.380W				Green can.	Private aid.
16405	- Buoy 8	41-36-12.300N 070-38-32.160W				Red nun.	Private aid.
16410	- Buoy 9	41-36-21.720N 070-38-53.100W				Green can.	Private aid.
16420	- Buoy 13	41-36-15.480N 070-38-35.520W				Green can.	Private aid.
16425	- Buoy 14	41-36-14.700N 070-38-36.120W				Red nun.	Private aid.
	BUZZARDS BAY						
	Wild Harbor						
16450	- *Lighted Buoy 1*	41-38-08.029N 070-39-16.964W	Fl G 4s		4	Green.	Removed when endangered by ice.
16460	- Buoy 4	41-38-06.742N 070-38-55.401W				Red nun.	
	Megansett Harbor						
16461	- *Lighted Buoy 1*	41-39-07.071N 070-40-04.914W	Fl G 4s		4	Green.	Maintained from Apr. 1 to Nov. 30.
16465	Seal Rocks Buoy 3	41-39-27.657N 070-39-29.225W				Green can.	
16475	Fiddlers Cove Marina Buoy 4FC	41-39-02.040N 070-38-08.040W				Red nun.	Private aid.
16480	Fiddlers Cove Marina Buoy 5FC	41-39-01.860N 070-38-07.020W				Green can.	Private aid.
16490	- Buoy 4	41-39-11.856N 070-38-48.141W				Red nun.	
16495	- Buoy 5	41-39-24.588N 070-38-19.463W				Green can.	
16497	- *Lighted Buoy 6*	41-39-11.206N 070-38-08.105W	Fl R 2.5s		4	Red.	Replaced by nun from Dec. 1 to Apr. 1.
16500	- Buoy 7	41-39-29.636N 070-37-47.676W				Green can.	
16501	- BREAKWATER LIGHT 8	41-39-28.622N 070-37-34.814W	Fl R 6s	25	5	TR on spindle on timber structure.	
16502	- Channel Buoy 8A	41-39-30.180N 070-37-36.600W				Red nun.	Maintained from May 1 to Oct. 15. Private aid.
16510	- Buoy 9	41-39-30.974N 070-37-33.635W				Green can.	
16512	- Buoy 10	41-39-30.262N 070-37-34.379W				Red nun.	
16515	- Buoy 11	41-39-30.000N 070-37-31.100W				Green can.	Maintained from May 15 to Oct. 15. Private aid.
	Squeteague Harbor						
16517	- Buoy 2	41-39-33.300N 070-37-16.920W				Red nun.	Private aid.
16518	- Buoy 3	41-39-38.820N 070-37-13.020W				Green can.	Private aid.
	Southwest Ledge						
16530	- Buoy 2	41-40-02.113N 070-40-09.928W				Red nun.	
	CAPE COD CANAL AND APPROACHES						
	Red Brook Harbor						
16535	Eustis Rock Buoy ER	41-40-28.730N 070-38-42.781W				Red and green; nun.	
16540	Bassetts Island Shoal South Buoy 1	41-40-19.998N 070-38-15.660W				Green can.	
16543	Hospital Cove Buoy 1A	41-40-12.187N 070-38-10.257W				Green can.	

(1) No.	(2) Name and Location	(3) Position	(4) Characteristic	(5) Height	(6) Range	(7) Structure	(8) Remarks

CAPE COD CANAL AND APPROACHES

Red Brook Harbor

16545	Scraggy Rocks Buoy 2	41-40-14.758N 070-38-12.402W				Red nun.	
16550	Hospital Cove Buoy 3	41-40-05.974N 070-38-06.830W				Green can.	
16555	Hospital Cove Buoy 5	41-40-03.562N 070-38-02.319W				Green can.	
16557	Hospital Cove Buoy 5A	41-40-03.934N 070-37-57.125W				Green can.	
16560	Hospital Cove Buoy 6	41-40-01.504N 070-37-59.859W				Red nun.	

Red Brook Harbor South Channel

16565	- Buoy 7	41-40-07.126N 070-37-52.073W				Green can.	
16570	- Buoy 8	41-40-08.016N 070-37-50.026W				Red nun.	
16575	- Buoy 9	41-40-18.028N 070-37-46.949W				Green can.	
16580	- Buoy 10	41-40-26.908N 070-37-44.171W				Red nun.	
16585	- Buoy 12	41-40-38.044N 070-37-40.805W				Red nun.	
16590	- Buoy 11	41-40-33.639N 070-37-43.161W				Green can.	

Red Brook Harbor

16595	- Buoy 14	41-40-39.118N 070-37-37.673W				Red nun.	
16600	Handy Point Shoal Buoy 13	41-40-31.560N 070-37-26.040W				Green can.	Private aid.
16601	- Buoy 16	41-40-30.600N 070-37-27.000W				Red nun.	Private aid.
16602	- Buoy 18	41-40-30.400N 070-37-17.400W				Red nun.	Private aid.
16603	- Buoy 20	41-40-30.000N 070-37-09.400W				Red nun.	Private aid.
16604	- Buoy 22	41-40-29.600N 070-37-01.700W				Red nun.	Private aid.
16604.1	Hen Cove Channel Buoy 1	41-40-53.940N 070-37-24.660W				Green can.	Private aid.
16604.2	Hen Cove Channel Buoy 2	41-40-52.320N 070-37-22.560W				Red nun.	Private aid.
16604.3	Hen Cove Channel Buoy 4	41-40-57.500N 070-37-20.400W				Red nun.	Private aid.

BUZZARDS BAY

Pocasset Harbor Approach

16605	Bassetts Island Buoy 2	41-40-47.465N 070-38-41.424W				Red nun.	

Pocasset Harbor

16610	- Buoy 1	41-41-05.034N 070-38-14.011W				Green can.	
16615	- Buoy 2 Marks northern edge of rock.	41-41-04.132N 070-38-10.133W				Red nun.	
16620	- Buoy 3	41-41-05.451N 070-38-07.040W				Green can.	
16625	- Buoy 4	41-41-14.834N 070-38-07.124W				Red nun.	
16630	- Buoy 5	41-41-19.734N 070-37-59.123W				Green can.	
16635	- Buoy 7 Off flat.	41-41-17.740N 070-37-51.143W				Green can.	
16640	- Buoy 8	41-41-14.421N 070-37-50.114W				Red nun.	

(1) No.	(2) Name and Location	(3) Position	(4) Characteristic	(5) Height	(6) Range	(7) Structure	(8) Remarks
			MASSACHUSETTS - First District				
	BUZZARDS BAY						
	Pocasset Harbor						
16645	- Buoy 9 Rocks just eastward of buoy.	41-41-13.416N 070-37-48.123W				Green can.	
16646	Bassetts Island East Shoals Danger Buoy	41-41-11.940N 070-37-49.320W				White with orange bands.	Private aid.
	CAPE COD CANAL AND APPROACHES						
	Red Brook Harbor						
16647	- Buoy 11	41-41-06.450N 070-37-50.678W				Green can.	
16648	- Buoy 12	41-40-55.495N 070-37-51.068W				Red nun.	
16649	- Buoy 13	41-40-48.929N 070-37-40.052W				Green can.	
	BUZZARDS BAY						
	Phinneys Harbor						
16650	- Buoy 2	41-41-19.234N 070-39-23.716W				Red nun.	
16655	- Buoy 3	41-41-26.958N 070-39-17.432W				Green can.	
16660	- Buoy 5	41-41-56.538N 070-38-24.935W				Green can.	
16665	- Buoy 6	41-42-15.196N 070-37-50.201W				Red nun.	
16670	- LIGHT 7	41-42-16.155N 070-37-56.393W	Fl G 4s	26	5	SG on spindle.	
16670.5	Little Bay Channel Buoy 1	41-42-10.800N 070-37-16.080W				Green Can.	Private aid.
16671	Little Bay Channel Buoy 2	41-42-08.580N 070-37-15.540W				Red nun.	Private aid.
16672	Little Bay Channel Buoy 3	41-42-11.040N 070-37-13.380W				Green can.	Private aid.
16673	Little Bay Channel Buoy 4	41-42-10.800N 070-37-11.760W				Red nun.	Private aid.
16675	- Buoy 9	41-42-36.964N 070-37-52.343W				Green can.	
16680	- Buoy 10	41-42-56.714N 070-37-33.054W				Red nun.	
16685	- Buoy 12	41-42-59.629N 070-37-15.336W				Red nun.	
16690	- Buoy 11	41-43-04.054N 070-37-24.813W				Green can.	
16695	- Buoy 13	41-43-01.983N 070-37-15.050W				Green can.	
16700	- Buoy 14	41-43-17.484N 070-37-24.704W				Red nun.	
	Slocums River Entrance						
16705	Slocums Ledge Buoy 2 Off west side of ledge.	41-30-53.912N 070-58-05.147W				Red nun.	
	New Bedford Harbor **Southwest Approach**						
16711	Salters Point Ledge Buoy 1	41-31-30.044N 070-56-08.472W				Green can.	
16716	- Buoy 2	41-31-37.778N 070-55-23.046W				Red nun.	
16721	*The Sandspit Lighted Bell Buoy 4* On west point of shoal.	41-31-53.085N 070-54-58.658W	Fl R 4s		4	Red.	Replaced by nun when endangered by ice.
16726	Dumpling Rocks Gong Buoy 5	41-32-05.004N 070-55-12.913W				Green.	
16731 16040	DUMPLING ROCKS LIGHT 7 On rock.	41-32-17.834N 070-55-17.111W	Fl G 6s	52	8	SG on skeleton tower.	
16736	*- Lighted Bell Buoy 8*	41-32-20.058N 070-54-24.989W	Fl R 2.5s		3	Red.	

155

(1) No.	(2) Name and Location	(3) Position	(4) Characteristic	(5) Height	(6) Range	(7) Structure	(8) Remarks
			MASSACHUSETTS - First District				
	BUZZARDS BAY						
	New Bedford Harbor						
	Southwest Approach						
16738	Great Ledge Buoy 8A	41-32-25.687N 070-53-55.843W				Red nun.	
	Apponaganset Bay						
16741	- *Lighted Gong Buoy AB*	41-33-10.024N 070-54-42.068W	Fl (2+1)R 6s		4	Red and green bands.	
16742	Fatal Rock Buoy DF East of rock.	41-32-44.682N 070-55-34.063W				Black and red bands with two black spherical topmarks.	
16745	Hussey Rock Buoy 1 East of rock.	41-33-21.242N 070-55-17.473W				Green can.	
16747	Barekneed Rocks Daybeacon B	41-33-19.604N 070-55-54.604W				NB on spindle.	
16750	Keel Rock Buoy 3	41-33-24.912N 070-55-43.824W				Green can.	
16756	Lone Rock Buoy 4	41-33-38.142N 070-54-55.573W				Red nun.	
16760	Bents Ledge Buoy 6	41-34-03.742N 070-54-52.893W				Red nun.	
16765	PADANARAM BREAKWATER LIGHT 8	41-34-26.858N 070-56-21.381W	Fl R 4s	25	5	TR on spindle.	
16771	Dartmouth Rock Buoy 10	41-34-36.368N 070-56-33.273W				Red nun.	
16774	South Dartmouth Channel Buoy 12	41-34-50.841N 070-56-45.242W				Red nun.	
16775	- Buoy 13	41-35-03.000N 070-56-46.000W				Green can.	Private aid.
	Southwest Approach						
16780	- Buoy 10	41-33-43.013N 070-53-34.218W				Red nun.	
16791	- Buoy 12	41-34-26.040N 070-53-35.032W				Red nun.	
16793	*Vineyard Wind Feeder Barge Lighted Mooring Buoy*	41-34-57.000N 070-53-51.000W	Q Y			Yellow.	Private aid.
16796	Old Bartlemy Buoy 13	41-35-38.367N 070-53-43.816W				Green can.	
	MARTHA'S VINEYARD TO BLOCK ISLAND						
	New Bedford Harbor						
	New Bedford Channel						
16805	- *Lighted Buoy 1*	41-31-44.029N 070-50-46.003W	Q G		3	Green.	
16810	- *Lighted Buoy 2*	41-31-46.003N 070-50-32.031W	Q R		4	Red.	
16815	- Buoy 3	41-32-56.340N 070-51-47.976W				Green can.	
16817	*Phinney Rock Lighted Buoy DP*	41-33-06.177N 070-53-05.189W	Fl (2)W 5s		4	Black and red bands with two black spherical topmarks.	
16820	- *Lighted Buoy 4*	41-33-36.059N 070-51-41.970W	Fl R 4s		3	Red.	
16825	- *Lighted Buoy 5*	41-33-30.063N 070-51-54.068W	Fl G 4s		3	Green.	
16830	- *Lighted Buoy 6* On southwest side of rock.	41-34-12.964N 070-52-15.912W	Fl R 2.5s		3	Red.	
16835	- *Lighted Gong Buoy 7* East of rock.	41-34-09.302N 070-52-28.734W	Fl G 2.5s		3	Green.	
16845	- *Lighted Buoy 8*	41-35-13.065N 070-52-55.534W	Fl R 6s		3	Red.	
16851	- *Lighted Buoy 9*	41-35-11.842N 070-53-00.359W	Fl G 6s		3	Green.	
16855	- *Lighted Buoy 10*	41-36-16.723N 070-53-32.577W	Fl R 2.5s		3	Red.	

(1) No.	(2) Name and Location	(3) Position	(4) Characteristic	(5) Height	(6) Range	(7) Structure	(8) Remarks
			MASSACHUSETTS - First District				

MARTHA'S VINEYARD TO BLOCK ISLAND
New Bedford Harbor
New Bedford Channel

(1) No.	(2) Name and Location	(3) Position	(4) Characteristic	(5) Height	(6) Range	(7) Structure	(8) Remarks
16860	- Lighted Buoy 11	41-36-15.220N 070-53-36.500W	Fl G 2.5s		3	Green.	
16870	- Buoy 12	41-36-38.791N 070-53-47.041W				Red nun.	
16875	- Buoy 13	41-36-38.166N 070-53-51.923W				Green can.	
16880	- Lighted Buoy 14	41-36-57.418N 070-53-59.091W	Fl R 4s		3	Red.	
16885	- Lighted Buoy 15	41-36-58.229N 070-54-04.487W	Fl G 4s		3	Green.	
16890	- Buoy 16	41-37-21.408N 070-54-14.504W				Red nun.	
16895	- Buoy 17	41-37-20.120N 070-54-18.907W				Green can.	
16896	NEW BEDFORD EAST BARRIER LIGHT	41-37-28.934N 070-54-19.411W	Q R	33	8	On pile.	
16897	NEW BEDFORD WEST BARRIER LIGHT	41-37-27.234N 070-54-22.011W	Q G	48	8	On pile.	HORN: 1 blast ev 10s (1s bl). MRASS-Fog signal is radio activated, during times of reduced visibility, turn marine VHF-FM radio to channel 83A/157.175Mhz. Key microphone 5 times consecutively, to activate fog signal for 45 minutes.
16898	PALMERS ISLAND LIGHT	41-37-37.020N 070-54-32.910W	Fl W 4s			White conical tower on stone pier.	Private aid.

New Bedford Harbor Channel

(1) No.	(2) Name and Location	(3) Position	(4) Characteristic	(5) Height	(6) Range	(7) Structure	(8) Remarks
16910	- Lighted Buoy 2	41-37-40.180N 070-54-26.816W	Fl R 4s		3	Red.	
16915	- Lighted Buoy 3	41-37-47.700N 070-54-39.277W	Fl G 4s		3	Green.	
16917	SOUTH TERMINAL HURRICANE BARRIER FRONT RANGE	41-37-13.420N 070-54-46.650W	F W	19			Private aid.
16918	SOUTH TERMINAL HURRICANE BARRIER REAR RANGE	41-37-07.210N 070-54-45.250W	F W	19			Private aid.
16920	South Terminal Approach Buoy 1	41-37-44.410N 070-54-50.147W				Green can.	
16925	South Terminal Approach Buoy 2	41-37-44.535N 070-54-59.307W				Red nun.	
16926	New Bedford South Terminal Buoy 1	41-37-17.580N 070-54-46.020W				Green can.	Private aid.
16926.1	New Bedford South Terminal Buoy 2	41-37-16.405N 070-54-48.106W				Red nun.	Private aid.
16926.2	New Bedford South Terminal Buoy 3	41-37-15.960N 070-54-46.860W				Green can.	Private aid.
16926.3	New Bedford South Terminal Buoy 4	41-37-15.240N 070-54-48.900W				Red nun.	Private aid.
16926.4	New Bedford South Terminal Buoy 5	41-37-14.940N 070-54-48.300W				Green can.	Private aid.
16926.5	New Bedford South Terminal Buoy 6	41-37-14.203N 070-54-50.461W				Red nun.	Private aid.
16926.6	New Bedford South Terminal Buoy 7	41-37-13.188N 070-54-49.914W				Green can.	Private aid.
16926.7	New Bedford South Terminal Buoy 8	41-37-13.590N 070-54-51.624W				Red nun.	Private aid.
16930	- Buoy 4	41-37-54.390N 070-54-26.216W				Red nun.	
16935	- Lighted Buoy 6	41-38-05.109N 070-54-48.857W	Fl R 4s		3	Red.	
16940	Crow Island Buoy 1	41-38-11.016N 070-54-33.208W				Green can.	

(1) No.	(2) Name and Location	(3) Position	(4) Characteristic	(5) Height	(6) Range	(7) Structure	(8) Remarks
			MASSACHUSETTS - First District				
MARTHA'S VINEYARD TO BLOCK ISLAND							
New Bedford Harbor							
New Bedford Harbor Channel							
16945	- *Lighted Buoy 8*	41-38-14.579N 070-54-56.837W	Fl R 4s		3	Red.	
16950	Fish Island Flats Buoy 2	41-38-11.079N 070-55-06.947W				Red nun.	
16955	- *Lighted Buoy 9*	41-38-14.749N 070-55-02.748W	Fl G 2.5s		3	Green.	
New Bedford Southeast Approach							
16960	- Bell Buoy 2SE	41-34-04.135N 070-48-45.226W				Red.	Removed when endangered by ice.
16963	*Buzzards Bay Environmental Monitoring Lighted Buoy*	41-33-59.400N 070-49-32.500W	Fl Y 4s			Yellow.	Marked: ENVIRONMENTAL MONITORING MODULE. Maintained 01 May - 31 Oct. Private aid.
16965	- Buoy 4SE	41-34-00.615N 070-50-31.796W				Red nun.	
16970	- Buoy 5SE	41-34-07.034N 070-51-19.011W				Green can.	
16975	- Daybeacon 6SE	41-34-41.364N 070-51-44.805W				TR on spindle.	
16980	- Buoy 8SE	41-34-38.863N 070-52-11.579W				Red nun.	
Nasketucket Bay							
17026.1	*Brant Island Cove Channel Lighted Buoy 1*	41-36-39.780N 070-48-10.020W	Fl G 2s			Green.	Private aid.
17026.2	*Brant Island Cove Channel Lighted Buoy 2*	41-36-42.060N 070-48-07.620W	Fl R 2s			Red.	Private aid.
17026.3	*Brant Island Cove Channel Lighted Buoy 3*	41-37-00.300N 070-48-32.040W	Fl G 2s			Green.	Private aid.
17026.4	*Brant Island Cove Channel Lighted Buoy 4*	41-37-03.000N 070-48-27.780W	Fl R 2s			Red.	Private aid.
17026.5	Brant Island Cove Channel Buoy 5	41-37-09.480N 070-48-39.540W				Green can.	Private aid.
17026.6	Brant Island Cove Channel Buoy 6	41-37-11.580N 070-48-35.580W				Red nun.	Private aid.
17026.7	Brant Island Cove Channel Buoy 7	41-37-32.220N 070-48-54.360W				Green can.	Private aid.
17026.8	Brant Island Cove Channel Buoy 8	41-37-34.080N 070-48-53.220W				Red nun.	Private aid.
CAPE COD CANAL AND APPROACHES							
Nasketucket Bay							
Round Cove Aquaculture							
17030	*Nasketucket Bay Aquaculture Lighted Buoy NW*	41-36-35.820N 070-50-37.560W	Fl Y 4s			Yellow.	Seasonal May-Sep. Private aid.
17035	*Nasketucket Bay Aquaculture Lighted Buoy NE*	41-36-50.100N 070-50-26.040W	Fl Y 4s			Yellow.	Seasonal May-Sep. Private aid.
17040	*Nasketucket Bay Aquaculture Lighted Buoy SE*	41-36-42.900N 070-50-13.380W	Fl Y 4s			Yellow.	Seasonal May-Sep. Private aid.
17045	*Nasketucket Bay Aquaculture Lighted Buoy SW*	41-36-27.540N 070-50-25.320W	Fl Y 4s			Yellow.	Seasonal May-Sep. Private aid.
17045.5	*Blue Stream Shellfish North Lighted Buoy*	41-36-44.640N 070-48-25.920W	Fl Y 2.5s			Yellow.	Private aid.
17045.6	*Blue Stream Shellfish East Lighted Buoy*	41-36-30.960N 070-48-16.920W	Fl Y 2.5s			Yellow.	Private aid.
17045.7	*Blue Stream Shellfish South Lighted Buoy*	41-36-25.920N 070-48-34.920W	Fl Y 2.5s			Yellow.	Private aid.
17045.8	*Blue Stream Shellfish West Lighted Buoy*	41-36-39.240N 070-48-43.920W	Fl Y 2.5s			Yellow.	Private aid.
West Island Channel *Aids maintained from May 1 to Nov. 30.*							
17046	- Buoy 1	41-36-17.640N 070-50-31.750W				Green can.	Private aid.
17046.1	- Buoy 2	41-36-19.570N 070-50-30.120W				Red nun.	Private aid.

(1) No.	(2) Name and Location	(3) Position	(4) Characteristic	(5) Height	(6) Range	(7) Structure	(8) Remarks
			MASSACHUSETTS - First District				

CAPE COD CANAL AND APPROACHES

West Island Channel
Aids maintained from May 1 to Nov. 30.

17046.2	- Buoy 3	41-36-17.600N 070-50-32.000W				Green can.	Private aid.
17046.3	- Buoy 4	41-36-18.300N 070-50-32.100W				Red nun.	Private aid.
17046.4	- Buoy 5	41-36-16.500N 070-50-33.600W				Green can.	Private aid.
17046.5	- Buoy 6	41-36-17.000N 070-50-34.300W				Red nun.	Private aid.
17046.6	- Buoy 7	41-36-15.600N 070-50-34.800W				Green can.	Private aid.
17046.7	- Buoy 8	41-36-15.000N 070-50-36.600W				Red nun.	Private aid.
17046.8	- Buoy 9	41-36-14.910N 070-50-35.430W				Green can.	Private aid.
17046.9	- Buoy 10	41-36-14.170N 070-50-37.960W				Red nun.	Private aid.
17047	- Buoy 11	41-36-12.270N 070-50-38.940W				Green can.	Private aid.
17047.1	- Buoy 12	41-36-13.370N 070-50-39.110W				Red nun.	Private aid.
17047.2	- Buoy 13	41-36-11.100N 070-50-39.270W				Green can.	Private aid.
17047.3	- Buoy 14	41-36-11.480N 070-50-40.030W				Red nun.	Private aid.
17047.4	- Buoy 15	41-36-09.860N 070-50-38.500W				Green can.	Private aid.
17047.5	- Buoy 16	41-36-09.810N 070-50-39.600W				Red nun.	Private aid.

Mattapoisett Harbor

17050	Cormorant Rock Daybeacon	41-36-17.026N 070-47-30.428W				NG on spindle.	
17055	*NYE Ledge Lighted Bell Buoy 1*	41-37-02.932N 070-46-10.278W	Fl G 4s		4	Green	Replaced by can when endangered by ice.
17065	- Approach Buoy 3	41-37-35.094N 070-46-48.194W				Green Can.	
17070	ANGELICA POINT LIGHT 2 On outer rock.	41-38-20.517N 070-45-45.996W	Fl R 2.5s	24	3	TR on spindle.	
17075	- Approach Buoy 5	41-37-58.283N 070-47-11.894W				Green can.	
17080	- Approach Buoy 6	41-38-15.468N 070-47-30.917W				Red nun.	
17085	- Approach Buoy 7	41-38-10.562N 070-47-42.715W				Green can.	
17086	- *Lighted Buoy 8*	41-38-45.960N 070-48-00.600W	Fl R 4s			Red.	Seasonal 01 Apr - 15 Nov. Private aid.
17087	- *Lighted Buoy 9*	41-38-42.810N 070-48-02.940W	Fl G 4s			Green.	Seasonal 01 Apr - 15 Nov. Private aid.
17088	- Buoy 10	41-38-58.140N 070-48-16.620W				Red nun.	Seasonal 01 Apr - 15 Nov. Private aid.
17089	- Buoy 11	41-38-57.780N 070-48-20.880W				Green can.	Seasonal 01 Apr - 15 Nov. Private aid.
17090	- Buoy 12	41-39-11.480N 070-48-31.670W				Red nun.	Seasonal 01 Apr - 15 Nov. Private aid.
17091	- Buoy 13	41-39-10.560N 070-48-33.540W				Green can.	Seasonal 01 Apr - 15 Nov. Private aid.
17095	**Ned Point Light**	41-39-03.167N 070-47-44.347W	Iso W 6s	41	12	White tower. 39	
17096	Mattapoisett Town Landing Buoy 1	41-38-53.640N 070-48-51.990W				Green can.	Seasonal 01 Apr - 15 Nov. Private aid.
17097	Mattapoisett Town Landing Buoy 2	41-38-56.270N 070-48-48.900W				Red nun.	Seasonal 01 Apr - 15 Nov. Private aid.

(1) No.	(2) Name and Location	(3) Position	(4) Characteristic	(5) Height	(6) Range	(7) Structure	(8) Remarks
			MASSACHUSETTS - First District				

CAPE COD CANAL AND APPROACHES

Mattapoisett Harbor

(1) No.	(2) Name and Location	(3) Position	(4) Characteristic	(5) Height	(6) Range	(7) Structure	(8) Remarks
17098	Mattapoisett Town Landing Buoy 3	41-39-04.440N 070-48-59.640W				Green can.	Seasonal 01 Apr - 15 Nov. Private aid.
17099	Mattapoisett Town Landing Buoy 4	41-39-08.220N 070-49-02.520W				Red nun.	Seasonal 01 Apr - 15 Nov. Private aid.

Sippican Harbor

(1) No.	(2) Name and Location	(3) Position	(4) Characteristic	(5) Height	(6) Range	(7) Structure	(8) Remarks
17105	BIRD ISLAND LIGHT	41-40-10.020N 070-43-02.400W	Fl W 6s			White tower.	Private aid.
17115	- *Lighted Buoy 2* Off southwest side of shoal.	41-39-44.004N 070-43-34.081W	Fl R 4s		4	Red.	Replaced by nun when endangered by ice.
17130	- *Lighted Buoy 3* East of rock.	41-40-29.042N 070-44-22.173W	Fl G 2.5s		4	Green.	Replaced by can when endangered by ice.
17135	- Buoy 5	41-40-49.801N 070-44-23.703W				Green can.	
17140	- Buoy 6	41-41-36.590N 070-45-00.135W				Red nun.	
17145	- Buoy 7	41-41-47.619N 070-45-10.906W				Green can.	
17150	- *Lighted Buoy 8*	41-41-54.352N 070-45-13.134W	Fl R 4s		4	Red.	Replaced by nun from Oct. 15 to May 1.
17155	- Buoy 9	41-42-00.854N 070-45-14.170W				Green can.	
17156	- *Lighted Buoy 10*	41-42-04.300N 070-45-13.320W	Fl R 4s			Red.	Private aid.

Sippican Harbor Upper Channel
Aids maintained from Apr. 15 to Oct. 15.

(1) No.	(2) Name and Location	(3) Position	(4) Characteristic	(5) Height	(6) Range	(7) Structure	(8) Remarks
17169	- *Lighted Buoy 11*	41-42-11.460N 070-45-22.380W	Fl G 4s			Green.	Private aid.
17170	- Lighted Buoy 13	41-42-21.420N 070-45-29.520W	Fl G 4s			Green.	Private aid.
17174	- Mid-Channel Lighted Buoy	41-42-18.060N 070-45-27.600W	Fl W 4s			Red and white.	Private aid.
17180	- Lighted Buoy 15	41-42-26.000N 070-45-34.000W	Fl G 4s			Green can.	Private aid.
17185	- Lighted Buoy 17	41-42-29.000N 070-45-37.000W	Fl G 4s			Green can.	Private aid.
17195	- Lighted Buoy 19	41-42-37.000N 070-45-47.000W	Fl G 4s			Green can.	Private aid.
17200	- Lighted Buoy 21	41-42-39.000N 070-45-49.000W	Fl G 4s			Green can.	Private aid.

Burr Brothers Boatyard Channel

(1) No.	(2) Name and Location	(3) Position	(4) Characteristic	(5) Height	(6) Range	(7) Structure	(8) Remarks
17201	- Buoy 1	41-42-38.300N 070-45-48.100W				Green can.	Private aid.
17201.05	- Buoy 2	41-42-48.000N 070-45-54.000W				Red nun.	Private aid.
17202	- Buoy 3	41-42-43.400N 070-45-53.300W				Green can.	Private aid.
17202.4	- Buoy 4	41-42-45.100N 070-45-54.300W				Red nun.	Private aid.
17202.6	- Buoy 6	41-42-47.200N 070-45-55.000W				Red nun.	Private aid.
17202.8	- Buoy 8	41-42-49.200N 070-45-54.700W				Red nun.	Private aid.

Sippican Harbor

(1) No.	(2) Name and Location	(3) Position	(4) Characteristic	(5) Height	(6) Range	(7) Structure	(8) Remarks
17205	Hammet Cove Buoy 2	41-42-38.760N 070-45-30.120W				Red nun.	Maintained from Apr. 15 to Oct. 15. Private aid.
17210	Hammet Cove Buoy 4	41-42-39.900N 070-45-27.780W				Red nun.	Maintained from Apr. 15 to Oct. 15. Private aid.

Wareham River

(1) No.	(2) Name and Location	(3) Position	(4) Characteristic	(5) Height	(6) Range	(7) Structure	(8) Remarks
17215	Dry Ledge Buoy 2	41-42-05.172N 070-41-37.730W				Red nun.	

(1) No.	(2) Name and Location	(3) Position	(4) Characteristic	(5) Height	(6) Range	(7) Structure	(8) Remarks

MASSACHUSETTS - First District

CAPE COD CANAL AND APPROACHES

Wareham River

17220	- Entrance Buoy 4	41-42-54.939N 070-42-58.900W				Red nun.	
17225	- Entrance Buoy 6	41-43-14.947N 070-43-06.677W				Red nun.	
17230	- Entrance Buoy 7	41-43-18.593N 070-43-07.609W				Green can.	
17235	- Entrance Buoy 9	41-43-29.359N 070-43-04.849W				Green can.	
17240	- Entrance Buoy 10	41-43-44.868N 070-43-04.659W				Red nun.	
17247	- Buoy 12	41-43-56.510N 070-42-59.298W				Red nun.	
17250	- Buoy 13 At upper part of flats	41-44-06.977N 070-42-43.032W				green can.	
17255	- Buoy 15	41-44-15.201N 070-42-36.114W				Green can.	
17260	- Buoy 16	41-44-22.967N 070-42-31.283W				Red nun.	
17265	- Buoy 17	41-44-32.337N 070-42-27.453W				Green can.	
17270	- Buoy 19	41-44-39.668N 070-42-26.554W				Green can.	
17275	- Buoy 20	41-44-47.098N 070-42-23.139W				Red nun.	
17280	- Buoy 22	41-44-57.858N 070-42-15.264W				Red nun.	Removed when endangered by ice.
17290	- Buoy 26	41-45-07.476N 070-42-18.074W				Red nun.	
17295	- Buoy 28	41-45-12.508N 070-42-30.565W				Red nun.	

Weweantic River
Private aids maintained from May to Nov. 1, unless otherwise noted.

17296	- Buoy 1	41-43-18.900N 070-43-26.280W				Green can.	Private aid.
17296.2	- Buoy 3	41-43-35.520N 070-43-43.620W				Green can.	Private aid.
17296.3	- Buoy 4	41-43-37.200N 070-43-47.760W				Red nun.	Private aid.
17296.4	- Buoy 5	41-43-36.660N 070-43-50.220W				Green can.	Private aid.
17296.5	- Buoy 6	41-43-37.080N 070-43-55.980W				Red nun.	Private aid.
17296.8	- Buoy 7	41-43-48.180N 070-44-10.290W				Green can.	Private aid.
17297	- Buoy 9	41-43-52.950N 070-44-15.920W				Green can.	Private aid.
17297.2	- Buoy 11	41-43-50.700N 070-44-27.830W				Green can.	Private aid.
17297.4	- Buoy 14	41-43-50.100N 070-44-36.660W				Red nun.	Private aid.
17297.5	- Buoy 15	41-43-56.580N 070-44-43.140W				Green can.	Private aid.
17297.8	- Buoy 16	41-44-01.290N 070-44-43.970W				Red nun.	Private aid.

Onset Bay

17300	- Channel Buoy 1	41-43-25.722N 070-38-27.152W				Green can.	
17302	- Channel Buoy 2	41-43-29.917N 070-38-28.690W				Red nun.	
17305	- Channel Buoy 3	41-43-33.732N 070-38-34.196W				Green can.	
17310	- Channel Buoy 4	41-43-33.942N 070-38-32.771W				Red nun.	

(1) No.	(2) Name and Location	(3) Position	(4) Characteristic	(5) Height	(6) Range	(7) Structure	(8) Remarks
			MASSACHUSETTS - First District				

CAPE COD CANAL AND APPROACHES

Onset Bay

(1) No.	(2) Name and Location	(3) Position	(7) Structure	(8) Remarks
17315	- Channel Buoy 5	41-43-44.741N 070-38-34.090W	Green can.	
17320	- Channel Buoy 6	41-43-47.004N 070-38-32.780W	Red nun.	
17325	- Channel Buoy 7	41-43-47.929N 070-38-36.237W	Green can.	
17330	- Channel Buoy 8	41-43-50.986N 070-38-39.429W	Red nun.	
17335	- Channel Buoy 9	41-43-54.694N 070-38-50.024W	Green can.	
17340	- Channel Buoy 10	41-43-55.730N 070-38-48.979W	Red nun.	
17345	- Channel Buoy 11	41-44-00.381N 070-39-00.706W	Green can.	
17350	- Channel Buoy 12	41-44-05.707N 070-39-13.987W	Red nun.	
17355	- Channel Buoy 13	41-44-04.552N 070-39-15.440W	Green can.	
17360	- Channel Buoy 14	41-44-13.751N 070-39-19.019W	Red nun.	
17365	- Channel Buoy 15	41-44-13.534N 070-39-21.006W	Green can.	
17370	- Channel Buoy 16	41-44-21.666N 070-39-23.827W	Red nun.	
17375	Sunset Cove Approach Buoy 1	41-44-19.500N 070-39-40.560W	Green can.	Maintained from June 1 to Oct. 1. Private aid.
17380	Sunset Cove Approach Buoy 2	41-44-25.380N 070-39-35.040W	Red nun.	Maintained from June 1 to Oct. 1. Private aid.
17380.1	Shell Point Channel Buoy 4	41-44-15.780N 070-39-43.500W	Red nun.	Maintained May 1 to Nov 1. Private aid.
17380.2	Shell Point Channel Buoy 6	41-44-10.680N 070-39-45.000W	Red nun.	Maintained May 1 to Nov 1. Private aid.
17380.3	Shell Point Channel Buoy 8	41-44-07.440N 070-39-47.640W	Red nun.	Maintained May 1 to Nov 1. Private aid.
17380.4	Shell Point Channel Buoy 10	41-44-06.660N 070-39-51.120W	Red nun.	Maintained May 1 to Nov 1. Private aid.
17380.5	Shell Point Channel Buoy 12	41-44-09.600N 070-39-55.800W	Red nun.	Maintained May 1 to Nov 1. Private aid.
17380.6	Shell Point Channel Buoy 13	41-44-15.960N 070-39-55.080W	Green can.	Maintained May 1 to Nov 1. Private aid.
17380.7	Shell Point Channel Buoy 14	41-44-12.720N 070-39-55.860W	Red nun.	Maintained May 1 to Nov 1. Private aid.
17381	Point Independence Yacht Club Buoy 1	41-44-11.160N 070-39-02.520W	Green can.	Maintained from 1 June to Oct 1. Private aid.
17382	Point Independence Yacht Club Buoy 2	41-44-11.340N 070-39-01.320W	Red nun.	Maintained from 1 June to Oct 1. Private aid.
17383.1	- Marina Buoy 1	41-44-09.480N 070-38-56.220W	Green can.	Maintained 1 June to Oct 1. Private aid.
17383.2	- Marina Buoy 2	41-44-09.180N 070-38-54.840W	Red nun.	Maintained 1 June to Oct 1. Private aid.
17384	East River Channel Buoy 2	41-44-23.178N 070-39-20.940W	Red Nun.	Maintained May 1 to Nov 1. Private aid.
17384.1	East River Channel Buoy 3	41-44-25.578N 070-39-18.570W	Green can.	Maintained May 1 to Nov 1. Private aid.
17384.2	East River Channel Buoy 4	41-44-25.536N 070-39-17.784W	Red nun.	Maintained May 1 to Nov 1. Private aid.
17384.3	East River Channel Buoy 5	41-44-28.872N 070-39-14.502W	Green can.	Maintained May 1 to Nov 1. Private aid.

(1) No.	(2) Name and Location	(3) Position	(4) Characteristic	(5) Height	(6) Range	(7) Structure	(8) Remarks
			MASSACHUSETTS - First District				
	CAPE COD CANAL AND APPROACHES						
	Onset Bay						
17384.4	East River Channel Buoy 6	41-44-29.634N 070-39-13.542W				Red nun.	Maintained May 1 to Nov 1. Private aid.
17384.5	East River Channel Buoy 7	41-44-31.104N 070-39-13.518W				Green can.	Maintained May 1 to Nov 1. Private aid.
	MARTHA'S VINEYARD TO BLOCK ISLAND						
	Buttermilk Bay Approach						
17385	- Buoy 1	41-44-01.634N 070-37-57.969W				Green can.	
17390	- Buoy 3	41-44-07.935N 070-38-04.036W				Green can.	
17395	- Buoy 4	41-44-12.311N 070-38-02.043W				Red nun.	
17405	- Buoy 5	41-44-16.807N 070-37-58.587W				Green can.	
17410	- Buoy 7	41-44-19.833N 070-37-54.022W				Green can.	
17415	- Daybeacon 9 On rocky foundation close to edge of channel	41-44-34.123N 070-37-42.798W				SG on spindle.	
	Buttermilk Bay						
17421	- Buoy 2	41-45-05.051N 070-37-27.502W				Red nun.	Private aid.
17421.2	- Buoy 2A	41-45-08.760N 070-37-29.700W				Red nun.	Private aid.
17421.4	- Buoy 4	41-45-17.940N 070-37-21.420W				Red nun.	Private aid.
17421.5	- Buoy 5	41-45-21.480N 070-37-17.880W				Green can.	Private aid.
	CAPE COD CANAL AND APPROACHES						
	Buttermilk Bay Approach						
	Little Buttermilk Bay						
17422.2	- Buoy 2	41-45-45.600N 070-36-48.060W				Red nun.	Private aid.
17422.3	- Buoy 3	41-45-51.420N 070-36-44.340W				Green can.	Private aid.
17422.4	- Buoy 4	41-45-57.240N 070-36-37.920W				Red nun.	Private aid.
	BUZZARDS BAY						
	Westport Harbor Approach						
17425	Gooseberry Neck Buoy 2	41-28-42.856N 071-01-33.423W				Red nun.	
17430	Gooseberry Rock Buoy 4	41-28-35.178N 071-02-07.338W				Red nun.	
17435	Lumber Rock Buoy 6	41-28-23.412N 071-02-52.005W				Red nun.	
17445	- *Lighted Bell Buoy 1*	41-29-15.360N 071-04-04.377W	Fl G 2.5s		4	Green.	
17450	Two Mile Rock Daybeacon 3 On northwest side of rock.	41-29-32.177N 071-04-34.126W				SG on spindle.	
17455	Westport Buoy 4	41-29-56.288N 071-04-23.284W				Red nun.	
17460	Dogfish Ledge Buoy 5	41-30-10.619N 071-04-58.363W				Green can.	
17462	Halfmile Rock Buoy 5A	41-30-20.125N 071-05-01.211W				Green can.	
17463	Halfmile Rock Buoy 5B	41-30-25.021N 071-05-05.045W				Green can.	
17465	Halfmile Rock Buoy 6	41-30-15.149N 071-04-53.181W				Red nun.	
	MARTHA'S VINEYARD TO BLOCK ISLAND						
	Westport Harbor						
17470	- ENTRANCE LIGHT 7	41-30-26.808N 071-05-16.962W	Fl G 6s	35	9	SG on skeleton tower.	

(1) No.	(2) Name and Location	(3) Position	(4) Characteristic	(5) Height	(6) Range	(7) Structure	(8) Remarks

MARTHA'S VINEYARD TO BLOCK ISLAND

Westport Harbor

(1) No.	(2) Name and Location	(3) Position	(4) Characteristic	(5) Height	(6) Range	(7) Structure	(8) Remarks
17475	- Channel Buoy 8	41-30-27.995N 071-05-03.299W				Red nun.	
17480	- Channel Buoy 10	41-30-29.507N 071-05-18.918W				Red nun.	
17485	- *Channel Lighted Buoy 12*	41-30-32.313N 071-05-33.354W	Q R		3	Red.	Removed when endangered by ice.
17490	- *Channel Lighted Buoy 14*	41-30-35.951N 071-05-36.476W	Fl R 2.5s		3	Red.	Replaced by nun when endangered by ice.
17495	- Channel Buoy 15	41-30-35.889N 071-05-39.537W				Green can.	Removed when endangered by ice.
17500	- Channel Buoy 16	41-30-39.075N 071-05-37.451W				Red nun.	Removed when endangered by ice.
17505	- Channel Buoy 17	41-30-39.956N 071-05-38.818W				Green can.	Maintained from 31 March to 01 December.
17507	- Channel Buoy 18	41-30-42.343N 071-05-37.094W				Red nun.	Removed when endangered by ice.
17510	- Channel Buoy 19	41-30-44.863N 071-05-39.076W				Green can.	Maintained from 31 March to 01 December.
17515	- Channel Buoy 20	41-30-51.708N 071-05-35.543W				Red nun.	Maintained from 31 March to 01 December.
17517	- Channel Buoy 21	41-30-53.874N 071-05-35.656W				Green can.	Removed when endangered by ice.
17520	- Channel Buoy 23	41-30-58.702N 071-05-27.798W				Green can.	Maintained from 31 March to 01 December.
17522	- Channel Buoy 24	41-31-00.578N 071-05-20.383W				Red nun.	Removed when endangered by ice.
17525	- Channel Buoy 26	41-31-01.378N 071-05-06.992W				Red nun.	Removed when endangered by ice.
17527	- Channel Daybeacon 27	41-31-01.248N 071-04-53.151W				SG on pile.	
17530	- Channel Buoy 29	41-30-54.258N 071-04-34.281W				Green can.	Removed when endangered by ice.
17535	- Channel Buoy 31	41-30-53.772N 071-04-22.012W				Green can.	Removed when endangered by ice.
17540	- Channel Buoy 32	41-30-52.905N 071-04-15.761W				Red nun.	Removed when endangered by ice.
17545	- Channel Buoy 34	41-30-54.209N 071-04-12.360W				Red nun.	Removed when endangered by ice.
17546	- Boat Ramp Entrance Buoy 2	41-30-54.700N 071-04-05.500W				Red nun.	Private aid.
17547	- Boat Ramp Entrance Buoy 3	41-30-55.100N 071-04-05.000W				Green can.	Private aid.
17548	- Boat Ramp Entrance Buoy 4	41-30-58.400N 071-04-07.700W				Red nun.	Private aid.

Westport River West Branch
Positions of buoys are frequently shifted with changing conditions. Use only with local knowledge.

(1) No.	(2) Name and Location	(3) Position	(4) Characteristic	(5) Height	(6) Range	(7) Structure	(8) Remarks
17550	- Channel Buoy 1	41-30-57.780N 071-05-34.080W				Green can.	Private aid.
17550.1	- Channel Buoy 2	41-30-57.600N 071-05-34.800W				Red nun.	Private aid.
17550.2	- Channel Buoy 3	41-30-59.700N 071-05-37.500W				Green can.	Private aid.

(1) No.	(2) Name and Location	(3) Position	(4) Characteristic	(5) Height	(6) Range	(7) Structure	(8) Remarks

MARTHA'S VINEYARD TO BLOCK ISLAND

Westport River West Branch
Positions of buoys are frequently shifted with changing conditions. Use only with local knowledge.

(1) No.	(2) Name and Location	(3) Position	(4) Characteristic	(5) Height	(6) Range	(7) Structure	(8) Remarks
17550.3	- Channel Buoy 4	41-31-01.900N 071-05-36.900W				Red nun.	Private aid.
17550.5	- Channel Buoy 6	41-31-06.800N 071-05-35.800W				Red nun.	Private aid.
17550.6	- Channel Buoy 7	41-31-17.600N 071-05-38.600W				Green can.	Private aid.
17550.7	- Channel Buoy 8	41-31-20.400N 071-05-36.200W				Red nun.	Private aid.
17550.8	- Channel Buoy 9	41-31-27.800N 071-05-43.600W				Green can.	Private aid.
17551	- Channel Buoy 11	41-31-36.300N 071-05-51.100W				Green can.	Private aid.
17551.1	- Channel Buoy 12	41-31-45.600N 071-06-02.200W				Red nun.	Private aid.

Westport River
Positions of buoys are frequently shifted with changing conditions. Use only with local knowledge.

(1) No.	(2) Name and Location	(3) Position	(4) Characteristic	(5) Height	(6) Range	(7) Structure	(8) Remarks
17551.18	- Channel Buoy 34A	41-31-10.500N 071-03-57.100W				Red nun.	Private aid.
17551.2	- Channel Buoy 34B	41-31-25.560N 071-03-49.140W				Red nun.	Private aid.
17551.3	- Channel Buoy 35	41-31-33.400N 071-03-43.500W				Green can.	Private aid.
17551.4	- Channel Buoy 36	41-31-40.020N 071-03-40.920W				Red nun.	Private aid.
17551.5	- Channel Buoy 38	41-31-51.000N 071-03-47.900W				Red nun.	Private aid.
17551.6	- Channel Buoy 39	41-31-56.580N 071-03-46.020W				Green can.	Private aid.
17551.7	- Channel Buoy 40	41-32-01.300N 071-03-37.700W				Red nun.	Private aid.
17551.9	- Channel Buoy 42	41-32-12.720N 071-03-27.000W				Red nun.	Private aid.
17552.1	- Channel Buoy 44	41-32-12.200N 071-03-25.600W				Red nun.	Private aid.
17552.2	- Channel Buoy 45	41-32-18.540N 071-03-32.760W				Green can.	Private aid.
17552.3	- Channel Buoy 46	41-32-25.300N 071-03-35.300W				Red nun.	Private aid.
17552.5	- Channel Buoy 48	41-32-35.040N 071-03-36.300W				Red nun.	Private aid.
17552.6	- Channel Buoy 49	41-32-43.800N 071-03-32.100W				Green can.	Private aid.
17552.7	- Channel Buoy 50	41-32-44.600N 071-03-28.700W				Red nun.	Private aid.
17552.9	- Channel Buoy 52	41-32-44.700N 071-03-24.900W				Red nun.	Private aid.
17553	- Channel Buoy 53	41-32-45.500N 071-03-17.800W				Green can.	Private aid.
17553.1	- Channel Buoy 54	41-32-37.600N 071-03-13.000W				Red nun.	Private aid.
17553.2	- Channel Buoy 55	41-32-38.400N 071-03-09.240W				Green can.	Private aid.
17553.3	- Channel Buoy 56	41-32-45.060N 071-03-06.780W				Red nun.	Private aid.
17553.4	- Channel Buoy 58	41-32-52.320N 071-03-07.860W				Red nun.	Private aid.
17553.5	- Channel Buoy 59	41-32-59.500N 071-03-11.800W				Green can.	Private aid.
17553.6	- Channel Buoy 61	41-33-08.280N 071-03-15.480W				Green can.	Private aid.
17553.65	- Channel Buoy 62	41-33-17.200N 071-03-25.500W				Red nun.	Private aid.

(1) No.	(2) Name and Location	(3) Position	(4) Characteristic	(5) Height	(6) Range	(7) Structure	(8) Remarks

MASSACHUSETTS - First District

MARTHA'S VINEYARD TO BLOCK ISLAND

Westport River

Positions of buoys are frequently shifted with changing conditions. Use only with local knowledge.

(1) No.	(2) Name and Location	(3) Position	(4) Characteristic	(5) Height	(6) Range	(7) Structure	(8) Remarks
17553.7	- Channel Buoy 64	41-33-16.600N 071-03-32.100W				Red nun.	Private aid.
17553.8	- Channel Buoy 65	41-33-15.400N 071-03-38.800W				Green can.	Private aid.
17553.9	- Channel Buoy 67	41-33-17.200N 071-03-47.000W				Green can.	Private aid.
17554	- Channel Buoy 69	41-33-20.200N 071-03-54.400W				Green can.	Private aid.
17554.1	- Channel Buoy 71	41-33-26.600N 071-04-01.400W				Green can.	Private aid.
17554.2	- Channel Buoy 73	41-33-33.500N 071-04-16.800W				Green can.	Private aid.
17554.3	- Channel Buoy 75	41-33-38.100N 071-04-18.300W				Green can.	Private aid.
17554.4	- Channel Buoy 77	41-33-42.840N 071-04-24.840W				Green can.	Private aid.
17554.5	- Channel Buoy 78	41-33-52.400N 071-04-22.400W				Red nun.	Private aid.
17554.6	- Channel Buoy 80	41-34-00.600N 071-04-20.940W				Red nun.	Private aid.

RHODE ISLAND - First District

NARRAGANSETT BAY

Sakonnet River

(1) No.	(2) Name and Location	(3) Position	(4) Characteristic	(5) Height	(6) Range	(7) Structure	(8) Remarks
17555	Elisha Ledge Buoy EL On small rocky ledge.	41-26-40.259N 071-09-27.825W				Green and red bands; can.	
17560	Schuyler Ledge Bell Buoy 2	41-26-24.369N 071-11-35.333W				Red.	
17577	SAKONNET LIGHT	41-27-11.264N 071-12-08.781W	Fl W 6s	70	W 7 R 5	White conical tower on granite base. b	Red from 195° to 350°.
17580	Cormorant Reef Bell Buoy 1 South of reef.	41-27-16.006N 071-14-41.592W				Green.	
17585	- Bell Buoy 2A	41-27-43.927N 071-12-54.588W				Red.	
17590	SAKONNET BREAKWATER LIGHT 2	41-28-00.306N 071-11-43.182W	Fl R 4s	29	6	TR on skeleton tower on concrete base.	
17595	- Buoy 3	41-29-13.205N 071-13-44.182W				Green can.	
17600	- Buoy 4	41-29-32.405N 071-12-42.180W				Red nun.	
17605	- Buoy 5	41-32-39.204N 071-13-31.592W				Green can.	
17610	- Buoy 6	41-33-10.513N 071-13-40.892W				Red nun.	
17615	- Buoy 7	41-34-39.323N 071-13-20.271W				Green can.	
17620	- Buoy 8	41-34-33.569N 071-13-10.071W				Red nun.	
17625	- Buoy 10	41-35-24.403N 071-13-06.181W				Red nun.	
17630	- Buoy 11	41-35-55.983N 071-13-11.081W				Green can.	
17635	- Buoy 12	41-36-11.423N 071-12-59.181W				Red nun.	
17640	- Buoy 13	41-36-46.391N 071-13-05.110W				Green can.	
17643	Gould Island Hazard Buoy On east side of rock.	41-36-56.471N 071-13-18.248W				White and orange with diamond marked DANGER ROCKS, can.	
17645	- Buoy 15 Marks western end of remains of stone bridge.	41-37-31.307N 071-13-02.639W				Green can.	

(1) No.	(2) Name and Location	(3) Position	(4) Characteristic	(5) Height	(6) Range	(7) Structure	(8) Remarks
			RHODE ISLAND - First District				
	NARRAGANSETT BAY						
	Sakonnet River						
17650	- Buoy 16 Marks eastern end of remains of stone bridge.	41-37-31.003N 071-12-59.853W				Red nun.	
17655	- Buoy 17	41-38-50.612N 071-12-51.260W				Green can.	
17660	- Buoy 19	41-39-23.812N 071-13-01.121W				Green can.	
	Narragansett Bay						
	Eastern Approach						
17675	*Narragansett Bay Entrance Lighted Whistle Buoy NB*	41-23-00.034N 071-23-21.482W	Mo (A) W		6	Red and white stripes with red spherical topmark.	RACON: B (- . . .) AIS: MMSI 993672153 (21)
17680	Seal Ledge Bell Buoy 2A South of Seal Rock.	41-26-01.732N 071-20-48.247W				Red.	
17685	*Brenton Point Lighted Whistle Buoy 2* Southwest of shoal.	41-25-56.664N 071-21-46.739W	Q R		3	Red.	
	East Passage						
17775	- Gong Buoy 4 Marks edge of reef.	41-26-34.724N 071-21-49.290W				Red.	
17780	**Beavertail Light**	41-26-57.750N 071-23-57.897W	Fl W 10s	64	15	Square granite tower, attached to white dwelling. 70	Obscured from 175° to 215°. Lighted throughout 24 hours. HORN: 1 blast ev 30s (3s bl). MRASS-Fog signal is radio activated, during times of reduced visibility, turn marine VHF-FM radio to channel 83A/157.175Mhz. Key microphone 5 times consecutively, to activate fog signal for 45 minutes.
17790	- Bell Buoy 6	41-27-27.149N 071-21-58.989W				Red.	
17795	CASTLE HILL LIGHT	41-27-43.834N 071-21-46.512W	Iso R 6s	40	9	Conical granite tower, upper half white.	HORN: 1 blast ev 10s (1s bl). MRASS Fog signal is radio activated, during times of reduced visibility, turn marine VHF-FM radio to channel 83A/157.175Mhz. Key microphone 5 times consecutively, to activate fog signal for 45 minutes.
17800	- *Lighted Gong Buoy 7*	41-28-18.402N 071-22-14.903W	Fl G 4s		4	Green.	
17805	- *Lighted Gong Buoy 9*	41-28-38.403N 071-21-14.204W	Fl G 2.5s		4	Green.	
17810	- *Lighted Bell Buoy 11*	41-29-00.402N 071-21-02.700W	Q G		4	Green.	
17815	FORT ADAMS LIGHT 2	41-28-54.302N 071-20-12.397W	Fl R 6s	32	7	TR on white skeleton tower.	HORN: 1 blast ev 15s (2s bl). MRASS-Fog signal is radio activated, during times of reduced visibility, turn marine VHF-FM radio to channel 83A/157.175Mhz. Key microphone 5 times consecutively, to activate fog signal for 45 minutes.
	Newport Harbor						
17820	- Buoy 4	41-28-52.003N 071-20-05.538W				Red nun.	
17825	Goat Island Southwest Buoy 1	41-28-56.903N 071-19-45.877W				Green can.	
17830	*Goat Island Lighted Bell Buoy 3*	41-28-54.133N 071-19-36.746W	Fl G 2.5s		3	Green.	
17840	Little Ida Lewis Rock Daybeacon 6	41-28-47.473N 071-19-10.865W				TR on spindle.	

(1) No.	(2) Name and Location	(3) Position	(4) Characteristic	(5) Height	(6) Range	(7) Structure	(8) Remarks
			RHODE ISLAND - First District				
	NARRAGANSETT BAY						
	Narragansett Bay						
	Newport Harbor						
17845	*Goat Island Southeast Lighted Buoy 7*	41-29-00.913N 071-19-31.046W	Fl G 4s		3	Green.	Removed when endangered by ice.
17846	RI STATE PIER NINE LIGHT 1	41-29-16.900N 071-19-20.500W	Fl G 5s			Wharf end dolphin.	Private aid.
17847	RI STATE PIER NINE LIGHT 2	41-29-17.100N 071-19-19.300W	Fl R 5s				Private aid.
17850	- LIGHT	41-29-35.970N 071-19-37.416W	F G	33	9	White stone tower.	
17853	- North Channel Buoy 1	41-29-30.290N 071-19-32.520W				Green can.	Maintained 15 May - 15 Nov. Private aid.
17853.1	- North Channel Buoy 2	41-29-30.920N 071-19-30.640W				Red nun.	Maintained 15 May - 15 Nov. Private aid.
17853.2	- North Channel Buoy 3	41-29-33.760N 071-19-33.080W				Green can.	Maintained 15 May - 15 Nov. Private aid.
17853.3	- North Channel Buoy 4	41-29-34.430N 071-19-31.200W				Red nun.	Maintained 15 May - 15 Nov. Private aid.
17853.4	- North Channel Buoy 5	41-29-34.850N 071-19-34.408W				Green can.	Maintained 15 May - 15 Nov. Private aid.
17853.5	- North Channel Buoy 6	41-29-39.306N 071-19-36.872W				Red nun.	Maintained 15 May - 15 Nov. Private aid.
	East Passage						
17855	*- Lighted Bell Buoy 12*	41-29-40.232N 071-20-40.850W	Fl R 4s		4	Red.	
17857	ROSE ISLAND LIGHT	41-29-43.680N 071-20-33.780W	Fl W 6s	48		White dwelling.	Private aid.
17860	Rose Island South Point Buoy 1	41-29-35.972N 071-20-24.459W				Green can.	
17865	Mitchell Rock Gong Buoy 3	41-29-33.402N 071-20-11.099W				Green.	
17870	Tracey Ledge Buoy 5	41-29-53.272N 071-20-01.569W				Green can.	
	Jamestown Harbor						
	Channel buoys located 20-60 feet outside channel limit.						
17891	- Channel Buoy 1	41-29-42.781N 071-21-39.841W				Green can.	Private aid.
17892	*- Channel Lighted Buoy 2*	41-29-44.520N 071-21-39.179W	Fl R 4s			Red nun.	Private aid.
17893	- Channel Buoy 3	41-29-43.680N 071-21-47.160W				Green can.	Private aid.
17894	- Channel Buoy 4	41-29-45.359N 071-21-47.459W				Red nun.	Private aid.
	East Passage						
17900	Gull Rocks South Buoy	41-30-00.660N 071-19-58.158W				Green can with red bands.	
17905	- Buoy 12A	41-29-59.721N 071-20-44.960W				Red nun.	
17906	Newport-Pell Bridge VAIS SW	41-30-19.943N 071-21-05.418W					AIS: MMSI 993672526 (21)
17907	Newport-Pell Bridge VAIS SE	41-30-15.300N 071-20-45.621W					AIS: MMSI 993672525 (21)
17908	Newport-Pell Bridge VAIS NW	41-30-20.697N 071-21-04.996W					AIS: MMSI 993672564 (21)
17909	Newport-Pell Bridge VAIS NE	41-30-16.190N 071-20-45.217W					AIS: MMSI 993672534 (21)
17910	**NEWPORT - PELL BRIDGE RACON**	41-30-17.890N 071-20-55.320W				On bridge.	RACON: N (- .) Private aid.
17911	**Newport - Pell Bridge Sound Signal**	41-30-20.000N 071-21-05.000W				On bridge abutment.	HORN: 2 blasts ev 20s (1s bl-1s si-1s bl-17s si). Private aid.
17913	Taylor's Point Outfall Buoy	41-30-26.000N 071-21-23.000W				White and orange can.	Private aid.

(1)No.	(2)Name and Location	(3)Position	(4)Characteristic	(5)Height	(6)Range	(7)Structure	(8)Remarks

RHODE ISLAND - First District

NARRAGANSETT BAY
Narragansett Bay
East Passage

(1)No.	(2)Name and Location	(3)Position	(4)Characteristic	(5)Height	(6)Range	(7)Structure	(8)Remarks
17920	Gull Rocks Shoal Buoy 7 Off north edge of shoal.	41-30-15.870N 071-19-58.753W				Green can.	
17925	Rose Island Shoal Northeast End Buoy 2	41-30-15.379N 071-20-12.547W				Red nun.	
17930	Seventeen-Foot Spot Buoy	41-30-24.466N 071-20-06.901W				Green can with red bands.	
17935	- *Channel Junction Lighted Bell Buoy EP*	41-30-40.594N 071-20-49.812W	Fl (2+1)G 6s		3	Green and red bands.	
17940	*East Pass Lighted Bell Buoy 14*	41-30-59.902N 071-20-03.199W	Fl R 4s		4	Red.	
17945	- Buoy 16	41-31-23.502N 071-19-44.948W				Red nun.	
17950	Coddington Point Buoy 2	41-31-27.401N 071-19-24.196W				Red nun.	
17960	GOULD ISLAND SOUTH LIGHT	41-31-45.923N 071-20-38.472W	Fl G 6s	34	6	NR on skeleton tower.	
17965	- *Lighted Buoy 17*	41-31-46.851N 071-20-07.329W	Q G		4	Green.	
18005	CODDINGTON COVE BREAKWATER LIGHT 18	41-31-56.652N 071-19-28.980W	Fl R 6s	30	7	TR on red skeleton tower.	White/orange dayboards for Naval Security Zone. HORN: 2 blasts ev 20s (2s bl-2s si-2s bl-14s si). Operates continuously.
18010	Coddington Cove Buoy 2	41-31-59.881N 071-18-55.845W				Red nun.	
18055	Halfway Rock Daybeacon	41-33-49.401N 071-19-56.198W				NR on spindle.	
18060	Fiske Rock Buoy	41-34-04.921N 071-19-42.158W				Green can with red bands.	
18062	*Salt Water Farms Aquaculture Lighted Buoy A*	41-33-29.280N 071-18-38.100W	Oc (4)W 30s			White with orange bands.	Private aid.
18062.3	*Salt Water Farms Aquaculture Lighted Buoy B*	41-33-44.640N 071-18-30.180W	Oc (4)W 30s			White with orange bands.	Private aid.
18065	Dyer Island East Shoal Buoy 5	41-35-04.001N 071-17-45.502W				Green can.	
18070	Dyer Island East Shoal Buoy 7	41-35-14.671N 071-17-50.673W				Green can.	
18080	Prudence Island Southend Buoy PI	41-34-34.971N 071-19-40.128W				Red nun with green bands.	
18084	- *Wreck Lighted Buoy WR21*	41-34-32.034N 071-18-59.012W	Q G		3	Green.	
18085	- Buoy 22	41-34-39.401N 071-18-25.694W				Red nun.	
18095	- *Lighted Bell Buoy 24*	41-35-25.714N 071-18-15.552W	Fl R 2.5s		3	Red.	Replaced by LIB when endangered by ice.
18100	- *Lighted Buoy 25*	41-36-00.528N 071-18-08.520W	Fl G 4s		3	Green.	
18105	- *Lighted Bell Buoy 26*	41-35-58.851N 071-18-00.353W	Fl R 4s		4	Red.	Replaced by LIB when endangered by ice.
18110	- Buoy 27	41-36-19.711N 071-18-03.613W				Green can.	
18113	NEBW Daybeacon 1	41-35-29.781N 071-17-13.848W				SG on pole.	Private aid.
18113.1	NEBW Daybeacon 2	41-35-28.734N 071-17-14.218W				TR on pole.	Private aid.
18113.2	NEBW Daybeacon 3	41-35-27.729N 071-17-09.247W				SG on pole.	Private aid.
18113.3	NEBW Daybeacon 4	41-35-26.188N 071-17-08.818W				TR on pole.	Private aid.
18113.4	NEBW Daybeacon 5	41-35-27.542N 071-17-08.548W				SG on pole.	Private aid.

(1) No.	(2) Name and Location	(3) Position	(4) Characteristic	(5) Height	(6) Range	(7) Structure	(8) Remarks

RHODE ISLAND - First District

NARRAGANSETT BAY
Narragansett Bay
East Passage

(1) No.	(2) Name and Location	(3) Position	(4) Characteristic	(5) Height	(6) Range	(7) Structure	(8) Remarks
18113.5	NEBW Daybeacon 6	41-35-24.457N 071-17-07.328W				TR on pole.	Private aid.
18115	Coggeshall Point Buoy 10	41-35-32.046N 071-17-19.870W				Red nun.	
18120	Coggeshall Point Shoal Buoy 12	41-35-54.261N 071-17-15.351W				Red nun.	
18125	PRUDENCE ISLAND LIGHT	41-36-21.134N 071-18-12.712W	Fl G 6s	28	6	White octagonal tower.	
18130	Sandy Point Junction Lighted Bell Buoy SP	41-36-55.421N 071-17-35.552W	Fl (2+1)R 6s		3	Red and green bands.	Replaced by LIB when endangered by ice.
	Mount Hope Bay Approach						
18131	Carnegie Abbey Yacht Club Buoy 1	41-37-03.420N 071-16-33.080W					Private aid.
18132	Carnegie Abbey Yacht Club Buoy 2	41-37-02.570N 071-16-33.050W					Private aid.
18133	CARNEGIE ABBEY YACHT CLUB CHANNEL LIGHT 3	41-37-03.240N 071-16-26.040W	F G				Private aid.
18134	CARNEGIE ABBEY YACHT CLUB CHANNEL LIGHT 4	41-37-02.400N 071-16-26.000W	F R				Private aid.
18135	- Lighted Buoy 2	41-37-07.834N 071-17-00.012W	Fl R 2.5s		3		
18140	- Lighted Bell Buoy 3	41-37-47.565N 071-16-17.416W	Fl G 4s		3		
18143	- Buoy 4	41-37-35.172N 071-16-25.363W					
18145	**Hog Island Shoal Light**	41-37-56.677N 071-16-23.686W	Iso W 6s	54	12	White conical tower on black cylindrical pier. 60	HORN: 2 blasts ev 30s (2sbl-2s si-2s bl-24s si) Fog signal is radio activated, during times of reduced visibility, turn marine VHF-FM radio to channel 83A/157.175Mhz. Key microphone 5 times consecutively, to activate fog signal for 45 minutes.
18150	MUSSELBED SHOALS LIGHT 6A	41-38-10.464N 071-15-36.076W	Fl R 6s	26	6		
18155	Musselbed Shoals Gong Buoy 6	41-38-12.411N 071-15-38.196W				Red.	
18160	MUSSELBED SHOALS DIRECTIONAL LIGHT	41-38-10.454N 071-15-36.064W	F W (R & G sectors)	26	W 9 G 7 R 7		
	Narragansett Bay **Bristol Harbor**						
18165	Bristol Point Rock Buoy 2	41-38-28.161N 071-15-57.097W				Red nun.	
18170	Hog Island Rock Buoy 3	41-38-44.741N 071-16-25.538W				Green can.	
18175	Middle Ground Buoy At north end of shoal.	41-39-40.211N 071-16-52.150W				Red nun with green bands.	
18180	CASTLE ISLAND LIGHT 2 On shoal.	41-39-13.826N 071-17-10.442W	Fl R 6s	26	3	TR on skeleton tower.	
18185	Usher Rocks Buoy 3	41-39-31.751N 071-17-20.971W				Green can.	
18190	- LIGHT 4	41-39-58.200N 071-16-41.789W	F R	25	11	TR on skeleton tower.	
18191	- LIGHT 6	41-40-00.500N 071-16-47.100W	Fl R 4s				Marks southwest corner of pier. Private aid.
18192	- Daybeacon 6A	41-40-03.900N 071-16-48.200W					Marks northwest corner of pier. Private aid.
18194	- East Channel Buoy 5	41-40-01.320N 071-16-49.020W				Green can.	Private aid.

(1) No.	(2) Name and Location	(3) Position	(4) Characteristic	(5) Height	(6) Range	(7) Structure	(8) Remarks
			RHODE ISLAND - First District				
	NARRAGANSETT BAY						
	Narragansett Bay						
	Bristol Harbor						
18194.1	- East Channel Buoy 7	41-40-12.280N 071-16-51.900W				Green can.	Private aid.
18194.2	- East Channel Buoy 9	41-40-19.860N 071-16-53.640W				Green can.	Private aid.
18195.4	- Channel Daybeacon 8	41-40-15.900N 071-16-49.500W				TR on monopile.	Private aid.
18195.6	- East Channel Buoy 10	41-40-23.367N 071-16-52.718W				Red nun.	Private aid.
18196	- West Channel Buoy 1	41-40-09.960N 071-17-05.400W				Green can.	Private aid.
18196.1	- West Channel Buoy 2	41-40-06.720N 071-17-01.380W				Red nun.	Private aid.
18196.2	- West Channel Buoy 3	41-40-17.160N 071-17-07.200W				Green can.	Private aid.
18196.3	- West Channel Buoy 4	41-40-19.740N 071-17-06.480W				Red nun.	Private aid.
18196.4	- West Channel Buoy 5	41-40-27.900N 071-17-12.600W				Green can.	Private aid.
18196.5	- West Channel Buoy 6	41-40-31.380N 071-17-12.720W				Red nun.	Private aid.
	Providence River Approach						
18200	- *Channel Lighted Buoy 1*	41-37-42.571N 071-18-05.073W	Fl G 2.5s	3		Green.	Replaced by can when endangered by ice.
18205	Hog Island Southwest Point Buoy 2	41-37-51.081N 071-17-21.451W				Red nun.	
18210	- *Channel Lighted Buoy 2*	41-38-14.331N 071-18-11.133W	Fl R 2.5s	3		Red.	
18215	Potter Cove Buoy 2	41-38-32.480N 071-19-49.378W				Red nun.	
18220	Potter Cove Buoy 4	41-38-25.750N 071-20-05.709W				Red nun.	
18225	Potter Cove Buoy 6	41-38-28.060N 071-20-17.820W				Red nun.	
18230	*Popasquash Point Lighted Bell Buoy PP*	41-38-47.951N 071-17-58.433W	Fl (2+1)R 6s	4		Red and green bands.	Replaced by nun when endangered by ice.
18235	- *Channel Lighted Buoy 3*	41-38-31.801N 071-18-27.074W	Fl G 4s	3		Green.	Replaced by can when endangered by ice.
18240	- *Channel Lighted Buoy 4*	41-38-52.333N 071-18-28.202W	Q R	3		Red.	Replaced by nun when endangered by ice.
18241	*Prudence Island Monitoring Lighted Buoy*	41-38-53.020N 071-19-09.420W	Fl Y 4s			Yellow.	Property of URI. Maintained from May 1 to Nov 30. Private aid.
18245	- *Channel Lighted Buoy 5*	41-39-05.440N 071-18-42.745W	Q G	3		Green.	Replaced by can when endangered by ice.
18250	- *Channel Lighted Buoy 6*	41-39-20.570N 071-18-35.955W	Fl R 2.5s	3		Red.	Replaced by LIB when endangered by ice.
18255	Fork Rock Buoy	41-40-33.199N 071-20-51.251W				Red nun with green bands.	
18257	*North Prudence Point Monitoring Lighted Buoy*	41-40-14.040N 071-21-19.080W	Fl Y 5s			Yellow.	Property of URI. Maintained from May 1 - Nov 30. Private aid.
18260	Ohio Ledge Bell Buoy OL	41-40-56.200N 071-19-18.677W				Green and red bands.	Removed when endangered by ice.
18265	- *Channel Lighted Buoy 7*	41-40-19.370N 071-18-47.825W	Fl G 4s	3		Green.	Replaced by can when endangered by ice.

(1) No.	(2) Name and Location	(3) Position	(4) Characteristic	(5) Height	(6) Range	(7) Structure	(8) Remarks

RHODE ISLAND - First District

NARRAGANSETT BAY
Narragansett Bay
Providence River Approach

18270	- *Channel Lighted Buoy 8*	41-40-19.480N 071-18-39.725W	Fl R 4s		3	Red.	Replaced by nun when endangered by ice.
18275	- *Channel Lighted Buoy 9*	41-41-19.250N 071-18-53.825W	Fl G 2.5s		3	Green.	Replaced by can when endangered by ice.
18280	- *Channel Lighted Bell Buoy 10*	41-41-21.080N 071-18-43.525W	Q R		3	Red.	Replaced by LIB when endangered by ice.
18285	- *Channel Lighted Buoy 11*	41-41-54.129N 071-19-28.969W	Fl G 2.5s		3	Green.	Replaced by can when endangered by ice.
18290	- *Channel Lighted Buoy 12*	41-41-58.328N 071-19-21.721W	Fl R 2.5s		3	Red.	Replaced by LIB when endangered by ice.
18295	- *Channel Lighted Buoy 13*	41-42-41.545N 071-20-16.969W	Fl G 4s		3	Green.	Replaced by can when endangered by ice.
18300	- *Channel Lighted Buoy 14*	41-42-45.409N 071-20-10.187W	Fl R 4s		3	Red.	Replaced by nun when endangered by ice.
18305	CONIMICUT LIGHT	41-43-01.272N 071-20-42.546W	Fl W 2.5s (R sector)	58	8 R 5	White conical tower on cylindrical pier.	Red from 322° to 349°, covers Ohio Ledge. HORN: 2 bl ev 30s (2s bl-2s si-2s bl-24s si). Fog signal is radio activated, during times of reduced visibility, turn marine VHF-FM radio to channel 83A/157.175Mhz. Key microphone 5 times consecutively, to activate fog signal for 45 minutes.
18307	*Conimicut Point Monitoring Lighted Buoy*	41-42-49.870N 071-20-37.890W	Fl Y 5s			Yellow.	Property of URI. Maintained May 1 - Nov 30. Private aid.

Providence River

18310	- *Channel Lighted Buoy 15*	41-43-05.331N 071-20-41.315W	Q G		3	Green.	
18315	- *Channel Lighted Buoy 16*	41-43-08.849N 071-20-34.460W	Q R		3	Red.	Replaced by nun when endangered by ice.
18320	- Channel Buoy 17	41-43-22.295N 071-21-16.988W				Green can.	
18325	- *Channel Lighted Buoy 18*	41-43-33.558N 071-21-24.533W	Fl R 2.5s		3	Red.	
18330	- *Channel Lighted Buoy 19*	41-43-39.168N 071-21-50.974W	Q G		3	Green.	
18335	- *Channel Lighted Buoy 20*	41-43-44.438N 071-21-40.324W	Q R		3	Red.	
18340	- *Channel Lighted Buoy 22*	41-43-58.258N 071-21-50.384W	Fl R 2.5s		3	Red.	
18345	BULLOCK POINT LIGHT BP 540 feet east of channel.	41-44-15.795N 071-21-51.114W	Oc W 4s	29	6	NR on skeleton tower.	

Bullock Cove

18350	- *Entrance Lighted Buoy 1*	41-44-15.790N 071-21-21.934W	Fl G 2.5s		3	Green.	Replaced by can when endangered by ice.
18360	- Entrance Buoy 2	41-44-16.418N 071-21-18.623W				Red nun.	
18370	- Entrance Buoy 3	41-44-25.647N 071-21-18.072W				Green can.	Removed when endangered by ice.
18375	- Entrance Buoy 4	41-44-26.495N 071-21-16.578W				Red nun.	Removed when endangered by ice.

(1) No.	(2) Name and Location	(3) Position	(4) Characteristic	(5) Height	(6) Range	(7) Structure	(8) Remarks
			RHODE ISLAND - First District				
	NARRAGANSETT BAY						
	Narragansett Bay						
	Bullock Cove						
18380	- Entrance Buoy 5	41-44-32.830N 071-21-16.254W				Green can.	Removed when endangered by ice.
18385	- Entrance Buoy 6	41-44-33.194N 071-21-15.027W				Red nun.	Removed when endangered by ice.
18390	- Daybeacon 7	41-44-37.700N 071-21-15.400W				SG on pile.	Private aid.
18395	- Daybeacon 8	41-44-42.240N 071-21-12.600W				TR on pile.	Private aid.
18400	- Daybeacon 9	41-44-45.180N 071-21-13.260W				SG on pile.	Private aid.
18403	- Daybeacon 10	41-44-51.300N 071-21-12.420W				TR on pile.	Private aid.
18405	- Daybeacon 11	41-44-51.300N 071-21-14.040W				SG on pile.	Private aid.
18410	- Daybeacon 12	41-44-54.000N 071-21-13.400W				TR on pile.	Private aid.
18415	- Daybeacon 13	41-44-55.860N 071-21-15.240W				SG on pile.	Private aid.
18420	- Daybeacon 14	41-44-59.700N 071-21-14.900W				TR on pile.	Private aid.
18425	- Daybeacon 15	41-45-00.660N 071-21-16.800W				SG on pile.	Private aid.
18430	- Daybeacon 16	41-45-01.980N 071-21-15.360W				TR on pile.	Private aid.
18431	- Daybeacon 17	41-45-09.480N 071-21-14.580W				SG on pile.	Private aid.
18431.1	- Daybeacon 18	41-45-10.100N 071-21-13.300W				TR on pile.	Private aid.
18431.2	- Daybeacon 19	41-45-14.160N 071-21-12.540W				SG on pile.	Private aid.
	Providence River						
18435	- *Channel Lighted Buoy 23*	41-44-20.216N 071-22-07.760W	Fl G 2.5s	3		Green.	
18440	- *Channel Lighted Buoy 25*	41-44-47.396N 071-22-18.956W	Fl G 4s	3		Green.	Replaced by can when endangered by ice.
18445	- *Channel Lighted Buoy 26*	41-44-47.798N 071-22-10.945W	Fl R 4s	3		Red.	
18450	- *Channel Lighted Buoy 27*	41-45-16.034N 071-22-30.944W	Fl G 2.5s	3		Green.	
18455	Sabin Point Daybeacon SP	41-45-43.389N 071-22-27.250W				NR on dolphin.	
18460	- *Channel Lighted Buoy 28*	41-45-28.410N 071-22-27.338W	Fl R 6s	3		Red.	
	Pawtuxet Cove						
18465	- Channel Approach Buoy 1	41-45-36.480N 071-22-48.270W				Green can.	
18470	- Channel Buoy 2	41-45-37.859N 071-22-54.290W				Red nun.	
18475	- Channel Buoy 3	41-45-36.671N 071-22-53.636W				Green can.	
18480	- Channel Buoy 4	41-45-36.155N 071-23-02.138W				Red nun.	Removed when endangered by ice.
18485	- Channel Buoy 5	41-45-34.610N 071-23-06.573W				Green can.	Removed when endangered by ice.
18490	- Channel Buoy 6	41-45-34.887N 071-23-09.929W				Red nun.	Removed when endangered by ice.

173

(1) No.	(2) Name and Location	(3) Position	(4) Characteristic	(5) Height	(6) Range	(7) Structure	(8) Remarks

RHODE ISLAND - First District

NARRAGANSETT BAY

Narragansett Bay

Providence River

18500	- *Channel Lighted Buoy 29*	41-45-43.977N 071-22-42.147W	Q G		3	Green.	
18505	- *Channel Lighted Buoy 30*	41-45-43.427N 071-22-30.757W	Q R		3	Red.	

Fields Point Channel

18510	- Buoy 1	41-46-09.867N 071-22-51.418W				Green can.	
18515	- Buoy 2	41-46-28.837N 071-22-57.129W				Red nun.	
18520	- Buoy 3	41-46-47.277N 071-23-06.699W				Green can.	
18525	- Buoy 5	41-46-52.946N 071-23-19.340W				Green can.	

Providence River

18530	- *Channel Lighted Buoy 32*	41-45-58.347N 071-22-27.257W	Fl R 4s		3	Red.	
18535	- *Channel Lighted Buoy 33*	41-46-17.657N 071-22-26.277W	Fl G 4s		3	Green.	
18540	- *Channel Lighted Buoy 34*	41-46-26.079N 071-22-13.805W	Fl R 2.5s		3	Red.	
18550	- *Channel Lighted Buoy 35*	41-46-30.397N 071-22-22.207W	Q G		3	Green.	
18555	POMHAM ROCKS LIGHT	41-46-39.096N 071-22-10.406W	F R	54	6	White square tower.attached to dwelling.	
18560	- *Channel Lighted Buoy 37*	41-46-45.897N 071-22-24.207W	Fl G 2.5s		3	Green.	
18565	- Channel Buoy 39	41-46-56.397N 071-22-29.708W				Green can.	
18570	- Channel Buoy 41	41-47-17.086N 071-22-44.299W				Green can.	
18575	- Channel Buoy 40	41-47-23.396N 071-22-34.208W				Red nun.	
18580	- CHANNEL LIGHT 42 Off rock.	41-47-38.844N 071-22-46.712W	Iso R 6s	31	4	TR on skeleton tower on granite pier.	
18585	Green Jacket Shoal Buoy 2	41-48-50.656N 071-23-45.161W				Red nun.	
18590	Green Jacket Shoal Buoy 4	41-48-55.821N 071-23-39.938W				Red nun.	
18595	Green Jacket Shoal Buoy 6	41-48-59.336N 071-23-30.896W				Red nun.	

Seekonk River

18600	- Channel Buoy 1	41-49-16.645N 071-23-13.811W				Green can.	
18605	- Channel Buoy 2	41-49-20.833N 071-23-10.170W				Red nun.	
18620	- Channel Buoy 6	41-50-04.775N 071-22-35.680W				Red nun.	Maintained from 1 May to 31 Oct.
18630	- Channel Buoy 8	41-50-16.385N 071-22-28.180W				Red nun.	Maintained from 1 May to 31 Oct.
18640	- Channel Buoy 13	41-50-36.765N 071-22-19.800W				Green can.	Maintained from 1 May to 31 Oct.
18650	- Channel Buoy 18	41-51-00.695N 071-22-26.610W				Red nun.	Maintained from 1 May to 31 Oct.
18655	- Channel Buoy 19	41-51-14.204N 071-22-32.191W				Green can.	Maintained from 1 May to 31 Oct.
18665	- Channel Buoy 22	41-51-29.454N 071-22-35.081W				Red nun.	Maintained from 1 May to 31 Oct.

(1) No.	(2) Name and Location	(3) Position	(4) Characteristic	(5) Height	(6) Range	(7) Structure	(8) Remarks
			RHODE ISLAND - First District				

NARRAGANSETT BAY
Narragansett Bay
Seekonk River

(1) No.	(2) Name and Location	(3) Position	(4) Characteristic	(5) Height	(6) Range	(7) Structure	(8) Remarks
18670	- Channel Buoy 23	41-51-39.944N 071-22-40.931W				Green can.	Maintained from 1 May to 31 Oct.
18675	- Channel Buoy 27	41-51-56.324N 071-22-46.612W				Green can.	Maintained from 1 May 50 31 Oct.
Warren River							
18680	- *Entrance Lighted Buoy 1* Off southeast end of Rumstick Shoal.	41-41-51.850N 071-18-01.633W	Fl G 4s		3	Green.	Replaced by can when endangered by ice.
18685	- Entrance Buoy 2	41-41-50.750N 071-17-40.512W				Red nun.	
18690	- Buoy 3	41-42-13.960N 071-17-54.813W				Green can.	
18691	Rumstick Ledge Danger Buoy	41-42-12.138N 071-18-33.625W				White with orange bands worded ROCK.	Removed when endangered by ice.
18695	- Buoy 5	41-42-20.120N 071-17-50.822W				Green can.	
18700	- Buoy 6	41-42-23.900N 071-17-51.252W				Red nun.	
18705	- Buoy 8	41-42-31.172N 071-17-52.116W				Red nun.	
18710	- Buoy 9	41-42-40.030N 071-17-50.622W				Green can.	
18715	- Buoy 10	41-42-39.340N 071-17-43.022W				Red nun.	
18720	ALLEN ROCK LIGHT 11	41-42-48.799N 071-17-35.191W	Fl G 6s	28	6	SG on spindle.	
18725	- Buoy 12	41-42-49.400N 071-17-29.991W				Red nun.	
18730	- Buoy 13	41-42-59.500N 071-17-18.191W				Green can.	
18735	- Buoy 14	41-43-02.100N 071-17-12.390W				Red nun.	
18740	- Buoy 15	41-43-09.000N 071-17-17.191W				Green can.	
18745	- Buoy 16	41-43-14.000N 071-17-16.391W				Red nun.	
18750	- Buoy 18	41-43-24.300N 071-17-16.391W				Red nun.	
18755	- Buoy 21	41-43-49.600N 071-17-14.891W				Green can.	
18760	- Buoy 23	41-43-53.500N 071-17-17.391W				Green can.	
Barrington River							
18775	- Buoy 1 Marks reef.	41-43-57.139N 071-17-27.816W				Green can.	
18776	- Buoy 2	41-43-57.574N 071-17-31.092W				Red nun.	Maintained from 31 March to 01 December.
18778	- Buoy 4	41-43-58.174N 071-17-36.132W				Red nun.	Maintained from 31 March to 01 December.
18779	- *Fairway Channel Lighted Buoy 6*	41-44-03.970N 071-17-40.670W	F R			Red.	Maintained 15 May to 1 Nov. Private aid.
18779.1	- *Fairway Channel Lighted Buoy 7*	41-44-03.170N 071-17-40.870W	F G			Green.	Maintained 15 May to 1 Nov. Private aid.
18779.2	- *Lighted Buoy 7A*	41-44-27.730N 071-17-58.310W	Q G			Green.	Private aid.
18780	- Buoy 8	41-44-37.620N 071-18-28.220W				Red nun.	Maintained 15 May to 1 Nov. Private aid.

(1) No.	(2) Name and Location	(3) Position	(4) Characteristic	(5) Height	(6) Range	(7) Structure	(8) Remarks
			RHODE ISLAND - First District				
	NARRAGANSETT BAY						
	Mount Hope Bay						
18785	**- BRIDGE RACON**	41-38-23.640N 071-15-28.260W				On bridge.	RACON: MH (- - ....) Private aid.
18786	**- Bridge Fog Signal**	41-38-28.920N 071-15-31.920W				On bridge abutment.	HORN: 1 blast ev 20s (2s bl). Private aid. Private aid.
18788	Roger Williams Obstruction Buoy	41-38-55.920N 071-15-19.380W				White and orange.	Private aid. Private aid.
	Tiverton Channel						
18790	*Mount Hope Bay Junction Lighted Gong Buoy MH*	41-39-32.434N 071-14-02.637W	Fl (2+1)R 6s	3		Red and green bands.	
18795	- Buoy 2	41-39-27.962N 071-14-02.022W				Red nun.	
18800	- Buoy 3	41-39-36.032N 071-13-14.791W				Green can.	
18805	- *Lighted Bell Buoy 4*	41-39-32.202N 071-13-08.291W	Fl R 4s	3		Red.	
	Tiverton Upper Channel						
18810	- Buoy 1	41-39-39.042N 071-12-38.330W				Green can.	
18815	- Buoy 2	41-39-31.902N 071-12-39.179W				Red nun.	
18820	- Buoy 4	41-39-43.002N 071-12-19.459W				Red nun.	
18825	- *Lighted Gong Buoy 3*	41-39-48.322N 071-12-24.700W	Fl G 4s	3		Green.	
18830	- Buoy 5	41-40-25.992N 071-12-08.109W				Green can.	
	Mount Hope Bay						
18835	Seal Rock Buoy 1	41-39-42.545N 071-14-46.486W				Green can.	
18840	- *Lighted Buoy 1*	41-39-48.769N 071-13-50.539W	Fl G 2.5s	3		Green.	
18845	- Buoy 2	41-39-45.322N 071-13-45.256W				Red nun.	
18850	- Channel Buoy 3	41-40-17.243N 071-13-12.007W				Green can.	
18855	- *Lighted Bell Buoy 4*	41-40-14.222N 071-13-07.728W	Fl R 4s	3		Red.	
18857	*Mt Hope Bay Monitoring Lighted Buoy*	41-40-48.840N 071-12-54.360W	Fl Y 5s			Yellow.	Property of URI. Maintained May 1 - Nov 30. Private aid.
18860	- *Lighted Buoy 5*	41-40-44.197N 071-12-36.433W	Fl G 4s	3		Green.	
18865	- Buoy 6	41-40-40.755N 071-12-33.057W				Red nun.	
18870	- Buoy 7	41-41-10.693N 071-12-01.321W				Green can.	
18875	- *Lighted Bell Buoy 8*	41-41-07.902N 071-11-57.179W	Fl R 4s	3		Red.	
18880	- Buoy 9	41-41-32.601N 071-11-32.078W				Green can.	
18885	- *Lighted Bell Buoy 10*	41-41-39.262N 071-11-15.648W	Fl R 4s	3		Red.	
18890	- *Lighted Buoy 11*	41-41-54.242N 071-10-55.177W	Fl G 4s	3		Green.	Replaced by LIB when endangered by ice.
18895	- Buoy 12	41-41-51.232N 071-10-51.537W				Red nun.	
	Brayton Point Channel						
18900	- *Lighted Buoy 1*	41-42-04.260N 071-10-50.760W	Fl G 4s			Green.	Private aid.
18905	- *Lighted Buoy 2*	41-42-23.280N 071-11-02.280W	Fl R 4s			Red.	Private aid.

(1) No.	(2) Name and Location	(3) Position	(4) Characteristic	(5) Height	(6) Range	(7) Structure	(8) Remarks
			RHODE ISLAND - First District				
	NARRAGANSETT BAY **Mount Hope Bay** **Brayton Point Channel**						
18910	- *Lighted Buoy 3*	41-42-21.017N 071-11-06.526W	Fl G 4s			Green.	Private aid.
18915	- FRONT RANGE LIGHT	41-42-43.036N 071-11-24.856W	F R	12		KRW on metal tower.	Private aid.
18917	- REAR RANGE LIGHT 131 yards, 324.6T from front light.	41-42-46.121N 071-11-27.760W	F R	18		KRW on metal tower.	Private aid.
	Mount Hope Bay						
18920	- *Channel Lighted Buoy 13*	41-42-00.542N 071-10-42.847W	Fl G 2.5s		3	Green.	Removed when endangered by ice.
18925	BORDEN FLATS LIGHT	41-42-16.020N 071-10-27.837W	Fl W 2.5s	47	9	White conical tower with red stripe, on brown cylindrical pier.	
18930	**Braga Bridge Sound Signal**	41-42-24.534N 071-09-58.506W					HORN: 1 blast ev 20s (2s bl-18s si). Fog signal is radio activated, during times of reduced visibility, turn marine VHF-FM radio to channel 83A/157.175Mhz. Key microphone 5 times consecutively, to activate fog signal for 45 minutes. Private aid.
18935	- *Channel Lighted Buoy 15*	41-42-27.602N 071-09-53.715W	Fl G 2.5s		3	Green.	Replaced by can from Dec 1 to Apr 1.
18945	- Channel Buoy 18	41-43-16.202N 071-09-28.675W				Red nun.	
18950	- *Channel Lighted Buoy 19*	41-43-18.182N 071-09-32.545W	Fl G 4s		3	Green.	Removed when endangered by ice.
18953	- Channel Buoy 20	41-43-40.534N 071-08-56.212W				Red nun.	
18955	- *Channel Lighted Buoy 21*	41-43-43.534N 071-08-59.412W	Fl G 4s		3	Green.	Replaced by can from Dec 1 to Apr 1.
18960	Spar Island Buoy 2	41-41-13.351N 071-13-22.091W				Red nun.	
18965	Old Bay Rock Buoy 1	41-41-47.221N 071-13-29.811W				Green can.	
18966	*URI Lighted Research Buoy CR*	41-42-06.682N 071-12-56.264W	Fl Y 5s			Yellow.	Property of URI. Maintained May 01 to Dec 01. Private aid.
18967	*URI Lighted Research Buoy TR*	41-42-03.582N 071-11-14.298W	Fl Y 2s			Yellow.	Property of URI. Maintained May 01 to Dec 01. Private aid.
	Kickamuit River						
18970	- Buoy 1	41-41-37.801N 071-14-38.112W				Green can.	Maintained from April 1 to December 1.
18975	- Buoy 2	41-41-41.172N 071-14-40.848W				Red nun.	Maintained from April 1 to December 1.
18980	- Buoy 4	41-41-47.921N 071-14-41.493W				Red nun.	Maintained from April 1 to December 1.
18985	- Buoy 6	41-41-54.391N 071-14-39.094W				Red nun.	Maintained from April 1 to December 1.
18987	- Buoy 7	41-41-57.607N 071-14-39.828W				Green can.	Maintained from April 1 to December 1.
	Taunton River						
18995	- Buoy 1	41-44-29.942N 071-08-05.353W				Green can.	

(1) No.	(2) Name and Location	(3) Position	(4) Characteristic	(5) Height	(6) Range	(7) Structure	(8) Remarks

RHODE ISLAND - First District

NARRAGANSETT BAY
Mount Hope Bay
Taunton River

19000	- Buoy 4	41-45-26.665N 071-07-48.996W				Red nun.	
19005	- Buoy 3	41-44-57.901N 071-07-50.672W				Green can.	
19010	- Buoy 6	41-46-06.621N 071-07-19.403W				Red nun.	
19015	- Channel Buoy 7	41-46-24.291N 071-07-03.172W				Green can.	
19020	- Channel Buoy 8	41-46-37.980N 071-07-06.616W				Red nun.	
19035	- Channel Buoy 12	41-47-09.421N 071-07-03.336W				Red nun.	Maintained from 15 Mar to 30 Nov.
19040	- Channel Buoy 14	41-47-27.115N 071-07-12.210W				Red nun.	Maintained from 15 Mar to 30 Nov.
19045	- Channel Buoy 15	41-47-39.319N 071-07-13.380W				Green can.	Maintained from 15 Mar to 30 Nov.
19050	- Channel Buoy 16	41-47-52.777N 071-07-06.246W				Red nun.	Maintained from 15 Mar to 30 Nov.
19055	- Channel Buoy 17	41-48-12.851N 071-07-13.350W				Green can.	Maintained from 15 Mar to 30 Nov.
19060	- Channel Buoy 19	41-48-31.162N 071-07-05.736W				Green can.	Maintained from 15 Mar to 30 Nov.
19070	- Channel Buoy 22	41-48-48.683N 071-06-54.002W				Red nun.	Maintained from 15 Mar to 30 Nov.

Cole River

19075	- Buoy 2	41-42-48.020N 071-13-08.786W				Red nun.	Removed when endangered by ice.

West Passage

19080	River Ledge Buoy 1 Marks rock.	41-26-06.345N 071-26-08.194W				Green can.	
19085	Newton Rock Bell Buoy NR	41-26-38.243N 071-24-09.266W				Green and red bands.	
19090	*Whale Rock Lighted Gong Buoy 3*	41-26-39.572N 071-25-13.899W	Fl G 4s		4	Green.	
19100	Jones Ledge Buoy 5 On east side of ledge.	41-27-43.613N 071-25-01.065W				Green can.	
19101	DUTCH ISLAND LIGHT	41-29-48.270N 071-24-15.350W	Fl R 6s			Brick building.	White square brick tower with black cupola Private aid.
19103	*- Wreck Lighted Buoy WR6*	41-29-13.634N 071-24-20.512W	Q R		3	Red.	Removed when endangered by ice.
19105	*Dutch Island South End Lighted Gong Buoy DI*	41-29-42.241N 071-24-17.810W	Fl (2+1)R 6s		4	Red and green bands.	
19110	Beaverhead Point Shoal Buoy 2 On north edge of shoal.	41-29-44.912N 071-23-53.566W				Red nun.	
19111	Dutch Island Harbor Channel Buoy 1	41-29-51.420N 071-23-27.660W				Green can.	Private aid.
19112	Dutch Island Harbor Channel Buoy 2	41-29-50.280N 071-23-28.500W				Red nun.	Private aid.
19113	Dutch Island Harbor Channel Buoy 3	41-29-49.980N 071-23-18.300W				Green can.	Private aid.
19114	Dutch Island Harbor Channel Buoy 4	41-29-48.960N 071-23-18.600W				Red nun.	Private aid.

(1) No.	(2) Name and Location	(3) Position	(4) Characteristic	(5) Height	(6) Range	(7) Structure	(8) Remarks
			RHODE ISLAND - First District				
	NARRAGANSETT BAY						
	West Passage						
19115	Dutch Island Bell Buoy 8	41-30-30.161N 071-24-08.090W				Red.	
19119	*American Mussel Harvesters Aquaculture Lighted Buoy A*	41-30-38.040N 071-23-31.200W	Fl W 6s			White with Orange bands.	Private aid.
19120	*American Mussel Harvesters Aquaculture Lighted Buoy B*	41-30-58.440N 071-23-40.380W	Fl W 6s			White with Orange bands.	Private aid.
19126	- Buoy 10	41-32-06.034N 071-23-37.012W				Red nun.	
19130	PLUM BEACH LIGHT	41-31-48.990N 071-24-18.810W	Fl W 5s			Brown over white conical tower.	Private aid.
	Wickford Harbor						
19135	- LIGHT 1	41-34-21.460N 071-26-12.552W	Fl G 6s	40	6	SG on square skeleton tower.	
19140	- Gong Buoy 2	41-34-24.864N 071-26-07.465W				Red.	
19145	- NORTH BREAKWATER LIGHT 4	41-34-27.634N 071-26-15.712W	Fl R 4s	16	5	TR on white skeleton tower.	
19150	- Buoy 7	41-34-27.202N 071-26-35.388W				Green can.	Maintained from 1 May to 31 Oct.
19155	- Buoy 8	41-34-30.238N 071-26-35.628W				Red nun.	
19160	- Buoy 9	41-34-36.129N 071-26-45.538W				Green can.	
19165	- Buoy 10	41-34-37.450N 071-26-45.540W				Red nun.	
	Quonset Channel						
19175	- *Lighted Bell Buoy 2*	41-34-40.250N 071-21-40.603W	Fl R 4s		3	Red.	
19180	- *Lighted Buoy 3*	41-34-35.020N 071-22-06.575W	Fl G 2.5s		3	Green.	Replaced by can when endangered by ice.
19185	- Buoy 4	41-34-51.200N 071-22-39.556W				Red nun.	
19190	- Buoy 5	41-34-44.510N 071-22-57.947W				Green can.	
19193	*URI Lighted Research Buoy CONPT*	41-34-12.000N 071-23-24.000W	Fl Y 6s			Yellow.	Property of URI. Private aid.
19195	- *Lighted Buoy 6*	41-35-01.949N 071-23-35.074W	Q R		4	Red.	
19200	- *Lighted Buoy 7*	41-34-53.694N 071-23-49.253W	Q G		3	Green.	
19205	Ten-Foot Shoal Buoy	41-34-45.570N 071-23-55.880W				Red nun with green bands.	
19210	- *Lighted Buoy 9*	41-35-26.980N 071-23-48.969W	Fl G 4s		4	Green.	
19215	- *Lighted Buoy 8*	41-35-10.068N 071-23-41.187W	Fl R 2.5s		3	Red.	Replaced by nun when endangered by ice.
19220	- Buoy 10	41-35-52.409N 071-23-41.289W				Red nun.	
19225	- *Lighted Buoy 11*	41-35-54.902N 071-23-48.469W	Fl G 6s		4	Green.	
19230	- *Lighted Buoy 12*	41-36-18.599N 071-23-41.279W	Fl R 4s		4	Red.	
19235	- *Lighted Buoy 13*	41-36-16.959N 071-23-48.056W	Fl G 2.5s		3	Green.	
19240	- *Lighted Buoy 14*	41-36-37.491N 071-23-41.332W	Fl R 2.5s		4	Red.	
19241	- Buoy 15	41-36-25.998N 071-23-53.119W				Green can.	
19245	- Buoy 16	41-36-44.633N 071-23-57.947W				Red nun.	

(1) No.	(2) Name and Location	(3) Position	(4) Characteristic	(5) Height	(6) Range	(7) Structure	(8) Remarks
			RHODE ISLAND - First District				
	NARRAGANSETT BAY						
	West Passage						
	Quonset Channel						
19250	Davisville Turning Basin Buoy 18	41-36-51.858N 071-24-00.458W				Red nun.	Private aid.
19255	Davisville Turning Basin Buoy 20	41-36-55.923N 071-24-05.218W				Red nun.	Private aid.
19260	*West Quonset Channel Lighted Buoy 2*	41-34-52.753N 071-24-30.436W	Fl R 4s			Red.	Private aid.
19261	*West Quonset Channel Lighted Buoy 3*	41-34-49.115N 071-24-40.267W	Fl G 4s			Green.	Private aid.
19262	*West Quonset Channel Lighted Buoy 4*	41-34-52.704N 071-24-37.524W	Fl R 4s			Red.	Private aid.
19263	*West Quonset Channel Lighted Buoy 5*	41-34-51.789N 071-24-49.865W	Fl G 2.5s			Green.	Private aid.
19264	*West Quonset Channel Lighted Buoy 6*	41-34-54.977N 071-24-48.221W	Fl R 2.5s			Red.	Private aid.
19265	*West Quonset Channel Lighted Buoy 7*	41-34-56.423N 071-25-07.679W	Fl G 2.5s			Green.	Private aid.
19266	*West Quonset Channel Lighted Buoy 8*	41-34-59.547N 071-25-06.069W	Fl R 2.5s			Red.	Private aid.
19267	*West Quonset Channel Lighted Buoy 9*	41-34-59.552N 071-25-20.490W	Fl G 2.5s			Green.	Private aid.
19268	*West Quonset Channel Lighted Buoy 10*	41-35-01.012N 071-25-08.712W	Fl R 2.5s			Red.	Private aid.
19269	*West Quonset Channel Lighted Buoy 12*	41-35-06.064N 071-25-08.829W	Fl R 4s			Red.	Private aid.
	West Passage						
19280	*Hope Island Lighted Buoy 2*	41-35-33.300N 071-22-47.406W	Fl R 6s		3	Red.	Replaced by nun when endangered by ice.
19283	*Quonset Point Monitoring Lighted Buoy*	41-35-20.300N 071-22-47.940W	Fl Y 5s			Yellow.	Property of URI. Maintained May 1 - Nov 30. Private aid.
19285	*Despair Island Lighted Buoy 1*	41-36-29.180N 071-21-36.073W	Fl G 4s		4	Green.	
	Allen Harbor						
19290	- Buoy 1	41-37-09.559N 071-24-08.800W				Green can.	
19295	- *Lighted Buoy 2*	41-37-10.877N 071-24-05.131W	Fl R 4s		3	Red.	Replaced by nun from Dec. 1 to Mar. 15.
19300	- Buoy 3	41-37-13.922N 071-24-17.739W				Green can.	Maintained from 1 May to October 31.
19305	- Buoy 4	41-37-14.644N 071-24-16.878W				Red nun.	Maintained from 1 May to October 31.
19310	- Buoy 5	41-37-16.726N 071-24-25.572W				Green can.	Maintained from 1 May to October 31.
19315	- Buoy 6	41-37-17.569N 071-24-25.341W				Red nun.	Maintained from 1 May to October 31.
	Greenwich Bay Approach						
19320	Calf Pasture Shoal Buoy 3	41-37-25.269N 071-23-31.209W				Green can.	
19333	*Mt. View Point Monitoring Lighted Buoy*	41-38-21.720N 071-23-38.460W	Fl Y 5s			Yellow.	Property of URI. Maintained from May 1 - Nov 30. Private aid.
19334	*URI Lighted Research Buoy GB*	41-38-32.910N 071-23-16.070W	Fl Y 6s			Yellow.	Property of URI. Private aid.
19335	*Round Rock Lighted Buoy 1* On east side of shoal.	41-39-24.424N 071-23-26.298W	Fl G 2.5s		3	Green.	Replaced by can when endangered by ice.
19340	*Patience Island Lighted Bell Buoy 8* On edge of shoal.	41-39-39.399N 071-22-22.066W	Fl R 4s		3	Red.	

180

(1) No.	(2) Name and Location	(3) Position	(4) Characteristic	(5) Height	(6) Range	(7) Structure	(8) Remarks
			RHODE ISLAND - First District				
	NARRAGANSETT BAY						
	Greenwich Bay Approach						
19345	**Warwick Light**	41-40-01.834N 071-22-41.912W	Oc G 4s	66	10	White conical tower. 51	Lighted throughout 24 hours. HORN: 1 blast ev 15s (2s bl). MRASS-Fog signal is radio activated, during times of reduced visibility, turn marine VHF-FM radio to channel 81A/157.075Mhz. Key microphone 5 times consecutively, to activate fog signal for 45 minutes.
	Greenwich Bay						
	Warwick Cove						
19350	- *Lighted Buoy 1*	41-40-38.020N 071-23-32.261W	Q G		3	Green can.	
19355	- Buoy 2	41-40-38.678N 071-23-30.079W				Red nun.	
19360	- Buoy 3	41-40-54.421N 071-23-32.207W				Green can.	Removed when endangered by ice.
19365	- *Lighted Buoy 4*	41-40-54.507N 071-23-29.935W	Fl R 2.5s		3	Red nun.	Removed when endangered by ice.
19370	- *Lighted Buoy 5*	41-40-58.864N 071-23-27.692W	Fl G 2.5s		3	Green can.	Removed when endangered by ice.
19373	- Buoy 6	41-41-02.399N 071-23-25.244W					Removed when endangered by ice.
19375	- Buoy 7	41-41-02.483N 071-23-26.966W				Green can.	Removed when endangered by ice.
19380	- Buoy 9	41-41-22.603N 071-23-34.188W				Green can.	Removed When Endangered By Ice.
19385	- Buoy 10	41-41-37.543N 071-23-22.758W				Red nun.	Removed When Endangered By Ice.
19390	- Buoy 12	41-41-43.394N 071-23-22.624W				Red nun.	Removed When Endangered By Ice.
	Greenwich Bay						
19395	- Buoy 3	41-40-15.228N 071-23-57.240W				Green can.	
19400	- *Lighted Buoy 5*	41-40-33.638N 071-25-28.205W	Fl G 2.5s		3	Green can.	
19402	*Sally Rock Monitoring Lighted Buoy*	41-40-31.920N 071-25-27.480W	Fl Y 4s			Yellow.	Property of URI. Private aid.
19405	- Buoy 6	41-40-14.431N 071-26-15.852W				Red nun.	
19410	- Buoy 7 On edge of shoal.	41-40-03.205N 071-26-36.342W				Green can.	
19415	- LIGHT 8	41-40-03.698N 071-26-41.423W	F R			On wooden pile.	Private aid.
19420	Apponaug Cove Approach Buoy 1	41-40-42.398N 071-26-15.217W				Green can.	
	Apponaug Cove						
19425	- Channel Buoy 3	41-41-11.656N 071-26-43.752W				Green can.	
19426	- Channel Buoy 4	41-41-16.594N 071-26-42.672W				Red nun.	Removed when endangered by ice.
19435	- Channel Buoy 6	41-41-30.256N 071-26-41.712W				Red nun.	Removed when endangered by ice.

(1) No.	(2) Name and Location	(3) Position	(4) Characteristic	(5) Height	(6) Range	(7) Structure	(8) Remarks
			RHODE ISLAND - First District				
	NARRAGANSETT BAY						
	Greenwich Bay						
	Apponaug Cove						
19440	- Channel Buoy 7	41-41-34.930N 071-26-47.322W				Green can.	Removed when endangered by ice.
19445	- Channel Buoy 8	41-41-39.888N 071-26-53.623W				Red nun.	Removed when endangered by ice.
	BLOCK ISLAND SOUND AND APPROACHES						
	West Passage						
19450	**Point Judith Light**	41-21-39.725N 071-28-53.037W	Oc (3)W 15s 5s fl 2s ec. 2s fl 2s ec. 2s fl 2s ec.	65	16	Octagonal tower, lower half white, upper half brown. 51	HORN: 1 blast ev 15s (2s bl). Fog signal is radio activated, during times of reduced visibility, turn marine VHF-FM radio to channel 83A/157.175Mhz. Key microphone 5 times consecutively, to activate fog signal for 45 minutes.
19460	*Point Judith Lighted Buoy 2*	41-18-27.693N 071-28-20.832W	Fl R 4s		4	Red.	
19465	Point Judith Bell Buoy 4	41-20-56.122N 071-30-25.505W				Red.	
19468	Quonochontaug Pond Buoy 1	41-20-15.900N 071-43-26.170W				Green can.	Maintained from Apr. 1 to Nov. 1 Private aid.
19469	Quonochontaug Pond Buoy 2	41-20-17.080N 071-43-23.550W				Red nun.	Maintained from Apr. 1 to Nov. 1 Private aid.
19469.1	Quonochontaug Pond Buoy 3	41-20-20.600N 071-43-27.000W				Green can.	Maintained from Apr. 1 to Nov. 1 Private aid.
19469.2	Quonochontaug Pond Buoy 4	41-20-26.790N 071-43-25.540W				Red nun.	Maintained from Apr. 1 to Nov. 1 Private aid.
19469.3	Quonochontaug Pond Buoy 5	41-20-27.900N 071-43-29.300W				Green.	Private aid.
19475	*Block Island North Reef Lighted Bell Buoy 1BI*	41-15-26.327N 071-34-33.358W	Fl G 4s		4	Green.	
19481	BLOCK ISLAND NORTH LIGHT	41-13-39.410N 071-34-33.060W	Fl W 5s	58		White tower atop a house structure.	.... Private aid.
	Point Judith Harbor of Refuge						
19485	- *East Entrance Lighted Buoy 2*	41-21-28.520N 071-29-37.470W	Fl R 4s		4	Red.	
19490	- EAST ENTRANCE LIGHT 3	41-21-35.434N 071-29-52.712W	Fl G 4s	39	5	SG on post on concrete base.	
19492	- *East Entrance Lighted Buoy 5*	41-21-35.341N 071-30-11.412W	Fl G 2.5s		3	Green.	
19500	- WEST ENTRANCE LIGHT 2	41-21-41.134N 071-30-47.612W	Fl R 4s	29	5	TR on post on concrete base.	
19505	- WEST ENTRANCE LIGHT 3	41-21-56.234N 071-30-53.012W	Fl G 6s	35	5	SG on post on concrete base.	HORN: 1 blast ev 30s (3s bl). Fog signal is radio activated, during times of reduced visibility, turn marine VHF-FM radio to channel 83A/157.175Mhz. Key microphone 5 times consecutively, to activate fog signal for 45 minutes.
19510	South Lump Buoy	41-21-48.673N 071-30-28.056W				Red nun with green bands.	
19515	Point Judith Harbor Buoy 2	41-22-02.845N 071-30-50.989W				Red nun.	
19520	Point Judith Harbor Buoy 4	41-22-07.506N 071-30-52.284W				Red nun.	
19525	Point Judith Harbor Buoy 6	41-22-19.607N 071-30-50.636W				Red nun.	
19530	POINT JUDITH INNER HARBOR LIGHT 8	41-22-27.209N 071-30-47.687W	Fl R 2.5s		4	TR on spindle.	
	Great Island Channel						
19535	- Buoy 1	41-22-53.651N 071-30-49.584W				Green can.	

(1) No.	(2) Name and Location	(3) Position	(4) Characteristic	(5) Height	(6) Range	(7) Structure	(8) Remarks
			RHODE ISLAND - First District				
	BLOCK ISLAND SOUND AND APPROACHES						
	Great Island Channel						
19540	- Buoy 3	41-23-00.647N 071-30-45.459W				Green can.	
19545	- Buoy 5	41-23-03.858N 071-30-30.707W				Green can.	
	Point Judith Pond						
19550	- Junction Buoy	41-22-40.962N 071-30-50.278W				Red nun with green bands.	
19555	- Channel Buoy 2	41-22-45.336N 071-30-52.822W				Red nun.	
19560	- Channel Buoy 4	41-22-47.095N 071-30-54.925W				Red nun.	
19565	- *Channel Lighted Buoy 6*	41-22-52.486N 071-30-57.090W	Fl R 2.5s		3	Red nun.	Removed when endangered by ice.
19570	- Channel Buoy 7	41-23-07.006N 071-30-59.674W				Green can.	Removed when endangered by ice.
19575	- Channel Buoy 8	41-23-10.108N 071-30-55.518W				Red nun.	Removed when endangered by ice.
19580	- Channel Buoy 9	41-23-23.802N 071-30-52.219W				Green can.	Removed when endangered by ice.
19582	- Channel Buoy 11	41-23-27.133N 071-30-50.868W				Green can.	Removed when endangered by ice.
19585	- Channel Buoy 12	41-23-32.545N 071-30-46.926W				Red nun.	Removed when endangered by ice.
19590	- Channel Buoy 14	41-23-39.719N 071-30-44.269W				Red nun.	Removed when endangered by ice.
19592	- Channel Buoy 15	41-23-42.601N 071-30-44.419W				Green can.	Removed when endangered by ice.
19600	- Channel Buoy 16	41-23-46.699N 071-30-41.418W				Red nun.	Removed when endangered by ice.
19602	- Channel Buoy 17	41-23-54.401N 071-30-42.220W				Green can.	Removed when endangered by ice.
19605	- Channel Buoy 18	41-23-56.497N 071-30-39.804W				Red nun.	Removed when endangered by ice.
19607	- Channel Buoy 19	41-24-09.101N 071-30-39.238W				Green can.	Removed when endangered by ice.
19620	- Channel Buoy 20	41-24-10.001N 071-30-38.020W				Red nun.	Removed when endangered by ice.
19630	- Channel Buoy 22	41-24-15.241N 071-30-37.158W				Red nun.	Removed when endangered by ice.
19635	- Channel Buoy 24	41-24-25.471N 071-30-27.328W				Red nun.	Removed when endangered by ice.
19636	Beach Island Oyster Culture Buoy NW	41-24-27.510N 071-30-10.190W				Yellow spar.	Private aid.
19637	Beach Island Oyster Culture Buoy NE	41-24-27.160N 071-30-07.470W				Yellow spar.	Private aid.
19638	Beach Island Oyster Culture Buoy SW	41-24-22.550N 071-30-11.570W				Yellow spar.	Private aid.
19639	Beach Island Oyster Culture Buoy SE	41-24-21.190N 071-30-08.610W				Yellow spar.	Private aid.
19640	- Channel Buoy 25	41-24-34.058N 071-30-19.702W				Green can.	Maintained from Apr. 1 to Oct. 31.

(1) No.	(2) Name and Location	(3) Position	(4) Characteristic	(5) Height	(6) Range	(7) Structure	(8) Remarks

RHODE ISLAND - First District

BLOCK ISLAND SOUND AND APPROACHES
Point Judith Pond

19645	- Channel Buoy 26	41-24-56.468N 071-30-09.432W				Red nun.	Maintained from Apr. 1 to Oct. 31.
19650	- Channel Buoy 28	41-25-02.204N 071-30-07.918W				Red nun.	Maintained from Apr. 1 to Oct. 31.
19655	- Channel Buoy 29	41-25-05.201N 071-30-02.282W				Green can.	Maintained from Apr. 1 to Oct. 31.
19660	- Channel Buoy 30	41-25-02.506N 071-29-51.258W				Red nun.	Maintained from Apr. 1 to Oct. 31.
19665	- Channel Buoy 31	41-25-03.844N 071-29-49.866W				Green can.	Maintained from Apr. 1 to Oct. 31.
19670	- Channel Buoy 32	41-25-20.428N 071-29-47.271W				Red nun.	Maintained from Apr. 1 to Oct. 31.
19675	- Channel Buoy 33	41-25-28.601N 071-29-47.209W				Green can.	Maintained from Apr. 1 to Oct. 31.

Billington Cove Marina

19676	- Channel Buoy 1	41-25-07.260N 071-30-09.300W				Green can.	Private aid.
19677	- Channel Buoy 2	41-25-07.080N 071-30-08.040W				Red nun.	Private aid.
19678	- Channel Buoy 3	41-25-14.100N 071-30-07.210W				Green can.	Private aid.
19679	- Channel Buoy 4	41-25-14.820N 071-30-06.780W				Red nun.	Private aid.

BLOCK ISLAND
Block Island

19685	- Northeast Whistle Buoy 5	41-12-36.615N 071-32-01.889W				Green.	
19690	- *Old Harbor Channel Lighted Bell Buoy 1*	41-11-06.542N 071-33-09.268W	Fl G 2.5s		3	Green.	
19695	- Old Harbor Channel Buoy 5 North end of shoal.	41-10-38.512N 071-33-16.575W				Green can.	Removed when endangered by ice.
19700	- Old Harbor Channel Buoy 6	41-10-34.164N 071-33-19.611W				Red nun.	Removed when endangered by ice.
19705	- Old Harbor Channel Buoy 7	41-10-30.770N 071-33-17.638W				Green can.	Removed when endangered by ice.
19718	Clay Head Buoy 7 Marks rock.	41-13-16.634N 071-33-10.072W				Green can.	
19720	- OLD HARBOR CHANNEL BREAKWATER LIGHT 3	41-10-38.525N 071-33-14.550W	Q G	27	6	SG on white skeleton tower on base.	HORN: 2 blasts ev 30s (2s bl-2s si-2s bl-24s si). Fog signal is radio activated, during times of reduced visibility, turn marine VHF-FM radio to channel 81A/157.075Mhz. Key microphone 5 times consecutively, to activate fog signal for 45 minutes.
19725	- BREAKWATER OUTER BASIN LIGHT 8	41-10-30.972N 071-33-20.358W	Fl R 2.5s	30	6	TR on skeleton tower.	
19730	Black Rock Point Buoy 2 On south side of rock.	41-08-25.406N 071-35-44.214W				Red nun.	
19735	*Southwest Point Lighted Whistle Buoy 4*	41-08-43.757N 071-37-20.888W	Fl R 6s		4	Red.	
19740	Dickens Point Shoal Bell Buoy 6	41-09-33.844N 071-37-08.039W				Red.	

Great Salt Pond

19745	- Entrance Bell Buoy 2	41-12-05.403N 071-35-39.218W				Red.	

(1) No.	(2) Name and Location	(3) Position	(4) Characteristic	(5) Height	(6) Range	(7) Structure	(8) Remarks
			RHODE ISLAND - First District				
	BLOCK ISLAND **Great Salt Pond**						
19750	- BREAKWATER LIGHT 4	41-11-57.518N 071-35-35.448W	F R	49	8	TR on skeleton tower.	HORN: 1 blast ev 10s (1s bl). Fog signal is radio activated, during times of reduced visibility, turn marine VHF-FM radio to channel 83A/157.175Mhz. Key microphone 5 times consecutively, to activate fog signal for 60 minutes.
19755	- Entrance Buoy 5	41-11-59.734N 071-35-29.567W				Green can.	
19760	- Entrance Lighted Buoy 7	41-11-51.594N 071-35-23.087W	Fl G 4s		4	Green.	Replaced by unlighted buoy when endangered by ice.
19765	- Entrance Lighted Buoy 8	41-11-51.294N 071-35-24.897W	Fl R 4s		3	Red.	Replaced by unlighted buoy when endangered by ice.
19770	- Buoy 10	41-11-42.654N 071-35-16.881W				Red nun.	
19775	- Buoy 11	41-11-38.564N 071-35-09.546W				Green can.	
19780	- Buoy 12	41-11-35.834N 071-35-11.716W				Red nun.	
19785	- Buoy 13	41-11-11.808N 071-34-37.430W				Green can.	
19790	- Buoy 14	41-11-11.385N 071-34-40.200W				Red nun.	
	BLOCK ISLAND SOUND AND APPROACHES						
19795	**Watch Hill Light**	41-18-14.032N 071-51-30.312W	Al RW 5s	61	14	Square, gray granite tower attached to white building. 61	Emergency light Fl W 2.5s of reduced intensity when main light is extinguished. Lighted throughout 24 hours. HORN: 1 blast ev 30s (3s bl). Fog signal is radio activated, during times of reduced visibility, turn marine VHF-FM radio to channel 83A/157.175Mhz. Key microphone 5 times consecutively, to activate fog signal for 45 minutes.
19800	URI Coastal Monitoring Lighted Research Buoy	41-20-40.200N 071-40-00.840W	Fl Y 2.5s			Yellow.	Property of URI Private aid.
			NEW YORK - First District				
	BLOCK ISLAND SOUND AND GARDINERS BAY						
19810	Cerberus Shoal Lighted Gong Buoy 9	41-10-27.512N 071-57-03.965W	Fl G 4s		4		
19815	**Race Rock Light**	41-14-36.542N 072-02-49.688W	Fl R 10s	67	14	Granite tower attached to dwelling, on granite pier. 45	Horn points southeast. HORN: 2 blasts ev 30s (2s bl-2s si-2s bl-24s si). MRASS-Fog signal is radio activated, during times of reduced visibility, turn marine VHF-FM radio to channel 83A/157.175Mhz. Key microphone 5 times consecutively, to activate fog signal for 45 minutes.
19820	Race Point Buoy 2	41-14-45.709N 072-02-27.298W					
			LONG ISLAND SOUND (Connecticut and New York) - First District				
	LONG ISLAND SOUND (Eastern Part)						
19823	USCG RDC Fishers Island Sound Lighted Research Buoy	41-15-14.380N 072-02-38.439W	Fl Y 4s			Yellow.	Private aid.
			NEW YORK - First District				
	BLOCK ISLAND SOUND AND GARDINERS BAY						
19825	Valiant Rock Lighted Whistle Buoy 11	41-13-46.388N 072-03-59.980W	Q G		3		RACON: B (- . . .)
19830	**Little Gull Island Light**	41-12-22.933N 072-06-24.712W	Fl (2)W 15s	91	14	81	HORN: 1 blast ev 15s (2s bl). Operates continuously.

(1) No.	(2) Name and Location	(3) Position	(4) Characteristic	(5) Height	(6) Range	(7) Structure	(8) Remarks
			NEW YORK - First District				
	BLOCK ISLAND SOUND AND GARDINERS BAY						
19840	Little Gull Island Reef Buoy 1	41-12-29.695N 072-06-08.694W					
19845	*Block Island Sound South Entrance Obstruction Lighted Buoy BIS*	41-06-57.032N 071-43-06.330W	Fl (2+1)G 6s		3	Green and red bands.	
19850	*Endeavor Shoals Lighted Gong Buoy 1*	41-06-05.900N 071-46-21.711W	Fl G 4s		4	Green.	
19855	Blackfish Rock Buoy 3	41-04-56.010N 071-52-57.124W				Green can.	
	Montauk Harbor Approach						
19860	*Shagwong Rock Lighted Buoy SR*	41-05-30.399N 071-53-43.256W	Fl (2+1)G 6s		3	Green and red bands.	
19865	*Shagwong Reef Lighted Bell Buoy 7SR*	41-07-02.256N 071-54-49.552W	Fl G 2.5s		4	Green.	
19870	*Montauk Harbor Entrance Lighted Bell Buoy M*	41-05-06.548N 071-56-23.223W	Mo (A) W		4	Red and white stripes with red spherical topmark.	
19875	MONTAUK EAST JETTY LIGHT 1	41-04-46.128N 071-56-14.180W	Fl G 4s	33	4	SG on skeleton tower.	
19880	MONTAUK WEST JETTY LIGHT 2	41-04-44.243N 071-56-20.320W	Fl R 2.5s	36	5	TR on skeleton tower.	
	Montauk Harbor *Aids replaced by spar buoys during winter months.*						
19895	- Buoy 1	41-04-23.220N 071-56-09.420W				Green can.	Private aid.
19900	- Buoy 3	41-04-20.280N 071-56-12.060W				Green can.	Private aid.
19905	- Buoy 4	41-04-13.080N 071-56-15.000W				Red nun.	Private aid.
19910	- Buoy 5	41-04-11.580N 071-56-13.080W				Green can.	Private aid.
19915	- Buoy 6	41-04-09.060N 071-56-14.580W				Red nun.	Private aid.
19920	- Buoy 8	41-04-05.640N 071-56-13.440W				Red nun.	Private aid.
	Lake Montauk *Aids replaced by spar buoys during winter months.*						
19925	- Buoy 1	41-04-20.040N 071-55-50.580W				Green can.	Private aid.
19930	- Buoy 3	41-04-13.980N 071-55-40.260W				Green can.	Private aid.
19940	- Buoy 5	41-04-08.460N 071-55-44.500W				Green can.	Private aid.
19945	- LIGHT 7	41-04-06.240N 071-55-50.220W	Fl G 2.5s			Green.	Private aid.
19950	- Daybeacon 8	41-04-06.240N 071-55-51.240W				TR on pile.	Private aid.
19955	- Daybeacon 9	41-03-59.580N 071-55-49.620W				SG on pile.	Private aid.
19960	- LIGHT 10	41-03-58.980N 071-55-50.520W	Fl R 4s			Red.	Private aid.
19965	- LIGHT 11	41-03-54.780N 071-55-48.900W	Q G			Green.	Private aid.
19970	- Daybeacon 12	41-03-53.820N 071-55-49.200W				TR on pile.	Private aid.
19975	- *Lighted Buoy 13*	41-03-48.000N 071-55-27.300W	Fl G 4s			Green.	Private aid.
19980	- *Lighted Buoy 14*	41-03-44.520N 071-55-27.240W	Fl R 4s			Red.	Private aid.
19981	*Montauk Oyster Site 415 Lighted Aquaculture Buoy NW*	41-04-17.040N 071-55-30.079W	Fl Y 4s			Yellow.	Private aid.
19981.1	*Montauk Oyster Site 415 Lighted Aquaculture Buoy NE*	41-04-17.169N 071-55-28.130W	Fl Y 4s			Yellow.	Private aid.
19981.2	*Montauk Oyster Site 415 Lighted Aquaculture Buoy SE*	41-04-13.590N 071-55-30.420W	Fl Y 4s			Yellow.	Private aid.

(1) No.	(2) Name and Location	(3) Position	(4) Characteristic	(5) Height	(6) Range	(7) Structure	(8) Remarks
			NEW YORK - First District				
	BLOCK ISLAND SOUND AND GARDINERS BAY						
	Montauk Harbor						
	Lake Montauk						
	Aids replaced by spar buoys during winter months.						
19981.3	*Montauk Oyster Site 415 Lighted Aquaculture Buoy SW*	41-04-13.470N 071-55-32.379W	Fl Y 4s			Yellow.	Private aid.
			CONNECTICUT - First District				
	FISHERS ISLAND SOUND						
	Southeast Entrance						
19990	Catumb Passage Buoy 1C Off rock.	41-17-23.927N 071-52-48.991W				Green can.	
19995	Catumb Passage Buoy 3C Northeast side of Catumb Rocks.	41-17-37.366N 071-52-58.001W				Green can.	
20000	Catumb Rocks Buoy 2 Southwest of reef.	41-17-24.033N 071-53-12.012W				Red nun.	
20005	*Lords Passage Lighted Whistle Buoy L*	41-17-24.082N 071-54-19.775W	Mo (A) W		4	Red and white stripes with red spherical topmark.	
20010	Lords Passage Buoy 2L	41-17-32.222N 071-54-02.124W				Red nun.	
20015	Wicopesset Passage Bell Buoy W	41-17-28.661N 071-54-58.476W				Red and white stripes with red spherical topmark.	
20020	Wicopesset Passage Rock Buoy 1 On north side of rock.	41-17-34.091N 071-55-04.606W				Green can.	
	Main Channel						
20025	*Watch Hill Lighted Bell Buoy 2*	41-17-58.702N 071-51-33.251W	Fl R 6s		4	Red.	Removed when endangered by ice.
20030	Watch Hill Reef Gong Buoy 1 On east side of reef.	41-17-43.953N 071-51-39.921W				Green.	
20035	Watch Hill Passage Buoy WH	41-17-53.582N 071-51-40.000W				Green and red can.	
20040	Sugar Reef Buoy 5	41-17-45.202N 071-52-36.682W				Green can.	
20045	*Napatree Point Ledge Lighted Bell Buoy 6*	41-18-01.332N 071-53-20.103W	Fl R 4s		4	Red.	
20050	Wicopesset Rock Buoy 7 Northeast of rock.	41-17-47.744N 071-54-20.574W				Green can.	
20055	Wicopesset Ledge Buoy 9	41-17-52.561N 071-54-38.836W				Green can.	
20060	Wicopesset Island Buoy 11	41-17-50.501N 071-55-05.237W				Green can.	
20065	Latimer Reef North Isolated Danger Buoy DL	41-18-33.578N 071-55-39.824W				Black and red bands with two black spherical topmarks; can.	
20070	Latimer Reef Buoy 12	41-18-15.429N 071-55-31.893W				Red nun.	
20075	Seal Rocks Northeast Buoy 13	41-17-57.421N 071-55-30.818W				Green can.	
20080	Seal Rocks Buoy 15 On north side of rocks.	41-17-48.661N 071-55-42.838W				Green can.	
20085	LATIMER REEF LIGHT	41-18-16.260N 071-55-59.949W	Fl W 6s	55	9	White conical tower, brown midway of height; brown cylinder.	BELL: 2 strokes ev 15s. Operates continuously.
20090	Youngs Rock Buoy 17 At north end of rock.	41-17-45.690N 071-56-15.989W				Green can.	
20095	Eel Grass Ground Southeast Buoy 16	41-18-30.570N 071-56-42.391W				Red nun.	
20100	East Clump Buoy 19	41-17-51.020N 071-57-36.172W				Green can.	
20105	Eel Grass Ground Northwest Buoy 18	41-18-39.020N 071-57-08.902W				Red nun.	

(1) No.	(2) Name and Location	(3) Position	(4) Characteristic	(5) Height	(6) Range	(7) Structure	(8) Remarks

CONNECTICUT - First District

FISHERS ISLAND SOUND

Main Channel

(1) No.	(2) Name and Location	(3) Position	(4) Characteristic	(5) Height	(6) Range	(7) Structure	(8) Remarks
20110	*Ram Island Reef Lighted Bell Buoy 20*	41-18-11.390N 071-58-23.314W	Fl R 4s		4	Red.	
20115	Ram Island Reef Daybeacon RI	41-18-22.622N 071-58-27.519W				NW on pipe worded DANGER ROCKS.	
20120	Middle Clump Buoy 21	41-17-42.840N 071-58-38.975W				Green can.	
20130	Intrepid Rock Isolated Danger Buoy DIR On southeast side of rock.	41-17-56.009N 072-00-15.117W				Black and red bands with two black spherical topmarks; can.	
20135	Groton Long Point Buoy 22 On southwest end of reef.	41-18-16.033N 072-00-21.012W				Red nun.	
20140	Groton Long Point Buoy 24 On southwest side of 1/2 foot spot.	41-18-20.889N 072-00-48.278W				Red nun.	
20145	NORTH DUMPLING LIGHT	41-17-16.708N 072-01-09.678W	F W (R sector)	94	W 9 R 7	Square house with light tower.	Red from 257° to 023°. HORN: 1 blast ev 30s (3s bl). MRASS-Fog signal is radio activated, during times of reduced visibility, turn marine VHF-FM radio to channel 83A/157.175Mhz. Key microphone 5 times consecutively, to activate fog signal for 45 minutes.
20150	Horseshoe Reef Buoy 26 On southwest side of reef.	41-18-22.737N 072-01-32.098W				Red nun.	
20155	SEAFLOWER REEF LIGHT On southwest part of reef.	41-17-45.643N 072-01-59.594W	Fl W 4s	27	7	NG on skeleton tower.	
20158	Vixen Ledge Buoy 28VL Marks south side of ledge.	41-18-23.306N 072-02-54.436W				Red nun.	

Stonington Harbor

(1) No.	(2) Name and Location	(3) Position	(4) Characteristic	(5) Height	(6) Range	(7) Structure	(8) Remarks
20160	- Approach Buoy 2	41-18-33.224N 071-54-35.884W				Red nun.	
20165	- Approach Gong Buoy 3 On southeast end of Noyes Shoal.	41-18-46.141N 071-54-49.407W				Green.	
20170	STONINGTON OUTER BREAKWATER LIGHT 4	41-18-59.733N 071-54-28.412W	Fl R 4s	46	5	TR on skeleton tower, small house, concrete base.	HORN: 1 blast ev 10s (1s bl). Operates continuously.
20175	STONINGTON BREAKWATER LIGHT 5	41-19-30.463N 071-54-47.246W	Fl G 4s	22	5	SG on skeleton tower, concrete base.	
20180	Stonington Point Junction Buoy SP	41-19-29.231N 071-54-22.437W				Red and green bands; nun.	
20185	STONINGTON INNER BREAKWATER LIGHT 8	41-19-50.124N 071-54-34.010W	Fl R 4s	27	4	TR on skeleton tower, concrete base.	
20190	- Buoy 7	41-19-44.431N 071-54-41.428W				Green can.	
20195	- Buoy 10 Marks end of outfall.	41-20-02.391N 071-54-39.268W				Red nun.	

Little Narragansett Bay

(1) No.	(2) Name and Location	(3) Position	(4) Characteristic	(5) Height	(6) Range	(7) Structure	(8) Remarks
20200	*Academy Rock Lighted Buoy 2* Marks west side of rock.	41-19-34.291N 071-54-13.366W	Fl R 4s		3	Red.	Replaced by nun when endangered by ice.
20205	- Entrance Buoy 4 Marks northwesterly edge of shoal.	41-19-47.391N 071-54-05.266W				Red nun.	
20210	- *Entrance Lighted Buoy 5*	41-19-58.215N 071-53-50.551W	Fl G 4s		3	Green.	Replaced by can from Nov. 15 to May 1.
20211	- Entrance Buoy 5A	41-19-55.260N 071-53-44.380W				Red nun.	
20215	- Buoy 7 On south side of rock.	41-19-54.347N 071-53-37.545W				Green can.	

(1) No.	(2) Name and Location	(3) Position	(4) Characteristic	(5) Height	(6) Range	(7) Structure	(8) Remarks
			CONNECTICUT - First District				
	FISHERS ISLAND SOUND						
	Little Narragansett Bay						
20220	- Buoy 9	41-19-54.314N 071-53-24.047W				Green can.	
20225	- Buoy 10	41-19-50.877N 071-53-13.586W				Red nun.	
20230	- Channel Buoy 11	41-19-53.291N 071-53-08.465W				Green can.	
20235	- *Channel Lighted Buoy 13* 180 feet outside channel limit.	41-19-50.891N 071-52-52.264W	Fl G 4s		3	Green.	Replaced by can from Nov. 15 to May 1.
20240	- Channel Buoy 14	41-19-41.391N 071-52-32.863W				Red nun.	Removed when endangered by ice.
20245	- Channel Buoy 16	41-19-35.392N 071-52-17.263W				Red nun.	Removed when endangered by ice.
20250	- Channel Buoy 16A	41-19-29.637N 071-52-00.668W				Red nun.	Removed when endangered by ice.
20255	- Channel Buoy 17	41-19-30.818N 071-52-00.262W				Green can.	Removed when endangered by ice.
20260	- Channel Buoy 18	41-19-27.392N 071-51-55.262W				Red nun.	Removed when endangered by ice.
20265	- *Channel Lighted Buoy 19*	41-19-20.840N 071-51-42.575W	Fl G 2.5s		3	Green.	Replaced by can from Nov. 15 to May 1.
20270	- Channel Buoy 20	41-19-20.042N 071-51-43.454W				Red nun.	Removed when endangered by ice.
20275	- Channel Buoy 22	41-19-16.361N 071-51-37.915W				Red nun.	Removed when endangered by ice.
20280	- *Channel Lighted Buoy 23* Marks south side of rock.	41-19-14.792N 071-51-32.521W	Fl G 4s		3	Green.	Replaced by can from Nov. 15 to May 1.
20285	- Buoy 24 Marks south side of rock.	41-19-02.612N 071-52-13.962W				Red nun.	Removed when endangered by ice.
	Pawcatuck River *Channel buoys located 20-30 feet outside channel limit.*						
20290	- Buoy 1 On south edge of shoal.	41-19-20.564N 071-51-17.812W				Green can.	Removed when endangered by ice.
20295	- Buoy 3 On south point of shoal.	41-19-27.590N 071-51-09.523W				Green can.	Removed when endangered by ice.
20300	- Channel Buoy 4 On south point of shoal.	41-19-35.692N 071-50-58.399W				Red nun.	
20305	- Channel Buoy 6	41-19-45.963N 071-50-46.863W				Red nun.	Removed when endangered by ice.
20310	- Channel Buoy 7	41-19-55.212N 071-50-35.336W				Green can.	
20315	- Channel Buoy 8	41-20-10.011N 071-50-13.299W				Red nun.	Removed when endangered by ice.
20320	- Channel Buoy 10	41-20-16.963N 071-50-07.775W				Red nun.	Removed when endangered by ice.
20325	- Channel Buoy 12 On west edge of rocky area.	41-20-29.500N 071-49-54.812W				Red nun.	
20330	- Channel Buoy 14	41-20-32.806N 071-49-47.561W				Red nun.	
20335	- Channel Buoy 16	41-20-46.097N 071-49-46.548W				Red nun.	

(1) No.	(2) Name and Location	(3) Position	(4) Characteristic	(5) Height	(6) Range	(7) Structure	(8) Remarks

FISHERS ISLAND SOUND

Pawcatuck River
Channel buoys located 20-30 feet outside channel limit.

20340	- Channel Buoy 17	41-20-48.154N 071-49-47.802W				Green can.	
20342	- Channel Daybeacon 18	41-20-56.000N 071-49-49.000W				TR on pile.	Private aid.
20345	- Channel Daybeacon 19	41-20-55.140N 071-49-49.800W				SG on pile.	Private aid.
20350	Thompson Cove Buoy 1	41-20-49.900N 071-49-45.600W				Green can.	Maintained from May 1 to Nov. 30. Private aid.
20355	Thompson Cove Buoy 3	41-20-50.800N 071-49-45.100W				Green can.	Maintained from May 1 to Nov. 30. Private aid.
20356	Thompson Cove Buoy 5	41-20-51.700N 071-49-44.500W				Green can.	Maintained from May 1 to Nov. 30. Private aid.
20357	Thompson Cove Buoy 7	41-20-52.900N 071-49-44.000W				Green can.	Maintained from May 1 to Nov. 30. Private aid.
20360	- Channel Daybeacon 20	41-21-00.900N 071-49-53.400W				TR on pile.	Private aid.
20363	- Channel Daybeacon 21	41-21-10.980N 071-50-07.680W				SG on pile.	Private aid.
20365	- Channel Daybeacon 22	41-21-06.420N 071-50-01.920W				TR on pile.	Private aid.
20367	- Channel Daybeacon 23	41-21-26.160N 071-50-14.760W				SG on pile.	Private aid.
20370	- Channel Daybeacon 24	41-21-10.900N 071-50-06.300W				TR on pile.	Private aid.
20385	- Channel Daybeacon 26	41-21-18.360N 071-50-10.200W				TR on pile.	Private aid.
20405	- Channel Daybeacon 28	41-21-25.800N 071-50-13.680W				TR on pile.	Private aid.
20407	- Channel Daybeacon 30	41-21-40.300N 071-50-16.500W				TR on pile.	Private aid.
20410	Gavitt Point Outfall Buoy	41-21-09.000N 071-50-07.000W				White with orange bands and diamond worded DANGER SUB PIPE.	Private aid.
	Watch Hill Cove						
20415	- *Channel Lighted Buoy 2*	41-18-53.042N 071-51-42.671W	Fl R 4s		3	Red.	Removed when endangered by ice.
20420	- Channel Buoy 1	41-18-52.182N 071-51-40.621W				Green can.	Removed when endangered by ice.
20425	- Channel Buoy 3	41-18-45.507N 071-51-41.060W				Green can.	
20430	- Channel Buoy 4	41-18-45.188N 071-51-42.004W				Red nun.	
20435	- Channel Buoy 5	41-18-38.302N 071-51-32.970W				Green can.	Removed when endangered by ice.
	Quiambog Cove Approach						
20440	Rock Island South Buoy 2R	41-19-43.940N 071-56-00.540W				Red nun.	
	Mystic Harbor						
20445	Red Reef Buoy 2	41-19-31.336N 071-56-23.082W				Red nun.	
20450	Dodge Island Buoy 4 On southwest end of reef.	41-19-26.390N 071-57-11.472W				Red nun.	
20455	Ellis Reef Daybeacon ER On rocks.	41-19-00.624N 071-57-18.949W				NW on pipe tower worded DANGER ROCKS.	
20460	Enders Island Buoy 6 On southeast edge of shoal.	41-19-22.790N 071-57-30.573W				Red nun.	

(1) No.	(2) Name and Location	(3) Position	(4) Characteristic	(5) Height	(6) Range	(7) Structure	(8) Remarks

CONNECTICUT - First District

FISHERS ISLAND SOUND
Mystic Harbor

(1) No.	(2) Name and Location	(3) Position	(4) Characteristic	(5) Height	(6) Range	(7) Structure	(8) Remarks
20465	- East Approach Buoy 7	41-19-09.569N 071-58-28.065W				Green can.	
20470	- East Approach Buoy 7A	41-19-07.541N 071-58-37.237W				Green can.	
20475	- East Approach Buoy 9	41-18-59.301N 071-58-50.213W				Green can.	
20480	- East Approach Buoy 10	41-18-58.989N 071-58-58.276W				Red nun.	
20485	- Junction Buoy MH	41-18-56.559N 071-59-06.086W				Red and green bands; nun.	
20490	- West Approach Buoy 1	41-18-23.652N 071-59-25.006W				Green can.	
20495	- West Approach Buoy 2	41-18-34.536N 071-59-25.311W				Red nun.	
20500	- West Approach Buoy 3	41-18-38.389N 071-59-29.546W				Green can.	
20505	- *West Approach Lighted Buoy 4*	41-18-50.979N 071-59-21.616W	Fl R 4s		3	Red.	Replaced by nun when endangered by ice.
20510	NOANK LIGHT 5 On East point shoal.	41-18-58.814N 071-59-13.832W	Q G	17	4	SG on skeleton tower.	
20515	- Buoy 6	41-19-00.659N 071-59-09.926W				Red nun.	
20520	- Buoy 8	41-19-04.959N 071-59-13.856W				Red nun.	
20522	- Buoy 10	41-19-08.440N 071-59-14.786W				Red nun.	
20523	- Buoy 12	41-19-12.470N 071-59-14.826W				Red nun.	
20525	- Buoy 14	41-19-17.122N 071-59-12.974W				Red nun.	
20530	- Buoy 16	41-19-29.832N 071-59-00.940W				Red nun.	
20530.5	Mystic River Fairway Channel Daybeacon 1	41-19-25.318N 071-58-33.065W				SG on pile.	Private aid.
20530.7	Mystic River Fairway Channel Daybeacon 2	41-19-25.861N 071-58-32.111W				TR on pile.	Private aid.
20531	Mystic River Fairway Channel Daybeacon 3	41-19-32.400N 071-58-40.200W				SG on pole.	Private aid.
20531.1	Mystic River Fairway Channel Daybeacon 4	41-19-32.520N 071-58-39.120W				TR on pole.	Private aid.
20531.2	Mystic River Fairway Channel Daybeacon 5	41-19-39.120N 071-58-46.860W				SG on pole.	Private aid.
20531.3	Mystic River Fairway Channel Daybeacon 6	41-19-39.300N 071-58-45.840W				TR on pole.	Private aid.
20531.4	Mystic River Fairway Channel Daybeacon 7	41-19-47.040N 071-58-46.560W				SG on pole.	Private aid.
20531.5	Mystic River Fairway Channel Daybeacon 8	41-19-47.460N 071-58-45.600W				TR on pole.	Private aid.
20535	- Buoy 18	41-19-42.706N 071-58-58.088W				Red nun.	
20540	- Buoy 19	41-19-47.199N 071-58-58.328W				Green can.	
20542	- Buoy 20	41-19-47.108N 071-58-54.609W				Red nun.	
20545	- Buoy 21	41-19-51.426N 071-58-42.149W				Green can.	
20550	- Buoy 22	41-19-49.394N 071-58-41.318W				Red nun.	
20555	- Buoy 23	41-19-58.168N 071-58-35.900W				Green can.	
20560	- Buoy 24	41-19-58.720N 071-58-33.044W				Red nun.	

(1) No.	(2) Name and Location	(3) Position	(4) Characteristic	(5) Height	(6) Range	(7) Structure	(8) Remarks

CONNECTICUT - First District

FISHERS ISLAND SOUND
Mystic Harbor

20565	- Buoy 26	41-20-07.779N 071-58-32.845W				Red nun.	
20570	- Buoy 27	41-20-14.708N 071-58-33.620W				Green can.	
20575	- Buoy 29	41-20-24.492N 071-58-27.042W				Green can.	
20580	- Buoy 30	41-20-34.258N 071-58-20.395W				Red nun.	
20585	- Buoy 31	41-20-38.965N 071-58-18.950W				Green can.	
20590	- Buoy 33	41-20-45.921N 071-58-11.130W				Green can.	
20595	- Buoy 35	41-20-50.132N 071-58-10.371W				Green can.	
20600	- Outfall Buoy	41-20-54.700N 071-58-10.000W				White with orange bands and diamond worded DANGER SUBMERGED PIPE.	Private aid.

Mystic River Auxiliary Channel

20601	- Daybeacon 1	41-20-33.720N 071-58-18.540W				SG on pile.	Private aid.
20602	- Daybeacon 2	41-20-33.120N 071-58-18.540W				TR on pile.	Private aid.
20603	- Daybeacon 3	41-20-32.280N 071-58-11.700W				SG on pile.	Private aid.
20604	- Daybeacon 4	41-20-30.660N 071-58-05.520W				TR on pile.	Private aid.
20605	- Daybeacon 5	41-20-31.700N 071-57-57.100W				SG on pile.	Private aid.
20610	- Daybeacon 7	41-20-32.615N 071-57-53.625W				SG on pile.	Private aid.
20615	- Daybeacon 8	41-20-36.383N 071-57-49.937W				TR on pile.	Private aid.
20617	- Daybeacon 9	41-20-36.600N 071-57-50.800W				SG on pile.	Private aid.
20620	- Daybeacon 10	41-20-40.505N 071-57-47.266W				TR on pile.	Private aid.
20625	- Daybeacon 11	41-20-40.733N 071-57-48.000W				SG on pile.	Private aid.
20630	- Daybeacon 12	41-20-45.494N 071-57-44.033W				TR on pile.	Private aid.
20635	- Daybeacon 13	41-20-45.747N 071-57-44.746W				SG on pile.	Private aid.
20640	- Daybeacon 14	41-20-49.037N 071-57-41.738W				TR on pile.	Private aid.
20645	- Daybeacon 15	41-20-49.247N 071-57-42.478W				SG on pile.	Private aid.
20650	- Daybeacon 16	41-20-51.212N 071-57-40.329W				TR on pile.	Private aid.
20651	- Daybeacon 17	41-20-51.426N 071-57-41.066W				SG on pile.	Private aid.
20652	- Daybeacon 18	41-20-52.869N 071-57-39.255W				TR on pile.	Private aid.
20653	- Daybeacon 19	41-20-53.095N 071-57-39.985W				SG on pile.	Private aid.

Mystic River
Channel buoys located 20 feet outside channel limit.

20670	- Channel Buoy 37	41-21-22.808N 071-58-04.995W				Green can.	Removed when endangered by ice.
20675	- Channel Buoy 38	41-21-27.592N 071-57-59.442W				Red nun.	
20680	- Channel Buoy 39	41-21-31.461N 071-57-58.814W				Green can.	

(1) No.	(2) Name and Location	(3) Position	(4) Characteristic	(5) Height	(6) Range	(7) Structure	(8) Remarks

CONNECTICUT - First District

FISHERS ISLAND SOUND

Mystic River

Channel buoys located 20 feet outside channel limit.

20685	- Channel Buoy 41	41-21-34.489N 071-57-58.075W				Green can.	
20695	- Channel Buoy 43	41-21-37.092N 071-57-58.600W				Green can.	
20700	- Channel Buoy 45	41-21-39.489N 071-58-01.976W				Green can.	Removed when endangered by ice.
20705	- Channel Buoy 47	41-21-41.876N 071-58-03.804W				Green can.	
20715	- Channel Buoy 49	41-21-44.984N 071-58-00.321W				Green can.	
20720	- Channel Buoy 51	41-21-48.817N 071-57-55.232W				Green can.	
20725	- Channel Buoy 53	41-21-53.878N 071-57-52.185W				Green can.	Removed when endangered by ice.

West Cove

20845	- Daybeacon 1	41-18-57.660N 071-59-34.020W				SG on pile.	Private aid.
20850	- Daybeacon 3	41-18-59.220N 071-59-33.600W				SG on pile.	Private aid.
20855	- Daybeacon 5	41-19-13.260N 071-59-35.700W				SG on pile.	Private aid.
20860	- Daybeacon 8	41-19-19.680N 071-59-34.080W				TR on pile.	Private aid.
20865	- Daybeacon 10	41-19-21.360N 071-59-33.360W				TR on pile.	Private aid.
20870	- Daybeacon 12	41-19-25.140N 071-59-31.680W				TR on pile.	Private aid.

Mumford Cove

Aids maintained from May 1 to Nov. 1 unless otherwise noted.

20875	VENETIAN HARBOR ENTRANCE LIGHT 1	41-18-53.806N 072-01-09.212W	Fl G 4s	14	4	SG on pile.	
20876	VENETIAN HARBOR LIGHT 2	41-18-55.300N 072-01-06.100W	Fl R 4s	6		Pile.	Private aid.
20880	- Daybeacon 1	41-18-57.710N 072-01-12.220W				SB on pile.	Private aid.
20885	- Daybeacon 2	41-18-57.160N 072-01-11.150W				TR on pile.	Private aid.
20890	- Daybeacon 3	41-19-01.780N 072-01-09.700W				SG on pile.	Private aid.
20895	- Daybeacon 4	41-19-01.250N 072-01-08.650W				TR on pile.	Private aid.
20900	- Daybeacon 5	41-19-10.400N 072-01-04.680W				SG on pile.	Private aid.
20905	- Daybeacon 6	41-19-09.200N 072-01-03.750W				TR on pile.	Private aid.
20910	- Daybeacon 7	41-19-10.500N 072-01-03.420W				SG on pile.	Private aid.
20925	- Daybeacon 8	41-19-10.560N 072-00-53.400W				TR on pile.	Private aid.
20930	- Daybeacon 9	41-19-11.400N 072-00-53.340W				SG on pile.	Private aid.

East Harbor

20970	- Buoy 1E	41-17-13.541N 071-56-50.130W				Green can.	
20975	- Buoy 2E	41-17-15.971N 071-57-04.481W				Red nun.	

West Harbor

20980	- East Channel Buoy 1W On northwest edge of shoal.	41-17-09.860N 071-58-05.583W				Green can.	
20985	- East Channel Buoy 2W	41-17-17.330N 071-58-14.003W				Red nun.	

CONNECTICUT - First District

(1) No.	(2) Name and Location	(3) Position	(4) Characteristic	(5) Height	(6) Range	(7) Structure	(8) Remarks
			CONNECTICUT - First District				

FISHERS ISLAND SOUND

West Harbor

(1) No.	(2) Name and Location	(3) Position	(4) Characteristic	(5) Height	(6) Range	(7) Structure	(8) Remarks
20990	- East Channel Buoy 4 On south side of shoal.	41-17-07.380N 071-59-28.715W				Red nun.	
20995	- East Channel Buoy 5 On northwest edge of Clay Point Shoal.	41-16-53.290N 071-59-33.375W				Green can.	
21010	Lewis Rock Buoy 7 On north side of rock.	41-16-12.600N 072-00-09.046W				Green can.	
21015	Pulpit Rock Buoy 1 Northwest of rock.	41-17-16.199N 071-59-50.616W				Green can.	
21020	Flat Hammock Buoy 2 On northeast end of shoal	41-17-10.689N 072-00-22.877W				Red nun.	
21025	- West Entrance Lighted Bell Buoy 2 Marks edge of ledge.	41-16-47.609N 072-01-23.068W	Fl R 2.5s		4	Red.	
21030	- West Entrance Buoy 3	41-16-52.159N 072-01-04.958W				Green can.	
21035	- West Entrance Channel Buoy 4 Marks northeast edge of shoal.	41-16-27.939N 072-00-50.667W				Red nun.	
21040	- Channel Lighted Buoy 6 Marks shoal off Hawks Nest Point.	41-16-18.279N 072-00-20.416W	Fl R 4s		3	Red.	Replaced by nun when endangered by ice.
21045	- Channel Buoy 8	41-16-07.210N 072-00-20.336W				Red nun.	
21050	- Channel Buoy 10	41-15-59.535N 072-00-30.251W				Red nun.	

Silver Eel Pond

(1) No.	(2) Name and Location	(3) Position	(4) Characteristic	(5) Height	(6) Range	(7) Structure	(8) Remarks
21055	- Entrance Lighted Whistle Buoy SE	41-15-37.026N 072-02-12.079W	Mo (A) W		4	Red and white stripes with red spherical topmark.	

| | | | **LONG ISLAND SOUND (Connecticut and New York) - First District** | | | | |

LONG ISLAND SOUND (Eastern Part)

(1) No.	(2) Name and Location	(3) Position	(4) Characteristic	(5) Height	(6) Range	(7) Structure	(8) Remarks
21060	UCONN Eastern Long Island Wave Lighted Buoy	41-15-51.918N 072-04-02.628W	Fl Y 2.5s			Yellow.	Property of UCONN. Private aid.
21065	Bartlett Reef Lighted Buoy 4	41-15-34.206N 072-08-21.258W	Fl R 4s		4	Red.	Removed when endangered by ice.
21070	BARTLETT REEF LIGHT On south end of reef.	41-16-28.333N 072-08-14.113W	Fl W 6s	35	8	NR on skeleton tower.	HORN: 2 blasts ev 60s (3s bl-3s si-3s bl-51s si). MRASS-Fog signal is radio activated, during times of reduced visibility, turn marine VHF-FM radio to channel 83A/157.175Mhz. Key microphone 5 times consecutively, to activate fog signal for 45 minutes.
21080	Plum Island Lighted Whistle Buoy PI	41-13-17.386N 072-10-48.292W	Mo (A) W		4	Red and white stripes with red spherical topmark.	
21085 27700	Plum Gut Lighted Bell Buoy 2PG	41-10-33.566N 072-13-05.897W	Fl R 4s		4	Red.	
21090 27695	PLUM GUT LIGHT	41-10-25.778N 072-12-42.150W	Fl W 2.5s	21	5	On skeleton tower.	
21095 27680	**Orient Point Light**	41-09-48.426N 072-13-25.027W	Fl W 5s	64	14	Black conical tower with white band in center. 64	HORN: 2 blasts ev 30s (2s bl-2s si-2s bl-24s si). MRASS-Fog signal is radio activated, during times of reduced visibility, turn marine VHF-FM radio to channel 83A/157.175Mhz. Key microphone 5 times consecutively, to activate fog signal for 45 minutes.
21100	Hatchett Reef Buoy 6 On south end of reef.	41-15-52.658N 072-16-00.930W				Red nun.	

194

(1) No.	(2) Name and Location	(3) Position	(4) Characteristic	(5) Height	(6) Range	(7) Structure	(8) Remarks
	LONG ISLAND SOUND (Connecticut and New York) - First District						
	LONG ISLAND SOUND (Eastern Part)						
21105	Saybrook Bar Lighted Bell Buoy 8 On south point of shoal.	41-14-51.285N 072-18-50.568W	Fl R 4s		4	Red.	
21110	Long Sand Shoal East End Buoy E	41-14-38.766N 072-19-21.329W				Red and green bands; nun.	
21115 22495	**Saybrook Breakwater Light**	41-15-47.633N 072-20-33.613W	Fl G 6s	58	11	White conical tower on brown cylindrical pier. 49	HORN: 1 blast ev 30s (3s bl). MRASS-Fog signal is radio activated, during times of reduced visibility, turn marine VHF-FM radio to channel 83A/157.175Mhz. Key microphone 5 times consecutively, to activate fog signal for 45 minutes.
21125	Orient Shoal Buoy 3 On northeast side of shoal.	41-08-58.450N 072-19-50.591W				Green can.	
21135	Long Sand Shoal Lighted Buoy 8A	41-13-30.388N 072-23-08.318W	Q R		3	Red.	
21145	Long Sand Shoal West End Lighted Gong Buoy W At west point of shoal.	41-13-35.461N 072-27-35.746W	Fl (2+1)R 6s		4	Red and green bands.	
21150	**Horton Point Light**	41-05-06.093N 072-26-44.053W	Fl G 10s	103	14	White square tower, dwelling attached. 103	
21155	Sixmile Reef Lighted Buoy 8C At southerly edge of reef.	41-10-47.143N 072-29-26.151W	Fl R 4s		4	Red.	
21160	Twenty-Eight Foot Shoal Lighted Whistle Buoy TE	41-09-15.953N 072-30-24.552W	Fl (2+1)R 6s		4	Red and green bands.	
21165	Kimberly Reef Lighted Bell Buoy KR	41-12-50.387N 072-37-25.349W	Fl (2+1)R 6s		3	Red and green bands.	
21170	**Falkner Island Light**	41-12-43.433N 072-39-13.113W	Fl W 10s	94	13	White octagonal tower. 94	
21171	UCONN Central Long Island Sound Research Lighted Buoy	41-08-15.401N 072-39-19.008W	Fl Y 4s			Yellow.	Private aid.
21175	Goose Island Lighted Bell Buoy 10GI Off south end of shoal.	41-12-07.985N 072-40-28.135W	Fl R 4s		4	Red.	
21180	SACHEM HEAD BREAKWATER LIGHT On rock.	41-14-44.160N 072-42-39.480W	Fl R 3s	8		Pile.	Maintained from June 1 to Oct. 1. Private aid.
21185	BRANFORD REEF LIGHT	41-13-16.727N 072-48-19.228W	Fl W 6s	22	7	NR on skeleton tower.	
21190	Townsend Ledge Lighted Buoy 10A Off south edge of ledge.	41-12-30.753N 072-51-47.174W	Fl R 4s		4	Red.	
21210 24060	**Southwest Ledge Light**	41-14-03.733N 072-54-43.813W	Fl R 5s	57	14	White octagonal house on brown cylindrical pier. 45	HORN: 1 blast ev 15s (2s bl). MRASS-Fog signal is radio activated, during times of reduced visibility, turn marine VHF-FM radio to channel 83A/157.175Mhz. Key microphone 5 times consecutively, to activate fog signal for 45 minutes.
21215 24075	NEW HAVEN LIGHT	41-13-16.372N 072-56-32.501W	Fl W 4s	27	7	NG on skeleton tower.	
21220	Pond Point Shoal Buoy 12 On south point of shoal.	41-11-52.555N 073-00-59.756W				Red nun.	
21225	Charles Island Lighted Buoy 16 South point of shoal.	41-11-01.444N 073-03-05.755W	Fl R 4s		4	Red.	
21230	**Stratford Point Light**	41-09-07.333N 073-06-11.614W	Fl (2)W 20s	52	14	White conical tower, dark red band midway of height. 35	

(1) No.	(2) Name and Location	(3) Position	(4) Characteristic	(5) Height	(6) Range	(7) Structure	(8) Remarks
	LONG ISLAND SOUND (Connecticut and New York) - First District						
	LONG ISLAND SOUND (Eastern Part)						
21240	Stratford Point Buoy 20 On south side of Point No Point Shoal.	41-07-50.334N 073-07-29.355W				Red nun.	
21245	*Stratford Point Lighted Buoy 18*	41-06-49.114N 073-08-09.417W	Fl R 4s		4	Red.	Removed when endangered by ice.
	Stratford Shoal						
21250	- Buoy 1	41-04-11.226N 073-05-11.558W				Green can.	
21255	- Buoy 3 Off north point of shoal.	41-04-35.936N 073-06-15.481W				Green can.	
21260	**- (Middle Ground) Light**	41-03-35.333N 073-06-04.714W	Fl W 5s	60	13	Gray, granite octagonal tower projection from house on pier. 35	HORN: 1 blast ev 15s (2s bl). Operates continuously.
21265	*- Middle Ground Lighted Bell Buoy 2* South of shoal.	41-03-04.036N 073-06-12.280W	Fl R 4s		4	Red.	
21270	Mount Misery Shoal Buoy 11 On northeast point of shoal.	40-59-12.255N 073-04-46.344W				Green can.	
	LONG ISLAND SOUND (Western Part)						
21275	**Old Field Point Light**	40-58-37.246N 073-07-06.817W	Al RG 20s 3s R fl 7s ec. 3s G fl 7s ec.	74	14	Black tower on granite house. 50	
21285	Old Field Point Gong Buoy 11A Off north point of shoal.	40-59-13.077N 073-07-17.432W				Green.	
21289	*The Little Cows Lighted Bell Buoy LC*	41-07-20.010N 073-12-52.016W	Fl G 4s		4	Green.	
21290	**Penfield Reef Light**	41-07-01.542N 073-13-19.539W	Fl R 6s	51	14	White tower on granite dwelling on pier. 51	HORN: 1 blast ev 15s (2s bl). MRASS-Fog signal is radio activated, during times of reduced visibility, turn marine VHF-FM radio to channel 83A/157.175Mhz. Key microphone 5 times consecutively, to activate fog signal for 45 minutes.
21295	*Pine Creek Point Lighted Buoy 22* On south point of shoal.	41-06-29.992N 073-15-47.005W	Fl R 4s		4	Red.	
21300	*Cockenoe Island Shoal Lighted Bell Buoy 24* Southeast of shoal.	41-04-31.692N 073-19-46.111W	Fl R 2.5s		4	Red.	Removed when endangered by ice.
21305	*Norwalk Islands Lighted Bell Buoy 26* Off southeast end of shoal.	41-03-41.152N 073-21-58.765W	Fl R 4s		4	Red.	Removed when endangered by ice.
21310	*Eatons Neck Point Lighted Gong Buoy 11B* On north end of shoal.	41-00-01.254N 073-23-41.666W	Fl G 4s		4	Green.	Replaced by smaller LIB when endangered by ice.
21312	*Eatons Neck Lighted Research Buoy*	41-00-36.197N 073-17-23.778W	Fl Y 4s			Yellow.	Maintained 15 Apr-15 Dec. Property of UCONN. Private aid.
21313	Eversource Energy Cable Marker NW1 VAIS	41-03-04.320N 073-24-26.760W					MMSI # - 993663039 Private aid.
21313.1	Eversource Energy Cable Marker NE2 VAIS	41-02-32.460N 073-23-50.400W					MMSI # - 993663040 Private aid.
21313.2	Eversource Energy Cable Marker E3 VAIS	41-00-10.980N 073-22-17.640W					MMSI # - 993663041 Private aid.
21313.3	Eversource Energy Cable Marker SE4 VAIS	40-57-30.720N 073-21-14.460W					MMSI # - 993663042 Private aid.
21313.4	Eversource Energy Cable Marker S5 VAIS	40-56-30.720N 073-20-42.000W					MMSI # - 993663043 Private aid.
21315	Eatons Neck Lump Buoy E On east side of shoal.	40-58-39.784N 073-24-32.159W				Green and red bands; can.	

(1) No.	(2) Name and Location	(3) Position	(4) Characteristic	(5) Height	(6) Range	(7) Structure	(8) Remarks
			LONG ISLAND SOUND (Connecticut and New York) - First District				
	LONG ISLAND SOUND (Western Part)						
21320	Eatons Neck Point Shoal Buoy 13 On north point of shoal.	40-58-11.834N 073-23-38.628W				Green can.	
21325	**Eatons Neck Light**	40-57-14.433N 073-23-43.414W	F W	144	14	White stone tower. 73	
21330	*Cable and Anchor Reef Lighted Bell Buoy 28C*	41-00-33.403N 073-25-08.429W	Fl R 4s		4	Red.	Replaced by smaller LIB when endangered by ice.
21335	*Great Reef Lighted Buoy 28* Marks south edge of reef.	41-02-23.853N 073-25-28.034W	Fl R 6s		4	Red.	
21336	*UCONN Western Long Island Sound Research Lighted Buoy*	40-57-23.825N 073-34-55.739W	Fl Y 4s			Yellow.	Maintained from 1 Apr. to 1 Oct. Private aid.
21340	**Greens Ledge Light** On north side of west end of ledge.	41-02-30.333N 073-26-37.614W	Al WR 20s 3s W fl 7s ec 3s R fl 7s ec	62	R 14 W 14	Conical tower, upper half white, lower half brown, on black cylindrical pier. 52	HORN: 2 blasts ev 20s (2s bl-2s si-2s bl-14s si). MRASS-Fog signal is radio activated, during times of reduced visibility, turn marine VHF-FM radio to channel 83A/157.175Mhz. Key microphone 5 times consecutively, to activate fog signal for 45 minutes.
21355	*Smith Reef Lighted Buoy 30* On southeast end of reef.	41-01-29.743N 073-29-30.929W	Fl R 4s		3	Red.	Removed when endangered by ice.
21360	*Lloyd Point Shoal Lighted Gong Buoy 15*	40-57-40.845N 073-29-15.749W	Fl G 4s		4	Green.	Removed when endangered by ice.
21365	*The Cows Lighted Bell Buoy 32* On south side of reef.	41-00-12.913N 073-31-26.203W	Fl R 2.5s		4	Red.	
21375 25210	STAMFORD HARBOR WEST BREAKWATER LIGHT 3	41-00-53.915N 073-32-17.349W	Fl G 2.5s	37	4	SG on tower.	
21380	*Twenty-Six Foot Spot Lighted Bell Buoy 32A*	40-58-07.075N 073-32-48.407W	Fl R 2.5s		4	Red.	
21385	Centre Island Reef Bell Buoy 17 East of point of shoal.	40-56-18.643N 073-31-57.923W				Green.	
21390	Oak Neck Point Buoy 19 Off northerly point of shoal.	40-55-27.407N 073-34-11.703W				Green can.	
21395	Woolsey Reef Buoy 34 Off shoals.	40-59-56.384N 073-33-54.459W				Red nun.	
21400	**Great Captain Island Light**	40-58-56.984N 073-37-23.268W	Al WR 12s	62	14 R 14	NR on skeleton tower. 62	HORN: 1 blast ev 15s (2s bl). MRASS-Fog signal is radio activated, during times of reduced visibility, turn marine VHF-FM radio to channel 83A/157.175Mhz. Key microphone 5 times consecutively, to activate fog signal for 45 minutes.
21405	Bluefish Shoal Bell Buoy 36	40-58-07.536N 073-38-47.192W				Red.	
21410	*Rye Beach Lighted Bell Buoy 38*	40-57-30.987N 073-39-35.974W	Fl R 4s		4	Red.	Replaced by nun if endangered by ice.
21415	*Parsonage Point Lighted Buoy 40* On southeast side of Porgy Shoal.	40-56-49.697N 073-40-29.897W	Fl R 6s		4	Red.	Removed when endangered by ice.
21420	*Matinecock Point Shoal Lighted Gong Buoy 21* Off north point of shoal.	40-54-31.478N 073-38-11.172W	Fl G 4s		4	Green.	Removed when endangered by ice.
21425	Milton Point Buoy 40A	40-56-07.758N 073-41-16.979W				Red nun.	
21430	*Scotch Caps Lighted Bell Buoy 42*	40-55-28.759N 073-42-09.061W	Fl R 2.5s		4	Red.	

(1) No.	(2) Name and Location	(3) Position	(4) Characteristic	(5) Height	(6) Range	(7) Structure	(8) Remarks

LONG ISLAND SOUND (Connecticut and New York) - First District

LONG ISLAND SOUND (Western Part)

(1) No.	(2) Name and Location	(3) Position	(4) Characteristic	(5) Height	(6) Range	(7) Structure	(8) Remarks
21435	*Prospect Point Lighted Gong Buoy 23* Marks northerly end of shoal.	40-52-54.362N 073-42-58.940W	Fl G 4s		4	Green.	
21436	*UCONN Execution Rocks Research Lighted Buoy*	40-52-56.004N 073-43-41.802W	Fl Y 4s			Yellow.	Private aid.
21440	**Execution Rocks Light**	40-52-41.333N 073-44-16.314W	Fl W 10s	62	14	White stone tower, brown band midway of height; granite dwelling attached. 55	RACON: X (- . . -)
21450	Execution Rocks Shoal North End Buoy 1	40-53-27.632N 073-44-09.497W				Green can.	
21455	Execution Rocks Shoal East Side Buoy 44	40-52-46.892N 073-44-06.486W				Red nun.	
21460	*Execution Rocks Lighted Gong Buoy 44A* Marks southeastern end of shoal.	40-52-23.513N 073-44-15.887W	Fl R 4s		4	Red.	
21465	Execution Rocks Shoal Southwest End Buoy ER	40-52-28.513N 073-44-33.488W				Red and green bands; nun.	
21470	Sands Point Daybeacon	40-52-01.733N 073-43-57.214W				NG on skeleton tower.	
21475	*Sands Point Reef Lighted Buoy 25* Marks northwest edge of shoal off point.	40-52-07.293N 073-44-15.387W	Fl G 2.5s		3	Green.	
21480	GANGWAY ROCK LIGHT 27A Near end of shoal.	40-51-29.232N 073-44-44.914W	Fl G 6s	40	6	SG on skeleton tower.	
21485	Gangway Rock Gong Buoy 27 On northwest point of shoal.	40-51-29.793N 073-44-48.488W				Green.	
21490	Success Rock Buoy	40-51-22.393N 073-44-35.488W				White with orange bands worded ROCK.	
21495	*Hewlett Point Lighted Buoy 29* Off northwest point of shoal.	40-50-30.264N 073-45-20.000W	Fl G 4s		4	Green.	
21500	HART ISLAND LIGHT 46	40-50-41.932N 073-45-59.914W	Fl R 4s	23	6	TR on skeleton tower, concrete base on rocks.	
21505	STEPPING STONES LIGHT Marks outer end of reef.	40-49-28.142N 073-46-28.735W	Oc G 4s	46	8	Red brick on granite pier; white band on southwest face of pier.	
21510	Locust Point Buoy 46A	40-49-26.621N 073-47-09.881W				Red nun.	
21515	*Throgs Neck Lighted Bell Buoy 48* Marks southern end of shoal.	40-48-11.032N 073-47-15.014W	Fl R 4s		4	Red.	
21520	THROGS NECK LIGHT	40-48-16.496N 073-47-26.126W	F R	60	9	NB on skeleton tower.	

WATCH HILL TO NEW HAVEN HARBOR
North Channel (Saybrook to New Haven)

(1) No.	(2) Name and Location	(3) Position	(4) Characteristic	(5) Height	(6) Range	(7) Structure	(8) Remarks
21525	Hatchett Reef Buoy 1 On northeast point of reef.	41-16-14.484N 072-15-44.600W				Green can.	
21530	*Cornfield Point Shoal Lighted Bell Buoy 2* South of shoal.	41-15-01.358N 072-23-03.258W	Fl R 4s		4	Red.	
21535	Hen and Chickens Buoy On southeast edge of shoal.	41-15-09.989N 072-24-13.311W				White can with orange bands and diamond worded ROCKS.	
21560	INDIAN TOWN EAST BREAKWATER LIGHT	41-16-34.406N 072-24-18.805W	Fl W 2s	28		On pile.	Private aid.
21565	Crane Reef Buoy 4 On south side of reef.	41-14-53.039N 072-25-22.324W				Red nun.	
21570	Duck Island Reef Buoy 6 On south end of reef.	41-14-51.031N 072-28-28.472W				Red nun.	

(1) No.	(2) Name and Location	(3) Position	(4) Characteristic	(5) Height	(6) Range	(7) Structure	(8) Remarks
		LONG ISLAND SOUND (Connecticut and New York) - First District					
	WATCH HILL TO NEW HAVEN HARBOR						
	North Channel (Saybrook to New Haven)						
21575	Stone Island Reef Buoy 8 On south side of reef.	41-14-14.401N 072-30-43.217W				Red nun.	
21580	Hammonasset Point Reef Buoy 10 On southwest side of shoal.	41-14-45.250N 072-33-13.822W				Red nun.	
21585	Charles Reef Buoy 14 Off south end of reef.	41-14-50.677N 072-37-26.719W				Red nun.	
21590	*Falkner Island Reef Lighted Gong Buoy 15* North of shoal.	41-13-22.996N 072-39-15.372W	Fl G 4s		4	Green.	
21595	Indian Reef Southwest Buoy 16 On south side of shoal.	41-14-24.024N 072-41-04.856W				Red nun.	
21600	Chimney Corner Reef Buoy 20 South side of reef.	41-14-19.914N 072-42-19.658W				Red nun.	
21610	*Goose Rocks Shoal Lighted Bell Buoy 22* Marks southwest end of shoal.	41-14-22.710N 072-43-28.245W	Fl R 4s		4	Red.	
21615	*Browns Reef Lighted Bell Buoy 26* South of reefs.	41-13-48.372N 072-46-15.344W	Fl R 4s		4	Red.	
21620	*Totoket Bar Lighted Buoy 28* On south end of reef.	41-14-04.106N 072-48-05.027W	Fl R 4s		4	Red.	Replaced by nun when endangered by ice.
21625	Five Foot Rock Buoy 32 On southwest side of rock.	41-14-25.403N 072-49-55.139W				Red nun.	
21630	*Cow and Calf Lighted Bell Buoy 34*	41-14-16.355N 072-50-33.184W	Fl R 2.5s		4	Red.	
21635	Round Rock Buoy 36 On south side of shoal.	41-13-43.611N 072-53-09.587W				Red nun.	
	LONG ISLAND SOUND (Eastern Part)						
	South Side						
	Mattituck Inlet						
21645	Mattituck Gong Buoy 3A	41-01-50.913N 072-33-58.277W					
21650	MATTITUCK BREAKWATER LIGHT MI	41-00-55.413N 072-33-39.553W	Fl W 4s	25	6	NR on skeleton tower.	
21653	- Buoy 1	41-00-55.588N 072-33-34.604W				Green Can.	
21655	- Lighted Buoy 2	41-00-55.656N 072-33-37.378W	Fl R 4s		3	Red.	
21657	- Lighted Buoy 2A	41-00-48.726N 072-33-30.780W	Q R		3	Red.	Marks edge of encroaching shoal.
21660	- Buoy 3	41-00-46.681N 072-33-26.755W				Green can.	
	Mattituck Creek						
21665	Mattituck Inner Creek Buoy 2	41-00-47.700N 072-32-59.760W				Red nun.	Maintained from May 1 to Oct. 31. Private aid.
21667	Mattituck Inner Creek Buoy 3	41-00-21.360N 072-32-49.140W				Green can.	Maintained from May 1 to Oct. 31. Private aid.
21670	Mattituck Inner Creek Buoy 5	41-00-11.400N 072-32-46.620W				Green can.	Maintained from May 1 to Oct. 31. Private aid.
21673	Mattituck Inner Creek Buoy 6	41-00-02.640N 072-32-42.600W				Red nun.	Maintained from May 1 to Oct. 31. Private aid.
21675	Mattituck Inner Creek Buoy 8	40-59-54.840N 072-32-38.700W				Red nun.	Maintained from May 1 to Oct. 31. Private aid.
21677	Mattituck Inner Creek Buoy 10	40-59-48.960N 072-32-35.460W				Red nun.	Maintained from May 1 to Oct. 31. Private aid.

199

(1) No.	(2) Name and Location	(3) Position	(4) Characteristic	(5) Height	(6) Range	(7) Structure	(8) Remarks

LONG ISLAND SOUND (Connecticut and New York) - First District

LONG ISLAND SOUND (Eastern Part)

South Side

Jacobs Point

21680	- PLATFORM LIGHTS (4)	41-00-01.102N 072-38-47.688W	Q W	25		On platform.	Lights flash in unison.HORN: 1 blast ev 20s (2s bl). Private aid.
21685	- Pipeline Buoy A	40-59-13.000N 072-38-43.000W				Yellow can.	Private aid.
21690	- Pipeline Buoy B	40-59-47.000N 072-38-48.000W				Yellow can.	Private aid.
21715	Roanoke Point Shoal Buoy 5 On northwest side of shoal.	41-00-13.859N 072-42-16.690W				Green can.	

South Side (Mattituck to Mt. Sinai)

21720	Herod Point Shoal Buoy 7 On north point of shoal.	40-59-41.686N 072-49-26.577W				Green can.	
21725	Rocky Point Buoy 9 On north end of shoal.	40-59-34.389N 072-57-52.982W				Green can.	

LONG ISLAND SOUND (Connecticut) - First District

APPROACHES TO NEW LONDON HARBOR

Pine Island Channel

21735	- *Lighted Bell Buoy 2* On southwest point of shoal.	41-18-36.878N 072-03-38.961W	Fl R 4s		3	Red.	
21740	- Buoy 3 On north side of reef.	41-18-35.488N 072-04-09.033W				Green can.	
21742	AVERY POINT LIGHT	41-18-54.900N 072-03-48.840W	Fl G 4s			White octagonal concrete tower.	Private aid.
21745	*Pine Island Lighted Buoy 1* On southern tip of shoal.	41-18-53.370N 072-03-40.562W	Fl G 4s		3	Green.	Replaced by can when endangered by ice.
21750	AVERY POINT BREAKWATER LIGHT 1A Marks end of breakwater.	41-18-57.600N 072-03-36.300W	Q G			SG on spindle.	Private aid.
21755	Pine Island Buoy 2 On northern tip of shoal.	41-18-54.938N 072-03-33.663W				Red nun.	

West Approach

21758	Bartlett Reef Buoy 1	41-16-28.966N 072-07-53.968W				Green can.	
21760	Little Goshen Reef Buoy 3 On south point of shoal.	41-17-20.767N 072-06-43.107W				Green can.	
21765	Goshen Ledge Buoy 5 On south end of ledge.	41-17-28.767N 072-06-17.385W				Green can.	
21770	Rapid Rock Buoy R On southeast side of rock	41-17-15.618N 072-06-05.567W				Green and red bands; can.	
21775	Cormorant Rock Ledge Buoy 7 On point of ledge east of rock.	41-17-56.967N 072-05-42.665W				Green can.	
21780	Sarah Ledge Buoy SL	41-17-42.387N 072-05-23.884W				Green and red bands; can.	

NEW LONDON HARBOR AND VICINITY

New London Harbor

21790	- *Channel Lighted Buoy 2*	41-17-37.409N 072-04-38.558W	Fl R 2.5s		4	Red.	
21795	- *Channel Lighted Buoy 1*	41-17-37.088N 072-04-46.783W	Fl G 2.5s		4	Green.	
21800	- *Channel Lighted Buoy 3*	41-18-28.387N 072-04-53.484W	Fl G 4s		4	Green.	
21805	- Channel Buoy 4	41-18-29.246N 072-04-44.786W				Red nun.	
21810	Black Ledge Buoy 2BL	41-18-01.178N 072-03-57.513W				Red nun.	
21815	Black Ledge Buoy 4BL	41-18-04.688N 072-04-15.843W				Red nun.	
21820	Black Ledge Buoy 6BL	41-18-17.493N 072-04-22.278W				Red nun.	

(1) No.	(2) Name and Location	(3) Position	(4) Characteristic	(5) Height	(6) Range	(7) Structure	(8) Remarks
			LONG ISLAND SOUND (Connecticut) - First District				
	NEW LONDON HARBOR AND VICINITY						
	New London Harbor						
21825	**New London Ledge Light** On west side of Southwest Ledge.	41-18-21.177N 072-04-38.793W	Fl (3+1) WR 30s 0.1s R fl 9.9s ec. 0.1s W fl 4.9s ec. 0.1s W fl 4.9s ec. 0.1s W fl 9.9s ec.	58	W 17 R 14	Red brick dwelling on square pier. 58	HORN: 2 blast ev 20s (2s bl-2s si-2s bl-14s si). MRASS-Fog signal is radio activated, during times of reduced visibility, turn marine VHF-FM radio to channel 83A/157.175Mhz. Key microphone 5 times consecutively, to activate fog signal for 45 minutes.
21840	Frank Ledge Buoy F On north side of ledge.	41-18-40.667N 072-04-32.854W				Green and red bands; can.	
21845	- Light	41-18-59.867N 072-05-23.135W	Iso W 6s (R sector)	90	W 17 R 14	White octagonal pyramidal tower. 89	Red from 000° to 041°. Covers Sarah Ledge and shoals westward.
21850	- *Channel Lighted Buoy 5*	41-19-19.594N 072-04-59.655W	Fl G 2.5s		4	Green.	
21855	- *Channel Lighted Buoy 6*	41-19-20.139N 072-04-51.258W	Fl R 2.5s		4	Red.	
21859	Greens Harbor Obstruction Buoy 2A	41-20-03.693N 072-05-24.741W				Red nun.	
21860	- LOWER WHARF LIGHT	41-20-06.900N 072-04-55.000W	Fl R 15s	15		Pile.	Private aid.
21865	- UPPER WHARF LIGHT	41-20-11.300N 072-04-55.900W	Fl R 15s			Pile.	Private aid.
21870	Groton Outfall Hazard Buoy	41-20-16.000N 072-04-57.000W				White with orange bands.	Private aid.
21875	- *Channel Lighted Buoy 7*	41-20-19.234N 072-05-07.275W	Fl G 6s		4	Green.	
21885	Melton Rocks Buoy On north side of Melton Ledge.	41-20-23.546N 072-05-24.754W				White can with orange bands and diamond worded ROCKS.	
21890	GRAVING DOCK SOUTH LIGHT	41-20-36.000N 072-04-58.860W	Q R	22		Pier dolphin.	Private aid.
21895	GRAVING DOCK CENTER LIGHT	41-20-36.720N 072-04-59.940W	Q R	22		Pier dolphin.	Private aid.
21900	GRAVING DOCK NORTH LIGHT	41-20-37.800N 072-05-01.320W	Q R	22		Pier dolphin.	Private aid.
21905	GRAVING DOCK 3 SOUTH LIGHT	41-20-50.220N 072-05-02.640W	Q R	24		Dual light fixture on pier.	Private aid.
21910	GRAVING DOCK 3 NORTH LIGHT	41-20-53.600N 072-05-03.100W	Q R				Private aid.
21915	- Buoy 9	41-20-35.287N 072-05-13.387W				Green can.	
21920	- Buoy 11	41-20-46.887N 072-05-15.487W				Green can.	
21922	Thames River Buoy EP	41-22-26.801N 072-05-23.281W				Green and red; can.	
21935	- *Channel Lighted Buoy 13*	41-21-05.987N 072-05-12.947W	Fl G 4s		4	Green.	
21940	- Buoy 14	41-21-06.698N 072-05-05.994W				Red nun.	
21943	- Buoy 16	41-21-26.283N 072-05-09.109W				Red nun.	
21944	STATE PIER LIGHT	41-21-26.600N 072-05-20.000W	F G	19		Green.	Private aid.
21948	- LEADING LIGHT	41-21-46.686N 072-05-14.287W	Oc R 4s	44	4	On southeast bridge abutment of railroad bridge.	Shows red from 353° to 356°. Higher intensity on 354.5°.
21956	THAMES RIVER LOWER RANGE FRONT LIGHT	41-23-26.952N 072-05-27.383W	Iso G 6s	26		On monopole.	"Visible 5.5° each side of rangeline. Lighted throughout 24 hours.

(1) No.	(2) Name and Location	(3) Position	(4) Characteristic	(5) Height	(6) Range	(7) Structure	(8) Remarks
			LONG ISLAND SOUND (Connecticut) - First District				
	NEW LONDON HARBOR AND VICINITY						
	New London Harbor						
21960	THAMES RIVER LOWER RANGE REAR LIGHT 452 yards, 354.7° from front light.	41-23-40.288N 072-05-29.035W	F G	88		On skeleton tower.	Visible 4° each side of rangeline. Lighted throughout 24 hours. Note: Does not mark center of channel at far end of range.
	Greens Harbor						
21970	- Buoy On southwest side of shoal.	41-20-08.513N 072-05-35.013W					White can with orange bands and diamond worded ROCKS.
	Shaw Cove Entrance						
21975	- Buoy 1	41-20-44.416N 072-05-24.800W					Green can.
21980	- Buoy 3	41-20-50.737N 072-05-36.627W					Green can.
	Thames River *Channel buoys located 30 feet outside channel limit.*						
21985	- Lighted Buoy 1	41-22-01.886N 072-05-20.887W	Fl G 2.5s		4		Green.	Replaced by can when endangered by ice.
21990	Academy Buoy 1A On north side of shoal.	41-22-18.407N 072-05-36.878W					Green can.
21995	BAILEY POINT LIGHT 2	41-22-40.076N 072-05-16.057W	Fl R 4s	13	3	TR on pile tower on concrete base.	
22000	- Lighted Buoy 3	41-22-51.517N 072-05-25.547W	Fl G 4s		4		Green.	Replaced by can when endangered by ice.
22010	- Lighted Buoy 5	41-23-15.217N 072-05-33.339W	Fl G 4s		3		
22020	- UPPER DIRECTIONAL LIGHT	41-23-34.297N 072-05-46.475W	F W (G & R sector)	21	W 7 R 5 G 5	On pile.	Shows green from 174.5 to 177.5; white from 177.5 to 180.5; red from 180.5 to 183.5; with a fixed white passing light.
22025	- Lighted Buoy 7	41-23-45.700N 072-05-51.349W	Fl G 4s		4		Green.	Replaced by can when endangered by ice.
22035	- MIDDLE RANGE FRONT LIGHT	41-23-55.795N 072-05-51.754W	Q G	15		on pile.	Visible all around; higher intensity on rangeline. Lighted throughout 24 hours.
22036	- MIDDLE RANGE REAR LIGHT 197 yards, 336.0° from front.	41-24-01.133N 072-05-54.917W	Iso G 6s	29			Visible 1.5° each side of rangeline. Lighted throughout 24 hours.
22040	- Buoy 9	41-24-04.087N 072-05-50.163W					Green can.
22055	SCOTCH CAP LIGHT 11	41-24-21.701N 072-05-50.305W	Fl G 4s	21	3	SG on skeleton tower on concrete base.	
22060	- Buoy 13	41-24-36.497N 072-05-45.780W					Green can.
22063	- Buoy 14	41-25-00.043N 072-05-25.492W					Red nun.
22065	ICE HOUSE LIGHT 15	41-25-04.371N 072-05-33.720W	Fl G 2.5s	13	3	SG on pipe tower pn consrete base.	
22070	- Buoy 16	41-25-26.967N 072-05-46.830W					Red nun.
22075	BARTLETT POINT LIGHT 17	41-25-33.565N 072-05-55.218W	Fl G 4s	13	3	SG on pipe tower on concrete base.	
22078	- Buoy 18	41-25-44.957N 072-05-48.350W					Red nun.
22080	- Buoy 20	41-26-05.214N 072-05-38.837W					Red nun.

(1) No.	(2) Name and Location	(3) Position	(4) Characteristic	(5) Height	(6) Range	(7) Structure	(8) Remarks
		LONG ISLAND SOUND (Connecticut) - First District					
	NEW LONDON HARBOR AND VICINITY						
	Upper Thames River						
22105	ALLYN POINT LIGHT 22	41-26-37.204N 072-05-02.611W	Fl R 4s	21	3	TR on pipe tower on concrete base.	
22110	Thames River Buoy 23	41-26-49.657N 072-05-07.130W				Green can.	
22115	LONG REACH LOWER LIGHT 24	41-26-53.894N 072-04-56.344W	Fl R 4s	13	3	TR on pipe tower on concrete base.	
22120	Thames River Buoy 25	41-27-00.197N 072-04-57.220W				Green can.	
22125	Thames River Buoy 26	41-27-02.577N 072-04-41.350W				Red nun.	
22130	LONG REACH UPPER LIGHT 27	41-27-10.828N 072-04-24.521W	Fl G 4s	21	3	SG on pipe tower on concrete base.	
22135	Thames River Buoy 29	41-27-18.687N 072-04-16.089W				Green can.	
22140	STODDARDS OLD DOCK LIGHT 30	41-27-38.453N 072-04-03.063W	Fl R 4s	21	3	TR on pipe tower on concrete base.	
22143	Thames River Wreck Buoy WR30A	41-27-41.287N 072-04-05.832W				Red nun.	
22145	Thames River Buoy 31	41-27-48.896N 072-04-06.889W				Green can.	
22150	WALDEN ISLAND LIGHT 32	41-28-05.046N 072-04-06.789W	Fl R 2.5s	14	3	TR on pipe tower on concrete base.	
22155	Thames River Buoy 33	41-28-05.756N 072-04-12.810W				Green can.	
22160	Thames River Buoy 34	41-28-22.076N 072-04-16.280W				Red nun.	
22165	Thames River Buoy 35	41-28-38.076N 072-04-23.010W				Green can.	
22170	MOHEGAN DIKE LIGHT 36	41-28-41.903N 072-04-19.865W	Fl R 4s	13	3	TR on pipe tower on concrete base.	
22180	Thames River Buoy 38	41-28-59.756N 072-04-32.221W				Red nun.	
22195	INDIAN HILL LIGHT 39	41-29-10.786N 072-04-46.658W	Fl G 4s	13	3	SG on pipe tower on concrete base.	
22200	PRIDE PIER LIGHT 40	41-29-28.678N 072-04-47.534W	Fl R 4s	13	3	TR on pipe tower on concrete base.	
22205	Thames River Buoy 41	41-29-33.246N 072-04-51.211W				Green can.	
22210	BURNT HOUSE PIER LIGHT 42	41-29-40.672N 072-04-48.560W	Fl R 2.5s	16	3	TR on skeleton tower on concrete base.	
22215	PERCHE ROCK LIGHT 43 On rock.	41-29-50.522N 072-04-57.117W	Fl G 4s	21	3	SG on pipe tower on concrete base.	
22220	Thames River Channel Buoy 44	41-29-56.896N 072-04-57.831W				Red nun.	
22225	Thames River Channel Buoy 45	41-30-06.650N 072-05-03.758W				Green can.	
22230	SAND PIER LIGHT 47	41-30-13.025N 072-05-05.031W	Fl G 2.5s	13	3	SG on pipe tower on concrete base.	
22235	Thames River Channel Buoy 48	41-30-21.386N 072-04-59.162W				Red nun.	
22240	LOWER COAL DOCK LIGHT 50	41-30-41.641N 072-04-40.134W	Fl R 4s	21	3	TR on pipe tower on concrete base.	
22245	Thames River Channel Buoy 51	41-30-44.064N 072-04-43.894W				Green can.	
22250	Thames River Channel Buoy 53	41-31-00.669N 072-04-43.318W				Green can.	
	NIANTIC BAY AND VICINITY						
22255	Bartlett Reef North End Buoy 1	41-17-45.406N 072-08-29.410W				Green can.	
22260	Two Tree Island Shoal Buoy 3	41-17-53.386N 072-09-15.691W				Green can.	
22265	Flat Rock Buoy 2 On southwest side of rock	41-18-15.007N 072-09-02.865W				Red nun.	

(1) No.	(2) Name and Location	(3) Position	(4) Characteristic	(5) Height	(6) Range	(7) Structure	(8) Remarks
		LONG ISLAND SOUND (Connecticut) - First District					
	NIANTIC BAY AND VICINITY						
22270	High Rock Buoy 4	41-18-17.096N 072-09-23.691W				Red nun.	
22275	*White Rock Lighted Bell Buoy 6*	41-18-00.375N 072-10-29.303W	Fl R 4s		3	Red.	
	Millstone Security Zone						
22276	- Buoy A	41-18-30.480N 072-10-19.320W				White and orange can.	Private aid.
22277	- Buoy B	41-18-27.900N 072-10-15.840W				White and orange can.	Private aid.
22278	- Buoy C	41-18-25.380N 072-10-12.300W				White and orange can.	Private aid.
22279	- Buoy D	41-18-22.860N 072-10-08.640W				White and orange can.	Private aid.
22279.1	Millstone Power Plant CG Mooring Buoy	41-18-22.945N 072-10-28.938W				White with blue band.	
22279.2	- Buoy E	41-18-27.660N 072-09-36.720W				White and orange can.	Private aid.
22279.3	- Buoy F	41-18-32.220N 072-09-37.380W				White and orange can.	Private aid.
22279.4	- Buoy G	41-18-37.380N 072-09-38.040W				White and orange can.	Private aid.
22279.5	- Buoy H	41-18-12.660N 072-09-59.280W				White and orange can.	Private aid.
22279.6	- Buoy I	41-18-16.200N 072-10-02.880W				White and orange can.	Private aid.
	NIANTIC BAY AND VICINITY						
22280	Threefoot Rock Buoy 7 On east side of rock.	41-18-21.865N 072-11-46.645W				Green can.	
22285	Black Rock Buoy 8 On west side of rock.	41-18-34.675N 072-10-42.923W				Red nun.	
22290	CRESCENT PARK BREAKWATER LIGHT	41-18-39.480N 072-12-03.060W	Fl W 6s	8		On pile.	Maintained from Apr. 15 to Nov. 15. Private aid.
22300	Wigwam Rock Buoy 9	41-18-55.377N 072-11-45.879W				Green can.	Removed when endangered by ice.
	Niantic River *Positions of buoys frequently shifted with changing conditions.*						
22305	- Channel Buoy 1	41-19-10.247N 072-10-55.187W				Green can.	
22310	- Channel Buoy 3	41-19-16.191N 072-10-45.532W				Green can.	
22315	- Channel Buoy 4	41-19-15.318N 072-10-44.880W				Red nun.	
22320	- Channel Buoy 6	41-19-31.585N 072-10-41.813W				Red nun.	Removed when endangered by ice.
22321	Mago Point West Daybeacon	41-19-34.600N 072-10-39.000W				SG on pile.	Private aid.
22322	Mago Point East Daybeacon	41-19-36.500N 072-10-33.300W				SG on pile.	Private aid.
22325	- Channel Daybeacon 7	41-19-33.544N 072-10-49.316W				SG on pile.	
22330	- Channel Daybeacon 8	41-19-35.200N 072-10-49.242W				TR on pile.	
22335	NIANTIC DOCKOMINIUM LIGHT D At end of dock.	41-19-38.500N 072-11-00.400W	Fl Y 2s	9		SY on pier.	Private aid.
22340	- Channel Buoy 10	41-19-38.585N 072-10-58.093W				Red nun.	Removed when endangered by ice.
22345	- Channel Buoy 11	41-19-40.685N 072-11-01.294W				Green can.	Removed when endangered by ice.
22350	- Channel Buoy 12	41-19-41.475N 072-10-59.935W				Red nun.	

(1) No.	(2) Name and Location	(3) Position	(4) Characteristic	(5) Height	(6) Range	(7) Structure	(8) Remarks
		LONG ISLAND SOUND (Connecticut) - First District					

NIANTIC BAY AND VICINITY

Niantic River

Positions of buoys frequently shifted with changing conditions.

(1) No.	(2) Name and Location	(3) Position	(4) Characteristic	(5) Height	(6) Range	(7) Structure	(8) Remarks
22355	- Channel Daybeacon 13	41-19-45.536N 072-10-57.432W				SG on pile.	
22360	- Channel Buoy 14	41-19-46.475N 072-10-54.973W				Red nun.	Removed when endangered by ice.
22365	- Channel Buoy 15	41-19-51.185N 072-10-52.802W				Green can.	Removed when endangered by ice.
22370	- Channel Buoy 16	41-19-52.585N 072-10-49.193W				Red nun.	Removed when endangered by ice.
22375	- Channel Daybeacon 17	41-19-55.720N 072-10-49.096W				SG on pile.	
22380	- Channel Buoy 18	41-20-01.118N 072-10-43.188W				Red nun.	Removed when endangered by ice.
22385	- Channel Buoy 19	41-20-01.331N 072-10-45.133W				Green can.	Removed when endangered by ice.
22390	- Channel Buoy 21	41-20-06.255N 072-10-43.423W				Green can.	Removed when endangered by ice.
22395	- Channel Buoy 21A	41-20-07.363N 072-10-53.070W				Green can.	Removed when endangered by ice.
22400	- Channel Buoy 22	41-20-06.711N 072-10-42.493W				Red nun.	Removed when endangered by ice.
22405	- Channel Buoy 22A	41-20-08.665N 072-10-52.484W				Red nun.	Removed when endangered by ice.
22410	- Channel Buoy 23	41-20-09.627N 072-10-56.766W				Green can.	Removed when endangered by ice.
22415	- Channel Buoy 24	41-20-09.873N 072-10-54.737W				Red nun.	Removed when endangered by ice.
22420	- Channel Buoy 25	41-20-11.435N 072-10-57.434W				Green can.	Removed when endangered by ice.
22425	- Channel Buoy 26	41-20-13.705N 072-10-55.774W				Red nun.	Removed when endangered by ice.
22430	- Channel Junction Daybeacon SC	41-20-18.685N 072-10-57.694W				JG on pile.	
22435	- Channel Daybeacon 28	41-20-22.315N 072-10-57.993W				TR on pile.	
22440	- Channel Buoy 29	41-20-25.945N 072-11-01.654W				Green can.	Removed when endangered by ice.
22445	- Channel Buoy 30	41-20-26.655N 072-10-59.944W				Red nun.	Removed when endangered by ice.

Smith Cove

(1) No.	(2) Name and Location	(3) Position	(4) Characteristic	(5) Height	(6) Range	(7) Structure	(8) Remarks
22449	- Daybeacon 1	41-20-18.200N 072-10-57.500W				SG on pile.	Private aid.
22450	- Daybeacon 1A	41-20-17.400N 072-11-05.500W				SG on pile.	Private aid.
22455	- Daybeacon 2	41-20-18.000N 072-11-05.880W				TR on pile.	Private aid.
22460	- Daybeacon 4	41-20-16.680N 072-11-10.380W				TR on pile.	Private aid.
22465	- Daybeacon 6	41-20-15.660N 072-11-14.160W				TR on pile.	Private aid.
22470	- Daybeacon 8	41-20-16.080N 072-11-18.000W				TR on pile.	Private aid.

(1) No.	(2) Name and Location	(3) Position	(4) Characteristic	(5) Height	(6) Range	(7) Structure	(8) Remarks
			LONG ISLAND SOUND (Connecticut) - First District				
	NIANTIC BAY AND VICINITY						
	Smith Cove						
22475	- Daybeacon 9	41-20-16.140N 072-11-19.920W				SG on pile.	Private aid.
	Pattaganset River						
22480	Blackboys Rocks Buoy 2 Marks southside of rock.	41-16-58.538N 072-13-29.108W				Red nun.	
22485	Long Rock Buoy 4 Marks southwest side of rocky shoal.	41-17-27.036N 072-13-48.236W				Red nun.	
22490	Seal Rock Buoy 5 Marks south end of rock.	41-17-40.517N 072-13-50.011W				Green can.	
	CONNECTICUT RIVER - LONG ISLAND SOUND TO DEEP RIVER						
	Connecticut River						
22495 21115	**Saybrook Breakwater Light**	41-15-47.633N 072-20-33.613W	Fl G 6s	58	11	White conical tower on brown cylindrical pier. 49	HORN: 1 blast ev 30s (3s bl). MRASS-Fog signal is radio activated, during times of reduced visibility, turn marine VHF-FM radio to channel 83A/157.175Mhz. Key microphone 5 times consecutively, to activate fog signal for 45 minutes.
22505	- *Lighted Buoy 2*	41-15-47.476N 072-20-28.911W	Fl R 2.5s		3	Red.	Replaced by nun when endangered by ice.
22510	Saybrook Daybeacon	41-16-07.382N 072-20-17.144W				White globe on granite structure.	
22515	- Buoy 4	41-16-11.306N 072-20-26.252W				Red nun.	
22520	**Lynde Point Light**	41-16-17.333N 072-20-34.913W	F W	71	14	White stone tower. 71	
22525	- *Lighted Buoy 5*	41-16-18.716N 072-20-30.001W	Fl G 4s		3	Green.	Replaced by can when endangered by ice.
22530	- Buoy 6 Marks west edge of shoal	41-16-31.716N 072-20-24.211W				Red nun.	
22535	- Buoy 7 Marks east edge of shoal	41-16-35.717N 072-20-37.162W				Green can.	
22540	- *Lighted Buoy 8* Marks shoal.	41-16-42.267N 072-20-37.432W	Fl R 4s		3	Red.	Replaced by nun when endangered by ice.
22545	- Buoy 10 Marks west edge of shoal.	41-16-58.845N 072-20-42.901W				Red nun.	
22550	- *Lighted Buoy 14*	41-17-20.418N 072-20-57.222W	Fl R 4s		3	Red.	Replaced by nun when endangered by ice.
22555	- Buoy 15	41-17-25.427N 072-21-03.863W				Green can.	
22565	Old Saybrook North Cove Buoy 2	41-17-27.000N 072-21-08.920W				Red nun.	Private aid.
22570	Old Saybrook North Cove Buoy 3	41-17-25.140N 072-21-12.180W				Green can.	Private aid.
22571	Old Saybrook North Cove Buoy 4	41-17-26.100N 072-21-15.060W				Red nun.	Private aid.
22572	Old Saybrook North Cove Buoy 5	41-17-23.040N 072-21-32.760W				Green can.	Private aid.
22573	Old Saybrook North Cove Buoy 6	41-17-24.360N 072-21-32.940W				Red nun.	Private aid.
22575	- Buoy 17	41-17-34.777N 072-21-01.923W				Green can.	
22580	- *Lighted Buoy 19*	41-17-52.676N 072-21-01.853W	Fl G 4s		3	Green.	Replaced by can when endangered by ice.
22585	Calves Island Bar South Junction Buoy CI On southwest end of shoal.	41-19-19.887N 072-20-42.913W				Red and green bands; nun.	

206

(1) No.	(2) Name and Location	(3) Position	(4) Characteristic	(5) Height	(6) Range	(7) Structure	(8) Remarks

LONG ISLAND SOUND (Connecticut) - First District

CONNECTICUT RIVER - LONG ISLAND SOUND TO DEEP RIVER

Connecticut River

22590	- Buoy 20 30 feet outside channel limit.	41-19-38.687N 072-20-53.313W				Red nun.	
22595	- LIGHT 22	41-19-51.547N 072-20-59.822W	Fl R 4s	26	3	TR on skeleton tower.	
22600	*- Lighted Buoy 23*	41-19-57.697N 072-21-10.153W	Fl G 4s		3	Green.	Replaced by can when endangered by ice.
22605	- Buoy 24 120 feet outside channel limit.	41-20-38.128N 072-22-16.436W				Red nun.	
22610	- LIGHT 25	41-20-42.541N 072-22-36.153W	Fl G 4s	26	3	SG on skeleton tower, concrete base.	

Essex Anchorage
Aids maintained from Apr. 1 to Nov. 30.

22615	- Buoy A	41-20-43.320N 072-22-37.500W				Yellow can.	Private aid.
22620	- Buoy B	41-20-52.080N 072-22-48.600W				Yellow can.	Private aid.
22625	- Daybeacon C	41-20-54.240N 072-23-02.400W				Yellow square on pile.	Private aid.
22630	- Buoy D	41-20-55.140N 072-22-59.940W				Yellow can.	Private aid.
22635	- Buoy E	41-20-54.060N 072-22-50.460W				Yellow can.	Private aid.
22640	- Buoy F	41-21-03.840N 072-22-51.000W				Yellow can.	Private aid.
22645	- Buoy G	41-21-06.840N 072-23-00.120W				Yellow can.	Private aid.
22650	- Buoy H	41-21-08.340N 072-22-59.520W				Yellow can.	Private aid.
22655	- Buoy I	41-21-05.820N 072-22-51.240W				Yellow can.	Private aid.
22660	- Buoy J	41-21-22.440N 072-22-51.060W				Yellow can.	Private aid.

Connecticut River

22665	*- Lighted Buoy 26*	41-20-55.877N 072-22-46.607W	Fl R 4s		3	Red.	Replaced by nun when endangered by ice.
22670	- Buoy 28 25 feet outside channel limit.	41-21-18.658N 072-22-46.248W				Red nun.	
22675	- LIGHT 29	41-22-07.567N 072-22-34.536W	Fl G 4s	26	3	SG on skeleton tower.	
22680	- Channel Buoy 29A	41-22-41.654N 072-22-39.899W				Green can.	
22685	Essex Meadows Anchorage Buoy A	41-22-21.540N 072-22-47.880W				White with Orange bands, can.	Maintained from Apr. 1 to Dec. 1. Private aid.
22690	Essex Meadows Anchorage Buoy B	41-22-29.220N 072-22-54.060W				Yellow can.	Maintained from Apr. 1 to Dec. 1. Private aid.

Hamburg Cove
Aids maintained from May 1 to Nov. 1 unless otherwise noted.

22695	- Entrance Buoy 1	41-22-28.245N 072-22-20.632W				Green can.	Maintained year round.
22700	- Entrance Buoy 2	41-22-27.152N 072-22-19.783W				Red nun.	Maintained year round.
22705	- Entrance Buoy 3	41-22-29.640N 072-22-09.120W				Green can.	Private aid.
22710	- Entrance Buoy 4	41-22-27.840N 072-22-16.320W				Red nun.	Private aid.
22715	- Entrance Buoy 5	41-22-30.720N 072-22-04.080W				Green can.	Private aid.
22720	- Entrance Buoy 6	41-22-27.840N 072-22-10.560W				Red nun.	Private aid.

(1) No.	(2) Name and Location	(3) Position	(4) Characteristic	(5) Height	(6) Range	(7) Structure	(8) Remarks

LONG ISLAND SOUND (Connecticut) - First District

CONNECTICUT RIVER - LONG ISLAND SOUND TO DEEP RIVER
Connecticut River
Hamburg Cove
Aids maintained from May 1 to Nov. 1 unless otherwise noted.

(1) No.	(2) Name and Location	(3) Position	(4) Characteristic	(5) Height	(6) Range	(7) Structure	(8) Remarks
22723	- Entrance Buoy 7	41-22-30.000N 072-21-57.600W				Green can.	Private aid.
22725	- Entrance Buoy 8	41-22-29.640N 072-22-04.080W				Red nun.	Private aid.
22727	- Entrance Buoy 9	41-22-34.320N 072-21-38.160W				Green can.	Private aid.
22735	- Entrance Daybeacon 11	41-22-36.840N 072-21-34.920W				SG on pile.	Private aid.
22740	- Entrance Daybeacon 13	41-22-39.000N 072-21-33.120W				SG on pile.	Private aid.
22745	- Daybeacon 15	41-22-40.800N 072-21-31.680W				SG on pile.	Private aid.
22750	- Daybeacon 17	41-22-42.960N 072-21-29.160W				SG on pile.	Private aid.
22755	- Daybeacon 19	41-22-45.480N 072-21-26.640W				SG on pile.	Private aid.
22760	- Buoy 21	41-22-48.360N 072-21-24.480W				Green can.	Private aid.
22765	- Buoy 23	41-22-50.520N 072-21-24.480W				Green can.	Private aid.
22767	- Buoy 24	41-22-57.360N 072-21-23.400W				Red nun.	Private aid.
22769	- Bouy 26	41-23-01.320N 072-21-18.360W				Red nun.	Private aid.
22780	- Daybeacon 29	41-23-02.040N 072-21-13.680W				SG on pile.	Private aid.
22785	- Daybeacon 31	41-23-02.040N 072-21-11.880W				SG on pile.	Private aid.
22790	- Daybeacon 33	41-23-02.040N 072-21-09.000W				SG on pile.	Private aid.
22792	- Daybeacon 35	41-23-04.200N 072-21-06.840W				SG on pile.	Private aid.
	Connecticut River						
22860	- Buoy 30	41-23-04.241N 072-22-45.068W				Red nun.	
22865	- Buoy 31	41-23-03.248N 072-22-47.758W				Green can.	
22870	- LIGHT 32 On northeast side of Brockaway Bar cut.	41-23-09.689N 072-22-51.619W	Fl R 4s	21	3	TR on skeleton tower.	
22875	- Buoy 33	41-23-11.388N 072-23-13.448W				Green can.	
22880	- LIGHT 35	41-23-22.214N 072-24-50.523W	Fl G 4s	26	3	SG on skeleton tower.	
	BODKIN ROCK TO HARTFORD **Connecticut River**						
22885	- Buoy 34	41-23-23.049N 072-24-33.171W				Red nun.	
22890	- LIGHT 36	41-23-59.608N 072-25-11.912W	Fl R 4s	21	3	TR on pipe tower on concrete base.	
22895	- Buoy 37 25 feet outside channel limit.	41-24-28.239N 072-25-23.123W				Green can.	
22900	- RANGE A FRONT LIGHT 40	41-25-01.838N 072-25-34.959W	Fl R 2.5s	36		KRW and TR on skeleton tower.	Visible all around higher intensity on range line.
22905	- RANGE A REAR LIGHT 94 yards, 343.2° from front light.	41-25-04.506N 072-25-36.029W	F R	50		KRW on skeleton tower.	Visible 1.5° each side of range line.
22910	- Buoy 39	41-24-42.939N 072-25-31.463W				Green can.	
22911	CHESTER FERRY DOCK NORTH LIGHT A	41-25-10.500N 072-25-57.500W	Fl W 2.5s	19		On dolphin center pile.	Private aid.

(1) No.	(2) Name and Location	(3) Position	(4) Characteristic	(5) Height	(6) Range	(7) Structure	(8) Remarks
		LONG ISLAND SOUND (Connecticut) - First District					
	BODKIN ROCK TO HARTFORD						
	Connecticut River						
22912	CHESTER FERRY DOCK SOUTH LIGHT B	41-25-09.000N 072-25-57.500W	Fl Y 2.5s	20		On dolphin center pile.	Private aid.
22913	HADLYME FERRY DOCK NORTH LIGHT A	41-25-12.500N 072-25-43.000W	Fl Y 2.5s	21		On dolphin center pile.	Private aid.
22914	HADLYME FERRY DOCK SOUTH LIGHT B	41-25-12.000N 072-25-43.000W	Fl W 2.5s	21		On dolphin center pile.	Private aid.
22915	- LIGHT 42	41-25-44.823N 072-26-11.375W	Fl R 4s	31	3	TR on skeleton tower.	
22920	- Buoy 44	41-26-08.290N 072-27-18.137W				Red nun.	
22925	- LIGHT 45	41-26-12.552N 072-27-31.869W	Fl G 4s	31	3	SG on skeleton tower.	
22930	- *Lighted Buoy 46*	41-26-24.390N 072-27-41.327W	Fl R 4s		3	Red.	Replaced by nun when endangered by ice.
22935	- Buoy 47 Marks east edge of flats.	41-27-44.400N 072-27-58.788W				Green can.	
22940	- LIGHT 48	41-27-53.893N 072-27-58.743W	Fl R 4s	36	3	TR on pipe tower.	
22945	- Buoy 49 Marks east edge of flats.	41-27-54.240N 072-28-08.158W				Green can.	
22950	- Buoy 50	41-28-19.009N 072-29-04.769W				Red nun.	Maintained from June 1 to Nov. 1.
22955	- Buoy 52 50 feet outside channel limit.	41-28-31.590N 072-29-55.061W				Red nun.	
22960	- LIGHT 53	41-28-33.128N 072-30-03.548W	Fl G 4s	26	3	SG on skeleton tower.	
22965	- HADAM ISLAND LIGHT	41-29-36.623N 072-30-48.273W	Fl W 2.5s	40		NR on skeleton tower.	Visible all around.
22975	- Buoy 55	41-29-36.654N 072-30-55.081W				Green can.	Maintained from June 1 to Nov. 1.
22980	- Buoy 57	41-29-43.509N 072-31-16.562W				Green can.	Maintained from June 1 to Nov. 1.
22985	- LIGHT 58	41-29-50.039N 072-31-23.463W	Fl R 4s	31	3	TR on skeleton tower.	
23000	- Buoy 59	41-29-49.968N 072-31-29.585W				Green can.	Maintained from June 1 to Nov. 1.
23005	- LIGHT 61	41-30-04.460N 072-32-59.609W	Fl G 4s	31	3	SG on skeleton tower.	
23010	- Buoy 62	41-30-24.334N 072-33-08.530W				Red nun.	Maintained from June 1 to Nov. 1.
23015	- Buoy 64	41-30-41.778N 072-33-16.919W				Red nun.	Maintained from June 1 to Nov. 1.
23020	- Buoy 66 100 feet outside channel limit.	41-30-58.494N 072-33-26.615W				Red nun.	Maintained from June 1 to Nov. 1.
23025	- LIGHT 67	41-31-12.374N 072-33-31.557W	Q G	31	4	SG on skeleton tower.	Visible all around.
23035	- Buoy 69	41-31-34.749N 072-33-19.197W				Green can.	Maintained from June 1 to Nov. 1.
23040	- LIGHT 70	41-32-04.845N 072-32-58.229W	Fl R 4s	27	3	TR on skeleton tower.	Higher intensity beam up and down river.
23045	MAROMAS PIER SOUTH LIGHT	41-32-28.800N 072-33-04.920W	F G	49		On pile.	Private aid.
23050	MAROMAS PIER NORTH LIGHT	41-32-29.280N 072-33-04.800W	F W	35		On pile.	Private aid.

(1) No.	(2) Name and Location	(3) Position	(4) Characteristic	(5) Height	(6) Range	(7) Structure	(8) Remarks
			LONG ISLAND SOUND (Connecticut) - First District				
	BODKIN ROCK TO HARTFORD						
	Connecticut River						
23060	- Buoy 71	41-32-55.299N 072-33-09.876W				Green can.	Maintained from June 1 to Nov. 1.
23065	- *Lighted Buoy 72*	41-33-06.995N 072-33-15.328W	Fl R 2.5s		3	Red.	Maintained from June 1 to Nov. 1.
23070	- Buoy 73	41-33-08.268N 072-33-24.472W				Green can.	Maintained from June 1 to Nov. 1.
23075	- Buoy 75	41-33-26.148N 072-34-21.298W				Green can.	Maintained from June 1 to Nov. 1.
23080	- LIGHT 76	41-33-32.279N 072-34-36.330W	Fl R 4s	31	3	TR on skeleton tower.	
23085	- Buoy 78	41-33-32.388N 072-35-50.841W				Red nun.	Maintained from June 1 to Nov. 1.
23090	- LIGHT 80	41-33-40.060N 072-36-09.349W	Fl R 4s	21	3	TR on skeleton tower.	
23095	STRAITS HILL LIGHT	41-33-49.001N 072-36-14.892W	Q W	23	7	NR on skeleton tower.	Higher intensity beam up river.
23100	- Buoy 84	41-33-46.830N 072-36-24.730W				Red nun.	Maintained from June 1 to Nov. 1.
23105	- Buoy 86 50 feet outside channel limit.	41-33-36.282N 072-37-11.176W				Red nun.	Maintained from June 1 to Nov. 1.
23110	- LIGHT 87	41-33-32.938N 072-37-15.254W	Fl G 2.5s	32	3	SG on skeleton tower.	
23115	- Buoy 88	41-33-38.466N 072-37-36.502W				Red nun.	Maintained from June 1 to Nov. 1.
23120	- Buoy 89	41-33-36.184N 072-38-07.885W				Green can.	Maintained from June 1 to Nov. 1.
23125	- Buoy 90	41-33-36.547N 072-38-21.039W				Red nun.	Maintained from June 1 to Nov. 1.
23130	- Buoy 92	41-33-46.861N 072-38-42.189W				Red nun.	Maintained from June 1 to Nov. 1.
23135	- LIGHT 94	41-34-43.263N 072-38-40.736W	Fl R 4s	14	3	TR on pipe tower on concrete base.	
23140	- LIGHT 95	41-35-46.826N 072-38-17.344W	Fl G 4s	21	3	SG on skeleton tower.	
23145	- Buoy 96	41-35-45.457N 072-38-08.871W				Red nun.	Maintained from June 1 to Nov. 1.
23150	- LIGHT 98	41-36-00.122N 072-37-30.551W	Fl R 2.5s	21	3	TR on skeleton tower.	
23155	- Buoy 99	41-36-02.219N 072-37-22.693W				Green can.	Maintained from June 1 to Nov. 1.
23160	- LIGHT 100	41-36-07.867N 072-36-56.183W	Fl R 4s	36	3	TR on skeleton tower.	
23165	- LIGHT 102	41-36-40.167N 072-36-42.732W	Fl R 2.5s	25	4	TR on skeleton tower.	Visible all around.
23175	- Buoy 104	41-36-55.059N 072-37-07.142W				Red nun.	Maintained from June 1 to Nov. 1.
23180	- LIGHT 105	41-37-09.655N 072-37-39.042W	Fl G 4s	21	3	SG on skeleton tower.	
23185	- Buoy 106	41-37-39.390N 072-37-49.344W				Red nun.	Maintained from June 1 to Nov. 1.
23190	- LIGHT 107	41-37-49.702N 072-37-58.023W	Fl G 2.5s	21	3	SG on skeleton tower.	

(1) No.	(2) Name and Location	(3) Position	(4) Characteristic	(5) Height	(6) Range	(7) Structure	(8) Remarks
		LONG ISLAND SOUND (Connecticut) - First District					
	BODKIN ROCK TO HARTFORD						
	Connecticut River						
23195	- Buoy 109	41-38-13.480N 072-37-47.163W				Green can.	Maintained from June 1 to Nov. 1.
23200	- RANGE F FRONT LIGHT 110	41-38-35.610N 072-37-24.697W	Fl R 2.5s	26		KRW and TR on skeleton tower.	Visible all around; higher intensity on rangeline.
23205	- RANGE F REAR LIGHT 177.1° 40 yards from front light.	41-38-34.441N 072-37-24.619W	F R	53		KRW on skeleton tower.	Visible 1.5° each side of range line.
23206	GLASTONBURY FERRY SLIP LIGHT	41-39-56.000N 072-37-36.000W	F G	24		On wood dolphin.	Private aid.
23207	ROCKYHILL FERRY SLIP SOUTH LIGHT	41-39-58.500N 072-37-46.300W	F G	24		On wood dolphin.	Private aid.
23208	ROCKYHILL FERRY SLIP NORTH LIGHT	41-39-58.900N 072-37-45.800W	F R	24		On wood dolphin.	Private aid.
23210	- LIGHT 113	41-40-05.204N 072-37-43.773W	Fl G 4s	15	3	SG on pile.	
23215	- Buoy 115	41-40-16.489N 072-37-06.387W				Green can.	Maintained from June 1 to Nov. 1.
23220	- LIGHT 116	41-40-24.854N 072-36-29.983W	Fl R 2.5s	47	4	TR on skeleton tower.	Visible all around.
23230	GLASTONBURY BAR LIGHT	41-40-32.035N 072-36-25.255W	Q W	21	5	NR on skeleton tower.	
23235	- LIGHT 120	41-41-07.822N 072-36-36.084W	Fl R 4s	36	3	TR on skeleton tower.	
23240	- Buoy 121	41-41-11.891N 072-36-47.340W				Green can.	Maintained from June 1 to Nov. 1.
23245	- LIGHT 122	41-41-18.880N 072-36-53.214W	Fl R 4s	36	3	TR on skeleton tower.	
23250	- Buoy 123	41-41-21.049N 072-37-15.561W				Green can.	Maintained from June 1 to Nov. 1.
23255	- Buoy 124	41-41-21.741N 072-37-34.271W				Red nun.	Maintained from June 1 to Nov. 1.
23260	- LIGHT 125	41-41-23.982N 072-38-09.039W	Fl G 4s	26	3	SG on skeleton tower.	
23265	- Buoy 126	41-41-51.727N 072-38-11.205W				Red nun.	Maintained from June 1 to Nov. 1.
23280	- Buoy 127	41-42-43.927N 072-37-12.207W				Green can.	Maintained from June 1 to Nov. 1.
23285	- LIGHT 129	41-42-43.011N 072-37-53.281W	Fl G 4s	31	3	SG on skeleton tower.	
23300	- LIGHT 135	41-43-27.142N 072-39-03.290W	Fl G 2.5s	21	3	SG on skeleton tower.	
23305	- Buoy 136	41-43-27.392N 072-38-57.344W				Red nun.	Maintained from June 1 to Nov. 1.
	Wethersfield Cove						
23310	- Daybeacon 1	41-43-31.364N 072-39-03.663W				SG on pile.	
23315	- Daybeacon 2	41-43-31.855N 072-39-03.297W				TR on pile.	
23320	- Daybeacon 3	41-43-30.614N 072-39-20.509W				SG on pile.	
23325	- Daybeacon 4	41-43-30.964N 072-39-23.280W				TR on pile.	
	Connecticut River						
23335	- Buoy 137	41-43-41.572N 072-38-51.783W				Green can.	Maintained from June 1 to Nov. 1.

(1) No.	(2) Name and Location	(3) Position	(4) Characteristic	(5) Height	(6) Range	(7) Structure	(8) Remarks
			LONG ISLAND SOUND (Connecticut) - First District				
	BODKIN ROCK TO HARTFORD						
	Connecticut River						
23340	- LIGHT 138	41-43-49.905N 072-38-37.397W	Fl R 4s	31	3	TR on skeleton tower.	
23345	- LIGHT 140	41-44-02.998N 072-38-26.700W	Fl R 4s	36	3	TR on skeleton tower.	
23360	- LIGHT 142	41-44-53.645N 072-38-39.365W	Fl R 4s	26	3	TR on skeleton tower.	
23365	HARTFORD JETTY LIGHT 143	41-45-03.690N 072-39-02.765W	Fl G 4s	26	3	SG on pipe tower.	
23375	Westbrook Harbor Buoy Marks south side of Lobster Rock.	41-16-11.216N 072-26-50.370W				Red with green band; nun.	
23380	West Beach Shoal Buoy	41-16-16.000N 072-27-08.000W				White with orange band; can.	Maintained from May. 1 to Nov. 1. Private aid.
23385	Menunketesuck Island Shoal Buoy	41-15-32.000N 072-27-35.000W				White with orange band; can.	Maintained from May. 1 to Nov. 1. Private aid.
23390	Menunketesuck Island Rock Buoy	41-15-39.000N 072-28-02.000W				White can with orange band.	Maintained from May. 1 to Nov. 1. Private aid.
	DUCK ISLAND TO MADISON REEF						
	Duck Island Roads						
23395	DUCK ISLAND NORTH BREAKWATER LIGHT	41-15-36.851N 072-28-29.849W	Fl W 4s	16	6	NR on skeleton tower.	
23400	DUCK ISLAND WEST BREAKWATER LIGHT 2DI	41-15-22.719N 072-29-06.569W	Fl R 4s	17	4	TR on skeleton tower.	
	Patchogue River						
23405	- BREAKWATER LIGHT 3A	41-16-07.114N 072-28-22.816W	Fl G 4s	21	4	SG on skeleton tower.	
23410	- *Channel Lighted Buoy 2*	41-15-58.777N 072-28-21.978W	Fl R 4s		3	Red.	Replaced by nun when edangered by ice.
23415	- Channel Buoy 3	41-16-01.451N 072-28-22.807W				Green can.	
23420	- Channel Buoy 4	41-16-05.056N 072-28-20.355W				Red nun.	
23425	- Channel Daybeacon 5	41-16-13.200N 072-28-19.900W				SG on pile	Private aid.
23430	Menunketesuck River Junction Daybeacon M	41-16-14.000N 072-28-20.000W				Green and red square.	Private aid. Maintained from Apr. 1 to Nov. 30. Private aid.
23435	- Channel Buoy 6	41-16-15.700N 072-28-17.700W				Red nun.	Private aid.
23440	- Daybeacon 7	41-16-26.300N 072-28-10.400W				SG on pile.	Private aid.
23445	- Daybeacon 8	41-16-30.850N 072-28-09.960W				TR on pile.	Private aid.
23450	- Channel Daybeacon 10	41-16-32.100N 072-28-03.800W				TR on pile.	Private aid.
23455	KELSEY POINT BREAKWATER LIGHT	41-14-36.614N 072-30-28.956W	Fl W 2.5s	22	7	NG on skeleton tower.	
	Clinton Harbor *Channel buoys located 20 feet outside channel limit.*						
23460	- Rock Buoy 2 West of rock.	41-15-07.341N 072-31-17.308W				Red nun.	
23465	- *Lighted Buoy 3*	41-15-23.271N 072-31-39.783W	Fl G 4s		3	Green.	Removed when endangered by ice.
23466	- Channel Buoy 4	41-15-24.071N 072-31-37.166W				Red nun.	
23470	- Channel Buoy 6	41-15-39.234N 072-31-36.249W				Red nun.	
23475	- Channel Buoy 5	41-15-39.581N 072-31-37.426W				Green can.	
23480	- Channel Buoy 8	41-15-46.923N 072-31-34.243W				Red nun.	

(1) No.	(2) Name and Location	(3) Position	(4) Characteristic	(5) Height	(6) Range	(7) Structure	(8) Remarks
			LONG ISLAND SOUND (Connecticut) - First District				

DUCK ISLAND TO MADISON REEF

Clinton Harbor

Channel buoys located 20 feet outside channel limit.

(1) No.	(2) Name and Location	(3) Position	(4) Characteristic	(5) Height	(6) Range	(7) Structure	(8) Remarks
23485	- Channel Buoy 9	41-15-47.071N 072-31-35.363W				Green can.	
23487	- Temporary Channel Buoy 10	41-15-54.180N 072-31-25.320W				Red nun.	Private aid.
23490	- Channel Buoy 11	41-15-57.048N 072-31-24.112W				Green can.	
23495	- Channel Buoy 11A	41-16-00.088N 072-31-24.000W				Green can.	
23500	- Channel Buoy 12	41-15-58.620N 072-31-21.480W				Red nun.	Maintained from May 1 to Dec. 1. Private aid.
23505	- Channel Buoy 13	41-16-03.180N 072-31-29.460W				Green can.	Maintained from May 1 to Dec. 1. Private aid.
23510	- Channel Buoy 14	41-16-03.300N 072-31-26.160W				Red nun.	Maintained from May 1 to Dec. 1. Private aid.
23513	- Channel Buoy 15	41-16-05.280N 072-31-33.960W				Green can.	Private aid.
23515	- Channel Buoy 16	41-16-06.600N 072-31-33.840W				Red nun.	Maintained from May 1 to Dec. 1. Private aid.
	Hammonasset River						
23520	- Daybeacon 1	41-15-59.468N 072-32-02.688W				SG on pile.	Private aid.
23530	- Daybeacon 3	41-15-57.260N 072-32-04.030W				SG on pile.	Private aid.
23535	- Daybeacon 4	41-15-57.692N 072-32-05.141W				TR on pile	Private aid.
23540	- Daybeacon 5	41-15-55.400N 072-32-06.083W				SG on pile.	Private aid.
23545	- Daybeacon 6	41-15-56.281N 072-32-07.359W				TR on pile.	Private aid.
23546	- Daybeacon 7	41-15-54.396N 072-32-08.296W				SG on pile.	Private aid.
23550	- Daybeacon 8	41-15-54.900N 072-32-09.300W				TR on pile.	Private aid.
23555	- Daybeacon 9	41-15-52.266N 072-32-10.841W				SG on pile.	Private aid.
23560	- Daybeacon 10	41-15-53.119N 072-32-11.863W				TR on pile.	Private aid.
23565	- Daybeacon 11	41-15-50.128N 072-32-14.080W				SG on pile.	Private aid.
23570	- Daybeacon 12	41-15-50.828N 072-32-15.164W				TR on pile.	Private aid.
23575	- Daybeacon 13	41-15-48.305N 072-32-15.508W				SG on pile.	Private aid.
23580	- Daybeacon 14	41-15-48.936N 072-32-17.035W				TR on pile.	Private aid.
23585	- Daybeacon 15	41-15-46.458N 072-32-17.472W				SG on pile.	Private aid.
23590	- Daybeacon 16	41-15-47.006N 072-32-18.379W				TR on pile.	Private aid.
23595	- Daybeacon 17	41-15-43.285N 072-32-20.994W				SG on pile.	Private aid.
23600	- Daybeacon 18	41-15-44.079N 072-32-21.654W				TR on pile.	Private aid.
23606	- Daybeacon 20	41-15-42.647N 072-32-22.963W				TR on pile.	Private aid.
23610	- Daybeacon 21	41-15-40.880N 072-32-23.238W				SG on pile.	Private aid.
23615	- Daybeacon 22	41-15-41.287N 072-32-24.223W				TR on pile.	Private aid.

(1) No.	(2) Name and Location	(3) Position	(4) Characteristic	(5) Height	(6) Range	(7) Structure	(8) Remarks
			LONG ISLAND SOUND (Connecticut) - First District				
	DUCK ISLAND TO MADISON REEF						
	Hammonasset River						
23620	- Daybeacon 23	41-15-38.087N 072-32-26.307W				SG on pile.	Private aid.
23625	- Daybeacon 24	41-15-38.755N 072-32-26.612W				TR on pile.	Private aid.
23630	- Daybeacon 25	41-15-37.400N 072-32-28.500W				SG on pile.	Private aid.
23635	- Daybeacon 26	41-15-37.893N 072-32-28.866W				TR on pile.	Private aid.
23640	- Daybeacon 27	41-15-36.678N 072-32-31.382W				SG on pile.	Private aid.
23645	- Daybeacon 28	41-15-37.291N 072-32-31.419W				TR on pile.	Private aid.
23650	- Daybeacon 29	41-15-35.830N 072-32-35.213W				SG on pile.	Private aid.
23655	- Daybeacon 30	41-15-36.513N 072-32-35.275W				TR on pile.	Private aid.
23660	- Daybeacon 31	41-15-35.630N 072-32-37.968W				SG on pile.	Private aid.
23665	- Daybeacon 32	41-15-36.510N 072-32-38.025W				TR on pile.	Private aid.
23670	- Daybeacon 33	41-15-36.424N 072-32-40.576W				SG on pile.	Private aid.
23675	- Daybeacon 34	41-15-37.205N 072-32-40.472W				TR on pile.	Private aid.
23680	- Daybeacon 35	41-15-36.940N 072-32-43.578W				SG on pile.	Private aid.
23685	- Daybeacon 36	41-15-38.000N 072-32-43.460W				TR on pile.	Private aid.
23690	- Daybeacon 37	41-15-38.249N 072-32-47.325W				SG on pile.	Private aid.
23695	- Daybeacon 38	41-15-38.900N 072-32-47.100W				TR on pile.	Private aid.
23700	- Daybeacon 39	41-15-39.710N 072-32-50.157W				SG on pile.	Private aid.
23705	- Daybeacon 40	41-15-39.600N 072-32-48.900W				TR on pile.	Private aid.
23706	- Daybeacon 41	41-15-40.690N 072-32-50.850W				SG on pile.	Private aid.
23706.1	- Daybeacon 42	41-15-41.000N 072-32-50.500W				TR on pile.	Private aid.
23706.2	- Daybeacon 43	41-15-42.319N 072-32-51.557W				SG on pile.	Private aid.
23706.3	- Daybeacon 44	41-15-42.400N 072-32-50.900W				TR on pile. TR on pile.	Private aid.
23706.4	- Daybeacon 45	41-15-45.542N 072-32-51.976W				SG on pile.	Private aid.
23706.5	- Daybeacon 46	41-15-45.581N 072-32-51.332W				Tr on pile.	Private aid.
23706.8	- Daybeacon 49	41-15-49.843N 072-32-52.266W				SG on pile.	Private aid.
23706.9	- Daybeacon 50	41-15-49.907N 072-32-51.654W				TR on pile.	Private aid.
23707	- Daybeacon 51	41-15-51.154N 072-32-52.496W				SG on pile.	Private aid.
23707.1	- Daybeacon 52	41-15-51.124N 072-32-51.681W				TR on pile.	Private aid.
23707.2	- Daybeacon 53	41-15-51.900N 072-32-52.100W				SG on pile.	Private aid.
23707.3	- Daybeacon 55	41-15-53.600N 072-32-50.800W				SG on pile.	Private aid.
23707.4	- Daybeacon 56	41-15-52.210N 072-32-51.119W				TR on pile.	Private aid.
23707.5	- Daybeacon 57	41-15-54.200N 072-32-49.800W				SG on pile.	Private aid.

(1) No.	(2) Name and Location	(3) Position	(4) Characteristic	(5) Height	(6) Range	(7) Structure	(8) Remarks
		LONG ISLAND SOUND (Connecticut) - First District					
	DUCK ISLAND TO MADISON REEF						
	Hammonasset River						
23707.6	- Daybeacon 58	41-15-52.863N 072-32-50.471W				TR on pile.	Private aid.
23708	- Daybeacon 60	41-15-54.300N 072-32-47.700W				TR on pile.	Private aid.
	GUILFORD HARBOR TO FARM RIVER						
	Guilford Harbor						
23715	- *Lighted Bell Buoy 4*	41-15-01.643N 072-39-13.320W	Fl R 4s		3	Red.	Replaced by nun when endangered by ice.
23720	Indian Reef Buoy 1 South of reef.	41-14-38.584N 072-40-30.484W				Green can.	
23725	- Buoy 3 On southeast side of Netties Reef.	41-15-03.745N 072-39-37.123W				Green can.	
23730	- Buoy 5 On east end of reef.	41-15-27.834N 072-39-38.543W				Green can.	
23735	- *Channel Lighted Buoy 7*	41-15-44.085N 072-39-50.453W	Fl G 4s		3	Green.	Removed when endangered by ice.
23740	- Channel Buoy 9	41-15-53.977N 072-39-59.336W				Green can.	
23745	- Channel Buoy 10	41-15-55.132N 072-39-58.228W				Red nun.	
23750	- Channel Buoy 11	41-15-58.263N 072-40-00.099W				Green can.	Removed when endangered by ice.
23755	- Channel Buoy 12	41-15-57.875N 072-39-59.424W				Red nun.	
23760	- Channel Buoy 13	41-16-05.386N 072-39-57.184W				Green can.	Removed when endangered by ice.
23765	- Channel Buoy 14	41-16-12.249N 072-39-53.489W				Red nun.	Removed when endangered by ice.
	West River Entrance *Aids maintained from May 1 to Oct. 1.*						
23770	- Buoy 1W	41-15-21.300N 072-39-56.400W				Green can.	Private aid.
23775	- Buoy 2W	41-15-22.600N 072-39-52.200W				Red nun.	Private aid.
23780	- Buoy 3W	41-15-32.400N 072-40-05.800W				Green can.	Private aid.
23785	- Buoy 4W	41-15-33.660N 072-40-04.080W				Red nun.	Private aid.
23790	- Buoy 5W	41-15-40.600N 072-40-13.100W				Green can.	Private aid.
23795	- Buoy 6W	41-15-41.200N 072-40-11.700W				Red nun.	Private aid.
23800	- Buoy 7W	41-15-45.800N 072-40-18.100W				Green can.	Private aid.
23805	- Buoy 8W	41-15-46.300N 072-40-17.000W				Red nun.	Private aid.
23806	- Daybeacon 9	41-15-48.400N 072-40-21.100W				SG on PVC pole.	Private aid.
23806.1	- Daybeacon 10	41-15-49.400N 072-40-20.400W				TR on PVC pole.	Private aid.
23806.2	- Daybeacon 11	41-15-50.700N 072-40-23.200W				SG on PVC pole.	Private aid.
23806.3	- Daybeacon 12	41-15-51.400N 072-40-22.600W				TR on PVC pole.	Private aid.
23806.4	- Daybeacon 13	41-15-53.200N 072-40-25.900W				SG on PVC pole.	Private aid.
23806.5	- Daybeacon 14	41-15-53.700N 072-40-25.100W				TR on PVC pole.	Private aid.

(1) No.	(2) Name and Location	(3) Position	(4) Characteristic	(5) Height	(6) Range	(7) Structure	(8) Remarks
		LONG ISLAND SOUND (Connecticut) - First District					
	GUILFORD HARBOR TO FARM RIVER						
	Guilford Harbor						
	West River Entrance						
	Aids maintained from May 1 to Oct. 1.						
23806.6	- Daybeacon 15	41-15-54.900N 072-40-27.600W				SG on PVC pole.	Private aid.
23806.7	- Daybeacon 16	41-15-56.800N 072-40-28.300W				TR on PVC pole.	Private aid.
23810	WEST RIVER RANGE FRONT LIGHT	41-16-07.600N 072-40-40.600W	Q W	16		KWR on pile.	Visible on range line only. Private aid.
23815	WEST RIVER RANGE REAR LIGHT 261 yards, 321° from front light.	41-16-13.600N 072-40-47.000W	Iso W 6s	30		KRW on pile.	Visible on range line only. Private aid.
	The Thimbles						
	Thimble Shoals						
23820	- Buoy 4 At southwest edge of rocky shoal.	41-14-59.820N 072-44-31.340W				Red nun.	
23825	- Buoy 6	41-15-09.110N 072-44-40.113W				Red nun.	
23830	- Buoy 8	41-15-15.518N 072-44-46.897W				Red nun.	
23835	- Buoy 10	41-15-12.576N 072-44-56.551W				Red nun.	
23840	- Buoy 11 On east side of shoal.	41-15-12.018N 072-45-04.787W				Green can.	
	Stony Creek						
23845	- Buoy 1	41-15-35.219N 072-45-15.140W				Green can.	
23850	- Buoy 3	41-15-46.181N 072-45-13.563W				Green can.	
23855	- Buoy 4	41-15-45.376N 072-45-12.280W				Red nun.	
23860	- Buoy 5	41-15-53.281N 072-45-13.080W				Green can.	
	The Thimbles						
23865	Commander Rocks Buoy 2CR Marks southwest end of rocks.	41-14-33.200N 072-45-04.389W				Red nun.	
23870	High Island East Shoal Buoy 1 South of shoal.	41-14-52.148N 072-45-28.199W				Green can.	
23875	East Reef Buoy 1 Marks east side of reef.	41-13-57.852N 072-45-48.464W				Green can.	
23880	Wheaton Reef Buoy 3 On north side of reef.	41-14-12.282N 072-46-13.015W				Green can.	
23885	Inner Reef North Buoy 5 Marks northeast side of rock.	41-14-31.732N 072-46-03.364W				Green can.	
23890	Gangway Rock Buoy 1 Marks southeast side of rock.	41-14-19.438N 072-47-21.552W				Green can.	
23895	Northwest Reef Buoy 2NW Marks southwest side of reef.	41-14-04.168N 072-46-37.227W				Red nun.	
23900	Hookers Rock Buoy 3 Southeast side of rock.	41-14-37.682N 072-46-57.366W				Green can.	
23905	Inner Reef South Buoy 4 Marks southwest end of reef.	41-14-26.892N 072-46-11.795W				Red nun.	
23910	*Pine Orchard Approach Lighted Buoy 4A* Southeast of Hookers Rock.	41-14-33.452N 072-46-40.795W	Fl R 4s	3		Red.	Replaced by nun when endangered by ice.
23915	Pork Rocks Buoy 5 East of rocks.	41-15-07.381N 072-46-31.114W				Green can.	
23920	Dick Rocks Buoy 6 West of rocks.	41-15-01.011N 072-45-51.783W				Red nun.	

(1) No.	(2) Name and Location	(3) Position	(4) Characteristic	(5) Height	(6) Range	(7) Structure	(8) Remarks

LONG ISLAND SOUND (Connecticut) - First District

GUILFORD HARBOR TO FARM RIVER

The Thimbles

(1) No.	(2) Name and Location	(3) Position	(4) Characteristic	(5) Height	(6) Range	(7) Structure	(8) Remarks
23925	*Pine Orchard Approach Lighted Buoy 8* Marks southwest edge of rocks.	41-15-17.852N 072-46-13.334W	Fl R 4s		3	Red.	Replaced by nun from Nov. 15 to May 1.

Duck Island Roads

(1) No.	(2) Name and Location	(3) Position	(4) Characteristic	(5) Height	(6) Range	(7) Structure	(8) Remarks
23930	JUNIPER POINT SOUTH OBSTRUCTION LIGHT	41-15-51.800N 072-46-00.200W	Q Y	11		On wood dolphin.	Private aid.
23931	JUNIPER POINT MIDDLE OBSTRUCTION LIGHT	41-15-52.300N 072-45-59.500W	Q Y			On wood dolphin.	Private aid.
23932	JUNIPER POINT NORTH OBSTRUCTION LIGHT	41-15-52.800N 072-45-58.800W	Q Y			On wood dolphin.	Private aid.
23935	QUARRY RANGE FRONT LIGHT	41-15-55.100N 072-45-56.400W	F R	20		KRW on metal pile.	Private aid.
23940	QUARRY RANGE REAR LIGHT 40 yards, 028° from front light.	41-15-56.300N 072-45-55.500W	F R			KRW attached to loading chute.	Private aid.

Pine Orchard Harbor
Buoys maintained from May 1 to Nov. 1.

(1) No.	(2) Name and Location	(3) Position	(4) Characteristic	(5) Height	(6) Range	(7) Structure	(8) Remarks
23946	- BREAKWATER LIGHT	41-15-44.000N 072-46-15.000W	Fl G 6s	6		SG on pile.	Private aid.
23946.1	- Buoy 1	41-15-43.500N 072-46-13.700W				Green can.	Private aid.
23946.2	- Buoy 2	41-15-44.100N 072-46-11.200W				Red nun.	Private aid.
23946.5	- Buoy 3	41-15-45.500N 072-46-16.400W				Green can.	Private aid.
23947	- Buoy 4	41-15-46.200N 072-46-16.000W				Red nun.	Private aid.
23947.3	- Buoy 5	41-15-47.900N 072-46-17.800W				Green can.	Private aid.
23947.5	- Buoy 6	41-15-48.100N 072-46-16.800W				Red nun.	Private aid.
23948	- East Channel Buoy 1E	41-15-47.600N 072-46-14.600W				Green can.	Private aid.
23948.1	- East Channel Buoy 2E	41-15-48.600N 072-46-13.000W				Red nun.	Private aid.
23948.2	- East Channel Buoy 4E	41-15-52.300N 072-46-14.900W				Red nun.	Private aid.
23948.3	- East Channel Buoy 6E	41-15-05.700N 072-46-16.500W				Red nun.	Private aid.

Branford Harbor

(1) No.	(2) Name and Location	(3) Position	(4) Characteristic	(5) Height	(6) Range	(7) Structure	(8) Remarks
23950	*Blyn Rock Lighted Buoy 2* On south side of rock.	41-14-48.939N 072-49-52.671W	Fl R 4s		3	Red.	Replaced by nun from Nov. 15 to May 1.
23955	Bird Rock Buoy 4 On west side of reef.	41-15-00.551N 072-49-49.640W				Red nun.	
23960	Lovers Island Rock Buoy 5 East of rock.	41-15-14.208N 072-49-50.476W				Green can.	
23965	Little Mermaid Rock Buoy 6 West of rock.	41-15-19.892N 072-49-41.030W				Red nun.	
23970	BIG MERMAID LIGHT 7	41-15-22.720N 072-49-40.457W	Fl G 4s	22	5	SG on skeleton tower.	

Farm River

(1) No.	(2) Name and Location	(3) Position	(4) Characteristic	(5) Height	(6) Range	(7) Structure	(8) Remarks
23975	- Approach Buoy 1	41-14-27.602N 072-51-30.613W				Green can.	
23980	- Approach Buoy 2	41-14-37.372N 072-51-29.193W				Red nun.	

NEW HAVEN HARBOR

New Haven Harbor

(1) No.	(2) Name and Location	(3) Position	(4) Characteristic	(5) Height	(6) Range	(7) Structure	(8) Remarks
23985	- East Entrance Buoy 1 On northeast side of shoal.	41-14-09.106N 072-53-47.453W				Green can.	
23990	- East Entrance Buoy 2 On southwest side of shoal.	41-14-12.813N 072-53-42.114W				Red nun.	

(1) No.	(2) Name and Location	(3) Position	(4) Characteristic	(5) Height	(6) Range	(7) Structure	(8) Remarks
		LONG ISLAND SOUND (Connecticut) - First District					
	NEW HAVEN HARBOR						
	New Haven Harbor						
23995	- East Entrance Buoy 4 On southwest side of shoal.	41-14-22.463N 072-53-59.987W				Red nun.	
24000	- East Entrance Buoy 5 On northeast end of Old Head Reef.	41-14-26.276N 072-54-14.364W				Green can.	
24005	Adams Fall Buoy A On southwest side of shoal.	41-14-36.366N 072-54-39.163W				Red and green bands; nun.	
24010	- East Entrance Channel Buoy 6 On southwest end of Lighthouse Point Shoal.	41-14-44.592N 072-54-22.747W				Red nun.	
24015	- Lighted Whistle Buoy NH	41-12-07.503N 072-53-47.147W	Mo (A) W		4	Red and white stripes with spherical marks.	
24020	- OUTER CHANNEL RANGE FRONT LIGHT	41-15-38.776N 072-56-05.077W	F G	34		On skeleton tower.	Visible 0.5° each side of range line. Lighted throughout 24 hours.
24025	- OUTER CHANNEL RANGE REAR LIGHT 839 yards, 333.6° from front light.	41-16-01.049N 072-56-19.754W	F G	68		On skeleton tower.	Visible 0.5° each side of range line. Lighted throughout 24 hours.
24030	- Channel Lighted Gong Buoy 1	41-13-17.623N 072-54-35.918W	Fl G 2.5s		3	Green.	
24035	- Lighted Buoy 2	41-13-20.163N 072-54-30.268W	Fl R 2.5s		3	Red.	
24040	- Buoy 3	41-13-38.793N 072-54-49.899W				Green can.	
24045	- Channel Lighted Buoy 4	41-13-41.063N 072-54-43.959W	Fl R 4s		3	Red.	
24050	- Channel Lighted Bell Buoy 6	41-14-00.273N 072-54-56.209W	Fl R 2.5s		3	Red.	Replaced by LIB of reduced intensity when endangered by ice.
24055	- Channel Lighted Buoy 7	41-14-02.923N 072-55-05.499W	Fl G 2.5s		3	Green.	Replaced by smaller LIB of reduced intensity when endangered by ice.
24060 21210	**Southwest Ledge Light**	41-14-03.733N 072-54-43.813W	Fl R 5s	57	14	White octagonal house on cylindrical pier. 45	HORN: 1 blast ev 15s (2s bl). MRASS-Fog signal is radio activated, during times of reduced visibility, turn marine VHF-FM radio to channel 83A/157.175Mhz. Key microphone 5 times consecutively, to activate fog signal for 45 minutes.
24065	NEW HAVEN MIDDLE BREAKWATER EAST END LIGHT	41-13-53.018N 072-55-23.716W	Fl G 4s	31	4	NG on skeleton tower.	
24070	NEW HAVEN MIDDLE BREAKWATER WEST END LIGHT	41-13-27.781N 072-56-09.545W	Fl R 4s	26	4	NR on skeleton tower.	
24075 21215	NEW HAVEN LIGHT	41-13-16.372N 072-56-32.501W	Fl W 4s	27	7	NG on skeleton tower.	
24080	NEW HAVEN WEST BREAKWATER WEST END LIGHT 2	41-13-32.322N 072-57-21.977W	Fl R 6s	21	4	TR on skeleton tower.	
24085	- Channel Lighted Buoy 8	41-14-09.913N 072-54-58.809W	Q R		3	Red.	Replaced by smaller LIB of reduced intensity when endangered by ice.
24090	- Channel Lighted Buoy 9	41-14-31.503N 072-55-00.499W	Fl G 4s		3	Green.	Replaced by can when endangered by ice.
24095	- Channel Buoy 9A	41-14-54.883N 072-54-56.519W				Green can.	
24100	- Channel Lighted Buoy 10	41-14-30.883N 072-54-55.179W	Fl R 4s		3	Red.	

(1) No.	(2) Name and Location	(3) Position	(4) Characteristic	(5) Height	(6) Range	(7) Structure	(8) Remarks
			LONG ISLAND SOUND (Connecticut) - First District				
	NEW HAVEN HARBOR						
	New Haven Harbor						
24105	- *Channel Lighted Buoy 10A*	41-14-54.583N 072-54-50.579W	Fl R 2.5s		3	Red.	Replaced by smaller LIB of reduced intensity when endangered by ice.
24110	- Channel Buoy 12	41-15-16.232N 072-54-47.039W				Red nun.	
24115	- *Channel Lighted Buoy 11*	41-15-16.942N 072-54-52.189W	Fl G 4s		3	Green.	Replaced by can when endangered by ice.
24120	- Channel Buoy 13	41-15-47.344N 072-54-48.498W				Green can.	
24125	SANDY POINT BREAKWATER LIGHT	41-15-44.398N 072-55-04.406W	Fl W 4s	17	7	NG on skeleton tower.	
24130	- *Channel Lighted Bell Buoy 14*	41-15-47.085N 072-54-43.293W	Fl R 4s		3	Red.	Replaced by nun when endangered by ice.
24135	Black Rock Buoy	41-16-04.033N 072-54-17.135W				White can with orange bands and diamond worded ROCK.	Removed when endangered by ice.
24140	- *Channel Lighted Buoy 15*	41-16-18.452N 072-54-44.719W	Fl G 2.5s		3	Green.	Replaced by can when endangered by ice.
24145	- Channel Buoy 16	41-16-22.315N 072-54-38.527W				Red nun.	
	Fort Hale Channel						
24150	- Buoy 1	41-16-17.371N 072-54-26.592W				Green can.	
24155	- Buoy 2	41-16-16.625N 072-54-25.918W				Red nun.	
24160	- Buoy 3	41-16-19.738N 072-54-23.124W				Green can.	
24165	- Buoy 4	41-16-19.065N 072-54-22.227W				Red nun.	
	New Haven Harbor						
24170	- Channel Buoy 17	41-16-45.473N 072-54-47.479W				Green can.	
24175	- *Channel Lighted Buoy 18*	41-16-46.482N 072-54-40.879W	Fl R 2.5s		3	Red.	
24185	- Channel Buoy 20	41-16-55.643N 072-54-39.179W				Red nun.	
24200	*New Haven Reach Turning Basin Lighted Buoy A*	41-17-29.683N 072-54-45.379W	Fl Y 2.5s		3	Yellow.	Replaced by can When endangered by ice.
24205	NEW HAVEN LONG WHARF LIGHT	41-17-33.764N 072-54-54.885W	Fl G 4s	19	4	NG on skeleton tower.	
	New Haven Wharf						
24230	Quinipiac River Buoy 1	41-18-03.108N 072-53-51.532W				Green can.	
	West Haven Channel						
	Channel buoys located 50 feet outside channel limit.						
24234	- *Lighted Buoy 1*	41-16-54.222N 072-54-58.299W	Fl G 4s		3	Green.	Replaced by can when endangered by ice.
24235	- Buoy 2	41-16-55.083N 072-55-05.310W				Red nun.	
24240	- Buoy 3	41-16-53.499N 072-55-11.473W				Green can.	
24245	- Buoy 4	41-16-54.703N 072-55-18.960W				Red nun.	
24250	- Buoy 5	41-16-53.132N 072-55-22.880W				Green can.	
24255	- Buoy 7	41-16-52.381N 072-55-31.590W				Green can.	
24260	- Buoy 9	41-16-50.853N 072-55-37.553W				Green can.	

(1) No.	(2) Name and Location	(3) Position	(4) Characteristic	(5) Height	(6) Range	(7) Structure	(8) Remarks
			LONG ISLAND SOUND (Connecticut) - First District				
	NEW HAVEN HARBOR						
	West Haven Channel						
	Channel buoys located 50 feet outside channel limit.						
24265	- Buoy 11	41-16-46.133N 072-55-46.811W				Green can.	
24270	- Buoy 12	41-16-40.583N 072-55-59.781W				Red nun.	
24275	- Buoy 13	41-16-41.383N 072-55-56.581W				Green can.	
24280	- Buoy 14 Marks channel limit.	41-16-39.693N 072-56-09.891W				Red nun.	
24285	- Buoy 16 Marks channel limit.	41-16-41.343N 072-56-13.932W				Red nun.	
24290	- Buoy 18 Marks channel limit.	41-16-45.009N 072-56-15.819W				Red nun.	
	HOUSATONIC RIVER AND MILFORD HARBOR						
	Milford Harbor						
	Channel buoys located 60 feet outside channel limit.						
24295	Welchs Point Buoy 2 Off south end of shoal.	41-11-55.334N 073-02-11.173W				Red nun.	
24300	Charles Island Buoy 1 At northeast edge of shoal.	41-11-36.483N 073-03-03.355W				Green can.	
24305	- *Channel Lighted Buoy 4*	41-12-15.753N 073-02-57.065W	Fl R 4s		4	Red.	Replaced by nun when endangered by ice.
24310	- Channel Buoy 5 Marks point of shoal.	41-12-21.620N 073-02-58.498W				Green can.	
24315	- Channel Buoy 6	41-12-23.990N 073-02-56.705W				Red nun.	
24318	- Channel Buoy 6A	41-12-31.191N 073-02-56.084W				Red nun.	
24320	- Channel Buoy 7 Marks outer end of submerged rocks.	41-12-34.583N 073-02-57.296W				Green can.	
24325	- Channel Buoy 8	41-12-35.921N 073-02-56.213W				Red nun.	
24330	- LIGHT 10	41-12-36.996N 073-02-54.224W	Fl R 4s	27	4	TR on skeleton tower.	
	Housatonic River						
24355	- *Entrance Channel Lighted Bell Buoy 1*	41-09-24.084N 073-05-26.401W	Fl G 2.5s		4	Green.	Replaced by can when endangered by ice.
24360	- BREAKWATER LIGHT 2A	41-09-38.690N 073-05-34.953W	Fl R 4s	27	5	TR on skeleton tower.	
24365	- Channel Buoy 1A	41-09-34.384N 073-05-45.202W				Green can.	
24370	- Channel Buoy 2	41-09-36.384N 073-05-42.202W				Red nun.	
24375	- *Channel Lighted Buoy 3*	41-09-47.584N 073-06-03.903W	Fl G 4s		3	Green.	Replaced by can when endangered by ice.
24380	- Channel Buoy 4	41-09-52.683N 073-06-08.602W				Red nun.	
24385	- LIGHT 7	41-10-06.225N 073-06-32.476W	Fl G 6s	21	3	SG on skeleton tower on concrete base.	
24390	- Channel Buoy 8	41-10-08.888N 073-06-30.355W				Red nun.	
24395	- Channel Buoy 9	41-10-18.483N 073-06-47.604W				Green can.	
24400	- Channel Buoy 10	41-10-19.863N 073-06-45.805W				Red nun.	
24405	- LIGHT 11	41-10-31.633N 073-07-15.555W	Fl G 4s	14	4	SG on pipe tower on concrete base.	
24410	- Channel Buoy 12	41-10-36.853N 073-07-16.446W				Red nun.	

(1) No.	(2) Name and Location	(3) Position	(4) Characteristic	(5) Height	(6) Range	(7) Structure	(8) Remarks

LONG ISLAND SOUND (Connecticut) - First District

HOUSATONIC RIVER AND MILFORD HARBOR

Housatonic River

24415	- Channel Buoy 14	41-10-42.629N 073-07-21.909W					Red nun.
24420	- Channel Buoy 16	41-10-57.832N 073-07-22.186W					Red nun.
24425	- Channel Buoy 18	41-11-12.969N 073-07-17.106W					Red nun.
24430	- Channel Buoy 19	41-11-22.412N 073-07-08.948W					Green can.
24435	- Channel Buoy 21	41-11-25.205N 073-06-58.223W					Green can.
24440	- Channel Buoy 23	41-11-30.372N 073-06-52.165W					Green can.
24445	- Channel Buoy 24	41-12-11.152N 073-06-32.005W					Red nun.
24450	- Channel Buoy 26	41-12-27.162N 073-06-35.030W					Red nun.
24455	- Channel Buoy 27	41-12-31.614N 073-06-37.442W					Green can.
24460	- Channel Buoy 29	41-12-52.770N 073-06-34.576W					Green can.
24465	- Channel Buoy 31	41-13-02.081N 073-06-30.087W					Green can.
24470	- Channel Buoy 32	41-13-13.632N 073-06-33.188W					Red nun.
24495	- Channel Buoy 34	41-13-19.560N 073-06-38.178W					Red nun.
24500	- Channel Buoy 36 50 feet outside channel limit.	41-13-32.665N 073-06-37.840W					Red nun.
24505	- Channel Buoy 37	41-13-37.801N 073-06-38.916W					Green can.
24510	- Channel Buoy 40	41-14-20.531N 073-06-15.405W					Red nun.
24515	- Channel Buoy 44	41-14-35.391N 073-05-46.944W					Red nun.
24520	- Channel Buoy 53	41-15-12.361N 073-05-08.982W					Green can.
24525	- Channel Buoy 54	41-15-20.991N 073-05-11.232W					Red nun.
24530	- Channel Buoy 58	41-15-59.381N 073-05-21.403W					Red nun.
24535	- Channel Buoy 62	41-16-18.075N 073-05-20.500W					Red nun.
24540	- Channel Buoy 68	41-16-55.283N 073-05-00.232W					Red nun.

STRATFORD POINT TO SHERWOOD POINT

Bridgeport Harbor

Channel buoys 2 through 13 are located 75 feet outside channel limit.

24575	- *Entrance Channel Lighted Buoy 1*	41-08-30.681N 073-11-02.672W	Fl G 2.5s		3		Green.
24580	- *Entrance Channel Lighted Buoy 2*	41-08-29.777N 073-10-57.475W	Fl R 2.5s		3		Red.
24585	- Entrance Channel Buoy 3	41-08-55.080N 073-10-55.029W					Green can.
24590	- *Entrance Channel Lighted Buoy 4*	41-08-54.112N 073-10-49.925W	Fl R 2.5s		3		Red.
24595	- Entrance Channel Buoy 5	41-09-13.876N 073-10-49.010W					Green can.
24600	- Entrance Channel Buoy 6	41-09-12.907N 073-10-44.036W					Red nun.
24605	- LIGHT 7	41-09-24.249N 073-10-47.335W	Q G	50	5		SG on skeleton tower.
24610	BRIDGEPORT EAST BREAKWATER LIGHT 8	41-09-17.426N 073-10-36.495W	Fl R 4s	21	4		TR on skeleton tower.

(1) No.	(2) Name and Location	(3) Position	(4) Characteristic	(5) Height	(6) Range	(7) Structure	(8) Remarks
		LONG ISLAND SOUND (Connecticut) - First District					

STRATFORD POINT TO SHERWOOD POINT

Bridgeport Harbor
Channel buoys 2 through 13 are located 75 feet outside channel limit.

24620	- Channel Buoy 10	41-09-26.756N 073-10-39.682W				Red nun.	
24625	- Channel Buoy 11	41-09-41.178N 073-10-40.483W				Green can.	
24630	- *Channel Lighted Buoy 12*	41-09-40.407N 073-10-35.326W	Fl R 2.5s		3	Red.	
24635	TONGUE POINT LIGHT	41-09-59.933N 073-10-39.014W	Fl G 4s	31	5	Black conical tower.	
24640	- *Channel Lighted Buoy 13*	41-09-59.841N 073-10-34.610W	Q G		3	Green.	
24645	- Channel Buoy 15	41-10-08.561N 073-10-36.949W				Green can.	
	Johnson Creek						
24650	- Channel Buoy 2	41-09-56.604N 073-10-12.504W				Red nun.	
24653	- Channel Buoy 2A	41-09-56.380N 073-10-04.010W				Red nun.	
24654	- Channel Buoy 3	41-09-58.640N 073-10-04.480W				Green can.	
24655	- Channel Buoy 4	41-09-56.382N 073-09-49.512W				Red nun.	
24660	- Channel Buoy 8	41-10-12.536N 073-09-47.859W				Red nun.	

Black Rock Harbor
Channel buoys located 30 to 80 feet outside the channel limit.

24671	*Black Rock Lighted Danger Buoy* Marks location of sunken tower.	41-07-09.655N 073-13-02.854W	Q W		3	White and orange can with diamond marked DANGER ROCKS.	Removed when endangered by ice.
24675	- ENTRANCE LIGHT 2A	41-08-13.562N 073-13-02.059W	Fl R 4s	27	4		
24680	- Channel Buoy 4	41-08-18.411N 073-13-11.210W				Red nun.	
24685	- Channel Buoy 6	41-08-30.871N 073-13-15.740W				Red nun.	
24690	- CHANNEL LIGHT 7	41-08-34.713N 073-13-21.302W	Fl G 4s	22	4	SG on skeleton tower.	
24695	- Channel Buoy 8	41-08-38.321N 073-13-15.980W				Red nun.	
24700	- Channel Buoy 9	41-08-50.571N 073-13-14.840W				Green can.	
24705	- Channel Buoy 10	41-09-03.911N 073-13-06.870W				Red nun.	
24710	- Channel Buoy 11	41-09-06.875N 073-13-08.147W				Green can.	
24715	- Channel Buoy 12	41-09-17.097N 073-12-55.760W				Red nun.	
24720	- Channel Buoy 13	41-09-21.668N 073-12-52.677W				Green can.	

Ash Creek
Aids maintained May 1 to Nov. 1

24725	- RANGE FRONT LIGHT	41-08-41.940N 073-14-10.140W	Fl G 3s	25		KWR on pile.	Private aid.
24730	- RANGE REAR LIGHT 285 yards, 314° from front light.	41-08-47.940N 073-14-17.880W	Fl G 6s	45		KRW on pile.	Private aid.
24735	- *Lighted Buoy 1*	41-08-23.940N 073-13-47.510W	Fl G 6s			Green	Private aid.
24740	- *Lighted Buoy 2*	41-08-25.860N 073-13-47.820W	Fl R 3s			Red	Private aid.
24745	- *Lighted Buoy 3*	41-08-27.720N 073-13-51.840W	Fl G 6s			Green	Private aid.
24750	- *Lighted Buoy 4*	41-08-28.560N 073-13-51.180W	Fl R 3s			Red	Private aid.

(1) No.	(2) Name and Location	(3) Position	(4) Characteristic	(5) Height	(6) Range	(7) Structure	(8) Remarks
		LONG ISLAND SOUND (Connecticut) - First District					
	STRATFORD POINT TO SHERWOOD POINT						
	Ash Creek						
	Aids maintained May 1 to Nov. 1						
24755	- *Lighted Buoy 5*	41-08-30.730N 073-13-56.240W	Fl G 6s			Green	Private aid.
24760	- *Lighted Buoy 6*	41-08-31.520N 073-13-54.760W	Fl R 3s			Red	Private aid.
	Southport Harbor						
24762	*Pine Creek Point Aquaculture Lighted Buoys (4)*	41-06-49.200N 073-15-14.000W	Fl Y 4s			Yellow.	Marks aquaculture farm. Maintained from Mar. 15 to Dec. 15. Private aid.
24765	- Entrance Buoy 2	41-07-10.671N 073-17-08.018W				Red nun.	
24770	- Channel Buoy 3	41-07-13.631N 073-17-11.238W				Green can.	
24775	- Channel Buoy 4	41-07-16.691N 073-17-09.818W				Red nun.	
24780	- Channel Buoy 5	41-07-16.471N 073-17-12.048W				Green can.	
24785	- LIGHT 7	41-07-18.792N 073-17-14.203W	Fl G 4s	21	4	SG on skeleton tower.	
24790	- Channel Buoy 8	41-07-23.281N 073-17-11.798W				Red nun.	
24795	- Channel Buoy 9	41-07-26.311N 073-17-14.678W				Green can.	
24797	*USGS Southport River Lighted Research Buoy*	41-07-28.884N 073-17-17.073W	Fl Y 4s			Yellow.	Property of USGS. Private aid.
24800	- Channel Buoy 10	41-07-31.291N 073-17-15.948W				Red nun.	
24805	- Channel Buoy 11	41-07-31.653N 073-17-17.335W				Green can.	
24810	SOUTHPORT BREAKWATER LIGHT 12	41-07-33.410N 073-17-13.944W	Fl R 4s	28	4	TR on skeleton tower.	
	SHERWOOD POINT TO STAMFORD HARBOR						
	Saugatuck River						
24815	*Georges Rock Lighted Buoy 1* On northeast side of rock.	41-05-12.232N 073-19-28.685W	Fl G 2.5s		4	Green.	Replaced by can when endangered by ice.
24820	- *Entrance Lighted Buoy 3*	41-05-52.382N 073-21-13.435W	Fl G 4s		3	Green.	Replaced by can when endangered by ice.
24825	- Buoy 5	41-05-55.332N 073-21-33.606W				Green can.	Removed when endangered by ice.
24830	- Buoy 6	41-06-01.992N 073-21-27.786W				Red nun.	Removed when endangered by ice.
24835	- Buoy 8	41-06-06.831N 073-21-32.376W				Red nun.	Removed when endangered by ice.
24840	- Buoy 9	41-06-09.481N 073-21-39.366W				Green can.	Removed when endangered by ice.
24845	- Buoy 10	41-06-12.771N 073-21-41.187W				Red nun.	Removed when endangered by ice.
24850	- Buoy 11	41-06-13.449N 073-21-48.612W				Green can.	Removed when endangered by ice.
24853	*USGS Saugatuck River Lighted Research Buoy*	41-06-13.932N 073-21-59.400W	Fl Y 4s			Yellow.	Property of USGS. Private aid.
24855	- Buoy 13	41-06-14.701N 073-21-58.897W				Green can.	Removed when endangered by ice.
24860	- Buoy 15	41-06-10.401N 073-22-05.277W				Green can.	Removed when endangered by ice.

(1) No.	(2) Name and Location	(3) Position	(4) Characteristic	(5) Height	(6) Range	(7) Structure	(8) Remarks

LONG ISLAND SOUND (Connecticut) - First District

SHERWOOD POINT TO STAMFORD HARBOR

Saugatuck River

No.	Name and Location	Position	Characteristic	Height	Range	Structure	Remarks
24865	- Buoy 16	41-06-01.711N 073-22-12.367W				Red nun.	Removed when endangered by ice.
24870	- Buoy 18	41-06-06.861N 073-22-26.038W				Red nun.	Removed when endangered by ice.
24875	- Buoy 20	41-06-13.751N 073-22-37.138W				Red nun.	Removed when endangered by ice.
24890	- Buoy 22	41-06-25.511N 073-22-41.239W				Red nun.	Removed when endangered by ice.
24895	- Buoy 24	41-06-35.624N 073-22-37.419W				Red nun.	Removed when endangered by ice.
24900	- Buoy 26	41-06-40.111N 073-22-29.669W				Red nun.	Removed when endangered by ice.
24905	- Buoy 27	41-06-44.681N 073-22-23.708W				Green can.	Removed when endangered by ice.
24910	- Buoy 29	41-06-49.481N 073-22-14.138W				Green can.	Removed when endangered by ice.
24911	Compo Yacht Basin Buoy 1	41-06-11.160N 073-21-33.300W				Green can.	Private aid.
24911.1	Compo Yacht Basin Buoy 2	41-06-10.600N 073-21-30.500W				Red nun.	Private aid.
24911.2	Compo Yacht Basin Buoy 3	41-06-14.760N 073-21-31.500W				Green can.	Private aid.
24911.3	Compo Yacht Basin Buoy 4	41-06-14.220N 073-21-29.580W				Red nun.	Private aid.
24911.4	Compo Yacht Basin Buoy 5	41-06-16.600N 073-21-30.000W				Green can.	Private aid.
24911.5	Compo Yacht Basin Buoy 6	41-06-17.520N 073-21-27.780W				Red nun.	Private aid.
24911.6	Compo Yacht Basin Buoy 7	41-06-19.300N 073-21-29.600W				Green can.	Private aid.
24911.7	Compo Yacht Basin Buoy 8	41-06-19.680N 073-21-26.760W				Red nun.	Private aid.
24912	Longshore Channel Buoy 1	41-06-21.960N 073-21-58.680W				Green can.	Maintained Apr. 1 to Dec 30. Private aid.
24912.1	Longshore Channel Buoy 2	41-06-21.600N 073-21-57.000W				Red nun.	Maintained Apr. 1 to Dec 30. Private aid.
24912.2	Longshore Channel Buoy 3	41-06-24.000N 073-21-58.380W				Green can.	Maintained Apr. 1 to Dec 30. Private aid.
24912.3	Longshore Channel Buoy 4	41-06-23.820N 073-21-56.580W				Red nun.	Maintained Apr. 1 to Dec 30. Private aid.
24912.4	Longshore Channel Buoy 5	41-06-25.920N 073-21-58.380W				Green can.	Maintained Apr. 1 to Dec 30. Private aid.
24912.5	Longshore Channel Buoy 6	41-06-25.560N 073-21-56.700W				Red nun.	Maintained Apr. 1 to Dec 30. Private aid.
24912.6	Longshore Channel Buoy 7	41-06-27.000N 073-21-58.800W				Green can.	Maintained Apr. 1 to Dec 30. Private aid.
24912.7	Longshore Channel Buoy 8	41-06-27.000N 073-21-56.940W				Red nun.	Maintained Apr. 1 to Dec 30. Private aid.

Norwalk East Approach

No.	Name and Location	Position	Characteristic	Height	Range	Structure	Remarks
24915	- Buoy 2	41-04-25.032N 073-20-44.083W				Red nun.	
24920	- Buoy 4 Marks southwest end of rock reef at Channel Rock.	41-04-36.292N 073-21-45.366W				Red nun.	
24925	- Buoy 5	41-04-33.592N 073-21-57.251W				Green can.	

(1) No.	(2) Name and Location	(3) Position	(4) Characteristic	(5) Height	(6) Range	(7) Structure	(8) Remarks
			LONG ISLAND SOUND (Connecticut) - First District				
	SHERWOOD POINT TO STAMFORD HARBOR						
	Norwalk East Approach						
24930	PECK LEDGE LIGHT	41-04-38.633N 073-22-10.914W	Fl G 2.5s	61	5	White conical tower, middle part brown, on black cylindrical pier.	
24935	GRASSY HAMMOCK LIGHT 8	41-04-35.766N 073-23-01.302W	Fl R 4s	22	5	TR on skeleton tower.	
24940	- Buoy 9 On point of shoal.	41-04-29.082N 073-23-15.738W				Green can.	
24945	- Buoy 11 Off end of shoal.	41-04-23.752N 073-23-49.970W				Green can.	
	Sheffield Island Harbor						
24950	Noroton Point Buoy 1A At east end of shoal.	41-02-56.382N 073-26-03.443W				Green can.	
24952	*Greens Ledge Lighted Buoy 2A*	41-02-47.022N 073-26-04.129W	Fl R 4s		3	Red.	
	Norwalk Channel						
	Channel buoys located 30 to 50 feet outside channel limit.						
24955	- Entrance Buoy 1	41-03-21.332N 073-25-26.971W				Green can.	
24960	- *Lighted Buoy 2*	41-03-30.702N 073-25-04.401W	Fl R 2.5s		3	Red.	Replaced by nun when endangered by ice.
24965	- Buoy 3	41-03-31.602N 073-25-07.151W				Green can.	
24970	- *Lighted Buoy 4*	41-03-46.062N 073-24-50.381W	Fl R 4s		3	Red.	Replaced by nun when endanged by ice.
24975	- Buoy 5	41-03-47.612N 073-24-52.601W				Green can.	
24980	- Buoy 7	41-03-59.122N 073-24-42.171W				Green can.	
24985	- Buoy 8 75 feet outside channel limit.	41-04-01.082N 073-24-35.640W				Red nun.	
24990	- LIGHT 10 200 yards north of rock.	41-04-08.953N 073-24-27.534W	Fl R 6s	27	4	TR on skeleton tower.	
25005	- Buoy 9	41-04-11.274N 073-24-32.208W				Green can.	
25010	- LIGHT 11	41-04-23.610N 073-24-20.581W	Fl G 4s	21	4	SG on skeleton tower.	
25015	- Buoy 11A	41-04-24.410N 073-24-18.661W				Green can.	
25020	- Buoy 12	41-04-33.562N 073-24-06.340W				Red nun.	
25025	- Buoy 13	41-04-36.532N 073-24-07.740W				Green can.	
25030	- LIGHT 14	41-04-42.561N 073-23-59.188W	Q R	26	4	TR on pipe tower on concrete base.	
25035	- Buoy 15	41-04-44.932N 073-24-04.340W				Green can.	
25040	- Buoy 17	41-04-57.749N 073-24-04.874W				Green can.	
25045	- Buoy 19 75 feet outside channel limit.	41-05-14.575N 073-24-15.213W				Green can.	
25050	- Buoy 21	41-05-26.590N 073-24-25.982W				Green can.	
	East Norwalk Channel						
25055	- Buoy 2	41-05-28.672N 073-24-18.451W				Red nun.	
25060	FITCH POINT LIGHT 1	41-05-30.832N 073-24-20.047W	Fl G 2.5s	29	4	SG on skeleton tower.	
25065	- Buoy 3	41-05-34.714N 073-24-17.646W				Green can.	
25070	- Buoy 5	41-05-40.364N 073-24-15.925W				Green can.	

(1) No.	(2) Name and Location	(3) Position	(4) Characteristic	(5) Height	(6) Range	(7) Structure	(8) Remarks
		LONG ISLAND SOUND (Connecticut) - First District					
SHERWOOD POINT TO STAMFORD HARBOR							
Fivemile River							
25075	Ballast Reef Buoy 2	41-03-13.243N 073-26-33.132W				Red nun.	
25080	Fish Island Buoy 1 On southeast side of reef.	41-03-04.033N 073-26-58.014W				Green can.	
25085	- *Entrance Lighted Buoy 3*	41-03-21.902N 073-26-48.995W	Fl G 4s		3	Green.	Replaced by can when endangered by ice.
25090	- Entrance Buoy 4	41-03-22.892N 073-26-46.255W				Red nun.	
25090.1	- Buoy 4A	41-03-31.000N 073-26-47.000W				Red nun.	Private aid.
25091	- Buoy 5	41-03-30.000N 073-26-49.000W				Green can.	Private aid.
25095	- Channel Buoy 6	41-03-40.620N 073-26-47.204W				Red nun.	
Goodwives River Approach							
25100	- *Lighted Buoy 1* Marks east side of shoal.	41-02-14.592N 073-29-00.758W	Fl G 4s		3	Green.	Replaced by can when endangered by ice.
25105	- Buoy 2	41-02-19.204N 073-28-56.397W				Red nun.	
25110	- Buoy 3 On east side of 3-foot spot.	41-02-21.932N 073-29-05.215W				Green can.	
25115	NOROTON RANGE FRONT LIGHT	41-02-39.000N 073-29-10.000W	F R	12		On pile.	Maintained from June 1 to Sept. 1. Private aid.
25120	NOROTON RANGE REAR LIGHT	41-02-41.000N 073-29-10.500W	F R			On pile.	Maintained from June 1 to 1 Sept. 65 yards, 352° from front light. Private aid.
25121	Goodwives River Mid-Channel Buoy A	41-02-28.080N 073-29-04.020W				Red and white.	Private aid.
25122	Goodwives River Mid-Channel Buoy B	41-02-32.340N 073-29-05.880W				Red and white.	Private aid.
25123	Goodwives River Mid-Channel Buoy C	41-02-39.240N 073-29-07.980W				Red and white.	Private aid.
25124	Goodwives River Mid-Channel Buoy D	41-02-45.240N 073-29-05.100W				Red and white.	Private aid.
Cove Harbor							
25125	Cove Mills Buoy 1	41-02-22.500N 073-30-11.500W				Green can.	Private aid.
25130	Cove Mills Buoy 2	41-02-25.000N 073-30-10.500W				Red nun.	Private aid.
Westcott Cove							
25135	- *East Entrance Lighted Buoy 1* On east side of shoal.	41-01-40.243N 073-30-36.381W	Fl G 4s		3	Green.	Replaced by can from Nov. 15 to May 1.
25140	- East Entrance Buoy 2 On south side of shoal.	41-01-46.193N 073-30-24.861W				Red nun.	
25145	- West Entrance Danger Buoy On northwest side of shoal.	41-01-40.723N 073-30-44.012W				White can with orange bands worded DANGER ROCKS.	
25150	- Buoy 3	41-01-51.513N 073-30-57.158W				Green can.	
25155	- *Lighted Buoy 4*	41-01-55.172N 073-30-55.692W	Fl R 4s		3	Red.	Replaced by nun from Nov. 15 to May 1.
25160	- Buoy 5	41-01-56.804N 073-31-05.699W				Green can.	
25165	- Buoy 6	41-01-57.546N 073-31-04.774W				Red nun.	
25170	- Buoy 7	41-02-00.641N 073-31-10.686W				Green can.	
25175	- Buoy 8	41-02-00.975N 073-31-07.922W				Red nun.	

(1) No.	(2) Name and Location	(3) Position	(4) Characteristic	(5) Height	(6) Range	(7) Structure	(8) Remarks

LONG ISLAND SOUND (Connecticut) - First District

SHERWOOD POINT TO STAMFORD HARBOR

Westcott Cove

| 25180 | - Buoy 9 | 41-02-10.122N
073-31-14.253W | | | | Green can. | |
| 25185 | - Buoy 10 | 41-02-11.409N
073-31-12.980W | | | | Red nun. | |

Stamford Harbor
Channel buoys located 30 to 60 feet outside of channel limit.

25195	- LEDGE OBSTRUCTION LIGHT On southwest end of Harbor Ledge.	41-00-49.000N 073-32-34.000W	Fl W 4s			White conical tower, on red cylindrical pier.	Private aid.
25200	- Entrance Gong Buoy 1 On southeast end of ledge.	41-00-41.523N 073-32-22.555W				Green.	
25205	- Entrance Buoy 2	41-00-44.633N 073-32-05.355W				Red nun.	
25210 21375	- WEST BREAKWATER LIGHT 3	41-00-53.915N 073-32-17.349W	Fl G 2.5s	37	4	SG on tower.	
25220	- West Approach Buoy 2	41-00-59.400N 073-32-56.400W				Red nun.	Private aid.
25221.2	Rocky Point Channel Buoy 3	41-00-54.720N 073-33-31.980W				Green can.	Maintained 1 May to Oct. 31. Private aid.
25221.4	Rocky Point Channel Buoy 5	41-00-59.640N 073-33-33.060W				Green can.	Maintained 1 May to Oct. 31. Private aid.
25221.5	Rocky Point Channel Buoy 6	41-00-59.640N 073-33-32.580W				Red nun.	Maintained 1 May to Oct. 31. Private aid.
25225	- EAST BREAKWATER LIGHT 4	41-00-54.209N 073-32-06.332W	Fl R 4s	21	4	TR on skeleton tower.	
25230	- RANGE FRONT LIGHT	41-01-48.917N 073-32-15.119W	Q W	26		KRW on skeleton tower.	Visible all around.
25235	- REAR RANGE LIGHT 211 yards, 356.8° from front light.	41-01-55.147N 073-32-15.582W	Iso R 6s	45		KRW on skeleton tower.	Visible all around; higher intensity on range line.
25240	- Channel Buoy 6	41-01-11.582N 073-32-10.905W				Red nun.	
25245	- Channel Buoy 7	41-01-19.932N 073-32-15.005W				Green can.	
25250	- Channel Buoy 9	41-01-32.563N 073-32-15.946W				Green can.	
25255	- Channel Buoy 10	41-01-34.702N 073-32-12.695W				Red nun.	
25260	- Channel Buoy 11	41-01-44.492N 073-32-16.305W				Green can.	
25265	- Channel Buoy 12	41-01-47.132N 073-32-13.545W				Red nun.	

Stamford East Branch

| 25270 | - CHANNEL LIGHT 1 | 41-02-06.882N
073-32-09.545W | Fl G 4s | 21 | 4 | SG on skeleton tower. | |

Stamford West Branch
Channel buoys located 30 to 60 feet outside of channel limit.

25275	- Channel Buoy 1	41-01-48.122N 073-32-18.665W				Green can.	
25280	- Channel Buoy 2	41-01-51.022N 073-32-21.145W				Red nun.	
25290	- Channel Buoy 3	41-01-51.743N 073-32-25.686W				Green can.	
25295	- Channel Buoy 4	41-01-54.912N 073-32-28.416W				Red nun.	
25300	- Channel Buoy 5	41-01-55.042N 073-32-31.836W				Green can.	
25305	- Channel Buoy 6	41-01-58.232N 073-32-31.306W				Red nun.	
25310	- Channel Buoy 7	41-02-02.602N 073-32-34.716W				Green can.	
25315	- Channel Buoy 9	41-02-10.243N 073-32-37.527W				Green can.	

(1) No.	(2) Name and Location	(3) Position	(4) Characteristic	(5) Height	(6) Range	(7) Structure	(8) Remarks
		LONG ISLAND SOUND (Connecticut) - First District					
	SHERWOOD POINT TO STAMFORD HARBOR						
	Stamford West Branch						
	Channel buoys located 30 to 60 feet outside of channel limit.						
25320	- Channel Buoy 10	41-02-15.968N 073-32-37.919W				Red nun.	
	GREENWICH POINT TO NEW ROCHELLE						
	Captain Harbor (From Eastward)						
25325	Flat Neck Point Shoal Buoy 2	40-59-44.934N 073-35-29.303W				Red nun.	
25330	*Little Captain Island East Reef Lighted Gong Buoy 1* Off east side of reef.	40-59-35.974N 073-35-51.984W	Fl G 2.5s		4	Green.	
25335	Hen and Chickens Buoy 1A	40-59-45.024N 073-36-17.025W				Green can.	
25340	*Newfoundland Reef Lighted Buoy 4* Marks southwest side of rock.	41-00-19.830N 073-36-01.274W	Fl R 4s		3	Red.	Replaced by nun when endangered by ice.
25345	Red Rock Buoy R On southeast side of rock.	41-00-19.078N 073-36-41.407W				Red and green bands; nun.	
	Captain Harbor (From Westward)						
25350	Great Captain Island West Reef Buoy 2 Marks southwest edge of shoal.	40-58-35.645N 073-37-56.740W				Red nun.	
25355	Fourfoot Rocks Buoy F On south side of rocks.	40-58-40.725N 073-38-31.621W				Green and red bands; can.	
25360	Calf Island Buoy 1 On southeast side of reef.	40-59-11.585N 073-38-12.280W				Green can.	
25365	JONES ROCK LIGHT 3 On rocks.	40-59-18.133N 073-38-05.314W	Fl G 4s	25	4	SG on skeleton tower.	
25370	Cormorant Reef Buoy 4 On northwest side of reef.	40-59-27.515N 073-37-52.429W				Red nun.	
25375	Cormorant Reef Buoy 1 Marks south side of reef.	40-59-08.955N 073-37-42.609W				Green can.	
	Captain Harbor						
	Greenwich Cove						
25380	Sugar Boat Buoy 2A West of wreck.	41-00-07.300N 073-35-26.700W				Red nun.	Maintained from May 15 to Nov. 1. Private aid.
25390	Cove Rock Buoy 2 On west side of rock.	41-00-32.268N 073-35-21.066W				Red nun.	
	Greenwich Point						
25395	- Buoy 1GP	41-00-35.700N 073-34-56.000W				Green spar.	Maintained from May 15 to Nov. 1. Private aid.
25400	- Buoy 2GP	41-00-36.800N 073-34-58.700W				Red spar.	Maintained from May 15 to Nov. 1. Private aid.
25405	- Buoy 3GP	41-00-30.200N 073-34-53.000W				Green spar.	Maintained from May 15 to Nov. 1. Private aid.
25410	- Buoy 4GP	41-00-32.900N 073-34-56.000W				Red spar.	Maintained from May 15 to Nov. 1. Private aid.
	Greenwich Cove						
25415	Inner Cove Rock Buoy 1 On east side of rock.	41-00-46.653N 073-34-52.161W				Green can.	
	Cos Cob Harbor						
25420	- *Lighted Buoy 2* Northwest side of rock.	41-00-37.934N 073-36-15.700W	Fl R 4s		3	Red.	
25425	- Buoy 3 South side of Peck Rock	41-00-46.854N 073-36-10.435W				Green can.	
25430	- Buoy 5 On southeast point of Saw Island Shoal.	41-00-51.703N 073-36-04.525W				Green can.	

(1) No.	(2) Name and Location	(3) Position	(4) Characteristic	(5) Height	(6) Range	(7) Structure	(8) Remarks

LONG ISLAND SOUND (Connecticut) - First District

GREENWICH POINT TO NEW ROCHELLE
Captain Harbor
Cos Cob Harbor

(1) No.	(2) Name and Location	(3) Position	(4) Characteristic	(5) Height	(6) Range	(7) Structure	(8) Remarks
25435	- Buoy 7	41-01-02.916N 073-35-49.489W				Green can.	
25440	Jake Reef Hazard Buoy J	41-00-54.600N 073-35-49.500W				White with Orange Bands.	Maintained from May 15 to Nov. 1. Private aid.
25445	- Channel Buoy 8	41-01-10.905N 073-35-44.338W				Red nun.	
25450	- Channel Buoy 9	41-01-14.608N 073-35-44.353W				Green can.	
25455	- Channel Buoy 10	41-01-24.778N 073-35-40.836W				Red nun.	
25460	- Channel Buoy 11	41-01-23.133N 073-35-41.764W				Green can.	
25465	- Channel Buoy 12	41-01-42.689N 073-35-40.790W				Red nun.	
25470	- Channel Buoy 13	41-01-42.233N 073-35-42.604W				Green can.	

Greenwich Harbor

(1) No.	(2) Name and Location	(3) Position	(4) Characteristic	(5) Height	(6) Range	(7) Structure	(8) Remarks
25480	- Channel Buoy 2	40-59-54.384N 073-37-16.367W				Red nun.	
25485	- Channel Buoy 3	41-00-11.284N 073-37-21.568W				Green can.	
25490	- Channel Buoy 4	41-00-11.785N 073-37-17.291W				Red nun.	
25495	- Channel Buoy 5	41-00-27.684N 073-37-23.068W				Green can.	
25500	- Channel Buoy 6 75 feet outside channel limit.	41-00-28.774N 073-37-20.628W				Red nun.	
25505	- Channel Buoy 8 75 feet outside channel limit.	41-00-37.120N 073-37-22.727W				Red nun.	
25510	- Channel Buoy 9	41-00-39.983N 073-37-24.968W				Green can.	

Byram Harbor

(1) No.	(2) Name and Location	(3) Position	(4) Characteristic	(5) Height	(6) Range	(7) Structure	(8) Remarks
25515	- Entrance Buoy 1 On end of reef.	40-59-51.369N 073-38-09.865W				Green can.	
25520	- Entrance Lighted Buoy 2 Marks southwest side of Otter Rocks.	40-59-54.444N 073-38-13.300W	Fl R 4s		3	Red.	Replaced by nun when endangered by ice.
25525	- Buoy 3 On east side of Wilson Head.	40-59-59.054N 073-38-20.740W				Green can.	
25530	- Reef Buoy 4 On southwest end of rocky reef.	41-00-03.564N 073-38-17.220W				Red nun.	

LONG ISLAND SOUND (New York) - First District

GREENWICH POINT TO NEW ROCHELLE
Port Chester Harbor

(1) No.	(2) Name and Location	(3) Position	(4) Characteristic	(5) Height	(6) Range	(7) Structure	(8) Remarks
25535	Great Captain Rocks Lighted Buoy 2 On south side of reef.	40-58-56.905N 073-39-04.392W	Fl R 4s		3	Red.	
25540	Manursing Island Reef Buoy 3 Off northeast point of reef.	40-58-59.435N 073-39-18.003W				Green can.	
25545	PORT CHESTER LIGHT 4	40-59-03.965N 073-39-23.393W	Fl R 2.5s	28	4	TR on skeleton tower.	
25550	- CHANNEL LIGHT 5	40-59-09.415N 073-39-35.533W	Fl G 4s	25	4	SG on skeleton tower.	
25555	- Channel Buoy 6 30 feet outside channel limit.	40-59-16.515N 073-39-34.503W				Red nun.	

Tide Mill Yacht Basin

(1) No.	(2) Name and Location	(3) Position	(4) Characteristic	(5) Height	(6) Range	(7) Structure	(8) Remarks
25556.1	- Channel Buoy 1	40-59-06.060N 073-39-33.780W				Green can.	Private aid.
25556.2	- Channel Buoy 2	40-59-06.840N 073-39-34.020W				Red nun.	Private aid.

(1) No.	(2) Name and Location	(3) Position	(4) Characteristic	(5) Height	(6) Range	(7) Structure	(8) Remarks
			LONG ISLAND SOUND (New York) - First District				
	GREENWICH POINT TO NEW ROCHELLE						
	Port Chester Harbor						
	Tide Mill Yacht Basin						
25556.3	- Channel Buoy 4	40-59-04.900N 073-39-37.500W				Red nun.	Private aid.
25556.4	- Channel Buoy 6	40-59-02.100N 073-39-42.100W				Red nun.	Private aid.
25556.5	- Channel Buoy 7	40-58-55.300N 073-39-47.400W				Green can.	Private aid.
25556.6	- Channel Buoy 8	40-58-55.700N 073-39-48.100W				Red nun.	Private aid.
25556.7	- Channel Buoy 9	40-58-49.740N 073-39-47.160W				Green can.	Private aid.
25556.8	- Channel Buoy 10	40-58-52.020N 073-39-48.180W				Red nun.	Private aid.
25556.9	- Channel Buoy 11	40-58-47.340N 073-39-47.340W				Green can.	Private aid.
25557	- Channel Buoy 12	40-58-47.940N 073-39-47.880W				Red nun.	Private aid.
25558	- Channel Buoy 13	40-58-45.300N 073-39-49.260W				Green can.	Private aid.
25559	- Channel Buoy 14	40-58-45.900N 073-39-50.460W				Red nun.	Private aid.
	Rye Beach						
25560	Forbes Rocks Outer Buoy 1 On east side of reef.	40-57-12.797N 073-40-08.156W				Green can.	
25565	Forbes Rocks North Gong Buoy 1A On east side of shoal.	40-57-30.037N 073-40-08.046W				Green can.	
25570	Transport Rock Buoy 2 Off west side of rock.	40-57-35.516N 073-40-05.631W				Red nun.	
	Oakland Beach						
25575	Forlies Rocks Buoy 2 South side of rock.	40-57-26.717N 073-40-29.847W				Red nun.	
	Coveleigh Yacht Club Channel *Private aids are maintained from 15 Apr. to 15 Oct.*						
25576	- *Lighted Buoy 1*	40-56-24.600N 073-41-09.000W	Fl G 4s			Green.	Private aid.
25576.5	- Buoy 4	40-56-32.580N 073-41-16.620W				Red nun.	Private aid.
25577	- Lighted Buoy 3	40-56-30.420N 073-41-16.020W	Fl G 2s			Green can.	Private aid.
25577.5	- Lighted Buoy 7	40-56-31.458N 073-41-31.200W	Q G			Green can.	Private aid.
25578	- Buoy 5	40-56-31.500N 073-41-24.960W				Green can.	Private aid.
25578.5	- Buoy 6	40-56-32.700N 073-41-24.120W				Red nun.	Private aid.
25579	- Buoy 8	40-56-32.460N 073-41-30.300W				Red nun.	Private aid.
25579.1	- Buoy 9	40-56-33.420N 073-41-31.680W				Green can.	Private aid.
25579.2	- Buoy 10	40-56-35.220N 073-41-31.320W				Red nun.	Private aid.
25579.3	- Buoy 12	40-56-36.420N 073-41-30.900W				Red nun.	Private aid.
25579.4	- Buoy 14	40-56-37.380N 073-41-30.660W				Red nun.	Private aid.
	Mamaroneck Harbor						
25580	- Entrance Buoy 1 Marks south edge of shoal.	40-55-19.659N 073-43-16.174W				Green can.	
25585	- Entrance Buoy 3 Marks southeast edge of shoal.	40-55-34.469N 073-43-07.753W				Green can.	
25590	- Entrance Buoy 2 Marks west end of rocks	40-55-49.340N 073-42-24.123W				Red nun.	

(1) No.	(2) Name and Location	(3) Position	(4) Characteristic	(5) Height	(6) Range	(7) Structure	(8) Remarks
		LONG ISLAND SOUND (New York) - First District					
	GREENWICH POINT TO NEW ROCHELLE						
	Mamaroneck Harbor						
25595	- *Lighted Buoy MM* Marks southwest side of Ship Rock.	40-55-52.433N 073-42-32.114W	Fl (2+1)R 6s		4	Red and green bands.	Replaced by nun when endangered by ice.
25600	- Buoy 6 Marks south end of Turkey Rock.	40-56-16.668N 073-42-45.182W				Red nun.	
25605	- *Channel Lighted Buoy 5* On northeast side of Outer Steamboat Rock.	40-56-14.139N 073-43-01.133W	Fl G 4s		4	Green.	Removed when endangered by ice.
25610	- Buoy 8 Southwest side of rock.	40-56-19.448N 073-42-53.582W				Red nun.	
25615	- Channel Buoy 7	40-56-24.678N 073-43-21.091W				Green can.	
25620	- *Channel Lighted Buoy 10*	40-56-25.263N 073-43-17.126W	Fl R 4s		4	Red.	Removed when endangered by ice.
25625	Little Nanhook Obstruction Buoy	40-56-24.000N 073-43-24.000W				White nun.	Maintained from May 1 to Nov. 15. Private aid.
25630	- Channel Buoy 12	40-56-30.119N 073-43-35.620W				Red nun.	
25635	- Junction Buoy A	40-56-30.342N 073-43-37.700W				Green and red bands; can.	
25640	- Buoy 9	40-56-37.822N 073-43-42.005W				Green can.	
25645	- Channel Buoy 11	40-56-40.188N 073-43-43.583W				Green can.	
25650	- Channel Buoy 14	40-56-43.596N 073-43-43.635W				Red nun.	
25655	- Channel Buoy 16	40-56-46.079N 073-43-46.248W				Red nun.	
	Milton Harbor						
25660	West Rock Obstruction Buoy	40-55-55.497N 073-42-08.454W				White can with orange bands and diamond worded ROCK.	
25665	- Buoy 3 Marks southeast side of rocks.	40-56-07.518N 073-42-22.302W				Green can.	
25670.1	- Buoy 5	40-56-32.194N 073-41-59.827W				Green can.	Private aid.
25675.1	- Buoy 6	40-56-31.263N 073-41-57.194W				Red nun.	Private aid.
25680.1	- Buoy 8	40-56-47.355N 073-41-50.653W				Red nun.	Private aid.
25685.1	- Buoy 9	40-57-02.458N 073-41-45.934W				Green can.	Private aid.
25690.1	- Buoy 10	40-57-02.729N 073-41-44.774W				Red nun.	Private aid.
25695.1	- Buoy 11	40-57-13.670N 073-41-43.708W				Green can.	Private aid. Private aid.
25700.1	- Buoy 12	40-57-13.280N 073-41-42.896W				Red nun.	Private aid.
25705.1	- Buoy 13	40-57-25.661N 073-41-32.282W				Green can.	Private aid.
25710.1	- Buoy 14	40-57-25.757N 073-41-31.048W				Red nun.	Private aid.
	Larchmont Harbor (East Entrance)						
25715	*Hen and Chickens Northeast Lighted Bell Buoy 1* On northeast point of shoal.	40-54-48.690N 073-44-04.386W	Fl G 4s		4	Green.	
25720	LARCHMONT HARBOR LIGHT 2	40-55-05.049N 073-43-52.365W	Fl R 4s	26	4	TR on skeleton tower.	
25725	Dauntless Rock Buoy 3 Northeast of rock.	40-54-59.450N 073-44-11.606W				Green can.	

(1) No.	(2) Name and Location	(3) Position	(4) Characteristic	(5) Height	(6) Range	(7) Structure	(8) Remarks
		LONG ISLAND SOUND (New York) - First District					
	GREENWICH POINT TO NEW ROCHELLE						
	Larchmont Harbor (South Entrance)						
25730	*Hen and Chickens South Lighted Buoy 2*	40-54-10.601N 073-44-19.847W	Fl R 4s		3	Red.	Replaced by nun when endangered by ice.
25735	Hicks Ledge Junction Buoy HL	40-54-10.391N 073-45-07.988W				Green and red bands; can.	
25740	Table Rock Buoy 3 On southeast side of shoals.	40-54-29.791N 073-45-01.888W				Green can.	
25745	Hen and Chickens West Buoy 4 Marks west side of shoal.	40-54-36.401N 073-44-35.637W				Red nun.	
25750	Hen and Chickens North Buoy 6 Marks northwest edge of reef.	40-54-58.350N 073-44-19.387W				Red nun.	
25755	Umbrella Rock Buoy 7 On southeast side of rock.	40-55-04.650N 073-44-24.257W				Green can.	
25765	North Ledge South Daybeacon	40-55-20.980N 073-44-32.860W				NW on spindle worded ROCKS.	Private aid.
25770	North Ledge North Daybeacon	40-55-23.620N 073-44-33.570W				NW on spindle worded ROCKS.	Private aid.
	Echo Bay						
25775	Middle Ground Buoy 1M	40-53-56.171N 073-45-31.479W				Green can.	
25780	*Bailey Rock Lighted Buoy 3BR*	40-54-13.571N 073-45-42.159W	Fl G 4s		4	Green.	
25785	Premium Point Buoy 4	40-54-21.691N 073-45-41.979W				Red nun.	
25790	- Channel Buoy 5	40-54-24.691N 073-46-00.610W				Green can.	
25795	- Channel Buoy 6	40-54-25.271N 073-45-58.810W				Red nun.	
25800	- Channel Buoy 8	40-54-31.511N 073-46-01.120W				Red nun.	
25805	- Channel Buoy 10	40-54-34.051N 073-46-06.330W				Red nun.	
	HEMPSTEAD HARBOR TO TALLMAN ISLAND						
	New Rochelle Harbor (North Approach)						
25810	Emerald Rock Buoy On northeast side of rock.	40-53-43.302N 073-45-49.630W				Green and red bands; can.	
25815	*Huckleberry Island Lighted Buoy 2* On southeast side of shoal.	40-53-26.522N 073-45-23.339W	Fl R 4s		3	Red.	Removed when endangered by ice.
25820	Old Tom Head Rocks Buoy 4 On south edge of shoal.	40-53-30.012N 073-46-05.150W				Red nun.	
25825	*Davids Island North Lighted Buoy 5* On north point of shoal.	40-53-25.222N 073-46-08.310W	Fl G 4s		4	Green.	Replaced by can when endangered by ice.
25830	Davids Island North Buoy 7	40-53-24.162N 073-46-16.081W				Green can.	
25835	Davenport Neck Buoy 8 25 yards, 089.5° from obstruction.	40-53-26.152N 073-46-20.601W				Red nun.	
25840	Spindle Rock Buoy 9 On west side of shoal.	40-53-22.292N 073-46-29.901W				Green can.	
	New Rochelle Harbor (Southeast Approach)						
25845	Pea Island Buoy 1	40-52-32.333N 073-46-01.730W				Green can.	
	New Rochelle Harbor (South Approach)						
25850	Hart Island East Side Gong Buoy 1 On east side of shoals.	40-51-25.093N 073-45-45.790W				Green.	
25855	Hart Island North Buoy 3 On north side of shoals.	40-51-42.193N 073-46-13.461W				Green can.	

(1) No.	(2) Name and Location	(3) Position	(4) Characteristic	(5) Height	(6) Range	(7) Structure	(8) Remarks
			LONG ISLAND SOUND (New York) - First District				
	HEMPSTEAD HARBOR TO TALLMAN ISLAND						
	New Rochelle Harbor (South Approach)						
25860	*South Nonations Reef Lighted Bell Buoy 4* On southwest end of shoal.	40-51-52.343N 073-46-16.341W	Fl R 4s		4	Red.	
	New Rochelle Harbor (Southwest Approach)						
25865	**City Island Ferry Sound Signal**	40-50-54.000N 073-46-54.000W				Wharf end dolphin.	HORN: 1 blast ev 15s (5s bl). Private aid.
25870	*Chimney Sweeps Lighted Buoy 1* On east side of shoal.	40-51-45.213N 073-46-47.332W	Fl G 4s		4	Green.	Replaced by can when endangered by ice.
25875	Orchard Beach Buoy 2 Marks southeast side of rock.	40-51-54.112N 073-47-11.062W				Red nun.	
25880	Orchard Beach Channel Buoy 2A	40-51-49.392N 073-47-19.493W				Red nun.	
25885	Orchard Beach Buoy 1 Marks northwest side of rocky shoal.	40-51-50.442N 073-47-08.762W				Green can.	
	Davids Island Channel						
25890	*Machaux Rock Lighted Bell Buoy 6* On west side of shoals.	40-52-24.372N 073-46-39.441W	Fl R 4s		4	Red.	
25895	Twin Island Buoy 7 East of shoal.	40-52-24.892N 073-46-46.392W				Green can.	
25900	- Buoy 7A	40-52-40.543N 073-46-40.391W				Green can.	
25905	- Buoy 7B	40-52-54.582N 073-46-35.371W				Green can.	
25910	Davids Island West Buoy 8 On edge of shoal.	40-52-54.202N 073-46-31.451W				Red nun.	
	Glen Island Channel						
25915	R.R. Stevens Rock Buoy On east side of rock.	40-52-52.822N 073-46-41.011W				Red and green bands; nun.	
25920	- Buoy 1 Marks northeast side of ledge of rocks.	40-52-50.986N 073-47-02.136W				Green can.	
25925	- Buoy 2	40-52-51.757N 073-47-01.470W				Red nun.	
25930	- Buoy 4	40-52-53.525N 073-47-07.341W				Red nun.	
25935	- Buoy 6	40-52-59.392N 073-47-15.492W				Red nun.	
	Middle Channel						
25940	Corning Rock Buoy 9 On east side of rock.	40-53-06.092N 073-46-32.901W				Green can.	
25945	AUNT PHEBE ROCK LIGHT 10 On ledge.	40-53-08.122N 073-46-30.621W	Fl R 4s	24	4	TR on skeleton tower.	
25950	Spindle Rock South Buoy 10A On southside of shoal.	40-53-16.302N 073-46-28.391W				Red nun.	
25955	Davenport Neck Buoy 12 On east side of shoal.	40-53-20.162N 073-46-35.461W				Red nun.	
25960	*Harbor Rock Lighted Buoy 14*	40-53-18.872N 073-46-42.121W	Q R		3	Red.	Replaced by nun when endangered by ice.
25965	GLEN ISLAND LIGHT 15	40-53-21.733N 073-46-49.114W	Fl G 4s	20	4	SG on tower on concrete base.	
	City Island						
25970	Big Tom Rock Buoy BT	40-50-08.094N 073-47-16.273W				White with orange bands; can.	
25975	- *Lighted Buoy 2*	40-49-58.284N 073-47-21.653W	Fl R 4s		4	Red.	
25980	- Buoy 4 On west side of shoal.	40-50-06.874N 073-47-32.663W				Red nun.	

(1) No.	(2) Name and Location	(3) Position	(4) Characteristic	(5) Height	(6) Range	(7) Structure	(8) Remarks
			LONG ISLAND SOUND (New York) - First District				
	HEMPSTEAD HARBOR TO TALLMAN ISLAND						
	City Island						
25985	- Wreck Buoy WR6	40-50-38.137N 073-47-44.243W				Red nun.	
25990	- Buoy 7 On east side of rock.	40-50-46.574N 073-47-58.864W				Green can.	
25995	- Buoy 8	40-51-05.893N 073-47-44.494W				Red nun.	
26000	*Cuban Ledge Junction Lighted Buoy CL*	40-50-05.032N 073-47-57.514W	Fl (2+1)R 6s		3	Red and green bands.	Replaced by nun when endangered by ice.
26005	Cuban Ledge Daybeacon	40-50-30.207N 073-48-13.748W				NW on spindle worded DANGER ROCK.	
	Eastchester Bay						
26007	*Bronxonia Yacht Club Lighted No Wake Buoy*	40-49-37.700N 073-48-33.300W	Fl W 2.5s			White with orange bands.	Private aid.
26010	*Cuban Ledge Lighted Buoy 2* Marks southwest edge of ledge.	40-50-26.253N 073-48-15.697W	Fl R 4s		3	Red.	Remove when endangered by ice.
26015	- *Shoal Lighted Buoy 4* Marks southwest edge of shoal.	40-50-50.373N 073-48-32.065W	Fl R 2.5s		3	Red.	
26020	- Channel Buoy 6	40-51-17.393N 073-48-32.495W				Red nun.	
26025	- *Channel Lighted Buoy 7*	40-51-33.373N 073-48-35.755W	Fl G 4s		4	Green.	Replaced by can when endangered by ice.
26030	- Channel Buoy 9 Marks northeast edge of rocky shoals.	40-51-35.773N 073-48-37.205W				Green can.	
26035	- Channel Buoy 11 On north side of Middle Rock.	40-51-40.232N 073-48-45.035W				Green can.	
	Hutchinson River						
26040	- Buoy 2	40-51-52.536N 073-49-08.111W				Red nun.	Removed when endangered by ice.
26045	- Buoy 3	40-52-00.092N 073-49-11.346W				Green can.	Removed when endangered by ice.
26050	- Buoy 4	40-52-13.752N 073-49-21.806W				Red nun.	Removed when endangered by ice.
26055	- Buoy 6	40-52-30.143N 073-49-21.092W				Red nun.	Removed when endangered by ice.
26060	- Buoy 7	40-52-42.881N 073-49-17.336W				Green can.	Removed when endangered by ice.
	PORT JEFFERSON AND MOUNT SINAI HARBORS						
	Mount Sinai Harbor						
26070	- BREAKWATER LIGHT	40-57-55.900N 073-02-33.906W	Fl G 5s	20		On concrete pedestal.	Private aid.
26071	- BREAKWATER LIGHT 2	40-57-58.000N 073-02-40.700W	Fl R 4s	15		On pile.	Private aid.
26075	- *Lighted Buoy 3*	40-57-46.400N 073-02-35.000W	Fl G 4s			Green.	Private aid.
26080	- Buoy 5	40-57-46.000N 073-02-30.100W				Green can.	Private aid.
26085	- Buoy 4	40-57-44.100N 073-02-27.400W				Red nun.	Private aid.
26090	- Buoy 7	40-57-44.400N 073-02-15.300W				Green can.	Private aid.
26095	- Buoy 6	40-57-43.600N 073-02-15.200W				Red nun.	Private aid.
26100	- Buoy 9	40-57-45.500N 073-02-06.600W				Green can.	Private aid.

(1) No.	(2) Name and Location	(3) Position	(4) Characteristic	(5) Height	(6) Range	(7) Structure	(8) Remarks
			LONG ISLAND SOUND (New York) - First District				
	PORT JEFFERSON AND MOUNT SINAI HARBORS						
	Mount Sinai Harbor						
26105	- Buoy 8	40-57-43.300N 073-02-01.200W				Red nun.	Private aid.
26110	- Buoy 10	40-57-43.600N 073-01-55.100W				Red nun.	Private aid.
26115	- Buoy 12	40-57-44.100N 073-01-46.400W				Red nun.	Private aid.
26120	- Buoy 14	40-57-43.400N 073-01-36.900W				Red nun.	Private aid.
26122	*Rock Head Lighted Hazard Buoy*	40-58-02.500N 073-03-36.600W	F W			White with Orange bands.	Private aid.
	Port Jefferson Harbor						
26125	*Port Jefferson Approach Lighted Whistle Buoy PJ*	40-59-16.387N 073-06-26.700W	Mo (A) W		4	Red and white stripes with red spherical topmark.	AIS: MMSI 993672155 (21)
26130	- *Entrance Lighted Buoy 1*	40-58-24.315N 073-05-38.348W	Fl G 2.5s		4	Green.	
26135	PORT JEFFERSON EAST BREAKWATER LIGHT	40-58-20.333N 073-05-29.643W	Fl W 4s	27	6	NG on skeleton tower.	
26140	- *Entrance Lighted Bell Buoy 2*	40-58-22.493N 073-05-41.631W	Fl R 2.5s		4	Red.	
26145	PORT JEFFERSON WEST BREAKWATER LIGHT 2A	40-58-13.468N 073-05-35.701W	Fl R 4s	22	4	TR on skeleton tower.	
26155	PORT JEFFERSON REAR RANGE LIGHT	40-56-47.434N 073-04-14.906W	Iso R 6s	63		On Tower.	Lighted throughout 24 hours.
26160	PORT JEFFERSON FRONT RANGE LIGHT	40-56-52.258N 073-04-19.157W	Q R	39		On Tower.	Lighted throughout 24 hours.
26165	- Buoy 4	40-57-52.838N 073-05-14.859W				Red nun.	
26170	- *Lighted Bell Buoy 5*	40-57-49.188N 073-05-06.879W	Fl G 4s		4	Green.	
26175	- Channel Buoy 7	40-57-17.984N 073-04-36.469W				Green can.	
26176	- Buoy 8	40-57-12.267N 073-04-40.526W				Red nun.	
26177	- Buoy 9	40-57-00.688N 073-04-17.197W				Green can.	
	Conscience Bay						
26179	- Narrows Channel Buoy CN1	40-57-51.060N 073-05-19.800W				Green can.	Private aid.
26180	- Narrows Channel Buoy CN2	40-57-55.620N 073-05-24.780W				Red nun.	Private aid.
26181	- Narrows Channel Buoy CN3	40-57-52.260N 073-05-33.420W				Green can.	Private aid.
26182	- Narrows Channel Buoy CN4	40-57-53.160N 073-05-33.960W				Red nun.	Private aid.
26183	- Narrows Channel Buoy CN5	40-57-54.240N 073-06-00.000W				Green can.	Private aid.
26184	- Narrows Channel Buoy CN6	40-57-55.260N 073-06-00.000W				Red nun.	Private aid.
26185	- Narrows Channel Buoy CN8	40-58-00.240N 073-06-11.700W				Red nun.	Private aid.
26186	- Narrows Channel Buoy CN9	40-58-05.520N 073-06-26.520W				Green can.	Private aid.
26187	- Narrows Channel Buoy CN10	40-58-10.020N 073-06-33.600W				Red nun.	Private aid.
26188	- Narrows Channel Buoy CN11	40-58-12.900N 073-06-42.420W				Green can.	Private aid.
26189	- Narrows Channel Buoy CN12	40-58-13.860N 073-06-41.940W				Red nun.	Private aid.
26190	- Narrows Channel Buoy CN13	40-58-13.200N 073-06-46.920W				Green can.	Private aid.
	Setauket Harbor						
26191	Conscience Bay Narrows Channel Buoy CN14	40-58-14.160N 073-06-45.240W				Red nun.	Private aid.

(1) No.	(2) Name and Location	(3) Position	(4) Characteristic	(5) Height	(6) Range	(7) Structure	(8) Remarks
			LONG ISLAND SOUND (New York) - First District				
	PORT JEFFERSON AND MOUNT SINAI HARBORS						
	Port Jefferson Harbor						
	Setauket Harbor						
26193	- Channel Buoy S1	40-57-27.720N 073-05-22.980W				Green can.	Private aid.
26194	- Channel Buoy S2	40-57-34.560N 073-05-12.540W				Red nun.	Private aid.
26195	- Channel Buoy S3	40-57-30.420N 073-05-36.480W				Green can.	Private aid.
26196	- Channel Buoy S4	40-57-30.000N 073-05-26.700W				Red nun.	Private aid.
26197	- Channel Buoy S5	40-57-30.540N 073-05-45.720W				Green can.	Private aid.
26198	- Channel Buoy S6	40-57-32.160N 073-05-38.520W				Red nun.	Private aid.
26199	- Channel Buoy S7	40-57-29.520N 073-05-50.040W				Green can.	Private aid.
26200	- Channel Buoy S8	40-57-30.000N 073-05-52.380W				Red nun.	Private aid.
26201	- Channel Buoy S9	40-57-22.980N 073-05-56.640W				Green can.	Private aid.
26202	- Channel Buoy S10	40-57-23.460N 073-05-59.220W				Red nun.	Private aid.
	Belle Terre						
26203	- Channel Buoy BT2	40-57-48.060N 073-04-40.200W				Red nun.	Private aid.
26204	- Channel Buoy BT4	40-57-40.980N 073-04-34.080W				Red nun.	Private aid.
26205	- Channel Buoy BT6	40-57-24.720N 073-04-23.040W				Red nun.	Private aid.
26206	- Channel Buoy BT8	40-57-13.980N 073-04-15.000W				Red nun.	Private aid.
26207	- Channel Buoy BT10	40-57-06.360N 073-04-06.300W				Red nun.	Private aid.
	LONG ISLAND SOUND (Western Part)						
	Smithtown Bay						
	Stony Brook Harbor						
26208	- *Entrance Lighted Buoy 1*	40-56-15.015N 073-09-46.429W	Fl G 4s	4		Green.	Remove when endangered by ice.
26210	- *Approach Channel Lighted Buoy 3*	40-56-15.960N 073-09-27.660W	Fl G 4s			Green.	Private aid.
26215	- *Approach Channel Lighted Buoy 5*	40-56-13.080N 073-09-12.780W	Fl G 4s			Green.	Private aid.
26220	- *Approach Channel Lighted Buoy 7*	40-56-10.600N 073-08-58.000W	Fl G 4s			Green.	Private aid.
26225	- *Approach Channel Lighted Buoy 9*	40-55-58.100N 073-08-48.400W	Fl G 4s			Green.	Private aid.
26230	- *Approach Channel Lighted Buoy 11*	40-55-48.800N 073-08-51.000W	Fl G 4s			Green.	Private aid.
26235	Stonybrook Channel Buoy 1	40-55-26.500N 073-08-55.000W				Green can.	Private aid.
	Porpoise Channel *Aids maintained from May 1 to Nov. 1.*						
26240	- *Lighted Buoy 1*	40-55-33.400N 073-08-57.300W	Fl G 4s			Green.	Private aid.
26245	- *Lighted Buoy 2*	40-55-34.400N 073-08-58.200W	Fl R 4s			Red.	Private aid.
26250	- *Lighted Buoy 3*	40-55-28.400N 073-09-06.000W	Fl G 4s			Green.	Private aid.
26255	- *Lighted Buoy 4*	40-55-29.500N 073-09-06.500W	Fl R 4s			Red.	Private aid.
26260	- Buoy 5	40-55-27.300N 073-09-16.700W				Green can.	Private aid.
26265	- *Lighted Buoy 6*	40-55-26.400N 073-09-19.500W	Fl R 4s			Red.	Private aid.

(1) No.	(2) Name and Location	(3) Position	(4) Characteristic	(5) Height	(6) Range	(7) Structure	(8) Remarks
			LONG ISLAND SOUND (New York) - First District				
	LONG ISLAND SOUND (Western Part)						
	Smithtown Bay						
	Porpoise Channel						
	Aids maintained from May 1 to Nov. 1.						
26270	- Buoy 7	40-55-26.100N 073-09-18.600W				Green can.	Private aid.
26275	- *Lighted Buoy 8*	40-55-18.210N 073-09-24.100W	Fl R 4s			Red.	Private aid.
26280	- Buoy 9	40-55-16.920N 073-09-23.400W				Green can.	Private aid.
26285	- *Lighted Buoy 10*	40-55-08.160N 073-09-43.680W	Fl R 4s			Red.	Private aid.
26290	- Buoy 11	40-55-07.200N 073-09-43.560W				Green can.	Private aid.
26295	- *Lighted Buoy 12*	40-55-01.600N 073-10-05.000W	Fl R 4s			Red.	Private aid.
26300	- Buoy 13	40-55-00.000N 073-10-04.000W				Green can.	Private aid.
26305	- *Lighted Buoy 14*	40-54-53.400N 073-10-27.780W	Fl R 4s			Red.	Private aid.
26310	- Buoy 15	40-54-52.200N 073-10-27.060W				Green can.	Private aid.
	Nissequogue River						
26315	- *Entrance Lighted Buoy NR*	40-55-23.352N 073-13-45.407W	Mo (A) W			Red and white stripes.	Private aid.
26320	- *Lighted Buoy 2*	40-55-03.000N 073-13-54.000W	Fl R 4s			Red.	Maintained from Apr. 1 to Nov. 30. Private aid.
26325	- *Lighted Buoy 4*	40-54-46.000N 073-14-03.000W	Fl R 4s			Red.	Maintained from Apr. 1 to Nov. 30. Private aid.
26330	- *Lighted Buoy 6*	40-54-32.000N 073-14-07.500W	Fl R 4s			Red.	Maintained from Apr. 1 to Nov. 30. Private aid.
26335	- *Lighted Buoy 8*	40-54-26.600N 073-14-01.000W	Fl R 4s			Red.	Maintained from Apr. 1 to Nov. 30. Private aid.
26340	- *Lighted Buoy 10*	40-54-18.800N 073-13-50.500W	Fl R 4s			Red.	Maintained from Apr. 1 to Nov. 30. Private aid.
26345	- *Lighted Buoy 12*	40-54-09.000N 073-13-29.900W	Fl R 4s			Red.	Maintained from Apr. 1 to Nov. 30. Private aid.
26350	- *Lighted Buoy 14*	40-53-58.500N 073-13-32.100W	Fl R 4s			Red.	Maintained from Apr. 1 to Nov. 30. Private aid.
	OYSTER AND HUNTINGTON BAYS						
	Northport						
26360	- PLATFORM EAST LIGHT	40-57-16.000N 073-20-26.000W	Q W	26		On pile platform.	Private aid.
26365	- PLATFORM WEST LIGHT	40-57-17.000N 073-20-31.500W	Q W	26		On pile platform.	HORN: 1 blast ev 20s (2s bl). Private aid.
	Lilco Basin						
	Aids maintained from Mar. 15 to Oct. 30.						
26380	- *Lighted Buoy 2*	40-55-41.430N 073-20-44.190W	Fl R 3s			Red.	Private aid.
26385	- *Lighted Buoy 3*	40-55-38.490N 073-20-42.170W	Fl G 3s			Green.	Private aid.
26390	- *Lighted Buoy 4*	40-55-32.800N 073-20-44.010W	Fl R 3s			Red.	Private aid.
26395	- *Lighted Buoy 5*	40-55-30.140N 073-20-42.320W	Fl G 3s			Green.	Private aid.
26400	- *Lighted Buoy 6*	40-55-26.570N 073-20-43.220W	Fl R 3s			Red.	Private aid.

(1) No.	(2) Name and Location	(3) Position	(4) Characteristic	(5) Height	(6) Range	(7) Structure	(8) Remarks
			LONG ISLAND SOUND (New York) - First District				
	OYSTER AND HUNTINGTON BAYS						
	Huntington Bay						
	Eatons Neck						
26420	- Lighted Buoy 1	40-56-49.978N 073-24-16.979W	Fl G 2.5s		3	Green.	Replaced by can when endangered by ice.
26425	- Buoy 2 Marks shoal.	40-56-49.961N 073-24-09.021W				Red nun.	Position frequently changed due to shoaling. Replaced by nun when endangered by ice.
26430	- Lighted Buoy 2A Marks shoal.	40-56-50.505N 073-24-06.541W	Q R		3	Red.	Position frequently changed due to shoaling. Replaced by nun when endangered by ice.
26435	- Basin Buoy 4	40-56-53.718N 073-24-04.018W				Red nun.	
26440	- Basin Buoy 5	40-56-56.138N 073-24-05.046W				Green can.	
26445	- Basin Buoy 6	40-57-03.140N 073-24-02.415W				Red nun.	
26450	- Basin Buoy 7	40-57-03.354N 073-24-03.650W				Green can.	
26455	- Basin Buoy 8	40-57-11.046N 073-24-00.104W				Red nun.	
26460	- Basin Buoy 9	40-57-11.293N 073-24-01.145W				Green can.	
26461	- Basin Coast Guard Mooring Buoy	40-57-12.721N 073-24-00.651W				White with blue band.	Marked CG.
	Huntington Bay						
26465	- Approach Buoy 2 On north side of rock reef.	40-57-18.035N 073-28-42.719W				Red nun.	
26470	Morris Rock Warning Buoy	40-56-53.385N 073-28-33.448W				White can with orange bands worded DANGER.	
26475	- Approach Buoy 4	40-56-46.145N 073-27-37.497W				Red nun.	
26480	- Approach Buoy 6 On northeast side of rock.	40-56-32.645N 073-26-21.825W				Red nun.	
26485	- Lighted Bell Buoy 8	40-55-51.595N 073-25-24.124W	Fl R 4s		3	Red.	
	Price Bend *Aids maintained from May 1 to Oct. 15.*						
26489	- No Wake Lighted Buoy A	40-55-36.100N 073-23-56.000W	Fl W 3s			White with Orange bands.	Private aid.
26490	- Lighted Buoy 1	40-55-37.000N 073-23-56.500W	Q G			Green.	Private aid.
26495	- Lighted Buoy 2	40-55-38.100N 073-23-54.000W	Q R			Red.	Private aid.
26500	- Lighted Buoy 3	40-55-40.000N 073-23-57.800W	Fl G 3s			Green.	Private aid.
26505	- Lighted Buoy 4	40-55-40.700N 073-23-56.100W	Fl R 3s			Red.	Private aid.
26510	- Lighted Buoy 5	40-55-41.100N 073-24-01.000W	Fl G 3s			Green.	Private aid.
26515	- Lighted Buoy 6	40-55-42.000N 073-23-58.900W	Fl R 3s			Red.	Private aid.
26520	- Lighted Buoy 7	40-55-41.400N 073-24-04.680W	Fl G 3s			Green.	Private aid.
26525	- Lighted Buoy 8	40-55-43.000N 073-23-58.000W	Fl R 2s			Red.	Private aid.
	Huntington Harbor						
26527	- Approach Lighted No Wake Buoy	40-54-50.160N 073-25-34.000W	Fl W 3s			White with Orange Band.	Seasonal April 15 - October 15. Private aid.

(1) No.	(2) Name and Location	(3) Position	(4) Characteristic	(5) Height	(6) Range	(7) Structure	(8) Remarks
			LONG ISLAND SOUND (New York) - First District				

OYSTER AND HUNTINGTON BAYS
Huntington Bay
Huntington Harbor

(1) No.	(2) Name and Location	(3) Position	(4) Characteristic	(5) Height	(6) Range	(7) Structure	(8) Remarks
26530	- LIGHT	40-54-38.733N 073-25-52.014W	Iso W 6s	42	9	Square concrete tower attached to dwelling on rectangular pier.	HORN: 1 bl ev 15s (2s bl). MRASS-Fog signal is radio activated, during times of reduced visibility, turn marine VHF-FM radio to channel 81A/157.075Mhz. Key microphone 5 times consecutively, to activate fog signal for 45 minutes.
26532	*Huntington Inlet Lighted No Wake Buoy A*	40-54-41.160N 073-25-48.960W	Fl W 4s			White with orange bands.	Maintained Apr. 15 to Nov. 15. Private aid.
26532.1	*Huntington Inlet Lighted No Wake Buoy B*	40-54-38.220N 073-25-44.640W	Fl W 4s			White with orange bands.	Maintained Apr. 15 to Nov. 15. Private aid.
26535	*- Entrance Lighted Buoy 1*	40-54-37.376N 073-25-46.155W	Fl G 4s		3	Green.	Replaced by can from Nov. 15 to May 1.
26540	- Entrance Buoy 2	40-54-34.646N 073-25-52.396W				Red nun.	
26545	- Channel Buoy 3	40-54-31.136N 073-25-51.546W				Green can.	
26550	*- Channel Lighted Buoy 4*	40-54-29.606N 073-25-56.083W	Fl R 4s		3	Red.	Replaced by nun from Nov. 15 to May 1.
26555	- LIGHT 6	40-54-19.686N 073-26-06.346W	Fl R 4s	5	4	TR on red cylindrical structure on pile.	
26560	*- Lighted Buoy 7*	40-54-06.046N 073-26-04.711W	Fl G 4s		3	Green.	Replaced by can from Nov. 15 to May 1.
26565	*- Channel Lighted Buoy 9*	40-53-56.000N 073-25-55.600W	Fl G 3s			Green.	Private aid.
26570	*- Channel Lighted Buoy 10*	40-53-49.800N 073-25-31.100W	Fl R 2s			Red.	Private aid.
26575	*- Channel Lighted Buoy 11*	40-53-51.100N 073-25-31.500W	Fl G 2.5s			Green.	Private aid.
26580	*- Channel Lighted Buoy 12*	40-53-45.000N 073-25-22.000W	Fl R 2s			Red.	Private aid.
26585	*- Channel Lighted Buoy 13*	40-53-37.000N 073-25-11.500W	Fl G 2s			Green.	Private aid.
26590	- Channel Junction Buoy	40-53-29.800N 073-25-08.300W				Red and green bands, nun.	Private aid.
26595	*- Channel Lighted Buoy 14*	40-53-21.000N 073-25-04.500W	Fl R 3s			Red.	Private aid.
26600	*- Channel Lighted Buoy 16*	40-53-17.000N 073-25-07.000W	Fl R 3s			Red.	Private aid.
26605	*- Channel Lighted Buoy 18*	40-53-10.500N 073-25-08.820W	Fl R 3s			Red.	Private aid.
26615	*- Inner Lighted Buoy 1*	40-53-27.600N 073-25-10.400W	Fl G 3s			Green.	Private aid.
26620	*- Inner Lighted Buoy 2*	40-53-30.900N 073-25-10.600W	Fl R 3s			Red.	Private aid.
26625	*- Inner Lighted Buoy 3*	40-53-24.400N 073-25-11.900W	Fl G 3s			Green.	Private aid.
26630	*- Inner Lighted Buoy 4*	40-53-27.200N 073-25-12.200W	Fl R 3s			Red.	Private aid.
26635	*- Inner Lighted Buoy 5*	40-53-20.900N 073-25-13.600W	Fl G 3s			Green.	Private aid.
26640	*- Inner Lighted Buoy 6*	40-53-24.600N 073-25-13.700W	Fl R 3s			Red.	Private aid.
26645	*- Inner Lighted Buoy 7*	40-53-17.900N 073-25-14.900W	Fl G 3s			Green.	Private aid.
26650	*- Inner Lighted Buoy 9*	40-53-15.300N 073-25-16.200W	Fl G 3s			Green.	Private aid.

(1) No.	(2) Name and Location	(3) Position	(4) Characteristic	(5) Height	(6) Range	(7) Structure	(8) Remarks
			LONG ISLAND SOUND (New York) - First District				

OYSTER AND HUNTINGTON BAYS
Huntington Bay
Lloyd Harbor

(1) No.	(2) Name and Location	(3) Position	(4) Characteristic	(5) Height	(6) Range	(7) Structure	(8) Remarks
26655	- Buoy 2 Marks south end of shoal.	40-54-52.325N 073-25-51.505W				Red nun.	
26660	- Buoy 3 Marks north point of shoal.	40-54-44.016N 073-26-03.975W				Green can.	
26665	- Buoy 4 Marks south point of shoal.	40-54-47.786N 073-26-08.046W				Red nun.	
26670	- West End Buoy 5	40-54-48.000N 073-26-58.000W				Green can.	Maintained from May 1 to Nov. 1. Private aid.
26675	- West End Buoy 6	40-54-51.000N 073-26-58.000W				Red nun.	Maintained from May 1 to Nov. 1. Private aid.
	Northport Bay						
26680	- *Entrance Lighted Buoy 1*	40-54-51.886N 073-24-21.442W	Fl G 4s		3	Green.	Replaced by can when endangered by ice.
26682	- *Channel Lighted No Wake Buoy B*	40-54-46.620N 073-24-18.300W	Fl W 4s			White with orange bands.	Maintained from Apr. 15 to Oct. 15. Private aid.
26683	*Sand City No Wake Lighted Buoy C*	40-55-15.300N 073-24-01.600W	Fl W 3s			White with Orange bands.	Private aid.
26685	- *Entrance Buoy 2*	40-54-47.786N 073-24-13.702W				Red nun.	
26690	- *Buoy 3*	40-54-52.216N 073-24-01.772W				Green can.	
26692	*Sand City Lighted No Wake Buoy H*	40-54-52.400N 073-24-01.100W	Fl W 3s			White with orange bands.	Maintained from Apr. 15 to Oct 15. Private aid.
26695	- *Buoy 4*	40-54-47.946N 073-23-52.702W				Red nun.	
26700	- *Lighted Buoy 6*	40-54-49.226N 073-23-34.181W	Fl R 4s		3	Red.	Replaced by nun from Nov. 15 to May 1.
26705	- *Lighted Buoy 8*	40-55-00.186N 073-22-32.039W	Fl R 4s		3	Red.	Replaced by nun from Nov. 15 to May 1.
26710	- *East Channel Lighted Buoy 1*	40-55-16.500N 073-21-14.400W	Fl G 3s			Green.	Maintained from Apr. 1 to Oct. 1. Private aid.
26715	- *East Channel Lighted Buoy 2*	40-55-14.400N 073-21-14.700W	Fl R 3s			Red.	Maintained from Apr. 1 to Oct. 1. Private aid.
26720	- *East Channel Lighted Buoy 3*	40-55-15.300N 073-21-11.600W	Fl G 3s			Green.	Maintained from Apr. 1 to Oct. 1. Private aid.
26725	- *East Channel Lighted Buoy 4*	40-55-13.700N 073-21-11.600W	Fl R 3s			Red.	Maintained from Apr. 1 to Oct. 1. Private aid.
	Northport Harbor *Aids maintained from Apr. 15 to Nov. 1.*						
26729	- *Lighted No Wake Buoy A*	40-54-43.800N 073-21-56.280W	Fl W 4s			White with orange bands.	Maintained from Apr. 15 to Nov. 15. Private aid.
26730	- *Channel Lighted Buoy 1*	40-54-45.300N 073-21-52.500W	Fl G 3s			Green.	Private aid.
26735	- *Channel Lighted Buoy 2*	40-54-43.300N 073-21-55.200W	Fl R 2s			Red.	Private aid.
26740	- Channel Lighted Buoy 3	40-54-35.200N 073-21-42.900W	Fl G 3s			Green.	Private aid.
26745	- *Channel Lighted Buoy 4*	40-54-32.700N 073-21-43.900W	Fl R 3s			Red.	Private aid.
26750	- *Channel Lighted Buoy 5*	40-54-25.000N 073-21-33.500W	Fl G 3s			Green.	Private aid.
26755	- *Channel Lighted Buoy 6*	40-54-20.000N 073-21-32.300W	Fl R 2s			Red.	Private aid.

(1) No.	(2) Name and Location	(3) Position	(4) Characteristic	(5) Height	(6) Range	(7) Structure	(8) Remarks

OYSTER AND HUNTINGTON BAYS

Huntington Bay

Northport Harbor
Aids maintained from Apr. 15 to Nov. 1.

No.	Name and Location	Position	Characteristic	Structure	Remarks
26760	- Channel Lighted Buoy 7	40-54-13.000N 073-21-22.600W	Fl G 3s	Green.	Private aid.
26765	- Channel Lighted Buoy 8	40-54-12.500N 073-21-24.500W	Fl R 3s	Red.	Private aid.
26767	- Channel Lighted Buoy 9	40-54-08.800N 073-21-19.000W	Fl G 3s	Green.	Private aid.
26770	- Channel Lighted Buoy 10	40-54-06.700N 073-21-18.400W	Fl R 2s	Red.	Private aid.
26775	- Channel Lighted Buoy 12	40-53-57.800N 073-21-13.500W	Fl R 2s	Red.	Private aid.
26780	- Channel Lighted Buoy 13	40-53-53.000N 073-21-19.600W	Fl G 3s	Green.	Private aid.
26781	- Channel Lighted Buoy 14	40-53-54.700N 073-21-21.600W	Fl R 3s	Red.	Private aid.

Northport Boatyard Channel
Aids maintained from Mar. 15 to Nov. 15.

No.	Name and Location	Position	Characteristic	Structure	Remarks
26785	- Lighted Buoy 15	40-53-51.300N 073-21-21.900W	Fl G 4s	Green.	Private aid.
26786	- Lighted Buoy 16	40-53-51.700N 073-21-24.100W	Fl R 4s	Red.	Private aid.
26787	- Lighted Buoy 17	40-53-46.500N 073-21-24.200W	Fl G 4s	Green.	Private aid.
26788	- Lighted Buoy 18	40-53-44.200N 073-21-26.100W	Fl R 4s	Red.	Private aid.
26789	- Lighted Buoy 19	40-53-44.800N 073-21-24.800W	Fl G 4s	Green.	Private aid.
26790	- Lighted Buoy 20	40-53-38.200N 073-21-28.700W	Fl R 4s	Red.	Private aid.
26791	- Lighted Buoy 21	40-53-40.600N 073-21-26.900W	Fl G 4s	Green.	Private aid.
26792	- Buoy 22	40-53-34.800N 073-21-30.200W		Red nun.	Private aid.
26793	- Buoy 23	40-53-30.900N 073-21-26.400W		Green can.	Private aid.
26794	- Lighted Buoy 24	40-53-31.100N 073-21-27.400W	Fl R 4s	Red.	Private aid.

Centerport Harbor Approach Channel
Aids maintained from Apr. 15 to Nov. 15.

No.	Name and Location	Position	Characteristic	Structure	Remarks
26835	- Lighted Buoy 1	40-54-21.600N 073-22-56.760W	Fl G 3s	Green.	Private aid.
26840	- Lighted Buoy 2	40-54-20.340N 073-22-57.600W	Q R	Red.	Private aid.
26842	Centerport Harbor Lighted No Wake Buoy A	40-54-21.480N 073-22-58.620W	Fl W 4s	White with orange bands.	Maintained Apr. 15 to Nov. 15. Private aid.
26845	- Lighted Buoy 3	40-54-13.380N 073-22-54.660W	Fl G 3s	Green.	Private aid.
26850	- Lighted Buoy 4	40-54-12.420N 073-22-56.040W	Fl R 3s	Red.	Private aid.
26855	- Lighted Buoy 5	40-54-03.240N 073-22-51.780W	Q G	Green.	Private aid.
26860	- Lighted Buoy 6	40-54-01.620N 073-22-52.920W	Q R	Red.	Private aid.
26861	- Lighted Buoy 7	40-54-00.300N 073-22-45.500W	Fl G 3s	Green.	Private aid.
26862	- Lighted Buoy 8	40-53-57.600N 073-22-44.280W	Fl R 3s	Red.	Private aid.
26863	- Lighted Buoy 9	40-53-52.320N 073-22-36.480W	Fl G 3s	Green.	Private aid.
26864	- Lighted Buoy 10	40-53-51.960N 073-22-37.260W	Fl R 3s	Red.	Private aid.

(1) No.	(2) Name and Location	(3) Position	(4) Characteristic	(5) Height	(6) Range	(7) Structure	(8) Remarks
		LONG ISLAND SOUND (New York) - First District					
	OYSTER AND HUNTINGTON BAYS						
	Oyster Bay						
	Aids maintained from Apr. 15 to Nov. 1.						
26865	- Gong Buoy 1 On northwest side of Northwest Bluff Shoals.	40-55-33.426N 073-30-14.654W				Green.	
26870	COLD SPRINGS HARBOR LIGHT On point of shoal.	40-54-51.333N 073-29-34.914W	F W (R sector)	37	W 8 R 6	NR on skeleton tower, on caisson.	Red from 039° to 125°; covers Plum Point and shoal off Rocky Point.
26875	- Buoy 2 South of shoal.	40-54-40.776N 073-30-08.434W				Red nun.	
26880	- Buoy 4 On east side of Plum Point Shoal.	40-54-07.216N 073-30-23.175W				Red nun.	
26885	- *Lighted Buoy 5* On northwest end of Cove Point Shoal.	40-53-50.847N 073-30-35.086W	Fl G 4s		3	Green.	Replaced by can when endangered by ice.
26890	- Buoy 6 On southwest point of Moses Point Shoal.	40-53-08.359N 073-31-05.879W				Red nun.	
26895	- Harbor Channel Junction Lighted Buoy B	40-53-00.200N 073-31-13.200W	Fl (2+1)G 6s			Green and red bands.	Private aid.
26900	- Harbor Channel Buoy 2	40-53-04.000N 073-31-12.000W				Red nun.	Private aid.
26905	- Harbor Channel Buoy 3	40-53-00.120N 073-31-31.100W				Green can.	Private aid.
26910	- Harbor Channel Buoy 4	40-53-02.400N 073-31-20.400W				Red nun.	Private aid.
26915	- Harbor Channel Buoy 5	40-53-00.000N 073-31-48.900W				Green can.	Private aid.
26920	- Harbor Channel Buoy 6	40-53-02.400N 073-31-39.400W				Red nun.	Private aid.
26925	- Harbor Channel Buoy 7	40-52-59.900N 073-32-16.400W				Green can.	Private aid.
26930	- Harbor Channel Buoy 8	40-53-02.400N 073-31-58.500W				Red nun.	Private aid.
26935	- Harbor Channel Buoy 9	40-52-48.696N 073-32-15.360W				Green can.	Private aid.
26940	- Harbor Channel Buoy 11	40-52-42.782N 073-32-14.727W				Green can.	Private aid.
26980	- Harbor Inner Channel Buoy 1	40-53-00.200N 073-31-10.300W				Green can.	Private aid.
26985	- Harbor Inner Channel Buoy 3B	40-52-50.600N 073-31-16.800W				Green can.	Private aid.
26990	- Harbor Inner Channel Buoy 2B	40-52-51.500N 073-31-19.100W				Red nun.	Private aid.
26995	- Harbor Inner Channel Buoy 5B	40-52-41.400N 073-31-23.430W				Green can.	Private aid.
27000	- *Harbor Inner Channel Lighted Buoy 4B*	40-52-42.700N 073-31-25.000W	Fl R 4s			Red.	Private aid.
27005	- Harbor Inner Channel Buoy 7B	40-52-41.844N 073-31-26.232W				Green can.	Private aid.
27020	- Harbor Inner Channel Buoy 9B	40-52-41.600N 073-31-48.700W				Green can.	Private aid.
27025	- Harbor Inner Channel Junction Buoy C	40-52-42.600N 073-31-48.700W				Red and green bands.	Private aid.
27030	- Harbor Alternate Channel Junction Buoy A	40-53-00.000N 073-31-50.200W				Green and red bands.	Private aid.
27035	- Harbor Alternate Channel Buoy 1A	40-52-50.800N 073-31-48.800W				Green can.	Private aid.
27040	- Harbor Alternate Channel Buoy 2A	40-52-50.800N 073-31-50.100W				Red nun.	Private aid.
27045	- Harbor Alternate Channel Buoy 4A	40-52-41.600N 073-31-50.000W				Red nun.	Private aid.

(1) No.	(2) Name and Location	(3) Position	(4) Characteristic	(5) Height	(6) Range	(7) Structure	(8) Remarks
		LONG ISLAND SOUND (New York) - First District					
	HEMPSTEAD HARBOR TO TALLMAN ISLAND						
	Hempstead Harbor						
27047	- Buoy 1	40-52-44.076N 073-39-30.024W				Green can.	
27050	- Buoy 2 On edge of shoal.	40-52-29.033N 073-42-44.014W				Red nun.	
27055	- Buoy 4 On north side of shoal.	40-52-12.812N 073-42-01.882W				Red nun.	
27060	Mott Point Bell Buoy 6 East of Picket Rock.	40-51-39.192N 073-40-25.679W				Red.	
27065	GLEN COVE BREAKWATER LIGHT 5	40-51-43.181N 073-39-37.247W	Fl G 4s	24	5	SG on skeleton tower.	
27070	- Buoy 8	40-51-19.682N 073-40-12.649W				Red nun.	
27075	- Anchorage Buoy A	40-51-09.492N 073-39-33.077W				Yellow can.	
27080	- Anchorage Buoy B	40-51-03.492N 073-39-32.577W				Yellow nun.	
27085	Glen Cove Entrance Buoy 1	40-51-14.492N 073-39-09.376W				Green can.	
27090	Glen Cove Entrance Buoy 2	40-51-13.092N 073-39-07.476W				Red nun.	
27095	- Buoy 9	40-50-24.593N 073-39-29.878W				Green can.	
27100	Tappen Beach Boat Basin Entrance Buoy 1	40-49-59.088N 073-39-12.630W				Green can.	Maintained from May 1 to Nov. 1. Private aid.
27105	Tappen Beach Boat Basin Entrance Buoy 2	40-49-56.900N 073-39-11.400W				Red nun.	Maintained from May 1 to Nov. 1. Private aid.
27110	BAR BEACH LIGHT 11	40-49-54.453N 073-39-11.974W	Fl G 4s	30	5	SG on skeleton tower.	
	Manhasset Bay						
27115	*Plum Point Lighted Buoy 1* Southwest side of shoals.	40-49-56.214N 073-43-43.236W	Fl G 4s		4	Green.	Replaced by can when endangered by ice.
27120	Plum Point Shoal Buoy 3	40-49-51.431N 073-43-19.503W				Green can.	
27140	- Buoy 4	40-49-46.024N 073-43-04.325W				Red nun.	
27145	Tom Point Inner Buoy 5	40-49-46.250N 073-42-17.750W				Green can.	Maintained from Mar. 1 to Dec. 1. Private aid.
27150	Tom Point Outer Buoy 6	40-49-45.000N 073-42-21.000W				Red nun.	Maintained from Mar. 1 to Dec. 1. Private aid.
	Little Neck Bay Approach						
27155	Elm Point Buoy 2 Marks south end of Stepping Stones Shoal.	40-49-06.116N 073-45-51.601W				Red nun.	
27160	Elm Point Buoy 4 Marks south end of Stepping Stones Shoal.	40-49-00.636N 073-46-03.271W				Red nun.	
27165	KINGS POINT LIGHT	40-48-42.000N 073-45-48.000W	Iso W 2s			White cylindrical structure.	Private aid.
27170	Willets Point Buoy 2	40-47-52.817N 073-46-32.052W				Red nun.	
27180	- Anchorage Buoy A	40-46-55.923N 073-45-51.098W				Yellow nun.	
27185	- Anchorage Buoy B	40-47-09.467N 073-45-18.358W				Yellow nun.	
	Little Bay						
27200	- Entrance Buoy 2	40-47-49.707N 073-47-15.863W				Red nun.	

(1) No.	(2) Name and Location	(3) Position	(4) Characteristic	(5) Height	(6) Range	(7) Structure	(8) Remarks
		LONG ISLAND SOUND (New York) - First District					
	HEMPSTEAD HARBOR TO TALLMAN ISLAND						
	Little Bay						
27205	- *Lighted Buoy 3*	40-47-42.767N 073-47-04.073W	Fl G 2.5s		4	Green.	Replaced by can when endangered by ice.
27210	- Buoy 4	40-47-37.777N 073-47-01.933W				Red nun.	
		NEW YORK - First District					
	HEMPSTEAD HARBOR TO TALLMAN ISLAND						
	East River Main Channel						
27215	WHITESTONE POINT LIGHT 1	40-48-06.396N 073-49-10.496W	Q G	56	3	SG on black skeleton tower.	
27216	Whitestone Point Buoy 1A	40-48-08.771N 073-49-11.020W				Green can.	
	TALLMAN ISLAND TO QUEENSBORO BRIDGE						
	East River Main Channel						
27220	COLLEGE POINT REEF LIGHT CP	40-47-51.526N 073-51-03.339W	Fl W 2.5s	29	7	NG on skeleton tower.	
27225	- Gong Buoy 3 On point of shoal.	40-47-54.546N 073-51-05.050W				Green.	
27230	- *Lighted Buoy 5*	40-47-47.106N 073-51-56.921W	Fl G 2.5s		4	Green.	
27235	- *Lighted Buoy 6*	40-47-56.096N 073-52-12.562W	Fl R 2.5s		3	Red.	
27240	- Buoy 7	40-48-08.456N 073-53-45.524W				Green can.	
27245	NORTH BROTHER ISLAND NORTH LIGHT 9	40-48-08.832N 073-53-54.614W	Fl G 4s	33	4	SG on tower.	
27246	EAST RIVER REGULATORY LIGHT A	40-48-18.350N 073-53-55.520W	Q W			On dolphin.	Private aid.
27246.1	EAST RIVER REGULATORY LIGHT B	40-48-20.090N 073-53-47.110W	Q W			On dolphin.	Private aid.
27246.2	EAST RIVER REGULATORY LIGHT C	40-48-21.170N 073-53-45.120W	Q W			On dolphin.	Private aid.
27246.3	EAST RIVER REGULATORY LIGHT D	40-48-21.720N 073-53-46.750W	Q W			On dolphin.	Private aid.
27246.4	EAST RIVER REGULATORY LIGHT E	40-48-21.490N 073-53-49.390W	Q W			On dolphin.	Private aid.
	Brother Island Channel						
27250	- Buoy 6	40-48-00.366N 073-53-44.014W				Red nun.	
27260	- Buoy 8	40-47-55.512N 073-53-53.848W				Red nun.	
27265	SOUTH BROTHER ISLAND LIGHT SB	40-47-50.832N 073-53-53.114W	Fl W 2.5s	20	5	NG on skeleton tower.	
27270	- Buoy 9	40-47-51.196N 073-53-58.805W				Green can.	
	East River Main Channel						
27275	- Buoy ER	40-47-39.536N 073-54-22.516W				Green and red bands; can.	
27280	- *Lighted Buoy 13* On edge of flats.	40-47-30.546N 073-54-38.456W	Fl G 2.5s		4	Green.	
27285	HOG BACK LIGHT 14	40-46-50.944N 073-55-55.214W	Fl R 4s	25	5	TR on skeleton tower.	
27290	HELL GATE LIGHT 15	40-46-40.768N 073-56-05.359W	Fl G 2.5s	33	4	SG on single pile.	
27295	MILL ROCK NORTH LIGHT 1 On ledge.	40-46-51.345N 073-56-17.625W	Fl G 4s	35	4	SG on skeleton tower on white base.	
27300	MILL ROCK SOUTH LIGHT 16 On south end of ledge.	40-46-46.486N 073-56-22.319W	Fl R 4s	37	4	TR on skeleton tower on white base.	
	HUDSON AND EAST RIVERS						
	East River Main Channel						
27305	*Roosevelt Island Reef Lighted Buoy B* Marks 29-foot shoal.	40-44-31.669N 073-58-04.013W	Fl (2+1)G 6s		4	Green and red bands.	

(1) No.	(2) Name and Location	(3) Position	(4) Characteristic	(5) Height	(6) Range	(7) Structure	(8) Remarks
			NEW YORK - First District				
	HUDSON AND EAST RIVERS						
	East River Main Channel						
27315	ROOSEVELT ISLAND REEF LIGHT 17	40-44-47.482N 073-57-51.994W	Fl G 4s	57		SG on skeleton tower on white base.	Higher intensity beam up and down stream.
27325	POORHOUSE FLATS RANGE FRONT LIGHT	40-43-27.888N 073-57-46.254W	Q R	25		KGR on skeleton tower.	Lighted throughout 24 hours.
27330	POORHOUSE FLATS RANGE REAR LIGHT 153 yards, 160.4° from front light.	40-43-23.782N 073-57-44.382W	Iso G 6s	48		KGR on skeleton tower.	Lighted throughout 24 hours.
27335	- Lighted Buoy 18 Marks southern end of Poorhouse Flats.	40-43-22.900N 073-58-05.013W	Fl R 2.5s		3	Red.	
27337	Brooklyn Bridge NYPD Mooring Buoy	40-42-30.432N 073-59-40.314W					
	HEMPSTEAD HARBOR TO TALLMAN ISLAND						
	East River Main Channel						
27340	Deep Water Channel Lighted Buoy 3	40-41-57.156N 074-00-30.464W	Fl G 2.5s		3	Green.	
27345	Deep Water Channel Lighted Buoy 2	40-41-46.762N 074-00-44.821W	Q R		3	Red.	
27350	Deep Water Channel Lighted Buoy 1	40-41-52.311N 074-01-16.144W	Q G		3	Green.	
27351	BROOKLYN PIER 5 MARINA LIGHT 1	40-41-52.370N 074-00-03.720W	Fl G 4s			Green	On floating dock. Private aid.
27352	BROOKLYN PIER 5 MARINA LIGHT 2	40-41-51.290N 074-00-04.400W	Fl R 4s			Red	On floating dock. Private aid.
27353	BROOKLYN PIER 5 MARINA LIGHT	40-41-44.870N 074-00-08.430W	Fl W 4s			White	On pier corner. Private aid.
	HUDSON AND EAST RIVERS						
	East River Main Channel						
	Whitehall Ferry						
27355	- EAST FOG LIGHT	40-42-00.000N 074-00-43.000W	STROBE			On dolphin.	Private aid.
27360	- WEST FOG LIGHT	40-42-00.000N 074-00-49.000W	STROBE			On dolphin.	Private aid.
27370	- **Rack A Fog Signal**	40-42-00.000N 074-00-48.000W				On wood platform.	HORN: 1 blast ev 13s (5s bl). Private aid.
27375	- **RACON**	40-42-00.000N 074-00-48.000W					RACON: W (.--) Private aid.
	HEMPSTEAD HARBOR TO TALLMAN ISLAND						
	Westchester Creek						
	Removed when endangered by ice. Channel buoys located 60 feet outside channel limit.						
27410	- Channel Buoy 1	40-48-23.379N 073-50-30.953W				Green can.	
27415	- Channel Buoy 2	40-48-22.306N 073-50-27.969W				Red nun.	
27420	- Channel Buoy 3	40-48-30.236N 073-50-34.449W				Green can.	
27425	- Channel Buoy 4	40-48-32.306N 073-50-33.709W				Red nun.	
27430	- Channel Buoy 5	40-48-40.552N 073-50-38.382W				Green can.	
27435	- Channel Buoy 6	40-48-40.808N 073-50-37.344W				Red nun.	
27440	- Channel Buoy 8	40-48-46.525N 073-50-38.139W				Red nun.	
27445	- Channel Buoy 10	40-48-52.975N 073-50-36.149W				Red nun.	
27450	- Channel Buoy 12	40-49-00.615N 073-50-31.669W				Red nun.	
27455	- Channel Buoy 13	40-49-05.585N 073-50-27.499W				Green can.	

(1) No.	(2) Name and Location	(3) Position	(4) Characteristic	(5) Height	(6) Range	(7) Structure	(8) Remarks

NEW YORK - First District

TALLMAN ISLAND TO QUEENSBORO BRIDGE

Flushing Bay

27460	- *Channel Lighted Buoy 1*	40-47-35.396N 073-51-25.501W	Fl G 2.5s		4	Green.	Replaced by can when endangered by ice.
27465	- Channel Buoy 2	40-47-36.396N 073-51-36.501W				Red nun.	
27470	- *Channel Lighted Buoy 3*	40-47-18.277N 073-51-42.831W	Fl G 4s		4	Green.	Replaced by can when endangered by ice.
27475	- *Channel Lighted Buoy 4*	40-47-01.067N 073-51-37.461W	Fl R 4s		4	Red.	Replaced by nun when endangered by ice.
27480	- *Channel Lighted Buoy 5*	40-46-54.127N 073-51-29.211W	Fl G 4s		4	Green.	Replaced by can when endangered by ice.
27485	- Channel Buoy 6	40-46-44.847N 073-51-28.091W				Red nun.	
27490	- Channel Buoy 7	40-46-38.217N 073-51-19.941W				Green can.	
27495	- LIGHT 8	40-46-28.607N 073-51-19.900W	Fl R 4s	23	4	TR on skeleton tower.	
27500	- Channel Buoy 9	40-46-22.208N 073-51-10.630W				Green can.	
27505	- Channel Buoy 10	40-46-13.028N 073-51-09.860W				Red nun.	
27507	*La Guardia Outfall Lighted Hazard Buoy 013*	40-46-13.000N 073-51-15.300W	Fl Y 4s				Private aid.
27510	- Channel Buoy 11	40-46-05.968N 073-51-01.060W				Green can.	
27515	- LIGHT 12	40-45-57.932N 073-51-01.314W	Fl R 4s	13	4	TR on tower on piles.	
27520	- Channel Buoy 13	40-45-54.695N 073-50-55.062W				Green can.	
27525	- *Channel Lighted Buoy 15*	40-45-52.338N 073-50-51.210W	Fl G 4s		4	Green.	Replaced by can when endangered by ice.
27530	- Channel Buoy 17	40-45-52.387N 073-50-44.727W				Green can.	
27535	- Channel Buoy 18	40-45-50.838N 073-50-42.420W				Red nun.	
27540	Flushing Harbor Buoy 1	40-45-44.948N 073-50-52.400W				Green can.	
27545	Flushing Harbor Buoy 2	40-45-48.388N 073-50-58.160W				Red nun.	
27547	*La Guardia Airport Security Zone Lighted Buoy A*	40-47-14.500N 073-52-03.050W	Fl W 4s			White and orange.	Marked RESTRICTED AREA. Private aid.
27547.1	*La Guardia Airport Security Zone Lighted Buoy B*	40-47-10.600N 073-52-06.700W	Fl W 4s			White and orange.	Marked RESTRICTED AREA. Private aid.
27547.2	*La Guardia Airport Security Zone Lighted Buoy C*	40-47-06.240N 073-52-04.540W	Fl W 4s			White and orange.	Marked RESTRICTED AREA. Private aid.
27547.3	*La Guardia Airport Security Zone Lighted Buoy D*	40-46-23.540N 073-51-16.680W	Fl W 4s			White and orange.	Marked RESTRICTED AREA. Private aid.
27547.4	*La Guardia Airport Security Zone Lighted Buoy E*	40-46-18.740N 073-51-14.020W	Fl W 4s			White and orange.	Marked RESTRICTED AREA. Private aid.
27547.5	*La Guardia Airport Security Zone Lighted Buoy F*	40-46-13.270N 073-51-10.940W	Fl W 4s			White and orange.	Marked RESTRICTED AREA. Private aid.
27547.6	*La Guardia Airport Security Zone Lighted Buoy G*	40-46-07.840N 073-51-07.920W	Fl W 4s			White and orange	Marked RESTRICTED AREA. Private aid.
27547.7	*La Guardia Airport Security Zone Lighted Buoy H*	40-46-02.410N 073-51-04.820W	Fl W 4s			White and orange	Marked RESTRICTED AREA. Private aid.
27547.8	*La Guardia Airport Security Zone Lighted Buoy I*	40-45-56.930N 073-51-01.800W	Fl W 4s			White and orange	Marked RESTRICTED AREA. Private aid.
27547.9	*La Guardia Airport Security Zone Lighted Buoy J*	40-45-51.200N 073-50-59.700W	Fl W 4s			White and orange	Marked RESTRICTED AREA. Private aid.

(1) No.	(2) Name and Location	(3) Position	(4) Characteristic	(5) Height	(6) Range	(7) Structure	(8) Remarks
		NEW YORK - First District					

TALLMAN ISLAND TO QUEENSBORO BRIDGE

Bronx River
Channel buoys located 60 feet outside channel limit.

(1)	(2)	(3)	(4)	(5)	(6)	(7)	(8)
27550	- Channel Buoy 1	40-48-04.256N 073-51-54.661W				Green can.	
27555	- Channel Buoy 2	40-48-04.936N 073-51-50.651W				Red nun.	
27560	- Channel Buoy 3	40-48-14.676N 073-51-58.151W				Green can.	Removed when endangered by ice.
27565	- Channel Buoy 4	40-48-16.396N 073-51-57.341W				Red nun.	Removed when endangered by ice.
27570	- Channel Buoy 5	40-48-26.106N 073-52-03.551W				Green can.	Removed when endangered by ice.
27575	- Channel Buoy 6	40-48-27.085N 073-52-02.491W				Red nun.	Removed when endangered by ice.
27580	- Channel Buoy 7	40-48-37.205N 073-52-08.842W				Green can.	Removed when endangered by ice.
27585	- Channel Buoy 8	40-48-36.135N 073-52-06.782W				Red nun.	Removed when endangered by ice.
	South Brother Island Channel						
27590	*- Lighted Buoy 1*	40-48-01.086N 073-53-29.644W	Fl G 2.5s		3	Green.	
27595	- Junction Buoy SB	40-47-56.119N 073-53-42.485W				Green and red bands; can.	
27600	*- Lighted Buoy 2*	40-47-51.528N 073-53-41.787W	Fl R 4s		3	Red.	
27605	*- Lighted Buoy 3*	40-47-51.710N 073-53-34.376W	Fl G 4s		3	Green.	
27610	- Buoy 4	40-47-30.771N 073-53-43.334W				Red nun.	
27615	*- Lighted Buoy 5*	40-47-29.076N 073-53-36.408W	Fl G 6s		3	Green.	
27620	*- Lighted Buoy 7*	40-47-18.085N 073-53-36.579W	Fl G 2.5s		3	Green.	
27625	*Rikers Island Basin Junction Lighted Buoy RI*	40-47-18.796N 073-53-42.605W	Fl (2+1)R 6s		3	Red and green bands.	
27630	- Buoy 9	40-47-07.097N 073-53-27.904W				Green can.	
27635	STEINWAY CREEK WHARF LIGHT	40-47-07.000N 073-53-45.000W	F R	20		Wharf end dolphin.	Private aid.
	Rikers Island Channel						
27639	*La Guardia Outfall Lighted Hazard Buoy 006*	40-46-52.600N 073-52-56.900W	Fl Y 4s			Yellow.	Private aid.
27640	LAWRENCE POINT LEDGE LIGHT LP On ledge.	40-47-35.526N 073-54-14.305W	Fl W 4s	25	5	NR on skeleton tower.	
27645	Lawrence Point Ledge Buoy 2	40-47-36.096N 073-54-05.635W				Red nun.	
27650	SOUTH BROTHER ISLAND LEDGE LIGHT 3 On ledge.	40-47-32.196N 073-53-54.864W	Fl G 4s	17	5	SG on skeleton tower.	
27651	LA GUARDIA AIRPORT SECURITY ZONE LIGHT A	40-46-31.100N 073-53-21.000W	Fl W 4s	18		On pile.	Marked RESTRICTED AREA. Private aid.
27652	LA GUARDIA AIRPORT SECURITY ZONE LIGHT B	40-46-41.960N 073-53-15.920W	Fl W 4s	18		On pile.	Marked RESTRICTED AREA. Private aid.
27653	LA GUARDIA AIRPORT SECURITY ZONE LIGHT C	40-46-52.000N 073-53-08.000W	Fl W 4s	14		On pile.	Marked RESTRICTED AREA. Private aid.
27653.1	LA GUARDIA AIRPORT SECURITY ZONE LIGHT D	40-46-54.800N 073-52-54.300W	Fl W 4s	14		On pile.	Marked RESTRICTED AREA. Private aid.
27653.2	LA GUARDIA AIRPORT SECURITY ZONE LIGHT E	40-47-13.200N 073-52-14.000W	Fl W 4s	14		On pile	Marked RESTRICTED AREA. Private aid.

(1) No.	(2) Name and Location	(3) Position	(4) Characteristic	(5) Height	(6) Range	(7) Structure	(8) Remarks

TALLMAN ISLAND TO QUEENSBORO BRIDGE

Rikers Island Channel

(1)	(2)	(3)	(4)	(5)	(6)	(7)	(8)
27653.3	LA GUARDIA AIRPORT SECURITY ZONE LIGHT F	40-47-16.400N 073-52-09.500W	Fl W 4s	14		On pile	Marked RESTRICTED AREA. Private aid.
27653.4	LA GUARDIA AIRPORT SECURITY ZONE LIGHT G	40-47-01.920N 073-52-02.480W	Fl W 4s	14		On pile	Marked RESTRICTED AREA. Private aid.
27653.5	LA GUARDIA AIRPORT SECURITY ZONE LIGHT H	40-46-56.000N 073-52-05.300W	Fl W 4s	14		On pile	Marked RESTRICTED AREA. Private aid.
27653.6	LA GUARDIA AIRPORT SECURITY ZONE LIGHT I	40-46-50.460N 073-52-08.050W	Fl W 4s	14		On pile	Marked RESTRICTED AREA. Private aid.
27653.7	LA GUARDIA AIRPORT SECURITY ZONE LIGHT J	40-46-44.100N 073-51-54.910W	Fl W 4s	14		On pile	Marked RESTRICTED AREA. Private aid.
27653.8	*La Guardia Airport Security Zone Light K*	40-46-37.800N 073-51-41.680W	Fl W 4s	14		On pile	Marked RESTRICTED AREA. Private aid.
27653.9	LA GUARDIA AIRPORT SECURITY ZONE LIGHT L	40-46-31.530N 073-51-28.420W	Fl W 4s	14		On pile	Marked RESTRICTED AREA. Private aid.
27654	LA GUARDIA AIRPORT SECURITY ZONE LIGHT M	40-45-58.770N 073-51-13.200W	Fl W 4s	14		On pile	Marked RESTRICTED AREA. Private aid.
27654.1	LA GUARDIA AIRPORT SECURITY ZONE LIGHT N	40-46-01.200N 073-51-20.000W	Fl W 4s	14		On pile	Marked RESTRICTED AREA. Private aid.
27654.2	LA GUARDIA AIRPORT SECURITY ZONE LIGHT O	40-45-52.790N 073-51-31.700W	Fl W 4s	14		On pile	Marked RESTRICTED AREA. Private aid.
27654.3	LA GUARDIA AIRPORT SECURITY ZONE LIGHT P	40-45-49.690N 073-51-35.740W	Fl W 4s	14		On pile	Marked RESTRICTED AREA. Private aid.

BLOCK ISLAND SOUND AND GARDINERS BAY

North Entrance

(1)	(2)	(3)	(4)	(5)	(6)	(7)	(8)
27655	Gardiners Island Shoal Buoy 1	41-07-18.112N 072-06-39.175W				Green can.	
27660	Constellation Rock Buoy 2 Marks 17-foot rock.	41-10-28.394N 072-06-35.726W				Red nun.	
27662	Old Silas Rock Buoy 1	41-11-25.033N 072-08-43.033W				Green can.	
27665	*Gardiners Island Lighted Gong Buoy 1GI*	41-08-59.619N 072-08-56.269W	Fl G 4s	4		Green.	
27670	Plum Island Rock Buoy 4 On south side of rock.	41-10-24.423N 072-10-38.954W				Red nun.	

Plum Gut

(1)	(2)	(3)	(4)	(5)	(6)	(7)	(8)
27675	*Midway Shoal Lighted Buoy MS* On east side of shoal.	41-09-44.852N 072-12-38.941W	Fl (2+1)G 6s		3	Green and red bands.	
27680 21095	**Orient Point Light**	41-09-48.426N 072-13-25.027W	Fl W 5s	64	14	Black conical tower with white band in center. 64	HORN: 2 blasts ev 30s (2s bl-2s si-2s bl-24s si). MRASS-Fog signal is radio activated, during times of reduced visibility, turn marine VHF-FM radio to channel 83A/157.175Mhz. Key microphone 5 times consecutively, to activate fog signal for 45 minutes.
27685	PLUM ISLAND HARBOR EAST DOLPHIN LIGHT	41-10-15.600N 072-12-22.200W	Q R			On dolphin.	Maintained by DHS. Private aid.
27690	PLUM ISLAND HARBOR WEST DOLPHIN LIGHT	41-10-15.800N 072-12-24.000W	Q G			On dolphin.	Maintained by DHS. Private aid.
27695 21090	- LIGHT	41-10-25.778N 072-12-42.150W	Fl W 2.5s	21	5	On skeleton tower.	
27700 21085	*- Lighted Bell Buoy 2PG*	41-10-33.566N 072-13-05.897W	Fl R 4s		4	Red.	

North Entrance

(1)	(2)	(3)	(4)	(5)	(6)	(7)	(8)
27705	CAR FERRY LIGHT	41-09-12.200N 072-14-20.800W	F W	18		On dolphin.	Private aid.

Research Basin
Aids are maintained by the U.S. Dept. of Agiculture.

(1)	(2)	(3)	(4)	(5)	(6)	(7)	(8)
27715	- Bay Daybeacon 1	41-09-02.460N 072-14-27.120W				SG on pile.	Private aid.
27720	- Bay Daybeacon 3	41-09-07.500N 072-14-29.880W				SG on pile.	Private aid.

(1) No.	(2) Name and Location	(3) Position	(4) Characteristic	(5) Height	(6) Range	(7) Structure	(8) Remarks
			NEW YORK - First District				

BLOCK ISLAND SOUND AND GARDINERS BAY
North Entrance
Research Basin
Aids are maintained by the U.S. Dept. of Agiculture.

(1) No.	(2) Name and Location	(3) Position	(4) Characteristic	(5) Height	(6) Range	(7) Structure	(8) Remarks
27725	- LIGHT	41-09-12.240N 072-14-31.080W	F R	10		On pile.	Maintained from sundown to 0130 daily. HORN: 1 blast ev 30s (1s bl). Private aid.
	Gardiners Bay South Entrance						
27730	- Lighted Bell Buoy S	41-02-11.437N 072-03-05.319W	Mo (A) W		4	Red and white stripes with red spherical topmark.	Removed when endangered by ice.
27735	- Buoy 2	41-01-30.137N 072-03-47.410W				Red nun.	
27745	- Buoy 4	41-00-54.547N 072-04-49.922W				Red nun.	
27747	Out East Oysters Lighted Aquaculture Buoy A	41-00-07.000N 072-05-24.000W	F Y			Yellow.	Maintained Apr 01 to Nov 01. Private aid.
27747.1	Out East Oysters Lighted Aquaculture Buoy B	41-00-10.000N 072-05-28.000W	F Y			Yellow.	Maintained Apr 01 to Nov 01. Private aid.
27747.2	Out East Oysters Lighted Aquaculture Buoy C	41-00-10.000N 072-05-20.000W	F Y			Yellow.	Maintained Apr 01 to Nov 01. Private aid.
27747.3	Out East Oysters Lighted Aquaculture Buoy D	41-00-04.000N 072-05-20.000W	F Y			Yellow.	Maintained Apr 01 to Nov 01. Private aid.
27748	Promised Land Shellfish Lighted Buoy NW	40-59-58.361N 072-06-04.990W	F Y			Yellow.	Private aid.
27748.1	Promised Land Shellfish Lighted Buoy NE	40-59-58.221N 072-05-56.385W	F Y			Yellow.	Private aid.
27748.2	Promised Land Shellfish Lighted Buoy SE	40-59-51.702N 072-05-56.568W	F Y			Yellow.	Private aid.
27748.3	Promised Land Shellfish Lighted Buoy SW	40-59-51.842N 072-06-05.177W	F Y			Yellow.	Private aid.
27749	Empire State Shellfish Aquaculture Lighted Buoy NW	41-00-07.581N 072-06-04.726W	F Y			Yellow.	Private aid.
27749.1	Empire State Shellfish Aquaculture Lighted Buoy NE	41-00-07.440N 072-05-56.119W	F Y			Yellow.	Private aid.
27749.2	Empire State Shellfish Aquaculture Lighted Buoy SE	41-00-00.921N 072-05-56.305W	F Y			Yellow.	Private aid.
27749.3	Empire State Shellfish Aquaculture Lighted Buoy SW	41-00-01.062N 072-06-04.914W	F Y			Yellow.	Private aid.
27749.4	Montauk Shellfish Company Lighted Aquaculture Buoy NW	41-00-33.613N 072-05-15.270W	Fl Y 4s			Yellow.	Private aid.
27749.5	Montauk Shellfish Company Lighted Aquaculture Buoy NE	41-00-33.472N 072-05-06.662W	Fl Y 4s			Yellow.	Private aid.
27749.6	Montauk Shellfish Company Lighted Aquaculture Buoy SE	41-00-26.952N 072-05-06.849W	Fl Y 4s			Yellow.	Private aid.
27749.7	Montauk Shellfish Company Lighted Aquaculture Buoy SW	41-00-27.093N 072-05-15.456W	Fl Y 4s			Yellow.	Private aid.
27750	- Buoy 6	41-00-52.941N 072-06-40.126W				Red nun.	
27755	- Buoy 8	41-01-18.995N 072-07-10.387W				Red nun.	
27756	Acabonack Harbor Entrance Buoy 1	41-01-28.560N 072-07-59.460W				Green can.	Private aid.
27756.5	Acabonack Harbor Entrance Buoy 2	41-01-29.100N 072-07-59.640W				Red nun.	Private aid.
27757	Acabonack Harbor Entrance Buoy 3	41-01-26.700N 072-08-10.300W				Green can.	Private aid.
27757.5	Acabonack Harbor Entrance Buoy 4	41-01-27.660N 072-08-11.340W				Red nun.	Private aid.
27760	- Buoy 11	41-02-44.994N 072-07-57.288W				Green can.	
27765	Lionhead Rock Buoy 13	41-03-24.092N 072-09-54.122W				Green can.	
27770	Crow Shoal Buoy 14 Southwest of shoal.	41-04-34.190N 072-10-36.323W				Red nun.	

(1) No.	(2) Name and Location	(3) Position	(4) Characteristic	(5) Height	(6) Range	(7) Structure	(8) Remarks

NEW YORK - First District

BLOCK ISLAND SOUND AND GARDINERS BAY

Gardiners Bay South Entrance

(1) No.	(2) Name and Location	(3) Position	(4) Characteristic	(5) Height	(6) Range	(7) Structure	(8) Remarks
27771	HOG CREEK CHANNEL EAST LIGHT 1	41-03-01.800N 072-10-04.800W	Fl G 2.5s			SG on pile.	Private aid.
27772	HOG CREEK CHANNEL EAST LIGHT 2	41-03-01.200N 072-10-05.400W	Fl R 2.5s			TR on pile.	Private aid.

Threemile Harbor
Aids maintained from May 1 to Nov. 1.

(1) No.	(2) Name and Location	(3) Position	(4) Characteristic	(5) Height	(6) Range	(7) Structure	(8) Remarks
27775	- Entrance Lighted Bell Buoy TM	41-02-39.371N 072-11-18.685W	Mo (A) W		4	Red and white stripes with red spherical topmark.	Removed when endangered by ice.
27780	- Entrance Buoy 1	41-02-16.228N 072-11-20.871W				Green can.	
27785	- Entrance Buoy 2	41-02-15.150N 072-11-24.789W				Red nun.	
27790	- EAST BREAKWATER LIGHT	41-02-05.580N 072-11-15.780W	Q G	27		On post on dolphin.	Private aid.
27795	- WEST BREAKWATER LIGHT	41-02-06.060N 072-11-19.560W	Q R	10		On dolphin.	Private aid.
27797	- Buoy 3	41-01-57.540N 072-11-10.980W				Green can.	Private aid.
27800	- Lighted Buoy 4	41-01-56.880N 072-11-12.840W	Fl R 2s			Red.	Private aid.
27805	- Buoy 5	41-01-53.700N 072-11-04.200W				Green can.	Private aid.
27810	- Lighted Buoy 6	41-01-52.380N 072-11-04.620W	Fl R 2s			Red.	Private aid.
27815	- Buoy 7	41-01-48.600N 072-10-57.600W				Green can.	Private aid.
27820	- Lighted Buoy 8	41-01-46.200N 072-10-57.960W	Fl R 2s			Red.	Private aid.
27825	- Buoy 9	41-01-43.920N 072-10-54.000W				Green can.	Private aid.
27830	- Lighted Buoy 10	41-01-43.000N 072-10-56.800W	Fl R 2s			Red.	Private aid.
27832	- Buoy 11	41-01-36.240N 072-10-52.680W				Green can.	Private aid.
27835	- Lighted Buoy 12	41-01-37.140N 072-10-55.020W	Fl R 2s			Red.	Private aid.
27840	- Buoy 13	41-01-30.600N 072-10-54.240W				Green can.	Private aid.
27845	- Lighted Buoy 14	41-01-31.500N 072-10-55.620W	Fl R 2s			Red.	Private aid.
27850	- Buoy 15	41-01-30.600N 072-10-54.240W				Green can.	Private aid.
27855	- Lighted Buoy 16	41-01-23.100N 072-10-56.580W	Fl R 2s			Red.	Private aid.
27860	- Buoy 17	41-01-19.860N 072-10-55.550W				Green can.	Private aid.
27865	- Lighted Buoy 18	41-01-17.280N 072-10-57.780W	Fl R 2s			Red.	Private aid.
27870	- Lighted Buoy 19	41-01-16.140N 072-10-55.320W	Fl G 2s			Green can.	Private aid.
27875	- Lighted Buoy 20	41-01-07.500N 072-10-57.840W	Fl R 2s			Red.	Private aid.
27880	- Buoy 21	41-01-09.480N 072-10-55.440W				Green can.	Private aid.
27885	- Lighted Buoy 22	41-01-02.280N 072-10-57.840W	Fl R 2s			Red.	Private aid.
27890	- Buoy 23	41-01-03.000N 072-10-55.380W				Green can.	Private aid.
27895	- Lighted Buoy 24	41-00-56.760N 072-11-00.120W	Fl R 2s			Red.	Private aid.
27900	- Buoy 25	41-00-56.640N 072-10-57.300W				Green can.	Private aid.

(1) No.	(2) Name and Location	(3) Position	(4) Characteristic	(5) Height	(6) Range	(7) Structure	(8) Remarks

BLOCK ISLAND SOUND AND GARDINERS BAY
Threemile Harbor
Aids maintained from May 1 to Nov. 1.

(1) No.	(2) Name and Location	(3) Position	(4) Characteristic	(5) Height	(6) Range	(7) Structure	(8) Remarks
27905	- Lighted Buoy 26	41-00-49.400N 072-11-01.700W	Fl R 2s			Red.	Private aid.
27910	- Buoy 27	41-00-50.900N 072-10-58.900W				Green can.	Private aid.
27915	- Lighted Buoy 28	41-00-43.100N 072-11-09.600W	Fl R 2s			Red.	Private aid.
27920	- Buoy 29	41-00-38.100N 072-11-09.600W				Green can.	Private aid.
27925	- Lighted Buoy 30	41-00-35.800N 072-11-11.300W	Fl R 2s			Red.	Private aid.
27927	- Buoy 31	41-00-30.200N 072-11-09.000W				Green can.	Private aid.
27929	- LIGHT 32	41-00-29.580N 072-11-10.200W	Fl R 2s			Red.	Private aid.
27930	- Buoy 33	41-00-19.080N 072-11-05.160W				Green can.	Private aid.
27935	- Lighted Buoy 34	41-00-20.280N 072-11-07.080W	Fl R 2s			Red.	Private aid.
27940	- Buoy 35	41-00-12.120N 072-11-02.340W				Green can.	Private aid.
27945	- Lighted Buoy 36	41-00-11.040N 072-11-04.260W	Fl R 2s			Red.	Private aid.
27950	- Buoy 37	41-00-07.380N 072-11-00.900W	Fl G 2s			Green can.	Private aid.
27955	- Lighted Buoy 38	41-00-05.400N 072-10-58.020W	Fl R 2s			Red.	Private aid.

SHELTER ISLAND SOUND AND PECONIC BAYS
Shelter Island Sound North Channel

(1) No.	(2) Name and Location	(3) Position	(4) Characteristic	(5) Height	(6) Range	(7) Structure	(8) Remarks
27960	- Lighted Whistle Buoy N	41-05-58.778N 072-15-41.463W	Mo (A) W		5	Red and white stripes with red spherical topmark.	Removed when endangered by ice.
27965	- Lighted Bell Buoy 2	41-06-10.974N 072-18-03.560W	Fl R 4s		3	Red.	Replaced by nun when endangered by ice.
27970	- Buoy 3	41-06-04.669N 072-18-23.258W				Green can.	
27975	LONG BEACH BAR LIGHT	41-06-35.133N 072-18-21.413W	Fl W 4s	58	8	White tower and dwelling on piles.	
28035	- Buoy 6	41-06-51.839N 072-19-00.639W				Red nun.	
28040	- Lighted Buoy 7	41-06-34.009N 072-19-19.729W	Fl G 4s		4	Green.	
28045	- Buoy 8	41-06-52.918N 072-20-01.851W				Red nun.	
28046	ROGERS POUND NET LIGHT A	41-07-17.930N 072-19-47.000W	Fl Y 4s				Maintained Mar 15 to Dec 23. Private aid.
28046.1	ROGERS POUND NET LIGHT B	41-07-15.690N 072-19-43.630W	Fl Y 4s				Maintained Mar 15 to Dec 23. Private aid.
28046.2	ROGERS POUND NET LIGHT C	41-07-22.060N 072-19-41.490W	Fl Y 4s				Maintained Mar 15 to Dec 23. Private aid.
28046.3	ROGERS POUND NET LIGHT D	41-07-19.380N 072-19-38.230W	Fl Y 4s				Maintained Mar 15 to Dec 23. Private aid.
28046.4	ROGERS POUND NET LIGHT E	41-06-48.580N 072-18-18.890W	Fl Y 4s				Maintained Mar 15 to Dec 23. Private aid.
28046.5	ROGERS POUND NET LIGHT F	41-08-21.560N 072-18-42.720W	Fl Y 4s				Maintained Mar 15 to Dec 23. Private aid.
28047	GULL POND LIGHT	41-06-41.860N 072-20-53.730W	Fl R 4s	6		Single pile.	Private aid.
28050	GREENPORT HARBOR LIGHT 8A	41-06-13.029N 072-20-51.552W	Fl R 4s	19	4	TR on skeleton tower.	
28052	- Lighted Buoy 10	41-05-26.341N 072-21-40.113W	Fl R 2.5s		4	Red.	Replaced by nun from 15 Nov. to 1 May.

(1) No.	(2) Name and Location	(3) Position	(4) Characteristic	(5) Height	(6) Range	(7) Structure	(8) Remarks

SHELTER ISLAND SOUND AND PECONIC BAYS
Shelter Island Sound North Channel
Stirling Basin

(1)	(2)	(3)	(4)	(5)	(6)	(7)	(8)
28055	- Buoy 1	41-06-12.360N 072-21-13.440W				Green can.	Maintained from May 1 to Oct. 31. Private aid.
28060	- Buoy 2	41-06-13.380N 072-21-05.760W				Red nun.	Maintained from May 1 to Oct. 31. Private aid.
28061	- Buoy 4	41-06-18.600N 072-21-11.400W				Red nun.	Maintained from May 1 to Oct. 31. Private aid.
28062	- Buoy 6	41-06-22.620N 072-21-13.440W				Red nun.	Maintained from May 1 to Oct. 31. Private aid.
28063	- Buoy 7	41-06-22.320N 072-21-18.660W				Green can.	Maintained from May 1 to Oct. 31. Private aid.
28064	- Buoy 9	41-06-24.000N 072-21-20.100W				Green can.	Private aid.

Dering Harbor

(1)	(2)	(3)	(4)	(5)	(6)	(7)	(8)
28075	- Buoy 1	41-05-23.340N 072-21-01.620W				Green can.	Private aid.
28080	- Buoy 2	41-05-23.280N 072-21-05.400W				Red nun.	Private aid.
28085	- Buoy 3	41-05-17.220N 072-21-03.000W				Green can.	Private aid.
28090	- Buoy 4	41-05-17.880N 072-21-05.520W				Red nun.	Private aid.
28093	- Buoy 5	41-05-09.600N 072-21-04.100W				Green can.	Private aid.
28095	- Buoy 6	41-05-09.540N 072-21-05.880W				Red nun.	Private aid.
28100	- Buoy 7	41-05-06.540N 072-21-05.100W				Green can.	Private aid.
28103	- Buoy 8	41-05-06.400N 072-21-06.100W				Red nun.	Private aid.

SHELTER ISLAND SOUND AND PECONIC BAYS
Aids maintained from May 1 to Oct. 31.

(1)	(2)	(3)	(4)	(5)	(6)	(7)	(8)
28105	*Mill Creek Lighted Buoy 1*	41-04-26.200N 072-23-53.800W	Fl G 2s			Green.	Private aid.
28110	Mill Creek Buoy 2	41-04-26.700N 072-23-52.100W				Red.	Private aid.
28115	Mill Creek Buoy 3	41-04-29.500N 072-23-56.500W				Green can.	Private aid.
28120	Mill Creek Buoy 4	41-04-28.500N 072-23-53.800W				Red nun.	Private aid.
28125	Mill Creek Buoy 5	41-04-33.000N 072-23-59.300W				Green spar.	Private aid.
28130	Mill Creek Buoy 6	41-04-34.900N 072-23-59.700W				Red spar.	Private aid.

Shelter Island Sound North Channel

(1)	(2)	(3)	(4)	(5)	(6)	(7)	(8)
28135	- *Lighted Buoy 11* Off Jennings Point Shoal.	41-04-19.732N 072-23-08.326W	Fl G 4s		3	Green.	Replaced by can from Nov. 15 to May 1.

Town Creek

(1)	(2)	(3)	(4)	(5)	(6)	(7)	(8)
28140	- Buoy 1	41-03-29.640N 072-24-47.160W				Green can.	Private aid.
28145	- *Lighted Buoy 2*	41-03-31.000N 072-24-41.000W	Fl R 4s			Red.	Private aid.
28155	- Buoy 4	41-03-32.400N 072-24-49.200W				Red nun.	Private aid.
28178	Southold Bay CG Mooring Buoy	41-03-19.973N 072-23-27.864W				White with blue band.	
28179	REYDON SHORES MARINA LIGHT	41-02-55.700N 072-23-46.970W	Fl Y 2.5s				Private aid.

(1) No.	(2) Name and Location	(3) Position	(4) Characteristic	(5) Height	(6) Range	(7) Structure	(8) Remarks
			NEW YORK - First District				
	SHELTER ISLAND SOUND AND PECONIC BAYS						
	Shelter Island Sound North Channel						
28179.5	ROGERS POUND NET LIGHT G	41-03-03.750N 072-23-39.890W	Fl Y 4s				Maintained Mar 15 to Dec 23. Private aid.
28180	- Lighted Buoy 12	41-02-57.769N 072-22-40.104W	Fl R 4s		3	Red.	Replaced by nun from Nov. 15 to May 1.
28185	- Buoy 14 Off southeastern point of Paradise Point Shoal.	41-02-24.892N 072-22-27.414W				Red nun.	
28190	- Buoy 15 West of Black Dog Rock.	41-02-26.392N 072-21-58.313W				Green can.	
28191	CLARK AQUACULTURE POUND TRAP LIGHT F	41-02-13.500N 072-23-12.840W	Fl Y 20s				Private aid.
	Coecles Harbor *Aids maintained from Apr. 1 to Nov. 30 unless otherwise noted.*						
28195	- ENTRANCE LIGHT	41-04-12.000N 072-16-48.000W	Fl R 4s	12		Red skeleton tower.	Maintained from Apr. 15 to Oct. 15. Private aid.
28200	- Lighted Buoy 1	41-04-05.100N 072-16-28.000W	Fl G 4s			Green.	Private aid.
28205	- Buoy 3	41-04-06.800N 072-16-39.100W				Green can.	Private aid.
28210	- Lighted Buoy 5	41-04-09.000N 072-16-55.000W	Q G			Green.	Private aid.
28215	- Buoy 7	41-04-14.000N 072-17-38.000W				Green can.	Private aid.
28220	- Buoy 10	41-04-19.000N 072-18-21.000W				Red nun.	Private aid.
28222	- Buoy 11	41-04-17.000N 072-18-30.000W				Green can.	Private aid.
28225	- Buoy 12	41-04-38.000N 072-18-53.000W				Red nun.	Private aid.
28226	- Marina Buoy 1	41-04-38.000N 072-19-01.000W				Green can.	Private aid.
28227	- Marina Buoy 3	41-04-40.000N 072-19-06.000W				Green can.	Private aid.
28228	- Marina Buoy 5	41-04-41.000N 072-19-10.000W				Green can.	Private aid.
	Shelter Island Sound South Channel						
28235	- Buoy 1	41-03-08.911N 072-14-01.301W				Green can.	
28240	- Buoy 3 On northwest point of shoal.	41-02-49.419N 072-15-11.294W				Green can.	
28242	Nicoll Point Buoy 4	41-03-02.084N 072-15-58.124W				Red nun.	
28245	CEDAR ISLAND LIGHT 3CI	41-02-25.204N 072-15-43.001W	Fl G 4s	25	5	SG on Spindle.	
28250	- Buoy 6	41-02-19.669N 072-16-11.825W				Red nun.	
28255	BARCELONA POINT LIGHT 7	41-01-00.783N 072-16-01.293W	Fl G 4s	28	4	SG on skeleton tower.	
28295	- Buoy 8	41-01-03.390N 072-16-15.306W				Red nun.	
28300	- Buoy 9	41-00-50.110N 072-16-33.586W				Green can.	
28303	- Buoy 9A	41-00-48.842N 072-17-06.242W				Green can.	
28305	Sand Spit Rock Buoy S	41-01-15.278N 072-16-46.609W				White can with orange bands and diamond worded DANGER ROCKS.	
28310	SAND SPIT LIGHT 10A	41-00-55.489N 072-16-57.019W	Fl R 4s	10	4	TR on monopole.	
28315	- Lighted Buoy 11	41-00-51.121N 072-17-21.187W	Fl G 4s		3	Green.	Replaced by can from Nov. 15 to May 1.

253

(1) No.	(2) Name and Location	(3) Position	(4) Characteristic	(5) Height	(6) Range	(7) Structure	(8) Remarks

NEW YORK - First District

SHELTER ISLAND SOUND AND PECONIC BAYS

Shelter Island Sound South Channel

28320	- Junction Buoy SH	41-00-53.701N 072-17-28.387W				Green and red bands; can.	

Sag Harbor
Private aids maintained from May 15 to Nov. 15.

28323	- Approach Channel Buoy 1	41-00-42.033N 072-17-32.013W				Green can.	
28325	- BREAKWATER LIGHT 3SH	41-00-32.140N 072-17-40.177W	Fl G 2.5s	12	4	SG on monopole.	
28331	- Channel Buoy 2	41-00-34.680N 072-17-43.200W				Red nun.	Private aid.
28332	- Channel Buoy 3	41-00-18.000N 072-17-42.000W				Green can.	Private aid.
28333	- Channel Buoy 4	41-00-22.920N 072-17-51.300W				Red nun.	Private aid.
28334	- Junction Buoy	41-00-21.120N 072-17-48.060W				Green and red can.	Private aid.
28335	- Channel Buoy 5	41-00-12.480N 072-17-33.000W				Green can.	Private aid.
28336	- Channel Buoy 6	41-00-16.980N 072-17-53.160W				Red nun.	Private aid.

Sag Harbor Cove
Aids maintained from May 15 to Nov. 15.

28350	- Buoy 4	41-00-09.840N 072-18-02.580W				Red nun.	Private aid.
28355	- *Lighted Buoy 6*	41-00-09.420N 072-18-07.740W	Fl R 5s			Red.	Private aid.
28360	- Buoy 6A	41-00-07.620N 072-18-18.720W				Red nun.	Private aid.
28365	- Buoy 7	41-00-07.380N 072-18-11.040W				Green can.	Private aid.
28370	- Buoy 7A	41-00-06.180N 072-18-16.920W				Green can.	Private aid.
28375	- *Lighted Buoy 8*	41-00-05.820N 072-18-33.180W	Fl R 5s			Red.	Private aid.
28380	- Buoy 9	41-00-02.460N 072-18-34.140W				Green can.	Private aid.
28385	- Buoy 11	40-59-59.220N 072-18-39.780W				Green can.	Private aid.
28390	- *Lighted Buoy 12*	41-00-00.900N 072-18-43.200W	Fl R 5s			Red.	Private aid.

Shelter Island Sound South Channel

28395	- Buoy 12 On west side of shoal.	41-01-10.421N 072-17-32.517W				Red nun.	
28400	- Buoy 14	41-02-00.950N 072-18-00.688W				Red nun.	
28405	- *Lighted Buoy 15*	41-02-34.890N 072-18-41.309W	Fl G 4s		3	Green.	Replaced by can from Nov. 15 to May 1.
28407	CLARK AQUACULTURE POND TRAP LIGHT A	41-03-06.950N 072-18-45.020W	Fl Y 4s			Yellow.	Seasonal 4/15 to 11/15. Private aid.
28410	- Danger Buoy	41-02-34.000N 072-19-32.000W				White with orange bands; can worded DANGER.	Maintained from June 1 to Nov. 1. Private aid.
28412	SHELL BEACH POINT LIGHT	41-02-49.400N 072-20-20.000W	Fl G 4s	6		Medal tower.	Private aid.
28415	*West Neck Harbor Entrance Lighted Buoy 2*	41-02-50.000N 072-20-18.000W	Fl R 4s			Red.	Private aid.
28425	West Neck Harbor Buoy 4	41-02-47.000N 072-20-34.000W				Red nun.	Maintained from May 15 to Oct. 15. Private aid.

Menantic Creek

28430	- Buoy 1	41-02-54.720N 072-20-44.400W				Green can.	Private aid.
28435	- Buoy 2	41-02-54.300N 072-20-40.920W				Red nun.	Private aid.

(1) No.	(2) Name and Location	(3) Position	(4) Characteristic	(5) Height	(6) Range	(7) Structure	(8) Remarks
			NEW YORK - First District				
	SHELTER ISLAND SOUND AND PECONIC BAYS						
	Shelter Island Sound South Channel						
	Menantic Creek						
28440	- Buoy 3	41-03-06.660N 072-20-40.860W				Green can.	Private aid.
28445	- Buoy 4	41-03-06.240N 072-20-39.720W				Red nun.	Private aid.
	Shelter Island Sound South Channel						
28450	- *Lighted Buoy 16* On south point of West Neck Point Shoal.	41-01-43.682N 072-21-16.512W	Fl R 4s		3	Red.	Replaced by nun from Nov. 15 to May 1.
28451.1	BENNETT AQUACULTURE LIGHT F	41-01-34.400N 072-19-55.700W	Fl Y 2s			On pile.	Maintained from 01 Apr to 15 Dec. Private aid.
	Mill Creek						
	Aids maintained from May 15 to Nov. 15.						
28455	- Buoy 1	41-00-03.102N 072-20-57.001W				Green can.	Private aid.
28460	- Buoy 1A	40-59-53.520N 072-20-58.380W				Green can.	Private aid.
28465	- Buoy 2A	41-00-04.440N 072-20-59.580W				Red nun.	Private aid.
28470	- *Lighted Buoy 2*	41-00-04.440N 072-21-00.660W	Fl R 5s			Red.	Private aid.
28475	- Buoy 3	40-59-44.520N 072-20-58.260W				Green can.	Private aid.
28480	- *Lighted Buoy 4*	40-59-44.820N 072-20-59.460W	Fl R 5s			Red.	Private aid.
28485	- Buoy 5	40-59-46.320N 072-20-51.960W				Green can.	Private aid.
28490	- Buoy 6	40-59-44.640N 072-20-51.300W				Red nun.	Private aid.
	Shelter Island Sound South Channel						
28495	Noyack Creek Buoy 1	40-59-54.600N 072-21-49.800W				Green can.	Maintained from May. 15 to Nov. 15. Private aid.
28500	*Noyack Creek Lighted Buoy 2*	40-59-47.760N 072-21-59.520W	Fl R 5s			Red.	Maintained from May. 15 to Nov. 15. Private aid.
28501	SEMLEAR AQUACULTURE EAST BUNKER LIGHT	41-00-33.600N 072-22-08.040W	Fl Y 2s			On pile.	Maintained from 01 Apr to 30 Sep. Private aid.
28501.1	SEMLEAR AQUACULTURE WEST BUNKER LIGHT	41-00-32.820N 072-21-58.200W	Fl Y 2s			On pile.	Maintained from 01 Apr to 30 Sep. Private aid.
28501.2	SEMLEAR AQUACULTURE JESSUPS LIGHT	41-00-41.880N 072-22-35.040W	Fl Y 2s			On pile.	Maintained from 01 Apr to 30 Sep. Private aid.
28501.3	SEMLEAR AQUACULTURE SOUTH LIGHT	41-00-14.520N 072-22-24.120W	Fl Y 2s			On pile.	Maintained from 01 Apr to 30 Sep. Private aid.
28502	CLARK AQUACULTURE POUND TRAP LIGHT A	41-02-20.000N 072-17-17.000W	Fl Y 4s			On pile.	Maintained from 01 Apr to 30 Nov. Private aid.
28502.1	CLARK AQUACULTURE POUND TRAP LIGHT B	41-01-06.000N 072-22-42.000W	Fl Y 4s			On pile.	Maintained from 01 Apr to 30 Nov. Private aid.
28502.2	CLARK AQUACULTURE POUND TRAP LIGHT C	41-03-17.000N 072-16-20.000W	Fl Y 4s			On pile.	Maintained from 01 Apr to 30 Nov. Private aid.
28502.3	CLARK AQUACULTURE POUND TRAP LIGHT D	41-02-36.000N 072-16-39.000W	Fl Y 4s			On pile.	Maintained from 01 Apr to 30 Nov. Private aid.
28502.4	*Clark Aquaculture Pond Trap Light E*	41-01-05.100N 072-19-39.070W	Fl Y 2.5s				Private aid.
28502.5	CLARK AQUACULTURE POUND TRAP LIGHT G	40-59-40.270N 072-22-28.850W	Fl Y 20s				Private aid.

(1) No.	(2) Name and Location	(3) Position	(4) Characteristic	(5) Height	(6) Range	(7) Structure	(8) Remarks
			NEW YORK - First District				

SHELTER ISLAND SOUND AND PECONIC BAYS

Shelter Island Sound South Channel

(1) No.	(2) Name and Location	(3) Position	(4) Characteristic	(5) Height	(6) Range	(7) Structure	(8) Remarks
28503	SCHELLINGER FISH TRAP LIGHT FN4	41-00-26.220N 072-19-06.780W	Fl Y 2s			On pile.	Maintained from 15 Apr to 15 Dec. Private aid.
28503.1	SCHELLINGER FISH TRAP LIGHT FN38	41-00-57.420N 072-22-17.160W	Fl Y 2s			On pile.	Maintained from 15 Apr to 15 Dec. Private aid.
28503.2	SCHELLINGER FISH TRAP LIGHT FN63	41-00-09.240N 072-21-54.360W	Fl Y 2s			On pile.	Maintained from 15 Apr to 15 Dec. Private aid.
28503.4	JBH of Peconic Aquaculture Buoy A	41-01-12.108N 072-22-17.216W				Yellow.	Private aid.
28503.41	JBH of Peconic Aquaculture Buoy B	41-01-11.989N 072-22-08.605W				Yellow.	Private aid.
28503.42	JBH of Peconic Aquaculture Buoy C	41-01-05.466N 072-22-08.767W				Yellow.	Private aid.

Little Peconic Bay

(1) No.	(2) Name and Location	(3) Position	(4) Characteristic	(5) Height	(6) Range	(7) Structure	(8) Remarks
28503.5	WENCZEL SEAFOOD FISH TRAP LIGHT A	41-00-51.270N 072-15-29.360W	Fl Y 2s				Maintained Mar 15 to Nov 15. Private aid.
28503.6	BATKY FISH TRAP LIGHT B	41-00-37.500N 072-16-04.000W	Fl Y 2s				Maintained Mar15 to Nov 15. Private aid.
28503.7	BATKY FISH TRAP LIGHT C	41-00-58.870N 072-15-45.600W	Fl Y 2s				Maintained Mar 15 to Nov 15. Private aid.
28503.8	BATKY FISH TRAP LIGHT D	41-02-37.030N 072-17-56.330W	Fl Y 2s				Maintained Mar 15 to Nov 15. Private aid.
28503.9	KOTULA AQUACULTURE LIGHT	41-02-42.430N 072-18-03.750W	Fl Y 2s	6			Maintained 15 May to 30 Nov. Private aid.
28504	CLARK AQUACULTURE POND TRAP LIGHT B	41-00-58.370N 072-22-42.730W	Fl Y 2s				Maintained Apr 01 to Nov 15. Private aid.
28505	- Lighted Buoy 17	41-01-29.373N 072-22-54.464W	Fl G 4s		3	Green.	Replaced by can from Nov. 15 to May 1.
28510	- Lighted Buoy 18	41-00-41.883N 072-23-53.675W	Fl R 4s		3	Red.	Replaced by nun from Nov. 15 to May 1.
28511	Stein Seafoods Lighted Aquaculture Buoy A	41-00-55.000N 072-25-01.850W	Fl Y 2.5s			Yellow.	Private aid.
28511.1	Stein Seafoods Lighted Aquaculture Buoy B	41-00-50.410N 072-25-04.380W	Fl Y 2.5s			Yellow.	Private aid.
28511.2	Stein Seafoods Lighted Aquaculture Buoy C	41-00-48.510N 072-24-58.260W	Fl Y 2.5s			Yellow.	Private aid.
28511.3	Stein Seafoods Lighted Aquaculture Buoy D	41-00-53.140N 072-24-55.810W	Fl Y 2.5s			Yellow.	Private aid.

Corey Creek Entrance
Aids maintained from May 1 to Oct. 31.

(1) No.	(2) Name and Location	(3) Position	(4) Characteristic	(5) Height	(6) Range	(7) Structure	(8) Remarks
28515	- Buoy 2	41-01-43.560N 072-25-33.480W				Red nun.	Private aid.
28520	- Buoy 1	41-01-43.320N 072-25-39.240W				Green can.	Private aid.
28523	- Buoy 3	41-01-55.800N 072-25-33.180W				Green can.	Private aid.
28525	- Buoy 4	41-01-50.940N 072-25-27.960W				Red nun.	Private aid.
28530	- Buoy 6	41-01-56.040N 072-25-26.220W				Red nun.	Private aid.

Shelter Island Sound South Channel

(1) No.	(2) Name and Location	(3) Position	(4) Characteristic	(5) Height	(6) Range	(7) Structure	(8) Remarks
28530.43	JBH of Peconic Aquaculture Buoy D	41-01-05.588N 072-22-17.374W				Yellow.	Private aid.

Little Peconic Bay

Richmond Creek
Aids maintained from May 1 to Oct. 31.

(1) No.	(2) Name and Location	(3) Position	(4) Characteristic	(5) Height	(6) Range	(7) Structure	(8) Remarks
28535	- Buoy 1	41-01-55.400N 072-26-08.700W				Green spar.	Private aid.
28540	- Buoy 2	41-01-55.500N 072-26-07.600W				Red spar.	Private aid.

(1) No.	(2) Name and Location	(3) Position	(4) Characteristic	(5) Height	(6) Range	(7) Structure	(8) Remarks

NEW YORK - First District

SHELTER ISLAND SOUND AND PECONIC BAYS

Little Peconic Bay

Richmond Creek
Aids maintained from May 1 to Oct. 31.

| 28545 | - Buoy 3 | 41-01-59.600N
072-26-11.500W | | | | Green spar. | Private aid. |
| 28550 | - Buoy 4 | 41-02-00.100N
072-26-10.700W | | | | Red spar. | Private aid. |

Little Peconic Bay

28555	BENNETT AQUACULTURE LIGHT A	40-59-16.410N 072-22-43.750W	Fl Y 2s			On pile.	Maintained from 01 Apr to 15 Dec. Private aid.
28555.2	BENNETT AQUACULTURE LIGHT C	40-59-11.550N 072-22-47.290W	Fl Y 2s			On pile.	Maintained from 01 Apr to 15 Dec. Private aid.
28555.3	BENNETT AQUACULTURE LIGHT D	40-59-07.800N 072-22-36.660W	Fl Y 2s			On pile.	Maintained from 01 Apr to 15 Dec. Private aid.
28560	*Fresh Pond Approach Lighted Buoy 1*	40-58-03.400N 072-23-39.000W	Fl G 5s			Green.	Maintained from May 15 to Nov. 15. Private aid.
28565	Fresh Pond Approach Buoy 2	40-58-02.300N 072-23-39.600W				Red nun.	Maintained from May 15 to Nov. 15. Private aid.
28567	*Dunne Aquaculture Lighted Buoy NE*	40-58-54.530N 072-23-12.843W	Fl Y 2s			Yellow.	Maintained Apr.1 to Dec 1. Private aid.
28567.1	*Dunne Aquaculture Lighted Buoy SE*	40-58-48.007N 072-23-13.001W	Fl Y 2s			Yellow.	Maintained Apr.1 to Dec 1. Private aid.
28567.2	*Dunne Aquaculture Lighted Buoy SW*	40-58-48.129N 072-23-21.606W	Fl Y 2s			Yellow.	Maintained Apr.1 to Dec 1. Private aid.
28567.3	*Dunne Aquaculture Lighted Buoy NW*	40-58-54.000N 072-23-21.000W	Fl Y 2s			Yellow.	Maintained Apr. 1 to Dec 1. Private aid.
28570	- *Lighted Buoy 20* Off south end of shoal.	40-58-33.984N 072-25-46.359W	Fl R 4s		3	Red.	Replaced by nun from Nov. 1 to Apr. 15.
28576	MASTAGLIO POUND TRAP LIGHT A	40-59-36.900N 072-26-49.300W	Fl Y 2s			On pole.	Maintained from 01 Feb to 31 Dec. Private aid.
28577	MASTAGLIO POUND TRAP LIGHT B	40-59-32.900N 072-25-57.200W	Fl Y 2s			On pole.	Maintained from 01 Feb to 31 Dec. Private aid.
28578	MASTAGLIO POUND TRAP LIGHT C	40-59-31.400N 072-26-04.000W	Fl Y 2s			On pole.	Maintained from 01 Feb to 31 Dec. Private aid.

Wooley Pond
Aids maintained from Apr. 15 to Nov. 15.

28590	- *Entrance Lighted Buoy 1*	40-57-32.600N 072-24-10.000W	Fl G 5s			Green.	Private aid.
28595	- Buoy 2	40-57-31.800N 072-24-10.600W				Red nun.	Private aid.
28600	- Buoy 4	40-57-17.880N 072-23-58.980W				Red nun.	Private aid.
28605	- Buoy 5	40-57-14.940N 072-23-45.540W				Green can.	Private aid.

North Sea Harbor
Aids maintained from Apr. 15 to Nov. 15.

28610	- *Lighted Buoy 2*	40-57-02.640N 072-24-59.160W	Fl R 5s			Red.	Private aid.
28615	- Buoy 1	40-57-07.020N 072-24-56.640W				Green can.	Private aid.
28620	- Buoy 3	40-56-54.780N 072-24-56.460W				Green can.	Private aid.
28625	- Buoy 4	40-56-47.900N 072-24-58.900W				Red nun.	Private aid.
28630	- Buoy 5	40-56-47.280N 072-24-57.300W				Green can.	Private aid.
28635	- Buoy 6	40-56-23.800N 072-24-54.600W				Red nun.	Private aid.

(1) No.	(2) Name and Location	(3) Position	(4) Characteristic	(5) Height	(6) Range	(7) Structure	(8) Remarks

NEW YORK - First District

SHELTER ISLAND SOUND AND PECONIC BAYS

Little Peconic Bay

North Sea Harbor
Aids maintained from Apr. 15 to Nov. 15.

28638	- Aquaculture Lighted Buoy B	40-56-24.900N 072-25-02.200W	Fl Y 4s			Yellow.	Private aid.

Wickham Creek
Aids maintained from May 1 to Nov. 1.

28640	- Entrance Buoy 1	41-00-05.400N 072-27-52.200W				Green can.	Private aid.
28645	- Entrance Buoy 2	41-00-08.220N 072-27-56.400W				Red nun.	Private aid.
28650	- Entrance Buoy 3	41-00-07.200N 072-27-58.000W				Green spar.	Private aid.
28655	- Entrance Lighted Buoy 4	41-00-09.420N 072-28-00.000W	Fl R 2s			Red spar.	Private aid.

East Creek
Maintained from May 1 to Oct. 31.

28660	- Buoy 1	41-00-17.820N 072-27-35.340W					Private aid.
28661	- Buoy 2	41-00-18.480N 072-27-34.500W					Private aid.
28662	- Buoy 3	41-00-24.600N 072-27-36.180W					Private aid.
28663	- Buoy 4	41-00-24.180N 072-27-35.520W					Private aid.

Little Peconic Bay

New Suffolk Channel

28665	- Buoy 1	40-59-41.000N 072-28-12.600W					Private aid.
28670	- Buoy 2	40-59-41.800N 072-28-12.900W					Private aid.
28675	- Buoy 3	40-59-40.600N 072-28-17.000W					Private aid.
28680	- Buoy 4	40-59-40.600N 072-28-18.700W					Private aid.

Little Peconic Bay

28685	North Race Buoy 1	40-59-12.285N 072-26-55.330W				Green can.	
28687	Peconic Gold Oysters Aquaculture Lighted Buoy A	40-59-34.901N 072-27-27.511W	Fl Y 2.5s			Yellow.	Private aid.
28687.1	Peconic Gold Oysters Aquaculture Lighted Buoy B	40-59-35.015N 072-27-36.115W	Fl Y 2.5s			Yellow.	Private aid.
28687.2	Peconic Gold Oysters Aquaculture Lighted Buoy C	40-59-28.381N 072-27-27.662W	Fl Y 2.5s			Yellow.	Private aid.
28687.3	Peconic Gold Oysters Aquaculture Lighted Buoy D	40-59-28.496N 072-27-36.266W	Fl Y 2.5s			Yellow.	Private aid.
28690	North Race Lighted Buoy 3	40-59-08.405N 072-28-17.364W	Fl G 4s		3	Green.	Replaced by can from Nov. 15 to Apr. 15.
28695	West Robins Oyster Aquaculture Lighted Buoy A	40-58-26.350N 072-28-39.380W	Fl Y 2.5s			Yellow	Seasonal. Maintained May 1st to Nov 15th. Private aid.
28696	West Robins Oyster Aquaculture Lighted Buoy B	40-58-35.980N 072-28-28.450W	Fl Y 2.5s			Yellow	Seasonal. Maintained May 1st to Nov 15th. Private aid.
28697	West Robins Oyster Aquaculture Lighted Buoy C	40-58-23.130N 072-28-28.700W	Fl Y 2.5s			Yellow	Seasonal. Maintained May 1st to Nov 15th. Private aid.
28698	West Robins Oyster Aquaculture Lighted Buoy D	40-58-21.570N 072-28-37.730W	Fl Y 2.5s			Yellow	Seasonal. Maintained May 1st to Nov 15th. Private aid.
28700	Davy Jones Shellfish Lighted Aquaculture Buoy NW	40-57-54.710N 072-29-03.623W	Fl Y 2.5s			Yellow.	Private aid.
28700.1	Davy Jones Shellfish Lighted Aquaculture Buoy NE	40-57-54.598N 072-28-55.019W	Fl Y 2.5s			Yellow.	Private aid.
28700.2	Davy Jones Shellfish Lighted Aquaculture Buoy SE	40-57-48.077N 072-28-55.171W	Fl Y 2.5s			Yellow.	Private aid.

(1) No.	(2) Name and Location	(3) Position	(4) Characteristic	(5) Height	(6) Range	(7) Structure	(8) Remarks

SHELTER ISLAND SOUND AND PECONIC BAYS

Little Peconic Bay

28700.3	*Davy Jones Shellfish Lighted Aquaculture Buoy SW*	40-57-48.189N 072-29-03.771W	Fl Y 2.5s			Yellow.	Private aid.
28705	North Race Buoy 4	40-58-27.256N 072-28-56.513W				Red nun.	

Marratrooka Point

28710	Marratooka Point Buoy 1	40-59-04.980N 072-29-54.000W				Green can.	Maintained from May 1 to Oct. 31. Private aid.
28715	Marratooka Point Buoy 2	40-59-06.900N 072-29-54.360W				Red nun.	Maintained from May 1 to Oct. 31. Private aid.
28720	Marratooka Point Buoy 3	40-59-06.480N 072-30-02.580W				Green spar.	Maintained from May 1 to Oct. 31. Private aid.
28725	Marratooka Point Buoy 4	40-59-10.800N 072-30-11.640W				Red nun.	Private aid.

James Creek
Aids maintained from May 1 to Oct. 31.

28730	- Buoy 1	40-58-35.100N 072-31-34.400W				Green can.	Private aid.
28735	- *Lighted Buoy 2*	40-58-35.800N 072-31-33.000W	Fl R 4s			Red.	Private aid.
28740	- Buoy 3	40-58-40.300N 072-31-36.600W				Green can.	Private aid.
28745	- Buoy 4	40-58-44.600N 072-31-38.200W				Red nun.	Private aid.

Great Peconic Bay

28750	- *Lighted Buoy 22* On south point of Robins Island Shoal.	40-57-09.088N 072-27-01.113W	Fl R 2.5s		3	Red.	Replaced by nun from Nov. 15 to May 1.

Robins Island

28755	- Rock Danger Buoy Marks west side of rock.	40-57-23.292N 072-28-17.160W				White with orange bands worded DANGER ROCKS.	

Great Peconic Bay

28786	MARAN AQUACULTURE POUND TRAP LIGHT A	40-55-48.680N 072-27-00.330W	Fl Y 2s			On wood pole.	Maintained Apr 1 to Dec 31. Private aid.
28787	MASTAGLIO POUND TRAP LIGHT D	40-55-34.200N 072-26-58.800W	Fl Y 2s	8		On pole.	Private aid.
28790	Rodgers Rock Danger Buoy On northeast side of rock.	40-56-22.285N 072-28-04.274W				White with orange bands worded DANGER ROCKS.	
28792	ROBINS ISLAND SE POUND TRAP LIGHT	40-57-33.270N 072-27-01.530W	Fl Y 2s			On pile.	Maintained from May 15 to Nov 1. Private aid.

Sebonac Creek
Aids maintained from May 15 to Nov. 15.

28795	- Buoy 1	40-55-10.020N 072-27-26.940W				Green can.	Private aid.
28800	- Buoy 1A	40-55-09.600N 072-27-24.840W				Green can.	Private aid.
28810	- Buoy 2A	40-55-07.620N 072-27-21.600W				Red nun.	Private aid.
28815	- Daybeacon 2B	40-55-05.580N 072-27-12.240W				TR on pile.	Private aid.
28820	- *Lighted Buoy 2*	40-55-09.240N 072-27-27.480W	Fl R 5s			Red.	Private aid.
28825	- *Lighted Buoy 3*	40-55-03.780N 072-27-01.380W	Fl G 5s			Green.	Private aid.
28830	- Buoy 4	40-55-01.000N 072-26-46.000W				Red nun.	Private aid.
28835	- *Lighted Buoy 5*	40-55-02.820N 072-26-35.040W	Fl G 5s			Green.	Private aid.
28840	- Buoy 7	40-55-02.400N 072-26-35.760W				Green can.	Private aid.

(1) No.	(2) Name and Location	(3) Position	(4) Characteristic	(5) Height	(6) Range	(7) Structure	(8) Remarks

NEW YORK - First District

SHELTER ISLAND SOUND AND PECONIC BAYS

Great Peconic Bay

Sebonac Creek

Aids maintained from May 15 to Nov. 15.

| 28845 | - Buoy 8 | 40-55-00.120N
072-26-29.400W | | | | Red nun. | Private aid. |

Great Peconic Bay

28847	*Manna Fish Farms* *Aquaculture Lighted Buoy NW*	40-54-41.065N 072-29-08.041W	Fl Y 2s			Yellow.	Private aid.
28847.1	*Manna Fish Farms* *Aquaculture Lighted Buoy NE*	40-54-40.953N 072-28-59.444W	Fl Y 2s			Yellow.	Private aid.
28847.2	*Manna Fish Farms* *Aquaculture Lighted Buoy SE*	40-54-34.434N 072-28-59.592W	Fl Y 2s			Yellow.	Private aid.
28847.3	*Manna Fish Farms* *Aquaculture Lighted Buoy SW*	40-54-34.546N 072-29-08.188W	Fl Y 2s			Yellow.	Private aid.
28850	COLD SPRING POND APPROACH LIGHT 1	40-53-56.200N 072-28-41.707W	Fl G 5s	6		SG on pile.	Maintained from May 1 to Nov. 1. Private aid.
28855	Cold Spring Pond Approach Buoy 2	40-53-55.200N 072-28-43.920W				Red nun.	Maintained from May 1 to Nov. 1. Private aid.

Shinnecock Canal Entrance

28860	- Buoy 1	40-53-56.033N 072-30-11.441W				Green can.	
28865	- Buoy 2	40-53-56.162N 072-30-14.274W				Red nun.	
28870	- LIGHT 3	40-53-50.692N 072-30-10.372W	Fl G 6s	25	5	SG on skeleton tower.	

Great Peconic Bay

28882	*East Creek Lighted Buoy 2*	40-56-19.440N 072-34-06.780W	Fl R 2s			Red.	Maintained from May 1 to Nov. 1. Private aid.
28883	*East Creek Lighted Buoy 3*	40-56-17.940N 072-34-06.720W	Fl G 2s			Green.	Maintained from May 1 to Nov. 1. Private aid.
28884	*East Creek Lighted Buoy 5*	40-56-19.320N 072-34-13.560W	Fl G 2s			Green.	Maintained from May 1 to Nov 1. Private aid.

Red Creek Pond Entrance

28885	- LIGHT 1	40-55-00.180N 072-33-14.880W	Fl G 5s	6		SG on pile.	Maintained from Apr. 15 to Nov. 15. Private aid.
28890	- Buoy 2	40-54-58.980N 072-33-15.780W				Red nun.	Maintained from May 15 to Nov. 1. Private aid.
28895	- Buoy 3	40-54-54.900N 072-33-11.040W				Green can.	Maintained from May 15 to Nov. 1. Private aid.
28900	- Buoy 4	40-54-52.860N 072-33-13.620W				Red nun.	Maintained from May 15 to Nov. 1. Private aid.

Flanders Bay

28903	*Spinelli's Sea Farms* *Aquaculture Lighted Buoy NE*	40-56-30.169N 072-33-19.165W	Fl Y 2.5s			Yellow.	Private aid.
28903.1	*Spinelli's Sea Farms* *Aquaculture Lighted Buoy SE*	40-56-23.650N 072-33-19.309W	Fl Y 2.5s			Yellow.	Private aid.
28903.2	*Spinelli's Sea Farms* *Aquaculture Lighted Buoy SW*	40-56-23.758N 072-33-27.906W	Fl Y 2.5s			Yellow.	Private aid.
28903.3	*Spinelli's Sea Farms* *Aquaculture Lighted Buoy NW*	40-56-30.277N 072-33-27.766W	Fl Y 2.5s			Yellow.	Private aid.
28905	- *Lighted Buoy 2*	40-55-45.764N 072-32-41.066W	Fl R 2.5s		3	Red.	Maintained from to May 1 to Nov 15.
28910	- *Lighted Buoy 4*	40-55-36.482N 072-34-21.988W	Fl R 4s		3	Red.	Maintained from 1 April to 15 Nov.
28915	- Buoy 5 On northwest point of shoal.	40-55-44.307N 072-34-40.774W				Green can.	Maintained from 1 April to 15 Nov.

(1) No.	(2) Name and Location	(3) Position	(4) Characteristic	(5) Height	(6) Range	(7) Structure	(8) Remarks

NEW YORK - First District

SHELTER ISLAND SOUND AND PECONIC BAYS
Flanders Bay

28920	- Buoy 7	40-55-43.144N 072-34-57.721W				Green can.	Maintained from 1 April to 15 Nov.
28925	- Lighted Buoy 8	40-55-22.626N 072-35-15.170W	Fl R 4s		3	Red.	Maintained from 1 April to 15 Nov.
28930	- Lighted Buoy 9	40-55-38.567N 072-36-11.357W	Fl G 4s		4	Green.	Maintained from 1 April to 15 Nov.

Meeting House
Aids maintained from May 1 to Nov. 15.

28955	Meetinghouse Creek Entrance Buoy 1	40-55-41.400N 072-36-48.000W				Green can.	Private aid.
28960	Meetinghouse Creek Entrance Buoy 2	40-55-41.000N 072-36-46.000W				Red nun.	Private aid.
28965	Meetinghouse Creek Entrance Buoy 3	40-55-41.880N 072-36-51.240W				Green can.	Private aid.
28970	Meetinghouse Creek Entrance Buoy 4	40-55-42.840N 072-36-51.240W				Red nun.	Private aid.
28971	Meetinghouse Creek Lighted Bouy 6	40-55-43.200N 072-36-54.480W	Fl R 2s			Red.	Maintained from May 1 to Nov 1. Private aid.
28972	Reeves Creek Buoy 2	40-55-45.240N 072-36-41.350W				Red nun.	Maintained from May 1 to Nov 1. Private aid.
28972.1	Reeves Creek Buoy 4	40-55-49.200N 072-36-39.840W				Red nun.	Maintained from May 1 to Nov 1. Private aid.
28972.2	Reeves Creek Buoy 6	40-55-51.540N 072-36-38.940W				Red nun.	Maintained from May 1 to Nov 1. Private aid.

Peconic River
Aids maintained from May 1 to Nov. 1.

28975	- Lighted Buoy 2	40-55-30.120N 072-36-50.220W	Fl R 2s			Red.	Private aid.
28977	- Lighted Buoy 3	40-55-29.000N 072-36-50.000W	Fl G 2s			Green.	Private aid.
28980	- Lighted Buoy 4	40-55-17.580N 072-37-11.220W	Fl R 2s			Red.	Private aid.
28985	- Lighted Buoy 6	40-55-14.040N 072-37-25.200W	Fl R 2s			Red.	Private aid.
28990	- Lighted Buoy 8	40-55-10.680N 072-37-40.020W	Fl R 2s			Red.	Private aid.
28995	- Lighted Buoy 10	40-55-06.120N 072-37-53.700W	Fl R 2s			Red.	Private aid.
28997	- Lighted Buoy 11	40-55-04.000N 072-38-02.000W	Fl G 2s			Green.	Private aid.
29000	- Lighted Buoy 12	40-55-05.220N 072-38-09.300W	Fl R 2s			Red.	Private aid.
29005	- Lighted Buoy 13	40-55-03.120N 072-38-33.300W	Fl G 2s			Green.	Private aid.
29010	- Lighted Buoy 14	40-55-02.280N 072-38-47.040W	Fl R 2s			Red.	Private aid.
29015	- Lighted Buoy 16	40-55-02.580N 072-39-08.460W	Fl R 2s			Red.	Private aid.
29020	- Lighted Buoy 17	40-55-01.620N 072-39-15.600W	Fl G 2s			Green.	Private aid.

SHINNECOCK BAY TO EAST ROCKAWAY INLET
Shinnecock Inlet

29025 675	**Shinnecock Light**	40-50-31.434N 072-28-41.690W	Fl (2)W 15s	75	11	Skeleton tower. 75	
29035 670	- Approach Lighted Whistle Buoy SH	40-49-00.194N 072-28-34.532W	Mo (A) W		4	Red and white stripes with red spherical topmark.	AIS: MMSI 993672254 (21)
29040	- BREAKWATER LIGHT 1	40-50-23.523N 072-28-40.135W	Fl G 2.5s	36	4	Green.	
29042	- BREAKWATER LIGHT 2	40-50-17.985N 072-28-29.023W	Fl R 2.5s	36	4	Red.	

(1) No.	(2) Name and Location	(3) Position	(4) Characteristic	(5) Height	(6) Range	(7) Structure	(8) Remarks

SHINNECOCK BAY TO EAST ROCKAWAY INLET

Shinnecock Inlet

(1) No.	(2) Name and Location	(3) Position	(4) Characteristic	(5) Height	(6) Range	(7) Structure	(8) Remarks
29045	- *Lighted Buoy 4*	40-50-39.625N 072-28-36.782W	Fl R 4s		3	Red.	Replaced by nun when endangered by ice.
29050	- Buoy 6	40-50-34.509N 072-29-07.100W				Red nun.	
29059	- *Lighted Buoy 8*	40-50-39.594N 072-29-33.732W	Fl R 4s		3	Red.	Replaced by nun when endangered by ice.
	Shinnecock Bay East Channel						
29060	- Buoy 1	40-50-38.923N 072-28-25.495W				Green can.	
29065	- Buoy 3	40-50-43.704N 072-28-19.194W				Green can.	
29070	- *Lighted Buoy 4*	40-50-48.131N 072-28-11.176W	Fl R 2.5s		3	Red.	Replaced by nun when endangered by ice.
29075	- Buoy 5	40-51-05.780N 072-28-10.481W				Green can.	
29080	- Buoy 6	40-51-09.992N 072-28-07.070W				Red nun.	
29085	- *Lighted Buoy 7*	40-51-29.193N 072-28-09.853W	Fl G 4s		4	Green.	Replaced by can when endangered by ice.
29090	- Buoy 8	40-51-30.896N 072-28-08.725W				Red nun.	
	Moriches Inlet						
29104	- BREAKWATER LIGHT 1	40-45-49.725N 072-45-21.732W	Fl G 2.5s	28	4	Skeleton tower.	
29105	- BREAKWATER LIGHT 2	40-45-47.796N 072-45-11.108W	Fl R 4s	30	4	On skeleton tower.	
29106	- West Cut Buoy 4W	40-46-12.783N 072-45-25.601W				Red nun.	Maintained from Apr. 15 to Dec. 1.
29106.1	- West Cut Buoy 6W	40-46-25.435N 072-45-58.182W				Red nun.	Maintained from Apr. 15 to Dec. 1.
29106.2	- West Cut Buoy 7W	40-46-19.963N 072-45-50.747W				Green can.	Maintained from Apr. 15 to Dec. 1.
29107	- East Cut Buoy 3E	40-46-04.989N 072-44-59.847W				Green can.	Maintained from Apr. 15 to Dec. 1.
29107.1	- East Cut Buoy 5E	40-46-06.681N 072-44-47.567W				Green can.	Maintained from Apr. 15 to Dec. 1.
29107.2	- East Cut Buoy 7E	40-46-09.189N 072-44-39.066W				Green can.	Maintained from Apr. 15 to Dec. 1.
29107.3	- East Cut Buoy 9E	40-46-19.304N 072-44-25.406W				Green can.	Maintained from Apr. 15 to Dec. 1.
29107.4	- Danger Rock Buoy West	40-46-08.874N 072-44-37.238W				White and orange marked DANGER ROCKS.	Removed when endangered by ice.
29107.5	- Danger Rock Buoy East	40-46-11.493N 072-44-31.933W				White and orange marked DANGER ROCKS	Removed when endangered by ice.
29108	- East Cut Buoy 11E	40-46-31.516N 072-44-24.601W				Green can.	Maintained from Apr. 15 to Dec. 1.
29109	- *East Cut Rock Lighted Hazard Buoy*	40-46-10.400N 072-44-34.100W	Fl W 4s			White with orange bands.	Private aid.

(1) No.	(2) Name and Location	(3) Position	(4) Characteristic	(5) Height	(6) Range	(7) Structure	(8) Remarks

SHINNECOCK BAY TO EAST ROCKAWAY INLET

Fire Island Inlet
Positions of buoys frequently shifted with changing conditions.

29110	- Lighted Whistle Buoy FI	40-36-08.111N 073-19-53.047W	Mo (A) W		4	Red and white stripes with red spherical topmark.	Replaced by can when endangered by ice.
29115	- Buoy 1	40-36-41.883N 073-19-55.774W				Green can.	Aid does not appear on navigational charts due to frequent shoaling and relocations.
29120	- Lighted Buoy 2	40-36-42.096N 073-19-48.611W	Fl R 4s		3	Red.	Aid does not appear on navigational charts due to frequent shoaling and relocations. Replaced by nun when endangered by ice.
29125	- Lighted Buoy 4	40-37-19.381N 073-19-48.049W	Fl R 2.5s		3	Red .	Aid does not appear on navigational charts due to frequent shoaling and relocations. Replaced by nun when endangered by ice.
29126	- Buoy 4A	40-37-37.734N 073-19-51.998W					Removed when endangered by ice.
29130	- Lighted Buoy 3	40-37-14.860N 073-19-54.450W	Fl G 4s		4	Green.	Aid does not appear on navigational charts due to frequent shoaling and relocations.Replaced by can when endangered by ice.
29135	- Lighted Buoy 6	40-37-51.057N 073-19-48.473W	Q R		3	Red.	Aid does not appear on navigational charts due to frequent shoaling and relocations.Replaced by nun when endangered by ice.
29137	- Buoy 6B	40-37-56.808N 073-19-34.419W					Removed when endangered by ice.
29140	- Buoy 5	40-37-56.977N 073-18-56.001W				Green can.	Aid does not appear on navigational charts due to frequent shoaling and relocations.
29145	- Lighted Buoy 8	40-37-45.719N 073-18-24.189W	Fl R 2.5s		3	Red.	Aid does not appear on navigational charts due to frequent shoaling and relocations.Replaced by nun when endangered by ice.
29155	- Channel Lighted Buoy 7	40-37-54.871N 073-18-24.706W	Fl G 4s		4	Green.	Replaced by can when endangered by ice.
29160	- Lighted Buoy 10	40-37-45.311N 073-17-43.969W	Q R		3	Red.	Replaced by nun when endangered by ice.
29165	- Buoy 9	40-37-54.280N 073-18-01.893W				Green can.	
29170	- Lighted Buoy 11	40-37-40.840N 073-17-31.114W	Fl G 2.5s		4	Green.	Replaced by can when endangered by ice.
29175	- Lighted Buoy 13	40-37-39.536N 073-16-43.314W	Q G		4	Green.	Replaced by can when endangered by ice.
29180	- Buoy 15	40-37-55.207N 073-16-31.916W				Green can.	
29190	- Buoy 16	40-37-48.665N 073-16-26.274W				Red nun.	
29191	COAST GUARD STATION FIRE ISLAND EAST ENTRANCE LIGHT	40-37-35.332N 073-15-35.349W	Fl W 4s		3		

(1) No.	(2) Name and Location	(3) Position	(4) Characteristic	(5) Height	(6) Range	(7) Structure	(8) Remarks
			NEW YORK - First District				

SHINNECOCK BAY TO EAST ROCKAWAY INLET

Fire Island Inlet
Positions of buoys frequently shifted with changing conditions.

(1) No.	(2) Name and Location	(3) Position	(4) Characteristic	(5) Height	(6) Range	(7) Structure	(8) Remarks
29192	COAST GUARD STATION FIRE ISLAND WEST ENTRANCE LIGHT	40-37-35.195N 073-15-36.306W	Fl W 4s		3		
29195	- *Lighted Buoy 18*	40-37-50.112N 073-15-29.047W	Fl R 4s		3	Red.	Replaced by nun when endangered by ice.
29196	- Buoy 19	40-37-58.380N 073-15-08.198W				Green can.	
29205	*Captree Boat Basin Entrance Lighted Buoy CB*	40-38-08.940N 073-14-30.495W	Fl (2+1)G 6s		4	Green and red bands.	Replaced by can when endangered by ice.

Great South Bay
Farm Shoals Channel

29210	- *Lighted Buoy 2*	40-38-01.980N 073-14-00.926W	Fl R 2.5s		3	Red.	Replaced by nun when endangered by ice.
29215	- Buoy 3	40-38-05.809N 073-13-31.545W				Green can.	
29220	- Buoy 5	40-38-15.074N 073-12-52.222W				Green can.	
29225	- Buoy 6	40-38-24.396N 073-12-23.633W				Red nun.	
29230	- *Lighted Buoy 7*	40-38-20.547N 073-12-30.726W	Q G		3	Green.	Replaced by can from Nov 15 to Apr. 1.
29233	SALTAIRE DOCK ENTRANCE LIGHT 1	40-38-28.260N 073-11-57.180W	Fl G 4s			SG on pile.	Private aid.
29234	SALTAIRE DOCK ENTRANCE LIGHT 2	40-38-27.900N 073-11-57.840W	Fl R 2.5s			TR on pile.	Private aid.

East Channel

29240	- *Junction Lighted Buoy EW*	40-38-46.202N 073-12-11.088W	Fl (2+1)G 6s		4	Green and red bands.	Replaced by can when endangered by ice.
29245	- *Lighted Buoy 8*	40-39-10.523N 073-11-21.472W	Fl R 2.5s		3	Red.	Replaced by nun from Nov. 15 to Apr. 1.
29250	FAIR HARBOR LIGHT 1	40-38-37.800N 073-11-06.000W	Fl G 4s	8		SG on pile.	Maintained from May. 1 to Nov. 25. Private aid.
29255	DUNEWOOD LIGHT 2	40-38-39.600N 073-10-47.400W	Fl R 4s			On pile.	Maintained from May 1 to Nov. 15. Private aid.
29260	- *Lighted Buoy 10*	40-39-03.038N 073-10-57.242W	Fl R 2.5s		3	Red.	Replaced by nun from Nov. 15 to Apr. 1.
29265	- Buoy 11	40-39-00.418N 073-10-33.952W				Green can.	
29267	Atlantique Entrance Buoy 1	40-38-43.800N 073-10-26.400W				Green can.	Maintained from Apr. 15 to Nov. 15. Private aid.
29268	Atlantique Entrance Buoy 2	40-38-43.800N 073-10-27.960W				Red nun.	Maintained from Apr. 15 to Nov. 15. Private aid.
29269	Atlantique Entrance Buoy 3	40-38-41.100N 073-10-26.100W				Green can.	Maintained from Apr. 15 to Nov. 15. Private aid.
29269.5	Atlantique Entrance Buoy 4	40-38-41.000N 073-10-27.000W				Red nun.	Private aid.
29270	- *Lighted Buoy 12*	40-38-52.192N 073-10-07.326W	Fl R 2.5s		3	Red.	Replaced by nun from Nov. 15 to Apr. 1.
29272	- Buoy 14	40-39-02.473N 073-09-36.486W				Red nun.	
29275	- Buoy 15	40-39-06.592N 073-09-23.125W				Green can.	

(1) No.	(2) Name and Location	(3) Position	(4) Characteristic	(5) Height	(6) Range	(7) Structure	(8) Remarks
			NEW YORK - First District				

SHINNECOCK BAY TO EAST ROCKAWAY INLET
Great South Bay
East Channel

(1) No.	(2) Name and Location	(3) Position	(4) Characteristic	(5) Height	(6) Range	(7) Structure	(8) Remarks
29280	- Buoy 17	40-39-06.692N 073-09-02.024W				Green can.	
29285	- Lighted Buoy 19	40-39-10.992N 073-08-31.123W	Fl G 2.5s		4	Green.	Replaced by can from Nov. 15 to Apr. 1.
29290	- Buoy 20	40-39-32.570N 073-08-15.354W				Red nun.	
29295	- Lighted Buoy 21	40-39-56.314N 073-08-04.322W	Fl G 2.5s		4	Green.	Replaced by can from Nov. 15 to Apr. 1.
29297	- Buoy 23	40-40-21.000N 073-08-06.415W				Green can.	
29300	- Lighted Buoy 24	40-40-35.129N 073-08-04.864W	Q R		3	Red.	Replaced by nun from Nov. 15 to Apr. 1.
29310	- Buoy 25	40-40-58.961N 073-07-44.028W				Green can.	
29325	- Buoy 27	40-41-14.086N 073-07-15.604W				Green can.	
29330	- Buoy 28	40-41-36.716N 073-07-00.312W				Red nun.	
29335	- Lighted Buoy EN	40-41-42.584N 073-06-58.800W	Fl (2+1)G 6s		4	Green and red bands.	Replaced by can from Nov. 15 to Apr. 1.

Great South Bay

(1) No.	(2) Name and Location	(3) Position	(4) Characteristic	(5) Height	(6) Range	(7) Structure	(8) Remarks
29340	- Buoy 30	40-41-55.089N 073-06-13.238W				Red nun.	
29341	STONY BROOK UNIVERSITY LIGHTED RESEARCH BUOY GSB1	40-41-57.228N 073-05-12.192W	Fl Y 6s			Yellow.	Private aid.
29342	- Buoy 32	40-42-18.370N 073-04-51.112W				Red nun.	
29344	- Lighted Buoy 34	40-42-41.612N 073-03-25.367W	Fl R 2.5s		3	Red.	Replaced by nun from Nov. 15 to Apr. 1.
29345	- Lighted Buoy 35	40-43-08.179N 073-01-56.323W	Fl G 4s		4	Green.	Replaced by can from Nov. 15 to Apr. 1.
29350	- Lighted Buoy 36	40-43-41.440N 072-59-47.417W	Fl R 6s		3	Red.	Replaced by nun from Nov. 15 to Apr. 1.
29355	- Buoy 37	40-43-50.646N 072-58-42.758W				Green can.	Maintained from 15 April to 1 Nov.
29360	- Lighted Buoy 38	40-43-57.469N 072-57-37.536W	Fl R 4s		3	Red.	Maintained from 15 April to 1 Nov.

Range Channel

(1) No.	(2) Name and Location	(3) Position	(4) Characteristic	(5) Height	(6) Range	(7) Structure	(8) Remarks
29365	- Buoy 1	40-39-34.491N 073-08-40.523W				Green can.	
29370	- Lighted Buoy 4	40-40-36.090N 073-08-42.523W	Fl R 2.5s		3	Red.	Replaced by nun from Nov. 15 to Apr. 1.

West Channel

(1) No.	(2) Name and Location	(3) Position	(4) Characteristic	(5) Height	(6) Range	(7) Structure	(8) Remarks
29371	- Buoy 1	40-38-50.079N 073-12-16.648W				Green can.	
29375	- Buoy 3	40-39-10.003N 073-12-25.640W				Green can.	
29380	- Lighted Buoy 4	40-39-28.392N 073-12-24.432W	Fl R 2.5s		3	Red.	Replaced by nun from Nov. 15 to Apr. 1.
29385	- Buoy WD	40-39-59.291N 073-12-49.433W				Green and red bands; can.	
29390	- Lighted Buoy 6	40-40-07.891N 073-12-46.832W	Fl R 4s		3	Red.	Replaced by nun from Nov. 15 to Apr. 1.

(1) No.	(2) Name and Location	(3) Position	(4) Characteristic	(5) Height	(6) Range	(7) Structure	(8) Remarks
			NEW YORK - First District				

SHINNECOCK BAY TO EAST ROCKAWAY INLET

Great South Bay

West Channel

(1) No.	(2) Name and Location	(3) Position	(4) Characteristic	(5) Height	(6) Range	(7) Structure	(8) Remarks
29395	- Lighted Buoy 7	40-40-28.091N 073-13-14.933W	Fl G 4s		4	Green.	Replaced by can from Nov. 15 to Apr. 1.
29400	- Buoy 8	40-40-48.351N 073-13-31.906W				Red nun.	
29405	- Lighted Buoy 10	40-41-11.914N 073-13-54.284W	Fl R 2.5s		3	Red.	Replaced by nun from Nov. 15 to Apr. 1.
29410	- Lighted Buoy 11	40-41-22.222N 073-14-14.856W	Fl G 4s		4	Green.	Replaced by can from Nov. 15 to Apr. 1.

Dickerson Channel

29420	- Buoy 2	40-39-55.091N 073-13-42.635W				Red nun.	Maintained from 1 April to 15 Nov.
29425	- Buoy 3	40-40-05.039N 073-14-38.166W				Green can.	Maintained from 1 Apr. to 15 Nov.
29430	- Buoy 4	40-40-18.091N 073-14-57.037W				Red nun.	Maintained from 1 April to 15 Nov.
29435	- Buoy 5	40-40-17.091N 073-15-09.937W				Green can.	Maintained from 1 Apr. to 15 Nov.
29440	- Buoy 6	40-40-39.251N 073-16-00.017W				Red nun.	Maintained from 1 April to 15 Nov.
29445	WEST ISLIP MARINA LIGHT 1	40-41-09.000N 073-17-26.000W	F G			On pile.	Private aid.

North Channel

29449	- Lighted Buoy 1	40-41-58.400N 073-14-14.200W	Fl G 2.5s		4	Green.	Replaced by can from Nov. 15 to Apr. 1.
29450	- Lighted Buoy 3	40-41-54.089N 073-12-52.532W	Fl G 4s		4	Green.	Replaced by can from Nov. 15 to Apr. 1.
29455	- Lighted Buoy 4	40-41-28.155N 073-11-42.082W	Fl R 4s		3	Red.	Replaced by nun from Nov. 15 to Apr. 1.
29460	- Buoy 6	40-41-28.118N 073-10-20.950W				Red nun.	
29465	- Lighted Buoy 8	40-41-27.180N 073-09-01.881W	Fl R 4s		3	Red.	Replaced by nun from Nov. 15 to Apr. 1.
29470	- Buoy 9	40-41-32.042N 073-08-00.189W				Green can.	

East-West Channel

Aids maintained from May 15 to Oct. 15 unless otherwise noted.

29475	- Lighted Buoy 2	40-40-36.600N 073-18-23.200W	Fl R 4s			Red.	Private aid.
29480	- Lighted Buoy 3	40-40-32.640N 073-18-23.400W	Fl G 4s			Green.	Private aid.
29485	- Buoy 4	40-40-22.380N 073-19-22.780W				Red nun.	Private aid.
29490	- Buoy 5	40-40-19.300N 073-19-21.700W				Green can.	Private aid.
29495	West Babylon Creek Lighted Buoy 6	40-40-15.000N 073-20-06.000W	Fl R 4s			Red.	Private aid.
29500	- Buoy 7	40-40-10.850N 073-20-01.440W				Green can.	Private aid.
29505	Santapogue River Buoy 8	40-40-04.680N 073-20-40.260W				Red nun.	Private aid.
29510	- Buoy 9	40-40-02.580N 073-20-38.760W				Green can.	Private aid.
29515	- Lighted Buoy 10	40-39-56.160N 073-21-05.700W	Fl R 4s			Red.	Private aid.

(1) No.	(2) Name and Location	(3) Position	(4) Characteristic	(5) Height	(6) Range	(7) Structure	(8) Remarks

NEW YORK - First District

SHINNECOCK BAY TO EAST ROCKAWAY INLET
Great South Bay
East-West Channel
Aids maintained from May 15 to Oct. 15 unless otherwise noted.

(1) No.	(2) Name and Location	(3) Position	(4) Characteristic	(5) Height	(6) Range	(7) Structure	(8) Remarks
29520	- Lighted Buoy 11	40-39-53.150N 073-21-04.100W	Fl G 4s			Green.	Private aid.
29525	- Buoy 12	40-39-44.250N 073-21-50.300W				Red nun.	Private aid.
29530	- Buoy 13	40-39-41.000N 073-21-48.000W				Green can.	Private aid.
29535	Lugano Canal Lighted Buoy 14	40-39-33.300N 073-22-20.520W	Fl R 4s			Red.	Private aid.
29540	- Buoy 15	40-39-31.500N 073-22-19.440W				Green can.	Private aid.
29545	Great Neck Creek Lighted Buoy 16	40-39-29.880N 073-22-34.500W	Fl R 4s			Red.	Private aid.
29550	- Buoy 17	40-39-26.000N 073-22-35.000W				Green can.	Private aid.
29555	Howell Creek Lighted Buoy 18	40-39-18.840N 073-23-23.160W	Fl R 4s			Red.	Private aid.
29560	- Buoy 19	40-39-17.770N 073-23-16.800W				Green can.	Private aid.
29565	Woods Creek Buoy 20	40-39-11.200N 073-24-11.300W				Red nun.	Private aid.
29570	- Buoy 21	40-39-08.280N 073-24-12.900W				Green can.	Private aid.
29575	AMITYVILLE CREEK ENTRANCE LIGHT 1	40-39-25.000N 073-24-52.000W	F G	25		On pile.	Maintained year round. Private aid.
29580	- Buoy 22	40-39-02.040N 073-25-06.000W				Red nun.	Private aid.
29585	- Buoy 23	40-38-59.160N 073-25-05.640W				Green can.	Private aid.

Fox Creek
Aids maintained from May 15 to Oct. 15 unless otherwise noted.

(1) No.	(2) Name and Location	(3) Position	(4) Characteristic	(5) Height	(6) Range	(7) Structure	(8) Remarks
29600	- Channel Lighted Buoy 1	40-38-54.000N 073-20-11.000W	Fl G 4s			Green.	Private aid.
29605	- Channel Lighted Buoy 2	40-38-56.820N 073-20-12.600W	Fl R 4s			Red.	Private aid.
29610	- Channel Buoy 3	40-39-15.540N 073-20-28.440W				Green can.	Private aid.
29615	- Channel Lighted Buoy 4	40-39-15.000N 073-20-25.000W	Fl R 4s			Red.	Private aid.
29620	- Channel Lighted Buoy 5	40-39-27.720N 073-20-36.720W	Fl G 4s			Green.	Private aid.
29621	East Fox Creek Outfall Lighted Buoy	40-39-38.460N 073-20-41.700W	Fl W 4s				Private aid.
29625	- Channel Lighted Buoy 6	40-39-28.000N 073-20-33.000W	Fl R 4s			Red.	Private aid.
29630	- Channel Buoy 7	40-39-42.420N 073-20-54.960W				Green can.	Private aid.
29635	- Channel Buoy 8	40-39-43.680N 073-20-49.440W				Red nun.	Private aid.
29640	- Channel Lighted Buoy 9	40-40-06.000N 073-21-15.000W	Fl G 4s			Green.	Private aid.
29645	- Channel Lighted Buoy 10	40-40-06.000N 073-21-11.000W	Fl R 4s			Red.	Private aid.

North Side

(1) No.	(2) Name and Location	(3) Position	(4) Characteristic	(5) Height	(6) Range	(7) Structure	(8) Remarks
29670	Bay Shore Lighted Buoy 2	40-42-30.609N 073-14-13.295W	Fl R 2.5s		3	Red.	Replaced by nun from Nov. 15 to Apr. 1.
29675	BAY SHORE MARINA LIGHT	40-42-44.000N 073-14-12.000W				On pile.	Private aid.
29685	Orowoc Creek Entrance Lighted Buoy 2	40-42-59.100N 073-13-31.500W	Fl R 4s			Red.	Maintained from Mar. 15 to Nov. 15. Private aid.
29687	Orowoc Creek Daybeacon 4	40-43-14.820N 073-13-26.460W				TR on pile.	Private aid.

(1) No.	(2) Name and Location	(3) Position	(4) Characteristic	(5) Height	(6) Range	(7) Structure	(8) Remarks
			NEW YORK - First District				

SHINNECOCK BAY TO EAST ROCKAWAY INLET

Great South Bay

North Side

29695	*Champlin Creek Entrance Lighted Buoy 2*	40-42-36.300N 073-12-17.100W	Fl R 4s			Red.	Maintained from Apr. 15 to Nov. 15. Private aid.
29705	*East Islip Lighted Buoy 2*	40-42-18.000N 073-11-18.000W	Fl R 4s			Red.	Maintained from Apr. 15 to Nov. 15. Private aid.
29710	*East Islip Lighted Buoy 4*	40-42-22.000N 073-11-15.000W	Fl R 4s			Red.	Private aid.
29715	TIMBER POINT BREAKWATER LIGHT WEST	40-42-42.840N 073-08-36.690W	Fl G 4s	6		On end of breakwater.	Private aid.
29720	TIMBER POINT BREAKWATER LIGHT EAST	40-42-44.080N 073-08-36.200W	Fl R 4s	6		On pile.	Private aid.
29721	GREAT RIVER ENTRANCE LIGHT 2	40-43-27.180N 073-07-47.520W	Fl R 15s			TR on pile.	Light maintained from Apr. 15 to Nov. 15. Private aid.
29722	Brick Kiln Lighted Buoy 2	40-43-36.180N 073-07-23.820W	Fl R 4s			Red.	Maintained from Apr. 15 to Nov. 15. Private aid.
29724	GREEN HARBOR LIGHT	40-43-11.000N 073-05-37.000W	F W	18		NG on pile.	Private aid.
29725	BROWN POINT WEST BREAKWATER LIGHT 1	40-43-18.968N 073-04-10.506W	Fl G 4s	18	5	SG on pile.	
29730	BROWN POINT EAST BREAKWATER LIGHT 2	40-43-21.633N 073-04-08.013W	Fl R 4s	20	3	TR on pile.	
29732	HOMANS CREEK LIGHT	40-43-40.000N 073-03-13.000W	Fl R 15s	18			Private aid.

Patchogue Bay

29740	- *Entrance Lighted Buoy 1*	40-43-46.388N 073-01-03.205W	Fl G 2.5s		4	Green.	Replaced by can from Nov. 15 to Apr. 15.
29745	- Channel Buoy 2	40-44-01.287N 073-00-58.605W				Red nun.	
29750	- Channel Buoy 3	40-44-12.787N 073-01-01.805W				Green can.	
29755	- Channel Buoy 4	40-44-30.287N 073-00-57.805W				Red nun.	
29760	PATCHOGUE BREAKWATER LIGHT 5	40-44-46.179N 073-01-00.595W	Fl G 2.5s	21	4	SG on skeleton tower.	
29765	PATCHOGUE RIVER LIGHT	40-44-50.340N 073-00-56.520W	Fl R 5s			On concrete pedestal.	Private aid.
29766	Sandspit Buoy 1	40-44-47.460N 073-00-46.740W				Green can.	Private aid.
29767	Sandspit Buoy 2	40-44-51.300N 073-00-46.740W				Red nun.	Private aid.
29770	*Swan River Entrance Lighted Buoy 1*	40-44-42.240N 072-59-50.760W	Fl G 4s			Green.	Maintained from Apr 15 to Nov. 15. Private aid.
29771	*Swan River Lighted Buoy 3*	40-44-47.100N 072-59-50.300W	Fl G 4s			Green.	Maintained from Apr 15 to Nov 15. Private aid.
29772	*Swan River Lighted Buoy 5*	40-44-50.900N 072-59-49.600W	Fl G 4s			Green.	Maintained from Apr 15 to Nov 15. Private aid.
29780	*Tuthills Creek Entrance Lighted Buoy 2*	40-44-46.500N 073-01-14.900W	Fl R 4s			Red.	Maintained from May 1 to Nov. 1. Private aid.
29785	COREY CREEK ENTRANCE LIGHT 1	40-44-36.720N 073-01-37.140W	Fl G 4s			SB on black skeleton tower.	Maintained from May 1 to Nov. 1. Private aid.
29790	COREY CREEK ENTRANCE LIGHT 2	40-44-38.160N 073-01-36.720W	Fl R 4s	12		TR on red skeleton tower.	Maintained from May 1 to Nov. 1. Private aid.
29794	*Mud Creek Entrance Lighted Buoy 1*	40-44-49.800N 072-59-16.820W	Fl G 4s			Green.	Private aid.

(1) No.	(2) Name and Location	(3) Position	(4) Characteristic	(5) Height	(6) Range	(7) Structure	(8) Remarks

NEW YORK - First District

SHINNECOCK BAY TO EAST ROCKAWAY INLET

Great South Bay

Patchogue Bay

29795	*Mud Creek Entrance Lighted Buoy 2*	40-44-51.870N 072-59-10.560W	Fl R 4s			Red.	Maintained from May 1 to Nov. 1. Private aid.
29796	Mud Creek Buoy 3	40-44-53.280N 072-59-14.480W				Green can.	Private aid.
29797	Mud Creek Buoy 4	40-44-53.520N 072-59-11.520W				Red nun.	Private aid.
29800	*Abets Creek Lighted Buoy 1* 50 feet, 183° from south end of sunken barge.	40-44-46.380N 072-58-40.980W	Fl G 4s			Green.	Maintained from May 1 to Nov. 1. Private aid.
29801	*Hampton Oyster Company Aquaculture Lighted Buoy A*	41-01-21.680N 072-26-20.490W	F Y			Yellow.	Private aid.
29801.1	*Hampton Oyster Company Aquaculture Lighted Buoy B*	41-01-24.570N 072-26-11.880W	F Y			Yellow.	Private aid.
29801.2	*Hampton Oyster Company Aquaculture Lighted Buoy C*	41-01-18.050N 072-26-12.040W	F Y			Yellow.	Private aid.
29801.3	Hampton Oyster Company Aquaculture Lighted Buoy D	41-01-18.160N 072-26-20.640W	F Y			Yellow.	Private aid.

South Side

29805	POINT O'WOODS DOCK LIGHT (2)	40-39-13.440N 073-08-14.100W	F R			On pile.	Private aid.

Sailors Haven Channel
Floating aids maintained from May 1 to Oct. 15.

29820	- Lighted Buoy 1	40-39-40.200N 073-06-20.700W	Fl G 2s			Green.	Private aid.
29825	- Lighted Buoy 2	40-39-39.300N 073-06-24.100W	Fl R 2s			Red.	Private aid.
29830	- Lighted Buoy 3	40-39-37.000N 073-06-19.400W	Fl G 2s			Green.	Private aid.
29835	- Lighted Buoy 4	40-39-35.700N 073-06-22.300W	Fl R 2s			Red.	Private aid.
29840	- Lighted Buoy 5	40-39-32.400N 073-06-17.900W	Fl G 2s			Green.	Private aid.
29845	- Lighted Buoy 6	40-39-31.200N 073-06-19.900W	Fl R 2s			Red.	Private aid.

Great South Bay
Aids maintained from May 1 to Nov. 1.

29855	*Cherry Grove Entrance Lighted Buoy 1*	40-40-02.280N 073-05-08.640W	Fl G 4s			Green.	Private aid.
29856	*Cherry Grove Entrance Lighted Buoy 2*	40-40-02.700N 073-05-10.800W	Fl R 4s			Red.	Private aid.
29860	*Cherry Grove Lighted Buoy 3*	40-39-45.300N 073-05-19.140W	Fl G 4s			Green.	Private aid.
29861	*Cherry Grove Lighted Buoy 4*	40-39-45.700N 073-05-21.000W	Fl R 4s			Red.	Private aid.

Sailors Haven Channel - Lone Hill Entrance
Aids maintained from May 1 to Nov. 1.

29870	*Fire Island Pines Lighted Buoy 1*	40-40-53.640N 073-03-47.400W	Fl G 4s			Green.	Private aid.
29872	*Fire Island Pines Lighted Buoy 2*	40-40-51.500N 073-03-52.100W	Fl R 4s			Red.	Private aid.
29875	*Fire Island Pines Lighted Buoy 3*	40-40-25.020N 073-04-02.040W	Fl G 4s			Green.	Private aid.
29877	*Fire Island Pines Lighted Buoy 4*	40-40-23.800N 073-04-06.100W	Fl R 4s			Red.	Private aid.
29885	*Fire Island Pines Lighted Buoy 5*	40-40-08.820N 073-04-12.600W	Fl G 4s			Green.	Private aid.
29887	*Fire Island Pines Lighted Buoy 6*	40-40-07.200N 073-04-16.000W	Fl R 4s			Red.	Private aid.

Barrett Beach
Aids maintained from May 1 to Nov. 15.

29910	- Lighted Buoy 1	40-40-46.700N 073-02-39.400W	Fl G 2s			Green.	Private aid.

(1) No.	(2) Name and Location	(3) Position	(4) Characteristic	(5) Height	(6) Range	(7) Structure	(8) Remarks

NEW YORK - First District

SHINNECOCK BAY TO EAST ROCKAWAY INLET

Great South Bay

Barrett Beach
Aids maintained from May 1 to Nov. 15.

29915	- Lighted Buoy 2	40-40-46.600N 073-02-40.800W	Fl R 2s			Red.	Private aid.
29920	- Lighted Buoy 3	40-40-39.000N 073-02-36.600W	Fl G 2s			Green.	Private aid.
29925	- Lighted Buoy 4	40-40-39.900N 073-02-38.400W	Fl R 2s			Red.	Private aid.
29930	- Lighted Buoy 5	40-40-32.000N 073-02-34.200W	Fl G 2s			Green.	Private aid.
29935	- Lighted Buoy 6	40-40-33.900N 073-02-36.400W	Fl R 2s			Red.	Private aid.

Great South Bay
Aids maintained from May 1 to Nov. 1.

29937	Water Island Channel Lighted Buoy 1	40-40-54.120N 073-01-51.900W	Fl G 4s			Green.	Private aid.
29937.5	Water Island Channel Lighted Buoy 2	40-40-52.800N 073-01-53.300W	Fl R 4s			Red.	Private aid.
29938	Water Island Channel Lighted Buoy 3	40-40-44.600N 073-01-49.100W	Fl G 4s			Green.	Private aid.
29939	Water Island Channel Lighted Buoy 4	40-40-43.600N 073-01-50.400W	Fl R 4s			Red.	Private aid.
29950	Porgy Bar Lighted Buoy 2 Marks north edge of shoal.	40-41-21.360N 073-01-35.340W	Fl R 4s			Red.	Private aid.

Davis Park
Aids maintained from May 1 to Nov. 1.

29955	- Entrance Lighted Buoy 1	40-41-21.660N 073-00-20.280W	Fl G 4s			Green.	Private aid.
29960	- Entrance Lighted Buoy 2	40-41-21.060N 073-00-22.380W	Fl R 4s			Red.	Private aid.
29965	- Entrance Buoy 3	40-41-17.700N 073-00-18.600W				Green.	Private aid.
29970	- Entrance Buoy 4	40-41-17.880N 073-00-20.520W				Red.	Private aid.
29975	- Entrance Lighted Buoy 5	40-41-14.820N 073-00-16.620W	Fl G 4s			Green.	Private aid.
29980	- Entrance Lighted Buoy 6	40-41-14.280N 073-00-18.420W	Fl R 4s			Red.	Private aid.
29981	- WAVE BREAK WARNING LIGHT A	40-41-12.600N 073-00-17.100W	Q Y			Yellow.	Private aid.
29982	- WAVE BREAK WARNING LIGHT B	40-41-12.100N 073-00-17.500W	Q Y			Yellow.	Private aid.
29983	- WAVE BREAK WARNING LIGHT C	40-41-11.600N 073-00-17.200W	Q Y			Yellow.	Private aid.
29984	- WAVE BREAK WARNING LIGHT D	40-41-11.300N 073-00-17.400W	Q Y			Yellow.	Private aid.
29985	- WAVE BREAK WARNING LIGHT E	40-41-10.800N 073-00-17.800W	Q Y			Yellow.	Private aid.
29986	- WAVE BREAK WARNING LIGHT F	40-41-10.300N 073-00-18.200W	Q Y			Yellow.	Private aid.

Watch Hill
Aids maintained from May 1 to Oct. 15.

29990	- Channel Lighted Buoy 1	40-42-12.000N 073-00-34.400W	Fl G 4s			Green.	Private aid.
29995	- Channel Lighted Buoy 2	40-42-10.100N 073-00-35.400W	Fl R 4s			Red.	Private aid.
30000	- Channel Lighted Buoy 3	40-42-04.800N 073-00-17.100W	Fl G 4s			Green.	Private aid.
30005	- Channel Lighted Buoy 4	40-42-03.800N 073-00-18.500W	Fl R 4s			Red.	Private aid.
30010	- Channel Lighted Buoy 5	40-41-55.700N 072-59-53.000W	Fl G 2s			Green.	Private aid.
30015	- Channel Lighted Buoy 6	40-41-54.800N 072-59-53.600W	Fl R 4s			Red.	Private aid.

(1) No.	(2) Name and Location	(3) Position	(4) Characteristic	(5) Height	(6) Range	(7) Structure	(8) Remarks
			NEW YORK - First District				

SHINNECOCK BAY TO EAST ROCKAWAY INLET
Great South Bay
Watch Hill
Aids maintained from May 1 to Oct. 15.

(1) No.	(2) Name and Location	(3) Position	(4) Characteristic	(5) Height	(6) Range	(7) Structure	(8) Remarks
30020	- *Channel Lighted Buoy 7*	40-41-48.900N 072-59-34.000W	Fl G 4s			Green.	Private aid.
30025	- *Channel Lighted Buoy 8*	40-41-47.900N 072-59-34.900W	Fl R 4s			Red.	Private aid.
30030	- *Channel Lighted Buoy 9*	40-41-45.100N 072-59-24.300W	Fl G 4s			Green.	Private aid.
30035	- *Channel Lighted Buoy 10*	40-41-43.800N 072-59-23.800W	Fl R 2s			Red.	Private aid.
30040	- WEST ENTRANCE LIGHT	40-41-41.400N 072-59-24.300W	F R			On pile.	Private aid.
30045	- EAST ENTRANCE LIGHT	40-41-41.400N 072-59-20.300W	F G			On pile.	Private aid.
30050	- CHANNEL RANGE FRONT LIGHT	40-41-43.680N 072-59-19.140W	F W			KWB on pile.	Private aid.
30055	- CHANNEL RANGE REAR LIGHT	40-41-41.580N 072-59-13.980W	F W			KWB on pile.	Private aid.

BELLPORT BEACH
Aids maintained from May 1 to Oct 1.

(1) No.	(2) Name and Location	(3) Position	(4) Characteristic	(5) Height	(6) Range	(7) Structure	(8) Remarks
30090	- Channel Buoy 1	40-43-56.880N 072-55-43.560W				Green can.	Private aid.
30095	- Channel Buoy 2	40-43-56.760N 072-55-45.900W				Red nun.	Private aid.
30100	- Channel Buoy 3	40-43-49.260N 072-55-42.300W				Green can.	Private aid.
30105	- Channel Buoy 4	40-43-48.660N 072-55-44.460W				Red nun.	Private aid.
30110	- Channel Buoy 5	40-43-43.740N 072-55-41.340W				Green can.	Private aid.
30115	- Channel Buoy 6	40-43-37.800N 072-55-41.220W				Red nun.	Private aid.
30120	- Channel Buoy 7	40-43-32.700N 072-55-39.360W				Green can.	Private aid.
30125	- Channel Buoy 8	40-43-25.500N 072-55-39.540W				Red nun.	Private aid.
30126	- Channel Buoy 9	40-43-25.860N 072-55-37.860W				Green can.	Private aid.
30126.5	- Channel Buoy 11	40-43-21.240N 072-55-37.260W				Green can.	Private aid.
30127	- Channel Buoy 10	40-43-21.360N 072-55-38.400W				Red nun.	Private aid.
30127.5	- Channel Buoy 13	40-43-15.660N 072-55-35.800W				Green can.	Private aid.
30128	- Channel Buoy 14	40-43-13.860N 072-55-37.140W				Red nun.	Private aid.
30128.5	- Channel Buoy 17	40-43-05.460N 072-55-34.380W				Green can.	Private aid.
30128.6	- Channel Buoy 16	40-43-09.180N 072-55-36.180W				Red nun.	Private aid.
30128.8	- Channel Buoy 18	40-43-04.260N 072-55-35.520W				Red nun.	Private aid.

Bellport Bay

(1) No.	(2) Name and Location	(3) Position	(4) Characteristic	(5) Height	(6) Range	(7) Structure	(8) Remarks
30130	- *Lighted Buoy 1*	40-43-57.436N 072-56-38.940W	Fl G 2.5s	4		Green.	Maintained from 15 Apr. to 1 Nov.
30135	- Buoy 2	40-44-14.288N 072-55-56.195W				Red nun.	Maintained from Apr. 15 to Nov. 1.
30140	- Buoy 4	40-44-34.648N 072-55-16.849W				Red nun.	Maintained from Apr. 15 to Nov. 1.
30145	- *Lighted Buoy 6*	40-44-58.202N 072-54-30.471W	Q R	3		Red.	Maintained from 15 April to 1 Nov.

271

(1) No.	(2) Name and Location	(3) Position	(4) Characteristic	(5) Height	(6) Range	(7) Structure	(8) Remarks
			NEW YORK - First District				

SHINNECOCK BAY TO EAST ROCKAWAY INLET
Great South Bay
Bellport Bay

(1) No.	(2) Name and Location	(3) Position	(4) Characteristic	(5) Height	(6) Range	(7) Structure	(8) Remarks
30150	- Buoy 7	40-44-48.870N 072-54-06.461W				Green can.	Maintained from Apr. 15 to Nov. 1.
30155	- Buoy 8	40-44-38.836N 072-53-45.647W				Red nun.	Maintained from Apr. 15 to Nov. 1.
30160	- Buoy 9	40-44-28.656N 072-53-19.517W				Green can.	Maintained from 15 April to 1 Nov.
30162	- Buoy 10	40-44-18.987N 072-52-57.828W				Red nun.	Maintained from Apr. 15 to Nov. 1.
30165	- *Lighted Buoy 11*	40-44-08.499N 072-52-32.365W	Q G		3	Green.	Maintained from 15 April to 1 Nov.
30166	Smith Point Marina Buoy 1	40-44-15.000N 072-52-24.480W					Private aid.
30167	Smith Point Marina Buoy 2	40-44-15.000N 072-52-22.500W					Private aid.
30168	Smith Point Marina Buoy 3	40-44-20.460N 072-52-27.120W					Private aid.
30169	Smith Point Marina Buoy 4	40-44-20.760N 072-52-25.860W					Private aid.

Beaverdam Creek Entrance
Aids maintained from May 1 to Nov. 1.

(1) No.	(2) Name and Location	(3) Position	(4) Characteristic	(5) Height	(6) Range	(7) Structure	(8) Remarks
30175	- *Lighted Buoy 2*	40-45-21.000N 072-55-22.080W	Fl R 4s			Red.	Private aid.
30180	- *Lighted Buoy 4*	40-45-33.060N 072-55-16.980W	Fl R 4s			Red.	Private aid.
30190	*Carmans River Entrance Lighted Buoy 1*	40-45-39.480N 072-53-27.120W	Fl G 4s			Green.	Private aid.
30195	*Carmans River Lighted Buoy 2*	40-46-04.699N 072-53-32.788W	Fl R 4s			Red.	Private aid.

Narrows Bay

(1) No.	(2) Name and Location	(3) Position	(4) Characteristic	(5) Height	(6) Range	(7) Structure	(8) Remarks
30200	*Johns Neck Creek Lighted Buoy 1*	40-44-42.700N 072-51-47.000W	Fl G 4s			Green.	Private aid.
30201	*Unchachogue Creek Lighted Buoy 2*	40-44-30.300N 072-51-58.200W	Fl R 4s			Red.	Private aid.
30201.1	Unchachogue Creek Buoy 4	40-44-36.800N 072-51-57.700W				Red nun.	Private aid.
30201.2	Unchachogue Creek Buoy 6	40-44-42.100N 072-51-59.300W				Red nun.	Private aid.
30205	- Buoy 2	40-44-23.433N 072-51-49.913W				Red nun.	Removed when endangered by ice.
30210	- Buoy 4	40-44-27.281N 072-51-33.040W				Red nun.	Maintained from Apr. 15 to Nov. 1.
30211	*Section Five Lighted Buoy 1*	40-44-41.160N 072-51-09.120W	Fl G 4s			Green.	Private aid.
30215	- *Lighted Buoy 5*	40-44-36.533N 072-50-56.213W	Fl G 4s		4	Green.	Removed when endangered by ice.
30220	- *Lighted Buoy 6*	40-45-03.333N 072-50-10.613W	Fl R 2.5s		3	Red.	Removed when endangered by ice.
30222	*Pattersquash Creek Lighted Buoy 1*	40-45-04.900N 072-50-30.400W	Fl G 4s			Green.	Private aid.
30223	*Pattersquash Creek Lighted Buoy 2*	40-45-10.000N 072-50-44.000W	Fl R 4s			Red.	Private aid.
30224	*Pattersquash Creek Lighted Buoy 4*	40-45-12.400N 072-50-46.800W	Fl R 4s			Red.	Private aid.
30225	- Buoy 8	40-45-15.533N 072-49-22.313W				Red nun.	Maitained from Apr. 15 to Nov. 1.

(1) No.	(2) Name and Location	(3) Position	(4) Characteristic	(5) Height	(6) Range	(7) Structure	(8) Remarks

SHINNECOCK BAY TO EAST ROCKAWAY INLET
Great South Bay
Narrows Bay

No.	Name and Location	Position	Characteristic	Height	Range	Structure	Remarks
30230	- Buoy 7	40-45-10.333N 072-49-47.513W				Green can.	Maintained from Apr. 15 to Nov. 1.
30231	Section One Lighted Buoy 2	40-45-24.800N 072-49-57.400W	Fl R 4s			Red.	Private aid.
30233	Narrow Bay Aquaculture Lighted Buoy C	40-45-29.950N 072-49-17.430W	Fl Y 2s			Yellow.	Private aid.
30233.1	Narrow Bay Aquaculture Lighted Buoy D	40-45-29.090N 072-49-15.820W	Fl Y 2s			Yellow.	Private aid.
30233.2	Narrow Bay Aquaculture Lighted Buoy E	40-45-29.090N 072-49-21.500W	Fl Y 2s			Yellow.	Private aid.
30235	- Lighted Buoy 9	40-45-24.513N 072-48-57.118W	Fl G 2.5s		4	Green.	Removed when endangered by ice.

Fire Island East End Channel
Aids maintained from May 1 to Nov. 1.

No.	Name and Location	Position	Characteristic	Height	Range	Structure	Remarks
30255	Great Gun Beach Channel Lighted Buoy 1	40-46-19.560N 072-47-09.420W	Fl G 4s			Green.	Private aid.
30260	Great Gun Beach Channel Lighted Buoy 2	40-46-19.260N 072-47-10.440W	Fl R 4s			Red.	Private aid.
30265	Great Gun Beach Channel Lighted Buoy 3	40-46-10.380N 072-47-04.080W	Fl G 4s			Green.	Private aid.
30268	Great Gun Beach Channel Lighted Buoy 4	40-46-09.800N 072-47-05.700W	Fl R 4s			Red.	Private aid.
30270	Great Gun Beach Channel Buoy 5	40-46-03.240N 072-46-59.220W				Green can.	Private aid.
30275	Great Gun Beach Channel Buoy 6	40-46-01.800N 072-47-00.200W				Red nun.	Private aid.
30276	Great Gun Beach Channel Lighted Buoy 7	40-45-59.100N 072-46-50.000W	Fl G 4s			Green.	Private aid.
30277	Great Gun Beach Channel Lighted Buoy 8	40-45-58.100N 072-46-51.600W	Fl R 4s			Red.	Private aid.
30278	Great Gun Beach Channel Lighted Buoy 9	40-45-53.400N 072-46-39.900W	Fl G 4s			Green.	Private aid.
30279	Great Gun Beach Channel Lighted Buoy 10	40-45-51.900N 072-46-41.000W	Fl R 4s			Red.	Private aid.

Moriches Bay

No.	Name and Location	Position	Characteristic	Height	Range	Structure	Remarks
30291	- Buoy 10	40-45-45.982N 072-48-31.485W				Red nun.	Maintained from Apr. 15 to Nov. 1.
30292	- Buoy 11	40-46-12.586N 072-48-02.529W				Green can.	Maintained from 15 April to 1 Nov.
30293	- Lighted Buoy 12	40-46-27.646N 072-47-46.584W	Q R		3	Red.	Maintained from 15 April to 1 Nov.
30294	- Buoy 14	40-46-29.920N 072-47-17.475W				Red nun.	Maitained from Apr. 15 to Nov. 1.
30295	- Lighted Buoy 15	40-46-37.415N 072-46-22.462W	Fl G 4s		4	Green.	Maintained from 15 April to 1 Nov.
30300	- Buoy 17	40-46-44.552N 072-45-46.127W				Green can.	Removed when endangered by ice.
30303	- Buoy 17A	40-46-48.935N 072-45-32.325W				Green can.	Removed when endangered by ice.
30304	- Danger Buoy West	40-46-40.713N 072-46-02.833W				White and orange diamond marked DANGER SEVERE SHOALING AHEAD.	Maintained from 15 Apr. to 15 Nov.
30305	- Lighted Buoy 18	40-46-45.313N 072-45-40.495W	Fl R 4s		3	Red.	Removed when endangered by ice.

(1) No.	(2) Name and Location	(3) Position	(4) Characteristic	(5) Height	(6) Range	(7) Structure	(8) Remarks
			NEW YORK - First District				
SHINNECOCK BAY TO EAST ROCKAWAY INLET							
Moriches Bay							
30315	- Buoy 21	40-46-52.166N 072-45-10.577W					
30320	- Buoy 20	40-46-48.946N 072-45-29.892W					
30323	- Tuthill Danger Buoy	40-46-53.318N 072-45-07.040W				White and orange diamond marked DANGER SEVERE SHOALING AHEAD.	Maintained from 15 Apr. to 15 Nov.
30325	- Lighted Buoy 23	40-46-55.295N 072-44-56.877W	Fl G 2.5s		4	Green.	Removed when endangered by ice.
30330	- Lighted Buoy 24	40-46-57.924N 072-44-42.999W	Fl R 2.5s		3	Red.	Removed when endangered by ice.
30333	- Danger Buoy East	40-47-13.838N 072-43-33.726W				White and orange diamond marked DANGER SEVERE SHOALING AHEAD.	Maintained from 15 Apr. to 15 Nov.
30335	- Buoy 26	40-47-04.698N 072-44-21.600W					
30340	- Buoy 27	40-47-05.126N 072-44-11.684W					
30341	- Buoy 28	40-47-09.687N 072-43-50.280W					
30345	Fish Creek Entrance Buoy 2	40-48-16.800N 072-43-22.200W				Red nun.	Maintained from Apr. 15 to Nov. 15. Private aid.
30350	Seatuck Cove Buoy 2	40-48-23.160N 072-43-37.560W				Red nun.	Maintained from May 15 to Nov. 1. Private aid.
30355	Seatuck Cove Buoy 4	40-48-45.600N 072-43-35.400W				Red nun.	Maintained from May 15 to Nov. 1. Private aid.
30360	Seatuck Cove Buoy 6	40-48-52.200N 072-43-28.300W				Red nun.	Maintained from May 15 to Nov. 1. Private aid.
30361	Heils Creek Lighted Entrance Buoy 1	40-48-24.360N 072-43-50.280W	Fl G 4s			Green.	Private aid.
30365	- Lighted Buoy 29	40-47-14.608N 072-43-30.480W	Fl G 2.5s		4		
30367	Hart Cove Lighted Buoy 1	40-47-54.300N 072-44-47.040W	Fl G 4s			Green.	Private aid.
30368	Hart Cove Lighted Buoy 2	40-48-05.100N 072-45-09.000W	Fl R 4s			Red.	Private aid.
30368.2	Hart Cove Lighted Buoy 3	40-47-58.700N 072-44-57.000W	Fl G 4s			Green.	Private aid.
30368.4	Hart Cove Lighted Buoy 5	40-48-01.600N 072-45-06.700W	Fl G 4s			Green.	Private aid.
30370	- Lighted Buoy 30	40-47-24.837N 072-42-46.495W	Fl R 4s		3	Red.	Removed when endangered by ice.
30375	- Lighted Buoy 31	40-47-42.542N 072-41-27.516W	Fl G 4s		4	Green.	Maintained from 15 April to 1 Nov.
30380	- Buoy 33	40-47-48.177N 072-41-01.095W				Green can.	Maintained from 15 April to 1 Nov.
30385	- Lighted Buoy 34	40-47-58.636N 072-40-12.145W	Q R		3	Red.	Removed when endangered by ice.
30390	Beaverdam Cove Buoy 1	40-48-15.000N 072-39-57.000W				Green can.	Maintained from Apr. 15 to Nov. 1. Private aid.
30395	Beaverdam Cove Buoy 2	40-48-20.400N 072-39-55.200W				Red nun.	Maintained from Apr. 15 to Nov. 1. Private aid.

(1) No.	(2) Name and Location	(3) Position	(4) Characteristic	(5) Height	(6) Range	(7) Structure	(8) Remarks

SHINNECOCK BAY TO EAST ROCKAWAY INLET

Moriches Bay

No.	Name and Location	Position	Characteristic	Height	Range	Structure	Remarks
30400	Beaverdam Cove Buoy 3	40-48-26.400N 072-39-55.200W				Green can.	Maintained from Apr. 15 to Nov. 1. Private aid.
30405	- Buoy 35	40-47-55.099N 072-39-44.486W				Green can.	Maintained from 15 April to 1 Nov.
30410	- Buoy 36	40-47-50.130N 072-39-15.450W				Red nun.	Maintained from 15 April to 1 Nov.
30415	- Lighted Buoy 37	40-47-48.194N 072-38-54.624W	Q G		3	Green.	Removed when endangered by ice.

Boat Basin
Aids maintained from Apr. 15 to Nov. 1.

No.	Name and Location	Position	Characteristic	Height	Range	Structure	Remarks
30425	- Buoy 2	40-47-55.800N 072-38-28.800W				Red nun.	Private aid.
30430	- LIGHT 3	40-47-56.400N 072-38-29.400W	Fl G 4s			On pile.	Private aid.
30435	- Buoy 4	40-48-07.200N 072-38-23.400W				Red nun.	Private aid.
30440	- LIGHT 6	40-48-12.600N 072-38-24.000W	Fl R 4s			On pile.	Maintained from Apr. 15 to Nov. 1. Private aid.

Forge River Channel
Aids maintained from May 1 to Nov. 1.

No.	Name and Location	Position	Characteristic	Height	Range	Structure	Remarks
30445	- Lighted Buoy 1	40-46-29.500N 072-48-36.900W	Fl G 4s			Green.	Private aid.
30450	- Lighted Buoy 2	40-46-30.700N 072-48-34.900W	Fl R 4s			Red.	Private aid.
30455	- Buoy 3	40-46-46.860N 072-48-53.580W				Green can.	Private aid.
30460	- Buoy 4	40-46-47.640N 072-48-52.620W				Red nun.	Private aid.
30465	- Buoy 5	40-47-06.420N 072-49-13.500W				Green can.	Private aid.
30470	- Lighted Buoy 6	40-47-06.900N 072-49-12.540W	Fl R 4s			Red.	Private aid.
30475	- Buoy 7	40-47-29.580N 072-49-35.520W				Green can.	Private aid.
30480	- Buoy 8	40-47-30.120N 072-49-34.680W				Red nun.	Private aid.

Moriches Bay

No.	Name and Location	Position	Characteristic	Height	Range	Structure	Remarks
30485	Senix Creek Entrance Lighted Buoy 1	40-46-57.420N 072-48-10.560W	Fl G 4s			Green.	Private aid.

Areskonk Creek Entrance
Aids maintained from May 1 to Nov. 1.

No.	Name and Location	Position	Characteristic	Height	Range	Structure	Remarks
30490	- Lighted Buoy 2	40-46-49.200N 072-47-50.760W	Fl R 4s			Red.	Private aid.
30495	Areskonk Creek Lighted Buoy 4	40-47-04.200N 072-47-48.700W	Fl R 4s			Red.	Private aid.

Moriches Bay

No.	Name and Location	Position	Characteristic	Height	Range	Structure	Remarks
30510	Orchard Neck Creek Entrance Lighted Buoy 1	40-46-55.920N 072-47-23.580W	Fl G 4s			Green.	Maintained from May 1 to Nov. 1. Private aid.

Tuthill Cove

No.	Name and Location	Position	Characteristic	Height	Range	Structure	Remarks
30515	- Buoy 2	40-47-02.568N 072-44-59.210W				Red nun.	Maintained from 15 April to 1 Nov.
30520	- Buoy 4	40-47-10.540N 072-45-03.196W				Red nun.	Maintained from 15 April to 1 Nov.

Quantuck Canal

No.	Name and Location	Position	Characteristic	Height	Range	Structure	Remarks
30559	- Daybeacon 3	40-47-52.952N 072-38-22.931W				SG on pile.	
30560	- Daybeacon 5	40-47-55.407N 072-38-08.034W				SG on pile.	

(1) No.	(2) Name and Location	(3) Position	(4) Characteristic	(5) Height	(6) Range	(7) Structure	(8) Remarks
			NEW YORK - First District				
	SHINNECOCK BAY TO EAST ROCKAWAY INLET						
	Moriches Bay						
	Quantuck Canal						
30565	- LIGHT 7 On edge of marsh.	40-48-10.177N 072-37-30.014W	Fl G 4s	14	4	SG on pile.	Removed when Endangered by ice.
30570	- Buoy 9	40-48-18.975N 072-37-08.533W				Green can.	Maintained from Apr. 15 to Nov. 1.
30575	- Lighted Buoy 10	40-48-23.801N 072-36-50.509W	Fl R 2.5s		3	Red.	Maintained from Apr. 15 to Nov. 1.
	Shinnecock Bay						
30580	- Buoy 1	40-49-07.028N 072-34-57.185W				Green can.	Maintained from 15 April to 1 Nov.
30583	- Buoy 3	40-49-19.761N 072-34-41.662W				Green can.	Maintained from 15 April to 1 Nov.
30585	QUANTUCK CANAL LIGHT 12 On edge of marsh.	40-48-50.113N 072-35-05.454W	Q R	14	3	TR on pile.	Removed when Endangered by ice.
30590	- LIGHT 2	40-49-06.897N 072-34-55.195W	Fl R 4s	16	3	TR on pile.	Removed when endangered by ice.
30600	- Buoy 4	40-49-31.259N 072-34-27.337W				Red nun.	Maintained from 15 April to 1 Nov.
	Daves Creek *Aids maintained from Apr. 15 to Nov. 15.*						
30605	- Buoy 1	40-50-12.780N 072-34-11.280W				Green can.	Private aid.
30610	- Buoy 2	40-50-13.620N 072-34-11.160W				Red nun.	Private aid.
30615	- Buoy 3	40-50-11.520N 072-34-16.800W				Green can.	Private aid.
30620	- Buoy 4	40-50-12.060N 072-34-16.800W				Red nun.	Private aid.
	Phillips Creek *Aids maintained from Apr. 15 to Nov. 15.*						
30625	- Buoy 1	40-49-42.600N 072-34-29.200W				Green can.	Private aid.
30630	- Buoy 2	40-49-42.060N 072-34-23.760W				Red nun.	Private aid.
30635	- Buoy 4	40-49-48.300N 072-34-38.500W				Red nun.	Private aid.
30640	- Buoy 5	40-49-50.800N 072-34-45.400W				Green can.	Private aid.
	Shinnecock Bay						
30645	Weesuck Creek Buoy 2	40-50-24.000N 072-34-07.800W				Red nun.	Maintained from Apr. 15 to Nov. 15. Private aid.
30650	Weesuck Creek Buoy 4	40-50-32.300N 072-34-11.000W				Red nun.	Maintained from Apr. 15 to Nov. 15. Private aid.
30655	Weesuck Creek Buoy 6	40-50-40.600N 072-34-14.300W				Red nun.	Maintained from Apr. 15 to Nov. 15. Private aid.
30660	- Lighted Buoy 6	40-49-48.193N 072-34-07.534W	Fl R 2.5s		3	Red.	Maintained from 15 Apr. to 1 Nov.
30670	- Buoy 8	40-49-57.681N 072-33-34.786W				Red nun.	Maintained from 15 Apr. to 1 Nov.
30675	- Lighted Buoy 9	40-50-10.091N 072-32-56.488W	Fl G 4s		4	Green.	Maintained from 15 Apr. to 1 Nov.
30680	- Buoy 10	40-50-33.462N 072-32-25.852W				Red nun.	Maintained from 15 Apr. to 1 Nov.

(1) No.	(2) Name and Location	(3) Position	(4) Characteristic	(5) Height	(6) Range	(7) Structure	(8) Remarks

NEW YORK - First District

SHINNECOCK BAY TO EAST ROCKAWAY INLET

Shinnecock Bay

(1) No.	(2) Name and Location	(3) Position	(4) Characteristic	(5) Height	(6) Range	(7) Structure	(8) Remarks
30685	- Lighted Buoy 13	40-50-39.164N 072-31-20.969W	Fl G 4s		4	Green.	Maintained from 15 Apr. to 1 Nov.
30690	- Lighted Buoy 12	40-50-50.529N 072-32-05.792W	Fl R 4s		3	Red.	Maintained from 15 Apr. to 1 Nov.
30695	- Buoy 16	40-50-37.123N 072-30-43.065W				Red nun.	Maintained from 15 Apr. to 1 Nov.
30700	Ponquogue South Channel Buoy 3S	40-50-55.020N 072-30-03.415W				Green can.	
30705	Ponquogue South Channel Buoy 2S	40-50-48.664N 072-29-58.896W				Red nun.	

Smith Creek
Aids maintained from May 15 to Nov. 1 unless otherwise noted.

(1) No.	(2) Name and Location	(3) Position	(4) Characteristic	(5) Height	(6) Range	(7) Structure	(8) Remarks
30710	- Buoy 1	40-50-43.900N 072-31-00.600W				Green can.	Private aid.
30715	- Buoy 1A	40-50-51.700N 072-31-04.300W				Green can.	Maintained from Apr. 15 to Nov. 15. Private aid.
30720	- Buoy 2	40-50-51.600N 072-31-03.600W				Red nun.	Private aid.
30725	- Buoy 3	40-50-57.900N 072-31-11.300W				Green can.	Private aid.
30730	- Buoy 4	40-51-06.600N 072-31-19.600W				Red nun.	Private aid.
30735	- Buoy 6	40-51-21.600N 072-31-30.100W				Red.	Private aid.

Shinnecock Bay

(1) No.	(2) Name and Location	(3) Position	(4) Characteristic	(5) Height	(6) Range	(7) Structure	(8) Remarks
30740	Wells Creek Entrance Buoy 1	40-51-01.000N 072-31-04.500W				Green can.	Maintained from Apr. 15 to Nov. 15. Private aid.
30745	Wells Creek Entrance Buoy 2	40-51-00.400N 072-31-03.600W				Red nun.	Maintained from Apr. 15 to Nov. 15. Private aid.
30750	Penny Pond Entrance Buoy 1	40-50-58.680N 072-30-48.180W				Green can.	Maintained from Apr. 15 to Nov. 15. Private aid.
30755	Penny Pond Entrance Buoy 2	40-50-58.380N 072-30-47.460W				Red nun.	Maintained from Apr. 15 to Nov. 15. Private aid.
30760	- Buoy 15	40-50-38.174N 072-30-56.441W				Green can.	Maintained from 15 Apr. to 1 Nov.
30765	- Buoy 19	40-50-41.391N 072-29-56.291W				Green can.	
30770	- Lighted Buoy 17	40-50-36.713N 072-30-13.135W	Fl G 2.5s		4	Green.	Replaced by can when endangered by ice.
30820	- Junction Lighted Buoy SI	40-50-40.800N 072-29-48.349W	Fl (2+1)G 6s		4	Green and red bands.	Replaced by can when endangered by ice.
30825	- Buoy 23	40-51-00.337N 072-29-46.562W				Green can.	
30830	- Buoy 22	40-50-44.394N 072-29-45.833W				Red nun.	
30835	- Buoy 24	40-51-01.943N 072-29-43.851W				Red nun.	
30845	Ponquogue Channel Buoy 4	40-50-59.819N 072-30-04.516W				Red nun.	
30847	Ponquogue Channel Buoy 6	40-51-02.985N 072-29-59.845W					
30850	- Lighted Buoy 25	40-51-10.391N 072-29-40.379W	Fl G 4s		4	Green.	Replaced by can from Nov. 1 to Apr. 15.
30855	- Buoy 26	40-51-11.346N 072-29-38.661W				Red nun.	

(1) No.	(2) Name and Location	(3) Position	(4) Characteristic	(5) Height	(6) Range	(7) Structure	(8) Remarks
			NEW YORK - First District				

SHINNECOCK BAY TO EAST ROCKAWAY INLET

Shinnecock Bay

(1) No.	(2) Name and Location	(3) Position	(4) Characteristic	(5) Height	(6) Range	(7) Structure	(8) Remarks
30860	- Buoy 27	40-51-50.895N 072-29-21.431W				Green can.	
30865	- *Lighted Buoy 29*	40-52-36.028N 072-29-02.073W	Fl G 4s		4	Green.	Replaced by can from Nov. 1 to Apr. 15.
30867	- Buoy 30	40-52-39.739N 072-29-23.231W				Red nun.	
30870	- Buoy 31	40-52-40.680N 072-29-30.838W				Green can.	
30872	- Buoy 32	40-52-44.300N 072-29-50.950W				Red nun.	
30875	- *Lighted Buoy 34*	40-52-45.581N 072-29-59.950W	Q R		3	Red.	Replaced by nun when endangered by ice.
30885	OLD FORT POND LIGHT 1	40-52-25.200N 072-26-35.880W	Fl G 6s	6		SB on pile.	Maintained from May 1 to Nov. 1. Private aid.

Jones Inlet
Positions of buoys frequently shifted with changing conditions.

(1) No.	(2) Name and Location	(3) Position	(4) Characteristic	(5) Height	(6) Range	(7) Structure	(8) Remarks
30890	- LIGHT	40-34-23.600N 073-34-32.378W	Fl W 2.5s	33	4	NR on white skeleton tower.	
30900	- *Lighted Whistle Buoy JI*	40-33-37.551N 073-35-13.094W	Mo (A) W		4	Red and white stripes with red spherical topmark.	
30905	- *Lighted Buoy 1*	40-33-58.788N 073-34-56.257W	Fl G 4s		3	Green.	
30910	- *Lighted Buoy 2*	40-33-58.285N 073-34-50.906W	Fl R 4s		3	Red.	
30920	- Buoy 3	40-34-21.594N 073-34-54.203W	Fl G 2.5s		3	Green can.	
30925	- *Lighted Buoy 4*	40-34-20.590N 073-34-46.893W	Q R		3	Red nun.	
30930	- *Lighted Buoy 5*	40-34-49.965N 073-34-48.933W	Q G		3		
30935	- *Lighted Buoy 6*	40-34-50.042N 073-34-42.826W	Fl R 2.5s		3	Red.	
30940	- *Lighted Buoy 7*	40-35-13.153N 073-34-22.733W	Fl G 6s		3	Green can.	Removed when endangered by ice.
30945	- Buoy 8	40-35-07.704N 073-34-23.118W				Red nun.	
30950	- Buoy 9	40-35-22.019N 073-34-16.850W				Green can.	
30951	- Buoy 11	40-35-32.445N 073-34-15.742W				Green can.	
30955	- Buoy 12	40-35-33.775N 073-34-08.153W				Red nun.	
30960	- Buoy 13	40-35-41.174N 073-34-11.919W				Green can.	
30961	Alder Island Shoal Buoy 1A	40-35-40.465N 073-34-18.267W				Green can.	
30962	Alder Island Shoal Buoy 2A	40-35-42.937N 073-34-16.005W				Red nun.	Removed when endangered by ice.
30965	- *Lighted Buoy 14*	40-35-46.485N 073-34-04.554W	Q R		3	Red.	Replaced by nun when endangered by ice.
30970	- Buoy 15	40-35-49.219N 073-34-08.315W				Green can.	
30975	- *Lighted Buoy 16*	40-36-04.727N 073-34-06.683W	Fl R 4s		3	Red.	Replaced by nun when endangered by ice.
30980	- Buoy 17	40-36-06.729N 073-34-10.141W				Green can.	

(1) No.	(2) Name and Location	(3) Position	(4) Characteristic	(5) Height	(6) Range	(7) Structure	(8) Remarks
			NEW YORK - First District				

SHINNECOCK BAY TO EAST ROCKAWAY INLET

Sloop Channel
Positions of buoys frequently shifted with changing conditions.

(1) No.	(2) Name and Location	(3) Position	(4) Characteristic	(5) Height	(6) Range	(7) Structure	(8) Remarks
30995	- *Junction Lighted Buoy SJ*	40-35-20.918N 073-34-11.849W	Fl (2+1)G 6s		4	Green and red bands.	
31000	- Entrance Buoy 2	40-35-18.450N 073-34-07.280W				Red nun.	
31005	- Entrance Buoy 3	40-35-28.842N 073-33-53.070W				Green can.	
31010	- LIGHT 4	40-35-30.343N 073-33-31.132W	Fl R 4s	12	3	TR on pile.	
31015	West End Boat Basin Buoy 1	40-35-31.853N 073-33-20.891W				Green can.	
31020	COAST GUARD STATION JONES BEACH BREAKWATER LIGHT 2	40-35-28.063N 073-33-19.082W	Fl R 2.5s	6	3	TR on breakwall.	
31025	- Buoy 5	40-35-42.307N 073-33-27.733W				Green can.	
31030	- *Lighted Buoy 6*	40-35-51.686N 073-33-03.916W	Fl R 2.5s		3	Red.	
31040	- *Lighted Buoy 8*	40-35-58.425N 073-31-40.736W	Fl R 4s		3	Red.	Remove when endangered by ice.
31045	- *Lighted Buoy 9*	40-36-02.210N 073-31-20.378W	Fl G 4s		4	Green.	Removed when endangered by ice.
31050	- Buoy 10	40-35-59.417N 073-31-10.615W				Red nun.	Removed when endangered by ice.
31055	- LIGHT 11	40-36-14.847N 073-31-02.597W	Q G	12	3	SG on pile.	
31070	- Buoy 12	40-36-33.278N 073-30-24.008W				Red nun.	Removed when endangered by ice.
31075	- *Lighted Buoy 15*	40-36-45.398N 073-30-14.406W	Q G		3	Green.	Removed when endangered by ice.
31085	- Daybeacon 18	40-37-08.036N 073-30-19.352W				TR on pile.	
31090	- Buoy 19	40-37-08.119N 073-30-24.153W				Green can.	
31095	- LIGHT 20	40-37-15.042N 073-30-23.048W	Q R	14	3	TR on pile.	
31100	- Daybeacon 21	40-37-17.684N 073-30-28.444W				SG on pile.	
31105	- Daybeacon 23	40-37-21.884N 073-30-19.391W				SG on pile.	

State Boat Channel
Positions of buoys frequently shifted with changing conditions.

(1) No.	(2) Name and Location	(3) Position	(4) Characteristic	(5) Height	(6) Range	(7) Structure	(8) Remarks
31110	- Daybeacon 1	40-37-23.848N 073-29-46.559W				SG on pile.	
31120	- Daybeacon 3	40-37-11.552N 073-29-53.774W				SG on pile.	
31125	- Buoy 5	40-36-54.134N 073-29-57.952W				Green can.	Maintained from 1 April to 15 Nov.
31130	- LIGHT 4	40-36-57.225N 073-30-01.532W	Fl R 2.5s	10	3	TR on pile.	
31145	- Daybeacon 9	40-36-41.722N 073-29-41.845W				SG on pile.	
31150	- LIGHT 10	40-36-35.286N 073-29-35.976W	Fl R 2.5s	12	3	TR on pile.	

Zach's Bay
Maintained from May 1 to Nov. 1.

(1) No.	(2) Name and Location	(3) Position	(4) Characteristic	(5) Height	(6) Range	(7) Structure	(8) Remarks
31151	- Channel Buoy ZB1	40-36-27.000N 073-29-20.880W				Green can.	Private aid.
31151.1	- Channel Buoy ZB2	40-36-27.240N 073-29-22.200W				Red nun.	Private aid.

(1) No.	(2) Name and Location	(3) Position	(4) Characteristic	(5) Height	(6) Range	(7) Structure	(8) Remarks
			NEW YORK - First District				

SHINNECOCK BAY TO EAST ROCKAWAY INLET
State Boat Channel
Zach's Bay
Maintained from May 1 to Nov. 1.

(1) No.	(2) Name and Location	(3) Position	(4) Characteristic	(5) Height	(6) Range	(7) Structure	(8) Remarks
31151.2	- Channel Buoy ZB3	40-36-22.980N 073-29-22.980W				Green can.	Private aid.
31151.3	- Channel Buoy ZB4	40-36-20.640N 073-29-25.020W				Red nun.	Private aid.
31151.5	- Channel Buoy ZB6	40-36-15.120N 073-29-26.820W				Red nun.	Private aid.

State Boat Channel
Positions of buoys frequently shifted with changing conditions.

(1) No.	(2) Name and Location	(3) Position	(4) Characteristic	(5) Height	(6) Range	(7) Structure	(8) Remarks
31160	- Daybeacon 13	40-36-28.430N 073-29-13.412W				SG on pile.	
31175	- *Lighted Buoy 15*	40-36-22.376N 073-29-00.056W	Q G		3	Green.	Maintained from 1 April to 15 Nov.
31180	- Buoy 16	40-36-26.551N 073-28-42.067W				Red nun.	Maintained from 1April to 15 Nov.
31185	- Daybeacon 17	40-36-37.967N 073-28-17.963W				SG on pile.	
31190	- LIGHT 19	40-36-49.856N 073-27-42.119W	Fl G 2.5s	15	4	SG on pile.	
31215	- LIGHT 25	40-37-00.483N 073-25-57.400W	Fl G 2.5s		3	SG on pile.	
31220	- LIGHT 29	40-37-15.652N 073-25-00.068W	Fl G 4s	12	4	SG on pile.	
31235	- *Lighted Buoy 35*	40-37-28.796N 073-23-58.838W	Fl G 2.5s		4	Green.	Maintained from 1 April to 15 Nov.
31245	- Daybeacon 38	40-37-41.106N 073-22-53.724W				TR on pile.	
31255	- LIGHT 42	40-37-57.863N 073-21-42.820W	Fl R 4s	12	3	TR on pile.	Removed when endangered by ice.
31260	- Daybeacon 44	40-38-07.500N 073-21-04.239W				TR on pile.	
31265	- LIGHT 47	40-38-17.839N 073-20-32.844W	Q G	12	3	SG on pile.	Removed when endangered by ice.
31270	- Daybeacon 48	40-38-29.218N 073-20-02.213W				TR on pile.	
31275	- LIGHT 49	40-38-38.662N 073-19-55.075W	Fl G 4s	12	4	SG on pile.	Removed when endangered by ice.
31280	- Daybeacon 50	40-38-37.944N 073-19-48.038W				TR on pile.	
31285	- Daybeacon 52	40-38-48.002N 073-19-28.955W				TR on pile.	
31295	- Buoy 54	40-38-53.374N 073-19-18.790W				Red nun.	Maintained from 1April to 15 Nov.
31300	- Buoy 55	40-38-56.450N 073-19-12.011W				Green can.	Maintained from 1April to 15 Nov.
31305	- Buoy 56	40-38-58.147N 073-18-55.732W				Red nun.	Maintained from 1April to 15 Nov.
31310	- *Lighted Buoy 57*	40-39-00.402N 073-18-53.517W	Fl G 2.5s		4	Green.	Removed when endangered by ice.
31315	- *Lighted Buoy 58*	40-38-59.303N 073-18-37.400W	Fl R 4s		3	Red.	Removed when endangered by ice.
31320	- Buoy 59	40-39-01.040N 073-18-34.934W				Green can.	Maintained from 1 April to 15 Nov.

(1)No.	(2)Name and Location	(3)Position	(4)Characteristic	(5)Height	(6)Range	(7)Structure	(8)Remarks
			NEW YORK - First District				

SHINNECOCK BAY TO EAST ROCKAWAY INLET
State Boat Channel
Positions of buoys frequently shifted with changing conditions.

(1)No.	(2)Name and Location	(3)Position	(4)Characteristic	(5)Height	(6)Range	(7)Structure	(8)Remarks
31325	- Buoy 61	40-39-00.638N 073-18-21.235W				Green can.	Maintained from 1 April to 15 Nov.
31330	- Daybeacon 62	40-38-58.957N 073-18-08.686W				TR on pile.	
31340	- *Lighted Buoy 64*	40-38-58.361N 073-17-52.235W	Fl R 4s		3	Red.	Maintained from 1 April to 15 Nov.
31350	- Daybeacon 66	40-38-53.976N 073-17-23.792W				TR on pile.	
31360	- LIGHT 68	40-38-44.872N 073-16-56.405W	Fl R 4s	12	3	TR on pile.	Light removed when endangered by ice.

Sloop Channel
Oak Island Channel
Positions of buoys frequently shifted with changing conditions.

31380	- JUNCTION LIGHT SO	40-39-00.388N 073-17-28.837W	Fl (2+1)G 6s	12	4	JG on pile.	Removed when endangered by ice.
31385	- Buoy 2	40-39-12.999N 073-17-36.315W				Red nun.	Maintained from 1 April to 15 Nov.
31390	- Buoy 3	40-39-22.424N 073-17-42.878W				Green can.	Maintained from 1 April to 15 Nov.
31395	- Buoy 4	40-39-29.683N 073-17-45.169W				Red nun.	Maintained from 1 April to 15 Nov.
31400	- Buoy 5	40-39-36.090N 073-17-50.295W				Green can.	Maintained from 1 April to 15 Nov.
31405	- Buoy 6	40-39-43.830N 073-17-52.597W				Red nun.	Maintained from 1 April to 15 Nov.
31410	- Buoy 7	40-39-55.983N 073-18-01.378W				Green can.	Maintained from 1 April to 15 Nov.
31415	- Buoy 8	40-40-01.037N 073-18-02.093W				Red nun.	Maintained from 1 April to 15 Nov.
31420	- *Entrance Lighted Buoy 9*	40-40-08.444N 073-18-08.821W	Fl G 2.5s		4	Green.	Maintained from 1 April to 15 Nov.

State Boat Channel
Positions of buoys frequently shifted with changing conditions.

31430	- Daybeacon 74	40-38-32.423N 073-16-08.019W				TR on pile.	
31435	- Buoy 75	40-38-39.990N 073-16-32.396W				Green can.	Maintained from Apr. 1 to Nov. 15.
31436	- Buoy 76	40-38-34.986N 073-15-56.405W				Red nun.	Maintained from 1 April to 15 Nov.
31440	- Buoy 77	40-38-35.143N 073-15-23.237W				Green can.	Maintained from Apr. 1 to Nov. 15.
31445	- Buoy 78	40-38-33.827N 073-15-33.409W				Red nun.	Maintained from Apr. 1 to Nov. 15.
31450	- Buoy 79	40-38-36.798N 073-15-14.961W				Green can.	Maintained from Apr. 1 to Nov. 15.
31455	- Buoy 80	40-38-36.523N 073-15-05.123W				Red nun.	Removed when endangered by ice.
31460	- Buoy 81	40-38-38.251N 073-14-57.011W				Green can.	Maintained from Apr 1 to Nov 15.

(1) No.	(2) Name and Location	(3) Position	(4) Characteristic	(5) Height	(6) Range	(7) Structure	(8) Remarks
			NEW YORK - First District				

SHINNECOCK BAY TO EAST ROCKAWAY INLET

Sloop Channel

State Boot Channel
Positions of buoys frequently shifted with changing conditions.

31462	- Buoy 82	40-38-36.376N 073-14-56.036W				Red nun.	Removed when endangered by ice.
31465	- Buoy 84	40-38-33.987N 073-14-50.453W				Red nun.	Removed when endangered by ice.
31470	- Buoy 86	40-38-31.385N 073-14-46.867W				Green.	Removed when endangered by ice.
31475	- Lighted Buoy 87	40-38-31.790N 073-14-43.045W	Q G		3	Green.	Maintained from 1 April to 15 Nov.
31480	- Buoy 88	40-38-27.920N 073-14-40.509W				Red nun.	
31485	- Buoy 89	40-38-25.988N 073-14-34.645W				Green can.	
31487	- Lighted Buoy 90	40-38-22.018N 073-14-31.969W	Fl R 4s		3	Red.	Maintained from 1 April to 15 Nov.
31490	- Buoy 91	40-38-19.219N 073-14-24.301W				Green can.	

East Rockaway Inlet
Positions of buoys frequently shifted with changing conditions.

31495	- Lighted Bell Buoy ER	40-34-17.026N 073-45-49.026W	Mo (A) W		5	Red and white stripes with red spherical topmark.	
31500	- BREAKWATER LIGHT	40-34-56.632N 073-45-17.214W	Fl W 4s	34	4	NR on skeleton tower.	
31515	- Lighted Buoy 2	40-34-42.542N 073-45-42.942W	Fl R 4s		3	Red.	Replaced by nun when endangered by ice.
31520	- Lighted Buoy 3	40-34-52.497N 073-45-41.515W	Fl G 4s		3		
31525	- Buoy 4	40-34-51.599N 073-45-37.776W				Red nun.	
31530	- Lighted Buoy 5	40-35-08.700N 073-45-32.195W	Fl G 4s		4	Green.	Replaced by can when endangered by ice.
31535	- Lighted Buoy 6	40-35-06.201N 073-45-30.721W	Q R		3	Red.	Replaced by nun when endangered by ice.
31540	- Buoy 7	40-35-16.050N 073-45-18.596W				Green can.	
31545	- Buoy 8	40-35-14.087N 073-45-16.661W				Red nun.	
31550	- Lighted Buoy 9	40-35-23.559N 073-45-05.917W	Fl G 4s		4	Green.	Replaced by can when endangered by ice.
31555	- Buoy 10	40-35-21.653N 073-45-03.880W				Red nun.	
31560	- Buoy 12	40-35-31.683N 073-44-48.522W				Red nun.	

Bannister Creek
Aids maintained from May 1 to Nov. 1.

31561	- Channel Buoy BC1	40-35-41.820N 073-44-07.860W				Green can.	Private aid.
31562	- Channel Buoy BC2	40-35-40.020N 073-44-07.320W				Red nun.	Private aid.
31563	- Channel Buoy BC3	40-35-44.880N 073-44-07.380W				Green can.	Private aid.
31564	- Channel Buoy BC4	40-35-44.460N 073-44-06.600W				Red nun.	Private aid.
31564.1	- Channel Buoy BC5	40-36-05.160N 073-44-03.600W				Green can.	Private aid.

(1) No.	(2) Name and Location	(3) Position	(4) Characteristic	(5) Height	(6) Range	(7) Structure	(8) Remarks

NEW YORK - First District

SHINNECOCK BAY TO EAST ROCKAWAY INLET

East Rockaway Inlet

Bannister Creek
Aids maintained from May 1 to Nov. 1.

(1) No.	(2) Name and Location	(3) Position	(4) Characteristic	(5) Height	(6) Range	(7) Structure	(8) Remarks
31564.2	- Channel Buoy BC6	40-36-03.960N 073-44-03.600W				Red nun.	Private aid.
31564.3	- Channel Buoy BC7	40-36-06.840N 073-44-00.360W				Green can.	Private aid.
31564.4	- Channel Buoy BC8	40-36-06.120N 073-43-59.400W				Red nun.	Private aid.

Hempstead Bay

Reynolds Channel

(1) No.	(2) Name and Location	(3) Position	(4) Characteristic	(5) Height	(6) Range	(7) Structure	(8) Remarks
31565	- *Lighted Buoy 1*	40-35-28.949N 073-43-35.098W	Fl G 2.5s		3	Green.	Replaced by can when endangered by ice.
31575	- *Lighted Buoy 3*	40-35-30.017N 073-42-47.353W	Fl G 4s		3	Green.	Replaced by can when endangered by ice.
31580	- *Lighted Buoy 5*	40-35-25.297N 073-41-45.215W	Fl G 6s		3	Green.	Replaced by can when endangered by ice.
31585	- LIGHT 7	40-35-25.176N 073-41-20.751W	Fl G 2.5s	16	4	SG on pile.	

Woodsburgh Channel
Aids maintained from May 1 to Nov. 1.

(1) No.	(2) Name and Location	(3) Position	(4) Characteristic	(5) Height	(6) Range	(7) Structure	(8) Remarks
31590	- Daybeacon A1	40-36-07.140N 073-41-09.180W				SG on pile.	Private aid.
31595	- Buoy A2	40-36-08.640N 073-41-08.340W				Red nun.	Private aid.
31600	- Daybeacon A4	40-36-12.780N 073-41-18.480W				TR on pile.	Private aid.
31605	- Buoy A5	40-36-12.120N 073-41-19.560W				Green can.	Private aid.
31610	- Buoy A6	40-36-17.940N 073-41-27.720W				Red nun.	Private aid.
31615	- Buoy A7	40-36-15.120N 073-41-27.720W				Green can.	Private aid.
31620	- Daybeacon A8	40-36-24.720N 073-41-29.880W				TR on pile.	Private aid.
31625	- Buoy A9	40-36-34.620N 073-41-30.120W				Green can.	Private aid.
31630	- Buoy A12	40-36-38.580N 073-41-28.680W				Red nun.	Private aid.
31635	- Buoy A13	40-36-42.000N 073-41-30.840W				Green can.	Private aid.
31640	- Buoy A14	40-36-43.680N 073-41-30.410W				Red nun.	Private aid.
31645	- Buoy A16	40-36-49.200N 073-41-35.880W				Red nun.	Private aid.
31650	- Buoy A17	40-36-48.240N 073-41-35.520W				Green can.	Private aid.
31653	- Buoy A18	40-36-52.080N 073-41-38.460W				Red nun.	Private aid.
31655	- Buoy A19	40-36-53.400N 073-41-40.500W				Green can.	Private aid.
31656	- Buoy A19-A	40-36-58.200N 073-41-43.020W				Green can.	Private aid.
31660	- Buoy A20	40-36-59.700N 073-41-44.100W				Red nun.	Private aid.
31665	- Buoy A21	40-37-01.200N 073-41-47.520W				Green can.	Private aid.
31670	- Buoy A22	40-37-02.580N 073-41-49.560W				Red nun.	Private aid.
31675	- Buoy A23	40-37-02.520N 073-41-52.380W				Green can.	Private aid.
31677	- Buoy A24	40-37-03.600N 073-41-54.540W				Red nun.	Private aid.

(1) No.	(2) Name and Location	(3) Position	(4) Characteristic	(5) Height	(6) Range	(7) Structure	(8) Remarks

NEW YORK - First District

SHINNECOCK BAY TO EAST ROCKAWAY INLET

Hempstead Bay

Woodsburgh Channel
Aids maintained from May 1 to Nov. 1.

(1)	(2)	(3)	(4)	(5)	(6)	(7)	(8)
31680	- Buoy A25	40-37-04.440N 073-42-00.360W				Green can.	Private aid.
31685	- Buoy A26	40-37-03.840N 073-42-01.440W				Red nun.	Private aid.
31690	- Buoy A27	40-36-59.160N 073-42-02.280W				Green can.	Private aid.
31695	- Buoy A28	40-37-00.960N 073-42-03.060W				Red nun.	Private aid.
31700	- Buoy A29	40-36-53.700N 073-42-01.860W				Green can.	Private aid.
31705	- Buoy A30	40-36-53.580N 073-42-03.240W				Red nun.	Private aid.
31710	- Buoy A31	40-36-51.660N 073-42-13.380W				Green can.	Private aid.
31715	- Buoy A32	40-36-52.620N 073-42-09.540W				Red nun.	Private aid.
31720	- Buoy A33	40-36-50.820N 073-42-19.620W				Green can.	Private aid.
31725	- Buoy A34	40-36-51.420N 073-42-19.920W				Red nun.	Private aid.
31730	- Buoy A38	40-36-55.200N 073-42-23.100W				Red nun.	Private aid.

Broseware Bay - North End
Aids maintained from May 1 to Nov. 1.

(1)	(2)	(3)	(4)	(5)	(6)	(7)	(8)
31735	Broseware Bay North End Buoy AB1	40-37-04.620N 073-41-55.680W				Green can.	Private aid.
31740	Broseware Bay North End Buoy AB2	40-37-06.600N 073-41-54.600W				Red nun.	Private aid.
31743	Broseware Bay North End Buoy AB3	40-37-07.800N 073-41-54.600W				Green can.	Private aid.
31745	Broseware Bay North End Buoy AB4	40-37-09.780N 073-41-52.680W				Red nun.	Private aid.

Broad Channel
Aids maintained from May 1 to Nov. 1.

(1)	(2)	(3)	(4)	(5)	(6)	(7)	(8)
31750	- Junction Buoy B	40-35-33.720N 073-41-05.460W				Green and red bands; can.	Private aid.
31755	- Buoy B4	40-35-45.060N 073-41-03.480W				Red nun.	Private aid.
31760	- Buoy B8	40-35-53.760N 073-41-04.380W				Red nun.	Private aid.
31762	- Buoy B10	40-36-02.940N 073-41-03.180W				Red nun.	Private aid.
31765	- Buoy B11	40-36-06.000N 073-41-03.000W				Green can.	Private aid.
31770	- Buoy B12	40-36-07.500N 073-40-58.500W				Red nun.	Private aid.
31775	- Daybeacon B13	40-36-12.600N 073-40-54.840W				SG on pile.	Private aid.
31780	- Buoy B14	40-36-14.700N 073-40-48.900W				Red nun.	Private aid.
31790	- Buoy B19	40-36-24.840N 073-40-39.180W				Green can.	Private aid.
31795	- Buoy B20	40-36-23.520N 073-40-38.940W				Red nun.	Private aid.
31800	- Buoy B22	40-36-32.880N 073-40-35.760W				Red nun.	Private aid.
31805	- Buoy B24	40-36-38.940N 073-40-33.960W				Red nun.	Private aid.
31810	- Buoy B25	40-36-42.060N 073-40-34.680W				Green can.	Private aid.
31815	- Buoy B26	40-36-49.560N 073-40-29.040W				Red nun.	Private aid.

(1) No.	(2) Name and Location	(3) Position	(4) Characteristic	(5) Height	(6) Range	(7) Structure	(8) Remarks

NEW YORK - First District

SHINNECOCK BAY TO EAST ROCKAWAY INLET

Hempstead Bay

Broad Channel

Aids maintained from May 1 to Nov. 1.

(1) No.	(2) Name and Location	(3) Position	(7) Structure	(8) Remarks
31820	- Buoy B27	40-36-53.160N 073-40-29.700W	Green can.	Private aid.
31825	- Buoy B28	40-36-57.060N 073-40-30.120W	Red nun.	Private aid.
31830	- Daybeacon B29	40-36-57.900N 073-40-31.440W	SG on pile.	Private aid.
31835	- Buoy B30	40-37-04.260N 073-40-32.280W	Red nun.	Private aid.
31836	- Daybeacon B31	40-37-04.980N 073-40-34.020W	SG on pile.	Private aid.
31839	- Daybeacon B33	40-37-07.500N 073-40-36.360W	SG on pile.	Private aid.
31845	- Daybeacon B35	40-37-07.380N 073-40-42.540W	SG on pile.	Private aid.
31846	- Buoy B36	40-37-08.100N 073-40-52.080W	Red nun.	Private aid.
31850	- Daybeacon B37	40-37-08.100N 073-40-53.940W	SG on pile.	Private aid.
31855	- Buoy B38	40-37-13.380N 073-40-56.580W	Red nun.	Private aid.
31860	- Daybeacon B39	40-37-18.780N 073-40-59.760W	SG on pile.	Private aid.
31865	- Buoy B40	40-37-17.820N 073-40-58.320W	Red nun.	Private aid.
31870	- Buoy B42	40-37-25.260N 073-41-04.680W	Red nun.	Private aid.
31875	- Buoy B43	40-37-24.240N 073-41-05.580W	Green can.	Private aid.
31885	- Buoy B47	40-37-31.320N 073-40-50.460W	Green can	Private aid.
31890	- Buoy B48	40-37-33.780N 073-40-42.360W	Red nun.	Private aid.

Hewlett Bay Extension

Aidsmaintained from May 1 to Nov. 1.

(1) No.	(2) Name and Location	(3) Position	(7) Structure	(8) Remarks
31900	- Buoy B50	40-37-36.420N 073-40-31.260W	Red nun.	Private aid.
31910	- Buoy B52	40-37-36.360N 073-40-22.560W	Red nun.	Private aid.
31915	- Buoy B53	40-37-37.500N 073-40-28.980W	Green can.	Private aid.
31920	- Buoy B54	40-37-36.300N 073-40-16.800W	Red nun.	Private aid.
31925	- Buoy B55	40-37-38.280N 073-40-16.500W	Green can.	Private aid.
31930	- Buoy B56	40-37-33.360N 073-40-11.580W	Red nun.	Private aid.
31935	- Buoy B57	40-37-34.500N 073-40-08.520W	Green can.	Private aid.
31940	- Buoy B58	40-37-31.860N 073-40-07.260W	Red nun.	Private aid.
31945	- Daybeacon B59	40-37-34.080N 073-40-03.960W	SG on pole.	Private aid.
31950	- Buoy B60	40-37-27.720N 073-40-07.080W	Red nun.	Private aid.
31955	- Buoy B61	40-37-27.240N 073-40-04.740W	Green can.	Private aid.
31960	- Buoy B62	40-37-22.560N 073-40-07.500W	Red nun.	Private aid.
31965	- Buoy B63	40-37-23.040N 073-40-04.800W	Green can.	Private aid.

(1) No.	(2) Name and Location	(3) Position	(4) Characteristic	(5) Height	(6) Range	(7) Structure	(8) Remarks
			NEW YORK - First District				
	SHINNECOCK BAY TO EAST ROCKAWAY INLET						
	Hempstead Bay						
	Reynolds Channel						
31970	- LIGHT 9	40-35-44.672N 073-40-25.957W	Fl G 4s	12	4	SG on pile.	
	Hog Island Channel *Aids maintainedfrom May 1 to Nov. 1.*						
31975	- Lighted Buoy C1	40-35-46.380N 073-39-55.860W	Fl G 4s			Green.	Private aid.
31980	- Lighted Buoy C2	40-35-47.100N 073-39-50.880W	Fl R 4s			Red.	Private aid.
31985	- Lighted Buoy C3	40-36-01.200N 073-40-10.260W	Fl G 4s			Green.	Private aid.
31990	- Lighted Buoy C5	40-36-10.440N 073-40-15.000W	Fl G 4s			Green.	Private aid.
31995	- Lighted Buoy C7	40-36-23.100N 073-40-04.320W	Fl G 4s			Green.	Private aid.
32000	- Lighted Buoy C9	40-36-25.440N 073-39-50.040W	Fl G 4s			Green.	Private aid.
32005	- Lighted Buoy C11	40-36-25.680N 073-39-38.340W	Fl G 4s			Green.	Private aid.
32010	- Lighted Buoy C13	40-36-28.020N 073-39-29.520W	Fl G 4s			Green.	Private aid.
32015	- Lighted Buoy C15	40-36-34.500N 073-39-22.500W	Fl G 4s			Green.	Private aid.
	East Rockaway Channel *Aids maintained from May 1 to Nov. 1.*						
32020	- Buoy D1	40-36-28.620N 073-40-02.160W				Green can.	Private aid.
32025	- Buoy D4	40-36-34.740N 073-39-57.900W				Red nun.	Private aid.
32030	- Buoy D7	40-36-48.240N 073-39-55.500W				Green can.	Private aid.
32035	- Daybeacon D8	40-36-48.360N 073-39-51.240W				TR on pile.	Private aid.
32040	- Daybeacon D9	40-36-57.240N 073-39-51.240W				SG on pile.	Private aid.
32045	- Buoy D10	40-36-55.380N 073-39-51.360W				Red nun.	Private aid.
32050	- Buoy D12	40-36-58.920N 073-39-43.680W				Red nun	Private aid.
32055	- Buoy D13	40-37-02.700N 073-39-38.880W				Green can.	Private aid.
32060	- Buoy D14	40-37-03.780N 073-39-36.240W				Red nun	Private aid.
32065	- Buoy D15	40-37-12.660N 073-39-39.000W				Green can	Private aid.
32070	- Buoy D16	40-37-21.420N 073-39-38.400W				Red nun	Private aid.
32075	- Buoy D17	40-37-18.840N 073-39-40.020W				Green can	Private aid.
	Reynolds Channel						
32085	- LIGHT 11	40-35-50.170N 073-38-39.088W	Fl G 4s	16	4	SG on pile.	
32090	- Buoy 14	40-35-49.232N 073-37-45.439W				Red nun.	Maintained from 1 Apr to 1 Dec.
	Garretts Lead *Aids maintained from May 1 to Nov. 1.*						
32100	- Buoy H1	40-35-51.540N 073-38-20.040W				Green can.	Private aid.
32105	- Buoy H2	40-35-52.200N 073-38-17.040W				Red nun.	Private aid.
32110	- Buoy H3	40-35-58.560N 073-38-14.220W				Green can.	Private aid.
32120	- Daybeacon H4	40-36-00.540N 073-38-10.320W				TR on pile.	Private aid.

(1) No.	(2) Name and Location	(3) Position	(4) Characteristic	(5) Height	(6) Range	(7) Structure	(8) Remarks

NEW YORK - First District

SHINNECOCK BAY TO EAST ROCKAWAY INLET
Hempstead Bay
Garretts Lead
Aids maintained from May 1 to Nov. 1.

32125	- Daybeacon H5	40-36-03.600N 073-38-10.500W				SG on pile.	Private aid.
32135	- Buoy H7	40-36-11.940N 073-38-02.940W				Green can.	Private aid.
32140	- Buoy H8	40-36-08.520N 073-38-03.600W				Red nun.	Private aid.
32145	- Buoy H9	40-36-16.980N 073-37-58.560W				Green can.	Private aid.
32150	- Buoy H10	40-36-17.760N 073-37-56.220W				Red nun.	Private aid.
32155	- Buoy H13	40-36-22.920N 073-37-58.980W				Green can.	Private aid.
32160	- Daybeacon H14	40-36-27.480N 073-37-56.760W				TR on pile.	Private aid.
32165	- Daybeacon H15	40-36-29.340N 073-37-59.640W				SG on pile.	Private aid.
32170	- Buoy H16	40-36-31.740N 073-37-57.420W				Red nun.	Private aid.
32175	- Buoy H17	40-36-39.960N 073-37-54.000W				Green can.	Private aid.
32180	- Buoy H19	40-36-41.820N 073-37-47.820W				Green can.	Private aid.
32185	- Buoy H20	40-36-39.960N 073-37-37.920W				Red nun.	Private aid.
32190	- Daybeacon H24	40-36-46.440N 073-37-25.500W				TR on pile.	Private aid.
32195	- Daybeacon H25	40-36-56.160N 073-37-29.040W				SG on pile.	Private aid.
32200	- Daybeacon H26	40-36-49.440N 073-37-24.000W				TR on pile.	Private aid.
32205	- Buoy H27	40-36-59.520N 073-37-24.000W				Green can.	Private aid.
32210	- Buoy H29	40-37-02.220N 073-37-20.400W				Green can.	Private aid.
32215	- Buoy H30	40-36-59.040N 073-37-18.300W				Red nun.	Private aid.
32220	- Daybeacon H31	40-37-02.760N 073-37-18.780W				SG on pile.	Private aid.
32225	- Buoy H32	40-37-06.120N 073-37-06.240W				Red nun.	Private aid.
32230	- Daybeacon H33	40-37-06.720N 073-37-11.520W				SG on pile.	Private aid.
32235	- Daybeacon H35	40-37-11.220N 073-37-03.480W				SG on pile.	Private aid.
32240	- Daybeacon H36	40-37-15.360N 073-36-57.600W				TR on pile.	Private aid.
32245	- Daybeacon H42	40-37-25.680N 073-36-57.960W				TR on pile.	Private aid.
32250	- Buoy H44	40-37-30.720N 073-37-00.600W				Red nun.	Private aid.

Hassock Channel
Aids maintained from May 1 to Nov. 1.

32255	- Buoy HK1	40-37-11.340N 073-36-55.080W				Green can.	Private aid.
32260	- Buoy HK2	40-37-10.380N 073-36-55.260W				Red nun.	Private aid.
32265	- Buoy HK3	40-37-13.020N 073-36-47.100W				Green can.	Private aid.
32270	- Buoy HK4	40-37-12.300N 073-36-44.280W				Red nun.	Private aid.
32273	- Buoy HK5	40-37-14.340N 073-36-37.800W				Green can.	Private aid.

(1) No.	(2) Name and Location	(3) Position	(4) Characteristic	(5) Height	(6) Range	(7) Structure	(8) Remarks

NEW YORK - First District

SHINNECOCK BAY TO EAST ROCKAWAY INLET
Hempstead Bay
Hassock Channel
Aids maintained from May 1 to Nov. 1.

32275	- Buoy HK6	40-37-13.380N 073-36-38.340W				Red nun.	Private aid.
32280	- Buoy HK7	40-37-15.360N 073-36-30.300W				Green can.	Private aid.
32285	- Buoy HK8	40-37-14.460N 073-36-30.180W				Red nun.	Private aid.

Reynolds Channel

| 32300 | - Daybeacon 13 | 40-35-51.769N
073-37-46.908W | | | | SG on pile. | |
| 32305 | - Buoy 16 | 40-35-48.784N
073-36-58.906W | | | | Red nun. | Maintained from 1 Apr to 1 Dec. |

Borrow Pit Channel
Aids maintained from May 1 to Nov. 1.

32310	- Buoy K1	40-37-12.300N 073-35-41.700W				Green can.	Private aid.
32315	- Buoy K3	40-37-12.180N 073-35-50.820W				Green can.	Private aid.
32320	- Buoy K6	40-37-14.460N 073-35-56.220W				Red nun.	Private aid.
32325	- Daybeacon K8	40-37-17.220N 073-36-04.140W				TR on pile.	Private aid.
32330	- Buoy K9	40-37-15.000N 073-36-06.480W				Green can.	Private aid.
32335	- Buoy K10	40-37-18.360N 073-36-12.120W				Red nun.	Private aid.
32340	- Buoy K11	40-37-16.860N 073-36-18.420W				Green can.	Private aid.
32345	- Buoy K12	40-37-19.200N 073-36-20.400W				Red nun.	Private aid.
32350	- Buoy K13	40-37-18.060N 073-36-30.600W				Green can.	Private aid.
32355	- Daybeacon K14	40-37-21.000N 073-36-30.240W				TR on pile.	Private aid.
32360	- Daybeacon K15	40-37-19.260N 073-36-35.460W				SG on pile.	Private aid.
32365	- Buoy K19	40-37-26.820N 073-36-48.000W				Green can.	Private aid.
32370	- Buoy K20	40-37-22.860N 073-36-39.120W				Red nun.	Private aid.
32375	- Daybeacon K22	40-37-32.640N 073-36-48.000W				TR on pile.	Private aid.
32380	- Daybeacon K23	40-37-27.360N 073-36-54.120W				SG on pile.	Private aid.
32385	- Daybeacon K25	40-37-30.360N 073-36-56.100W				SG on pile.	Private aid.
32390	- Daybeacon K26	40-37-42.960N 073-36-54.420W				TR on pile.	Private aid.
32395	- Buoy K27	40-37-35.760N 073-36-58.740W				Green can.	Private aid.

Oakwood Channel
Aids maintained from May 1 to Nov. 1.

32400	- Buoy KK1	40-37-18.960N 073-36-02.580W				Green can.	Private aid.
32405	- Buoy KK2	40-37-19.680N 073-36-01.320W				Red nun.	Private aid.
32407	- Buoy KK 3	40-37-22.320N 073-36-04.440W				Green can.	Private aid.
32409	- Buoy KK4	40-37-22.620N 073-36-03.240W				Red nun.	Private aid.
32410	- Daybeacon KK5	40-37-24.360N 073-36-06.660W				SG on pile.	Private aid.
32412	- Buoy KK6	40-37-24.420N 073-36-05.520W				Red nun.	Private aid.

288

(1) No.	(2) Name and Location	(3) Position	(4) Characteristic	(5) Height	(6) Range	(7) Structure	(8) Remarks
			NEW YORK - First District				

SHINNECOCK BAY TO EAST ROCKAWAY INLET

Hempstead Bay

Bellmore Creek Channel
Aids maintained from May 1 to Nov. 1.

(1) No.	(2) Name and Location	(3) Position	(4) Characteristic	(5) Height	(6) Range	(7) Structure	(8) Remarks
32415	- Buoy M1	40-38-18.360N 073-31-17.940W				Green can.	Private aid.
32420	- Buoy M2	40-38-06.480N 073-31-11.760W				Red nun.	Private aid.
32425	- Buoy M3	40-38-17.700N 073-31-12.900W				Green can.	Private aid.
32430	- Buoy M4	40-38-11.820N 073-31-10.740W				Red nun.	Private aid.
32435	- Daybeacon M5	40-38-19.200N 073-31-09.660W				SG on pile.	Private aid.
32440	- Buoy M6	40-38-18.360N 073-31-07.500W				Red nun.	Private aid.
32445	- Buoy M7	40-38-26.400N 073-31-07.200W				Green can.	Private aid.
32450	- Daybeacon M8	40-38-25.920N 073-31-05.700W				TR on pile.	Private aid.
32455	- Buoy M9	40-38-30.840N 073-31-00.960W				Green can.	Private aid.
32460	- Buoy M10	40-38-30.900N 073-30-57.720W				Red nun.	Private aid.
32465	- Buoy M11	40-38-34.740N 073-30-57.240W				Green can.	Private aid.

Baldwin Bay
Aids maintained from May 1 to Nov. 1.

(1) No.	(2) Name and Location	(3) Position	(4) Characteristic	(5) Height	(6) Range	(7) Structure	(8) Remarks
32475	- Buoy N1	40-37-17.580N 073-35-42.480W				Green can.	Private aid.
32480	- Buoy N2	40-37-17.760N 073-35-37.980W				Red nun.	Private aid.
32485	- Buoy N3	40-37-24.000N 073-35-38.400W				Green can.	Private aid.
32490	- Buoy N4	40-37-27.360N 073-35-35.700W				Red nun.	Private aid.
32495	- Buoy N5	40-37-28.380N 073-35-36.180W				Green can.	Private aid.
32500	- Buoy N6	40-37-32.880N 073-35-34.500W				Red nun.	Private aid.
32505	- Buoy N8	40-37-41.760N 073-35-35.220W				Red nun.	Private aid.
32510	- Buoy N10	40-37-47.820N 073-35-36.360W				Red nun.	Private aid.
32515	- Buoy N12	40-37-55.380N 073-35-44.520W				Red nun.	Private aid.
32520	- Buoy N13	40-37-58.560N 073-35-45.420W				Green can.	Private aid.
32525	- Buoy N14	40-37-59.700N 073-35-43.680W				Red nun.	Private aid.

Reynolds Channel

(1) No.	(2) Name and Location	(3) Position	(4) Characteristic	(5) Height	(6) Range	(7) Structure	(8) Remarks
32530	- Buoy 15 On edge of marsh.	40-35-48.769N 073-37-20.961W				Green can.	Maintained from 1 Apr to 1 Dec.
32550	- Buoy 21	40-35-47.340N 073-36-38.382W				Green can.	Maintained from 1 Apr to 1 Dec.
32555	- *Lighted Buoy 24*	40-35-44.033N 073-35-56.076W	Fl R 4s		3	Red.	Maintained from 1 Apr to 15 Nov.
32565	POINT LOOKOUT WEST MARINA LIGHT	40-35-39.030N 073-35-29.790W	Q R	8		On pile.	Maintained from Apr. 1 to Nov. 1. Private aid.

Sea Dog Creek
Aids maintained from May 1 to Nov. 1.

(1) No.	(2) Name and Location	(3) Position	(4) Characteristic	(5) Height	(6) Range	(7) Structure	(8) Remarks
32580	- Buoy SD3	40-35-44.880N 073-35-26.880W				Green can.	Private aid.
32585	- Buoy SD4	40-35-46.800N 073-35-25.080W				Red nun.	Private aid.

(1) No.	(2) Name and Location	(3) Position	(4) Characteristic	(5) Height	(6) Range	(7) Structure	(8) Remarks

NEW YORK - First District

SHINNECOCK BAY TO EAST ROCKAWAY INLET

Hempstead Bay

Sea Dog Creek
Aids maintained from May 1 to Nov. 1.

32590	- Buoy SD5	40-35-49.740N 073-35-26.280W				Green can.	Private aid.
32595	- Buoy SD6	40-35-54.000N 073-35-24.780W				Red nun	Private aid.
32600	- Buoy SD7	40-35-59.580N 073-35-23.580W				Green can.	Private aid.
32603	- Buoy SD8	40-35-59.820N 073-35-22.680W				Red nun.	Private aid.
32604	- Buoy SD8A	40-36-04.740N 073-35-19.800W				Red nun.	Private aid.
32605	- Buoy SD9	40-36-04.500N 073-35-21.060W				Green can.	Private aid.
32610	- Daybeacon SD10	40-36-08.040N 073-35-15.840W				TR on pile.	Private aid.
32613	- Buoy SD11	40-36-08.220N 073-35-18.660W				Green can.	Private aid.
32615	- Buoy SD12	40-36-13.740N 073-35-09.000W				Red nun.	Private aid.
32620	- Daybeacon SD13	40-36-15.480N 073-35-10.500W				SG on pile.	Private aid.
32630	- Daybeacon SD16	40-36-19.560N 073-34-54.720W				TR on pile.	Private aid.
32635	- Daybeacon SD17	40-36-24.600N 073-34-39.840W				SG on pile.	Private aid.
32636	- Buoy SD17A	40-36-26.040N 073-34-30.480W				Green can.	Private aid.
32637	- Buoy SD18	40-36-26.160N 073-34-25.740W				Red nun.	Private aid.
32640	- Buoy SD19	40-36-27.480N 073-34-23.400W				Green can.	Private aid.
32645	- Buoy SD20	40-36-27.000N 073-34-20.640W				Red nun.	Private aid.
32646	- Buoy SD21	40-36-28.980N 073-34-17.220W				Green can.	Private aid.

Swift Creek
Aids maintained from May 1 to Nov. 1.

32650	- Buoy SW1	40-36-02.100N 073-33-00.360W				Green can.	Private aid.
32655	- Buoy SW2	40-36-01.800N 073-32-57.360W				Red nun.	Private aid.
32660	- Buoy SW3	40-36-10.560N 073-33-04.740W				Green can.	Private aid.
32665	- Buoy SW4	40-36-16.320N 073-33-02.500W				Red nun.	Private aid.
32670	- Buoy SW5	40-36-39.300N 073-33-21.360W				Green can.	Private aid.
32675	- Buoy SW6	40-36-45.300N 073-33-19.140W				Red nun.	Private aid.
32685	- Buoy SW7	40-36-52.320N 073-33-30.720W				Green can.	Private aid.
32690	- Buoy SW8	40-36-50.640N 073-33-24.420W				Red nun.	Private aid.
32695	- Buoy SW9	40-37-01.740N 073-33-48.360W				Green can.	Private aid.
32700	- Buoy SW10	40-37-07.560N 073-33-54.900W				Red nun.	Private aid.
32705	- Daybeacon SW11	40-37-15.420N 073-34-17.100W				SG on pile.	Private aid.
32710	- Daybeacon SW12	40-37-24.660N 073-34-29.520W				TR on pile.	Private aid.
32715	- Buoy SW13	40-37-24.480N 073-34-35.100W				Green can.	Private aid.

290

(1) No.	(2) Name and Location	(3) Position	(4) Characteristic	(5) Height	(6) Range	(7) Structure	(8) Remarks

SHINNECOCK BAY TO EAST ROCKAWAY INLET
Hempstead Bay
Crow Island Haunts Creek
Aids maintained from May 1 to Nov. 1.

No.	Name and Location	Position	Characteristic	Structure	Remarks
32720	Haunt's Creek Buoy R1	40-36-08.520N 073-31-34.020W		Green can.	Private aid.
32725	Haunt's Creek Buoy R3	40-36-15.360N 073-31-30.000W		Green can.	Private aid.
32730	Haunt's Creek Buoy R4	40-36-21.360N 073-31-24.120W		Red nun.	Private aid.
32735	Haunt's Creek Buoy R5	40-36-23.460N 073-31-29.280W		Green can.	Private aid.
32740	Haunt's Creek Buoy R6	40-36-27.660N 073-31-25.920W		Red nun.	Private aid.
32745	Haunt's Creek Buoy R7	40-36-35.460N 073-31-29.940W		Green can.	Private aid.
32750	Haunt's Creek Buoy R8	40-36-35.520N 073-31-25.500W		Red nun.	Private aid.
32755	Haunt's Creek Buoy R9	40-36-44.760N 073-31-28.080W		Green can.	Private aid.
32760	Haunt's Creek Buoy R10	40-36-43.860N 073-31-23.100W		Red nun.	Private aid.

Fundy Channel
Aids maintained from May 1 to Nov. 1.

No.	Name and Location	Position	Characteristic	Structure	Remarks
32763	- Junction Buoy FB	40-36-45.600N 073-33-25.080W		Green and red bands; can.	Private aid.
32764	- Buoy FB1	40-36-29.160N 073-34-10.380W		Green can.	Private aid.
32765	- Buoy FB2	40-36-27.240N 073-34-07.440W		Red nun.	Private aid.
32770	- Buoy FB3	40-36-33.780N 073-33-55.740W		Green can.	Private aid.
32775	- Buoy FB4	40-36-34.020N 073-33-47.400W		Red nun.	Private aid.
32780	- Daybeacon FB5	40-36-37.500N 073-33-45.720W		SG on pile.	Private aid.
32785	- Daybeacon FB6	40-36-38.640N 073-33-35.040W		TR on pile.	Private aid.
32786	- Buoy FB7	40-36-40.920N 073-33-36.420W		Green can.	Private aid.
32787	- Buoy FB9	40-36-45.840N 073-33-29.160W		Green can.	Private aid.

Long Creek
Aids maintained from May 1 to Nov. 1.

No.	Name and Location	Position	Characteristic	Structure	Remarks
32795	- Junction Lighted Buoy P	40-36-36.660N 073-34-19.080W	Fl (2+1)G 6s	Green and red bands.	Private aid.
32800	- Lighted Buoy P1	40-36-41.820N 073-34-29.640W	Fl G 4s	Green.	Private aid.
32805	- Lighted Buoy P2	40-36-43.740N 073-34-25.080W	Fl R 4s	Red.	Private aid.
32810	- Lighted Buoy P4	40-36-50.100N 073-34-34.800W	Fl R 4s	Red.	Private aid.
32815	- Lighted Buoy P6	40-36-58.260N 073-34-44.640W	Fl R 4s	Red.	Private aid.
32820	- Lighted Buoy P8	40-37-07.800N 073-34-46.680W	Fl R 4s	Red.	Private aid.
32825	- Lighted Buoy P9	40-37-29.040N 073-34-41.940W	Fl G 4s	Green.	Private aid.
32830	- Lighted Buoy P10	40-37-23.040N 073-34-41.580W	Fl R 4s	Red.	Private aid.
32835	- Lighted Buoy P11	40-37-36.720N 073-34-45.300W	Fl G 4s	Green.	Private aid.
32840	- Buoy P12	40-37-36.180N 073-35-11.700W		Red nun.	Private aid.
32847	- Buoy P14	40-37-42.000N 073-35-12.000W		Red nun.	Private aid.

(1) No.	(2) Name and Location	(3) Position	(4) Characteristic	(5) Height	(6) Range	(7) Structure	(8) Remarks

NEW YORK - First District

SHINNECOCK BAY TO EAST ROCKAWAY INLET

Hempstead Bay

Long Creek
Aids maintained from May 1 to Nov. 1.

| 32850 | - Buoy P15 | 40-37-51.600N
073-35-12.720W | | | | Green can. | Private aid. |
| 32852 | - Buoy P17 | 40-37-56.340N
073-35-27.600W | | | | Green can | Private aid. |

Scow Creek Channel
Aids maintained from May 1 to Nov. 1.

32855	- Buoy PP1	40-36-36.000N 073-34-25.800W				Green can.	Private aid.
32860	- Buoy PP2	40-36-37.380N 073-34-28.620W				Red nun.	Private aid.
32865	- Buoy PP4	40-36-38.820N 073-34-36.840W				Red nun.	Private aid.
32870	- Buoy PP5	40-36-37.740N 073-34-43.860W				Green can.	Private aid.
32875	- Buoy PP6	40-36-39.240N 073-34-44.700W				Red nun.	Private aid.
32880	- Buoy PP8	40-36-37.800N 073-34-51.060W				Red nun.	Private aid.
32885	- Buoy PP10	40-36-36.960N 073-34-59.700W				Red nun.	Private aid.
32890	- Buoy PP12	40-36-37.980N 073-35-05.820W				Red nun.	Private aid.
32895	- Buoy PP14	40-36-41.460N 073-35-09.480W				Red nun.	Maintained from Apr. 1 to Nov. 1. Private aid.
32900	- Buoy PP17	40-36-54.060N 073-35-09.180W				Green can.	Private aid.
32905	- Buoy PP18	40-36-56.309N 073-35-09.180W				Red nun.	Private aid.
32910	- Buoy PP19	40-36-59.700N 073-35-14.820W				Green can.	Private aid.
32915	- Buoy PP21	40-37-01.980N 073-35-21.780W				Green can.	Private aid.
32920	- Buoy PP22	40-37-03.360N 073-35-33.660W				Red nun.	Private aid.
32925	- Buoy PP23	40-37-02.340N 073-35-34.320W				Green can.	Private aid.
32930	- Buoy PP24	40-37-05.760N 073-35-38.100W				Red nun.	Private aid.
32933	- Buoy PP24A	40-37-08.220N 073-35-39.720W				Red nun.	Private aid.
32935	- Buoy PP25	40-37-07.980N 073-35-40.380W				Green can.	Private aid.
32940	- Buoy PP26	40-37-12.000N 073-35-40.620W				Red nun.	Private aid.

Freeport Narrows
Aids maintained from May 1 to Nov. 1.

32945	- Buoy Q1	40-37-28.860N 073-34-19.560W				Green can..	Private aid.
32950	- Buoy Q2	40-37-27.720N 073-34-18.060W				Red nun.	Private aid.
32955	- Buoy Q3	40-37-38.580N 073-34-14.940W				Green can.	Private aid.
32960	- Buoy Q4	40-37-36.660N 073-34-13.500W				Red nun.	Private aid.
32965	- Buoy Q5	40-37-44.640N 073-34-08.280W				Green can.	Private aid.
32970	- Buoy Q6	40-37-41.760N 073-34-08.940W				Red nun.	Private aid.
32975	- Buoy Q7	40-37-50.880N 073-33-55.740W				Green can.	Private aid.
32980	- Daybeacon Q8	40-37-48.000N 073-33-55.860W				TR on pile.	Private aid.

Light List corrected through LNM week: 52/23

(1) No.	(2) Name and Location	(3) Position	(4) Characteristic	(5) Height	(6) Range	(7) Structure	(8) Remarks

NEW YORK - First District

NEW YORK - First District

SHINNECOCK BAY TO EAST ROCKAWAY INLET

Hempstead Bay

Freeport Narrows
Aids maintained from May 1 to Nov. 1.

32985	- Buoy Q9	40-37-54.840N 073-33-54.120W				Green can.	Private aid.
32990	- Buoy Q10	40-37-50.700N 073-33-52.200W				Red nun.	Private aid.
32995	- Buoy Q13	40-38-21.000N 073-33-55.380W				Green can.	Private aid.
32996	- Buoy Q14	40-38-42.720N 073-34-24.420W				Red nun.	Private aid.

Great Sand Creek
Aids maintained from May 1 to Nov. 1.

33005	Cedar Swamp Creek Buoy S3	40-38-20.000N 073-31-48.480W				Green can	Private aid.
33010	Cedar Swamp Creek Buoy S5	40-38-27.480N 073-31-40.800W				Green can	Private aid.
33015	Cedar Swamp Creek Buoy S7	40-38-52.440N 073-32-00.240W				Green can.	Private aid.
33020	- Buoy F2	40-37-06.600N 073-33-11.760W				Red nun.	Private aid.
33025	- Buoy F3	40-37-03.120N 073-33-15.600W				Green can.	Private aid.
33030	- Buoy F4	40-37-11.220N 073-33-12.360W				Red nun.	Private aid.
33035	- Buoy F5	40-37-09.240N 073-33-16.200W				Green can.	Private aid.
33040	- Buoy F6	40-37-17.940N 073-33-22.020W				Red nun.	Private aid.
33045	- Buoy F7	40-37-13.740N 073-33-19.800W				Green can.	Private aid.
33050	- Buoy F8	40-37-24.600N 073-33-31.140W				Red nun.	Private aid.
33055	- Buoy F10	40-37-29.400N 073-33-34.080W				Red nun.	Private aid.
33060	- Junction Buoy FF	40-37-14.640N 073-33-14.700W				Red and green bands; nun.	Private aid.

Dog Channel
Aids maintained from May 1 to Nov. 1.

33063	- Buoy T2	40-37-43.200N 073-33-34.920W				Red nun.	Private aid.
33075	- Buoy T7	40-38-07.860N 073-33-19.260W				Green can.	Private aid.
33085	- Daybeacon T10	40-38-14.340N 073-33-18.180W				TR on pile.	Private aid.
33090	- Daybeacon T11	40-38-14.340N 073-33-19.800W				SG on pile.	Private aid.
33095	- Daybeacon T12	40-38-21.240N 073-33-19.860W				TR on pile.	Private aid.
33100	- Buoy T13	40-38-20.220N 073-33-22.320W				Green can.	Private aid.
33105	- Buoy T14	40-38-26.340N 073-33-18.420W				Red nun.	Private aid.
33110	- Daybeacon T15	40-38-28.620N 073-33-22.200W				SG on pile.	Private aid.
33115	- Daybeacon T16	40-38-22.080N 073-33-12.240W				TR on pile	Private aid.
33120	- Daybeacon T17	40-38-30.960N 073-33-22.920W				SG on pile.	Private aid.
33155	- Daybeacon T18	40-38-18.120N 073-33-03.720W				TR on pile.	Private aid.
33160	- Daybeacon T20	40-38-13.860N 073-32-55.800W				TR on pile.	Private aid.
33165	- Daybeacon T22	40-38-09.900N 073-32-51.960W				TR on pile.	Private aid.

293

(1) No.	(2) Name and Location	(3) Position	(4) Characteristic	(5) Height	(6) Range	(7) Structure	(8) Remarks

NEW YORK - First District

SHINNECOCK BAY TO EAST ROCKAWAY INLET

Hempstead Bay

Neds Creek West Branch
Aids maintained from May 1 to Nov. 1.

33170	- Buoy G1	40-37-19.020N 073-33-13.260W				Green can.	Private aid.
33175	- Buoy G2	40-37-19.020N 073-33-11.700W				Red nun.	Private aid.
33180	- Buoy G3	40-37-22.020N 073-33-12.120W				Green can.	Private aid.
33185	- Buoy G4	40-37-23.940N 073-33-10.680W				Red nun.	Private aid.
33186	- Buoy G5	40-37-25.920N 073-33-11.340W				Green can.	Private aid.
33190	- Buoy G6	40-37-29.400N 073-33-05.880W				Red nun.	Private aid.
33195	- Buoy G7	40-37-36.900N 073-33-00.420W				Green can.	Private aid.
33200	- Buoy G8	40-37-37.020N 073-32-58.320W				Red nun.	Private aid.
33205	- Buoy G9	40-37-41.520N 073-32-59.280W				Green can.	Private aid.
33210	- Buoy G10	40-37-47.400N 073-32-58.920W				Red nun.	Private aid.
33214	- Buoy G11	40-37-46.800N 073-32-59.400W				Green can.	Private aid.
33215	- Buoy G12	40-37-53.040N 073-33-00.300W				Red nun.	Private aid.
33219	- Buoy G13	40-38-06.360N 073-32-52.140W				Green can.	Private aid.
33220	- Buoy G14	40-38-01.020N 073-32-54.660W				Red nun.	Private aid.
33225	- Buoy G15	40-38-16.320N 073-32-44.760W				Green can	Private aid.
33230	- Buoy G16	40-38-09.840N 073-32-49.500W				Red nun.	Private aid.

Merrick Point
Aids maintained from May 1 to Nov. 1.

33237	- Buoy G17	40-38-17.880N 073-32-41.460W				Green can	Private aid.
33240	- Daybeacon G18	40-38-11.340N 073-32-45.660W				TR on pile	Private aid.
33245	- Daybeacon G19	40-38-22.020N 073-32-40.080W				SG on pile.	Private aid.
33250	- Buoy G20	40-38-19.200N 073-32-37.200W				Red nun	Private aid.

East Bay
Aids maintained from May 1 to Nov. 1.

33260	Carmen Cut Buoy G22	40-38-26.820N 073-32-37.860W				Red nun	Private aid.
33265	Carmen Cut Buoy G23	40-38-28.920N 073-32-36.480W				Green can.	Private aid.
33266	Carmen Cut Daybeacon G24	40-38-27.120N 073-32-21.780W				TR on pile.	Private aid.
33270	Carmen Cut Buoy G25	40-38-29.700N 073-32-25.200W				Green can.	Private aid.
33271	Carmen Cut Buoy G26	40-38-25.260N 073-32-15.840W				Red nun.	Private aid.
33274	WhaleNeck Point Buoy G28	40-38-20.040N 073-32-10.200W				Red nun.	Private aid.
33285	WhaleNeck Point Buoy G29	40-38-21.180N 073-32-07.500W				Green can.	Private aid.
33286	WhaleNeck Point Buoy G30	40-38-14.880N 073-32-03.780W				Red nun.	Private aid.
33290	WhaleNeck Point Buoy G31	40-38-14.820N 073-31-55.800W				Green can.	Private aid.

(1) No.	(2) Name and Location	(3) Position	(4) Characteristic	(5) Height	(6) Range	(7) Structure	(8) Remarks

SHINNECOCK BAY TO EAST ROCKAWAY INLET

Hempstead Bay

East Bay
Aids maintained from May 1 to Nov. 1.

| 33291 | WhaleNeck Point Buoy G32 | 40-38-10.320N 073-31-58.320W | | | | Red nun. | Private aid. |

Broad Creek Channel
Aids maintained from May 1 to Nov. 1.

33314	- Junction Buoy W	40-38-06.660N 073-31-56.100W				Green and red bands, can.	Private aid.
33315	- Buoy W1	40-36-54.240N 073-31-24.840W				Green can	Private aid.
33320	- Buoy W2	40-36-56.340N 073-31-23.880W				Red nun.	Private aid.
33323	- Buoy W3	40-36-59.460N 073-31-26.100W				Green can.	Private aid.
33325	- Daybeacon W4	40-36-59.100N 073-31-23.760W				TR on pile.	Private aid.
33330	- Buoy W5	40-37-03.360N 073-31-28.260W				Green can.	Private aid.
33335	- Buoy W6	40-37-04.500N 073-31-27.900W				Red nun	Private aid.
33340	- Buoy W7	40-37-10.080N 073-31-34.500W				Green can.	Private aid.
33345	- Daybeacon W8	40-37-11.340N 073-31-34.440W				TR on pile.	Private aid.
33350	- Buoy W9	40-37-12.180N 073-31-40.320W				Green can.	Private aid.
33355	- Daybeacon W10	40-37-12.960N 073-31-40.320W				TR on pile.	Private aid.
33360	- Buoy W11	40-37-13.080N 073-31-52.800W				Green can.	Private aid.
33365	- Buoy W12	40-37-14.160N 073-31-50.940W				Red nun.	Private aid.
33370	- Buoy W13	40-37-16.620N 073-31-55.860W				Green can.	Private aid.
33375	- Buoy W14	40-37-17.760N 073-31-54.180W				Red nun.	Private aid.
33380	- Buoy W15	40-37-23.100N 073-31-59.400W				Green can.	Private aid.
33385	- Buoy W16	40-37-30.120N 073-32-05.880W				Red nun.	Private aid.
33387	- Buoy W17	40-37-33.840N 073-32-11.160W				Green can.	Private aid.
33390	- Buoy W18	40-37-35.280N 073-32-10.620W				Red nun.	Private aid.
33395	- Buoy W19	40-37-43.200N 073-32-16.140W				Green can.	Private aid.
33400	- Buoy W20	40-37-45.360N 073-32-15.840W				Red nun.	Private aid.
33405	- Buoy W21	40-37-48.360N 073-32-16.200W				Green can.	Private aid.
33410	- Buoy W22	40-37-48.180N 073-32-15.300W				Red nun.	Private aid.
33413	- Buoy W23	40-37-54.600N 073-32-09.180W				Green can	Private aid.
33415	- Buoy W24	40-37-55.560N 073-32-06.240W				Red nun.	Private aid.
33420	- Buoy W26	40-38-00.060N 073-32-00.960W				Red nun.	Private aid.
33425	- Buoy W27	40-38-01.200N 073-32-03.180W				Green can.	Private aid.
33435	- Buoy W30	40-38-05.820N 073-31-51.300W				Red nun.	Private aid.

(1) No.	(2) Name and Location	(3) Position	(4) Characteristic	(5) Height	(6) Range	(7) Structure	(8) Remarks

NEW YORK - First District

SHINNECOCK BAY TO EAST ROCKAWAY INLET

Hempstead Bay

Racehorse Channel
Aids maintained from May 1 to Nov. 1.

33475	- Buoy X1	40-37-20.580N 073-30-26.640W				Green can.	Private aid.
33480	- Buoy X2	40-37-20.040N 073-30-25.320W				Red nun	Private aid.
33485	- Buoy X3	40-37-27.660N 073-30-29.100W				Green can.	Private aid.
33490	- Buoy X4	40-37-28.920N 073-30-27.300W				Red nun.	Private aid.
33495	- Buoy X5	40-37-37.380N 073-30-32.640W				Green can.	Private aid.
33500	- Buoy X7	40-37-42.780N 073-30-34.740W				Green can.	Private aid.
33505	- Buoy X8	40-37-43.020N 073-30-32.400W				Red nun.	Private aid.
33510	- Daybeacon X9	40-37-54.840N 073-30-38.280W				SG on pile	Private aid.
33515	- Buoy X10	40-37-53.340N 073-30-35.100W				Red nun.	Private aid.
33520	- Daybeacon X11	40-37-58.740N 073-30-37.920W				SG on pile	Private aid.
33525	- Buoy X12	40-37-58.320N 073-30-34.800W				Red nun	Private aid.
33530	- Daybeacon X13	40-38-02.280N 073-30-36.540W				SG on pile.	Private aid.
33535	- Daybeacon X15	40-38-08.460N 073-30-33.480W				SG on pile.	Private aid.
33540	- Daybeacon X16	40-38-10.380N 073-30-30.840W				TR on pile.	Private aid.
33545	- Daybeacon X17	40-38-14.160N 073-30-32.760W				SG on pile.	Private aid.
33550	- Buoy X18	40-38-19.800N 073-30-30.600W				Red nun.	Private aid.
33555	- Buoy X19	40-38-19.620N 073-30-33.840W				Green can.	Private aid.

Olivers Channel
Aids maintained from May 1 to Nov. 1.

33605	- Buoy L2	40-38-04.320N 073-31-04.800W				Red nun.	Private aid.
33607	- Buoy L3	40-38-06.180N 073-31-06.000W				Green can.	Private aid.
33610	- Buoy L4	40-38-06.660N 073-30-57.300W				Red nun.	Private aid.
33615	- Daybeacon L5	40-38-11.400N 073-30-50.340W				SG on pile.	Private aid.
33620	- Daybeacon L6	40-38-09.300N 073-30-41.520W				TR on pile.	Private aid.
33625	- Daybeacon L7	40-38-14.040N 073-30-42.600W				SG on pile.	Private aid.
33626	- Buoy L8	40-38-10.740N 073-30-35.760W				Red nun.	Private aid.
33627	- Buoy L9	40-38-17.040N 073-30-35.760W				Green can.	Private aid.

Great Island Channel
Aids maintained from May 1 to Nov. 1.

33630	- Buoy Z1	40-37-36.660N 073-29-47.940W				Green can	Private aid.
33635	- Buoy Z2	40-37-37.500N 073-29-44.460W				Red nun	Private aid.
33640	- Buoy Z4	40-37-46.560N 073-29-42.600W				Red nun	Private aid.
33645	- Buoy Z5	40-37-50.760N 073-29-46.920W				Green can.	Private aid.

(1) No.	(2) Name and Location	(3) Position	(4) Characteristic	(5) Height	(6) Range	(7) Structure	(8) Remarks
			NEW YORK - First District				

SHINNECOCK BAY TO EAST ROCKAWAY INLET

Hempstead Bay

Great Island Channel
Aids maintained from May 1 to Nov. 1.

33650	- Buoy Z6	40-37-53.580N 073-29-41.580W				Red nun.	Private aid.
33655	- Buoy Z7	40-37-59.580N 073-29-44.460W				Green can.	Private aid.
33660	- Buoy Z8	40-37-59.220N 073-29-39.780W				Red nun.	Private aid.
33665	- Buoy Z9	40-38-09.480N 073-29-41.340W				Green can.	Private aid.
33670	- Buoy Z10	40-38-08.100N 073-29-35.820W				Red nun.	Private aid.
33675	- Buoy Z11	40-38-16.620N 073-29-34.320W				Green can.	Private aid.
33680	- Buoy Z12	40-38-14.280N 073-29-29.220W				Red nun.	Private aid.
33685	- Buoy Z13	40-38-22.980N 073-29-25.620W				Green can.	Private aid.
33690	- Buoy Z14	40-38-21.000N 073-29-19.860W				Red nun.	Private aid.
33695	- Buoy Z15	40-38-30.840N 073-29-20.460W				Green can.	Private aid.
33700	- Buoy Z-16	40-38-28.260N 073-29-15.960W				Red nun.	Private aid.
33705	- Buoy Z-18	40-38-37.140N 073-29-12.960W				Red nun.	Private aid.
33710	- Buoy Z19	40-38-41.700N 073-29-14.760W				Green can.	Private aid.
33713	- Buoy Z20	40-38-44.760N 073-29-09.900W				Red nun.	Private aid.
33715	- Buoy Z21	40-38-45.540N 073-29-13.440W				Green can.	Private aid.
33720	- Buoy Z22	40-38-56.940N 073-29-06.480W				Red nun.	Private aid.

South Oyster Bay

North Channel
Buoys in channel are maintained from May 1 to Nov. 1 unless otherwise noted.

33730	- Junction Buoy S	40-39-00.000N 073-29-07.000W				Green and red bands; can.	Private aid.
33735	SOUTH OYSTER BAY NORTH CHANNEL LIGHT 2	40-39-00.060N 073-28-58.920W	Fl R 4s			TR on pile.	Private aid.
33740	SOUTH OYSTER BAY NORTH CHANNEL LIGHT 4	40-38-53.880N 073-28-47.940W	Fl R 4s			TR on pile.	Private aid.
33745	SOUTH OYSTER BAY NORTH CHANNEL LIGHT 6	40-38-54.000N 073-28-33.420W	Fl R 4s			TR on pile.	Private aid.

Massapequa Creek
Buoys in channel are maintained from May 1 to Nov. 1 unless otherwise noted.

33755	- Daybeacon 8	40-38-59.800N 073-28-23.300W				TR on pile.	Private aid.
33760	- LIGHT 10	40-39-05.160N 073-28-18.060W	Fl R 4s			TR on pile.	Private aid.
33765	- LIGHT 12	40-39-07.680N 073-28-14.400W	Fl R 4s			TR on pile.	Private aid.
33770	- Light 14	40-39-04.440N 073-28-10.200W	Fl R 4s			TR on pile.	Private aid.

North Channel
Buoys in channel are maintained from May 1 to Nov. 1 unless otherwise noted.

33775	- LIGHT 16	40-38-56.280N 073-28-04.920W	Fl R 4s			TR on pile.	Private aid.
33780	- LIGHT 18	40-38-46.680N 073-27-58.260W	Fl R 4s			TR on pole.	Private aid.
33785	- Buoy 19	40-38-49.200N 073-27-54.600W				Green can.	Private aid.
33790	- LIGHT 20	40-38-45.420N 073-27-43.560W	Fl R 4s			TR on pole.	Private aid.

(1) No.	(2) Name and Location	(3) Position	(4) Characteristic	(5) Height	(6) Range	(7) Structure	(8) Remarks
		NEW YORK - First District					

SHINNECOCK BAY TO EAST ROCKAWAY INLET

South Oyster Bay

North Channel

Buoys in channel are maintained from May 1 to Nov. 1 unless otherwise noted.

(1) No.	(2) Name and Location	(3) Position	(4) Characteristic	(5) Height	(6) Range	(7) Structure	(8) Remarks
33795	- LIGHT 22	40-38-46.620N 073-27-31.920W	Fl R 4s			TR on pile.	Private aid.
33800	- LIGHT 24	40-38-51.120N 073-27-23.940W	Fl R 4s			TR on pile.	Private aid.
33805	- Buoy 25	40-38-54.000N 073-27-26.400W				Green can.	Private aid.
33810	- LIGHT 26	40-38-58.320N 073-27-18.000W	Fl R 4s			TR on pile.	Private aid.
33815	- LIGHT 28	40-39-02.100N 073-27-10.560W	Fl R 4s			TR on pile.	Private aid.
33820	- Buoy 29	40-39-04.800N 073-27-12.600W				Green can.	Private aid.
33825	- LIGHT 30	40-39-07.380N 073-27-01.200W	Fl R 4s			TR on pile.	Private aid.
33827	- Buoy 31	40-39-09.000N 073-27-03.000W				Green can.	Private aid.
33830	- LIGHT 32	40-39-10.080N 073-26-52.380W	Fl R 4s			TR on pile.	Private aid.
33832	- Buoy 33	40-39-12.000N 073-26-56.400W				Green can.	Private aid.
33835	- LIGHT 34	40-39-09.960N 073-26-41.340W	Fl R 4s			TR on pile.	Private aid.
33840	- LIGHT 36	40-39-08.460N 073-26-29.160W	Fl R 4s			TR on pile.	Private aid.
33845	- LIGHT 38	40-39-04.080N 073-26-22.800W	Fl R 4s			TR on pile.	Private aid.
33850	- LIGHT 40	40-39-00.420N 073-26-05.040W	Fl R 4s			TR on pile.	Private aid.
33855	- Buoy 42	40-38-56.400N 073-25-45.000W				Red nun.	Private aid.
33860	- Buoy 43	40-38-59.400N 073-25-45.600W				Green can.	Private aid.
33865	- Buoy 44	40-38-54.600N 073-25-32.400W				Red nun.	Private aid.
33867	- Buoy 45	40-38-57.000N 073-25-32.400W				Green can.	Private aid.

Amity Channel

Buoys in channel are maintained from May 1 to Nov. 1 unless otherwise noted.

(1) No.	(2) Name and Location	(3) Position	(4) Characteristic	(5) Height	(6) Range	(7) Structure	(8) Remarks
33875	- LIGHT 51	40-37-37.500N 073-28-45.000W	Fl G 4s			On pile.	Private aid.
33880	- LIGHT 52	40-37-33.780N 073-28-45.300W	Fl R 4s			TR on pile.	Private aid.
33885	- LIGHT 53	40-37-39.720N 073-28-34.620W	Fl G 4s			SG on pole.	Private aid.
33890	- LIGHT 54	40-37-36.480N 073-28-33.600W	Fl R 4s			TR on pole.	Private aid.
33895	- LIGHT 55	40-37-42.360N 073-28-24.300W	Fl G 4s			On pile.	Private aid.
33900	- LIGHT 56	40-37-37.560N 073-28-24.060W	Fl R 4s			TR on pile.	Private aid.
33905	- LIGHT 57	40-37-38.160N 073-28-13.620W	Fl G 4s			SG on pole.	Private aid.
33907	- LIGHT 58	40-37-35.760N 073-28-15.600W	Fl R 4s			TR on pole.	Private aid.
33910	- LIGHT 59	40-37-33.300N 073-28-03.540W	Fl G 4s			SG on pole.	Private aid.
33915	- LIGHT 60	40-37-29.220N 073-28-03.300W	Fl R 4s			TR on pile.	Private aid.
33920	- LIGHT 61	40-37-28.140N 073-27-50.580W	Fl G 4s			On pile.	Private aid.
33925	- LIGHT 62	40-37-25.380N 073-27-51.120W	Fl R 4s			TR on pile.	Private aid.

(1) No.	(2) Name and Location	(3) Position	(4) Characteristic	(5) Height	(6) Range	(7) Structure	(8) Remarks
			NEW YORK - First District				

SHINNECOCK BAY TO EAST ROCKAWAY INLET

South Oyster Bay

Amity Channel

Buoys in channel are maintained from May 1 to Nov. 1 unless otherwise noted.

(1) No.	(2) Name and Location	(3) Position	(4) Characteristic	(5) Height	(6) Range	(7) Structure	(8) Remarks
33930	- LIGHT 63	40-37-21.660N 073-27-41.520W	Fl G 4s			On pile.	Private aid.
33935	- LIGHT 64	40-37-19.560N 073-27-40.800W	Q R			TR on pile.	Private aid.
33940	- LIGHT 65	40-37-23.760N 073-27-27.360W	Fl G 4s			SG on pole.	Private aid.
33945	- LIGHT 66	40-37-21.300N 073-27-24.780W	Q R			TR on pile.	Private aid.
33950	- LIGHT 67	40-37-25.980N 073-27-20.100W	Fl G 4s			SG on pole.	Private aid.
33953	- Buoy 67A	40-37-30.240N 073-27-06.360W				Green can.	Private aid.
33955	- LIGHT 68	40-37-25.320N 073-27-13.440W	Fl R 4s			TR on pole.	Private aid.
33960	- LIGHT 69	40-37-36.840N 073-27-01.980W	Fl G 4s			On pile.	Private aid.
33965	- LIGHT 70	40-37-35.340N 073-26-58.260W	Fl R 4s			TR on pile.	Private aid.
33970	- LIGHT 71	40-37-43.980N 073-26-36.720W	Fl G 4s			On pile.	Private aid.
33975	- Daybeacon 72	40-37-41.460N 073-26-37.320W				TR on pile.	Private aid.
33980	- Daybeacon 74	40-37-49.080N 073-26-26.460W				TR on pile.	Private aid.
33985	- LIGHT 75	40-37-49.980N 073-26-28.740W	Fl G 4s			SG on pole.	Private aid.
33990	- Daybeacon 76	40-37-54.660N 073-26-21.060W				TR on pile.	Private aid.
33995	- Buoy 77	40-37-56.160N 073-26-22.980W				Green can.	Private aid.
34000	- Buoy 79	40-38-04.800N 073-26-19.800W				Green can.	Private aid.
34005	- Daybeacon 80	40-38-05.400N 073-26-15.840W				TR on pile.	Private aid.
34010	- Buoy 81	40-38-10.200N 073-26-22.260W				Green can.	Private aid.
34015	- LIGHT 82	40-38-10.140N 073-26-20.040W	Fl R 4s			TR on pole.	Private aid.
34020	- Buoy 83	40-38-15.000N 073-26-23.400W				Green can.	Private aid.
34025	- LIGHT 84	40-38-19.860N 073-26-22.560W	Fl R 4s			TR on pole.	Private aid.
34030	- Buoy 85	40-38-19.800N 073-26-24.420W				Green can.	Private aid.
34035	- LIGHT 86	40-38-22.380N 073-26-21.360W	Fl R 4s			TR on pole.	Private aid.
34040	- Buoy 87	40-38-25.800N 073-26-22.200W				Green can.	Private aid.
34045	- LIGHT 88	40-38-26.940N 073-26-16.140W	Fl R 4s			TR on pole.	Private aid.
34050	- Buoy 89	40-38-31.200N 073-26-11.400W				Green can.	Private aid.
34055	- LIGHT 90	40-38-30.600N 073-26-07.620W	Fl R 4s			TR on pole.	Private aid.
34060	- Buoy 91	40-38-35.400N 073-25-59.400W				Green can.	Private aid.
34065	- LIGHT 92	40-38-33.660N 073-25-58.680W	Fl R 4s			TR on pole.	Private aid.
34070	- Buoy 93	40-38-37.200N 073-25-45.600W				Green can.	Private aid.
34075	- LIGHT 94	40-38-35.400N 073-25-45.600W	Fl R 4s			TR on pole.	Private aid.

(1) No.	(2) Name and Location	(3) Position	(4) Characteristic	(5) Height	(6) Range	(7) Structure	(8) Remarks
			NEW YORK - First District				
	SHINNECOCK BAY TO EAST ROCKAWAY INLET						
	South Oyster Bay						
	Carman Creek						
34150	- Daybeacon D6	40-39-08.000N 073-25-45.000W				TR on pile.	Private aid.
34155	- Daybeacon D8	40-39-13.000N 073-25-44.000W				TR on pile.	Private aid.
34160	- Daybeacon D10	40-39-16.000N 073-25-46.000W				TR on pile.	Private aid.
	Tobay Boat Basin Entrance						
34180	- Daybeacon 1	40-37-00.000N 073-25-52.000W				Green arrow on pile.	Private aid.
	Massapequa Cove						
34190	- Buoy 1	40-39-19.440N 073-28-12.600W				Green can.	Private aid.
34195	- Daybeacon 2	40-39-19.560N 073-28-17.700W				Red arrow on pile.	Private aid.
34200	- Daybeacon 4	40-39-23.160N 073-28-21.720W				Red arrow on pile.	Private aid.
	JAMAICA BAY AND ROCKAWAY INLET						
	Rockaway Inlet						
34210	- *Lighted Bell Buoy 2*	40-31-45.614N 073-56-35.409W	Fl R 4s		4	Red.	
34215	- Buoy RI Marks southeast side of shoal.	40-31-57.390N 073-56-46.839W				Red and green bands.	
34220	ROCKAWAY POINT BREAKWATER LIGHT 4	40-32-25.232N 073-56-26.514W	Fl R 4s	34	5	TR on skeleton tower on piles.	
34225	- Buoy 5	40-32-26.228N 073-56-41.266W				Green can.	
34230	- Buoy 7	40-33-16.916N 073-56-47.375W				Green can.	
34235	- *Lighted Bell Buoy 8*	40-33-13.412N 073-56-34.509W	Fl R 2.5s		4	Red.	
34240	- *Lighted Buoy 9*	40-33-29.192N 073-56-32.902W	Fl G 4s		4	Green.	
34245	- Buoy 10	40-33-25.812N 073-56-19.709W				Red nun.	
34250	- *Lighted Bell Buoy 12*	40-33-40.402N 073-55-50.368W	Fl R 4s		4	Red.	
34255	- Buoy 13	40-33-49.412N 073-55-53.108W				Green can.	
34260	- Buoy 15	40-34-03.051N 073-55-15.547W				Green can.	
34265	- Buoy 16	40-33-53.684N 073-55-01.175W				Red nun.	
34270	- *Lighted Buoy 20*	40-34-11.311N 073-53-54.705W	Fl R 6s		4	Red.	
34285	**Marine Parkway Bridge Sound Signal**	40-34-24.000N 073-53-12.000W				On bridge abutment.	HORN: 1 blast ev 60s (10s bl). Private aid.
	Rockaway Inlet West Channel						
34290	- Buoy 4	40-32-54.213N 073-57-29.511W				Red nun.	
	Gerritsen Inlet						
34295	- *Lighted Buoy 2*	40-34-14.001N 073-55-03.217W	Fl R 4s		3	Red.	Removed when endangered by ice.
34300	- *Lighted Buoy 4*	40-34-29.531N 073-55-01.987W	Fl R 4s		3	Red.	Replaced by nun when endangered by ice.
34305	- Buoy 5	40-34-32.561N 073-55-03.957W				Green can.	
34310	- Buoy 7	40-34-36.671N 073-54-45.227W				Green can.	
34315	- Buoy 10	40-34-48.851N 073-54-29.246W				Red nun.	

(1) No.	(2) Name and Location	(3) Position	(4) Characteristic	(5) Height	(6) Range	(7) Structure	(8) Remarks
			NEW YORK - First District				
	JAMAICA BAY AND ROCKAWAY INLET						
	Gerritsen Inlet						
34320	- *Lighted Buoy 9*	40-34-49.501N 073-54-31.376W	Fl G 4s		3	Green.	Removed when endangered by ice.
	Sheepshead Bay						
34325	- Approach Buoy 1	40-34-04.230N 073-56-13.239W				Green can.	
34330	- Approach Buoy 2	40-34-03.761N 073-56-06.419W				Red nun.	
34335	OUTFALL GATE HOUSE LIGHT On shoal northerly of Rockaway Point.	40-33-57.973N 073-55-50.851W	F W	24		Tower on gate house.	Private aid.
34340	- Approach Buoy 3	40-34-19.281N 073-55-56.238W				Green can.	
34345	- *Approach Lighted Buoy 4*	40-34-18.411N 073-55-45.508W	Fl R 4s		3	Red.	Removed when endangered by ice.
34350	- *Lighted Buoy 6*	40-34-31.006N 073-55-41.034W	Fl R 4s		3	Red.	Replaced by nun when endangered by ice.
34355	- Buoy 7	40-34-34.479N 073-55-43.126W				Green can.	
34360	KINGSBOROUGH COMMUNITY COLLEGE LIGHT	40-34-34.500N 073-55-53.640W	Fl W 4s			On metal tower.	Private aid.
34365	- Buoy 8	40-34-41.221N 073-55-45.908W				Red nun.	
34370	- *Lighted Buoy 12*	40-34-53.230N 073-55-51.998W	Fl R 2.5s		3	Red.	Replaced by nun when endangered by ice.
34375	- Buoy 16	40-34-54.760N 073-56-14.979W				Red nun.	
34380	- Buoy 18	40-34-54.620N 073-56-24.829W				Red nun.	
	Beach Channel						
34385	*Nova Scotia Bar Junction Lighted Buoy N*	40-34-39.911N 073-52-10.502W	Fl (2+1)G 6s		3	Green and red bands.	Replaced by can when endangered by ice.
34390	- Buoy 1	40-34-55.910N 073-51-40.001W				Green can.	
34395	- Buoy 2	40-34-57.400N 073-51-17.611W				Red nun.	
34400	- *Lighted Buoy 3*	40-35-11.692N 073-51-09.894W	Fl G 2.5s		3	Green.	Replaced by can when endangered by ice.
34405	- *Lighted Buoy 5*	40-35-03.000N 073-50-14.514W	Fl G 4s		4	Green.	Replaced by can when endangered by ice.
34410	- Buoy 7	40-35-15.650N 073-49-45.078W				Green can.	
34412	*Jamaica Bay Water Quality Monitoring Lighted Buoy BC*	40-35-19.360N 073-49-24.754W	Fl W 2.5s			White with Orange Bands.	Seasonal 01 Apr - 31 Oct. Private aid.
34415	- Buoy 9	40-35-24.690N 073-49-24.498W				Green can.	
34420	Long Bar Buoy L	40-35-33.659N 073-49-04.177W				Green and red bands; can.	
34430	- Buoy 11	40-35-39.509N 073-48-52.527W				Green can.	
34431	- Buoy 12	40-35-50.052N 073-48-30.499W				Red nun.	
34445	- *Lighted Buoy W*	40-36-02.759N 073-48-15.834W	Fl (2+1)G 6s		3	Green and red bands.	Removed when endangered by ice.
	Grass Hassock Channel						
34450	- Buoy 14	40-36-00.269N 073-48-13.796W				Red nun.	

(1) No.	(2) Name and Location	(3) Position	(4) Characteristic	(5) Height	(6) Range	(7) Structure	(8) Remarks

JAMAICA BAY AND ROCKAWAY INLET

Grass Hassock Channel

34460	- Buoy 16	40-36-02.619N 073-47-57.235W				Red nun.	
34465	- Buoy 17	40-36-05.453N 073-47-48.504W				Green can.	
34470	- Buoy 19	40-36-24.671N 073-47-21.852W				Green can.	
34475	- Buoy 20	40-36-45.418N 073-46-37.443W				Red nun.	
34480	- Buoy 22	40-36-52.848N 073-46-24.143W				Red nun.	
34485	- Lighted Buoy 23	40-36-54.631N 073-46-25.565W	Fl G 4s		3	Green.	Replaced by can when endangered by ice.
34490	- Buoy M	40-36-54.631N 073-46-20.042W				Red and green bands; nun.	
34495	- Buoy 25	40-37-14.177N 073-46-10.242W				Green can.	
34500	- Buoy 27	40-37-32.587N 073-45-56.301W				Green can.	

Motts Basin

34505	- Buoy 1	40-36-54.928N 073-45-56.722W				Green can.	
34510	- Buoy 2	40-36-52.748N 073-45-55.422W				Red nun.	
34515	- Buoy 3	40-36-51.118N 073-45-49.112W				Green can.	
34535	Inwood Channel Buoy 2	40-36-54.868N 073-45-48.902W				Red nun.	

Head of Bay

34540	- Buoy 29	40-37-41.877N 073-45-49.862W				Green can.	
34543	Jamaica Bay Water Quality Monitoring Lighted Buoy HB	40-38-17.732N 073-44-48.804W	Fl W 2.5s			White with Orange Bands.	Seasonal 01 Apr - 31 Oct. Private aid.
34545	- Buoy 30	40-37-49.667N 073-45-17.631W				Red nun.	
34550	- Buoy NP	40-38-05.523N 073-44-52.016W				Red and green bands; nun.	

Winhole Channel

34555	- Buoy 1	40-36-19.469N 073-48-21.976W				Green can.	
34560	- Lighted Buoy 2	40-36-35.408N 073-48-20.996W	Fl R 2.5s		3	Red.	Replaced by nun when endangered by ice.
34565	- LIGHT 3	40-36-46.132N 073-48-28.114W	Fl G 4s	12	4	SG on pile.	
34570	- Buoy 5	40-37-04.208N 073-48-31.496W				Green can.	
34575	- Buoy 6	40-37-15.808N 073-48-30.696W				Red nun.	
34580	- Lighted Buoy 8	40-37-41.878N 073-48-37.472W	Fl R 4s		3	Red.	Replaced by nun when endangered by ice.
34590	- Lighted Buoy 9	40-37-48.457N 073-48-42.167W	Q G		3	Green.	

Grassy Bay

34593	Jamaica Bay Water Quality Monitoring Lighted Buoy BB	40-38-58.900N 073-49-21.400W	Fl W 2.5s			White with Orange Bands.	Seasonal 10 Apr - 31 Oct. Private aid.
34595	Bergen Basin Buoy 2	40-38-43.987N 073-49-14.131W				Red nun.	
34600	Bergen Basin Buoy 3	40-38-44.076N 073-49-17.538W				Green can.	
34605	Jamaica Bay Water Quality Monitoring Lighted Buoy GB	40-38-02.870N 073-48-27.972W	Fl W 2.5s			White with Orange Bands.	Seasonal 01 Apr - 31 Oct. Private aid.

(1) No.	(2) Name and Location	(3) Position	(4) Characteristic	(5) Height	(6) Range	(7) Structure	(8) Remarks
			NEW YORK - First District				
	JAMAICA BAY AND ROCKAWAY INLET						
	Grassy Bay						
34610	KENNEDY AIRPORT DOCK LIGHT F	40-37-05.400N 073-46-32.640W	F R			Red conical pipe structure.	Private aid.
	Runway Channel						
34615	- Buoy 1R	40-35-19.545N 073-51-16.081W				Green can.	
34620	- East Junction Lighted Buoy R	40-35-27.256N 073-51-03.458W	Fl (2+1)R 6s		3	Red and green bands.	Replaced by nun when endangered by ice.
34625	- Buoy 3R	40-35-28.070N 073-51-52.362W				Green can.	
34630	- Junction Lighted Buoy RC	40-35-39.139N 073-52-27.583W	Fl (2+1)R 6s		3	Red and green bands.	Replaced by nun when endangered by ice.
	The Raunt Channel						
34635	- Buoy 2	40-35-54.668N 073-50-53.615W				Red nun.	
34640	- Buoy 3	40-36-00.579N 073-50-54.040W				Green can.	
34645	- Buoy 5	40-36-12.709N 073-50-33.500W				Green can.	
34650	- Buoy 6	40-36-04.009N 073-50-13.999W				Red nun.	
34655	- Buoy 7	40-35-58.066N 073-49-47.988W				Green can.	
	North Channel						
34665	- LIGHT N	40-36-40.288N 073-52-51.403W	Fl W 4s	20	5	NR on four pile structure with pipe tower.	
34670	- Buoy 2	40-35-10.090N 073-52-19.753W				Red nun.	
34675	- Buoy 4	40-36-02.017N 073-52-35.919W				Red nun.	
34680	- Lighted Buoy 5	40-36-01.229N 073-52-48.013W	Fl G 2.5s		3	Green.	Replaced by can when endangered by ice.
34685	- Lighted Buoy 6 75 yards, 160° from obstruction.	40-36-17.435N 073-52-45.835W	Fl R 6s		3	Red.	
34695	- Lighted Buoy 9	40-36-26.012N 073-52-59.560W	Fl G 4s		4	Green.	Replaced by can when endangered by ice.
34700	Mill Basin Channel Buoy M	40-36-32.469N 073-53-10.774W				Green and red bands; can.	
34705	Mill Basin Channel Buoy 2	40-36-25.389N 073-53-27.024W				Red nun.	
34710	- Buoy 10	40-36-49.208N 073-53-07.754W				Red nun.	
34715	- Lighted Buoy 12	40-37-04.838N 073-53-16.924W	Fl R 2.5s		3	Red.	Replaced by nun when endangered by ice.
34720	- Buoy 13	40-37-02.478N 073-53-31.535W				Green can.	
34725	- Buoy 15	40-37-18.698N 073-53-33.075W				Green can.	
34730	- Buoy 16	40-37-18.388N 073-53-13.894W				Red nun.	
34735	- Lighted Buoy 20	40-37-43.927N 073-52-42.963W	Fl R 4s		3	Red.	Replaced by nun when endangered by ice.
34740	- Buoy 21	40-38-02.207N 073-52-25.303W				Green can.	
34750	- Lighted Buoy 24	40-38-17.154N 073-51-52.882W	Fl R 2.5s		3	Red.	Replaced by nun when endangered by ice.

(1) No.	(2) Name and Location	(3) Position	(4) Characteristic	(5) Height	(6) Range	(7) Structure	(8) Remarks
			NEW YORK - First District				
	JAMAICA BAY AND ROCKAWAY INLET						
	North Channel						
34755	- Lighted Buoy 26	40-38-28.430N 073-51-17.177W	Fl R 4s		3	Red.	Replaced by nun when endangered by ice.
34757	Jamaica Bay Water Quality Monitoring Lighted Buoy NC	40-38-28.630N 073-50-44.084W	Fl W 2.5s			White with Orange Bands.	Seasonal 01 Apr - 31 Oct. Private aid.
34760	- Buoy 29	40-38-37.156N 073-50-40.890W				Green can.	
34765	- Buoy 30	40-38-35.416N 073-50-34.260W				Red nun.	
34770	- Buoy 31	40-38-38.762N 073-50-23.433W				Green can.	
34775	- Lighted Buoy 32	40-38-37.386N 073-50-23.049W	Fl R 6s		4	Red.	Replaced by nun when endangered by ice.
34780	- Buoy 33	40-38-37.446N 073-49-44.588W				Green can.	
34781	Howard Beach Entrance Buoy 2	40-38-44.387N 073-50-00.482W				Red nun.	Removed when endangered by ice.
	NEW YORK HARBOR						
	Ambrose Channel						
34785	- Lighted Whistle Buoy A	40-27-28.023N 073-50-12.242W	Mo (A) W		6	Red and white stripes with red spherical topmark.	AIS: MMSI 993672056 (21)
34790	WEST BANK FRONT RANGE LIGHT	40-32-16.689N 074-02-34.319W	Iso W 6s (R Sector)	69		Brown conical tower on black cylindrical pier.	White from 181° to 004°, red from 004° to 181°, white higher intensity beam visible 4° each side of range line (297°). Range light is lighted throughout 24 hours. HORN: 2 blasts ev 20s (2s bl-2s si-2s bl-14s si). Operates continuously.
34795	STATEN ISLAND REAR RANGE LIGHT 10,221 yards, 297.0° from front light.	40-34-33.916N 074-08-28.511W	F W	234		Octagonal brick tower, gray limestone base.	Visible on range line only.Lighted throughout 24 hours.
34796	- Lighted Buoy 1	40-28-07.524N 073-52-20.018W	Fl G 2.5s		4	Green.	
34797	- Lighted Bell Buoy 2	40-28-22.545N 073-52-03.183W	Fl R 2.5s		4	Red.	
34798	- Lighted Buoy 3	40-29-04.041N 073-54-45.797W	Fl G 4s		4	Green.	
34799	- Lighted Buoy 4	40-29-08.256N 073-53-59.104W	Fl R 4s		4	Red.	AIS; MMSI 993672057 (21)
34800	- Lighted Buoy 5	40-29-23.775N 073-55-38.077W	Fl G 2.5s		4	Green.	
34805	- Lighted Buoy 6	40-29-41.173N 073-55-25.903W	Fl R 2.5s		3	Red.	
34807	- Alternate Departure Lane Lighted Buoy 1A	40-28-08.324N 073-53-57.896W	Q G		3	Green.	
34815	- Lighted Buoy 7	40-30-03.581N 073-57-20.741W	Fl G 4s		4	Green.	AIS: MMSI 993672058
34825	- Lighted Buoy 8	40-30-21.551N 073-57-09.251W	Fl R 4s		3	Red.	
34830	- Lighted Buoy 9	40-30-30.032N 073-58-28.754W	Fl G 2.5s		3	Green.	
34835	- Lighted Buoy 10	40-30-47.372N 073-58-17.114W	Fl R 2.5s		3	Red.	
34840	- Lighted Buoy 11	40-30-56.552N 073-59-36.794W	Fl G 4s		3	Green.	
34845	- Lighted Buoy 11A	40-31-09.758N 074-00-10.144W	Fl G 2.5s		3	Green.	
34850	- Lighted Buoy 12	40-31-14.372N 073-59-25.154W	Fl R 4s		3	Red.	

(1) No.	(2) Name and Location	(3) Position	(4) Characteristic	(5) Height	(6) Range	(7) Structure	(8) Remarks
			NEW YORK - First District				
	NEW YORK HARBOR						
	Ambrose Channel						
34855	- Lighted Buoy 12A	40-31-27.392N 073-59-58.934W	Fl R 2.5s		3	Red.	
34860	- Lighted Gong Buoy 13	40-31-25.960N 074-00-53.016W	Q G		3	Green.	AIS: MMSI 993672059
34865	- Lighted Bell Buoy 14	40-31-40.652N 074-00-33.734W	Q R		3	Red.	AIS: MMSI 993672060
34870	- Lighted Buoy 15	40-31-49.702N 074-01-13.604W	Fl G 2.5s		3	Green.	
34875	- Lighted Buoy 16	40-32-00.199N 074-00-52.686W	Fl R 2.5s		3	Red.	
34880	- Lighted Gong Buoy 17	40-32-14.090N 074-01-36.512W	Q G		3	Green.	AIS: MMSI 993672061
34885	- Lighted Bell Buoy 18	40-32-22.232N 074-01-11.954W	Q R		3	Red.	AIS: MMSI 993672062
34890	- Lighted Buoy AC	40-33-07.675N 074-01-51.058W	Fl (2+1)G 6s		3	Green and red bands.	
34895	- Lighted Buoy 20	40-33-11.687N 074-01-25.861W	Fl R 2.5s		3	Red.	
34903	- Lighted Gong Buoy 21	40-33-57.332N 074-02-05.354W	Fl G 4s		3	Green.	AIS: MMSI 993672063
34905	- Lighted Buoy 22	40-34-01.296N 074-01-39.628W	Fl R 4s		3	Red.	AIS:MMSI 993672064
	Main Channel						
34910	**Coney Island Light**	40-34-35.780N 074-00-42.336W	Fl R 5s	75	16	White square skeleton tower. 75	Lighted throughout 24 hours.
34920	Craven Shoal Lighted Buoy 23	40-35-07.810N 074-02-28.819W	Q G		3	Green.	
34925	**The Verrazano-Narrows Bridge Sound Signal**	40-36-31.080N 074-02-18.540W					HORN: 1 blast ev 15s (2s bl). One oriented upstream and one downstream. Private aid.
34930	COAST GUARD STATION SOUTH ENTRANCE LIGHT	40-36-46.067N 074-03-36.744W	Fl G 4s	20	3	On Pole.	
34935	COAST GUARD STATION NORTH ENTRANCE LIGHT	40-36-46.882N 074-03-36.339W	Fl R 6s	20	3	On pole.	
34945	Gowanus Flats Lighted Bell Buoy 26	40-38-03.406N 074-03-02.020W	Fl R 2.5s		4	Red.	
34946	CROMWELL PIER SOUTH HAZARD LIGHT	40-38-13.750N 074-04-13.800W	F W	20		On metal pole.	Private aid.
34946.1	CROMWELL PIER NORTH HAZARD LIGHT	40-38-14.860N 074-04-14.000W	F W	20		On metal pole.	Private aid.
34949	ST. GEORGE FERRY TERMINAL FOG LIGHT	40-38-38.880N 074-04-15.000W	STROBE			Marks wharf dolphin.	Private aid.
34955	**St. George Ferry Terminal Slip 4 Sound Signal**	40-38-41.000N 074-04-18.000W				On wharf dolphin.	HORN: (two-tone) 1 blast ev 15s (3s bl). Private aid.
34961	**ST. GEORGE FERRY RACON**	40-38-38.880N 074-04-15.000W					RACON: S (. . .) Private aid.
34965	Gowanus Flats Lighted Bell Buoy 28	40-38-38.805N 074-03-14.022W	Q R		3	Red.	
34970	Robbins Reef Lighted Gong Buoy 29	40-39-10.004N 074-03-49.823W	Q G		3	Green.	
34975	ROBBINS REEF LIGHT	40-39-26.544N 074-03-55.292W	Fl G 6s	56	7	Conical tower, lower half brown, upper half white, white base.	
34980	Gowanus Flats Lighted Bell Buoy 30	40-39-19.704N 074-03-01.821W	Fl R 2.5s		3	Red.	
34985	Gowanus Flats Lighted Gong Buoy 31	40-39-54.104N 074-03-09.321W	Fl G 2.5s		4	Green.	
34990	Gowanus Flats Lighted Buoy 32	40-40-19.003N 074-02-24.020W	Fl R 4s		3	Red.	
34995	Liberty Island Lighted Gong Buoy 33	40-41-02.102N 074-02-24.721W	Fl G 2.5s		3	Green.	

(1) No.	(2) Name and Location	(3) Position	(4) Characteristic	(5) Height	(6) Range	(7) Structure	(8) Remarks
			NEW YORK - First District				
	NEW YORK HARBOR						
	Main Channel						
35005	*Ellis Island Lighted Gong Buoy 35*	40-41-39.602N 074-02-00.320W	Fl G 4s		4	Green.	
35006	Ellis Island Security Zone Buoy ELSZ1	40-42-00.570N 074-02-37.620W				White with orange bands.	Private aid.
35006.1	Ellis Island Security Zone Buoy ELSZ2	40-41-53.670N 074-02-46.200W				White with orange bands.	Private aid.
35006.2	Ellis Island Security Zone Buoy ELSZ3	40-41-47.010N 074-02-38.150W				White with orange bands.	Private aid.
35006.3	Ellis Island Security Zone Buoy ELSZ4	40-41-41.040N 074-02-30.460W				White with orange bands.	Private aid.
35006.4	Ellis Island Security Zone Buoy ELSZ5	40-41-46.200N 074-02-22.960W				White with orange bands.	Private aid.
35006.5	Ellis Island Security Zone Buoy ELSZ6	40-41-51.000N 074-02-13.500W				White with orange bands.	Private aid.
35006.6	Ellis Island Security Zone Buoy ELSZ7	40-41-57.430N 074-02-07.440W				White with orange bands.	Private aid.
35006.7	Ellis Island Security Zone Buoy ELSZ8	40-42-02.590N 074-02-14.320W				White with orange bands.	Private aid.
35006.8	Ellis Island Security Zone Buoy ELSZ9	40-42-09.290N 074-02-23.860W				White with orange bands.	Private aid.
35006.9	Ellis Island Security Zone Buoy ELSZ10	40-42-06.500N 074-02-27.740W				White with orange bands.	Private aid.
35010	GOVERNORS ISLAND LIGHT	40-41-34.632N 074-01-10.814W	Iso R 6s	75	7	Red skeleton tower, gallery at top.	
			NEW YORK AND NEW JERSEY - First District				
	APPROACHES TO NEW YORK - FIRE ISLAND LIGHT TO SEA GIRT						
	Main Channel South Approach						
35020	Shrewsbury Rocks Buoy 1SR East end of rocky shoal.	40-20-31.232N 073-56-45.519W				Green can.	
35025	HIGHLANDS LIGHT	40-23-47.640N 073-59-09.000W	Iso W 10s			Brown octagonal shaped tower.	Obscured from 334° to 140°. Private aid.
	NEW YORK HARBOR						
	Swash Channel						
35030	- RANGE FRONT LIGHT	40-33-28.777N 074-06-26.595W	F W	80		White tower.	
35035	- RANGE REAR LIGHT 3,825 yards, 305.0° from front light.	40-34-33.842N 074-08-28.372W	F W	225		On same structure as Staten Island Light.	
35040	**Sandy Hook Light**	40-27-42.209N 074-00-07.323W	F W	88	19	88	Lighted throughout 24 hours.
35045	- Bell Buoy 2S	40-29-25.017N 073-58-23.112W				Red.	
35050	- Buoy 4S On southwest side of shoal.	40-29-48.117N 073-59-14.713W				Red nun.	
35055	- Bell Buoy 6S On southwest side of Romer Shoal.	40-30-09.332N 074-00-08.114W				Red.	
35060	- Buoy 7S Marks edge of shoal.	40-29-52.907N 074-00-18.875W				Green can.	
35065	- *Lighted Bell Buoy 8S* Marks southwest edge of shoal.	40-30-36.405N 074-01-01.686W	Fl R 2.5s		4	Red.	
35070	**Romer Shoal Light**	40-30-46.855N 074-00-48.686W	Fl (2)W 15s	54	15	Conical tower, lower part white upper part brown; on black cylindrical pier. 54	Emergency light of reduced intensity when main light is extinguished. HORN: 2 blasts ev 30s (2s bl-2s si-2s bl-24s si) Operates continuously.
35075	- Buoy 9S	40-30-50.215N 074-01-57.718W				Green can.	
35080	- Buoy 10S	40-31-25.532N 074-02-06.914W				Red nun.	

(1) No.	(2) Name and Location	(3) Position	(4) Characteristic	(5) Height	(6) Range	(7) Structure	(8) Remarks
			NEW YORK AND NEW JERSEY - First District				
	NEW YORK HARBOR						
	Sandy Hook Channel						
35085	*Scotland Lighted Whistle Buoy S*	40-26-32.820N 073-55-00.605W	Mo (A) W		6	Red and white stripes with red spherical topmark.	RACON: M (- -) RACON: M (- -)
35090	*- Lighted Gong Buoy 1*	40-27-10.560N 073-56-16.906W	Fl G 2.5s		3	Green.	
35095	*- Lighted Buoy 2*	40-27-17.765N 073-56-10.919W	Fl R 2.5s		3	Red.	
35100	*- Lighted Buoy 3*	40-27-43.119N 073-57-10.609W	Fl G 4s		3	Green.	
35105	*- Lighted Buoy 4*	40-27-49.899N 073-57-04.316W	Fl R 4s		3	Red.	
35110	*- Lighted Buoy 5*	40-28-13.249N 073-57-59.404W	Fl G 2.5s		3	Green.	
35115	*- Lighted Buoy 6*	40-28-19.912N 073-57-53.254W	Fl R 2.5s		3	Red.	
35120	*- Lighted Bell Buoy 8*	40-28-50.718N 073-58-44.812W	Fl R 4s		3	Red.	
35125	*- Lighted Buoy 7*	40-28-44.181N 073-58-51.596W	Q G		3	Green.	
35130	*- Buoy 10*	40-29-08.704N 073-59-15.808W				Red nun.	
35135	*- RANGE FRONT LIGHT*	40-29-15.136N 073-59-35.136W	Q W (G sector) (R sector)	45	W 6 G 4 R 4	KGB (E section) KRW (Main section) on skeleton tower.	RACON: C (- . - .) Red from 063.0° to 073.0°. Green from 300.5° to 315.5°.
35140	*- RANGE REAR LIGHT (EAST SECTION)* 1,729 yards, 308.1° from front light.	40-29-46.783N 074-00-27.969W	Iso G 6s	94		KGB on skeleton tower.	Range light visible 4° each side of rangeline. Passing light Fl Y 4s, nominal range 5 miles.
35145	*- RANGE REAR LIGHT (MAIN SECTION)* 315 yards, 067.5° from front light.	40-29-18.448N 073-59-24.311W	Iso R 6s	68		KRW on skeleton tower.	Passing light Fl Y 4s, nominal range 5 miles.
35150	*- Lighted Buoy 12*	40-29-09.404N 074-00-13.352W	Fl R 2.5s		3	Red.	Replaced by LIB of reduced intensity when endangered by ice.
35155	*- Lighted Gong Buoy 11*	40-28-59.636N 074-00-14.914W	Fl G 2.5s		3	Green.	Replaced by can when endangered by ice.
35157	*- Lighted Buoy 11A*	40-28-57.658N 074-00-28.385W	Fl G 4s		3		MMSI: 993672779
35160	*- Lighted Buoy 14*	40-29-02.191N 074-00-44.510W	Q R		3		
35165	*- Lighted Gong Buoy 13*	40-28-51.895N 074-00-39.773W	Q G		3	Green.	Replaced by LIB of reduced intensity when endangered by ice.
35170	*- Lighted Buoy 16*	40-28-46.508N 074-01-22.096W	Fl R 2.5s		3	Red.	
35175	*- Lighted Gong Buoy 17*	40-28-32.118N 074-01-40.617W	Fl G 2.5s		3	Green.	Replaced by LIB of reduced intensity when endangered by ice.
35180	*- Lighted Bell Buoy 18*	40-28-34.065N 074-02-02.059W	Fl R 4s		3	Red.	Replaced by LIB of reduced intensity when endangered by ice.
35185	*- Lighted Buoy 20*	40-28-33.618N 074-02-17.918W	Fl R 2.5s		3	Red.	Replaced by LIB of reduced intensity when endangered by ice.
35190	SANDY HOOK POINT LIGHT	40-28-14.732N 074-01-07.214W	Iso W 6s	38	7	NB on skeleton tower.	

(1) No.	(2) Name and Location	(3) Position	(4) Characteristic	(5) Height	(6) Range	(7) Structure	(8) Remarks

NEW YORK HARBOR

Chapel Hill South Channel

(1) No.	(2) Name and Location	(3) Position	(4) Characteristic	(5) Height	(6) Range	(7) Structure	(8) Remarks
35195	*Southwest Spit Junction Lighted Gong Buoy SP*	40-28-45.673N 074-03-17.819W	Fl (2+1)R 6s		3	Red and green bands.	Replaced by LIB of reduced intensity when endangered by ice.
35200	- Buoy 2	40-28-46.498N 074-02-39.648W				Red nun.	
35205	- *Lighted Buoy 3*	40-28-55.709N 074-02-57.139W	Q G		3	Green.	Replaced by can when endangered by ice.
35210	- Buoy 4	40-29-04.487N 074-02-42.598W				Red nun.	
35215	- Buoy 5	40-29-40.466N 074-02-50.737W				Green can.	
35220	- Buoy 6	40-29-36.797N 074-02-38.168W				Red nun.	
35225	- Buoy 7	40-30-12.026N 074-02-46.289W				Green can.	
35230	- Buoy 8	40-30-08.976N 074-02-33.688W				Red nun.	
35235	- *Lighted Bell Buoy 10*	40-30-44.207N 074-02-28.868W	Fl R 4s		3	Red.	Replaced by nun when endangered by ice.
35240	- Buoy 11	40-30-53.615N 074-02-41.219W				Green can.	
35245	- Junction Buoy CH	40-31-17.815N 074-02-24.118W				Red and green bands; nun.	
35250	- Buoy 13	40-31-22.114N 074-02-37.019W				Green can.	

Chapel Hill North Channel

(1) No.	(2) Name and Location	(3) Position	(4) Characteristic	(5) Height	(6) Range	(7) Structure	(8) Remarks
35255	- Buoy 14	40-31-57.792N 074-02-13.956W				Red nun.	
35260	- *Lighted Buoy 15*	40-31-59.286N 074-02-27.322W	Fl G 2.5s		3	Green.	
35265	- *Lighted Bell Buoy 17*	40-32-48.032N 074-02-20.014W	Fl G 4s		3	Green.	

Coney Island Channel

(1) No.	(2) Name and Location	(3) Position	(4) Characteristic	(5) Height	(6) Range	(7) Structure	(8) Remarks
35285	- Buoy 1 On northeast point of shoal.	40-33-51.543N 073-57-49.164W				Green can.	
35286	- Buoy 2	40-33-55.532N 073-57-26.514W				Red nun.	
35290	- Buoy 3 On north side of shoal.	40-33-55.127N 073-58-25.528W				Green can.	
35295	- Buoy 5 On north side of shoal.	40-33-50.032N 073-58-59.014W				Green can.	
35305	- *Lighted Buoy 6*	40-33-59.532N 073-59-16.014W	Fl R 4s		4	Red.	
35310	- Buoy 7 On north side of shoal.	40-33-59.032N 073-59-46.514W				Green can.	
35315	- Buoy 8	40-34-09.210N 074-00-06.591W				Red nun.	
35320	- Buoy 9	40-34-03.843N 074-00-30.404W				Green can.	
35330	- *Lighted Bell Buoy 10*	40-34-09.426N 074-00-37.618W	Fl R 4s		3	Red.	

Coney Island Creek Entrance

(1) No.	(2) Name and Location	(3) Position	(4) Characteristic	(5) Height	(6) Range	(7) Structure	(8) Remarks
35335	- Buoy 1 On south side of 6-foot shoal.	40-34-58.610N 074-00-20.216W				Green can.	
35340	- Buoy 3 On south side of 5-foot shoal.	40-34-57.711N 074-00-07.815W				Green can.	

Gravesend Bay

(1) No.	(2) Name and Location	(3) Position	(4) Characteristic	(5) Height	(6) Range	(7) Structure	(8) Remarks
35345	- Anchorage Buoy A	40-35-52.032N 074-01-42.514W				Yellow nun.	AIS: MMSI 993672068 (21)

(1) No.	(2) Name and Location	(3) Position	(4) Characteristic	(5) Height	(6) Range	(7) Structure	(8) Remarks
			NEW YORK AND NEW JERSEY - First District				
	NEW YORK HARBOR						
	Gravesend Bay						
35350	- Channel Buoy 1	40-35-19.302N 074-01-02.711W				Green can.	
35360	- Channel Buoy 2	40-35-05.510N 074-00-21.216W				Red nun.	
35370	- Channel Buoy 3	40-35-13.432N 074-00-08.514W				Green can.	
35375	- Channel Buoy 4	40-35-17.432N 073-59-57.014W				Red nun.	
35380	- Channel Buoy 5	40-35-21.210N 074-00-00.415W				Green can.	
35385	- Anchorage Buoy C	40-34-58.210N 074-01-21.517W				Yellow nun.	AIS: MMSI 993672069 (21)
35390	- Anchorage Buoy B	40-35-25.532N 074-01-32.514W				Yellow nun.	AIS: MMSI 993672070 (21)
	Old Orchard Shoal *Racing buoys are maintained from June 1 to Oct. 1.*						
35395	- LIGHT	40-30-44.304N 074-05-55.383W	Fl W 6s	20	4	Spindle on rocks.	
	Great Kills Harbor *Channel buoys located 50 feet outside channel limit.*						
35450	GREAT KILLS LIGHT On end of shoal.	40-31-17.832N 074-07-53.815W	Fl W 4s	35	6	NR on skeleton tower, red base.	
35455	GREAT KILLS ENTRANCE LIGHT A	40-32-06.999N 074-08-32.030W	Fl W 2.5s	27	5	NG on skeleton tower.	
35460	- Channel Buoy 2	40-31-21.017N 074-08-01.720W				Red nun.	
35465	- Channel Buoy 3	40-31-34.446N 074-08-13.239W				Green can.	
35470	- Channel Buoy 4	40-31-35.013N 074-08-11.428W				Red nun.	
35475	- Channel Buoy 5	40-31-45.971N 074-08-24.245W				Green can.	
35480	- Channel Buoy 6	40-31-47.997N 074-08-24.003W				Red nun.	Remove when endangered by ice.
35485	- Channel Buoy 8	40-31-57.530N 074-08-27.153W				Red nun.	
35488	- Channel Buoy 9	40-32-01.322N 074-08-30.910W				Green can.	
35490	- Channel Buoy 10	40-32-02.886N 074-08-28.547W				Red nun.	
35495	- Channel Buoy 11	40-32-19.412N 074-08-24.528W				Green can.	
35500	- Channel Buoy 12	40-32-19.412N 074-08-22.328W				Red nun.	
35510	- Channel Buoy 14	40-32-28.112N 074-08-24.928W				Red nun.	
35515	- Channel Buoy 16	40-32-38.811N 074-08-11.928W				Red nun.	
35517	Great Kills Danger Buoy	40-32-41.721N 074-08-08.131W				White can with orange bands worded ROCK.	
			NEW JERSEY - First District				
	NEW YORK HARBOR						
	Sandy Hook Bay						
35520	Sandy Hook Point Obstruction Buoy 1 On west side of obstruction.	40-28-19.009N 074-01-20.906W				Green can.	
35525	Anchorage Buoy E	40-27-57.869N 074-03-00.008W				Yellow can.	
	Leonardo Channel *Aids maintained from June 1 to Nov. 15.*						
35560	- Buoy 1	40-25-42.500N 074-03-24.500W				Green can.	Private aid.

309

(1) No.	(2) Name and Location	(3) Position	(4) Characteristic	(5) Height	(6) Range	(7) Structure	(8) Remarks
			NEW JERSEY - First District				

NEW YORK HARBOR
Sandy Hook Bay
Leonardo Channel
Aids maintained from June 1 to Nov. 15.

(1) No.	(2) Name and Location	(3) Position	(4) Characteristic	(5) Height	(6) Range	(7) Structure	(8) Remarks
35565	- Lighted Buoy 2	40-25-43.200N 074-03-26.100W	Fl R 4s			Red.	Private aid.
35570	- Buoy 3	40-25-37.400N 074-03-29.100W				Green can.	Private aid.
35575	- Buoy 4	40-25-37.800N 074-03-30.300W				Red nun.	Private aid.
35580	- Buoy 5	40-25-31.600N 074-03-33.900W				Green can.	Private aid.
35585	- Buoy 6	40-25-31.800N 074-03-35.000W				Red nun.	Private aid.
35590	- LIGHT 7	40-25-26.900N 074-03-37.000W	Fl G 2.5s			On pile.	Private aid.
	Sandy Hook Bay						
35595	ATLANTIC HIGHLANDS BREAKWATER LIGHT	40-25-07.263N 074-01-10.439W	Fl W 4s	33	7	NR on skeleton tower.	
35596.2	ATLANTIC HIGHLANDS LIGHT 2	40-25-04.300N 074-01-14.400W	Fl R 5s			On pile.	Private aid.
35596.3	ATLANTIC HIGHLANDS LIGHT 3	40-25-00.000N 074-01-23.200W	Fl G 5s			On pile.	Private aid.
35596.4	ATLANTIC HIGHLANDS LIGHT 4	40-25-02.000N 074-01-23.600W	Fl R 5s			On pile.	Private aid.
35596.5	Atlantic Highlands Lighted Buoy 5	40-25-01.900N 074-01-41.300W	Fl G 5s			Green.	Private aid.
35596.6	Atlantic Highlands Lighted Buoy 6	40-25-03.000N 074-01-41.300W	Fl R 5s			Red.	Private aid.
35596.7	ATLANTIC HIGHLANDS LIGHT 7	40-25-02.200N 074-01-49.000W	Fl G 5s			On pile.	Private aid.
35597	Atlantic Highlands West Entrance Lighted Buoy 2	40-25-17.100N 074-01-59.000W	Fl R 5s			Red.	Private aid.
35597.1	Atlantic Highlands West Entrance Lighted Buoy 4	40-25-15.400N 074-01-59.100W	Fl R 5s			Red.	Private aid.
35597.2	ATLANTIC HIGHLANDS WEST ENTRANCE LIGHT 6	40-25-14.700N 074-01-59.800W	Fl R 5s			On pile.	Private aid.
35597.3	ATLANTIC HIGHLANDS WEST ENTRANCE LIGHT 8.	40-25-13.300N 074-02-01.400W	Fl R 5s			On pile.	Private aid.
35597.4	ATLANTIC HIGHLANDS WEST ENTRANCE LIGHT 10	40-25-12.200N 074-02-02.800W	Fl R 5s			On pile.	Private aid.
35597.5	ATLANTIC HIGHLANDS WEST ENTRANCE LIGHT 11	40-25-12.000N 074-02-02.000W	Fl G 5s			On pile.	Private aid.
	Terminal Channel						
35610	- Junction Lighted Buoy TC	40-28-22.408N 074-02-18.677W	Fl (2+1)G 6s		3	Green and red bands.	Replaced by LIB of reduced intensity when endangered by ice.
35615	- DOCK RANGE FRONT LIGHT	40-27-08.000N 074-03-09.000W	F R	33		KRW on pile.	Lighted throughout 24 hours. Private aid.
35620	- DOCK RANGE REAR LIGHT 800 yards, 207.5° from front light.	40-26-42.000N 074-03-22.000W	F G			KRW on pile.	Lighted throughout 24 hours. Private aid.
35625	- Lighted Buoy 1	40-28-08.033N 074-02-20.238W	Fl G 4s		3	Green.	
35630	- Lighted Buoy 3	40-27-37.326N 074-02-41.375W	Fl G 2.5s		3	Green.	
35635	- Lighted Buoy 4	40-27-43.232N 074-02-43.214W	Fl R 2.5s		3	Red.	
35640	- Buoy 5	40-27-26.119N 074-02-41.118W				Green can.	
35645	- Buoy 6	40-27-36.419N 074-03-06.518W				Red nun.	
35650	- Buoy 7	40-27-09.620N 074-02-49.518W				Green can.	

(1) No.	(2) Name and Location	(3) Position	(4) Characteristic	(5) Height	(6) Range	(7) Structure	(8) Remarks
			NEW JERSEY - First District				
	NEW YORK HARBOR						
	Terminal Channel						
35655	- Buoy 8	40-27-17.111N 074-03-21.410W				Red nun.	
35660	*Naval Weapon Station Earle* *Security Zone Lighted Buoy 1*	40-27-35.349N 074-02-28.260W	Q W		2	White with orange diamond marked SECURITY ZONE KEEP OUT.	Aid maintained by U.S. Navy.
35665	*Naval Weapon Station Earle* *Security Zone Lighted Buoy 2*	40-27-47.432N 074-03-00.614W	Q W		2	White with orange diamond marked SECURITY ZONE KEEP OUT.	Aid maintained by U.S. Navy.
35670	*Naval Weapon Station Earle* *Security Zone Lighted Buoy 3*	40-27-27.832N 074-02-10.314W	Q W		2	White with orange diamond marked SECURITY ZONE KEEP OUT.	Aid maintained by U.S. Navy.
35675	*Naval Weapon Station Earle* *Security Zone Lighted Buoy 4*	40-27-56.032N 074-03-24.014W	Q W		2	White with orange diamond marked SECURITY ZONE KEEP OUT.	Aid maintained by U.S. Navy.
35680	*Naval Weapon Station Earle* *Security Zone Lighted Buoy 5*	40-27-00.032N 074-02-29.514W	Q W		2	White with orange diamond marked SECURITY ZONE KEEP OUT.	Aid maintained by U.S. Navy.
35685	*Naval Weapon Station Earle* *Security Zone Lighted Buoy 6*	40-27-25.551N 074-03-44.676W	Q W		2	White with orange diamond marked SECURITY ZONE KEEP OUT.	Aid maintained by U.S. Navy.
35686	*Naval Weapon Station Earle* *Security Zone Lighted Buoy 7*	40-26-29.502N 074-02-51.146W	Q W		2	White with orange diamond marked SECURITY ZONE KEEP OUT.	Aid maintained by U.S. Navy.
35687	*Naval Weapon Station Earle* *Security Zone Lighted Buoy 8*	40-26-57.992N 074-04-03.014W	Q W		2	White with orange diamond marked SECURITY ZONE KEEP OUT.	Aid maintained by U.S. Navy.
35688	*Naval Weapon Station Earle* *Security Zone Lighted Buoy 9*	40-26-06.332N 074-03-12.494W	Q W		2	White with orange diamond marked SECURITY ZONE KEEP OUT.	Aid maintained by U.S. Navy.
	Compton Channel						
35690	- Buoy 2	40-27-09.539N 074-04-31.510W				Red nun.	
35695	- Lighted Buoy 1	40-27-08.729N 074-04-29.770W	Fl G 4s		4	Green.	Removed when endangered by ice.
35700	- Buoy 4	40-26-50.650N 074-04-39.921W				Red nun.	
35705	- Buoy 3	40-26-49.910N 074-04-38.170W				Green can.	
35710	- Buoy 6	40-26-30.400N 074-04-48.981W				Red nun.	
35715	- Buoy 5	40-26-29.980N 074-04-47.111W				Green can.	
35720	- Buoy 8	40-26-19.629N 074-04-53.134W				Red nun.	
35725	- Lighted Buoy 9	40-26-10.900N 074-04-55.711W	Q G		3	Green.	
	SANDY HOOK TO LITTLE EGG HARBOR						
	Shrewsbury River *Buoys in river are maintained from Apr. 15 to Dec. 1 unless otherwise noted.*						
35740	- Channel Lighted Buoy 2	40-25-12.920N 074-00-19.258W	Fl R 4s		3	Red.	Replaced by nun when endangered by ice.
35745	- Channel Lighted Buoy 3	40-25-01.115N 074-00-09.619W	Fl G 4s		3	Green.	Replaced by can when endangered by ice.
35750	- Channel Buoy 4	40-24-56.685N 074-00-12.139W				Red nun.	Removed when endangered by ice.

(1) No.	(2) Name and Location	(3) Position	(4) Characteristic	(5) Height	(6) Range	(7) Structure	(8) Remarks

NEW JERSEY - First District

SANDY HOOK TO LITTLE EGG HARBOR

Shrewsbury River

Buoys in river are maintained from Apr. 15 to Dec. 1 unless otherwise noted.

(1) No.	(2) Name and Location	(3) Position	(4) Characteristic	(5) Height	(6) Range	(7) Structure	(8) Remarks
35755	- *Channel Lighted Buoy 5*	40-24-49.513N 074-00-07.212W	Fl G 2.5s		3	Green.	Removed when endangered by ice.
35760	- Channel Buoy 6	40-24-43.855N 074-00-06.382W				Red nun.	Maintained year round.
35765	- *Channel Lighted Buoy 7*	40-24-42.258N 073-59-56.780W	Fl G 4s		3	Green.	Removed when endangered by ice.
35775	- *Channel Lighted Buoy 9*	40-24-38.052N 073-59-45.329W	Fl G 6s		3	Green.	Removed when endangered by ice.
35780	- Channel Buoy 10	40-24-23.824N 073-59-16.011W				Red nun.	
35785	- *Channel Lighted Buoy 11*	40-24-23.166N 073-59-04.175W	Fl G 2.5s		3	Green.	Removed when endangered by ice.
35786	- *Channel Lighted Buoy 11A*	40-23-56.508N 073-58-47.796W	Fl G 4s		3	Green.	Removed when endangered by ice.
35800	- Channel Buoy 12	40-23-25.440N 073-58-47.679W				Red nun.	
35805	- Channel Buoy 13	40-23-16.060N 073-58-39.439W				Green can.	Maintained year round.
35810	- *Junction Lighted Buoy NS*	40-23-13.760N 073-58-42.979W	Fl (2+1)R 6s		3	Red and green bands.	Removed when endangered by ice.
35815	- Channel Buoy 15	40-23-06.917N 073-58-37.585W				Green can.	
35820	- Channel Buoy 14	40-23-10.325N 073-58-40.710W				Red nun.	
35823	- Channel Buoy 16	40-22-54.256N 073-58-40.144W				Red nun.	
35825	- Channel Buoy 17	40-22-50.826N 073-58-37.409W				Green can.	Maintained year round.
35830	- *Channel Lighted Buoy 18*	40-22-41.926N 073-58-39.209W	Fl R 4s		3	Red.	Removed when endangered by ice.
35835	- *Channel Lighted Buoy 19*	40-22-24.659N 073-58-32.211W	Fl G 2.5s		3	Green.	Removed when endangered by ice.
35840	- Channel Buoy 20	40-22-21.726N 073-58-35.709W				Red nun.	
35845	- Channel Buoy 22	40-22-03.355N 073-58-31.916W				Red nun.	
35850	- Channel Buoy 24	40-21-42.369N 073-58-37.284W				Red nun.	
35851	- *Channel Lighted Buoy 26*	40-21-27.684N 073-58-36.139W	Fl R 2.5s		3	Red.	Maintained from Apr. 15 to Dec. 1.
35860	- *Channel Lighted Buoy 28*	40-21-17.049N 073-58-41.510W	Fl R 4s		3	Red.	Maintained from Apr. 15 to Dec. 1.
35870	- Channel Buoy 29	40-21-04.675N 073-59-09.634W				Green can.	
35872	- Channel Buoy 29A	40-20-57.862N 073-59-24.194W				Green can.	
35875	- *Channel Lighted Buoy 30*	40-21-06.074N 073-59-10.892W	Fl R 4s		3	Red.	Maintained from Apr. 15 to Dec. 1.
35877	- Channel Buoy 30A	40-20-59.089N 073-59-25.201W				Red nun.	
35885	- Channel Buoy 32	40-20-49.861N 073-59-44.402W				Red nun.	
35890	- *Channel Lighted Buoy 31*	40-20-48.451N 073-59-43.352W	Fl G 4s		3	Green.	Maintained from Apr. 15 to Dec. 1.

(1) No.	(2) Name and Location	(3) Position	(4) Characteristic	(5) Height	(6) Range	(7) Structure	(8) Remarks
			NEW JERSEY - First District				

SANDY HOOK TO LITTLE EGG HARBOR

Shrewsbury River
Buoys in river are maintained from Apr. 15 to Dec. 1 unless otherwise noted.

(1) No.	(2) Name and Location	(3) Position	(4) Characteristic	(5) Height	(6) Range	(7) Structure	(8) Remarks
35900	- Channel Buoy 33	40-20-30.038N 074-00-01.086W				Green can.	
35905	- Channel Buoy 35	40-20-24.869N 074-00-03.529W				Green can.	
35910	*- Channel Lighted Buoy 34*	40-20-27.922N 074-00-05.954W	Fl R 4s	3		Red.	Maintained from Apr. 15 to Dec. 1.
35915	*- Channel Lighted Buoy 38*	40-20-17.593N 074-00-05.520W	Fl R 2.5s	3		Red.	Maintained from Apr. 15 to Dec. 1.
35920	- Channel Buoy 37	40-20-16.851N 074-00-04.066W				Green can.	
35930	- Channel Buoy 39	40-19-50.328N 073-59-49.723W				Green can.	
35935	*- Channel Lighted Buoy 40*	40-19-50.543N 073-59-51.340W	Fl R 4s	3		Red.	Maintained from Apr. 15 to Dec. 1.
35940	- Channel Buoy 42	40-19-31.988N 073-59-50.604W				Red nun.	
35945	- Channel Buoy 44	40-19-22.830N 073-59-45.610W				Red nun.	
35950	- Channel Buoy 46	40-19-00.431N 073-59-51.410W				Red nun.	
35955	- Channel Buoy 47	40-18-51.031N 074-00-02.010W				Green can.	
35960	- Channel Buoy 49	40-18-44.531N 074-00-12.210W				Green can.	

Navesink River
Buoys in river are maintained from Apr. 15 to Dec. 1 unless otherwise noted.

(1) No.	(2) Name and Location	(3) Position	(4) Characteristic	(5) Height	(6) Range	(7) Structure	(8) Remarks
35965	- Buoy 3	40-23-02.427N 073-58-46.709W				Green can.	
35970	- Buoy 4	40-23-02.924N 073-58-49.508W				Red nun.	
35975	- Buoy 1	40-23-06.427N 073-58-46.510W				Green can.	
35980	- Buoy 2	40-23-10.725N 073-58-50.110W				Red nun.	
35985	- Danger Buoy A Marks end of submerged breakwater.	40-23-04.925N 073-58-43.010W				White with orange bands.	Maintained year round.
35990	- Danger Buoy B	40-23-03.333N 073-58-43.290W				White with orange bands.	
35995	- Danger Buoy C	40-22-59.638N 073-58-45.724W				White with orange bands.	
36000	*- Lighted Buoy 5*	40-22-57.026N 073-58-52.510W	Fl G 2.5s	3		Green.	
36005	- Buoy 6	40-22-56.066N 073-59-00.500W				Red nun.	
36010	*- Lighted Buoy 8*	40-22-52.877N 073-59-24.157W	Fl R 2.5s	3		Red.	
36020	- Channel Buoy 10	40-22-55.320N 073-59-39.898W				Red nun.	
36025	*- Channel Lighted Buoy 11*	40-22-57.747N 073-59-49.995W	Fl G 2.5s	3		Green.	
36030	*- Channel Lighted Buoy 13*	40-22-56.558N 074-00-12.081W	Fl G 4s	3		Green.	
36035	*- Channel Lighted Buoy 14*	40-22-57.626N 074-00-16.491W	Fl R 4s	3		Red.	
36049	- Channel Buoy 15	40-22-54.382N 074-00-29.550W				Green can.	
36050	*- Channel Lighted Buoy 15A*	40-22-55.136N 074-00-44.178W	Fl G 2.5s	3		Green.	
36055	*- Channel Lighted Buoy 17*	40-22-43.654N 074-01-24.186W	Fl G 4s	3		Green.	

(1) No.	(2) Name and Location	(3) Position	(4) Characteristic	(5) Height	(6) Range	(7) Structure	(8) Remarks
			NEW JERSEY - First District				
	SANDY HOOK TO LITTLE EGG HARBOR						
	Navesink River						
	Buoys in river are maintained from Apr. 15 to Dec. 1 unless otherwise noted.						
36057	- Channel Buoy 16	40-22-56.119N 074-00-44.805W				Red nun.	
36060	- *Lighted Buoy 18*	40-22-25.793N 074-02-15.471W	Fl R 2.5s		3	Red.	
36065	- Channel Buoy 19	40-22-12.773N 074-02-44.328W				Green can.	
36070	- *Lighted Buoy 20*	40-22-07.518N 074-03-05.361W	Fl R 4s		3	Red.	
36075	- *Lighted Buoy 21*	40-21-56.115N 074-03-22.794W	Fl G 2.5s		3	Green.	
36090	- Channel Buoy 22	40-21-40.322N 074-03-37.419W				Red nun.	
36095	- Channel Buoy 23	40-21-28.487N 074-03-45.686W				Green can.	
36100	- Channel Buoy 24	40-21-24.719N 074-03-50.216W				Red nun.	
			NEW YORK AND NEW JERSEY - First District				
	NEW YORK HARBOR						
	Raritan Bay						
36110	- *Channel Lighted Buoy 1*	40-28-33.227N 074-02-59.204W	Fl G 2.5s		3	Green.	
36115	- Channel Buoy 4	40-28-52.782N 074-03-49.754W				Red nun.	
36120	- *Channel Lighted Buoy 6*	40-29-03.862N 074-04-40.193W	Fl R 2.5s		3	Red.	
36125	- Channel Buoy 8	40-29-15.134N 074-05-30.634W				Red nun.	
36130	- *Channel Lighted Buoy 9*	40-29-20.531N 074-06-23.329W	Fl G 4s		3	Green.	
36135	- *Channel Lighted Bell Buoy 10*	40-29-26.130N 074-06-21.252W	Fl R 2.5s		3	Red.	
36140	- Channel Buoy 12	40-29-37.462N 074-07-11.663W				Red nun.	
36145	- *Channel Lighted Buoy 14*	40-29-48.313N 074-08-00.569W	Fl R 2.5s		3	Red.	
36150	- Channel Buoy 16	40-29-57.415N 074-08-42.443W				Red nun.	
36155	- Channel Bell Buoy 18	40-30-07.174N 074-09-25.599W				Red.	
36160	- *Channel Lighted Gong Buoy 19*	40-30-05.737N 074-09-47.098W	Fl G 4s		3	Green.	
36165	- LIGHT 20	40-30-12.574N 074-09-44.259W	Fl R 4s	30	6	TR on skeleton tower.	
36170	- Channel Buoy 25	40-30-17.528N 074-10-40.670W				Green can.	
36175	- *Channel Lighted Bell Buoy 26*	40-30-23.200N 074-10-38.428W	Fl R 2.5s		3	Red.	
36180	- *Channel Lighted Buoy 27*	40-30-22.816N 074-11-04.647W	Q G		3	Green.	
36185	- Channel Buoy 28	40-30-30.536N 074-11-10.279W				Red nun.	
36190	PRINCES BAY RANGE FRONT LIGHT	40-30-27.717N 074-12-44.389W	Q R	75		KRW on white skeleton tower.	Visible all around with higher intensity on range line.
36195	PRINCES BAY RANGE REAR LIGHT 63 yards, 266.8° from front light.	40-30-27.613N 074-12-46.818W	Iso G 6s	89		KRW on grey monopole.	Visible all around with higher intensity on range line.
36200	- *Channel Lighted Bell Buoy 30*	40-30-34.141N 074-11-31.171W	Fl R 2.5s		3	Red.	
36205	- *Channel Lighted Buoy 31*	40-30-26.313N 074-11-45.234W	Fl G 2.5s		3	Green.	
36210	- *Channel Lighted Buoy 33*	40-30-25.098N 074-12-11.578W	Q G		3	Green.	

(1) No.	(2) Name and Location	(3) Position	(4) Characteristic	(5) Height	(6) Range	(7) Structure	(8) Remarks
			NEW YORK AND NEW JERSEY - First District				
NEW YORK HARBOR							
Raritan Bay							
36215	- Channel Lighted Buoy 34	40-30-31.888N 074-12-24.979W	Q R		3	Red.	
36220	- Channel Lighted Buoy 35	40-30-17.305N 074-12-33.449W	Q G		3	Green.	
36225	- Channel Lighted Buoy 36	40-30-17.882N 074-12-44.040W	Fl R 2.5s		3	Red.	
36230	- Channel Buoy 38	40-30-08.882N 074-12-56.349W				Red nun.	
36235	- Channel Buoy 39	40-30-04.478N 074-12-50.588W				Green Can.	
36240	- Channel Buoy 40	40-29-57.962N 074-13-10.881W				Red nun.	
36245	- LIGHT 42	40-29-47.332N 074-13-27.315W	Fl R 4s	30	4	TR on square skeleton tower.	
36250	- Channel Lighted Buoy 41	40-29-53.607N 074-13-05.238W	Fl G 4s		3	Green.	
36260	- Channel Lighted Bell Buoy 46	40-29-30.295N 074-13-47.420W	Q R		3	Red.	
36265	- Channel Lighted Buoy 47	40-29-25.922N 074-13-42.078W	Fl G 4s		3	Green.	
36270	- Channel East Junction Buoy E	40-29-16.485N 074-14-06.186W				Green and red bands; can.	
36275	- Channel Lighted Buoy 49	40-29-15.251N 074-14-16.643W	Fl G 2.5s		3	Green.	
36280	- Channel Lighted Buoy 50	40-29-22.955N 074-14-17.289W	Q R		3	Red.	
36285	- LIGHT 52	40-29-25.932N 074-14-25.215W	Fl R 4s	24	4	TR on skeleton tower with base.	
36287	- BREAKWATER LIGHT A	40-29-37.984N 074-14-48.697W	Fl Y 2.5s	16			Private aid.
36287.1	- BREAKWATER LIGHT B	40-29-39.199N 074-14-44.126W	Fl Y 4s	16			Private aid.
36287.2	- BREAKWATER LIGHT C	40-29-40.258N 074-14-40.141W	Fl W 2.5s	15			Private aid.
36287.3	- BREAKWATER LIGHT D	40-29-41.474N 074-14-35.570W	Fl W 4s	15			Private aid.
36287.4	- BREAKWATER LIGHT E	40-29-41.247N 074-14-29.263W	Fl Y 2.5s	15			Private aid.
36287.5	- BREAKWATER LIGHT F	40-29-42.025N 074-14-26.340W	Fl Y 4s	15			Private aid.
36287.6	- BREAKWATER LIGHT G	40-29-43.015N 074-14-22.528W	Fl W 2.5s	15			Private aid.
36287.7	- BREAKWATER LIGHT H	40-29-43.792N 074-14-19.608W	Fl W 4s	15			Private aid.
36288	- BREAKWATER LIGHT J	40-29-43.728N 074-14-13.279W	Fl Y 2.5s	18			Private aid.
36288.1	- BREAKWATER LIGHT K	40-29-45.679N 074-14-10.291W	Fl Y 4s	18			Private aid.
36290	- Channel Lighted Buoy 53	40-29-16.309N 074-14-36.084W	Fl G 2.5s		3	Green.	
36295	- Channel Buoy 54	40-29-24.057N 074-14-33.524W				Red nun.	
36300	- Channel West Junction Buoy W	40-29-20.798N 074-14-50.422W				Green and red bands; can.	
36305	- Channel Lighted Buoy 55	40-29-23.247N 074-14-58.069W	Fl G 2.5s		3	Green.	
36310	- Channel Lighted Buoy 56	40-29-35.356N 074-15-01.838W	Fl R 2.5s		3	Red.	
36315	- LIGHT 58	40-29-44.132N 074-15-06.215W	Fl R 4s	30	5	TR on skeleton tower with red base.	
36319	- Channel Buoy 60	40-30-12.648N 074-15-23.667W				Red nun.	

315

(1) No.	(2) Name and Location	(3) Position	(4) Characteristic	(5) Height	(6) Range	(7) Structure	(8) Remarks
			NEW YORK AND NEW JERSEY - First District				
	NEW YORK HARBOR						
	Raritan Bay						
	Ward Point Secondary Channel						
36320	- Buoy 1	40-29-13.014N 074-14-02.836W				Green can.	
36325	- Buoy 4	40-29-06.014N 074-14-20.436W				Red nun.	
36330	- Buoy 3	40-29-02.014N 074-14-19.636W				Green can.	
36335	- LIGHT W	40-29-07.632N 074-14-27.615W	Fl W 4s	30	5	NR on spindle.	
36340	- Buoy 5 Marks 12-foot spot.	40-29-04.014N 074-14-43.137W				Green can.	
36345	- Buoy 6	40-29-09.014N 074-14-43.037W				Red nun.	
36350	Ward Point Anchorage Buoy A	40-29-14.514N 074-15-24.038W				Yellow can.	
36355	Ward Point Anchorage Buoy B	40-29-22.014N 074-15-28.538W				Yellow can.	
	Raritan Bay						
36360	*Point Comfort Shoal Lighted Buoy 11A* On north edge of shoal.	40-29-01.416N 074-07-32.726W	Fl G 4s		4	Green.	Replaced by can when endangered by ice.
	Keyport Harbor						
36370	- *Entrance Lighted Buoy 1*	40-28-27.216N 074-11-00.531W	Fl G 2.5s		3	Green.	Replaced by can when endangered by ice.
36375	- *Channel Lighted Buoy 3*	40-27-07.618N 074-11-49.633W	Fl G 4s		3	Green.	Replaced by can when endangered by ice.
36380	- Channel Buoy 5	40-26-52.418N 074-11-53.033W				Green can.	
36385	- *Channel Lighted Buoy 8*	40-26-37.418N 074-11-59.633W	Fl R 4s		3	Red.	Replaced by nun when endangered by ice.
36390	- Channel Buoy 7	40-26-36.618N 074-11-57.233W				Green can.	
36395	- Channel Buoy 9	40-26-29.018N 074-12-02.533W				Green can.	
36400	- Channel Buoy 10	40-26-28.818N 074-12-05.433W				Red nun.	
36405	- Channel Buoy 12	40-26-22.218N 074-12-14.033W				Red nun.	Replaced by nun when endangered by ice. .
	Cheesequake Creek						
36415	- LIGHT 1	40-27-54.805N 074-15-23.338W	Fl G 4s	26	4	SG on skeleton tower.	
36420	- LIGHT 2	40-27-56.325N 074-15-25.988W	Fl R 4s	28	5	TR on skeleton tower.	Higher intensity beam toward Red Bank Reach.
			NEW JERSEY - First District				
	RARITAN RIVER						
	Raritan River *Private aids maintained from 05/01 to 10/31.*						
36425	- Channel Bell Buoy 2	40-29-06.514N 074-14-56.337W				Red.	
36430	GREAT BEDS LIGHT	40-29-11.993N 074-15-10.937W	Fl R 6s	61	6	White conical tower on black conical pier.	
36435	- Channel Buoy 3	40-29-03.600N 074-15-38.494W				Green can.	
36440	- LIGHT 4	40-29-08.083N 074-15-35.658W	Fl R 4s	22	3	TR on skeleton tower.	
36445	- *Channel Lighted Buoy 6*	40-29-54.012N 074-16-58.241W	Fl R 4s		3	Red.	Replaced by nun when endangered by ice.

(1) No.	(2) Name and Location	(3) Position	(4) Characteristic	(5) Height	(6) Range	(7) Structure	(8) Remarks
			NEW JERSEY - First District				
	RARITAN RIVER						
	Raritan River						
	Private aids maintained from 05/01 to 10/31.						
36450	- Channel Buoy 5	40-29-51.712N 074-17-04.842W				Green can.	
36455	- Channel Buoy 7	40-30-14.712N 074-17-11.442W				Green can.	
36460	- *Channel Lighted Buoy 8*	40-30-27.723N 074-17-13.732W	Fl R 4s		3	Red.	Replaced by nun when endangered by ice.
36465	- Channel Buoy 9 North side of wreck.	40-30-37.611N 074-17-47.943W				Green can.	
36470	- Channel Buoy 11	40-30-35.011N 074-18-18.744W				Green can.	
36475	- Channel Buoy 13	40-30-25.904N 074-18-39.027W				Green can.	
36480	- LIGHT 14	40-30-24.530N 074-18-53.025W	Fl R 4s	26	3	TR on skeleton tower.	
36490	- *Channel Lighted Buoy 15*	40-30-14.011N 074-19-00.946W	Fl G 4s		3	Green.	Removed when endangered by ice.
36495	- *Channel Lighted Buoy 17*	40-29-51.711N 074-19-27.147W	Fl G 4s		3	Green.	Replaced by can when endangered by ice.
36500	- *Lighted Buoy 25* Marks sunken end of drydock.	40-29-30.048N 074-19-44.377W	Q G		3	Green.	Removed when endangered by ice.
36505	- LIGHT 27	40-29-13.932N 074-19-58.515W	Fl G 2.5s	25	3	SG on skeleton tower.	
36510	- Channel Buoy 28	40-29-13.312N 074-20-09.348W				Red nun.	
36515	- LIGHT 29	40-29-03.471N 074-20-37.218W	Fl G 4s	25	4	SG on skeleton tower.	
36520	- Channel Buoy 30	40-29-05.012N 074-20-43.949W				Red nun.	
36525	- Channel Buoy 31	40-29-03.912N 074-21-07.650W				Green can.	
36530	- LIGHT 32	40-29-03.871N 074-21-20.820W	Fl R 2.5s	25	3	TR on skeleton tower.	
36535	- Channel Buoy 33	40-29-00.422N 074-21-17.249W				Green can.	
36540	- LIGHT 35	40-28-18.532N 074-22-03.415W	Q G	25	3	SG on skeleton tower.	
36545	- Daybeacon 37 On edge of flats.	40-28-42.371N 074-21-58.581W				SG on skeleton tower.	
36550	- Daybeacon 39 On edge of flats.	40-28-39.291N 074-22-37.773W				SG on skeleton tower.	
36555	- Daybeacon 41 On edge of flats.	40-29-02.920N 074-23-00.514W				SG on skeleton tower.	
36560	- Daybeacon 43 On edge of flats.	40-29-06.420N 074-23-35.385W				SG on iron spindle.	
	Raritan River Cutoff Channel						
36585	*Perth Amboy Port Authority No Wake Lighted Buoy A*	40-30-16.500N 074-15-41.500W	Fl W 4s			White and orange.	Seasonal. Private aid.
36586	*Perth Amboy Port Authority No Wake Lighted Buoy B*	40-30-17.400N 074-15-40.200W	Fl W 4s			White and orange.	Seasonal. Private aid.
36587	*Perth Amboy Port Authority No Wake Lighted Buoy C*	40-30-16.400N 074-15-38.400W	Fl W 4s			White and orange.	Seasonal. Private aid.
36588	*Perth Amboy Port Authority No Wake Lighted Buoy D*	40-30-15.300N 074-15-38.400W	Fl W 4s			White and orange.	Seasonal. Private aid.
36590	- LIGHT 1 Northerly point of Great Bed Shoals.	40-29-54.232N 074-15-40.915W	Fl G 4s	33	4	SG on skeleton tower.	
36595	Raritan River Cutoff Buoy 2	40-30-01.913N 074-15-44.539W				Red nun.	

317

(1) No.	(2) Name and Location	(3) Position	(4) Characteristic	(5) Height	(6) Range	(7) Structure	(8) Remarks
	NEW JERSEY - First District						
	RARITAN RIVER						
	Raritan River Cutoff Channel						
36600	- Buoy 3	40-29-48.813N 074-15-46.339W				Green can.	
36605	- Buoy 6	40-29-36.032N 074-16-09.015W				Red nun.	
36610	- Buoy 5 100 feet outside channel limit.	40-29-36.713N 074-15-57.439W				Green can.	
36615	- LIGHT 8	40-29-34.532N 074-16-14.515W	Fl R 4s	29	4	TR on skeleton tower.	
36620	- Junction Lighted Buoy R	40-29-24.213N 074-16-08.740W	Fl (2+1)R 6s		3	Red and green bands.	Replaced by nun when endangered by ice.
	NEW YORK AND NEW JERSEY - First District						
	NEW YORK HARBOR						
	Arthur Kill						
36625	- Channel Lighted Buoy 2	40-31-16.912N 074-14-47.137W	Fl R 2.5s		3	Red.	
36635	**Outerbridge Crossing Sound Signal**	40-31-29.000N 074-14-49.000W				On bridge abutment.	HORN: 1 blast ev 15s (5s bl). Private aid.
36640	OUTERBRIDGE REACH RANGE FRONT LIGHT	40-33-06.477N 074-15-12.681W	Q G	24		KRW on small white house on piles.	Visible on range line only.
36645	OUTERBRIDGE REACH RANGE REAR LIGHT 243 yards, 351.6° from front light.	40-33-13.612N 074-15-14.068W	Iso G 6s	55		KRW on black skeleton tower.	Visible on range line only.
36650	- Channel Lighted Buoy 4	40-31-56.111N 074-14-54.838W	Fl R 2.5s		3	Red.	
36665	MAURER NORTH RANGE FRONT LIGHT	40-32-04.920N 074-15-14.760W	F R			KRW on orange pile.	Private aid.
36670	MAURER NORTH RANGE REAR LIGHT 120 yards, 230° from front light.	40-32-02.640N 074-15-18.060W	F G			KRW on orange pole.	Private aid.
36675	Maurer Rock Lighted Buoy A	40-32-12.000N 074-15-12.000W	Fl W 5s			White with orange bands worded ROCK.	Private aid.
36680	Maurer Rock Lighted Buoy B	40-32-15.000N 074-15-07.000W	Fl W 5s			White with orange bands worded ROCK.	Private aid.
36700	- Channel Lighted Buoy 5	40-32-15.410N 074-15-06.538W	Fl G 2.5s		3	Green.	
36705	- Channel Lighted Buoy 6	40-32-21.510N 074-14-59.838W	Fl R 4s		3	Red.	
36710	SHELL OIL SEWAREN LIGHT 1	40-32-26.000N 074-15-14.000W	Fl G 4s			On steel pole.	Private aid.
36725	- Channel Buoy 8	40-32-36.410N 074-15-03.138W				Red nun.	
36730	- Channel Lighted Buoy 10	40-32-45.780N 074-15-04.388W	Fl R 4s		3	Red.	
36735	- Channel Lighted Buoy 11	40-33-03.309N 074-15-04.939W	Fl G 4s		3	Green.	
36740	- Channel Lighted Buoy 12	40-33-04.009N 074-14-53.538W	Fl R 2.5s		3	Red.	
36745	- Channel Lighted Buoy 13	40-33-20.409N 074-14-34.538W	Fl G 4s		3	Green.	
36750	- CHANNEL LIGHT 14	40-33-14.532N 074-14-28.315W	Fl R 4s	33	4	TR on skeleton tower.	
36755	- Channel Buoy 14A	40-33-16.683N 074-14-31.029W				Red nun.	
36760	- Channel Lighted Buoy 15	40-33-29.909N 074-14-01.037W	Fl G 2.5s		3	Green.	
36765	- Channel Lighted Buoy 16	40-33-24.609N 074-13-57.937W	Fl R 4s		3	Red.	
36770	- Channel Lighted Buoy 17	40-33-31.909N 074-13-09.736W	Q G		3	Green.	

(1) No.	(2) Name and Location	(3) Position	(4) Characteristic	(5) Height	(6) Range	(7) Structure	(8) Remarks
			NEW YORK AND NEW JERSEY - First District				
	NEW YORK HARBOR						
	Arthur Kill						
36775	- Channel Lighted Buoy 18 Marks barge.	40-33-27.009N 074-13-07.436W	Q R		3	Red.	
36780	- Channel Lighted Buoy 20	40-33-32.409N 074-12-55.535W	Fl R 2.5s		3	Red.	
36785	- Channel Lighted Buoy 21	40-33-40.109N 074-12-57.936W	Fl G 4s		3	Green.	
36786	CARTERET MARINA SOUTH LIGHT	40-34-06.895N 074-12-48.395W	Fl W 2s			On black metal pole.	Private aid.
36787	CARTERET MARINA NORTH LIGHT	40-34-07.955N 074-12-47.965W	Fl W 2s			On black metal pole.	Private aid.
36790	- Channel Lighted Buoy 24	40-34-13.908N 074-12-37.835W	Fl R 4s		3	Red.	
36795	CARTERET DOCK LIGHT A	40-35-07.200N 074-12-34.620W	Q W			On yellow pyramid tower.	Private aid.
36800	CARTERET DOCK LIGHT C	40-35-09.420N 074-12-33.240W	Q W	31		On steel pyramidal tower.	Private aid.
36805	- Channel Lighted Buoy 30	40-35-17.247N 074-12-23.305W	Fl R 4s		3	Red.	
36815	- Channel Lighted Buoy 32	40-35-30.540N 074-12-14.263W	Fl R 2.5s		3	Red.	
36820	- Channel Lighted Buoy 34	40-35-50.977N 074-11-56.335W	Fl R 4s		3	Red.	
36825	- Channel Lighted Buoy 36	40-36-02.306N 074-11-54.945W	Q R		3	Red.	
36830	PRALLS ISLAND CHANNEL RANGE FRONT LIGHT	40-36-13.244N 074-12-17.701W	Q R	32		KRW on tower.	Visible 4° each side of range line.
36835	PRALLS ISLAND CHANNEL RANGE REAR LIGHT 189 yards, 185.2° from front light.	40-36-07.662N 074-12-18.363W	Iso R 6s	36		KRW on red tower.	Visible 4° each side of range line.
36840	- Channel Lighted Buoy 38	40-36-17.166N 074-12-07.783W	Fl R 4s		3	Red.	
36845	- Channel Lighted Buoy 43	40-37-23.577N 074-12-15.599W	Fl G 4s		3	Green.	
36850	GULFPORT PILE LIGHT A	40-37-38.820N 074-12-15.660W	F W	5		On dolphin.	Private aid.
36855	GULFPORT PILE LIGHT B	40-37-39.180N 074-12-15.300W	F W	5		On dolphin.	Private aid.
36860	GULFPORT PILE LIGHT C	40-37-40.800N 074-12-14.580W	F W	5		On dolphin.	Private aid.
36865	GULFPORT PILE LIGHT D	40-37-41.340N 074-12-14.580W	F W	5		On dolphin.	Private aid.
	Upper Bay						
	Bay Ridge Channel						
36870	- Lighted Gong Buoy 3	40-38-03.406N 074-02-47.720W	Fl G 2.5s		3	Green.	
36872	- Lighted Buoy 2	40-37-21.620N 074-02-48.675W	Q R		3	Red.	
36880	- Lighted Bell Buoy 5	40-38-44.505N 074-02-28.520W	Fl G 2.5s		3	Green.	
36885	- Buoy 7	40-39-16.805N 074-01-54.719W				Green can.	
36888	NYPD Buoy 1	40-38-45.000N 074-01-49.000W				Green can.	Private aid.
36889	NYPD Buoy 2	40-38-45.000N 074-01-51.000W				Red nun.	Private aid.
36890	- Lighted Buoy 9	40-39-49.304N 074-01-21.318W	Q G		3	Green.	
36891	- Lighted Gong Buoy 11	40-40-20.804N 074-01-26.718W	Fl G 2.5s		3	Green.	
	Erie Basin						
36895	- ENTRANCE LIGHT 2	40-40-18.023N 074-01-09.203W	Fl R 2.5s	14	3	TR on spindle.	

(1) No.	(2) Name and Location	(3) Position	(4) Characteristic	(5) Height	(6) Range	(7) Structure	(8) Remarks
			NEW YORK AND NEW JERSEY - First District				

NEW YORK HARBOR
Upper Bay
Bay Ridge Channel

(1) No.	(2) Name and Location	(3) Position	(4) Characteristic	(5) Height	(6) Range	(7) Structure	(8) Remarks
36955	- Anchorage Lighted Buoy A	40-40-00.604N 074-01-46.219W	Fl Y 4s		3	Yellow.	
36960	- Anchorage Lighted Buoy C	40-39-03.405N 074-02-24.519W	Fl Y 4s		3	Yellow.	
36965	GOWANUS BAY WHARF LIGHT	40-39-53.100N 074-00-27.360W	Fl W 5s	12		On wharf piling.	HORN: 1 blast ev 5s (1s bl). Private aid.
	Buttermilk Channel						
36975	- RANGE FRONT LIGHT	40-40-51.787N 074-00-59.937W	Q G	26		KRW on skeleton tower.	Visible 1.5° each side of range line.
36980	- RANGE REAR LIGHT 238 yards, 068.9° from front light.	40-40-54.324N 074-00-51.290W	Iso G 6s	76		KRW on skeleton tower.	Visible 1.5° each side of range line.
36985	- Entrance Lighted Gong Buoy 1	40-40-48.112N 074-01-43.571W	Fl G 4s		4	Green.	
36990	- Buoy 5	40-41-13.343N 074-00-46.446W				Green can.	
36995	- Buoy 7	40-41-18.402N 074-00-41.517W				Green can.	
	Constable Hook Channel						
37000	- Buoy 2	40-39-17.624N 074-04-51.992W				Red nun.	
	New Jersey Pierhead						
37010	- South Entrance Lighted Buoy 1	40-39-16.204N 074-04-42.424W	Q G		3	Green.	
37015	- South Entrance Lighted Buoy 2	40-39-09.159N 074-04-26.815W	Q R		3	Red.	
37020	- South Entrance Lighted Buoy 5	40-39-25.506N 074-04-20.601W	Fl G 2.5s		3	Green.	
37025	- South Entrance Buoy 4	40-39-22.322N 074-04-13.025W				Red nun.	
37030	- South Channel Buoy 7	40-39-31.204N 074-04-18.024W				Green can.	
37031	- South Channel Buoy 8	40-39-30.832N 074-04-06.515W				Red nun.	
37032	- South Channel Lighted Buoy 12	40-39-51.718N 074-03-54.328W	Fl R 4s		3	Red.	
37033	- South Channel Lighted Buoy 13	40-39-56.308N 074-03-58.831W	Fl G 4s		3	Green.	
37034	- South Channel Buoy 14	40-40-01.603N 074-03-48.223W				Red nun.	
37035	- South Channel Lighted Buoy 16	40-40-11.498N 074-03-41.242W	Fl R 4s		3	Red.	
37036	- South Channel Buoy 18	40-40-17.392N 074-03-37.305W				Red nun.	
37037	- South Channel Buoy 19	40-40-20.603N 074-03-41.623W				Green can.	
37038	- South Channel Lighted Buoy P	40-40-26.703N 074-03-37.223W	Fl (2+1)G 6s		3	Green and red bands.	
	New Jersey Pierhead Channel						
37039	- North Entrance Lighted Buoy 1	40-40-39.103N 074-02-49.621W	Fl G 4s		3	Green.	
37040	- North Entrance Bell Buoy 2	40-40-44.831N 074-02-40.405W				Red.	
37045	- North Entrance Buoy 3	40-40-38.503N 074-02-58.522W				Green can.	
37050	- North Entrance Buoy 4	40-40-43.203N 074-03-06.522W				Red nun.	
37055	- North Entrance Lighted Buoy 6	40-40-30.470N 074-03-31.778W	Fl R 4s		3	Red.	
	Port Jersey Channel						
37100	- Lighted Buoy 1	40-39-23.412N 074-03-29.345W	Fl G 4s		3	Green.	

(1) No.	(2) Name and Location	(3) Position	(4) Characteristic	(5) Height	(6) Range	(7) Structure	(8) Remarks
			NEW YORK AND NEW JERSEY - First District				

NEW YORK HARBOR
Upper Bay
Port Jersey Channel

(1) No.	(2) Name and Location	(3) Position	(4) Characteristic	(5) Height	(6) Range	(7) Structure	(8) Remarks
37103	- Lighted Buoy 2	40-39-37.322N 074-03-20.315W	Fl R 4s		3	Red.	
37110	SEWER TERMINAL LIGHT	40-39-29.660N 074-03-52.029W	Fl Y 4s	30		Gray house on terminal chamber.	Private aid.
37115	- Buoy 3	40-39-34.138N 074-03-54.226W				Green can.	
37145	- South Buoy 1	40-39-40.712N 074-04-29.079W				Green can.	
37150	Bayonne Golf Club Lighted Buoy 1	40-39-53.160N 074-04-59.220W	Fl G 4s			Green.	Private aid.
37151	Bayonne Golf Club Lighted Buoy 2	40-39-54.540N 074-04-58.820W	Fl R 4s			Red.	Private aid.
37152	Bayonne Golf Club Lighted Buoy 3	40-39-53.700N 074-05-04.440W	Fl G 4s			Green.	Private aid.
37153	Bayonne Golf Club Lighted Buoy 4	40-39-54.540N 074-05-03.600W	Fl R 4s			Red.	Private aid.
37154	Bayonne Golf Club Lighted Buoy 5	40-39-53.700N 074-05-18.120W	Fl G 4s			Green.	Private aid.
37155	Bayonne Golf Club Lighted Buoy 6	40-39-54.540N 074-05-16.680W	Fl R 4s			Red.	Private aid.
37180	Port Jersey North Basin Buoy B	40-40-27.303N 074-05-25.126W				White with orange bands; can.	
37181	- RANGE FRONT LIGHT	40-40-28.448N 074-05-26.643W	Q R			KRW on skeleton tower.	Private aid.
37182	- RANGE REAR LIGHT 429 yards, 299° from front light.	40-40-34.601N 074-05-41.115W	Iso G 6s			KRW on monopole tower.	Private aid.
37185	Port Jersey North Basin Buoy C	40-40-28.103N 074-05-11.725W				White with orange bands; can.	
37190	Greenville Channel Shoal Buoy G	40-40-31.259N 074-04-07.501W				Yellow can.	

Claremont Terminal Channel

(1) No.	(2) Name and Location	(3) Position	(4) Characteristic	(5) Height	(6) Range	(7) Structure	(8) Remarks
37195	- Lighted Buoy 1	40-40-10.003N 074-03-13.422W	Fl G 4s		4	Green.	
37200	- Lighted Buoy 2	40-40-13.803N 074-03-06.122W	Fl R 4s		3	Red.	
37203	- Lighted Buoy 5	40-40-24.609N 074-03-30.308W	Fl G 2.5s		3	Green.	
37205	- Lighted Buoy 4	40-40-24.703N 074-03-22.822W	Fl R 2.5s		3	Red.	
37208	- Lighted Buoy 8	40-40-44.126N 074-03-55.009W	Fl R 6s		3	Red.	
37208.5	PVSC Research Lighted Buoy UNYB	40-40-33.540N 074-04-08.280W	Fl Y 4s				Maintained 01 Jul-30 Oct. Private aid.
37209	- FRONT RANGE LIGHT	40-41-17.000N 074-04-50.000W	Iso Y 6s			On pile.	Range light is only activated when ships are actively docking. Private aid.
37209.1	- REAR RANGE LIGHT	40-41-29.000N 074-05-09.000W	Iso Y 6s			On Pile.	Range light is only activated when ships are actively docking. Private aid.

National Dock Channel

(1) No.	(2) Name and Location	(3) Position	(4) Characteristic	(5) Height	(6) Range	(7) Structure	(8) Remarks
37210	- Buoy 2	40-41-09.402N 074-02-39.821W				Red nun.	
37215	- Buoy 3	40-41-09.902N 074-02-48.121W				Green can.	
37220	- Buoy 5	40-41-13.602N 074-02-54.622W				Green can.	
37225	- Buoy 4	40-41-15.802N 074-02-50.021W				Red nun.	
37230	- Buoy 7	40-41-18.302N 074-03-01.922W				Green can.	
37235	- Buoy 6	40-41-19.584N 074-02-58.390W				Red nun.	

(1) No.	(2) Name and Location	(3) Position	(4) Characteristic	(5) Height	(6) Range	(7) Structure	(8) Remarks
			NEW YORK AND NEW JERSEY - First District				
NEW YORK HARBOR **Upper Bay** **National Dock Channel**							
37237	- Buoy L	40-41-23.407N 074-02-55.582W					Yellow nun.
Liberty Island							
37247	- Security Zone Buoy LISZ1	40-41-24.320N 074-02-29.370W				White with orange bands.	Security Zone. Private aid.
37247.1	- Security Zone Buoy LISZ2	40-41-18.880N 074-02-31.300W				White with orange bands.	Security Zone. Private aid.
37247.2	- Security Zone Buoy LISZ3	40-41-14.970N 074-02-35.840W				White with orange bands.	Security Zone. Private aid.
37247.3	- Security Zone Buoy LISZ4	40-41-15.070N 074-02-44.930W				White with orange bands.	Security Zone. Private aid.
37247.4	- Security Zone Buoy LISZ5	40-41-26.000N 074-02-58.000W				White with orange bands.	Security Zone. Private aid.
37247.5	- Security Zone Buoy LISZ6	40-41-32.000N 074-02-53.000W				White with orange bands.	Security Zone. Private aid.
37247.6	- Security Zone Buoy LISZ7	40-41-32.950N 074-02-44.400W				White with orange bands.	Security Zone. Private aid.
37247.7	- Security Zone Buoy LISZ8	40-41-30.180N 074-02-38.610W				White with orange bands.	Security Zone. Private aid.
37247.8	- Security Zone Buoy LISZ9	40-41-27.850N 074-02-33.700W				White with orange bands.	Security Zone. Private aid.
Kill Van Kull							
37250	CONSTABLE HOOK RANGE FRONT LIGHT	40-39-12.319N 074-05-16.746W	F R	50		KRW on skeleton tower.	Visible 5.5° each side of range line. Lighted throughout 24 hours.
37255	CONSTABLE HOOK RANGE REAR LIGHT 134 yards, 289.6° from front light.	40-39-13.652N 074-05-21.673W	F G	75		KRW on skeleton tower.	Visible 5.5° each side of range line. Lighted throughout 24 hours.
37261	- Channel Lighted Buoy 1	40-38-51.632N 074-04-19.615W	Fl G 4s		3	Green.	
37263	- Channel Lighted Buoy 3	40-38-57.532N 074-04-37.815W	Q G		3	Green.	
37265	- Channel Junction Lighted Whistle Buoy KV	40-39-02.474N 074-03-50.834W	Fl (2+1)R 6s		3	Red and green bands.	MMSI # 993676008
37270	- Channel Lighted Buoy 5	40-38-59.232N 074-04-55.415W	Fl G 2.5s		3	Green.	
37271	- Channel Lighted Buoy 6	40-39-10.323N 074-04-54.626W	Fl R 4s		3	Red.	
37275	- Channel Lighted Buoy 7	40-38-57.842N 074-05-09.455W	Fl G 4s		3	Green.	
37280	- Channel Lighted Buoy 8	40-38-54.319N 074-05-40.596W	Fl R 2.5s		3	Red.	
37285	- Channel Lighted Buoy 9	40-38-46.772N 074-06-26.163W	Fl G 6s		3	Green.	
37286	- Channel Lighted Buoy 11	40-38-31.869N 074-07-55.122W	Fl G 2.5s		3	Green.	
37290	PORT RICHMOND DOCK LIGHT A	40-38-29.300N 074-07-32.300W	F G			Green.	Private aid.
37295	PORT RICHMOND DOCK LIGHT B	40-38-29.100N 074-07-34.600W	F G			Green.	Private aid.
37300	- Channel Lighted Buoy 10	40-38-39.422N 074-07-32.605W	Q R		3	Red.	
37305	- Channel Lighted Buoy 13	40-38-31.654N 074-08-07.611W	Fl G 4s		3	Green.	
37310	- Channel Lighted Buoy 12	40-38-39.422N 074-07-50.405W	Fl R 4s		3	Red.	
37313	- Channel Buoy 12A	40-38-40.761N 074-08-01.787W					Removed when endangered by ice.
37315	- Channel Lighted Buoy 14	40-38-37.046N 074-08-21.056W	Fl R 2.5s		3	Red.	

(1) No.	(2) Name and Location	(3) Position	(4) Characteristic	(5) Height	(6) Range	(7) Structure	(8) Remarks
			NEW YORK AND NEW JERSEY - First District				
	NEW YORK HARBOR						
	Kill Van Kull						
37320	- Channel Lighted Buoy 15	40-38-28.192N 074-08-27.576W	Fl G 4s		3	Green.	
37325	- Channel Lighted Buoy 16	40-38-33.948N 074-08-41.321W	Q R		3	Red.	
37327	- Channel East Junction Lighted Buoy E	40-38-31.036N 074-09-15.375W	Fl (2+1)G 6s		3	Green with red band.	
37332	- Channel Lighted Buoy 17	40-38-25.091N 074-09-00.151W	Fl G 2.5s		3	Green.	
37335	- Channel Lighted Buoy 18	40-38-49.228N 074-09-20.080W	Fl R 4s		3	Red.	
37340	- Channel Lighted Buoy 20	40-38-51.964N 074-09-33.253W	Fl R 4s		3	Red.	
37345	- Channel Lighted Buoy 19	40-38-38.786N 074-09-21.873W	Fl G 4s		3	Green.	
37350	- Channel Junction Lighted Buoy A	40-38-44.819N 074-10-06.570W	Fl (2+1)G 6s		3	Green and red bands.	
37355	ELIZABETHPORT DIRECTIONAL LIGHT	40-38-47.313N 074-11-20.104W	F W R G	60	W 13 R 10 G 9	On skeleton tower.	Shows red from 267.25° to 268.8°; white from 268.8° to 269.2°; green from 269.2° to 270.75°.
37360	- LIGHT 22	40-38-51.392N 074-10-18.233W	Fl R 4s	25	5	TR on skeleton tower.	
37365	- Channel Buoy 21	40-38-44.550N 074-10-17.783W				Green can.	
37370	- Channel Buoy 24	40-38-50.261N 074-10-35.051W				Red nun.	
37371	ELIZABETH MARINA NE LIGHT	40-38-46.400N 074-11-10.300W	Q R			Atop fendering dolphin.	Private aid.
37372	ELIZABETH MARINA SW LIGHT	40-38-46.100N 074-11-10.700W	Q G			Atop fendering dolphin.	Private aid.
	Shooters Island Channel						
37374	Shooters Island South Channel Wreck Lighted Buoy WR1	40-38-27.500N 074-09-38.800W	Q G			Green.	Marks wreck in channel. Private aid.
37375	SHOOTERS ISLAND LIGHT 2	40-38-28.532N 074-09-36.115W	Fl R 4s	19	3	TR on spindle.	
37380	- Buoy 4	40-38-36.824N 074-09-55.242W				Red nun.	
37381	Mariners Harbor Yacht Club Daybeacon 1	40-38-39.120N 074-10-12.000W				SG on pile.	Private aid.
37382	Mariners Harbor Yacht Club Daybeacon 2	40-38-39.360N 074-10-12.480W				TR on pile.	Private aid.
			NEW JERSEY - First District				
	NEW YORK HARBOR						
	Newark Bay						
37385	- Channel Lighted Buoy 2	40-38-39.503N 074-08-52.896W	Fl R 2.5s		3	Red.	
37390	- Channel Lighted Buoy 3	40-38-57.884N 074-09-10.965W	Fl G 4s		3	Green.	
37395	- Channel Lighted Buoy 4	40-38-50.549N 074-08-54.892W	Fl R 4s		3	Red.	
37400	- Channel Lighted Buoy 5	40-39-07.656N 074-08-58.612W	Fl G 2.5s		3	Green.	
37405	- Channel Lighted Buoy 7	40-39-19.042N 074-08-51.821W	Fl G 2.5s		3	Green.	
37410	- Channel Lighted Buoy 6	40-39-17.516N 074-08-38.402W	Fl R 2.5s		3	Red.	
	Newark Bay Channel						
37425	South Elizabeth Channel Buoy 1	40-39-28.412N 074-08-59.265W				Green can.	
37427	IMTT DOLPHIN LIGHT WEST	40-39-05.000N 074-05-22.000W	Q Y				Private aid.
37428	IMTT DOLPHIN LIGHT EAST	40-39-10.230N 074-05-10.550W	Q Y				Private aid.

(1) No.	(2) Name and Location	(3) Position	(4) Characteristic	(5) Height	(6) Range	(7) Structure	(8) Remarks
			NEW JERSEY - First District				

NEW YORK HARBOR
Newark Bay
Newark Bay Channel

(1) No.	(2) Name and Location	(3) Position	(4) Characteristic	(5) Height	(6) Range	(7) Structure	(8) Remarks
37430	- Buoy 8	40-39-34.067N 074-08-28.231W					Red nun.
37435	*- Lighted Buoy 10*	40-39-48.930N 074-08-19.154W	Fl R 4s		3		Red.
37440	- Buoy 12	40-40-04.871N 074-08-09.454W					Red nun.

Port Elizabeth Channel

| 37445 | - Buoy 2 | 40-40-33.698N 074-08-11.906W | | | | | Red nun. |
| 37450 | - Buoy 4 | 40-40-44.531N 074-08-30.167W | | | | | Red nun. |

Port Newark Pierhead Channel

37455	- Buoy 6	40-40-50.433N 074-08-30.340W					Red nun.
37460	- Buoy 8	40-41-01.650N 074-08-20.242W					Red nun.
37465	- Buoy 10	40-41-13.377N 074-08-09.273W					Red nun.

Newark Bay

37470	*- Channel Lighted Buoy 14*	40-40-20.226N 074-07-59.858W	Fl R 2.5s		3		Red.
37475	- CHANNEL LIGHT 15	40-40-36.632N 074-08-06.815W	Fl G 2.5s	20	6	SG on skeleton tower.	
37477	- Channel Buoy 15A	40-40-35.878N 074-08-03.873W					Green can.
37480	- Channel Buoy 16	40-40-40.772N 074-07-50.776W					Red nun.
37485	*- Channel Lighted Buoy 17*	40-40-54.455N 074-07-55.685W	Fl G 6s		3		Green.
37490	*- Channel Lighted Buoy 18*	40-41-01.192N 074-07-41.762W	Q R		3		Red.
37495	*Port Newark Terminal Channel Lighted Buoy 1*	40-41-03.294N 074-07-55.680W	Fl G 2.5s		3		Green.
37500	Port Newark Terminal Channel Buoy 3	40-41-13.799N 074-08-05.555W					Green can.
37505	- LIGHT 19	40-41-11.332N 074-07-48.115W	Fl G 4s	20	5	SG on skeleton tower.	
37507	- Channel Buoy 19A	40-41-10.299N 074-07-45.575W					Green can.
37510	*- Channel Lighted Buoy 20*	40-41-12.010N 074-07-36.960W	Fl R 4s		3		Red.
37515	- Channel Buoy 21	40-41-38.449N 074-07-25.935W					Green can.
37520	- LIGHT 22	40-41-35.532N 074-07-18.615W	Fl R 4s	26	5	TR on skeleton tower.	
37525	- Channel Buoy 24	40-42-07.800N 074-07-00.529W					Red nun.
37530	- LIGHT NB	40-42-27.632N 074-07-08.015W	Fl (2+1)R 6s	30	4	JR on skeleton tower on white base.	

PASSAIC AND HACKENSACK RIVERS
Hackensack River

37535	- Channel Buoy 2	40-42-24.400N 074-06-59.629W					Red nun.
37540	- Channel Buoy 4	40-42-33.900N 074-06-55.029W					Red nun.
37545	- LIGHT 5	40-42-43.659N 074-06-56.058W	Fl G 2.5s	34	4	SG on skeleton tower on green base.	
37550	- Channel Buoy 6	40-42-40.800N 074-06-49.228W					Red nun.
37555	- Channel Buoy 7	40-42-52.499N 074-06-39.128W					Green can.

324

(1) No.	(2) Name and Location	(3) Position	(4) Characteristic	(5) Height	(6) Range	(7) Structure	(8) Remarks
			NEW JERSEY - First District				
	PASSAIC AND HACKENSACK RIVERS						
	Hackensack River						
37560	- Channel Buoy 8	40-42-48.799N 074-06-35.428W				Red nun.	
37565	- LIGHT 9	40-42-58.332N 074-06-31.115W	Fl G 4s	34	5	SG on skeleton tower on green base.	
37570	- Channel Buoy 10	40-42-58.199N 074-06-19.928W				Red nun.	
37575	- Channel Buoy 11	40-44-15.698N 074-05-32.627W				Green can.	
37580	- Buoy 12	40-45-05.103N 074-04-41.341W				Red nun.	
37585	- Buoy 13	40-44-56.897N 074-04-46.025W				Green can.	
37590	- Buoy 15	40-44-58.597N 074-05-02.626W				Green can.	
37595	- Buoy 16	40-46-17.296N 074-05-18.126W				Red nun.	
37600	- Buoy 18	40-47-44.095N 074-04-33.125W				Red nun.	
37605	- Buoy 20	40-48-14.494N 074-03-47.623W				Red nun.	
37610	- Buoy 22	40-48-27.394N 074-02-18.520W				Red nun.	
37615	- Buoy 24	40-49-10.094N 074-01-51.319W				Red nun.	
37620	- Buoy 26	40-49-36.993N 074-02-07.420W				Red nun.	
	Passaic River						
37625	- *Channel Lighted Buoy 2*	40-42-44.799N 074-07-17.529W	Fl R 4s		3	Red.	Replaced by nun when endangered by ice.
37630	- Channel Buoy 4	40-43-03.599N 074-07-17.529W				Red nun.	
	HUDSON & EAST RIVERS - GOVERNORS ISLAND TO 67th STREET						
	Hudson River						
37645	NORTH COVE MARINA LIGHT N	40-42-47.000N 074-01-04.000W	F Y			On pile.	Private aid.
37650	NORTH COVE MARINA LIGHT S	40-42-46.000N 074-01-04.000W	F Y			On pile	Private aid.
37655	Morris Canal Wreck Buoy WR2A	40-42-38.001N 074-02-03.220W				Red nun.	
37660	Morris Canal Entrance Buoy 1	40-42-33.801N 074-01-53.520W				Green can.	
37661	*Newport Associates Hazard Lighted Buoy A*	40-43-57.300N 074-01-30.800W	Fl W 4s			White with Orange bands.	Private aid.
37661.1	*Newport Associates Hazard Lighted Buoy B*	40-43-54.310N 074-01-34.000W	Fl W 4s			White with Orange bands.	Private aid.
37661.2	*Newport Associates Hazard Lighted Buoy C*	40-43-51.800N 074-01-34.900W	Fl W 4s			White with Orange Bands.	Private aid.
37664	*PVSC Research Lighted Buoy HR*	40-46-47.320N 074-00-14.220W	Fl Y 4s				Maintained 01 Jul-30 Oct. Private aid.
37665	GUTTENBERG OUTFALL LIGHT	40-47-16.000N 073-59-53.000W	Q Y			On end of walkway over outfall pipe.	Private aid.
37666	- Anchorage 16 CG Mooring Buoy	40-50-36.922N 073-57-36.854W				White with blue band.	
			HUDSON RIVER (New York) - First District				
	NEW YORK TO WAPPINGER CREEK						
	Hudson River						
37667	- *Channel Lighted Buoy 2*	40-51-12.468N 073-56-48.456W	Fl R 2.5s		3	Red.	Replaced by LIB when endangered by ice.
37668	JEFFERY'S HOOK LIGHT	40-51-00.750N 073-56-49.100W	Fl R 3s	40		Red lighthouse.	Private aid.

(1) No.	(2) Name and Location	(3) Position	(4) Characteristic	(5) Height	(6) Range	(7) Structure	(8) Remarks
			HUDSON RIVER (New York) - First District				
	NEW YORK TO WAPPINGER CREEK						
	Hudson River						
37669	- *Lighted Buoy 3*	40-53-19.337N 073-55-38.752W	Fl G 2.5s		4	Green.	Replaced by LIB when endangered by ice.
37670	- *Lighted Buoy 4*	40-53-35.190N 073-55-19.206W	Fl R 4s		3	Red.	Replaced by nun when endangered by ice.
37675	- *Lighted Buoy 5*	40-58-06.033N 073-54-12.014W	Fl G 4s		4	Green.	Year round radar reflective LIB.
37676	EXXON MOBIL DOCK LIGHT B	40-59-18.780N 073-53-13.990W	Fl W 4s			On dolphin.	Private aid.
37677	EXXON MOBIL DOCK LIGHT A	40-59-15.000N 073-53-13.990W	Fl W 4s			On dolphin.	Private aid.
37690	- *Lighted Buoy 7*	41-02-12.033N 073-53-06.015W	Fl G 2.5s		4	Green.	Year round radar reflective LIB.
37695	**TAPPAN ZEE BRIDGE RACON**	41-04-17.400N 073-52-51.600W				On bridge.	RACON: B (- . . .) Morse Code B (-...) Private aid.
	Tarrytown South Channel						
37715	- Buoy 1	41-04-25.581N 073-52-26.302W				Green can.	
37720	- Buoy 2	41-04-23.711N 073-52-24.212W				Red nun.	
37725	- Buoy 3	41-04-32.931N 073-52-15.622W				Green can.	
37730	- Buoy 4	41-04-29.371N 073-52-14.882W				Red nun.	
37731	TBC MARINA ENTRANCE LIGHT 1	41-04-31.720N 073-52-07.032W	Fl G 2s	10		On pile.	Private aid.
37732	TBC MARINA ENTRANCE LIGHT 2	41-04-29.721N 073-52-07.752W	Fl R 2s	10		On pile.	Private aid.
	Tarrytown North Channel						
37735	- Buoy 3	41-04-58.240N 073-52-29.403W				Green can.	
37740	- Buoy 4	41-04-51.840N 073-52-19.993W				Red nun.	
	Hudson River						
37743	*Nyack YC Race Course Lighted Buoy E*	41-06-12.000N 073-52-33.300W	Fl W 4s			White with Orange Bands.	Maintained 01 Apr - 01 Nov. Private aid.
37745	- *Lighted Buoy 8*	41-05-00.033N 073-52-48.015W	Fl R 4s		3	Red.	Year round radar reflective LIB.
37746	TARRYTOWN LIGHT	41-05-03.180N 073-52-28.380W	Fl W 6s	54		Tower.	White cast iron and concrete tower. Private aid.
37746.5	*Nyack Boat Club Mid Channel Buoy A*	41-05-31.824N 073-54-20.184W	Mo (A) W			Red and white vertically striped.	Flashes Mo (A) every 10 seconds. Seasonal aid, April 15 to 01 Nov. Private aid.
37747	*Hook Mountain Yacht Club Lighted Buoy 1*	41-05-39.000N 073-54-25.000W	Fl G 2s			Green.	Private aid.
37747.1	*Hook Mountain Yacht Club Lighted Buoy 2*	41-05-42.000N 073-54-25.000W	Fl R 2s			Red.	Private aid.
37747.2	Hook Mountain Yacht Club Buoy 3	41-05-39.000N 073-54-32.000W				Green can.	Private aid.
37747.3	Hook Mountain Yacht Club Buoy 4	41-05-42.000N 073-54-32.000W				Red nun.	Private aid.
37747.4	Hook Mountain Yacht Club Buoy 5	41-05-39.000N 073-54-37.000W				Green can.	Private aid.
37747.5	Hook Mountain Yacht Club Buoy 6	41-05-42.000N 073-54-37.000W				Red nun.	Private aid.
37748	*Hook Mountain Yacht Club Hazard Lighted Buoy A*	41-05-50.520N 073-54-47.220W	Fl W 6s			White with orange bands.	Private aid.
37749	*Hook Mountain Yacht Club Hazard Lighted Buoy B*	41-05-50.520N 073-54-38.460W	Fl W 6s			White with orange bands.	Private aid.
37750	- *Lighted Buoy 10*	41-06-47.059N 073-52-35.544W	Fl R 2.5s		4	Red.	Year round radar reflective LIB.

(1) No.	(2) Name and Location	(3) Position	(4) Characteristic	(5) Height	(6) Range	(7) Structure	(8) Remarks
			HUDSON RIVER (New York) - First District				
	NEW YORK TO WAPPINGER CREEK						
	Hudson River						
37755	- Lighted Buoy 11	41-07-32.618N 073-52-51.985W	Fl G 4s		4	Green.	Year round radar reflective LIB. AIS: MMSI 993672032
37758	- Lighted Buoy 13	41-08-15.628N 073-52-56.848W	Q G		3	Green.	Year round radar reflective LIB.
37760	- LIGHT 14	41-08-17.177N 073-52-44.504W	Q R	38	4	TR on tower, small house at base.	
37765	- Lighted Buoy 15	41-08-46.977N 073-53-18.356W	Fl G 2.5s		4	Green.	Year round radar reflective LIB. AIS:MMSI 993672033
37770	- Lighted Buoy 16	41-08-48.467N 073-53-02.926W	Fl R 2.5s		4	Red.	Year round radar reflective LIB.
37775	ROCKLAND LAKE LIGHT On shoal.	41-08-51.333N 073-54-17.215W	Fl W 6s	50	4	NG on skeleton tower.	
37780	- Lighted Buoy 18	41-09-51.746N 073-54-29.699W	Fl R 4s		3	Red.	Year round radar reflective LIB.
37785	- LIGHT 19	41-09-50.133N 073-55-20.315W	Fl G 4s	35	4	SG on same structure as Haverstraw Bay South Reach Range Front Light.	Visible all around.
37790	HAVERSTRAW BAY SOUTH REACH RANGE FRONT LIGHT	41-09-48.549N 073-55-20.240W	Q W	20		KRW on skeleton tower.	Visible 4° each side of rangeline.
37795	HAVERSTRAW BAY SOUTH REACH RANGE REAR LIGHT 295 yards, 155.5° from front light.	41-09-40.566N 073-55-15.530W	Iso W 6s	47		KRW on skeleton tower.	Visible 4° each side of rangeline.
37800	- LIGHT 21	41-10-34.733N 073-56-08.415W	Fl G 4s	38	4	SG on skeleton tower.	
37805	- Lighted Buoy 22	41-11-03.865N 073-55-59.512W	Q R		3	Red.	Year round radar reflective LIB.
37810	HALF MOON BAY SOUTH BREAKWATER LIGHT	41-11-46.100N 073-53-24.700W	Iso W 2s			On metal pole.	Private aid.
37815	HALF MOON BAY NORTH BREAKWATER LIGHT	41-11-54.500N 073-53-21.300W	Oc Y 4s			On metal pole.	Private aid.
37817	Croton Yacht Club Lighted Buoy 1	41-12-12.420N 073-53-36.300W	Fl G 4s			Green.	Seasonally maintained 01 Apr to 30 Nov. Private aid.
37817.1	Croton Yacht Club Lighted Buoy 2	41-12-11.520N 073-53-34.500W	Fl R 4s			Red.	Seasonally maintained 01 Apr to 30 Nov. Private aid.
37817.2	Croton Yacht Club Buoy 4	41-12-12.780N 073-53-33.300W				Red nun.	Seasonally maintained 01 Apr to 30 Nov. Private aid.
37817.3	Croton Yacht Club Buoy 6	41-12-14.160N 073-53-33.180W				Red nun.	Seasonally maintained 01 Apr to 30 Nov. Private aid.
37820	- Lighted Buoy 23	41-12-07.444N 073-56-47.154W	Fl G 2.5s		4	Green.	Year round radar reflective LIB. AIS:MMSI 993672034
37825	- Lighted Buoy 24	41-12-11.904N 073-56-39.154W	Fl R 2.5s		3	Red.	Year round radar reflective LIB.
	Bowline Point						
37830	- MARINE TERMINAL SOUTH DOLPHIN LIGHT	41-12-10.000N 073-57-20.600W	Q W	15		On mooring dolphin.	Private aid.
37835	- MARINE TERMINAL NORTH DOLPHIN LIGHT	41-12-16.700N 073-57-22.600W	Q W	15		On mooring dolphin.	Private aid.
37840	- Outfall Buoy A	41-12-18.000N 073-57-27.000W				White nun with orange bands worded DANGER SUBMERGED OUTFALL.	Maintained from Apr. 1 to Nov. 15. Private aid.
37845	- Outfall Buoy B	41-12-22.000N 073-57-27.000W				White nun with orange bands worded DANGER SUBMERGED OUTFALL.	Maintained from Apr. 15 to Nov. 15. Private aid.

(1) No.	(2) Name and Location	(3) Position	(4) Characteristic	(5) Height	(6) Range	(7) Structure	(8) Remarks
			HUDSON RIVER (New York) - First District				
	NEW YORK TO WAPPINGER CREEK						
	Hudson River						
37850	- Lighted Buoy 25	41-13-16.292N 073-57-16.522W	Fl G 4s		4	Green	Year round radar reflective LIB. AIS: MMSI 993672035
37860	- Lighted Buoy 26	41-13-18.473N 073-57-07.616W	Fl R 4s		3	Red.	Year round radar reflective LIB.
	Stony Point Bay Channel *Aids maintained from Apr. 15 to Nov. 15.*						
37865	- Lighted Buoy 1	41-13-36.000N 073-57-53.900W	Q G			Green.	Private aid.
37870	- Lighted Buoy 2	41-13-36.800N 073-57-54.400W	Q R			Red.	Private aid.
37872	- Lighted Buoy 2A	41-13-37.500N 073-57-58.000W	Q R			Red.	Private aid.
37875	- Lighted Buoy 3	41-13-37.200N 073-57-59.700W	Q G			Green.	Private aid.
37877	- Lighted Buoy 4	41-13-38.200N 073-58-00.900W	Q R			Red.	Private aid.
37880	- Lighted Buoy 5	41-13-38.700N 073-58-04.600W	Fl G 6s			Green.	Private aid.
37883	- Lighted Buoy 6	41-13-39.300N 073-58-04.900W	Q R			Red.	Private aid.
37885	- Lighted Buoy 7	41-13-39.700N 073-58-08.200W	Q G			Green.	Private aid.
37890	- Lighted Buoy 8	41-13-40.700N 073-58-09.400W	Q R			Red.	Private aid.
	Hudson River						
37895	STONY POINT LIGHT SP	41-14-27.611N 073-58-09.378W	Fl W 4s	58	5	NG on skeleton tower, central column, small house, concrete base.	
37900	HAVERSTRAW BAY NORTH REACH RANGE FRONT LIGHT	41-14-46.077N 073-57-48.305W	Q R	25		KRW on skeleton tower.	Visible on range line only.
37905	HAVERSTRAW BAY NORTH REACH RANGE REAR LIGHT 422 yards, 342.6° from front light.	41-14-58.003N 073-57-53.243W	Iso R 6s	49		KRW on skeleton tower.	Visible on range line only.
	Greens Cove Channel *Aids maintained from Apr. 1 to Dec. 1.*						
37910	- Lighted Buoy 1	41-14-47.400N 073-57-32.000W	Fl G 2s			Green.	Private aid.
37915	- Lighted Buoy 2	41-14-51.060N 073-57-23.520W	Q R			Red.	Private aid.
37920	- LIGHT 3	41-14-53.400N 073-57-22.620W	Fl G 4s			On pile.	Private aid.
37925	- LIGHT 4	41-14-51.660N 073-57-21.060W	Fl R 4s			On pile.	Private aid.
37926	Cortlandt Yacht Club Channel Lighted Buoy 1	41-14-41.880N 073-57-27.060W	Fl G 2s			Green.	Seasonal. Private aid.
37926.1	Cortlandt Yacht Club Channel Lighted Buoy 2	41-14-40.680N 073-57-26.940W	Fl R 2s			Red.	Seasonal. Private aid.
37926.2	Cortlandt Yacht Club Channel Lighted Buoy 3	41-14-43.800N 073-57-18.180W	Fl G 4s			Green.	Seasonal. Private aid.
37926.3	Cortlandt Yacht Club Channel Lighted Buoy 4	41-14-42.096N 073-57-17.400W	Fl R 4s			Red.	Seasonal. Private aid.
	Hudson River						
37930	- Lighted Buoy 27	41-16-34.271N 073-57-35.017W	Fl G 2.5s		4	Green.	Year round radar reflective LIB. AIS: MMSI 993672036
	Indian Point Security Zone						
37931	- Buoy A	41-16-08.000N 073-57-29.000W				White and orange.	Maintained from Apr. 15 to Nov. 15. Private aid.
37931.1	- Lighted Buoy B	41-16-11.500N 073-57-34.500W	Fl W 4s			White and orange.	Maintained from Apr. 15 to Nov. 15. Private aid.

(1) No.	(2) Name and Location	(3) Position	(4) Characteristic	(5) Height	(6) Range	(7) Structure	(8) Remarks
		HUDSON RIVER (New York) - First District					
	NEW YORK TO WAPPINGER CREEK						
	Hudson River						
	Indian Point Security Zone						
37931.2	- *Lighted Buoy C*	41-16-16.920N 073-57-25.680W	Fl W 4s			White and orange.	Maintained from Apr. 15 to Nov. 15. Private aid.
37931.3	- *Lighted Buoy D*	41-16-20.100N 073-57-22.260W	Fl W 4s			White and orange.	Maintained from Apr. 15 to Nov. 15. Private aid.
37931.4	- *Lighted Buoy E*	41-16-23.580N 073-57-18.600W	Fl W 4s			White and orange.	Maintained from Apr. 15 to Nov. 15. Private aid.
37931.5	- *Lighted Buoy F*	41-16-27.060N 073-57-14.100W	Fl W 4s			White and Orange.	Maintained from Apr. 15 to Nov. 15. Private aid.
37931.6	- *Buoy G*	41-16-23.160N 073-57-10.860W				White and orange.	Maintained from Apr. 15 to Nov. 15. Private aid.
	Hudson River						
37935	CHARLES POINT MARINA LIGHT A	41-16-33.700N 073-56-42.800W	Oc W 4s			White.	Private aid.
37945	PEEKSKILL BAY LIGHT P	41-16-56.633N 073-56-36.915W	Fl (2)W 6s	47	4	NB on skeleton tower.	
37950	Peekskill Bay South Channel Buoy 2	41-16-52.781N 073-56-36.605W				Red nun.	Maintained from Apr. 1 to Nov. 1.
37955	Peekskill Bay South Channel Buoy 3	41-17-02.301N 073-56-19.224W				Green can.	Maintained from Apr. 1 to Nov. 1.
37960	Peekskill Bay South Channel Buoy 4	41-16-59.991N 073-56-19.654W				Red nun.	Maintained from Apr. 1 to Nov. 1.
37963	- *Lighted Buoy 28*	41-17-55.812N 073-57-35.178W	Fl R 4s		3	Red.	Maintained from Apr. 1 to Nov. 1.
37965	- LIGHT 29	41-18-35.733N 073-58-41.815W	Fl G 4s	52	4	SG on skeleton tower.	
37970	- *Lighted Buoy 31*	41-18-46.241N 073-58-51.355W	Q G		3	Green.	Year round radar reflective LIB. AIS: MMSI 993672037
37975	- *Lighted Buoy 33* Southeast side of rocky shoal.	41-20-46.371N 073-57-50.516W	Fl G 2.5s		4	Green.	Year round radar reflective LIB. AIS: MMSI 993672038
37980	- LIGHT 35	41-21-08.633N 073-57-44.315W	Fl G 4s	46	4	SG on skeleton tower, small house.	
37990	GARRISON MARINA LOWER LIGHT	41-22-55.600N 073-56-53.600W	F R			Gray rectangular structure.	Maintained from May 15 to Oct. 15. Private aid.
37995	GARRISON MARINA UPPER LIGHT	41-22-55.600N 073-56-53.600W	F G			Gray rectangular structure.	Maintained from May 15 to Oct. 15. Private aid.
38000	- LIGHT 37	41-23-36.933N 073-57-02.415W	Fl G 4s	26	4	SG on skeleton tower.	
38005	- LIGHT 39	41-23-45.933N 073-57-04.115W	Q G	39	4	SG on skeleton tower.	
38010	- *Lighted Buoy 40* On west edge of flats.	41-23-53.566N 073-56-50.990W	Fl R 2.5s		3	Red.	Replaced by nun from Nov. 1 to Apr. 1.
38015	- LIGHT 44	41-24-13.433N 073-57-34.815W	Fl R 4s	61	4	TR on skeleton tower.	
38020	- *Lighted Buoy 46* On west side of rocks.	41-24-29.371N 073-57-43.515W	Fl R 2.5s		3	Red.	Year round radar reflective LIB. AIS: MMSI 993672039
38025	- LIGHT 48	41-27-19.333N 073-59-29.515W	Fl R 4s	45	4	TR on skeleton tower.	
38027	*Beacon Harbor South Hazard Lighted Buoy*	41-30-26.067N 073-59-29.303W	Fl W 2s			White and orange.	Seasonal 04/15 - 10/31 Private aid.

(1) No.	(2) Name and Location	(3) Position	(4) Characteristic	(5) Height	(6) Range	(7) Structure	(8) Remarks
			HUDSON RIVER (New York) - First District				
	NEW YORK TO WAPPINGER CREEK						
	Hudson River						
38028	*Beacon Harbor North Hazard Lighted Buoy*	41-30-30.956N 073-59-29.303W	Fl W 2s			White and orange.	Seasonal 04/15 - 10/31 Private aid.
38035	*- Buoy 51*	41-31-29.711N 074-00-03.058W				Green can.	
38050	**Newburgh-Beacon Bridge Sound Signal**	41-31-12.000N 073-59-58.000W				On bridge.	RACON: N (- .) HORN: 1 blast ev 20s (2s bl). Private aid.
38055	*- Lighted Buoy 52*	41-32-19.370N 073-59-12.516W	Fl R 2.5s		3	Red.	Year round radar reflective LIB.
38060	*HMM Intake Hazard Lighted Buoy A*	41-32-52.000N 073-58-44.000W	Fl (2)W 5s			White with orange bands. Can.	Private aid.
38061	*HMM Intake Lighted Hazard Buoy B*	41-32-51.000N 073-58-41.000W	Fl (2)W 5s			White with orange bands. Can.	Private aid.
38062	*HMM Intake Lighted Hazard Buoy C*	41-32-50.000N 073-58-37.000W	Fl (2)W 5s			White with orange bands. Can.	Private aid.
38063	*HMM Intake Lighted Hazard Buoy D*	41-32-49.000N 073-58-33.000W	Fl (2)W 5s			White with orange bands. Can.	Private aid.
38064	*HMM Intake Lighted Hazard Buoy E*	41-32-48.000N 073-58-29.000W	Fl (2)W 5s			White with orange bands. Can.	Private aid.
38074	*Chelsea Yacht Club Anchorage Lighted Buoy N*	41-33-21.000N 073-58-16.000W	Fl W 2s			White and orange.	Private aid.
38074.3	*Chelsea Yatch Club Anchorage Lighted Buoy W*	41-32-54.000N 073-58-40.000W	Fl W 2s			White and orange.	Private aid.
38074.4	*Chelsea Yacht Club Obstruction Lighted Buoy S*	41-33-14.000N 073-58-24.000W	Fl W 2s			White and orange.	Private aid.
38075	*- Buoy 54*	41-34-35.870N 073-57-22.513W				Red nun.	
	WAPPINGER CREEK TO HUDSON RIVER						
	Hudson River						
38080	*- Lighted Buoy 56* On west side of rock.	41-35-05.670N 073-57-20.212W	Fl R 2.5s		3	Red.	Year round radar reflective LIB.
38085	*- Buoy 58*	41-35-37.070N 073-57-16.912W				Red nun.	
38090	*- Shoal Lighted Buoy A* On south side of shoal.	41-38-39.370N 073-56-54.511W	Fl (2+1)R 6s		3	Red and green bands.	Permanent ice hull. AIS: MMSI 993672040
38095	*- Shoal Lighted Buoy B* On south side of shoal.	41-40-43.370N 073-56-36.510W	Fl (2+1)R 6s		3	Red and green bands.	Replaced by nun from Nov. 1 to Apr. 1. AIS: MMSI 993672041
38100	**Mid Hudson Bridge Fog Signal**	41-42-12.000N 073-56-44.000W				On bridge abutment.	RACON: M (- -) HORN: 1 blast ev 20s. Private aid.
38110	*- Lighted Buoy 59*	41-42-30.205N 073-56-44.981W	Fl G 2.5s		3	Green.	Year round radar reflective LIB.
38115	*- Lighted Buoy 60*	41-42-53.476N 073-56-36.317W	Fl R 2.5s		3	Red.	Year round radar reflective LIB.
38120	*- LIGHT 62*	41-46-09.233N 073-56-49.215W	Fl R 4s	46	4	TR on skeleton tower.	
38125	ROGERS POINT LIGHT RP	41-46-23.733N 073-56-53.415W	Fl W 4s	50	4	NR on skeleton tower.	
38130	ESOPUS ISLAND LIGHT EI	41-49-23.633N 073-56-52.315W	Fl W 4s	57	4	NR on skeleton tower.	
38131	*Poughkeepsie Yacht Club Lighted Buoy A*	41-49-24.100N 073-56-42.700W	Fl W 4s			White and orange.	Private aid.
38132	*Poughkeepsie Yacht Club Lighted Buoy B*	41-49-01.200N 073-56-45.100W	Fl W 4s			White and orange.	Private aid.
38135	*Esopus Island North Shoal Lighted Buoy EN* North of Esopus Island Shoal.	41-49-50.798N 073-56-50.560W	Fl (2+1)R 6s		3	Red and green bands.	Replaced by nun from Nov. 15 to Apr. 1.
38140	INDIAN KILL SOUTH LIGHT	41-50-06.000N 073-56-36.000W	F R	6		On pile.	Maintained from May 1 to Oct. 15. Private aid.

(1) No.	(2) Name and Location	(3) Position	(4) Characteristic	(5) Height	(6) Range	(7) Structure	(8) Remarks
		HUDSON RIVER (New York) - First District					
	WAPPINGER CREEK TO HUDSON RIVER						
	Hudson River						
38145	INDIAN KILL NORTH LIGHT	41-50-06.000N 073-56-36.200W	F G	6		On pile.	Maintained from May 1 to Oct. 15. Private aid.
38150	- *Lighted Buoy 63*	41-51-19.567N 073-56-43.708W	Fl G 2.5s		4	Green.	Year round radar reflective LIB.
38155	ESOPUS MEADOWS LIGHT	41-52-06.336N 073-56-29.721W	Fl W 2.5s	52	6	White conical tower on white dwelling.	
38160	- *Lighted Buoy 66*	41-52-14.734N 073-56-03.507W	Fl R 2.5s		3	Red.	Year round radar reflective LIB.
38165	- *Lighted Buoy 67*	41-52-29.787N 073-56-38.098W	Fl G 4s		3	Green.	Replaced by can from Nov. 15 to Apr. 1. AIS: MMSI 993672042
38170	- *Lighted Buoy 68*	41-53-00.330N 073-56-42.773W	Fl R 4s		3	Red.	Replaced by nun from Nov. 15 to Apr. 1.
38175	- *Lighted Buoy 70*	41-53-52.372N 073-57-21.551W	Q R		3	Red.	Year round radar reflective LIB.
38180	- *Lighted Buoy 71*	41-54-21.386N 073-57-50.510W	Fl G 2.5s		3	Green.	Replaced by can from Nov. 15 to Apr. 1. AIS: MMSI 993672043
38182	- *Lighted Buoy 72*	41-54-23.757N 073-57-30.159W	Fl R 2.5s		3	Red.	Replaced by nun from Dec. 1 to Apr. 1. AIS: MMSI 993672044
38183	- *Lighted Buoy 73*	41-54-59.745N 073-57-36.141W	Q G		3	Green.	Replaced by can from Dec. 1 to Apr. 1.
	Rondout Creek *Maintained from May 1 to November 1.*						
38185	- LIGHT 1	41-55-10.473N 073-57-45.195W	Fl G 4s	25	4	SG on skeleton tower.	Year round aid.
38187	- West Jetty Warning Daybeacon	41-55-10.479N 073-57-45.201W				NW on dike worded DANGER SUBMERGED JETTY.	
38190	- LEADING LIGHT	41-55-14.769N 073-57-44.967W	Fl W 6s	52	9		DANGER SUBMERGED JETTY
38195	- East Jetty Daybeacon A	41-55-17.728N 073-57-45.494W				NW on dike worded DANGER SUBMERGED JETTY.	
38200	- East Jetty Daybeacon B	41-55-19.440N 073-57-46.111W				NW on dike worded DANGER SUBMERGED JETTY.	
38205	- East Jetty Daybeacon C	41-55-21.462N 073-57-46.661W				NW on dike worded DANGER SUBMERGED JETTY.	
38210	- East Jetty Daybeacon D	41-55-23.430N 073-57-47.751W				NW on dike worded DANGER SUBMERGED JETTY.	
38215	- Daybeacon 3	41-55-12.874N 073-57-49.645W				SG on dike.	
38220	- Daybeacon 4	41-55-15.798N 073-57-47.686W				TR on dike.	
38225	- Daybeacon 5	41-55-14.282N 073-57-52.127W				SG on dike.	
38230	- Daybeacon 6	41-55-17.393N 073-57-51.212W				TR on dike.	
38235	- Daybeacon 7	41-55-15.394N 073-57-55.291W				SG on dike.	
38240	- Daybeacon 8	41-55-18.846N 073-57-55.011W				TR on dike.	

(1) No.	(2) Name and Location	(3) Position	(4) Characteristic	(5) Height	(6) Range	(7) Structure	(8) Remarks
			HUDSON RIVER (New York) - First District				
	WAPPINGER CREEK TO HUDSON RIVER						
	Hudson River						
	Rondout Creek						
	Maintained from May 1 to November 1.						
38245	- Daybeacon 9	41-55-16.444N 073-57-58.880W				SG on dike.	
38250	- Daybeacon 10	41-55-20.520N 073-58-01.446W				TR on dike.	
	Rondout Creek Channel						
	Maintained from May 1 to Nov. 1.						
38255	- Buoy 12	41-54-51.213N 073-59-10.270W				Red nun.	Year round aid.
38260	- Buoy 13	41-54-47.119N 073-59-14.250W				Green can.	Year round aid.
38265	- Buoy 15	41-54-08.466N 074-00-45.410W				Green can.	
38270	- Buoy 16	41-54-07.465N 074-00-50.318W				Red nun.	
38275	- Buoy 17	41-54-04.387N 074-00-53.325W				Green can.	
38280	- Buoy 19	41-53-57.672N 074-00-59.828W				Green can.	
	Hudson River						
38285	- *Lighted Buoy 74*	41-55-45.596N 073-57-33.930W	Fl R 2.5s		3	Red.	Year round radar reflective LIB.
38290	KINGSTON FLATS LIGHT KF	41-56-15.356N 073-57-28.486W	Fl W 4s	38	4	NR on skeleton tower.	
38295	- *Lighted Buoy 76*	41-56-17.270N 073-57-41.847W	Fl R 2.5s		3	Red.	Year round radar reflective LIB.
38300	- *Lighted Buoy 77*	41-56-33.319N 073-57-47.427W	Q G		3	Green.	Year round radar reflective LIB.
38305	- *Lighted Buoy 78* On west side of The Flat.	41-56-43.817N 073-57-39.311W	Fl R 4s		4	Red.	Year round radar reflective LIB. AIS: MMSI 993672045
38310	- *Lighted Buoy 80*	41-57-39.199N 073-57-20.491W	Fl R 2.5s		3	Red.	Year round radar reflective LIB.
38315	**Kingston Bridge Sound Signal**	41-58-45.000N 073-57-03.180W				On bridge abutment.	RACON: K (- . -) HORN (2): 2 blast ev 30s (2s bl-2s si-2s bl-24s si). Private aid.
38320	ASTOR POINT LIGHT	41-59-25.233N 073-56-02.215W	Fl W 4s	40	5	NR on skeleton tower.	Obscured from the north.
38325	- *Lighted Buoy 82* At north end of flat.	41-59-55.439N 073-56-32.585W	Fl R 4s		3	Red.	Year round radar reflective LIB.
38330	- LIGHT 83	42-00-50.633N 073-56-20.315W	Fl G 2.5s	38	4	SG on skeleton tower.	
38335	- *Lighted Buoy 84*	42-00-47.363N 073-56-05.503W	Fl R 2.5s		3	Red.	Year round radar reflective LIB.
38340	*Hogs Back North Lighted Buoy N* On north edge of Hogs Back.	42-01-20.435N 073-55-56.222W	Fl (2+1)R 6s		3	Red and green bands.	Permanent ice hull.
38345	- *Lighted Buoy 85* On south end of Saddle Bags Shoal.	42-01-46.203N 073-56-06.410W	Fl G 4s		3	Green.	Year round radar reflective LIB.
38350	- LIGHT 86	42-02-02.919N 073-55-46.059W	Fl R 2.5s	28	4	TR on skeleton tower.	
38355	- *Lighted Buoy 87*	42-02-15.169N 073-55-56.872W	Fl G 2.5s		3	Green.	Replaced by can from Nov. 15 to Apr. 15. AIS: MMSI 993672046
38360	- *Lighted Buoy 89*	42-03-04.341N 073-55-42.489W	Fl G 2.5s		3	Green.	
38365	- *Lighted Buoy 91*	42-04-05.082N 073-55-40.484W	Q G		3	Green.	Replaced by can from Nov. 15 to Apr. 15.

(1) No.	(2) Name and Location	(3) Position	(4) Characteristic	(5) Height	(6) Range	(7) Structure	(8) Remarks
	HUDSON RIVER (New York) - First District						
	WAPPINGER CREEK TO HUDSON RIVER						
	Hudson River						
38370	- LIGHT 93	42-04-16.633N 073-55-46.115W	Fl G 4s	28	4	SG on skeleton tower.	
38375	SAUGERTIES LIGHT	42-04-19.197N 073-55-46.779W	Oc W 4s	41	6	White.	
38380	- Lighted Buoy 94	42-04-34.429N 073-55-36.687W	Fl R 2.5s		3	Red.	Year round radar reflective LIB.
38385	- Lighted Buoy 95	42-05-10.878N 073-55-53.947W	Fl G 2.5s		3	Green.	Replaced by can from Nov. 15 to Apr. 15. AIS: MMSI 993672047
38390	- LIGHT 96	42-05-22.641N 073-55-39.513W	Fl R 2.5s	24	4	TR on skeleton tower.	
38395	- Lighted Buoy 98	42-06-00.678N 073-55-37.696W	Fl R 4s		3	Red.	Year round radar reflective LIB.
38400	- Lighted Buoy 99	42-06-21.907N 073-55-37.035W	Fl G 4s		4	Green.	Year round radar reflective LIB.
38403	WANTON ISLAND DIRECTIONAL LIGHT	42-07-42.333N 073-55-01.115W	Oc W 4s	20	R 2 G 2 W 2	On skeleton tower.	Shows red from 015.25° to 016.75°; white from 016.75° to 017.25°; green from 017.25° to 018.75°.
38405	- LIGHT 101	42-07-42.833N 073-55-00.115W	Fl G 2.5s	24	4	SG on skeleton tower.	
38410	- Lighted Buoy 102 On southwest side of flats.	42-07-39.742N 073-54-51.614W	Fl R 2.5s		3	Red.	Replaced by nun from Nov. 15 to Apr. 15.
	Rondout Creek Channel *Maintained from May 1 to Nov. 1.*						
38413	LEHIGH MOORING DOLPHIN LIGHT 1	42-08-33.200N 073-54-31.500W	Fl Y 4s	10		On dolphin.	Private aid.
38414	LEHIGH MOORING DOLPHIN LIGHT 2	42-08-19.300N 073-54-40.100W	Fl Y 4s	10		On dolphin.	Private aid.
	Hudson River						
38415	- Lighted Buoy 104 Marks lower end of shoal.	42-08-21.695N 073-54-27.470W	Fl R 4s		3	Red.	Replaced by nun from Nov. 15 to Apr. 15. AIS: MMSI 993672048
38420	UPPER COALS BED LIGHT CB On south end of shoal.	42-08-44.475N 073-54-03.687W	Fl W 6s	27	5	NG on skeleton tower.	
38425	- Lighted Buoy 106	42-08-45.779N 073-54-13.916W	Q R		4	Red.	Year round radar reflective LIB.
38430	SILVER POINT RANGE FRONT LIGHT	42-08-44.197N 073-54-25.646W	Q G	30		On skeleton tower.	Lighted throughout 24 hours.
38435	SILVER POINT RANGE REAR LIGHT 164 yards, 219.4° from front light.	42-08-40.435N 073-54-29.802W	Iso G 6s	50		On skeleton tower.	Lighted throughout 24 hours.
38436	- Lighted Buoy 107	42-08-58.494N 073-54-14.533W	Q G		3	Green.	Year round radar reflective LIB.
38440	- Lighted Buoy 108	42-09-00.871N 073-54-03.725W	Fl R 2.5s		3	Red.	Replaced by nun from Nov. 15 to Apr. 15.
38445	- Lighted Buoy 109	42-09-13.034N 073-53-57.388W	Fl G 2.5s		3	Green.	Replaced by can from Nov. 15 to Apr. 15.
38450	- Lighted Buoy 110 Marks upper end of shoal.	42-09-25.621N 073-53-36.602W	Fl R 2.5s		3	Red.	Replaced by nun from Nov. 15 to Apr. 1.
38455	- Lighted Buoy 111	42-09-51.006N 073-53-16.259W	Fl G 4s		3	Green.	Replaced by can from Nov. 15 to Apr. 1. AIS: MMSI 993672049
38457	- Lighted Buoy 112	42-09-48.883N 073-53-10.147W	Fl R 4s		3	Red.	Replaced by nun from Nov. 15 to Apr. 1.

(1) No.	(2) Name and Location	(3) Position	(4) Characteristic	(5) Height	(6) Range	(7) Structure	(8) Remarks
			HUDSON RIVER (New York) - First District				
	WAPPINGER CREEK TO HUDSON RIVER						
	Hudson River						
38460	INBOCHT BAY LIGHT IB	42-10-14.233N 073-52-59.715W	Fl W 4s	26	4	NG on skeleton tower.	
38465	- *Lighted Buoy 113*	42-10-21.500N 073-52-42.777W	Fl G 2.5s		3	Green.	Replaced by can from Nov. 15 to Apr. 1. AIS: MMSI 993672050
38470	- *Lighted Buoy 114*	42-10-18.634N 073-52-38.400W	Fl R 2.5s		3	Red.	Replaced by nun from Nov. 15 to Apr. 15.
38475	- LIGHT 116	42-10-52.731N 073-51-52.239W	Fl R 4s	17	4	TR on skeleton tower.	
38480	- *Lighted Buoy 117*	42-11-10.504N 073-51-38.076W	Q G		3	Green.	Year round radar reflective LIB.
38485	- *Lighted Buoy 118*	42-11-07.498N 073-51-32.577W	Q R		3	Red.	Replaced by nun from Nov. 15 to Apr. 15.
38490	BURDEN DOCK LIGHT BD	42-11-36.933N 073-51-08.915W	Fl W 4s	28	5	NR on skeleton tower.	
38495	- *Lighted Buoy 119*	42-12-21.430N 073-51-05.548W	Q G		4	Green.	Year round radar reflective LIB.
38500	Catskill Creek Buoy 1	42-12-32.334N 073-51-15.479W				Green can.	Maintained from 1 May to 1 Nov.
38505	Catskill Creek Buoy 3	42-12-34.963N 073-51-19.846W				Green can.	Maintained from 1 May to 1 Nov.
38510	- *Lighted Buoy 120* Marks south end of Rogers Island Shoal.	42-12-21.436N 073-50-58.122W	Q R		3	Red.	Replaced by nun from Nov. 15 to Apr. 1.
38515	- LIGHT 121	42-12-53.974N 073-51-16.680W	Fl G 4s	31	4	SG on skeleton tower.	
38520	- *Lighted Buoy 122*	42-13-04.690N 073-51-07.517W	Fl R 4s		3	Red.	Replaced by nun from Nov. 15 to Apr. 15. AIS: MMSI 993672051
38525	**RIP VAN WINKLE BRIDGE RACON (X)**	42-13-27.000N 073-51-07.000W				Center bridge span.	RACON: X (- . . -) Private aid.
38530	- LIGHT 123	42-13-45.333N 073-51-08.215W	Fl G 2.5s	24	4	SG on skeleton tower.	
38535	- *Lighted Buoy 124*	42-13-46.762N 073-50-54.471W	Fl R 2.5s		3	Red.	Replaced by nun from Nov. 15 to Apr. 15.
38540	- LIGHT 126	42-14-11.333N 073-50-28.615W	Q R	28	4	TR on skeleton tower.	
38545	- *Lighted Buoy 128*	42-14-24.736N 073-50-12.793W	Fl R 2.5s		3	Red.	Replaced by nun from Nov. 15 to Apr. 1. AIS: MMSI 993672052
38546	New Athens Intake Hazard Buoy	42-14-27.580N 073-50-22.740W					Private aid.
38550	- LIGHT 129 On edge of shoal.	42-14-44.733N 073-49-45.815W	Fl G 4s	31	4	SG on skeleton tower.	
38555	- *Lighted Buoy 130*	42-14-52.330N 073-49-01.215W	Fl R 4s		3	Red.	Replaced by nun from Nov. 15 to Apr. 15.
38560	HUDSON CITY LIGHT	42-15-08.133N 073-48-31.915W	Fl G 2.5s	46	4		
38580	MIDDLE GROUND FLATS WEST CHANNEL LIGHT 2	42-16-11.733N 073-47-53.615W	Fl R 4s	28	3	TR on skeleton tower.	
38585	- *Lighted Buoy 133*	42-15-21.346N 073-48-03.668W	Q G		3	Green.	Replaced by can from Nov. 15 to Apr. 15.
38590	- *Lighted Buoy 135*	42-15-44.006N 073-47-39.507W	Fl G 2.5s		3	Green.	Replaced by can from Nov. 15 to Apr. 1.
38595	- Channel Buoy 137	42-16-02.345N 073-47-26.767W				Green can.	

(1) No.	(2) Name and Location	(3) Position	(4) Characteristic	(5) Height	(6) Range	(7) Structure	(8) Remarks
			HUDSON RIVER (New York) - First District				
	WAPPINGER CREEK TO HUDSON RIVER						
	Hudson River						
38600	- Lighted Buoy 138	42-16-01.283N 073-47-20.984W	Fl R 2.5s		4	Red.	Year round radar reflective LIB.
38605	- Buoy 139	42-16-28.936N 073-47-13.572W				Green can.	
38610	- LIGHT 140	42-16-43.782N 073-46-58.992W	Q R	24	4	TR on skeleton tower.	
38614	- Buoy 141	42-16-45.523N 073-47-08.274W				Green can.	
38615	- Lighted Buoy 143	42-17-14.813N 073-47-01.625W	Fl G 4s		3	Green.	Replaced by can from Nov. 15 to Apr. 1. AIS: MMSI 993672053
38620	- Lighted Buoy 144	42-17-17.343N 073-46-55.465W	Fl R 4s		3	Red.	Replaced by nun from Nov. 15 to Apr. 15.
38625	Four Mile Point Anchorage Buoy A	42-17-26.033N 073-47-05.075W				Yellow can.	
	COXSACKIE TO TROY						
	Hudson River						
38630	HUDSON ANCHORAGE LIGHT HA	42-17-32.433N 073-47-10.115W	Fl W 6s	35	4	NG on skeleton tower.	
38635	Four Mile Point Anchorage Buoy B	42-17-38.463N 073-47-03.675W				Yellow can.	
38640	- Lighted Buoy 145	42-17-49.864N 073-46-57.569W	Fl G 2.5s		3	Green.	Replaced by can from Nov. 15 to Apr. 1.
38645	- LIGHT 147	42-18-13.133N 073-46-57.515W	Q G	46	4	SG on skeleton tower.	
38647	- Buoy 148	42-18-14.481N 073-46-48.165W				Red nun.	
38650	- Buoy 150	42-18-37.653N 073-46-52.761W				Red nun.	
38655	- Lighted Buoy 151	42-19-11.379N 073-47-05.045W	Fl G 4s		3	Green.	Replaced by can from Nov. 15 to Apr. 15.
38660	- LIGHT 152	42-19-16.333N 073-46-58.815W	Fl R 4s	26	4	TR on skeleton tower.	
38665	- LIGHT 153	42-19-54.433N 073-47-09.915W	Fl G 6s	52	4	SG on skeleton tower.	
38670	- Lighted Buoy 154	42-20-01.909N 073-47-01.210W	Fl R 2.5s		4	Red.	Year round radar reflective LIB.
38675	- Lighted Buoy 155	42-20-11.434N 073-47-10.018W	Fl G 2.5s		3	Green.	Replaced by can from Nov. 15 to Apr. 1.
38680	- LIGHT 157	42-20-30.834N 073-47-18.115W	Fl G 4s	26	4	SG on skeleton tower.	
38690	- Lighted Buoy 158	42-20-45.459N 073-47-14.623W	Fl R 4s		3	Red.	Replaced by nun from Nov. 15 to Apr. 15.
38695	- Lighted Buoy 159	42-21-01.020N 073-47-28.122W	Fl G 2.5s		3	Green.	Replaced by can from Nov. 15 to Apr. 15. AIS: MMSI 993672054
38697	- Lighted Buoy 160	42-21-24.251N 073-47-24.273W	Fl R 2.5s		3	Red.	Replaced by nun from Nov. 15 to Apr. 1.
38699	- Hazard Buoy	42-21-22.170N 073-47-33.346W				White and orange diamond. Marked "ROCKS".	Maintained from 1 May to 1 Nov.
38700	- Lighted Buoy 161	42-21-24.466N 073-47-29.838W	Q G		3	Green.	Year round radar reflective LIB.
38705	- Lighted Buoy 163	42-21-50.271N 073-47-31.370W	Fl G 2.5s		3	Green.	Replaced by can from Nov. 15 to Apr. 1.

(1) No.	(2) Name and Location	(3) Position	(4) Characteristic	(5) Height	(6) Range	(7) Structure	(8) Remarks
		HUDSON RIVER (New York) - First District					
	COXSACKIE TO TROY						
	Hudson River						
38710	- Lighted Buoy 164	42-22-06.201N 073-47-26.370W	Fl R 2.5s		3	Red.	Replaced by nun from Nov. 15 to Apr. 1.
38715	- LIGHT 166 On flats.	42-22-37.222N 073-47-32.265W	Q R	24	3	TR on skeleton tower.	
38720	RATTLESNAKE ISLAND LEADING LIGHT RI	42-22-47.091N 073-47-41.181W	Fl W 4s	41	6	NG on skeleton tower.	
38725	- Lighted Buoy 168	42-22-59.418N 073-47-31.042W	Fl R 2.5s		4	Red.	Year round radar reflective LIB.
38730	- Buoy 168A	42-23-28.734N 073-47-17.982W				Red nun.	
38735	- LIGHT 169	42-23-46.108N 073-47-18.177W	Fl G 4s	14	4	SG on pile.	
38740	- Lighted Buoy 170	42-24-03.744N 073-47-03.711W	Fl R 4s		3	Red.	Replaced by nun from Nov. 15 to Apr. 15.
38745	Stuyvesant Upper Hudson River Anchorage Buoy A	42-24-13.744N 073-46-53.800W				Yellow nun.	
38750	Stuyvesant Upper Hudson River Anchorage Buoy B	42-24-25.754N 073-46-48.420W				Yellow nun.	
38755	- LIGHT 171	42-24-29.934N 073-47-00.115W	Fl G 4s	26	4	SG on skeleton tower.	
38757	- Buoy 173	42-24-40.405N 073-46-53.813W				Green can.	
38760	- Buoy 174	42-24-37.951N 073-46-48.670W				Red nun.	
38765	MILL CREEK LIGHT MC	42-24-41.134N 073-46-41.115W	Fl W 4s	48	5	NR on skeleton tower.	
38770	- Lighted Buoy 176	42-24-52.640N 073-46-42.608W	Q R		3	Red.	Replaced by nun from Nov. 15 to Apr. 15.
38775	- Lighted Buoy 177	42-25-05.333N 073-46-49.120W	Q G		4	Green spar buoy.	Year round radar reflective LIB.
38780	- Lighted Buoy 178	42-25-15.670N 073-46-45.338W	Fl R 2.5s		3	Red.	Replaced by nun from Nov. 15 to Apr. 1.
38785	- LIGHT 180	42-25-27.262N 073-46-44.179W	Fl R 4s	30	4	TR on skeleton tower.	
38790	- Lighted Buoy 181	42-25-49.150N 073-46-54.044W	Fl G 4s		4	Green spar buoy.	Year round radar reflective LIB.
38795	- Lighted Buoy 182	42-25-49.716N 073-46-48.505W	Fl R 4s		3	Red.	Replaced by nun from Nov. 15 to Apr. 15.
38800	STONEHOUSE BAR CHANNEL NORTH END RANGE FRONT LIGHT	42-27-14.077N 073-47-11.942W	Q G	32		KRW on skeleton tower.	Visible on 4deg each side of range line.
38805	STONEHOUSE BAR CHANNEL NORTH END RANGE REAR LIGHT 276 yards, 350.1° from front light.	42-27-22.123N 073-47-13.832W	Iso G 6s	45		KRW on skeleton tower.	Visible on 4deg each side of range line.
38810	- LIGHT 184	42-26-38.530N 073-46-58.281W	Fl R 2.5s	27	4	TR on skeleton tower.	
38815	- Lighted Buoy 185 150 feet outside channel limit.	42-26-49.930N 073-47-09.139W	Q G		3	Green.	Replaced by can from Nov. 15 to Apr. 15.
38820	- Lighted Buoy 187	42-27-42.290N 073-47-02.822W	Fl G 2.5s		3	Green.	Replaced by can from Nov. 15 to Apr. 15.
38825	- LIGHT 188	42-27-48.638N 073-46-53.967W	Q R	27	4	TR on skeleton tower.	
38830	- LIGHT 189	42-28-16.072N 073-47-12.495W	Fl G 4s	24	4	SG on skeleton tower.	

(1) No.	(2) Name and Location	(3) Position	(4) Characteristic	(5) Height	(6) Range	(7) Structure	(8) Remarks
		HUDSON RIVER (New York) - First District					

COXSACKIE TO TROY

Hudson River

Coeymans Dike
Aids maintained from Apr. 15 to Nov. 15.

(1) No.	(2) Name and Location	(3) Position	(4) Characteristic	(5) Height	(6) Range	(7) Structure	(8) Remarks
38835	- Buoy A	42-28-19.058N 073-47-12.548W				White and orange.	Worded DANGER SUBMERGED JETTY.
38840	- Buoy B	42-28-24.288N 073-47-13.841W				White and orange.	Worded DANGER SUBMERGED JETTY.
38845	- Buoy C	42-28-28.937N 073-47-14.962W				White and orange.	Worded DANGER SUBMERGED JETTY.
38850	- Buoy D	42-28-34.967N 073-47-16.487W				White and orange.	Worded DANGER SUBMERGED JETTY.

Hudson River

(1) No.	(2) Name and Location	(3) Position	(4) Characteristic	(5) Height	(6) Range	(7) Structure	(8) Remarks
38860	- *Lighted Buoy 190*	42-28-33.710N 073-47-08.059W	Fl R 2.5s		3	Red.	Replaced by nun from Nov. 15 to Apr. 15.
38865	- LIGHT 191	42-28-42.134N 073-47-19.115W	Q G	26	4	SG on skeleton tower.	
38870	- *Lighted Buoy 192*	42-28-46.693N 073-47-09.294W	Q R		3	Red.	Replaced by nun from Nov. 15 to Apr. 15.
38875	- LIGHT 193	42-29-11.900N 073-47-13.743W	Q G	26	4	SG on skeleton tower.	
38880	- *Lighted Buoy 194*	42-29-17.327N 073-47-05.887W	Fl R 2.5s		3	Red.	Replaced by nun from Nov. 15 to Apr. 15.
38885	- *Lighted Buoy 196*	42-29-41.194N 073-46-54.608W	Fl R 4s		3	Red.	Replaced by nun from Nov. 15 to Apr. 15.
38890	- LIGHT 197	42-30-04.288N 073-46-49.377W	Fl G 4s	25	4	SG on skeleton tower.	
38895	- *Lighted Buoy 199*	42-31-04.665N 073-46-01.464W	Fl G 4s		4	Green spar buoy.	Year round radar reflective LIB.
38900	- LIGHT 200	42-31-04.888N 073-45-52.629W	Q R	24	4	TR on skeleton tower.	
38903	- *Lighted Buoy 201*	42-31-23.182N 073-45-48.336W	Fl G 2.5s		3	Green.	Replaced by can from Nov. 15 to Apr. 15. AIS: MMSI 993672055
38905	- *Lighted Buoy 202*	42-31-21.552N 073-45-42.880W	Fl R 2.5s		3	Red.	Replaced by nun from Nov. 15 to Apr. 15.
38910	- LIGHT 204	42-32-15.934N 073-45-19.335W	Q R	28	4	TR on skeleton tower.	
38915	- *Lighted Buoy 205*	42-32-18.869N 073-45-27.664W	Q G		3	Green.	Replaced by can from Nov. 15 to Apr. 15.
38920	- *Lighted Buoy 207*	42-33-10.104N 073-45-22.237W	Fl G 2.5s		3	Green.	Replaced by can from Nov. 15 to Apr. 15.
38925	- LIGHT 209	42-33-26.934N 073-45-20.715W	Fl G 4s	25	4	SG on skeleton tower.	
38930	- *Lighted Buoy 210*	42-33-26.008N 073-45-12.915W	Fl R 4s		3	Red.	Replaced by nun from Nov. 15 to Apr. 15.
38935	- *Lighted Buoy 211*	42-34-12.183N 073-45-08.761W	Fl G 4s		3	Green.	Replaced by can from Nov. 15 to Apr. 15.
38940	- LIGHT 212	42-34-17.534N 073-45-02.015W	Fl R 4s	24	4	TR on skeleton tower.	
38945	- *Lighted Buoy 213*	42-34-25.661N 073-45-08.923W	Fl G 2.5s		3	Green.	Replaced by can from Nov. 15 to Apr. 15.
38950	- LIGHT 214	42-34-39.334N 073-45-02.415W	Q R	26	4	TR on skeleton tower.	

(1) No.	(2) Name and Location	(3) Position	(4) Characteristic	(5) Height	(6) Range	(7) Structure	(8) Remarks
			HUDSON RIVER (New York) - First District				
	COXSACKIE TO TROY						
	Hudson River						
38955	- LIGHT 215	42-35-05.704N 073-45-28.119W	Fl G 4s	21	4	SG on skeleton tower.	
38960	- *Lighted Buoy 216*	42-35-16.637N 073-45-27.453W	Fl R 2.5s		3	Red.	Replaced by nun from Nov. 15 to Apr. 15.
38965	- Buoy 217	42-35-29.249N 073-45-35.170W				Green can.	
38970	- LIGHT 219	42-36-10.134N 073-45-46.515W	Fl G 4s	29	4	SG on skeleton tower.	
38985	- LIGHT 221	42-36-49.378N 073-45-43.905W	Fl G 4s	28	4	SG on skeleton tower.	
39000	PORT OF ALBANY MOORING DOLPHIN LIGHT	42-37-32.280N 073-45-11.040W	Q W			On pile.	Private aid.
39010	- LIGHT 223	42-39-31.930N 073-44-18.387W	Fl G 4s	30	4	SG on skeleton tower.	
39015	- LIGHT 224	42-40-12.718N 073-43-24.801W	Fl R 4s	30	4	TR on skeleton tower.	
39025	- Buoy 226	42-42-18.534N 073-42-09.665W				Red nun.	
39030	- Buoy 228	42-43-15.966N 073-41-55.802W				Red nun.	
39035	Adams Island Obstruction Buoy	42-44-23.812N 073-41-17.985W					
39045	- Buoy 229	42-44-40.265N 073-41-17.161W				Green can.	
39050	- Buoy 231 100 feet outside channel limit.	42-44-55.615N 073-41-09.820W				Green can.	
	Troy Dam *Buoys mark turbulent area below dam. Aids maintained from May 1 to Nov. 1.*						
39055	- East Danger Buoy	42-44-58.970N 073-41-11.228W				White can with orange bands and diamond.	
39060	- Central Danger Buoy	42-44-58.669N 073-41-13.962W				White can with orange bands and diamond.	
39065	- West Danger Buoy	42-44-58.139N 073-41-16.378W				White can with orange bands and diamond.	
	NEW YORK STATE BARGE CANAL SYSTEM						
	Hudson River (Above Troy Lock) *Aids Maintained from May 1 to Nov. 1.*						
39070	*Hudson River Lighted Buoy 233*	42-45-23.018N 073-41-05.515W	Fl G 4s		3	Green.	Maintained from May 1 to Nov. 1.
39075	Hudson River Buoy 235	42-45-47.528N 073-40-59.015W				Green can.	Maintained from May 1 to Nov. 1.
39080	Hudson River Buoy 236	42-45-49.710N 073-40-57.090W				Red nun.	Maintained from 1 May to 1 Nov.
39085	Hudson River Buoy 237	42-45-59.482N 073-40-58.770W				Green can.	Maintained from 1 May to 1 Nov.
39090	Hudson River Buoy 238	42-46-05.544N 073-40-55.996W				Red nun.	Maintained from 1 May to 1 Nov.
39095	Hudson River Buoy 239	42-46-36.838N 073-40-47.364W				Green can.	Maintained from 1 May to 1 Nov.
39100	Hudson River Buoy 241	42-46-50.736N 073-40-42.280W				Green can.	Maintained from 1 May to 1 Nov.
39105	Hudson River Buoy 242	42-46-54.371N 073-40-37.022W				Red nun.	Maintained from 1 May to 1 Nov.
			LAKE CHAMPLAIN (New York and Vermont) - First District				
	RIVIERE RICHELIEU TO SOUTH HERO ISLAND						
	Main Passage						
39110	Kelly Bay Shoal Buoy 1	44-59-58.652N 073-20-48.458W				Green can.	

338

(1) No.	(2) Name and Location	(3) Position	(4) Characteristic	(5) Height	(6) Range	(7) Structure	(8) Remarks

LAKE CHAMPLAIN (New York and Vermont) - First District

RIVIERE RICHELIEU TO SOUTH HERO ISLAND

Main Passage

39115	Rouses Point Shoal Buoy 2 At east side of 4 foot shoal.	44-59-33.476N 073-21-10.294W				Red nun.	
39120	Railroad Bridge South Shoal Buoy 3 At southwest end of 3-foot shoal.	44-59-06.843N 073-21-04.483W				Green can.	
39130	WINDMILL POINT LIGHT	44-58-54.521N 073-20-30.436W	Fl W 4s	80	7	Grey conical tower.	.
39135	STONY POINT BREAKWATER LIGHT 4	44-58-25.935N 073-21-00.916W	Fl R 4s	19	5	TR on skeleton tower.	
39140	Windmill Point Reef Buoy 7 At west side of reef.	44-57-26.678N 073-20-08.692W				Green can.	
39145	Windmill Point Reef Buoy 9 At west side of 7-foot spot.	44-56-41.878N 073-20-13.792W				Green can.	
39150	Motte Reef Buoy 11 At northwest side of 2-foot reef.	44-56-02.079N 073-20-12.392W				Green can.	
39155	Point Au Fer Reef Buoy 12	44-55-55.479N 073-20-46.193W				Red nun.	
39160	Point Au Fer Reef Buoy 16 At east side of 1-foot reef.	44-55-18.279N 073-20-41.093W				Red nun.	
39163	Point Au Fer Reef Junction Buoy AF	44-54-54.035N 073-21-24.016W				Red and green bands; nun.	
39165	ISLE LA MOTTE LIGHT	44-54-23.424N 073-20-36.416W	Fl W 4s	46	7	Red conical tower.	

King Bay

Great Chazy River Boat Channel
Aids maintained from May 15 to Oct. 15.

39170	- Lighted Buoy 1	44-55-38.220N 073-22-37.200W	Fl G 4s			Green.	Private aid.
39175	- Lighted Buoy 2	44-55-39.120N 073-22-36.540W	Fl R 4s			Red.	Private aid.
39180	- Buoy 3	44-55-41.760N 073-22-44.400W				Green can.	Private aid.
39185	- Buoy 4	44-55-42.780N 073-22-42.900W				Red nun.	Private aid.
39190	- Buoy 5	44-55-44.940N 073-22-48.900W				Green can.	Private aid.
39195	- Buoy 6	44-55-45.900N 073-22-48.120W				Red nun.	Private aid.
39200	- Buoy 7	44-55-47.820N 073-22-52.860W				Green can.	Private aid.
39205	- Buoy 8	44-55-48.420N 073-22-52.320W				Red nun.	Private aid.
39210	- Buoy 9	44-55-50.640N 073-22-57.000W				Green can.	Private aid.
39215	- Buoy 10	44-55-51.120N 073-22-55.980W				Red nun.	Private aid.

La Motte Passage

39220	Pelots Point North Railroad Daybeacon 1	44-50-27.060N 073-17-58.560W				SG on metal pile.	Private aid.
39225	Pelots Point South Railroad Daybeacon 2	44-50-26.690N 073-17-59.680W				TR on metal pile.	Private aid.
39230	Horseshoe Shoal South End Buoy 3	44-50-16.984N 073-19-00.691W				Green can.	
39235	Townes Reef West Side Buoy 2 At northwest side of 4-foot reef.	44-49-50.333N 073-18-51.719W				Red nun.	
39240	Hills Shoal Buoy 1	44-49-43.950N 073-19-16.983W				Green can.	

Main Passage

| 39250 | La Roche Reef Lighted Buoy 20 | 44-47-56.188N
073-21-06.605W | Fl R 4s | | 3 | Red. | Replaced by nun from Nov. 1 to May 1. |

(1) No.	(2) Name and Location	(3) Position	(4) Characteristic	(5) Height	(6) Range	(7) Structure	(8) Remarks
		LAKE CHAMPLAIN (New York and Vermont) - First District					
	RIVIERE RICHELIEU TO SOUTH HERO ISLAND						
	The Gut North Entrance						
39255	Middle Reef Northeast End Buoy 2 At northeast side of reef.	44-45-54.187N 073-19-43.693W				Red nun.	
	South Entrance						
39260	Sister Shoal Buoy 1 On east side of 3-foot shoal.	44-44-06.789N 073-20-33.093W				Green can.	
	Main Channel						
39265	Middle Reef South Shoal Buoy 1 At south end of reef.	44-45-15.115N 073-19-59.324W				Green can.	
39270	SOUTH HERO LIGHT 2	44-45-03.797N 073-19-00.844W	Fl R 2.5s	25	5	TR on skeleton tower.	
39275	The Gut Western Entrance Buoy 3	44-45-06.189N 073-19-04.492W				Green can.	
39280	Simm Point South Buoy 4 At west side of 4-foot shoal.	44-45-11.989N 073-18-44.592W				Red nun.	
39285	Simm Point Buoy 6 At northwest end of 4-foot shoal.	44-45-18.288N 073-18-44.891W				Red nun.	
39290	Bow Arrow Point North Railroad Daybeacon	44-45-06.120N 073-18-59.040W				SG on pile.	Private aid.
39295	Tromp Point South Railroad Daybeacon	44-45-03.180N 073-18-58.260W				TR on pile.	Private aid.
39300	NORTH HERO LIGHT 8 On edge of shoal.	44-45-52.769N 073-17-32.350W	Fl R 4s	23	5	TR on skeleton tower.	
39305	Sandy Point Buoy 9	44-45-55.762N 073-17-33.117W				Green can.	
	St. Albans Bay						
39310	Ball Island South End Buoy 1 At southwest point of shoal.	44-45-21.193N 073-13-12.293W				Green can.	
39315	Hathaway Point Buoy 3 At south side of 2-foot spot.	44-46-40.319N 073-10-11.523W				Green can.	
39320	BURTON ISLAND LIGHT	44-46-38.860N 073-11-47.750W	Fl W 2.5s	14			Maintained from May 15 to Sept. 15. Private aid.
39321	Burton Island Pass Buoy 1	44-46-39.300N 073-11-31.700W				Green can.	Maintained from May 1 to Nov. 1. Private aid.
39322	Burton Island Pass Buoy 2	44-46-39.100N 073-11-31.900W				Red nun.	Maintained from May 1 to Nov. 1. Private aid.
	City Bay						
39325	City Reef Buoy 1 At east side of reef.	44-48-38.716N 073-16-36.094W				Green can.	
39330	- Buoy 2 At south point of shoal.	44-48-45.087N 073-16-54.788W				Red nun.	
	Gull Island Reef						
39335	- South Buoy GS At south point of reef.	44-50-40.687N 073-14-14.986W				Red and green bands; nun.	
39340	- North Buoy GN At north point of reef.	44-51-52.087N 073-13-27.886W				Red and green bands; nun.	
	Missisquoi Bay						
39345	- Buoy 2 Marks Northwest edge of Sandy Point Ledge.	44-59-06.181N 073-12-08.980W				Red nun.	Maintained from May 1 to Nov. 1.
39350	- Buoy 4 Marks Northwest point of shoal.	45-00-46.580N 073-10-11.879W				Red nun.	Maintained from May 1 to Nov. 1.
	Maquam Bay						
39351	- Danger Buoy DM	44-54-16.603N 073-10-18.213W				White and orange.	Maintained from May 1 to Nov. 1.

(1) No.	(2) Name and Location	(3) Position	(4) Characteristic	(5) Height	(6) Range	(7) Structure	(8) Remarks
		LAKE CHAMPLAIN (New York and Vermont) - First District					
	RIVIERE RICHELIEU TO SOUTH HERO ISLAND						
	Treadwell Bay						
39355	Rocky Point Reef Buoy 2 At south end of reef.	44-45-12.986N 073-23-13.997W				Red nun.	
39360	Four Foot Reef Buoy 3 At east side of 4-foot reef.	44-45-36.386N 073-23-43.998W				Green can.	
39361	*Bay Saint Armand Lighted Buoy 1*	44-44-52.000N 073-24-41.000W	Fl G 4s			Green.	Maintained from May 1 to Oct. 1. Private aid.
39362	*Bay Saint Armand Lighted Buoy 2*	44-44-54.000N 073-24-41.000W	Fl R 4s			Red.	Maintained from May 1 to Oct. 1. Private aid.
	CUMBERLAND HEAD TO FOUR BROTHERS ISLANDS						
	Main Passage						
	Cumberland Head						
39365	**- Ferry Dock Sound Signal**	44-41-57.840N 073-22-48.840W				On wharf piling.	Maintained from Apr. 1 to Dec. 30. HORN: 1 blast ev 30s (2s bl). Private aid.
39370	- FERRY DOCK NORTH SLIP SOUTH LIGHT	44-41-57.780N 073-22-48.540W	F G	22		On piling.	Private aid.
39375	- FERRY DOCK MIDDLE SLIP NORTH LIGHT	44-41-57.720N 073-22-48.480W	F R	19		On piling.	Private aid.
39380	- LIGHT	44-41-29.688N 073-23-06.894W	Fl W 4s	75	7	On Grey conical tower.	
	Main Passage						
39385	**Grand Isle Ferry Dock Fog Signal**	44-41-16.320N 073-20-58.680W				On wharf piling.	Maintained from Apr. 1 to Dec. 30. HORN: 2 blasts ev 30s (1s bl-1s si-1s bl-27s si). Private aid.
39390	GRAND ISLE FERRY DOCK SOUTH SLIP NORTH LIGHT	44-41-18.540N 073-21-00.930W	F G	18		On dolphin.	Private aid.
39395	GRAND ISLE FERRY DOCK SOUTH SLIP SOUTH LIGHT	44-41-18.160N 073-21-01.900W	F R	18		On dolphin.	Private aid.
39400	GORDON LANDING BREAKWATER LIGHT	44-41-18.569N 073-21-06.586W	Fl W 4s	18	7	NW on skeleton tower worded DANGER JETTY.	
39405	GRAND ISLE FERRY DOCK NORTH SLIP SOUTH LIGHT	44-41-18.660N 073-21-00.810W	F R			On pile cluster.	Maintained from Apr. 1 to Jan. 15. Private aid.
39410	GRAND ISLE FERRY DOCK NORTH SLIP NORTH LIGHT	44-41-19.220N 073-21-00.180W	F G			On pile cluster.	Maintained from Apr. 1 to Jan. 15. Private aid.
	Cumberland Bay						
39415	PLATTSBURGH BREAKWATER SOUTHWEST LIGHT	44-41-35.735N 073-26-23.016W	Fl W 2.5s	10	5	NW on skeleton tower.	
39420	PLATTSBURGH BREAKWATER NORTHEAST LIGHT	44-41-45.135N 073-26-09.116W	Fl W 4s	29	6	NW on skeleton tower worded DANGER JETTY.	
39425	Plattsburgh Buoy 1	44-42-02.289N 073-26-00.499W				Green can.	
39428	Gunboat Rock Hazard Buoy	44-43-13.193N 073-25-05.628W				White with orange bands marked DANGER ROCKS.	Maintained from May 1 to Nov. 1.
	Canal Terminal						
39430	- BREAKWATER LIGHT	44-42-25.560N 073-26-28.680W	Q R	20		On pile.	Private aid.
39435	- PIER LIGHT	44-42-29.580N 073-26-35.280W	Q R	15		On pile.	Private aid.
	Main Passage						
39450	Crab Island Buoy 24 East side of 2-foot shoal.	44-39-58.593N 073-24-43.497W				Red nun.	
39455	Valcour East Shoal Buoy 26	44-38-00.598N 073-24-12.806W				Red nun.	At east side of shoal.

(1) No.	(2) Name and Location	(3) Position	(4) Characteristic	(5) Height	(6) Range	(7) Structure	(8) Remarks
		LAKE CHAMPLAIN (New York and Vermont) - First District					
	CUMBERLAND HEAD TO FOUR BROTHERS ISLANDS						
	Valcour Island Channel						
39460	Valcour Shoal Buoy 2 At east side of 5-foot shoal.	44-38-12.818N 073-25-49.929W				Red nun.	
39465	Bluff Point Shoal Buoy 3 At north west side of 5-foot spot.	44-37-39.596N 073-25-56.198W				Green can.	
39470	BLUFF POINT LIGHT	44-37-22.152N 073-25-52.506W	Fl W 4s	95	7	In abandoned light house tower.	
39475	Au Sable Point Northwest Shoal Buoy 4	44-35-14.182N 073-25-31.801W				Red nun.	At north east side of shoal.
39480	Garden Island Ledge Buoy 28 At east side of 7-foot ledge.	44-36-12.281N 073-24-15.495W				Red nun.	
39482	*Lake Champlain Research Institute Data Lighted Buoy A*	44-36-09.000N 073-23-37.000W	Fl Y 4s			Yellow.	Maintained from Apr 15 to Dec 15. Private aid.
	Stave Island to Mallets Bay Channel						
39485	Stave Island Rock Buoy 2 At northeast side of rock.	44-35-55.841N 073-20-13.722W				Red nun.	
39490	ALLEN POINT RAILROAD SOUTH LIGHT 2	44-35-28.580N 073-18-44.940W	Q R			TR on spindle.	Maintained from May 15 to Nov. 15. Private aid.
39495	ALLEN POINT RAILROAD NORTH LIGHT 1	44-35-30.280N 073-18-44.400W	Q G			SG on spindle.	Maintained Apr 15 to Nov 15. Private aid.
39500	Allen Point Buoy 1 At south end of 1-foot shoal.	44-35-29.991N 073-18-20.834W				Green can.	Maintained from 1 May to 1 Nov.
39503	*Lake Champlain Research Institute Data Lighted Buoy B*	44-34-55.000N 073-16-53.000W	Fl Y 4s			Yellow.	Maintained from 01 May to 30 Nov. Private aid.
39505	Mallets Bay Rock Buoy Marks south side of submerged rock.	44-34-26.909N 073-12-23.626W				White with orange bands.	Maintained from 1 May to 1 Nov.
39507	Robinson Point Hazard Buoy	44-36-34.199N 073-16-29.663W				White and orange can.	Marked DANGER
39510	Coates Island Warning Buoy	44-33-31.855N 073-13-41.295W				White with orange bands; can.	Maintained from 1 May to 1 Nov.
	Main Passage						
39515	Stave Island Buoy 29 At west side of 4-foot ledge.	44-35-00.408N 073-20-24.792W				Green can.	Maintained from May 1 to Nov. 1.
39520	Jones Rock Buoy 31	44-34-42.784N 073-20-24.955W				Green can.	Maintained from May 1 to Nov. 1.
39525	Au Sable Point Buoy 32 At east side of shoal.	44-34-12.869N 073-24-46.576W				Red nun.	
39530	Hogback Reef Danger Buoy	44-33-32.961N 073-19-31.768W				White and orange.	Maintained from May 1 to Nov. 1.
39535	Au Sable River Flats Buoy 34 Marks east side of shoal.	44-33-02.929N 073-24-13.109W				Red nun.	
39540	COLCHESTER REEF LIGHT	44-33-18.435N 073-19-44.316W	Fl W 4s	51	6	NW on skeleton tower.	
39565	*Colchester Shoal Lighted Buoy 35* At northwest point of shoal.	44-32-58.105N 073-20-05.588W	Fl G 2.5s		3	Green.	Maintained from May 1 to Nov. 1.
39570	Colchester Shoal Buoy 37 At Southwest side of shoal.	44-32-47.955N 073-19-57.729W				Green can.	Maintained from May 1 to Nov. 1.
39575	*Ferris Rock Isolated Danger Lighted Buoy DFR*	44-31-23.915N 073-21-33.475W	Fl (2)W 5s		3	Black and red bands with two black spherical topmarks.	Maintained from May 1 to Nov. 1.
39585	The Pigs Shoal Buoy 39	44-30-09.308N 073-16-44.881W				Green can.	
39590	SCHUYLER ISLAND LIGHT S	44-29-55.397N 073-22-14.998W	Fl W 4s	27	7	NB on tower on concrete base.	

(1) No.	(2) Name and Location	(3) Position	(4) Characteristic	(5) Height	(6) Range	(7) Structure	(8) Remarks

LAKE CHAMPLAIN (New York and Vermont) - First District

CUMBERLAND HEAD TO FOUR BROTHERS ISLANDS

Main Passage

(1) No.	(2) Name and Location	(3) Position	(4) Characteristic	(5) Height	(6) Range	(7) Structure	(8) Remarks
39595	Schuyler Reef Buoy SR At northeast end of reef.	44-29-23.638N 073-20-52.922W				Red and green bands; nun.	Maintained from May 1 to Nov. 1.
39600	*NOAA Wave Research Lighted Buoy*	44-29-15.720N 073-20-20.760W	Fl Y 5s			Yellow.	Maintained from May1 to Nov 1. Private aid.
Appletree Bay							
39605	Appletree Point Buoy 1 Souteast of rock awash.	44-29-47.209N 073-16-05.979W				Green can.	
39610	*Appletree Shoal Lighted Buoy AS*	44-29-21.461N 073-15-58.830W	Fl (2+1)G 6s		3	Green and red bands.	Replaced by can from Nov 1 to May 1.
39612	Lake Champlain Yacht Club Racing Mark A	44-28-54.000N 073-16-40.800W				Yellow can.	Maintained May 01 to Oct 31. Private aid.
Burlington Bay							
39615	- BREAKWATER NORTH LIGHT	44-28-50.428N 073-13-46.788W	Fl R 2.5s	35	12	White square lighthouse on end of breakwater.	Maintained from 01 May to 01 Nov.
39617	Lake Champlain Yacht Club Racing Mark B	44-28-35.400N 073-13-48.600W				Yellow can.	Maintained May 01 to Oct 31. Private aid.
39625	BURLINGTON BREAKWATER LIGHT	44-28-46.998N 073-13-45.294W	Q W	13	3	NW on pile worded DANGER BREAKWATER.	
39630	- JETTY LIGHT	44-28-45.071N 073-13-22.846W	Fl W 2.5s		3	NW on pile worded DANGER BREAKWATER.	
39631	BURLINGTON HARBOR MARINA ENTRANCE LIGHT 1	44-28-43.165N 073-13-28.407W	F G			Green.	On floating docks. Seasonal 01 May - 01 Nov. Private aid.
39632	BURLINGTON HARBOR MARINA ENTRANCE LIGHT 2	44-28-44.268N 073-13-28.648W	F R			Red.	On floating docks. Seasonal from May 01 - Nov 01. Private aid.
Lake Champlain Underwater Preserve							
Aids maintained from June 1 to Nov. 1. Aids mark historic shipwreck diving sights.							
39635	- Buoy A	44-28-18.000N 073-13-43.000W				Yellow sphere.	Private aid.
39640	- Buoy B	44-28-08.000N 073-13-43.000W				Yellow sphere.	Private aid.
39645	- Buoy C	44-27-00.000N 073-14-42.000W				Yellow sphere.	Private aid.
39650	- Buoy D	44-27-12.000N 073-14-39.000W				Yellow sphere.	Private aid.
39655	- Buoy E	44-33-01.000N 073-19-48.000W				Yellow sphere.	Private aid.
39656	- Buoy F	44-28-42.600N 073-14-26.400W				Yellow sphere.	Maintained from Jun. 1 to Nov. 1. Private aid.
Burlington Bay							
39660	BURLINGTON FERRY DOCK NORTH SLIP NORTH LIGHT	44-28-30.120N 073-13-18.480W	F G	16		On dolphin.	Private aid.
39665	BURLINGTON FERRY DOCK NORTH SLIP SOUTH LIGHT	44-28-29.070N 073-13-18.240W	F R			On dolphin.	Private aid.
39680	- BREAKWATER SOUTH LIGHT	44-28-12.285N 073-13-32.717W	Fl W 4s	12	10	White triangular lighthouse on end of breakwater.	Maintained from 01 May to 01 Nov.
39681	CSC FLOATING BREAKWATER NORTH LIGHT	44-28-56.700N 073-13-34.620W	Q W			On end of breakwater.	Replaced by unlighted Danger Buoy when breakwater is submerged during ice. Private aid.
39682	CSC FLOATING BREAKWATER LIGHT N1	44-28-56.100N 073-13-34.740W	F W			On end of breakwater.	Aid discontinued when breakwater is endangered by ice. Private aid.
39683	CSC FLOATING BREAKWATER LIGHT N2	44-28-55.620N 073-13-34.860W	F W			On end of breakwater.	Aid discontinued when breakwater is endangered by ice. Private aid.
39684	CSC FLOATING BREAKWATER LIGHT S2	44-28-55.020N 073-13-34.920W	F W			On end of breakwater.	Aid discontinued when breakwater is endangered by ice. Private aid.

(1) No.	(2) Name and Location	(3) Position	(4) Characteristic	(5) Height	(6) Range	(7) Structure	(8) Remarks
			LAKE CHAMPLAIN (New York and Vermont) - First District				

CUMBERLAND HEAD TO FOUR BROTHERS ISLANDS

Burlington Bay

(1) No.	(2) Name and Location	(3) Position	(4) Characteristic	(5) Height	(6) Range	(7) Structure	(8) Remarks
39685	CSC FLOATING BREAKWATER LIGHT S1	44-28-54.360N 073-13-35.040W	F W			On end of breakwater.	Aid discontinued when breakwater is endangered by ice. Private aid.
39686	CSC FLOATING BREAKWATER SOUTH LIGHT	44-28-54.000N 073-13-34.980W	Q W			On end of breakwater.	Replaced by unlighted Danger Buoy when breakwater is submerged during ice. Private aid.

South Entrance (Burlington Bay)

39705	Juniper Ledge Buoy 1 At south side of ledge.	44-26-13.684N 073-16-24.911W				Green can.	Maintained from May 1 to Nov. 1.
39710	JUNIPER ISLAND LIGHT	44-26-58.343N 073-16-34.486W	Fl W 4s	125	7	On white skeleton tower.	
39715	Juniper Island Reef Buoy 3 At east side of reef.	44-26-56.132N 073-16-16.250W				Green can.	Maintained from May 1 to Nov. 1.
39720	Juniper Island Rock Buoy 5 Northeast side of 5-foot rock.	44-27-11.355N 073-16-26.577W				Green can.	Maintained from May 1 to Nov. 1.
39725	Proctor Shoal Buoy PS Northwest side of shoal.	44-27-07.113N 073-14-38.573W				Red and green bands; nun.	Maintained from May 1 to Nov. 1.
39727	Lake Champlain Yacht Club Racing Mark P	44-26-58.200N 073-14-58.800W				Yellow can.	Maintained May 01 to Oct 31. Private aid.

Main Passage

39730	Shelburne Point Shoal Buoy 2 At north end of shoal.	44-26-44.088N 073-14-53.974W				Red nun.	
39740	Shelburne Point Buoy 4 150 feet east of 3 charted wrecks.	44-26-10.704N 073-14-41.135W				Red nun.	
39741	Lake Champlain Yacht Club Racing Mark S	44-26-01.200N 073-14-24.600W				Yellow can.	Maintained May 01 to Oct 31. Private aid.
39742	Lake Champlain Yacht Club Racing Mark W	44-25-29.400N 073-14-39.000W				Yellow can.	Maintained May 01 to Oct 31. Private aid.
39743	Lake Champlain Yacht Club Racing Mark E	44-25-36.000N 073-13-27.000W				Yellow can.	Maintained May 01 to Oct 31. Private aid.
39751	Lake Champlain Yacht Club Racing Mark C	44-24-38.400N 073-13-53.400W				Yellow can.	Maintained May 01 to Oct 31. Private aid.
39755	Pumpkin Reef Buoy 40 At east side of reef.	44-26-47.508N 073-22-19.561W				Red nun.	
39760	The Four Brothers Islands Reef Buoy FB At north end of reef.	44-26-21.712N 073-19-43.282W				Red and green bands; nun.	Maintained from May 1 to Nov. 1.

FOUR BROTHERS ISLANDS TO BARBER POINT

Main Passage

39765	Saxton Reef Buoy 41 At west side of reef.	44-24-04.915N 073-17-04.275W				Green can.	Maintained from May 1 to Nov. 1.
39770	Four and One Half Foot Shoal Buoy 44 At east side of 4-foot reef.	44-23-36.414N 073-22-02.083W				Red nun.	
39775	*Quaker Smith Reef Lighted Buoy 47* At southwest side of reef.	44-23-05.116N 073-17-45.275W	Fl G 4s		3	Green.	Replaced by can from Nov. 1 to May 1.
39780	Quaker Smith Point Shoal Buoy 49 At west end of shoal.	44-22-57.614N 073-17-12.924W				Green can.	
39785	Bouquet River Buoy 50 At east end of shoal.	44-21-19.881N 073-20-41.466W				Red nun.	Maintained from May 1 to Nov. 1.
39787	*McNeil Cove Lighted Hazard Buoy*	44-18-04.920N 073-18-02.540W	Fl W 2.5s			White with orange band.	Private aid.
39790	ESSEX FERRY DOCK NORTH LIGHT	44-18-39.480N 073-21-01.140W	F R	14		On dolphin.	Private aid.
39795	ESSEX FERRY DOCK SOUTH LIGHT	44-18-38.700N 073-21-01.140W	F G	14		On dolphin.	Private aid.

(1) No.	(2) Name and Location	(3) Position	(4) Characteristic	(5) Height	(6) Range	(7) Structure	(8) Remarks
			LAKE CHAMPLAIN (New York and Vermont) - First District				
	FOUR BROTHERS ISLANDS TO BARBER POINT						
	Main Passage						
39800	CHARLOTTE FERRY DOCK NORTH SLIP NORTH LIGHT	44-18-04.230N 073-17-52.060W	F G			On dolphin.	Private aid.
39805	CHARLOTTE FERRY DOCK NORTH SLIP SOUTH LIGHT	44-18-03.690N 073-17-51.600W	F R	14		On dolphin.	Private aid.
39810	SPLIT ROCK POINT LIGHT	44-16-05.929N 073-19-19.363W	Fl W 4s	93	7		
39820	One Foot Spot Buoy 2 On west side of shoal.	44-15-58.124N 073-17-08.066W				Red nun.	
39825	DIAMOND ISLAND LIGHT	44-14-11.463N 073-20-03.168W	Fl W 2.5s	37	6	Gray skeleton tower.	
39830	Summer Point Shoal Buoy 51 At northwest edge of flats.	44-13-36.563N 073-20-15.130W				Green can.	
39835	Basin Harbor Reef Buoy 53 At west side of 9 oot rock.	44-11-39.005N 073-22-21.845W				Green can.	
39840	BARBER POINT LIGHT B	44-09-15.627N 073-24-14.669W	Fl W 4s	72	7	NB on skeleton tower.	
	BARBER POINT TO WHITEHALL						
	Main Passage						
39845	*Crane Point Shoal Lighted Buoy 55* At west end of shoal.	44-02-51.484N 073-26-09.663W	Fl G 4s		3	Green.	Replaced by can from Nov. 1 to May 1.
	Port Henry						
39850	- CANAL PIER LIGHT	44-03-01.500N 073-27-02.400W				On post.	Maintained from May 1 to Dec. 1. Private aid.
39855	- Buoy 2 Marks south end of shoal.	44-02-32.433N 073-27-16.465W				Red nun.	
	Main Passage						
39860	Crown Point Shoal Buoy 56 At northeast side of shoal.	44-02-06.135N 073-25-41.462W				Red nun.	
39865	*Crown Point Lighted Buoy 58*	44-01-42.236N 073-24-57.460W	Fl R 4s		3	Red.	Replaced by nun from Nov. 1 to May 1.
39870	Crown Point Buoy 60	44-00-35.838N 073-24-35.958W				Red nun.	
39875	YELLOW HOUSE POINT LIGHT Y	43-58-31.540N 073-24-25.452W	Fl W 4s	33	6	NB on black skeleton tower.	
39880	*Putnam Creek Lighted Buoy 62*	43-57-27.347N 073-24-24.686W	Fl R 2.5s		3	Red.	Replaced by nun from Nov. 1 to May 1.
39885	*Lake Champlain Main Channel Lighted Buoy 65*	43-56-07.243N 073-24-24.452W	Fl G 4s		3	Green.	Replaced by can from Nov. 1 to May 1.
39890	*Fivemile Point Lighted Buoy 67*	43-54-12.846N 073-23-43.147W	Fl G 4s		3	Green.	Replaced by can from Nov. 1 to May 1.
39895	FIVEMILE POINT LIGHT	43-54-14.686N 073-24-01.293W	Fl W 4s	25	7	NR on skeleton tower.	
39900	WATCH POINT LIGHT WP	43-53-08.992N 073-22-28.935W	Fl W 4s	20	6	NG on gray skeleton tower.	
39905	Kerby Middle Ground Buoy 68 At east side of middle ground.	43-52-38.148N 073-22-36.244W				Red nun.	
39910	Larabees Point Buoy 69	43-51-16.350N 073-22-43.042W				Green can.	
39915	TICONDEROGA LIGHT 70	43-50-53.087N 073-22-37.521W	Fl R 4s	30	4	TR on skeleton tower.	Higher intensity toward Watch Point.
39920	Fort Ticonderoga Buoy 72 At edge of shoal.	43-50-28.051N 073-22-42.341W				Red nun.	
39925	Montcalm Landing Buoy 73	43-49-13.052N 073-23-27.541W				Green can.	
39930	Wright Point Buoy 74 At edge of shoal.	43-48-36.753N 073-23-03.239W				Red nun.	

(1) No.	(2) Name and Location	(3) Position	(4) Characteristic	(5) Height	(6) Range	(7) Structure	(8) Remarks
		LAKE CHAMPLAIN (New York and Vermont) - First District					
	BARBER POINT TO WHITEHALL						
	Main Passage						
39935	WRIGHT POINT LIGHT 76	43-48-03.796N 073-22-45.359W	Fl R 4s	33	5	TR on skeleton tower.	
39940	Gourlie Point Buoy 78	43-47-19.855N 073-21-46.136W				Red nun.	
39945	ORWELL BLUFF LIGHT OB	43-46-41.122N 073-20-59.321W	Fl W 4s	38	6	NG on gray skeleton tower.	
39950	- Buoy 80	43-46-00.257N 073-21-28.434W				Red nun.	
39955	*Stony Point Lighted Buoy 81* West side of shoal.	43-44-32.077N 073-22-07.906W	Fl G 4s		3	Green.	Replaced by can from Nov. 1 to May 1.
	Whitehall Narrows						
39960	- LIGHT 1	43-43-20.476N 073-22-08.939W	Fl G 2.5s	25	4	SG on skeleton tower.	
39965	- Channel Buoy 2	43-43-18.857N 073-22-16.379W				Red nun.	
39970	- Channel Buoy 3	43-43-02.514N 073-22-38.405W				Green can.	
39975	- LIGHT 4	43-42-47.278N 073-23-05.207W	Fl R 4s	25	3	TR on skeleton tower.	
39980	- LIGHT 6	43-41-51.352N 073-23-43.295W	Fl R 2.5s	25	4	TR on skeleton tower.	
39985	- Channel Buoy 7	43-41-42.663N 073-23-50.231W				Green can.	
39990	- LIGHT 9	43-41-29.494N 073-24-11.681W	Fl G 2.5s	25	4	SG on skeleton tower.	
40000	- LIGHT 13	43-41-18.166N 073-24-15.503W	Fl G 4s	25	4	SG on skeleton tower.	
40005	- LIGHT 14	43-41-02.836N 073-24-14.495W	Fl R 4s	25	3	TR on skeleton tower.	
40010	- Channel Buoy 15	43-40-38.616N 073-24-18.400W				Green can.	
40015	- *Lighted Buoy 16*	43-40-13.364N 073-24-29.887W	Fl R 2.5s		3	Red.	Replaced by nun from Nov. 1 to May 1.
40020	- Channel Buoy 17	43-39-32.179N 073-24-49.684W				Green can.	
40025	- LIGHT 18	43-39-16.161N 073-24-56.699W	Fl R 4s	25	4	TR on skeleton tower on concrete base.	
40030	- Channel Buoy 20	43-39-03.466N 073-25-00.828W				Red nun.	
40035	- LIGHT 21	43-38-50.871N 073-25-09.515W	Fl G 2.5s	25	4	SG on skeleton tower on concrete base.	
40040	- LIGHT 22	43-38-11.985N 073-25-45.623W	Fl R 2.5s	25	4	TR on skeleton tower on concrete base.	
40045	- LIGHT 24	43-37-41.535N 073-25-22.553W	Fl R 4s	25	3	TR on skeleton tower on concrete base.	
40050	- LIGHT 26	43-37-19.011N 073-25-05.795W	Fl R 2.5s	25	4	TR on skeleton tower on concrete base.	
40055	- Channel Buoy 27	43-37-02.570N 073-25-12.325W				Green can.	
40060	- LIGHT 28	43-36-40.449N 073-25-27.983W	Fl R 4s	25	3	TR on skeleton tower on concrete base.	
40065	- LIGHT 30	43-36-10.839N 073-25-20.567W	Fl R 2.5s	25	4	TR on skeleton tower on concrete base.	
40070	- LIGHT 32	43-35-24.537N 073-25-52.595W	Fl R 4s	25	3	TR on skeleton tower.	
40075	- Channel Buoy 33	43-35-07.173N 073-25-47.423W				Green can.	

(1) No.	(2) Name and Location	(3) Position	(4) Characteristic	(5) Height	(6) Range	(7) Structure	(8) Remarks
		LAKE CHAMPLAIN (New York and Vermont) - First District					
	BARBER POINT TO WHITEHALL						
	Whitehall Narrows						
40080	- LIGHT 35	43-34-56.860N 073-25-17.163W	Fl G 4s	25	4	SG on skeleton tower on concrete base.	
40085	- Channel Buoy 37	43-34-46.187N 073-25-06.955W				Green can.	
		VERMONT - First District					
	LAKE MEMPHREMAGOG						
	Aids maintained from Jun 15 to Oct 1 unless otherwise noted.						
40095	- Lighted Buoy 2	44-56-30.600N 072-12-56.500W	Fl R 4s			Red nun.	Private aid.
40100	WHIPPLE POINT LIGHT	44-57-48.202N 072-13-52.384W	Fl W 4s	25	6	On grey skeleton tower.	Maintained year round.
40105	Scott's Points Buoy 1	44-56-56.800N 072-13-05.500W				Green can.	Private aid.
40110	*Indian Point Lighted Buoy 3*	44-57-18.700N 072-13-25.700W	Fl G 4s			Green.	Private aid.

INDEX

INDEX

INDEX

INDEX

INDEX

CROSS REFERENCE - INTERNATIONAL VS. U.S. LIGHT NUMBER

Inter.	U.S.	Inter.	U.S.	Inter.	U.S.	Inter.	U.S.
J0024.00	1120	J0152.00	6070	J0270.80	9740	J0384.00	13285
J0028.00	1390	J0156.00	6100	J0271.00	9765	J0384.20	13290
J0030.00	1305	J0157.00	6120	J0271.20	9795	J0386.00	485
J0034	1735	J0158	6125	J0272.00	9835	J0390.00	500
J0038.00	1785	J0160.00	6135	J0274.00	290	J0394.00	525
J0040.00	1865	J0160.10	6140	J0276.00	295	J0404.00	545
J0046.00	2045	J0166.00	6145	J0280.00	330	J0406.00	555
J0048.00	5	J0172.00	6440	J0282.00	9855	J0412.00	15150
J0052.00	2295	J0173.00	6580	J0284.00	9895	J0414.00	15205
J0054.00	2335	J0176.00	40	J0288.00	350	J0416.00	15160
J0056.00	2595	J0178.00	6845	J0290	10000	J0416.10	15165
J0058.00	2700	J0180.00	7145	J0290.10	10005	J0422	13860
J0062.00	2750	J0182.00	7280	J0294.00	10090	J0423	14050
J0064.00	3325	J0191.00	7690	J0295.00	10100	J0424.00	14065
J0068.00	3360	J0194.00	7620	J0306.00	10580	J0425.00	14085
J0072.00	3070	J0195.00	7610	J0306.20	10585	J0425.40	14170
J0074.00	3885	J0198.00	7605	J0306.40	10595	J0426.00	14450
J0078.00	3455	J0200.00	7225	J0306.60	10615	J0428.00	14540
J0080.00	3510	J0204.00	7575	J0306.80	10620	J0432.00	14741.21
J0082.00	3530	J0206.00	7565	J0310.00	390	J0438.00	13715
J0086.00	3585	J0208.00	60	J0314.00	425	J0440.00	15420
J0090.00	4405	J0214.00	95	J0318.00	11430	J0444.00	15460
J0094.00	4340	J0218.00	105	J0322.00	11440	J0446.00	13745
J0096.00	4310	J0220.00	8165	J0324.00	10795	J0448.00	15480
J0100.00	4280	J0222.20	8210	J0333.00	10890	J0449.00	15525
J0102.00	4130	J0226.00	125	J0337.00	10800	J0450.00	13775
J0104.00	4105	J0228.00	155	J0340.00	11065	J0451.00	14830
J0110.00	3965	J0233.00	8305	J0346.00	11675	J0452.00	15030
J0112.00	3760	J0233.10	8310	J0350.00	11710	J0454.00	15110
J0113.00	3715	J0234.00	8330	J0351.00	11715	J0456.00	15560
J0114.00	3235	J0235.00	8345	J0356.00	11650	J0460.00	15725
J0115.00	3250	J0237.00	8355	J0360.00	440	J0461.20	15740
J0116.00	10	J0237.10	8360	J0361.00	12185	J0463.00	15750
J0120.00	4540	J0238.00	8375	J0361.20	12195	J0464.00	15775
J0122.00	4580	J0239.00	8460	J0361.40	12205	J0465.00	15810
J0124.00	4780	J0240.2	8470	J0361.60	12215	J0470.00	15580
J0128.00	20	J0242.00	8520	J0362.00	465	J0472.00	15955
J0132.00	4980	J0242.20	8525	J0366.00	12545	J0480.00	630
J0134.00	5145	J0242.40	8530	J0368.00	12580	J0484	16295
J0136.00	5420	J0244.00	8785	J0369.00	12925	J0490.00	17470
J0140.00	5520	J0248	8880	J0369.20	12955	J0492.00	16040
J0142.00	5485	J0256.00	9070	J0372.00	13050	J0500.00	16830
J0144.00	5665	J0266.00	9315	J0374	13080	J0502.00	16085
J0145.00	5565	J0268.00	9615	J0374.10	13085	J0504.00	17095
J0145.40	5705	J0270.00	9660	J0376.00	13135	J0510.00	16095
J0146.00	35	J0270.20	9675	J0377.00	13150	J0510.10	16100
J0148.00	6025	J0270.40	9695	J0382.00	13275	J0512.00	16145
J0150.00	6050	J0270.6	9715	J0383.00	13270	J0512.40	16150

CROSS REFERENCE - INTERNATIONAL VS. U.S. LIGHT NUMBER

Inter.	-	U.S.	Inter.	-	U.S.	Inter.	-	U.S.	Inter.	-	U.S.
J0512.80		16165	J0681.00		20875	J0767.00		21680	J0890.00		25195
J0513.00		16170	J0690.00		660	J0771.00		23935	J0892.00		21375
J0514.00		16185	J0694.00		19880	J0771.10		23940	J0894.00		25225
J0515.00		16205	J0696.00		19875	J0773.00		21180	J0896		25230
J0516.00		16225	J0698.00		27790	J0774.00		21185	J0896.10		25235
J0517.00		16250	J0699.00		27795	J0775.00		23970	J0898.00		25270
J0520.00		16670	J0701.00		28195	J0778.00		24020	J0904.00		21400
J0524.00		17590	J0702.00		28245	J0778.10		24025	J0906.00		25365
J0530.00		17795	J0704.00		28255	J0780.00		21210	J0908.00		25545
J0532.00		17815	J0706.00		28310	J0782.00		24065	J0910.00		25550
J0540.00		17850	J0708.00		28325	J0782.20		24070	J0914.00		27065
J0547.00		17910	J0708.20		28355	J0784.00		21215	J0915.00		27110
J0552.00		17960	J0708.40		28375	J0786.00		24080	J0916.00		21440
J0555.00		18005	J0710.00		28050	J0790.00		24125	J0920.00		21480
J0566.00		18125	J0716.00		28870	J0794.00		24205	J0922.00		21500
J0570.00		18145	J0716.30		28885	J0798.60		24230	J0923.00		21505
J0572.00		18150	J0717.00		27725	J0804.00		24330	J0924.00		27165
J0576.00		18925	J0717.40		27705	J0808.00		24360	J0926.00		25720
J0577.00		18930	J0718.00		21095	J0808.40		24385	J0927.00		25765
J0580.00		18190	J0722.00		21090	J0808.60		24405	J0927.40		25770
J0582.00		18180	J0730.00		21825	J0810.00		21230	J0929.00		25945
J0583.00		18240	J0732.00		21845	J0812.00		21260	J0930.00		25965
J0584.00		18275	J0737.2		21860	J0816.00		26070	J0934.00		21520
J0590.00		18305	J0737.4		21865	J0818.00		26135	J0936.00		27215
J0592.00		18345	J0737.50		21890	J0819.00		26145	J0940.00		27250
J0600.00		18455	J0737.52		21895	J0820.10		26155	J0944		27495
J0602.00		18555	J0737.54		21900	J0828.00		24610	J0946.00		27515
J0604.00		18580	J0737.55		21905	J0830.00		24605	J0952.00		27635
J0608.00		19345	J0737.66		21960	J0832.00		24635	J0958.00		27265
J0610.00		19135	J0737.70		21995	J0836.00		24675	J0962.00		27650
J0612.00		19145	J0737.80		22055	J0838.00		24690	J0964.00		27640
J0628.00		19450	J0738.00		21070	J0839.00		24725	J0976.00		27285
J0631.00		19485	J0744.00		21115	J0839.10		24730	J0978.00		27290
J0632.00		19490	J0746.00		22520	J0840.00		21290	J0982.00		27300
J0636.00		19500	J0747.00		22595	J0842.00		24785	J0984.00		27295
J0638.00		19505	J0748.00		22610	J0844.00		24800	J0990.00		27315
J0644.00		19720	J0749.00		22675	J0850.00		24930	J0994.00		27325
J0646.00		19725	J0750.00		22870	J0852.00		24935	J0994.10		27330
J0650.00		640	J0750.10		22880	J0856.00		25030	J0998.00		675
J0654.00		19750	J0751.40		22890	J0858.00		25060	J1000.00		29040
J0658.00		19795	J0752.00		21560	J0860.00		25010	J1005.00		29105
J0664.00		20170	J0754.00		23400	J0862.00		24990	J1021.00		30890
J0665.00		20175	J0756.00		23395	J0867.00		26360	J1024.00		31500
J0666.00		20185	J0757.00		23405	J0867.20		26365	J1032.00		35025
J0671.00		20085	J0758.00		23455	J0879.00		26555	J1036.00		35040
J0676.00		20510	J0762.00		21170	J0880.00		26870	J1040.00		35190
J0678.00		20155	J0764.00		21150	J0884.00		25115	J1046.00		35595
J0680.00		20145	J0766.00		21650	J0884.10		25120	J1053.00		35560

CROSS REFERENCE - INTERNATIONAL VS. U.S. LIGHT NUMBER

Inter.	-	U.S.	Inter.	-	U.S.	Inter.	-	U.S.	Inter.	-	U.S.
J1053.10		35590	J1138.30		37790	J1141.10		38680			
J1054.00		35615	J1138.31		37795	J1141.20		38715			
J1054.10		35620	J1138.35		37785	J1141.25		38720			
J1057.00		36190	J1138.40		37800	J1141.30		38735			
J1057.10		36195	J1138.45		37830	J1141.35		38755			
J1057.20		36165	J1138.50		37835	J1141.40		38765			
J1057.30		36245	J1138.60		37895	J1141.45		38785			
J1057.40		36265	J1138.65		37900	J1141.50		38800			
J1057.60		36285	J1138.66		37905	J1141.51		38805			
J1057.70		36315	J1138.70		37945	J1141.55		38810			
J1057.80		36335	J1138.75		37965	J1141.60		38825			
J1058.00		36430	J1138.80		37980	J1141.65		38830			
J1061.00		36590	J1138.90		37990	J1141.70		38865			
J1062.00		36615	J1138.95		37995	J1141.75		38875			
J1062.20		36480	J1139.00		38000	J1141.80		38890			
J1062.25		36500	J1139.10		38015	J1141.85		38900			
J1064.00		36635	J1139.15		38025	J1141.90		38915			
J1066.00		36640	J1139.35		38100	J1141.95		38925			
J1066.10		36645	J1139.45		38120	J1142.00		38940			
J1067.50		36665	J1139.50		38125	J1142.10		38955			
J1067.51		36670	J1139.55		38130	J1142.15		38970			
J1068.20		36730	J1139.60		38140	J1142.30		38985			
J1068.50		36795	J1139.65		38145	J1154.00		37110			
J1068.52		36800	J1139.70		38155	J1156.00		34975			
J1068.60		36850	J1139.75		38185	J1161.00		34955			
J1070.00		35450	J1139.80		38190	J1164.00		37250			
J1072.00		35455	J1139.85		38290	J1164.10		37305			
J1074.00		35395	J1139.90		38315	J1166.00		37290			
J1081.90		34790	J1139.95		38320	J1166.20		37295			
J1082.00		34795	J1140.00		38335	J1173.00		37335			
J1082.10		35030	J1140.15		38390	J1174.00		37340			
J1090.00		35070	J1140.20		38405	J1176.00		37360			
J1092.00		34220	J1140.25		38420	J1177.00		37375			
J1096.00		34335	J1140.30		38430	J1177.50		37355			
J1097.00		34285	J1140.31		38435	J1177.70		36830			
J1100.00		34485	J1140.35		38460	J1177.71		36835			
J1103.80		34610	J1140.40		38475	J1178.00		37385			
J1106.00		34910	J1140.45		38490	J1179.00		36440			
J1108.00		34925	J1140.50		38515	J1184.00		37505			
J1114.00		36965	J1140.60		38530	J1186.00		37520			
J1118.00		36975	J1140.65		38540	J1188.00		37530			
J1118.10		36980	J1140.70		38545	J1189.00		37545			
J1126.00		35010	J1140.75		38560	J1189.40		37565			
J1134.20		27355	J1140.80		38580	J8236.00		21275			
J1134.40		27360	J1140.85		38610						
J1135.40		27370	J1140.90		38630						
J1138.20		37760	J1140.95		38645						
J1138.25		37775	J1141.00		38660						

Made in the USA
Columbia, SC
05 September 2024

41840578R10224